Educational Psychology

Educational Psychology

AN INTRODUCTION

SECOND EDITION

Steven V. Owen
UNIVERSITY OF CONNECTICUT

Robin D. Froman
UNIVERSITY OF CONNECTICUT

Henry Moscow

Little, Brown and Company   BOSTON   TORONTO

Library of Congress Catalog Card No. 80–82948

ISBN 0–316–677299

9 8 7 6 5 4 3 2 1

HAL

Published simultaneously in Canada
by Little, Brown & Company (Canada) Limited

Printed in the United States of America

Acknowledgments

Photographs by Bohdan Hrynewych and Lou Jones.

Tonia Noell-Roberts, Art Editor.

Teacher interviews by Kathy Kelzer and Ann McQueen.

All photographs, except as noted below, were taken especially for this book in the Boston public school system. Special thanks to Ms. Marion J. Fahey, Superintendent of Schools, without whose help this project would have been impossible, and to her assistant Jim Walsh for the many hours he contributed in coordinating and expediting access to the schools and classrooms. We're also most grateful to the following principals and headmasters who welcomed us into their schools: Barbara Jackson, of the William Monroe Trotter Elementary School; Marilyn Keily, of the Warren Prescott Elementary School; Joseph Bage, of the Thomas A. Edison Middle School; Mike Donato, of Hyde Park High School; and Donald Burgess, of West Roxbury High.

Most of all we thank those teachers who opened their classrooms to us, allowed us to observe, and shared their thoughts on teaching with us: Ruth O'Rourke, Harold Robinson, Barbara Chasen, Joseph Bonales, Peter Bernstein, Alma Wright, Barbara Sherman, Doreen R. Kelly, Rosalind Hoey, Barbara Fragone, Adam Artis, David P. Conroy, Mary Gonski, Myrna Michel, Cirstene Flygare, Angelo Giacalone, Denise Goldman, Henry Maffel, Judith Williams, Vincent Donovan, Neia Millan, and many others.

Art credits

Chapter 1. Page 16: Figure 1.1, from *Human Characteristics and Social Learning* by B. S. Bloom. Copyright © 1976 by B. S. Bloom. Used by permission of McGraw-Hill Book Company.

Chapter 3. Page 70: Figure 3.1, from *The Nature of Human Intelligence* by J. P. Guilford. Copyright © 1967 by J. P. Guilford. Used by permission of McGraw-Hill Book Company.

Chapter 6. Page 199: From "Verbal Learning and Verbal Behavior" by Gordon Bower. *Cognitive Psychology*, vol. 1, no. 1, 1970, p. 38. Reprinted with permission of the author.

Chapter 8. Page 255: Figure 8.1, from *A New History of the United States* by I. Bartlett et al. Copyright © 1969 Holt, Rinehart and Winston, Publishers.

Page 257: Figure 8.2, from *Modern Science, Level One* by H. A. Smith, M. K. Blecha, and H. Pless, 1974. Used by permission of Laidlaw Brothers, a division of Doubleday and Company, Inc.

Page 258: Figure 8.3, Dunbar poem reprinted by permission of Dodd, Mead, and Company, Inc. from *The Complete Poems of Paul Laurence Dunbar*. Hovey poem reprinted by permission of Dodd, Mead and Company, Inc. from *Poems* by Richard Hovey. Millay poem from *Collected Poems*, Harper and Row. Copyright 1921, 1948 by Edna St. Vincent Millay.

Page 259: Figure 8.4, from *Our Working World: Families* by Lawrence Senesh. © 1973, Science Research Associates, Inc. Reproduced by permission of the publisher.

Page 260: Figure 8.5, from B. J. Weiss, P. S. Rosenbaum, A. M. Shaw, and M. J. Tolbert, *Great Waves Breaking*. Copyright © 1977 by Holt, Rinehart and Winston, Publishers. Reprinted by permission.

Chapter 11. Page 360: From *Project Math*, used by permission of Educational Progress, a division of Educational Development Corporation, Tulsa, Oklahoma.

Page 363: Figure 11.1, adapted from M. Reynolds, "A Framework

(credits continue on p. 582)

Preface

We address this book primarily to future teachers, to working teachers bent on enhancing their professional capacities, and to everyone else concerned with the processes of teaching and learning, from nursery school through adulthood. The book should prove useful also to those who deal with learners outside the school setting. We have written in everyday language, not the commonly formidable language of college texts, and we explain essential technical terms when we use them.

Our purpose is threefold: to impart concisely what is now known or believed about the way students learn, to indicate how that information may serve in the classroom, and to stimulate the reader to further pursuit in a field of inquiry that predates Aristotle and is currently developing and changing prodigiously. In surveying what is known or believed, we have taken pains to present fairly three major approaches—behaviorism, cognitivism, and humanism—whose premises must await definition in the text. We have devoted several chapters each to behaviorism and cognitivism, and we have treated humanism implicitly throughout the book. We have tried also to establish that no one of the three theories provides all the answers to the mysteries of human behavior and that an approach embracing all three may be more profitable.

Users of the book provided detailed critiques that shaped the second edition, and new research on teaching and learning provided direction. We have added material on self-control, adult learning and teaching, cognitive functions beyond adolescence, cooperative learning arrangements, aggression, teacher effectiveness, and information processing. All of these topics have relatives in the first edition, and we have integrated most new ideas with earlier material. A major exception occurs with the original chapter on motivation and classroom management. The importance of these topics invited an expansion and separation into two chapters.

The book is organized in what seems to us logical sequence. In the first chapter we examine educational psychology's origins and growth. In Part I, which follows, we focus on the characteristics of children and how they develop; in Part II we consider the application of psychology to teaching them; in Part III we describe methods of determining whether or not they have learned; and in Part IV we report on rapidly changing trends in educational psychology.

We have not tampered with the special organization of the first edition. This sequence permitted concurrent and complementary treatment of two major schools of thought in educational psychology: behaviorism and cognitivism. Chapters in the first part cover individual differences of learners. The second part begins with chapters on behavioral and cognitive theories about the events of learning. A discussion of goals and objectives in teaching follows, which leads naturally to the application of the learning theories to teaching in the classroom. Six chapters in this part concentrate on the job of teaching. There we emphasize the importance of adapting teaching techniques to the needs of all learners. This comprehensive treatment of the characteristics of the learner and the process of learning and teaching provides the framework for the last two parts of the book: measuring learning outcomes and the call for accountability.

To make the book generally more useful and provocative, we have supplemented the text with:

1. informative and entertaining illustrations;
2. outlines preceding each chapter to put the content in perspective and permit the reader to see the topic whole;
3. questions in the margins of pages to facilitate absorption of the material;
4. quiz material following each chapter to assist in self-evaluation;
5. suggested readings to shed additional light on specific subjects that especially interest the reader; and
6. at the book's end, a large glossary.

Three of these features deserve fuller introduction. The photos and their captions represent real teachers, students, their problems and solutions. Sometimes the solutions reflect straightforward principles of educational psychology; occasionally they represent clever little experiments.

The glossary has been substantially expanded beyond the first edition. In an introductory course where basic vocabulary is extremely important, a glossary should be more than a handy dictionary of terms. We have endeavored to make it a teaching tool, to give new examples, and to show the interrelatedness of content. To help the glossary serve its purpose, each chapter concludes with a list of important terms that are explicitly defined in the glossary.

In this edition, we have expanded the number of questions in the page margins. We have also color-coded the questions to help direct reading and review. Questions in black require some further thought or synthesis of material. They generally cannot be answered by locating a simple phrase or sentence in the text. Questions in color are more factual and may be answered directly from the text. Both types of questions, and their answers, are important. Which type you profit from will depend on your own style of study and on the focus of your educational psychology course.

In the development of this edition, we owe more thanks to collaborators behind the scenes than we can possibly give here. Special credit is deserved by Mylan L. Jaixen, who as senior education editor contributed so much that he should probably be listed as a co-author. Book editor Elizabeth Schaaf gave expert supervision in the many steps of transforming a manuscript into a book. Tonia Noell-Roberts, art editor, conceived imaginative illustrations that enhance the written word. Cara Owen sorted, sequenced, and alphabetized awesome stacks of paper.

The critiques of scholars who reviewed our draft manuscript provided scores of suggestions that we have adopted. Those who read the entire manuscript included Thomas J. Shuell, State University of New York at Buffalo; Barry J. Wilson, University of Northern Iowa; James C. Shepard, Emporia State College; and Shawn M. Glynn, University of Georgia. Basic plans for the revision work were influenced by the comments and suggestions of a number of users of the first edition. We wish to extend a special note of appreciation to Marjorie Bayes, formerly of Yale University, who assisted in the writing of chapters 2 and 4.

S.V.O.
R.D.F.

Contents

12 Motivation 382

13 Coping with Misbehavior 409

The Nature and Nurture of Educational Psychology

You may have opened this book hesitantly, with a mixture of awe, curiosity, and dread. If you are a future teacher, you may view the study of educational psychology simply as part of the price for a license to teach. But possibly you wonder whether you will learn anything that you will be able to apply in the classroom. Some of your fellow students too—future pediatricians, speech therapists, counselors, and social workers among them, perhaps—may approach the subject as an obligation to be fulfilled, rather than an exciting and stimulating mental exploration. Too bad!

The doubts and preconceptions go pretty much like this: Teachers taught and pupils learned for centuries before the development of educational psychology, didn't they? Teaching and learning are natural processes, aren't they? Isn't it true that everyone teaches and everyone—or almost everyone—learns all the time? Your roommate teaches you and you teach your roommate and children teach each other, even if the subject is only hopscotch. Anyway, teaching is an art, not a science, isn't it? In *The Art of Teaching*, Gilbert Highet, himself a famous teacher and a professor of literature at Columbia University, wrote:

> I believe that teaching is an art, not a science. It seems to me very dangerous to apply the aims and methods of science to human beings as individuals.... Teaching involves emotions, which cannot be systematically appraised and employed, and human values, which are quite outside the grasp of science.... Teaching is not like inducing a chemical reaction: it is much more like painting a picture or making a piece of music.... You must realize that it cannot all be done by formulas, or you will spoil your work, and your pupils, and yourself (1950, p. vii).

If you want to teach, it is because you love children or because you love mathematics or history or French and would delight to share your enthusiasm. And if teaching is an art, who needs a course in educational psychology?

Is teaching an art or a science?*

The answer is implicit in the dictum of Edward L. Thorndike, who devoted many decades to developing theories of how living organisms learn:

> The efficiency of any profession depends in large measure upon the degree to which it becomes scientific. The profession of teaching will improve (i) in proportion as its members direct their daily work by the scientific spirit and methods, that is by honest, open-minded consideration of facts, by freedom from superstitions, fancies or unverified guesses and (ii) in proportion as the leaders in education direct their choices of methods by the results of scientific investigation rather than by general opinion (1962, p. 63).

Both Highet and Thorndike, it seems to us, are right. Teaching is both an art and a science. It takes more than a love of youngsters or of a field of human knowledge to make one a good teacher. Those attributes are essential for teaching, of course, but they are to be expected in a teacher: anyone who lacks them ought to choose another line of work. (The hard-bitten comic W. C. Fields, for example, probably would not have been a good teacher; he claimed

* The two types of questions in the margin are described in the Preface.

2

We asked a high school student, "What do you think would make a really effective teacher? what qualities do you like in teachers?" and the answer we got was, "A teacher that's strict, not too strict, though, you know. A teacher that helps you learn. A lot of teachers they'll just sit there—if the kids don't want to learn—and they'll just say 'Oh, well,' and they won't do anything. They make me want to get in a class that wants to learn. So, I guess I mean a teacher that more or less will teach."

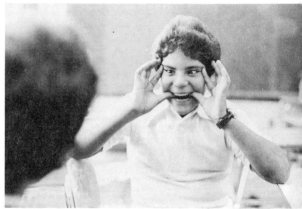

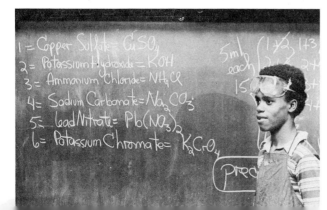

to tolerate children only when they were well-done and splattered with mustard.) Beyond love, good teaching demands among other things a mastery of techniques. Great teaching derives in large part from the imagination, versatility, and *understanding* with which the techniques are applied to the complex and diverse young human beings who attend school. The objective of educational psychology is to foster the understanding.

What Educational Psychology Is

Psychology, as you know, is the study of behavior in its broadest sense, that is, everything that people do or do not do and why they do or do not do it. Educational psychology

What are the general concerns of educational psychology?

is a very broad field of applied psychology that utilizes the theories, findings, methods and instruments of psychological science for educational purposes. Educational psychologists engage in a wide variety of activities, including research, educational testing, counseling and guidance, consultation with teachers and parents, and working with handicapped children (Elkind, 1973, pp. 420–421).

Despite its encompassing scope, educational psychology concerns itself with two basic questions:

1. How do people learn?
2. What are the best ways to teach them?

Learning and teaching are not automatic counterparts. Much learning occurs in the absence of teaching, and teaching can occur without much learning (as you have no doubt discovered). Those basic questions of educational psychology—How do people learn? and What are the best ways to teach them?—open additional issues, among them: Do youngsters develop by stages that control the rate at which they learn? What is intelligence? Can teaching enhance intelligence? What role do attitudes play in teaching and learning? Can we measure accurately how much a student has learned, or how much has been taught?

Responses to such questions fill the thousands of books and articles published each year by psychologists, learning theorists (who specialize, as Thorndike did, in the processes of learning), and educators. Some of the most important developments in psychology in this century have come about in the course of studying the problems involved in instructing youngsters and adults (Wittrock and Lumsdaine, 1977). Not surprisingly there are some difficulties.

Despite the hundreds of thousands—and perhaps millions—of hours that have been devoted to research, thought, and discussion, the answers to many of the questions remain fuzzy. Part of the difficulty originates in the nature of the object under study—humankind. People are complex creatures, and each of us is unique. So it obviously is impossible to predict accurately the behavior of any individual—much less that of a classroom full of individuals. Another part of the difficulty lies in the fact that educational psychology, like any other expanding science, incorporates various theories. A theory attempts to explain an observed behavior or phenomenon, and frequently there are several theories or explanations, all plausible. Disagreements among thinkers are inevitable.

GENERAL PRINCIPLES VERSUS INDIVIDUAL DIFFERENCES

No theory of human behavior is universally accepted. A major problem in constructing plausible theories about that behavior is that people are not, of course, all alike, and in an identical situation they react differently. For example, when an exam is announced for the near future, some students immediately start cramming and absorb what they read; others start cramming but are so worried about the exam that the cramming does them little good. Still others go off to a movie or make a date rather than face their books.

How are principles and individual differences complementary?

Does this mean that there is no general rule about what students will do before a test? Not at all. A few study little, we know; a few study extensively, and most of them study moderately. Therefore, we can develop a rule: students in general study moderately. Tests aside, much human behavior can be graphed in the same way, and variability in behavior does not invalidate the principle; but we must temper faith in broad principles. The principles are good guidelines about most people. But individual differences challenge educators to discover more exact principles to deal with the exceptions.

Often enough, principles seem to conflict, and student teachers confronting contradictory principles invariably demand, "But which is right?" The answer usually has to be, "We don't know—yet. Research so far has produced inconclusive results." Research may never produce laws that govern every teaching and learning situation. But two principles that seem contradictory can both actually be valid, for different circumstances or for different learners. We can favor one principle of behavior over another, but we should not trap ourselves into thinking that that principle governs all situations. Have we confused you? Relax. Educational psychology obviously is not so exact a science as physics, chemistry, or mathematics. It does represent, though, a great body of fact and theory about how youngsters develop and progress from diapers to gym suits, how they react to their environment, how they learn, how they can be taught as both a science and an art, adapting what science offers to your knowledge of your students' individual needs and characteristics. When you can do that, you will have become a good teacher.

This book will not make you a great teacher. We doubt that any book can. If you become great, you will do it on your own. But in this book we shall try to present, as fairly and as objectively as we can, the dominant and diverse ideas of the best minds in the field. You may accept some totally and discard some totally. Or you may, and probably will, contrive your own special and ever-changing blend. Whatever you do, we intend that this book should make you a better teacher than you would have been if you had not read it.

IN THE BEGINNING

Up to a little more than a century ago, you did not have to know much to teach. If you had been through sixth grade you qualified. Things had changed little since Thomas Jefferson formulated his radical plan for educating everyone for the good of the country. Jefferson proposed that all youngsters be sent to district schools free for three years to learn reading, writing, and arithmetic. At the end of the three years, all but the one brightest boy in each school were to be sent back to their father's ploughs or their mothers' kitchens or parlors. The brightest boy—girls were not in the running—was to be sent on free to boarding school, where classes of similar boys were to be weeded at the end of every year. The brightest of the bright would survive for a full six years of schooling. On their graduation after the sixth year, the top half of the class would go on to college, from which its members would emerge, it was hoped, to become leading citizens or to govern. The lower half of the class were to become teachers.

Jefferson's scheme never caught on. In any case, his college graduates would not have been specifically trained to teach. The first special schooling for teachers did not come until much later. New York State led the way in 1854 by subsidizing teacher training in special classes in private academies, and Massachusetts established the first true normal school in 1839. Then things speeded up. By 1897, more than half the country's colleges and universities offered courses in teaching, which included what was then called "child study."

"I buy John Locke's idea that these kids enter the world with an empty noodle. I try to load it up by having them practice, practice, practice with stimulating activities."

The Father of Educational Psychology?

So many thinkers have been identified as the father of educational psychology that one may wonder, says Charles (1976), about the legitimacy of the offspring. But a strong case can be made for Juan Luis Vives, a Spaniard born in 1492 who lectured in Paris and Bruges before settling in England at the court of King Henry VIII, where he was a good friend of Catherine of Aragon. When Henry divorced Catherine, Vives left England in a hurry and never returned. Vives expounded his ideas on educational psychology in his book *De Tra-*

dendis Disciplinus (1531). Among those ideas:

Facts should be arranged in orderly fashion to impress them on the memory.

Practice is essential to learning, and material to be learned should be repeated aloud and written down.

Interest in material is vital to learning it.

Teaching should take into account individual differences in children, and pay special attention to the retarded, the blind, and the deaf.

Students should be evaluated on the basis of their own achievements, rather than by comparison with others. ■

The Early Thinkers. Fascination with the development of youngsters and its relation to education, however, is as old as western civilization. In the fifth century B.C., the Greek philosopher Democritus wrote of the advantages of education and of how home environment influenced children. A century later, Aristotle and Plato considered many of the questions that still concern educational psychologists and teachers. What were the purposes of education? How did students learn? How much did home environment influence learning? Should different kinds of youngsters be educated differently? How much could instruction accomplish in moral, physical, and emotional development?

Closer to our own times, the Frenchman René Descartes (1596–1650) opened up an argument yet to be settled: he contended that true knowledge derived from ideas with which we are born, rather than from experience. The Englishman John Locke (1652–1704) stressed in *Some Thoughts Concerning Education* a dramatically different position. Locke believed that people began life equipped with only a body: the mind was a *tabula rasa* or blank tablet, on which experience would etch knowledge. The opposing contentions of Descartes and Locke foreshadowed the continuing, current debate over the relative influences of heredity and environment or, as psychologists put it, *nature* versus *nurture.* The Swiss-born thinker Jean Jacques Rousseau (1712–78) proposed in his novel *Émile* a system of education designed to make youngsters morally and intellectually self-reliant and therefore free. (He never tried it on his own five illegitimate children, whom he gave away for adoption.)

Borrowing some ideas from Descartes, Locke, and Rousseau, the Swiss educational reformer Johann Heinrich Pestalozzi (1746–1827) argued that teaching ought to focus on drawing out students' ideas and capabilities, rather than on drilling information into children. But a German named Johann Friedrich Herbart, who had met Pestalozzi, was the first to devise an approach

How did forerunners lay the groundwork for present-day educational psychology?

to education that had psychology as its avowed basis. To Herbart, the human mind was an arena in which ideas contended actively for supremacy. Herbart's work remained almost unknown for two decades after he died in 1841, but by 1890 it had become the pervasive influence in American education.

The Pioneers. Thus, educational psychology's seeds did not suddenly sprout in an intellectual desert: the philosophical ground was fertile and well tilled. The seeds began to germinate in the 1880s. Sir Francis Galton, who turned to anthropology after reading Darwin, started measuring the speed of human reactions and devising psychological tests. G. Stanley Hall, president of Clark University, began to employ questionnaires to discover how children's minds work. James McKeen Cattell, an admirer of Galton, devised mental tests for his students at the University of Pennsylvania and later at Columbia. The tests' results had no bearing on his students' standing in class, Cattell discovered, and that outcome discouraged further testing for a while. The philosopher William James wrote *Talks to Teachers* (1899), a book you would find still lively and useful because of its intriguing mix of philosophy and psychology. (Psychology as a science was sired by the study of philosophy. Nearly all contemporary theories in psychology rest on philosophical assumptions, though the assumptions may be unstated. Ancient philosophical disagreements reappear today in competing theories about the psychology of human behavior.)

What distinguished the work of the "pioneers"?

Meanwhile, Alfred Binet, working at the Sorbonne in Paris, with the help of Theophile Simon, devised the Binet Scale for measuring intelligence. Intended for sorting out retarded children so that they could be given special instruction, the Binet Scale, which was first published in 1905–08, developed into the widely used Stanford-Binet tests that yield those controversial IQs (intelligence quotients). The Binet Scale became the Stanford-Binet Test when Lewis M. Terman adapted it for America and renamed it for the university at which he was based.

But the first true, full-time American educational psychologist—albeit within a limited scope—was Thorndike, who devoted his more than forty years at Columbia University's Teachers College to searching for laws of learning. He conducted his research as rigidly as though he were a physicist, and he did establish a number of laws of learning. Although Thorndike was concerned with applying his research methodology to classroom problems, he was more interested in how people learned than in applying the information to teaching.

What Is Happening Now

Since Thorndike, and especially within the last decade or so, developments in education have come faster than ever before in the nation's or the world's history. Some result from advances in scholarly research and psychological theory. Some reflect the mood of the times, expressed in judicial decisions and new laws. All will affect your teaching career. The following list shows only a few of the major developments:

1. A surge of interest in cognitive psychology, which concerns itself with what goes on in people's heads, rather than with their observable behavior. One leader in this area has been the Swiss child psychologist Jean Piaget (1896–1980). Piaget held that all children develop by the same series of stages, which appear in unvarying order, although the timing of the stages differs among individuals. Other recent research has shed new light on how the brain functions and how its working relates to intelligent behavior. Still other studies have focused on the learning and use of concepts. These topics are discussed in chapters 2, 3, 6, and 8.

2. Increased attention to the nature of intelligence. From a narrow interest in IQ tests, research and theory have begun to change direction and turn to consideration of new views of intelligence. For example, much research now focuses on mental processes that underlie intelligent behavior, in a field called "information processing." Here, psychologists explore the relationships among memory, language, problem-solving, and thinking. Accompanying interest in the nature of intelligence is rising doubt about the way we have been measuring intelligence. Skepticism about the IQ score and new theories about intelligence are considered more fully in Chapter 3.

3. Increased influence on educators of the philosophy of behaviorism and of the principles of behavior modification, which derives from the philosophy. Behaviorism holds that all human and animal activity consists of reactions—called responses—to external forces, i.e., stimuli from the environment. Behavior modification puts that principle to practical use: it seeks to change behavior by changing the environment. Behavior modification and its classroom application are considered in chapters 5 and 10.

Are new developments related to old concerns?

4. Advances in educational technology. Computers have been enlisted in recent years as teacher aides: they keep records, program instruction, even serve as more or less private tutors. One computerized instructional system, for example, breaks down the curriculum of a course into scores of units: students are tested to determine their levels of knowledge, are individually assigned appropriate units and stick with their units until they master them. In another system, which applies the philosophy of behaviorism, the computer asks multiple-choice questions, the student presses a button in response, and the computer indicates whether the response is right or wrong.

5. Benjamin S. Bloom's (1964) conclusions that (a) general intelligence apparently increases as much between conception and age four as it does between ages five and eighteen; (b) environment, a child's home life, has its greatest effect on a child's characteristics when the child is changing fastest, in the first four years, and the least effect when the child is changing least

rapidly; (c) a child's mental growth appears to relate more to the child's environment than to the child's initial endowment of brains.*

6. Innovations in teaching theory. Among these is the approach to teaching procedures embodied in Bloom's Theory of School Learning, which is discussed later in this chapter.

All these developments relate directly to teaching and learning. Of equal importance are developments in the field of education that reflect changes in society's views. Among these developments are:

1. The Coleman Report (1966) on racial segregation in schools and two 1975 follow-up studies by the 1966 report's chief author. The new work significantly modifies the original conclusions. The 1966 survey determined that black pupils were segregated in varying degrees everywhere in the country and almost totally in the South. It also showed that the greater the rate of segregation, the lower the achievements of minority group students. The report's findings have been frequently cited in support of integration.

   In his 1975 studies, James S. Coleman determined that schools in the Southeast, where the black population is proportionally largest, were the least segregated. But segregation has increased slightly in New England and the Middle Atlantic states (1975a).

   Coleman suggests that "forced desegregation" may intensify segregation in big cities with large black populations because middle-class whites are moving to all-white suburbs, and to a lesser extent, are enrolling their children in private schools (1975b).

   Though he continues to support integration, Coleman proposes reconsideration of present methods of striving for complete integration. He suggests that students choose their schools, with the schools' racial balance constituting the only limitation (1975b). This alternative to court-ordered busing is discussed in Chapter 16, under the heading *Magnet Schools*.

Does educational psychology relate to broad societal issues?

2. Federal legislation, passed late in 1975, that is directly affecting 8 million "handicapped" children and virtually every classroom in the country. The legislation, officially known as Public Law 94–142, is intended to provide "full equality of opportunity" for education to youngsters who have been described as "learning disabled" or "emotionally disturbed" or "educable mentally retarded" or who have other disabilities. The law requires that such children be given all the special help they may need to fulfill their potential. It also requires that they get their help, as much as possible, in the least restrictive environment. That practice is called *mainstreaming* be-

---

* Bloom's findings greatly influenced the establishment of Head Start, a program of preschool instruction intended to compensate for deficiencies in children's home environment. The findings also inspired public and professional interest in nursery schools and kindergarten, and moved parents and educators to look afresh at primary education. But Head Start has become highly controversial because its results have been less impressive than its supporters had predicted.

"Back to the basics. It's fashionable right now, thanks to media that make a big deal about it. Some of us never left the basics; we kept hitting away right through all the fads. It's a good thing, too, because I'm not worried about getting my kids into non-basic things. They're already competent in reading and math."

cause it is supposed to draw the handicapped into the mainstream of schooling. You will probably encounter two or three such "exceptional" students in any class you teach. Their distinguishing characteristics and the ways such students may be taught are considered in Chapter 11.

3. Intensive pressure on educators to show results. A movement toward what is called *accountability* demands that teachers and school administrators produce visible evidence of the success of their efforts. A related development called *back-to-basics* is now widespread and often misused. The theme of accountability underlies many of the topics covered in Part IV of this book.

POPULAR AND UNPOPULAR OPINION

Have the changes improved education, or will they improve it in the future? What does the public, which pays the bill, think of current American education?

In a barbershop not long ago, one of us overheard the following from a man getting a haircut:

> Yeah. Yuh know? My boy Joe is in the fifth grade and last night he asks me, "Pop, how do you divide 265 by 22?" Whatsa matter with teachers? I bet they make more than I do and they don't teach the kids nothin'. That school board oughta make 'em shape up or go look for another job.

How does the public view today's education?

Barbershop one-person surveys do not constitute scientific evidence, we know. But the man's opinion reflected the changing public sentiment about education. The first Gallup poll on education, taken in 1969, concluded, "The teaching profession probably has never been held in higher esteem in this nation" (Elam, 1973, p. 23). For example, one question asked that year was, "Would you like to have a child of yours take up teaching in the public schools as a career?" Seventy-five percent said yes and 15 percent said no. But, in each year since 1974, the Gallup poll asked, "Students are often given the grades A, B, C, D, and Fail to denote the quality of their work. Suppose the *public* schools themselves, in this community, were graded in the same way. What grade would you give the public schools here—A, B, C, D, or Fail?" The results were:

Ratings	1974	1975	1976	1977	1978	1979	1980
A	18%	13%	13%	11%	9%	8%	10%
B	30	30	29	26	27	26	25
C	21	28	28	28	30	30	29
D	6	9	10	11	11	11	12
Fail	5	7	6	5	8	7	6
Don't know/no answer	20	13	14	19	15	18	18

The figures could be worse, you may say. After all, 48 percent in 1974 and 43 percent in 1975 marked the schools A or B. But among people between 18 and 29 years of age, 40 percent rated the schools A or B in 1974 and only 27 percent did in 1980. Perhaps even more significant, 40 percent of the college-educated gave the schools Cs or Ds in 1980, compared with 29 percent in 1974 (Gallup, 1980, p. 35).

The Problems. People polled in 1980 ranked the schools' ten most pressing problems thus:

1. Lack of discipline
2. Use of dope/drugs
3. Poor curriculum/poor standards
4. Lack of proper financial support

5. Integration/busing
6. Large schools/too many classes/overcrowding
7. Difficulty in getting good teachers
8. Parents' lack of interest
9. Teachers' lack of interest
10. Pupils' lack of interest/truancy (Gallup, 1980, p. 34).

There was a time when social and technological change was synonymous with progress. Today that equation is doubtful, and when unwanted change happens, we search out reasons and lay blame. As one of the most populated institutions, schools are easy to blame. But in the swirl of criticism directed toward schools and teachers, positive outcomes of the schools are often overlooked. For example, in 1950, less than half of the students finished high school. Today over three-fourths do (Hodgkinson, 1979).

Moreover, the problems felt by the public do not all originate in the schools. In the 1972 Gallup poll on education, 57 percent of those questioned blamed poor schoolwork on the students' homes (Elam, 1973). The schools, however, are expected to cope with these problems.

The problems have been around a long time. Even in 1661, when New York was still New Amsterdam, the city's Latin schoolmaster, Alexander Carolus Curtius, was called on the carpet by the burgomasters. The charge against him was that he "did not keep strict discipline over the boys in his school, who fight among themselves and tear the clothes from each other's bodies, which he should prevent and punish." Curtius replied that "some people do not wish to have their children punished" and he asked for a law to back him up. He did not get it, and he quit (Stokes, 1922, p. 210).

Are schools doing anything right?

Remedies. George Gallup has also asked the public to recommend ways in which the school might improve. In 1979, they responded:

1. Improve the quality of teachers
2. Increase discipline
3. Set higher standards
4. Give students more individual attention
5. Put more emphasis on the basics—the three Rs
6. [Improve] management and direction of schools
7. Establish closer relations with parents (Gallup, 1979, p. 36).

The list represents a tall order. And yet, major objectives of educational psychology are to reduce problems and to help with improvements. That is not so far-fetched as it sounds, and the situation is not so bleak as it looks.

Educational psychologists, sometimes thought to be afloat in irrelevant theory and research, do shape theory and research findings into practical applications for the classroom. The applications discussed throughout this text have resulted from closing the gap between theory and practice. For example, inserting questions into written passages is one simple technique repeatedly

"I like a busy class. I like children to come into a class where it looks like there's going to be a lot going on. Not after they've been here two or three weeks but the day they walk in. I think the physical environment is going to dictate the psychological environment to the kids. If they come in here and find nothing and I just waste time for a day they get the idea. 'Oh, this is going to be a laugh.' New teachers ask me, 'What do you suggest I do the first day?' and I say, 'Establish a discipline the first five minutes, and if you don't, you can forget it. You're in charge.'

I spend most of the first day just explaining my philosophy of education to them. What they can expect from me. What they can expect from themselves. I'm not going to demand their respect, I hope to earn it—if I haven't already done so from what they know about me. And I always give them a sheet with a list of incomplete questions—'I think this room will be. . .'—and they have to finish the statements. 'I hope the year turns out to be. . . .'; 'Our teacher seems to. . . .' Then at the end of the year I give them a sheet, 'I wish Mr. Robinson would. . . .' It's amazing the answers you get; they're honest too. And I tell them there are no correct answers."

shown to improve achievement; this practice began as esoteric research on how humans process information in their heads. That same line of research has now developed a large number of classroom applications, described further in chapters 6 and 8.

With the combined efforts of theorists, researchers, and practitioners, 85 percent of American children are doing "quite well" in school (Havighurst and Neugarten, 1975). But the other 15 percent cannot be dismissed as uneducable: the law would not permit that even if some uptight school board wanted to try. The national philosophy of equality of opportunity for all demands that the 15 percent be given every chance to learn all that they are capable of absorbing—and what they *can* absorb under certain conditions may surprise you. In dealing with them—and with the other 85 percent—the schools are not without their faults. But many of the schools' failures might be turned into successes, we believe, by educational psychology.

THE TEACHER'S ROLE

One of your most important and challenging—and enjoyable—tasks as a teacher will involve the application of educational psychology to create a classroom environment that will elicit desirable behavior on the part of your students. Let's say that desirable behavior means an eagerness to learn (though of course it means much more). Simple, isn't it? No!

What is the role of educational psychology? the teacher's role?

Educational psychology, remember, is not an exact science. Too many variables are embodied in every student and every class. Teaching, as Gilbert Highet put it, is not like inducing a chemical reaction. Students are more than combinations of chemicals. You will have to experiment constantly and to ask yourself constantly whether or not your experiment is working. Any serious experiment in an exact science starts with the premise that, on the basis of what we know, doing so-and-so should produce such-and-such a result. But educational psychology constitutes what we know and what we *think* we know. Thus, you can never be certain that a given way of teaching a given lesson will work. It may have been successful last year, but this year's class is different. This year's class may even be different today from yesterday. The brightest child in the class, whose questions stimulate most of the others, may have had a run-in at breakfast with Mother or Dad and be in no mood to concentrate on social studies.

Thus, the best way to discover whether or not a lesson will work is to try it. If it isn't working, two or three or half a dozen of the findings and theories you will encounter in this book will suggest alternative approaches.

But you—and no one else in the classroom and no theories—must determine whether and when and how to shift gears. The theories are your tools, not your manual of standard operating procedure; you and not your students must take responsibility for decision in the classroom. At this point in any educational psychology course someone is certain to protest, "But that's not democratic!" Let's face it. The classroom is not the place to practice pure democracy. Even the best of democracies set a minimum age for voters, and you won't have many voters in your classes. Even the best of democracies demand leadership. From Village Hall to White House, we choose leaders. In the classroom, you are the leader. Educational psychology should keep you from becoming a dictator.

Many responsibilities of teachers are determined by the teachers' particular jobs and environments. An eleventh-grade home economics teacher in a rural school has a quite different role from a playground supervisor in a large city. No book can prescribe specifics for every such situation. But this book *can* offer some guidance that should apply in any teaching job.

Learning is a responsibility shared by teacher and students. The teacher introduces materials, lectures, manages discussions, asks questions—in effect manipulating the environment to encourage learning. When students demonstrate their intention to learn, the teacher takes the credit—as human beings do in every field of endeavor—for success. But when students fail, the teacher places the blame—as other human beings do—on external causes, such as student incapacity.

The balance of shared responsibility does not shift when things don't work out; it then is time to acknowledge that the instructional environment might have been better designed, to try harder, to experiment more. (Many of the ideas and applications throughout this text are aimed toward teacher responsibility in planning, arranging, and evaluating learning environments, and toward helping students to develop a sense of responsibility.)

Is a teacher responsible for too many things?

Another important component of the teacher's role deals with the nature of learning. Instruction is usually intended to produce two rather different results. One is the acquisition of facts, definitions, rules, concepts—a body of knowledge. Sometimes the urgency of acquiring the facts obscures the equal importance of knowing what to do with them. In instructional planning, teachers must contrive techniques to achieve both results, and that requires considerable forethought. Without it, the shrewd matching of individual needs and teaching tactics remains hard to achieve. But plans must not be rigid rules, for unexpected events may demand their modification. Successful teaching is thus a constant interplay between planning for the future and working in the present.

A Practical Way to Work

However you apply the principles of educational psychology, you will want and need to organize your approach to actual teaching. There is a method that can succeed in countless classrooms. Its title, Bloom's Theory of School Learning (1976), sounds a little imposing. But its design is fairly simple and commonsensical. It is built on several major developments in instructional theory over the past twenty years, most notably Robert Glaser's (1976) model

Figure 1.1. Bloom's Theory of School Learning

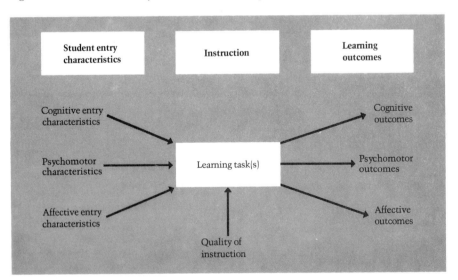

Constructs: The Terms of the Trade

Many of the terms of psychology involve *hypothetical constructs,* or abstract summaries of invisible processes. These processes are assumed to occur somewhere within the human being, but they cannot be seen, touched, or measured directly. The processes must be inferred from their observable results. Learning, motivation, self-control, and intelligence are constructs, for example. We see the outcomes of learning, in the form of behavior, but we cannot see the learning itself. It goes on mysteriously under the cover of our skulls and probably involves hundreds of minute chemical and physical changes in the brain. When we observe changes in behavior, we take this as evidence of the construct called *learning.*

As you will see in Chapter 5, some scientists try not to use constructs in their analysis of human behavior. They rely strictly on observable evidence and avoid speculation about a human's inner workings. For most of us, though, constructs are part of our day-to-day language, and it is difficult to dispense with them.

Constructs can be handy shortcuts in communicating about complicated internal events. They permit the exchange of ideas in the field without long explanations. But their definitions should be fairly clear. When the meaning of a construct is fuzzy, its use can lead to misunderstandings and disagreements about the processes of learning and teaching. In this book, many constructs are introduced, and we shall define them as we use them for the first time. The Important Terms lists at the ends of chapters and the Glossary at the end of the book will help you to get a grip on slippery constructs. ■

of instruction originally published in 1962, and John Carroll's model of school learning, which appeared in 1963. Figure 1.1 provides a visual overview of Bloom's theory. Don't let the terms intimidate you.

Student entry characteristics are the characteristics that a student brings to a learning task *and* that are important to the accomplishment of the task. (The color of a student's eyes is a characteristic but it is irrelevant to learning, so it does not qualify as an entry characteristic.) Another way to describe these characteristics is to say that they *interact* with instruction and influence what gets learned and how. For example, if an assessment of entry characteristics shows that Wayne has a short attention span and does not respond well to oral instruction, you will have to alter your methods to match Wayne's needs. Student entry characteristics divide conveniently into three groups: *cognitive, affective,* and *psychomotor. Cognitive* entry characteristics include such abilities as knowing, understanding, comprehending, and achieving. These characteristics determine the extent to which learning can take place. *Affective* entry characteristics include a student's feelings, emotions, attitudes, interests, values, and deep-seated self-concepts and aspects of personality. They help determine the conditions under which the learner will engage in learning. *Psychomotor* characteristics are observable movement skills. Dancing, holding a pencil, and catching a ball typify psychomotor behaviors. Bloom's theory acknowledges affective and psychomotor characteristics, but he focuses sharply on the cognitive domain because "such learning constitutes a major part of schooling." (Bloom, 1976, p. 69). On the other hand, Simpson (1972) argues that psychomotor skills are exceedingly important in art and music, business and industrial education, agriculture, home economics, and of course, physical education.

What are the components of Bloom's Theory of School Learning?

Learning task, in a general sense, means whatever is supposed to be learned in school. It is the learning activity, project, or course with which the learner must deal. A learning task may contain a variety of ideas, procedures, or behaviors to be learned over a fairly short time. The elements may be unrelated, or they may be highly interdependent.

Quality of instruction relates to what the teacher does; that is, how the teacher arranges the classroom environment so that students may learn. The quality of instruction determines the efficiency with which the learner will accomplish a learning task. *Quality of instruction* is considerably more complex than merely "good" or "bad" instruction. Offering cues to learners, requiring student participation, and providing feedback exemplify things teachers can do that contribute to the quality of instruction. Part II of this text considers many of these techniques in detail.

Learning outcomes, of course, refer to the level of accomplishment in a learning task. The tasks, then, can be regarded as goals to be achieved, and the outcomes as indications of whether or not the goals are met. Like entry characteristics, learning outcomes are of three general types, cognitive, affective, and psychomotor.

In applying Bloom's theory, the teacher strives to understand *who* the students are and what they are capable of learning, develops goals to be achieved and instructional procedures to be followed, and determines how well the goals have been met. Bloom's model describes a process that continually unfolds. The evaluation of learning outcomes gives us hints about the quality of instruction, the appropriateness of learning tasks, and the care with which we assessed entry characteristics. As students change, we will naturally adapt the model to fit the unique needs of the class.

Because the theory has so much potential for guiding teaching and learning, we have used it to help structure some of this book. In this chapter, we have introduced you to a developing science that should aid you to teach. In Part I we will consider student entry characteristics, both affective and cognitive. In Part II we will treat issues related to learning tasks and to quality of instruction. In Part III we will introduce theory and technique for measuring learning outcomes. Finally, in Part IV we will discuss how accountability has given rise to several new directions in educational psychology.

Summary

Teaching is both an art and a science. The artistry must be supplied by the teacher. Educational psychology provides a body of fact and theory about the workings of the human mind and facilitates the practice of the art. It concerns itself primarily with two questions: (1) How do people learn? and (2) What is the best way to teach them?

Educational psychology offers no single set of answers. That is partly because educational psychologists differ sharply among themselves. Also, educational psychology remains and probably will remain an inexact science because it deals with the mental processes of human beings and no two human beings are precisely alike.

The public's opinion of school systems has become more critical in recent years, and there is considerable demand that teachers be held responsible for the quality and quantity of students' learning. Yet most people agree that education is better than it was when they went to school.

If educational psychology is to help reduce the problems that confront educators, teachers must be willing to experiment and constantly to scrutinize results. Experimentation is best conducted within the broad framework called Bloom's Theory of School Learning. Under that system, a teacher determines what students already know, who they are, and what they are expected to accomplish. In another step, the teacher employs instructional procedures that seem appropriate to the students' abilities and the teacher's objectives. In the next step, the teacher considers whether the objectives have been attained, and if not, why not.

Other important aspects of a teacher's role include acceptance of shared responsibility for their students' achievement or nonachievements, and a commitment to planning and forethought, to help learners not only to acquire knowledge but to understand how to use it.

Chapter Study Guide

CHAPTER REVIEW

1. If you believe that teaching is an art rather than a science, you would be most likely to

   a. systematically try different approaches to teaching an area such as reading, and then comparatively evaluate each approach.
   b. practice until you have mastered the various techniques for motivating students, and then select a single technique for use in your classroom.

    c. improvise or combine different methods of presenting material to a class until you find a method both you and your students are satisfied with.

    d. teach in an unstructured rather than a structured classroom.

    e. b and d above.

2. Jefferson's plan for the education of the nation

    a. assumed that all individuals were equally capable in the area of academics.

    b. did not provide specific training to individuals who were going to become teachers.

    c. was so widely accepted that it has had a great influence on our present system of education.

    d. included specific instruction in farming and homemaking to ensure the development of the emerging nation.

    e. involved "rotating" teachers, so that everyone would take a turn at teaching.

3. It is correct to assume that educational psychology

    a. has received some attention in the past, but has flourished most in the twentieth century.

    b. is concerned primarily with the testing and evaluation of abilities.

    c. is essentially an American field of study, and has received limited attention in other countries.

    d. regards teaching as a science that can be mastered rather than as an art that must be practiced.

    e. can solve most classroom problems if applied carefully.

4. Teaching and learning are often companions, but

    a. teaching does not necessarily lead to learning and learning does not always require teaching.

    b. they must be separated to study the effects of each.

    c. only teaching is influenced by attitudes; learning generally is not.

    d. only learning can enhance intelligence; teaching cannot.

    e. a and b above.

5. The more recent developments in educational psychology show that

    a. secondary school teachers have a greater effect on their students than do primary and preprimary school teachers.

    b. racial integration has been effective in providing equal educational environments for the students in the United States.

    c. intelligence is far less complex than psychologists had thought, and computer technology can help accurately measure human intelligence.

    d. classroom teachers will need to know and understand more about the needs of exceptional or handicapped students.

    e. cognitive psychology, though an important approach to thought at the turn of the century, now contributes little to the understanding of behavior.

6. Educational psychology

    a. is limited in classroom applications because of its research orientation.

    b. is built on the results of controlled experiments with objective outcomes.

    c. is composed of a series of related principles and theories that can help enhance teaching.

    d. as a science describes *what* learning is, and as an art describes *who* students are.

    e. is an art developed during the late nineteenth and early twentieth centuries, and is currently devoted primarily to experimentation and research.

7. The problem with many theories, particularly those that apply to human behavior, is that

    a. they do not work.

    b. they cannot account for some of the individual differences found in people.

    c. they are only general rules and cannot be used to predict actions.

    d. variability in the theory leads to inaccurate prediction.

    e. they often conflict with or contradict the principles applied in classrooms.

FOR FURTHER THOUGHT

1. Why, according to Gilbert Highet, is teaching an art rather than a science? How do the authors attempt to reconcile Highet's views on this subject with Thorndike's? From your classroom experience to date, who seems closest to the truth—Highet, Thorndike, or the authors?

2. Was Jefferson's goal of "educating everyone for the good of the country" a legitimate one? Other purposes of education frequently cited are to prepare students for job roles, to help them realize their personal potential, and to perpetuate a cultural or academic tradition. To which of these purposes do you attach the most significance?

3. What difference might it make in your teaching approach if you believed, with Locke, that all learning comes through experience? If you believed, with Descartes, that true knowledge comes from inborn ideas? Which school of thought would be most likely to make use of student self-expression? learning through discovery? teacher exposition? a back-to-basics approach? drill?

4. How good a judge is the general public of the quality of educational programs or developments? Do you agree generally with the public's assessment of the schools' biggest problems, as registered in the 1980 Gallup Poll (pp. 12–13)?

5. What is the value of an instructional model like Bloom's Theory of School Learning? Are there circumstances in which such a theory might limit a teacher?

6. How has legislation changed school segregation, both theoretically and in practice? What are some alternatives to busing students to integrate schools? Why has segregation increased, proportionately, in the New England and Middle Atlantic states, even though these areas are traditionally thought of as politically liberal?

IMPORTANT TERMS

educational psychology

Bloom's Theory of School Learning

entry characteristics

cognitive characteristics

affective characteristics

psychomotor characteristics

construct

SUGGESTED READINGS

BLOOM, B. S. *Human characteristics and school learning.* New York: McGraw-Hill, 1976. A review of studies that form the background for Bloom's Theory of School Learning.

COLADARCI, A. P. The relevancy of educational psychology. *Educational Leadership*, 1956, 13(8), 489–492. In a short article many regard as a classic, Coladarci argues that the effective teacher is an experimenter. Yet, he reminds us, scientific scrutiny cannot answer all our questions about teaching, and we must be ingenious—as an artist—in improving our effectiveness.

ELAM, S. (ed.). *A decade of Gallup polls of attitudes toward education 1969–1978.* Bloomington, IN: Phi Delta Kappa, 1978. Outcomes of the first ten Gallup polls on education. A quick means of comparing changes in public attitude over the years. The annual Gallup polls continue, and are published with Gallup's commentary each year in an issue of the professional journal *Phi Delta Kappan.*

WATSON, R. I. A brief history of educational psychology. *Psychological Record*, 1961, 11, 209–242. A detailed record of the wandering origins of educational psychology from the early Greek philosophers to about 1945.

ANSWER KEY

1. c; 2. b; 3. a; 4. a; 5. d; 6. c; 7. b

PART

I

Student Entry Characteristics

Every human being is endowed—or burdened—with unique characteristics that distinguish him or her from all other people. Those characteristics influence the ways in which the individual confronts challenges and responds to external pressures such as instruction. Whether your future pupils are kindergartners recently emerged from the toddling stage or hulking high school seniors, each one will be different and will behave differently. But although there are countless variations in the ways that people—including youngsters in school—react to circumstances and interpret and acquire information, there are also many similarities. The similarities manifest themselves in both personality characteristics and in stages of human development. In the next three chapters, which constitute Part I of this book, we shall consider the similarities and the differences. Specifically, we shall explore: *Cognitive development* and the major theories that seek to explain how thinking germinates and matures in a systematic, stepwise fashion. *Intelligence* and what different psychologists think it is, how we attempt to measure it, and how it relates (or does not relate) to language.

Personality and affective and moral development, which concern how people get the way they are and what if anything can be done about it. In short, we shall be looking at "entry characteristics."

Our major objective in this exploration is to help you as a teacher to distinguish between behavior that is rooted deeply in personality and behavior that reflects a stage of development. Or, to put it another way, to distinguish between the differences and the similarities. Does that seemingly bright pupil, for example, really have extraordinary intelligence, or is he or she simply in a higher period of cognitive development than the rest of the class? It is important to know: the good teacher tailors instruction to students' similarities as well as to their differences and individual needs. You will make it easier for your students to learn if you know who and what they are. For that, you will have to look into their minds as well as at their performance in class. The three chapters of Part I are designed to guide the looking.

2

Cognitive Development

Is a child simply a miniature adult who has not yet acquired exerience, information, and a driver's license? Until well into this century, hardly anybody doubted that the answer was yes. Once children had reached what was called the *age of reason* at six or seven, it was accepted that they thought in the same way that grown-ups did. The educator John Dewey recalled that a boy was considered "a little man and his mind a little mind—in everything but size the same as that of the adult" (1956, p. 103).

Are children simply miniature adults?

But children do not perceive the world and organize knowledge as adults do, the Swiss scientist Jean Piaget and the American psychologist Jerome Bruner have concluded, and both Piaget and Bruner have some important things to say about the divergences.

To Piaget, a child differs from adults as much, we venture to say, as the caterpillar from the butterfly or the tadpole from the frog. Early in his sixty or so years of studying children—by sitting beside their cribs, joining them in their sandboxes, and cheating with them at marbles—Piaget concluded:

Children reason differently from adults.
They look at the world differently.
They live by a different philosophy.

So Piaget concentrated his investigations, and the vast amount of writing in which he reported their results, on the development of *cognition*. Cognition here means not merely *knowing*, which is its everyday definition, but how human intelligence organizes and utilizes knowledge. Piaget sought to deter-

"We assume that adolescents surge into abstract thought. So we usually give them a mountain of abstractions and see who can climb it. The whole class is offered the same mountain, and when the end of the unit comes, we measure how far each kid has climbed. There are two serious problems here. One is that thinking

mine what intelligence is, how children employ it to adjust to the world around them, and how children change with growth.

Piaget's interest in cognition led him to work briefly at Alfred Binet's institute in Paris in 1920. Piaget was asked to develop a standardized French version of reasoning tests, a task requiring him to question and interview children. He became convinced that the children's wrong, often zany, answers to questions revealed more about the children's thought processes than did their "right" answers. He came to believe that cognitive development is not simply a matter of acquiring more facts, but that young children think in a totally different way from older children and adults.

From his research, Piaget derived a theory of how cognition develops. Because Piaget's findings provide penetrating insight into the behavior and characteristics of youngsters from birth through adolescence, the implications of his theory are tremendous for parents and anyone else who works with children. Because his work is provocative, Piaget has both faithful followers and faithful critics.

Piaget's Theory of Cognitive Development

In Piaget's view, heredity, environment, and maturation—the process of growing up—all interact in the development of intelligence. Children—and adults—strive continually to adapt to their environments. Adaptation, Piaget

about abstractions takes far more practice than we give most kids. The second is that there is enormous variety in cognitive development. Some of them just aren't ready; others need more than we give them."

believed, represents a never-ending attempt to achieve a state of equilibrium or balance between individual and environment. Piaget called that the *equilibration factor*. Because none of us is ever static, a perfect, *continuing* balance remains beyond our reach; but in Piaget's view we keep trying for it.

ASSIMILATION AND ACCOMMODATION

Achievement of equilibrium even briefly involves, Piaget said, two complementary processes that he called *assimilation* and *accommodation*, which are essential to mental growth. Each of us has what Piaget called *cognitive structures* or *schemas* that represent what we know and how we look at our world. A schema is an organized pattern of thought or action, and our schemas determine how we respond at a given moment to people, objects, or occurrences.

How do assimilation and accommodation operate?

Assimilation is the process of internal organization whereby an individual fits new information into existing schemas. But much information and experience does not fit an existing schema, and disequilibrium results. So we then use the process of accommodation, which is a method of coping with new information by modifying existing schemas. Without accommodation, one would resemble a secretary who discards an important document because it falls under no category in the existing filing system. Absurd as that analogy may seem, lots of people *do* behave like that, rejecting information ("I don't believe it!"), not because it is false or incredible but because it does not fit into their schemas. They refuse to accommodate it in their already assimilated knowledge and beliefs.

Piaget applied the concept of equilibrium to knowledge in general. Each new piece of information either is assimilated, because it fits with existing schemas, or leads to modification of a schema through accommodation, the development of new patterns of thought and action. It is the equilibration process that determines where information is mentally routed.

For example, Steve, an eight-year-old, has always lived in Florida, and he has developed a schema for *snow* based on reading, on hearing about it, and on seeing it on television. Then, on a visit to Colorado, he encounters a snowstorm and runs out to play in it. As soon as he touches it, he exclaims in amazement, "It's *wet!*" He had known that snow was white, cold, and soft but had thought that it felt like cotton. He now has to change his schema for snow to accommodate this new and astonishing information.

How does the equilibration process promote growth?

Exercise on the seesaw of assimilation and accommodation, according to Piaget, produces cognitive growth. And this happens not only in children: assimilation and accommodation are part of the cognitive processes of adults as well.

Here is another example: Suppose one of your schemas involves identifying a particular person as a trusted friend. Every instance of his behavior toward you that is kindly is consistent with this understanding of him and is readily assimilated. Then one day you find that he has betrayed your confidence. You cannot assimilate this new information into your existing schema of "trusted friend." You may decide that he is, in fact, not a friend. Or you may accommodate your schema to include an occasional lapse on a friend's part and decide that a trusted friend will usually but not always be trustworthy. In one way or another you would have to incorporate the new information into the schema or modify the schema.

Most activities involve both assimilation and accommodation. Intelligent behavior is a type of biological adaptation that involves constructing a balance between the individual and the external environment, wherein the person both adapts to and changes the environment. A child actively explores, discovers, and, in a way, constructs reality. The end product of cognitive development is the capacity for logical, symbolic thought.

PERIODS OF DEVELOPMENT

Do cognitive periods emerge in strict sequence?

It is a major premise of Piaget's theory that *all* children *everywhere* progress from birth through adolescence by four separate periods of cognitive development (Figure 2.1). The periods, each of which is divided into stages, never vary in the order of their appearance, but children vary in the ages at which they enter the different periods. Even among mentally retarded youngsters, the progression from period to period differs from that of normal children only in that, as MacMillan (1977) has stated, its pace is slower.

Of these periods and stages, Piaget and his colleague Barbel Inhelder said, "Their order of succession is constant, although the average ages at which they occur may vary with the individual, according to his degree of intelligence or with the social milieu. . . . Each stage is characterized by an overall structure in terms of which the main behavior patterns can be explained. . . . These overall structures are integrative and non-interchangeable. Each results from the preceding one, integrating it as a subordinate structure, and prepares for the subsequent one, into which it is sooner or later itself integrated" (Piaget and Inhelder, 1969, p. 153). Biological maturation is the preeminent force that dictates the emergence of stages. Experience determines the extent to which a person's intellectual potential is realized.

What are Piaget's periods of mental development?

In each period, thought processes differ from those of past and future periods. Yet no definite boundaries set off one period from another. Progress from period to period resembles not a steady march along a highway but the probing of an army fighting in mountainous country. Children do not go to bed one evening in period 2, say, and awake the next morning in period 3.

Does each developmental period involve egocentrism?

Movement through the periods is characterized by a change in the structure of thinking, not just in the number of facts a child knows. There are changes in one's picture of the world and changes in logical thought processes. Thinking becomes more complex, more objective, less egocentric.

Egocentrism, which is present in each of the periods of growth, is the belief that one's own point of view is the only possible reality. As used here, the term does not mean selfish or arrogant behavior. It means that children cannot

Figure 2.1. Piaget's Theory: Four Periods of Cognitive Development

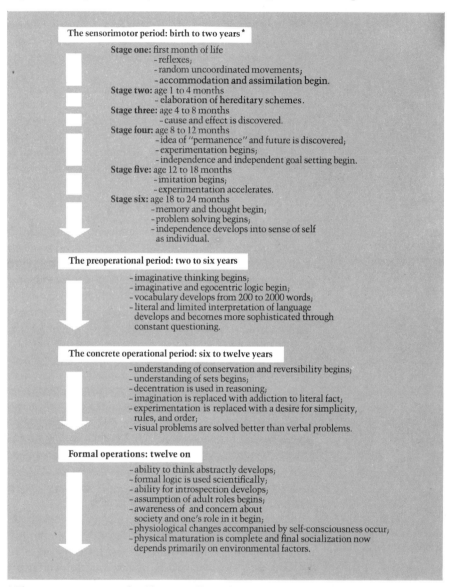

The sensorimotor period: birth to two years *

Stage one: first month of life
- reflexes;
- random uncoordinated movements;
- accommodation and assimilation begin.

Stage two: age 1 to 4 months
- elaboration of hereditary schemes.

Stage three: age 4 to 8 months
- cause and effect is discovered.

Stage four: age 8 to 12 months
- idea of "permanence" and future is discovered;
- experimentation begins;
- independence and independent goal setting begin.

Stage five: age 12 to 18 months
- imitation begins;
- experimentation accelerates.

Stage six: age 18 to 24 months
- memory and thought begin;
- problem solving begins;
- independence develops into sense of self
  as individual.

The preoperational period: two to six years

- imaginative thinking begins;
- imaginative and egocentric logic begin;
- vocabulary develops from 200 to 2000 words;
- literal and limited interpretation of language
  develops and becomes more sophisticated through
  constant questioning.

The concrete operational period: six to twelve years

- understanding of conservation and reversibility begins;
- understanding of sets begins;
- decentration is used in reasoning;
- imagination is replaced with addiction to literal fact;
- experimentation is replaced with a desire for simplicity,
  rules, and order;
- visual problems are solved better than verbal problems.

Formal operations: twelve on

- ability to think abstractly develops;
- formal logic is used scientifically;
- ability for introspection develops;
- assumption of adult roles begins;
- awareness of and concern about
  society and one's role in it begin;
- physiological changes accompanied by self-consciousness occur;
- physical maturation is complete and final socialization now
  depends primarily on environmental factors.

* These age categories are flexible, especially in the sensorimotor period.

distinguish their own thoughts and perceptions from objective, complex reality. They assume, therefore, that their personal perceptions are valid: other viewpoints must be mistaken. As we shall see, there are different levels and versions of egocentrism in each period, which give way to more objective forms of understanding of the world.

The Sensorimotor Period. Piaget calls the first period, which extends roughly from birth to two years of age, the *sensorimotor period*. The name derives from the fact that infants explore the world at first only by *senses* such as touch, and *motions* such as thrusting their fingers into their mouths. The child does not, at first, recognize him- or herself as a separate organism; infants cannot distinguish themselves from their environment. This is the most extensive stage of egocentricity. From the beginning, though, according to Piaget, the child is capable of initiating the action of which intelligence is born. In support of that contention, Piaget cited his son Laurent: on Laurent's second day of life, he began opening and closing his lips on a nipple that was not there. The child was not hungry; he had been fed. He was too young to have become addicted to the taste of milk or to the pleasure of being nursed. Piaget explained that Laurent was initiating action by practicing one of the few capibilities—sucking—with which he had been born.

The sensorimotor period, like subsequent periods of development, divides into stages. In the sensorimotor period, the first stage lasts only a month or so and is marked by hereditary reflexes such as sucking and crying, uncoordinated movements, and by rudimentary forms of assimilation and accommodation. The sucking reflex is a scheme, and the infant will suck a number of different things, exercising this scheme and assimilating objects—fingers, clothing—but he will also raise or turn his head to search for the breast or bottle when it is near; that is, he accomomodates, actively changing his behavior to obtain food by sucking.

By the second stage, from one to four months of age, the infant elaborates the basic hereditary schemes to include new objects. A baby will accommodate to strange new things such as a spoon or a thumb, and assimilate them into the sucking scheme. The baby can now repeat a sequence of movements (such as thumb-sucking), thereby establishing a habit. By beginning to listen rather than merely hearing, and by beginning to look rather than merely seeing, the child is launching a life based on learning. In the third stage, four to eight months, most children begin to discover cause and effect. "If I shake my crib, those whachamaycallems will jiggle." The baby knows the mobile will jiggle, because it jiggled the last time when the baby shook the crib accidentally. His or her striking, rubbing, shaking, and kicking seem to make interesting or pleasurable events happen over and over again. In short, cognition develops from experience, and the more experience, the more cognition. Piaget related that his daughter Lucienne, at five months, moved a foot to shake the doll hanging from the hood of her bassinet. When the doll shook, Lucienne looked at her foot—an indication of the beginning of understanding of cause and effect (1963, p. 158). In the same third stage, children start to follow moving objects with their eyes, often compulsively. But most babies in this stage have yet to comprehend that when something vanishes from view it still exists. Out of sight, out of mind. The stages are no more sharply defined by ages, however, than are the four major periods of development. Piaget's son Laurent was a mere six months and three days old when he began searching for a small box that Piaget had dropped to a sofa on which Laurent was lying. Laurent had not been able to follow the box's fall with his eyes because of the way Piaget deliberately had dropped it (1954, pp. 14–15). Laurent thus demonstrated that "out of sight, out of mind" no longer applied to him.

In the first three or so stages, most children know only *here* and *now*. "Yowl! yowl! I want my milk!" No amount of assurance that the bottle of milk is coming up will silence the squawking. It is not merely that the child does not understand speech. The child does not understand that there is a future—even an immediate future. A few months later, when the baby sees Mama warming the bottle, he or she realizes that help is on the way: the child has

What are the characteristics of the sensorimotor period?

Jean Piaget

Jean Piaget, the person who revolutionized the world's view of developmental psychology, was born in 1896 in Neuchâtel, Switzerland. The son of a highly organized and intellectual father and a religious, intense mother, Piaget preferred serious work to play even as a child. His lifelong preference for science and empiricism has been underscored by his repeated remarks about the foolishness of departures from "reality." By the age of ten, Piaget had published a paper on a part-albino sparrow he had seen in a park and was started on his way to a career in biology. By the age of fifteen, Piaget was considered to be an expert in the field of mollusk study and was invited to be the curator of the mollusk collection in the Musée d'Historie of Geneva. He decided to continue his education instead.

When Piaget was fifteen, his mother enrolled him in a six-week course in religious study. It was then that he faced what he described as one of the crises of his life. While never doubting the existence of God, Piaget was struck that intellectual people could accept church dogma that contradicted biological fact.

seen Mama warm the bottle many times before and now recalls what has followed.

It is in the fourth stage, from about eight to twelve months, that most children—despite the precocious Laurent—begin to search for vanished things and manifest a sense of *object permanence.* It is that sense that makes them fans of peek-a-boo games. Object permanence is the understanding that things exist apart from the self. This is the first step away from complete egocentricity. The fourth stage is also a time of experimentation such as throwing things. It is a time too for setting goals independently, such as reaching for the pipe Daddy left on a bedside ashtray and for pushing aside obstacles such as Daddy's restraining hand.

In the fifth stage, twelve to eighteen months, experimentation accelerates. Novelty becomes attractive. Infants try new ways of doing things that they have done many times before. Dolls, balls, rattles, and blocks go flying in different directions, by the child's intent, and their varying trajectories are watched by the infant with fascination. Imitation begins. Touch your eyebrow and the child will reach for his or her own.

The effect of the crisis was that Piaget developed a passion for philosophy and eventually decided to devote his life to developing a biological explanation of knowledge.

Piaget set about solving the problem in a highly organized fashion, undoubtedly modeling himself on his father. By the age of twenty-one, he had received his Ph.D. in biological science. He devoured literature in many fields, and went to work in Alfred Binet's laboratory helping to standardize an intelligence test. Claiming to be bored with the standardization routine, he was intrigued by children's *wrong* answers to test questions. He set about developing strategies and interview techniques that might allow more understanding of why wrong answers are produced. This occasion marked the beginning of Piaget's fifty years of research on the development of thinking.

Even in his eighties, Piaget continued to work diligently. He often arose at 4:00 A.M. and wrote, by hand, at least four publishable pages before attending classes and meetings. In the afternoon he walked or rode the bicycle which had become one of his trademarks, and contemplated new problems. Piaget once remarked, "I always like to think about a problem before reading about it" (Elkind, p. 14).

Piaget spent his summers "relaxing" in a spartan farmhouse in the Alps. No one knew of the location of the farmhouse except for his immediate family and a few intimate friends. It was here that Piaget isolated himself yearly and interpreted and summarized the research he had supervised in the previous year as the Director of the International Centre of Genetic Epistemology in Geneva. In the fall of 1980 Piaget's contribution ceased. ∎

Sources
Campbell, S. F. *Piaget sampler.* New York: John Wiley and Sons, 1976.
Elkind, D. Giant in the nursery—Jean Piaget. *New York Times Magazine*, May 26, 1968.
Hall, E. A conversation with Jean Piaget and Barbel Inhelder. *Psychology Today*, 1970, 3(12), p. 25.

In the sixth stage, from eighteen to twenty-four months, children become able to *think about doing things* instead of just doing things when the fancy strikes. They can form mental pictures of people and objects that are not present. With that newly acquired facility, they will imitate someone's action from a day or so before. They begin to solve problems, opening a bureau drawer and then opening the box within it in which Mama keeps a necklace. They are now thoroughly aware of themselves as individuals.

They are almost ready to enter the second major period of development. Their passage through the six stages of the sensorimotor period has not been a series of unrelated episodes. They entered each new stage only because they were armed with the experience and cognition they had gained in all the preceding substages. In those six stages, Piaget believed, they have laid the whole foundations on which they will build their intellects.

The Preoperational Period. The second major period of cognitive development Piaget called preoperational. It runs roughly from age two to age six. It derives its name from the sense in which Piaget used *operations* to mean mental activities or routines by which one combines or transforms information. The preoperational child is increasing in ability to reason and can perceive relationships, such as cause and effect, but the logic is still imprecise. During this period, the child is building a foundation for later periods; he or she now uses mental symbols, increases the use of language, and engages in imaginative play, but uses a kind of logic that is rudimentary and subjective.

Through symbols, children free themselves from confining realities and contrive worlds in which they are masters of all they survey. When a child refers to a wooden block as a fire truck, that block is a symbol and can be manipulated as if it were a miniature fire truck. When a child bathes and cooks for a doll, the doll is treated as if it were a living being.

Among the symbols the child employs are words, which are being acquired at a tremendous rate. Children enter the first stage of the period—from about two to about four—with a vocabulary of about 200 words. When they emerge from the second stage, at about six, their vocabulary will encompass perhaps 2000 words. But preoperational children use words differently from older children. Because the words are symbols, children use them to shape their world: as in *Alice's Adventures in Wonderland*, words mean only what the child wants them to mean, and the meanings may differ from those that you or we attribute to them.

Always literal in their interpretations of what they hear or read, children about to emerge from the preoperational period may sing *The Star-Spangled Banner* lustily without ever wondering why we would want to watch a ram's parts; in Sunday school, such children may take it for granted that Pontius Pilate worked for an airline. At other times, particularly in the earlier years of the preoperational period, an object's name is as much a part of the object as its shape, size, weight, and color. We recently asked a small boy why the Spaghetti-os he was eating were called Spaghetti-os. The answer: "Cause they're round like Spaghetti-os, and they taste like Spaghetti-os." And why is a duck called a duck? Because, "It *looks* like a duck, and it quacks like a duck."

The increasing use of mental symbols allows children to develop active imaginations. Patrick, at four, demonstrates this characteristic often. When his brothers and sisters were off at school, he would join them in his imagination. He began to tell what had supposedly occurred when he went to his imaginary school. One day he said that he had drawn the best picture at school that day. When his father said, "You did, huh?" he answered, "Yes, I nearly always do."

During the preoperational period the child is still quite egocentric. A. A. Milne's Winnie-the-Pooh expressed the child's egocentricity aptly: Sitting in a forest, Pooh heard a buzz.

> That buzzing-noise means something. You don't get a buzzing-noise like that, just buzzing and buzzing, without its meaning something. If there is a buzzing-noise, somebody's making a buzzing-noise, and the only reason for making a buzzing-noise that *I* know of is because you're a bee . . . and the only reason for being a bee that I know of is for making honey . . . and the only reason for making honey is so as *I* can eat it (1926, p. 4).

But when Pooh falls into a bush that proves prickly, he accepts the mishap as punishment for "*liking* honey so much." To the child at this age, justice is as much an inevitable part of life as having to go to bed. The child who plays with matches after being warned not to is going to get burned for disobedience, not because flame can be dangerous.

Because children are egocentric, they are impervious to adult reasoning: they will not remain quiet because Daddy is tired and wants to take a nap, because they cannot put themselves in Daddy's place. The only point of view the child knows is his or her own; there cannot be any other. That is why half a dozen children playing on the kindergarten jungle gym will all babble at once, none of them paying any attention to what the others are saying. That is why, too, the child cannot pass on information clearly: the child knows something, so you must know it too. If you explain to a child how a water faucet works (as Piaget has done) and ask the child to instruct another, the "instruction" will be incomprehensible. The first child will lack understanding of the second child's need for specifics. Or, if you are facing a child and ask that child to indicate his or her right and left hands, the child may reply correctly. But if you ask the same child, whom you are still facing, to indicate *your* right and left hands, the child will probably fail. The child cannot put him- or herself in your place.

The youngster of this age also cannot grasp the fact that quantity does not change with changing shape, a principle that Piaget called *conservation*. For example, at dinner, ten-year-old Tiffany cut up her baked potato and squashed the pieces, covering a good deal of her plate with mutilated potato. Five-year-old Andrea remarked, "I don't think I will cut up my potato the way Tiffany did because then it will be too big and I won't be able to eat it all."

"When I introduce new concepts I always like to include some common thing that the children can really identify with—in other words, something where they've already half-assimilated the idea without realizing it. As I do in this class: OK. Now there are three, *you might call these* properties, *or characteristics of air. It has weight. You saw that. It exerts a pressure. You saw that. . .and it takes up space. Now, can anyone spare me a lunch bag? . . . You've probably done this a thousand times. I'm going to* inflate *the bag. I'm going to blow it up, that's right—but we're going to say* inflate. *You won't be able to really tell a change in weight, but which of the three properties will you definitely* see *here? Right. Take a chip [token]. The air occupying space. And by blowing more in I'm putting air under pressure. [Blows more in, then quickly breaks bag, surprising students.] Now you know a tremendous force just occurred there. Look what it did to the bag. Imagine if we'd used the Goodyear blimp or something like that. Look at that. What caused that? Now you've probably done this many times and thought nothing of it —you just bang on the bag and that's the end of it. But by doing this we put the air under tremendous force and this is what happens."*

What are the characteristics of the preoperational period?

If you show a group of preoperational children like Andrea a short, broad glass of water and then pour the water into a tall, narrow glass, most of the children—as Piaget found—will tell you that the tall glass has more water in it. In short, preoperational children cannot reason abstractly; they can only judge by appearances.

Because they cannot reason abstractly, they also do not comprehend that if the water were poured back into the short, broad glass, it would rise only to its old level in that glass. Piaget called this concept *reversibility*. A grasp of reversibility, Piaget held, is the key to the understanding of conservation. Conservation and reversibility require children to deal with proportions as abstractions. If they lack that cognitive ability, they find it difficult to grasp concepts involving proportions, as in mathematics. Children can memorize, of course, how to add or subtract. But if children are to comprehend more fully the relationships between numbers, they must do more than memorize. Consider, for example, the problem of $2 + ? = 8$. To solve it the child must "see" numbers as proportions in space and realize that those proportions can be arranged in various configurations: the child then can detect the relationship between adding and subtracting in the problem. The manipulation of numbers that way—as distinct from calculations based on memorization—

requires abstract thinking, much as does the comprehension that the quantity of water does not change with the shape of the glass. Equipment that can be examined and manipulated is often of great value for teaching children of this age. Cuisenaire rods, for example, are sometimes used for teaching arithmetic, especially addition in the first grade.

In their drive to assimilate and accommodate, children ask questions endlessly. Near the end of the preoperational period, children are well able to remember information, storing it in their heads for future use. To their recognition of a past and a future, of which they are well aware, they have added a sense of time, although it may distort the clock and the calendar. ("Once upon a time, a very long time ago now, about last Friday" begins a story for Christopher Robin.) They not only benefit from experience, as they did in their sensorimotor period, but they can now recall and reenact experiences. A six-year-old boy whom we know will happily demonstrate for you how he trudged the last mile of the long climb from the bottom of Grand Canyon a few months ago. (He drags his feet.) Late in the preoperational period, children no longer believe that a duck is called a duck because it looks like a duck: they understand that a name is not part of an object but a label for it (and, presumably, that a rose by any other name would smell as sweet). Their application of the information often lacks formal logic, though. A man whom we know lived until he was six years old in a house that was heated only by a pot-bellied stove. Then his parents announced that they had bought a house with steam heat. To the six-year-old, steam heat meant steam locomotives, which he adored. He spent the whole first day at the new house waiting on the porch for a steam locomotive to go by. The absence of tracks in front of the house did not bother him a bit. In his preoperational, literal style of logic, his reasoning was perfectly sensible.

The Concrete Operational Period. The third period of cognitive development spans the ages of six or seven to about eleven or twelve. Children are now able to use mental operations such as classifying, seeing relationships, and comprehending concepts of number and spatial relations, but they use them only with particular objects that they can experience and manipulate. They have not yet reached the final stage of more abstract thought—hence the name of this period, concrete operations. As in all periods of development, the transition from preoperational to concrete operational thinking is gradual, but it is also revolutionary. When the transition has been completed, children think in an entirely new way.

What is meant by a cognitive operation?

Children at this age now have a concept of categories, or logical classes, and can comprehend *sets*, which crop up in arithmetic and mathematics courses at every level. First graders, presented with a jumble of marbles, buttons, and snips of paper, all in varying colors, will know what to do if you ask them to put together everything that is of the same color; blue marbles, blue buttons, and blue slips of paper will land in the same pile. Concrete operational children often have "collections" of various things, an activity made possible by the understanding of categories.

These children are now more capable of *decentration*. They have become able to consider two or more attributes of an object at the same time; they no longer *center* on a single attribute. Now if you give them the little problem of the short, broad glass and the tall, thin glass, they realize immediately that the water's quantity does not change. They can consider both height and width, and they can mentally reverse the operation of pouring the liquid.

What are the characteristics of the concrete operational period?

Because of their ability to decenter, they can now understand that an object may fit into two sets at once. Piaget once showed a group of five-, six-, and seven-year-olds a box that held twenty white and seven brown wooden beads. He asked each child in turn whether there were more white or brown beads. All got the answer right. Next Piaget inquired, "Are there more white or more wooden beads?" The younger children, still preoperational, replied, "There are more white than brown beads." They could not comprehend that beads could be both wooden and white or brown. The concrete operational children responded: "There are more wooden than white beads because all of the beads are wooden and only some are white."

Because children in the concrete operational period can reason abstractly only about things they have experienced, they solve visual problems more readily than verbal problems. Say to a fourth-grade class, "I have three trees in my yard, a pine, a fir, and a hemlock. The pine is taller than the hemlock but smaller than the fir. Which tree is the tallest?" Chances are most of the class will be baffled. But if you drew the three trees on the blackboard, you would not even have to ask the question.

The world expands for these children; now they can read, go places by themselves, and spend more time with other children. Through their increasing social interaction with others, they become more able to see the world from another's standpoint. This is a move away from the egocentric point of view. These children can explain the rules of a game so that another person can understand them. It is a period involving social cooperation—"cheating at a game so that I can win is not fair to others." Rules are for everybody. But, from the world of imagination and *Alice in Wonderland*, they turn to an addiction to literal fact. When they learn one way of doing things, they are likely to insist that it is the only way. "No, Daddy, you *can't* divide like that. Teacher said to do it like this!" A substitute teacher whom we know, taking over a second-grade class, called the children to order at the beginning of the day. The babble continued. She raised her voice. Chaos still reigned. Then one small boy said, "You have to flick the lights." The substitute teacher flicked the lights. The children snapped to attention in their seats, and quiet prevailed. Flicking the lights was what their regular teacher did, and that was the way things had to be done.

Pupils in this period, lacking the capacity for abstract thought, cannot accept anything but reality. If you say to the same fourth-grade class, "Suppose milk were black . . . ," they might protest, "But milk *isn't* black." If you asked,

"Suppose we discovered we could eat petroleum—what do you think would happen?" the class might answer immediately, "But we *can't* eat petroleum." Things are as they seem. Even if they came up with other responses, the answers would all be based on the children's concrete experience—for instance, "You would get sick." Until they are in the next and last period of development, youngsters are still egocentric in that they are unable to accept your assumptions and reason from them, if the assumptions are contrary to their own experience.

The Formal Operational Period. Piaget designated the fourth period of cognitive development as that of formal operations because youngsters now acquire the ability to perform operations using formal logic. Formal in the Piagetian sense does not mean stiff or aloof, but rather comprehensive and sophisticated. In this period, which begins at eleven or twelve years of age and runs into adulthood, students become able to think abstractly as well as logically. Unlike the boys and girls of the concrete operations level, they are able to "put it all together."

Piaget observed that adolescents do not always use formal operations in their thinking, but that most adolescents are capable of doing so. They may use formal operations in some areas but not in others. The ability to use advanced stages of logical thinking depends at least in part on opportunities to practice the new capabilities.

Parents and teachers, of course, can help youngsters exercise their new mental muscles. The key is equilibration. When new information is geared to a learner's present style of thought and is mildly provocative, the learner tries to balance—to equilibrate—the complementary processes of assimilation and accommodation. This search for cognitive balance results in growth. Let's match these abstract principles with a concrete example.

Roy is an avid runner, and today his thoughts are a mile away from the physics lecture. Ms. Robertson undertakes one last effort to make her discussion more stimulating.

"The soles of running shoes," she remarks, "follow the same principles of friction. Their durability depends on such things as the type of shoe tread, the runner's weight, and the road surface."

Now upright in his chair, Roy suddenly listens to catch every word. Parts of Ms. Robertson's talk can be assimilated easily—runner, shoe tread, road surface. But the idea of friction requires some accommodation when Roy combines it with his more familiar schemas. Immediately motivating, mild disequilibrium should result in more sustained cognitive growth.

What are the characteristics of the formal operational period?

Because students in formal operations can think abstractly, they are able to construct hypotheses and test them scientifically. Adolescents begin to think like adults (or as adults ought to think). The concrete operations child is more limited to thoughts about what she or he perceives. The formal operations student can consider various possibilities that cannot be observed at the moment. This student can also think in more complex ways, keeping in mind a variety of combinations of events that might occur and mentally comparing them.

Because of their new capabilities, adolescents often become deeply involved in abstract, theoretical, and philosophical issues: religious philosophy, for example, or political theory conversations can become a series of challenges to parents or teachers, with heated arguments resulting. A nineteen-year-old college student returned for spring vacation immersed in Buddhism and set out to convert her Methodist grandparents, who were unprepared for this phenomenon. One seventeen-year-old announced that he had become an anarchist, leaving his surprised teacher at a loss as to how to continue the discussion. Although a teacher may be tempted to say, "That's nice, John. Are you going to burn down the school today or tomorrow?" or "Not in *this* classroom you won't!" such responses denigrate serious efforts at new ways of thinking and analyzing systems of belief.

In a case such as that of the young anarchist, a teacher can encourage the development of formal operational thought by saying, "It sounds like you're doing some serious thinking about important political issues. Tell me more about what you think."

Early in the period of formal operations, preoccupation with newly found ideals may lead to temporary loss of touch with the real world. Or, if the student compares the real world with the ideal, he or she is likely to feel frustrated and depressed. And yet, this new ability, and the energy invested in exercising it, can be harnessed and used by teachers as instructional motivation. It can lead, for example, to realistic analysis of social problems and to community action projects.

How are adolescent and adult thought different?

Adolescents can ponder, and sometimes brood about, other people's thinking. They dream of changing society to conform to their own utopias. They think about their own future and their roles in society as adults. They are also able to think about their own thinking, to evaluate their own reasoning. That can keep them from flying off into the stratosphere of idealism and allow them to notice the constraints of the real world. Thinking about one's own thinking is a major thrust forward in cognitive development and logical reasoning, for here, finally, is the opportunity to examine critically one's ideas, ideals, and creations. In earlier stages of cognitive development, children must rely on others for corrective feedback; in formal operations, one can regulate one's own thought. A teacher may, for example, ask a formal operations student to evaluate his or her own classwork and to decide what grade it merits, and then to compare it with the teacher's evaluation. A fifteen-year-old student in a French class can say, "I've done well on translations in class, but I have to guess at a lot of words because I haven't spent much time memorizing vocabulary. I still have trouble with verb forms. I've been active in class discussions of the stories we read. My work on the written tests wasn't too great; I get in a hurry to finish and don't check what I've done. I guess a B– would be fair." The teacher may have had in mind a C, but may also completely agree with the student's evaluation of his or her work in the different areas.

Concerning adolescent egocentrism, psychologist David Elkind (1967) has noted two characteristic forms. The first embodies a sense of being always on stage and in the spotlight, playing to an imaginary audience. Youngsters of thirteen or fourteen, say, are convinced and often fearful that everyone is looking at them, judging their appearance and their behavior. They assume that other people are as much interested in them as they are in themselves—an interest that derives from the physiological changes they are undergoing. Because they feel "on stage," they act for audiences that are not paying attention. The acting accounts for much of the rambunctious conduct that teachers encounter in junior high school students and high school freshmen and sophomores. If you should find yourself teaching in those grades, bear with the kids: they will grow up, probably. We say "probably" because maturation and the onset of formal operations do not guarantee that they will: maturation offers the potential for growing up, but only the youngsters' social environment will bring about growing up.

The second form of egocentric thinking Elkind calls the "personal fable." This refers to an adolescent's belief that he or she is special and unique. No one else has ever felt this way, loved so deeply, or been so persecuted by parents, so misunderstood by teachers. The sense of being special can lead to risk-taking. An adolescent can drive too fast and recklessly because automobile accidents happen only to other people. Birth control measures are not necessary, because unwanted pregnancies happen only to other people.

The imaginary audience and the personal fable are dispelled through social interaction. As an adolescent establishes intimate relationships with others, he or she learns about real commonalities and differences. With increasing competence in using formal operations and with the wealth of information about other people gained through social contacts, adolescents move toward adulthood and a more accurate understanding of the real world.

THE IMPLICATIONS

The term *learning* was used by Piaget in two senses: (1) the acquisition of specific information, and (2) the acquisition of mental structures—characteristic ways of perceiving and organizing information (Ginsburg and Opper, 1979). In the first, the child absorbs knowledge relative to the society in which he or she lives. In the second, children acquire more general thought structures, applicable to many situations. It is learning in this second sense, transcending specific facts, that Piaget considered the more fundamental, the more truly developmental.

Piaget viewed the child as an active seeker of knowledge. The internal processes of assimilation, accommodation, and equilibration make development possible. In addition, physical maturation influences cognitive functioning. Maturation of the body, and particularly of the central nervous system—the physical equipment—is an important factor in development. The immature nervous system, if nothing else, restricts the infant from exploring the world and consequently restricts knowledge. At the same time, Piaget pointed out how little we know about physical maturational processes, and he was careful to say that development is not based on maturation alone.

It is experience with the environment that puts assimilation, accommodation, and equilibration to work. The child learns from interacting with the environment. He or she may learn about dogs, for example, from the family dog, a patient and friendly instructor. The young child finds out what the dog feels and looks like, how it sounds, how it eats, and that it doesn't like to have its ears pinched. But beyond this specific learning, the child also learns how animals differ from humans and begins to develop ideas that transcend any concrete experience with dogs.

The environment also offers to the child information through social transmission—the transmission of ideas, values, and beliefs of the culture. The child learns from the experience of others, through both formal and informal instruction. Consequently, each youngster is not required to experience everything anew but benefits from the accumulated wisdom of earlier arrivals. But this learning, like all other learning, cannot take place until the child possesses adequate cognitive structures to assimilate the information.

The school curriculum can be specifically designed to help children prog-

"One thing I try to do is provide as large a variety of experiences as I can—for instance, if a child gets a good score in reading and gets a reward, I let them go and count out their own jelly bean reward. That way I sneak in an additional experience in math. Also, I think if you put things out that you feel are for an advanced group, or even just one child, if you put special things out for that one child I don't think the other children feel threatened. I think they become quite interested. Especially if you have a dialogue with this child and you're both talking about it, I think it arouses the curiosity of the other children, even though some of them aren't capable of understanding it. They do become interested and

ress through the series of periods and the stages within them (e.g., Furth and Wachs, 1975). It is the school's and the teacher's job to provide the opportunity for experience. But the experience must be suitable to the child's period of cognitive development. "Teaching children concepts that they have not attained in their spontaneous development ... is completely useless," Piaget cautioned (Hall, 1970a, p. 30). You can tell kindergartners that Washington, D.C., is the capital of the United States, and they can parrot the information back to you. But unless they can conceive the United States, its expanse, and the numbers of its people (which children of that age cannot), the fact means nothing to them.

From a Piagetian viewpoint, what is the role of the teacher?

For teachers, one of the problems is that you cannot measure cognitive development accurately by the calendar. Children and growing youngsters, remember, enter each period at varying ages. It may seem that you can say with some confidence that ten-year-old Tommy is in the concrete operational period. But Tommy has difficulty with conservation and often with decentration. Those difficulties hint at the preoperational. What period, then, is Tommy really in? Because biological forces are so important in the emergence of periods, we would have to say that Tommy probably has the *capability* of concrete operational thought. But because of, perhaps, an impoverished envi-

curious about what's going on. And later some of them will go back and try it on their own. The more they have of this the more chance there is for them to practice, to discover, to reinforce what they are learning in different ways. And they need these experiences every step of the way, as they move along from grade to grade."

(Shown here is a whole gamut of experiences in math from the concrete to the abstract: jelly beans, felt board, a smiling [or frowning] self-correcting math computer, a math "bingo" game, an exercise in "mental" math, and the abstract principles of math as applied to high school chemistry.)

ronment, Tommy cannot *demonstrate* some of the characteristics that show concrete operations.

The disparities in behavior in a single individual reflect the experience or lack of experience the individual has had in an area. The area may be either educational, in the limited sense of curricular, or social. A child may get As and Bs in school, yet fail socially out of insufficient contact with other children and with adults. Learning from others—by *social transmission*—is a major factor in development.

Any teacher's profile of a typical student will include both the student's strong and weak points of cognitive development. If you are going to work on a weak point, consider the student's *wrong* answers, as Piaget did with small children. They will provide clues to why the student goes astray. But above all, remember that no one can learn—that is, assimilate and accommodate—anything without having attained the necessary level of cognitive development. Learning by rote, or memorization, is only one type of learning. The importance of memorization will be discussed in Chapter 6.

THE PROS AND CONS

What do critics say about Piaget's work?

Piaget's work has sometimes been criticized on the ground that his studies have been conducted with a limited number of children, among them his own three, and that his methods were casual: he did not set, it is complained, the laboratory-like conditions for his experiments that are considered essential by many psychologists in the United States. However, when his experiments have been repeated under laboratory-like conditions, as they have been in a number of studies, the results generally confirm Piaget's findings. His theory has been criticized by other researchers who suggest that the ages at which children pass through the various stages vary more than Piaget thought, that he underestimated the abilities of infants in the sensorimotor period, that cognitive development may be more influenced by education and environment than Piaget believed, and that development may be different in different cultures. These disagreements can be resolved by continuing research. In any case, his research constitutes the most monumental body of fact and theory centered on the cognitive development of children.

COGNITIVE DEVELOPMENT IN ADULTHOOD

The number of adults participating in educational programs is increasing. Many of you readers may eventually find yourselves working in some aspect of adult education. Educational programs designed for young people almost certainly will need to be adjusted for adult learners.

Piaget studied cognitive development only through adolescence, but he had some ideas about adult cognition. His theory states that no qualitative structural changes in mental operations occur after adolescence, but that the refinement of formal operational thought should continue through adulthood

(Piaget and Inhelder, 1969). He also believed that adults as well as adolescents operate at different cognitive levels at different times and in different areas, depending on their education, aptitudes, and occupations (Piaget, 1972). He said that he himself functioned at the highest levels of logic only sporadically: "I am for example at an operatory level for only a small part of the day. . . . The rest of the time I am dealing with empirical trial and error" (1960, p. 126). This should reassure those of us who sometimes feel that our cognitive functioning does not surpass that of the nearest six-year-old.

Recently, other researchers have been interested in testing Piaget's ideas about adult thought processes and have studied the performance of adults of different ages on Piagetian tasks involving concrete and formal operational thought. The findings can be summarized in the following three areas:

1. Most adults are capable of formal operational thought, but as Piaget has suggested, they do not always use it and show great variability on some Piagetian tasks (e.g., Papalia and Bielby, 1973).
2. During young and middle adulthood the quality of thought processes changes little. Most studies find few differences among adults between the ages of twenty and sixty. Such adults can engage in both concrete and formal operations and are not markedly egocentric; they are well able to decenter (consider more than one aspect of a situation) and they can understand the viewpoints of others.

   Does cognitive growth continue in adulthood?

   Some psychologists disagree with this concept of adult cognitive stability. Psychologist Klaus Riegel (1973) has proposed a fifth stage of cognitive development, arising in adulthood, which he calls *dialectic operations*. This describes a way of thinking in which the adult can accept contradictory information or ideas, not as something to be resolved or balanced, but as a part of reality and as a foundation for creative thought.

   We really know little about the development of cognition in this period of adulthood. It is an area open to research; with society's increasing interest in adult development, much may be discovered within the next few years.
3. Elderly adults do not perform as well on Piagetian tasks as do younger adults. The elderly do best on tasks requiring those abilities which appear earliest in the developmental periods, and they are less able to do tasks requiring more complicated mental operations (Papalia, 1972; Rubin et al., 1973). For example, when asked to classify objects, the elderly use strategies more like those of young children. In formal operational tests of logic and reasoning, the elderly as a group are less successful than younger adults. And older people are more egocentric (Bielby and Papalia, 1975).

How can we explain these differences? Old age may present another cognitive period, not yet understood, a period of decline rather than of growth or stability. Perhaps biological changes in aging result in cognitive decline. Perhaps the social isolation and restricted environment of many elderly people cause their skills to become rusty. Sometimes the differences seem to stem from disparities in education; as a group, younger adults have had more schooling than people now much older. Or are the test items, developed for use with children, inappropriate for older people? It is possible that the elderly lack the motivation to participate in game-like activities with blocks and pictures and glasses of water; or perhaps they feel nervous about unfamiliar testing situations. There is evidence to support all of these suggestions. One piece of such evidence is the finding that older people can improve their performance of the tasks after specific training in cognitive strategies (Denney and Denney, 1974; Hornblum and Overton, 1976). This indicates that the capacity remains available and can be refreshed; the skills merely have become rusty from disuse. Research so far tells us only about age differences, comparing groups of people of different ages. The research does not tell us about age changes; that information would have to come from study of the *same* people as they grow older, and such study is needed if we are to answer our questions.

Since there is so much that we do not know about adult cognitive development within the Piagetian framework, it is not easy even to think about designing adult education curricula. We can expect that adults will be able to use formal operations as adolescents do, in some areas better than in others. We can expect wide individual differences among adults, depending on their education and occupation. And, finally, we can expect that elderly students may need some preliminary exercise in cognitive strategies as they apply to new content material. Other issues of adult abilities will be discussed in Chapter 3.

Bruner's Approach to Teaching and Cognitive Development

Among American psychologists who adhere to a cognitive development theory of learning, Jerome S. Bruner has for many years been one of the most influential. Bruner, who spent a year with Piaget, builds on Piaget's work. But Bruner differs with Piaget in important ways.

Piaget is primarily concerned with understanding how children develop intellectually. Bruner is primarily concerned with understanding how intellectual development relates to learning and teaching. Theories of development serve little purpose, Bruner argues, unless they can be linked to education.

Piaget believed that children and young people can learn only to the limits of their period of cognitive development. Bruner has said that "any subject can be taught effectively in some intellectually honest form to any child at any stage of development" (1960, p. 33). The subject merely has to be explained in terms the learner can comprehend, and those terms must take into account the learner's way of viewing things at the time.

CHARACTERISTICS OF COGNITIVE DEVELOPMENT

Bruner (1966) identifies six characteristics, which he calls benchmarks, of cognitive growth or intellectual development. (See Figure 2.2.) His benchmarks follow in italics:

1. *Growth is characterized by increasing independence of responses from the immediate nature of the stimulus* (p. 5).

   Youngsters use mediating processes, which may loosely be called thinking, to diminish the degree of control that environmental stimuli exercise over them. Children think about the influence of events on their behavior and of the behavior's influence on the environment.

2. *Growth depends upon internalizing events into a "storage system" that corresponds to the environment* (p. 5).

   When a child gains information from an experience, the "storage system" enables the child to generalize from the information and to make "predictions and extrapolations from his stored model of the world."

3. *Intellectual growth involves an increasing capacity to say to oneself and others, by means of words or symbols, what one has done or will do* (p. 5).

4. *Intellectual development depends upon a systematic and contingent interaction between a tutor and a learner* (p. 6).

   Hence, the importance of parents, teachers, cultural heroes, and other models as tutors.

5. *Teaching is vastly facilitated by the medium of language, which ends by being not only the medium for exchange but the instrument that the learner can then use himself in bringing order into the environment* (p. 6).

6. *Intellectual development is marked by increasing capacity to deal with several alternatives simultaneously, to tend to several sequences during the same period of time, and to allocate time and attention in a manner appropriate to these multiple demands* (p. 6).

What are Bruner's "benchmarks" of cognitive development?

THREE FORMS OF KNOWING

The last benchmark especially points to the similarities between Piaget and Bruner, and indeed to the bond common to all cognitive developmental psychologists. But of course opinions differ on how stages and periods of development progress and on the nature of cognitive development at various chronological ages. Bruner agrees with Piaget, for example, that children develop by periods, but Bruner's periods are unlike Piaget's. In each of Bruner's periods, a child has or acquires different ways of looking at and responding to the world, or in Bruner's word, of *representing* the world, a process directly related to his first two benchmarks. There are three "modes of representation," Bruner holds, and though they are arrived at one by one, the characteristics of each remain with us throughout our lives. The three, as identified by Bruner, are:

1. *Enactive*, in which responses to objects and events take the form of physical activity, and in which words and pictures are of little value. It occurs developmentally from birth to about age three, and in this period children consider things primarily in terms of action on their part. A little girl can't tell you how a swing works or how to use it, but she can demonstrate her ability to make it go higher and higher. For teachers, the implication is this: if you are instructing enactive children in any physical or motor activity, you have to do more showing than telling; you have to demonstrate the activity instead of merely describing it and encourage the child to practice.

What characterizes Bruner's periods of mental growth?

2. *Iconic*, which gets its name from *icon*, an image—the image in this sense representing a past occurrence or a familiar object. In this period, which extends from about age three to age seven or eight, children can use images in thinking. They can store images in memory. They can substitute images for action; that is, they can imagine action without experiencing it, as children in the enactive period, according to Bruner, cannot. The images may be visual or mental, but whatever their character, they are understood to represent the relevant knowledge; thus, an older child can depict the enactive little girl's swing as a pendulum.

3. *Symbolic*, in which symbols (usually words) are employed to represent people, objects, and events. Children begin to think with symbols at about

Jerome S. Bruner

Although the name Jerome S. Bruner is most often linked to the field of developmental psychology, his areas of professional research and personal interest also include linguistics, cultural anthropology, infant perception, phenomenology, and education. Why the diversity of interests? Perhaps the character of his preprofessional experiences offers some clue:

World War II propaganda analysis and, later, European political intelligence work for the Office of War Information and the Department of State served to broaden his earlier training in social and experimental psychology. Or the diversity might have been a reaction to spending most of his professional career at Harvard, where Bruner took his Ph.D. in 1941, and where he helped to found the Harvard Center for Cognitive Studies.

As has every theorist in the field of cognitive development, Bruner has continually been confronted with the pioneering work of Swiss psychologist Jean Piaget. In fact, Bruner's views have been considered as an alternative to those of Piaget. It would be unfortunate, however, to limit one's picture of Bruner to "the one who disagrees with Piaget." Bruner's investigations into infant behavior, although less well known by the general public, have contributed much to the field of developmental psychology. Another area to which he has devoted some time and writing effort is the field of creativity. *On*

Figure 2.2. Bruner's Six Benchmarks of Cognitive Development

1. Independency of response
2. Internalizing events
3. Increased capacity for language
4. Systematic and contingent tutor-learner relationship
5. Language as an instrument for ordering the environment
6. Increasing capacity to deal with multiple demands

Knowing: Essays for the Left Hand explores myth, creativity, the novel, and art. Certainly Bruner has not put on the "intellectual blinders" worn by many theorists specializing in a particular field.

Bruner's theories of cognitive growth, especially his suggested applications in educational settings, have met with occasional resistance. His influence in shaping *Man: A Course of Study* (MACOS), a well-known social science curriculum, has helped to make the material the target of much criticism. On the other hand, it is encouraging to find a researcher concerned with bridging the gap between theory and practice. ∎

Sources
Jones, R. M. *Fantasy and feeling in education.* New York: Harper and Row, 1968.
Hall, E. Bad education—A conversation with Jerome Bruner. *Psychology Today*, 1970, 4(7), 50–57, 70–74.

age seven or eight, and the symbols permit *abstract* thinking. Children are no longer restricted to imagining single objects or events. Abstractly, they can group objects and events in classes and think about those classes in terms of symbolic labels. They can talk abstractly about dogs, for example, and include all the breeds that they have seen and all the breeds that they might see sometime, rather than individual dogs—to which children in the earlier stages would limit themselves. With the symbols of language, they can question statements about reality as they could not with the symbols of action.

Although the three ways of looking at and responding to the world develop at different ages in children, all three are available to us after about age eight and most of us use them all the time in varying degrees. As adults, we probably employ the symbolic mode most (as you are doing in reading this passage), but the other modes come in handy on occasion. Here, for example, is a situation in which any of the three modes may be used: You enter a restaurant, take off your coat, and enter a cloakroom. You spot a free hanger on the left of the rack, hang your coat, and leave the room. After the meal, you will need some sort of representation to recall where your coat is. In an enactive mode, you will probably turn your body to the left. In an iconic mode, you may visualize the coat rack and "see" your coat on the left. In a symbolic mode, you may say, "My coat hangs on the left."

Would a symbolic thinker use enactive or iconic representation?

The essence of the educational process, Bruner believes, is to provide tools and methods for translating one's experiences into symbols and organizing them systematically. This means using the symbolic mode of representation—mainly language—in varied ways of "seeing" knowledge and experience. It means "recoding" experiences in new forms, so that we say "I see what I'm doing now" or "So that's what the thing is." The new models are formed in increasingly powerful representational systems (Bruner, 1966, p. 21).

TWO FORMS OF USING KNOWLEDGE

Learning, Bruner says, should be *useful*. One form of learning involves specific skills that can be applied to a variety of similar tasks. When you have learned to hammer nails, Bruner points out, you will be better able later to learn how to hammer tacks. Psychologists call that *specific transfer of training*. Another form of learning consists of acquiring a general idea rather than a skill. The general idea can later serve as a basis for recognizing new problems as mere variations of an old problem with which the idea already has dealt. That kind of learning is called *nonspecific transfer*, or the *transfer of principles* and attitudes. That form of transfer, which involves a continual broadening and deepening of knowledge in terms of basic and general ideas, represents in Bruner's view the core of education and teaching (Bruner, 1966). Both forms are shown in Figure 2.3.

Figure 2.3. Transfer of Learning

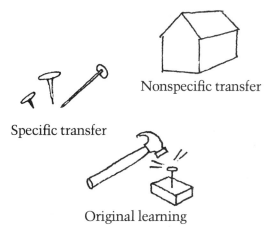

Nonspecific transfer

Specific transfer

Original learning

Figure 2.4. Spiral Curriculum

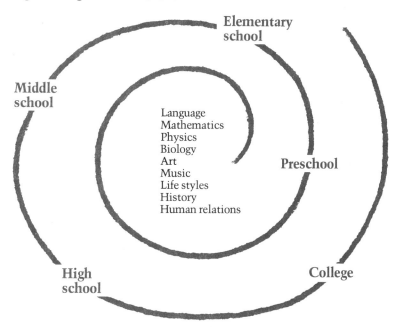

Elementary school

Middle school

Language
Mathematics
Physics
Biology
Art
Music
Life styles
History
Human relations

Preschool

High school

College

THE SPIRAL CURRICULUM

Bruner's theories have led him to propose a revolutionary change in the construction of school curricula. If young people can be taught any subject at any age—if the material is put into their language—and because learning con-

"Sometimes I wish we could put youngsters, you know, at 13 or 14 on ice for a couple of years until their minds catch up with their bodies. You'll notice the difference between seventh or eighth and ninth grade—all of a sudden they're two feet taller. They're growing like weeds, and suddenly they don't look like kids

sists of a continual broadening and deepening of knowledge, he suggests that every subject, including physics and mathematics, should be taught at every level of development. (See Figure 2.4.) Physics, for example, might be taught in the first grade, the fifth grade, and the ninth grade. The curriculum would present basic principles repeatedly through the years, first in simple forms, then in increasing complexity until the student comprehends them in a sophisticated way. What children learn about physics in the first, fifth, and ninth grades would enhance their comprehension and accelerate their learning when and if they go on to college.

Why a "spiral" curriculum?

Teaching children in that manner, Bruner contends, is possible because any complex idea can be presented in simpler form. As an example of a complex idea translated, Bruner cites Snell's Law in physics, which deals with the "pressure" of light. Does light hit film in a camera with any pressure, or is light pressureless? Complex as the question is, Bruner argues that the existence of the problem can be made comprehensible even to seven-year-olds. How? By using two balls, Bruner says, to demonstrate that if a moving object strikes a stationary object, it passes on the force of its velocity to the object it hits.

Bruner says that he has known preoperational children, presented with the problems posed by Snell's Law, to suggest construction of a "light windmill" to measure the pressure of light. Then they argued, he says, about whether it would be a "heat mill" or a "light mill" because starlight was cool (Hall, 1970b).

TEACHING METHODS

Although teachers talk more about teaching *methods*, all teachers organize their instruction, if only implicitly, by some theory. On the basis of the theory, we choose methods and decide, for instance, to use one set of examples rather than another. Bruner (1966) believes any theory of instruction should include

anymore—*they look like* adults! *It's hard to remember they're only 13 or 14 or 15 —Hey! Joe, where's that paper you owe me? Come in here!—Well, you know I've got to grab them when I can.*"

four broad features, and his suggestions provide a basis for such a theory that can prove immeasurably helpful in planning day-to-day teaching:

1. A theory of instruction should tell us what kind of preschool experiences provide a foundation for learning and wanting to learn when a child enters school. Teachers obviously cannot change the preschool experiences of youngsters in their classes, but they can take those experiences into account in teaching.

2. A theory should tell us how to structure subject matter so that the student can most easily understand it. Any body of knowledge has a structure: the issue Bruner raises is how that knowledge should be structured for optimum learning, for your students, your goals and objectives, and your students' goals and objectives. The structuring process involves the enactive, iconic, and symbolic modes of representation.

What should a theory of instruction say?

3. A theory should tell us how to present material in the most effective sequence. Bruner suggests that this sequence might follow the pattern of the three modes of representation, but he adds that no one sequence is most effective for all learners. A teacher must consider such factors as the kind of material and the individual differences among learners. You will find guidance on sequencing instruction in Chapter 8, in the discussion of concept learning.

4. A theory should tell us how and when to reward or to punish a student throughout the learning process. This point is of particular importance, and we shall discuss it and elaborate on it in various places in this book, specifically in chapters 5 and 10. Related to the same point, motivation will be examined in Chapter 12 and the importance of how students feel about themselves in Chapter 4.

In sum, Bruner sees cognitive and intellectual development as involving both the learner and a teacher, who may be a classroom instructor, a parent, or a friend, and who presents the structure of a body of knowledge by one of

  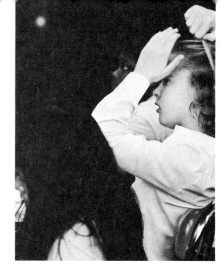

Although Piaget developed his theory of egocentricity for the young child, egocentricity spans all ages and is a strong element at work in self-concept and the development of self-concept—from the two-year-old toddler (top, left) who says, "Mine!" and reaches for a square on the floor in the middle of a lesson; to the next youngster, age nine, who's become preoccupied with the outside world and her every experience in it, needing to relate it over and over again to anyone who will listen; to the thirteen-year-old, who's suddenly self-conscious and constantly dwells on her appearance; to the fourteen-year-old who, growing into adulthood, is ready to take on the world; to the young adult, the seventeen-year-old who feels she's "arrived" as an adult. As her dance instructor puts it: "It's a paradox. You're telling a kid, 'You can't be an individual—but you're supposed to be an individual.' I tell them they have to move away from themselves. Toward the aesthetics. What does the piece mean? Not, 'How do I look in this number?' What does the piece command. Not, 'Is everybody watching me?' It gets real tricky.

Bruner's three modes. The effectiveness and power of the consequent learning and, ultimately, of intellectual development, depend on the relationship of the body of knowledge, the teacher, and the learner. It is not simply a matter of having the learner memorize the material; rather the teacher engages the learner in the intellectual activity that generated the subject material and that will generate new knowledge.

You will find it helpful, we believe, to think of Bruner's four points concerning a theory of instruction as a model, like the Bloom model presented in Chapter 1. Doing so can serve you in two ways. It can help you structure and organize, as Bruner intends, the body of knowledge that we call educational psychology. And, it can guide you in planning your actual instruction of your students.

Summary

Until this century, it was generally believed that once children reached the *age of reason*, they were simply small adults in their thinking. Jean Piaget has been a major factor in changing that belief: Piaget concluded that children reason differently from adults, look at the world differently, and live by a different philosophy.

Piaget's analysis of cognitive development led him to identify two complementary processes, *assimilation* and *accommodation*, which are used to construct *schemas*. Through these processes, the individual develops the ability to think logically and builds an understanding of the world.

A major premise of Piaget's theory is that all children develop by four stages, which he called the *sensorimotor*, the *preoperational*, the *concrete operational*, and the *formal operational*. Children can learn only when subject matter is presented in forms appropriate to their stage of development. Adults continue to refine their abilities to use formal operations, with no further changes in the basic form of thought until old age. Many elderly people become less able to use the more complicated formal operations and are likely to return to using concrete operations, at least in testing situations.

Jerome S. Bruner, who also has contributed importantly to current understanding of children, agrees with Piaget that children develop by stages. But his stages differ from Piaget's: he describes them as *enactive, iconic*, and *symbolic*. In a further difference, Bruner holds that any child can be taught anything at any age if the subject matter is presented in terms that the child can understand. He therefore proposes a *spiral curriculum*, in which a subject such as physics might be part of the curriculum in the first, fifth, and ninth grades and be taught in an increasingly sophisticated manner each time. Bruner suggests that any theory of instruction should be based on four broad features which may be abbreviated to *entry characteristics, structure of knowledge, sequence of presentation*, and *rewards and punishments.*

Chapter Study Guide

CHAPTER REVIEW

1. According to Bruner, "Intellectual development is marked by increasing capacity to deal with several alternatives simultaneously, to tend to several sequences

during the same period of time, and to allocate time and attention in a manner appropriate to these multiple demands." It follows from this statement that good teaching will, at the appropriate time,

a. provide several tasks for the student to perform at once.
b. let the student determine his or her own curriculum.
c. encourage more able students to help tutor the less able.
d. provide opportunities for students to choose and plan learning tasks in advance.

2. Though biological maturation is the preeminent force controlling the emergence of Piaget's various stages of development, cognitive growth can be nurtured by

a. paying proper attention to exercise and diet.
b. providing the proper experience.
c. providing for abundant drill and practice.
d. developing internal motivation.

3. When thinking is changed because of some new experience, Piaget called this

a. experiential learning.
b. reciprocity.
c. equalizing.
d. assimilation.
e. accomodation.

4. Each of the stages of cognitive growth as described by Piaget is characterized by

a. rigid age boundaries.
b. development through experience and physical actions.
c. attempts to apply new schemas to broader contexts.
d. a growing importance of action and operation on the environment.
e. lower levels of disequilibrium than found in preceding stages.

5. In each case, what period of Piagetian development has been reached by a child who has just learned to

a. invent fantasy stories involving imaginary playmates?
b. realize that a toy car is both blue and made of metal?
c. look for a lost ball?
d. figure how many fluid ounces there are in a gallon?
e. get Daddy's hat out of the closet and give it to him when he needs it?
f. identify trees by looking at the shapes of their leaves?
g. hypothesize what would happen if the angle of the earth's axis should begin to change?

6. A child in Piaget's sensorimotor period of development could be expected to be able to _____ , but not to be able to _____ . (Repeat for each of the four periods, in each case naming first an ability just acquired in that period followed by one acquired in the following period.)

7. When people first realized that the apparent motion of the sun across the sky from east to west was caused by the earth's rotation on its own axis rather than by the movement of the sun, what was required in their thinking, accommodation or assimilation?

8. From what we know about cognitive development in adults, we might assume that
   a. most adults are adept at theorizing and almost always plan mentally before actually responding.
   b. grown-ups, like children, show development through separate cognitive stages occurring between the ages of twenty and sixty.
   c. the older the person, the more adept he or she is at performing tasks requiring logical reasoning and formal operations.
   d. although adults can hypothesize about possible alternatives they do not regularly do so.

9. Bruner's six benchmarks of cognitive development are characterized by
   a. a continuing decrease in disequilibrium.
   b. movement from external to internal control.
   c. greater and more sophisticated use of language.
   d. less emphasis on language and more on thought.
   e. both b and c.

FOR FURTHER THOUGHT

1. Much classroom practice based on Piaget's theories is called *active learning*. Explain why this term is appropriate in light of Piaget's concepts of equilibrium, assimilation, and accommodation.

2. Piaget's and Bruner's theories of cognitive development parallel each other at several points: both posit an active period in early life; Bruner's "iconic" period evokes Piaget's imaginative and visually oriented "preoperational" period; and both theories culminate in a period of symbolic, abstract thought. What differences did you notice? At how many points does language (verbal or mathematical) provide a distinctive emphasis in Bruner's theory? What is the role of experience in each, and how does it differ?

3. Does Bruner's theory of instruction conflict with, or complement, Bloom's in Chapter 1? Using Bruner's model and his concept of a "spiral curriculum," outline the essentials for teaching a topic you have a special interest in. Show how you would approach the topic at the elementary, junior high, and high school levels.

4. For some time educational psychologists have used the term *readiness* to indicate the time at which it is feasible to try to teach a person a particular thing. How do Piaget's and Bruner's "periods of cognitive growth" lend specificity to the idea of readiness? Which theory do you think would be more useful to the classroom teacher? Why?

5. If the thoughts and understandings of children are qualitatively different from adults', as Piaget suggests, then who is the better teacher for a child, his or her peers or an adult?

6. What is the most recent experience you had that produced what Piaget calls disequilibrium? How did you adjust your thinking to deal with it? How do you think you will respond in similar situations in the future?

7. Piaget suggests that language and experience contribute to the degree to which children develop their cognitive structures. Do you think that bilingual children develop their cognitive abilities to a greater degree or lesser degree than children who speak only one language?

8. Can you identify some situations in which your thoughts continue to be egocentric and it is difficult for you to understand the views of others? Is egocentric thought a benefit or a liability to politicians? to salespeople? to teachers?

IMPORTANT TERMS

cognition	conservation
equilibration	reversibility
assimilation	decentration
accomodation	personal fable
cognitive structure	social transmission
schema	dialectic operations
egocentrism	modes of representation
sensorimotor period	enactive mode
preoperational period	iconic mode
concrete operational period	symbolic mode
formal operational period	specific transfer
object permanence	transfer of principles
operation	spiral curriculum

SUGGESTED READINGS

BRAINERD, C. J. *Piaget: A description and evaluation*. Englewood Cliffs, NJ: Prentice-Hall, 1978. A comprehensive introduction, with a chapter devoted to each of the four major developmental periods. The section on formal operations is as complete as exists today.

BRUNER, J. S. *The relevance of education*. New York: W. W. Norton, 1973. A series of short essays depicting Bruner's position on cognitive development and the process of schooling. Also included are arguments in favor of discovery learning (see Chapter 9 of this text).

BRUNER, J. S. *The process of education*. New York: Vintage Books, 1960. In this series of essays, Bruner lays out the fundamental pieces of his ideas about cognitive development, learning, and teaching.

ELKIND, D. *Children and adolescents* (2nd ed.). New York: Oxford University Press, 1974. A student of Piagetian theory, Elkind develops several essays about some of the more intriguing portions of the theory. The writing is considerably less technical than many texts on cognitive development.

FLAVELL, J. H. *Cognitive development*. Englewood Cliffs, NJ: Prentice-Hall, 1977. A comprehensive introduction to cognitive development, dominated by Piagetian concepts.

GINSBURG, H., AND OPPER, S. *Piaget's theory of intellectual development* (2nd ed.). Englewood Cliffs, NJ: Prentice-Hall, 1979. This is a moderate-level and fairly comprehensive explanation of Piaget's work.

LABINOWICZ, E. *The Piaget primer.* Menlo Park, CA: Addison-Wesley, 1980. Dozens of comprehensible, simple experiments and ideas for developing a Piagetian curriculum.

LEFRANCOIS, G. R. *Of children* (2nd ed.). Belmont, CA: Wadsworth, 1977. A highly readable and entertaining account of physical, social, and intellectual development in humans.

LEFRANCOIS, G. R. *Adolescents.* Belmont, CA: Wadsworth, 1976. A companion volume to *Of children,* with the focus on people from the ages of eleven to twenty.

PHILLIPS, J. L., JR. *The origins of intellect: Piàget's theory* (2nd ed.). San Francisco: W. H. Freeman, 1975. One of the best introductory primers on Piagetian theory, it also provides extensive discussions of teaching applications derived from the theory.

SCHAIE, K. W., AND WILLIS, S. L. Life-span development: Implications for education. In Shulman, L. S. (ed.), *Review of research in education, vol. 6.* Itasca, IL: F. E. Peacock, 1978, pp. 120–156. Thorough review of alternative theories and research on adult development.

WADSWORTH, B. J. *Piaget for the classroom teacher.* New York: Longman, 1978. Background and rationale for Piagetian curriculum, with assessment examples.

ANSWER KEY

1. d; 2. b; 3. e; 4. c; 5a. preoperational, b. concrete operational, c. sensorimotor, d. formal operations, e. sensorimotor, f. concrete operational, g. formal operations; 8. d; 9. e

3

Intelligence and Language Development

Among topics that are widely discussed and poorly understood, intelligence ranks with arms limitation and inflation. Since 95 percent of all schoolchildren undergo some form of intelligence test, it is likely that you have taken one some time. But do you know your own IQ (intelligence quotient) score? Perhaps not, because schools do not report IQ scores as they do grades.

If you did know your score, what would you do with it? Most of us may reveal our height, weight, allowance from Dad, and the size of our college loan, but an IQ is not the kind of thing one shares with friends.

Some of us are even frightened by intelligence testing. Jack Fincher (1976) reports that when a team of psychologists and psychiatrists went into San Francisco's Haight-Ashbury district, the loose-hanging, free-living acid freaks, dropouts, and hippies of the 1960s and 1970s discussed with apparent candor their sex lives, their drug experiments and habits, and even their fantasies, but they became disturbed and in some cases violent when asked to participate in an intelligence test. What is intelligence, anyway?

What was the fuss about? Perhaps some day people writing a book like this one will be able to start a sentence "Intelligence is . . . " and finish it authoritatively, on the basis of indisputable scientific findings. We cannot. Neither, yet, can anyone else. If you visit your doctor for a checkup, the nurse can stick a needle into a vein in your arm and extract a few cubic centimeters of your blood to send to a laboratory. In a few days the doctor can report that your hemoglobin and cholesterol levels are normal, your liver is functioning satisfactorily, and your blood sugar is a little high, so watch your diet. No comparable procedure exists for assessing the health and components of intelligence.

Why can't intelligence be defined precisely?

Intelligence, the presence of which seems evident everywhere, remains as elusive as the Loch Ness monster or the Northwest's Bigfoot. There are many definitions of it and many theories about what it is. We shall discuss them later in this chapter. But "the only evidence we have that a person is more or less intelligent," Robert L. Ebel points out, "is that he behaves more or less intelligently" (1974, p. 486). This is not to suggest that all intelligent actions are observable! We cannot directly watch the thinking, learning, and problem solving that go on in our heads. Yet we base our perceptions of intelligence on how smart one appears.

Such reasoning may sound circular, but it embodies an important message. Intelligence is an abstraction or *construct*, which is inferred from assorted behaviors that a given culture happens to value. (A *construct* is an internal process such as learning, the existence of which is assumed on the basis of performances.) Because cultural values are diverse, intelligence is related to whatever behaviors are demanded at a particular time and place. An individual who is considered to behave intelligently in a great American or European city might seem retarded or a bit odd, at least, in, say, a jungle village in mid-Africa. Further, intelligence is not a single *thing*, as IQ scores appear to hint, but a composite of behaviors or skills.

Whatever intelligence is, the ability to measure it accurately would have great practical importance for teaching. Intelligence tests are intended to fill that need, and to a certain extent, they do. For example, because IQ scores and school achievement have proven clearly related, the tests warn teachers and counselors that some students may be headed for problems in learning and need special attention to preclude failure in school. The tests also help to identify gifted students who may not be challenged by the regular curriculum; in those cases teachers can think up ways to offer additional intellectual stimulation.

The applications in education and the potential usefulness generally of accurate yardsticks for intelligence have involved scientists and psychologists for more than eighty years in developing and refining intelligence tests. Yet our measures of intelligence remain indirect and relatively crude.

Scientists used to hope that they might determine one's intelligence by weighing one's brain. Apart from the obvious technical difficulties, the

"I keep very accurate records when they answer questions—like today we went through the math multiplication cards. If they answer the card they get the card. When the lesson is all over they go up to the girl and they say, 'I have seven correct answers—here are my seven correct cards.' She gives them seven tabs and they love this. So—when the term is all over I'll go back to my math section in my book and I'll look over here on the tabs. If Pamela has 154 mental math tabs, that gives me a good indication that she's been involved in mental math and has become a pretty good observer and fast thinker. But if I didn't keep a record, a lot of it's left to guesswork. I imagine a lot of people, you know, say, 'She's good in written math. She must be good in mental math.' That's not so. I've had children who could do the written work just fine, but when they come up here and are giving the answers without the paper they have an awful job! So, I keep very accurate records. I only have these kids for one year. I want to be sure when they leave here they're as strong as they can be right across the board—all around."

method did not work; why did Cromwell and Lord Byron have brains twice as heavy as that of Anatole France, the writer who won an early Nobel Prize? Scientists were similarly bewildered when they found that many women's brains weighed as much as men's.

By the late 1800s, Sir Francis Galton, Charles Darwin's cousin, was seeking to show that mental capacity was inherited. In extending his cousin's theories of biological evolution, Galton had come to believe that genius ran in families. To prove that, he knew, he would need a test of intellectual ability, so he devised supposed methods of measuring sensory and motor functions and memory. But his techniques failed to distinguish even between high and low achievers, much less to document the inheritance of intellectual traits. Galton's theory of the heritability of intelligence, however, has been revived in the twentieth century.

Modern intelligence tests possess more sophistication than such efforts as Galton's and the brain-weighers'. In particular, they are designed to minimize subjective judgments in the measurement of mental ability or agility. Since 1905, when Alfred Binet and Theophile Simon first published their test, intelligence tests have been administered in America by the hundreds of millions, not only in schools but in business, industry, and the military services. A great many people have viewed the tests as providing accurate, unchanging indices of intellect and as predicting performance in the classroom, the laboratory, the office, the driver's seat in a garbage truck, and practically everywhere else.

The tests have been denounced, on the other hand, as weapons of racial bigotry, serving to guard privilege for the white middle class. They have been dismissed by some psychologists and educators as worthless or worse. They have been defended by others as valuable when they are not misinterpreted. Many nonprofessionals deride them, especially if they or their children have scored lower than they expected. The United States Supreme Court has restricted their application in employment (*Griggs* v. *Duke Power Company*, 1971), and the State of California, the City of New York and the District of Columbia have forbidden group IQ tests. Much of the furor generates in ignorance of what intelligence tests measure and what they can and cannot do.

In Pursuit of the Intellect

Binet and Simon could not foresee the controversy when they began work on measuring intelligence. France's education ministry had asked Binet to find some way to search out retarded children in the schools so that they could be given special instruction. To be precise and fair, the method would have to distinguish the truly dull from the merely lazy or unmotivated. It would have to circumvent teachers' subjectivity, so that a normal enough child would not be shunted off to a school for the backward because the child was unruly, or a slow student retained because the teacher feared to offend influential parents. Implicit in Binet's assignment was that he would have to accomplish the seemingly impossible, measuring the intangible, invisible, unknown quality or qualities that make some people smarter than other people.

What led Binet to develop the first intelligence test?

Binet was the obvious choice for the task: for more than a decade before the government enlisted him, he had been trying to determine just how the mind worked. In his research, he had looked for clues in everything from mental arithmetic to reading bumps on heads, deciphering handwriting, and studying wrinkles on the palms of hands. He sensed that he was seeking an overall attribute, intelligence, rather than an assortment of individual faculties such as reasoning and memory, which much of the psychological wisdom of the day believed constituted the mind. Intelligence resembled a yet unsighted planet that astronomers had ascertained must be out there; intelligence had to be *in* there because children who demonstrated generally good judgment and common sense were the same children who possessed broad vocabularies, paid attention in class, and earned high marks.

For the task at hand, Binet concentrated not on the nature of intelligence but on how to find it and measure it. His approach had to be empirical. He and his coworkers devised hundreds of minitests for the psychological functions he described as "judgment, otherwise called good sense, practical sense, initiative, . . . adapting oneself to circumstances" (Binet and Simon, 1916, p. 42).

The minitests included: Copy this square. What is silly about this picture? What does this word mean? What is this boy doing? What would you do if . . . ? Dozens of the minitests had to be discarded as proving nothing. But finally Binet had an assortment of nonacademic brainteasers that academically successful children tackled handily, average children managed moderately well, and slower students found nearly impossible. The intelligence test had been born.

THE MENTAL AGE CONCEPT

Binet borrowed an important concept from a German colleague, Wilhelm Stern. That idea was that children's intelligence, whatever it was, increased with age, like height and weight. Thus there must be a mental age as well as a chronological age. But because some six-year-olds, say, were obviously brighter and some were duller than average, mental age and chronological age did not necessarily coincide. Binet's test was contrived to match the mental capacities of average children at various age levels. So a six-year-old who outshone other six-year-olds could then be tested at higher levels until the child's mental age was established.

A CHANGING PACE OF DEVELOPMENT

Binet concluded that intelligence was not an originally fixed quantity that grew steadily at a preset rate. He also disagreed with Galton's proposition that intelligence was rigidly determined by ancestry. The development of intelligence, Binet believed, could be accelerated by training, instruction, and mental exercise. When a delegation from the French Chamber of Deputies visited a school for retarded children which Binet directed, he offered some evidence. A card to which nine objects were attached was flashed before the youngsters for five seconds. Then the children were asked to write down the objects' names. Two-thirds of the class, which had been given exercises in memory and observation, got all nine right. Then, for fun, the deputies tried the feat. All, to their understandable embarrassment, failed (Binet, 1975, p. 80).

THE TESTS IN AMERICA

What were early intelligence tests used for in America?

The Binet-Simon Test was brought to America in 1908 by H. H. Goddard, who had seen Binet's work in Paris. Goddard, who translated the Binet test and published his version in 1910, first applied it at a training school for the retarded at Vineland, New Jersey. The tests were later used by Goddard in assessing the mental abilities of European immigrants passing through Ellis Island. The tests usually were administered in English to Jews, Italians, Hungarians, and Russians who understood the language poorly or not at all, and on the basis of the results Goddard reported that more than three-quarters of the immigrants entering the United States were feebleminded (Jacobson, 1976). He proclaimed support for the theory of inherited intellect, and his influence led to the Immigration Act of 1924, which virtually banned Eastern Europeans from settling in the United States. That surely constituted one of the grossest misuses of intelligence testing, and psychologists recall it with horror.

The Stanford-Binet Test. Lewis M. Terman further revised the original Binet-Simon Test in 1916, because what worked for Parisian schoolchildren did not necessarily work for Kansas farm boys and girls. (Recognition of that limitation presaged current protests, to be discussed later, that a test on which white middle-class youngsters do well may be unfair to black pupils from a ghetto, Navajos from a reservation, or members of other minority groups.)

Terman named his version the Stanford-Binet Test for the university where he was based. He incorporated in the test the then new intelligence quotient, the computation of which is explained elsewhere in this chapter.

The Army Alpha Test. The Binet-Simon Test and the Stanford-Binet Test were administered to one individual at a time, but by 1917 some experimenting had begun in group testing, in which many youngsters were given the same examination simultaneously. When the United States entered World War I, group testing seemed to offer a fast, efficient, and economical system for screening drafted men. The potential foul-ups could be rejected immediately, and the remaining majority could be categorized, on the basis of their test scores, as future privates, noncoms, and officers. So psychologists contrived what became known as the Army Alpha Test, the first group "intelligence" test.

These four photographs show a high school English class exploring both divergent and convergent thinking. The class is preparing for a playwriting project— script-writing for video or film. The first three photographs show students and teacher demonstrating and discussing many different positions for the actors and the filming camera (divergent thinking). In the last photograph the teacher has handed another student a cutout "frame"; through this "frame" the student focuses in on the exact view that he would see on camera (convergent thinking). Both of these exercises, and others, were done as preparation before any actual writing was done to aid the students in considering all aspects of the presented project, the broad as well as detailed points.

What was distinctive about the Army Alpha Test?

It was not truly an intelligence test, because it sought to determine not a draftee's potential but what a draftee already knew. For an army whose job was to win a war and not to reform an educational system, the Alpha Test seemed to work very well. It worked so well, in fact, that after the war, civilian versions of the test were enthusiastically adopted by schools and industry. On the basis of test scores, school administrators and guidance counselors categorized pupils as "fast" or "slow" and put them in classes for the bright or the dull. Many schools still do that despite growing evidence that grouping by ability is undesirable for most students (Findley and Bryan, 1975). With intelligence testing and the IQ firmly established in the American credo, school psychologists found themselves after World War I spending most of their working days administering intelligence tests and calculating IQ scores.

Intelligence tests now abound, in many versions. Two that are widely used and esteemed are the Stanford-Binet and the Wechsler scales.

Wechsler's Scales. The Wechsler scales were devised because the Stanford-Binet tests were designed for children and adolescents: they originally stopped at age fifteen.* The Stanford-Binet tests, therefore, proved of limited use to David Wechsler, a clinical psychologist at New York City's Bellevue Hospital. The patients who came into Wechsler's office ranged from the Bowery alcoholic to the senile and the psychotic. Wechsler had to determine their capacities and incapacities before recommending their therapy. So in 1944 he devised the Wechsler-Bellevue Test. Unlike the Stanford-Binet Test, which measured overall "intelligence," Wechsler's sought to appraise specific mental abilities. Refined into the Wechsler Adult Intelligence Scale (WAIS) in 1955, it developed also into the Wechsler Intelligence Scale for Children (WISC) from ages six to sixteen in 1949 (which was revised in 1974) and the Wechsler Preschool-Primary Scale of Intelligence (WPPSI) for ages four to six and a half in 1967.

What needs were served by Wechsler's tests of mental abilities?

The Wechsler tests vary in difficulty but not in design. All the tests are divided into two categories of minitests. One group of minitests, the *verbal*, encompasses general information, vocabulary, comprehension, arithmetic, and the like. The second group, *performance*, requires arrangement of a series of pictures in logical order, assemblage of a simple jigsaw puzzle of a familiar object, the tracking of a pencil through a maze, and other such tasks. Oddly, both the Stanford-Binet and the Wechsler tests are employed most often for purposes contrary to those for which they were intended. Binet's test operates to select the brightest rather than the retarded, and Wechsler's to evaluate the young rather than the adult.

The Nature of Intelligence

Before we consider the merits and demerits of intelligence tests, let us return to what it is that they are intended to test. The precise nature of intelligence, as we indicated at the beginning of this chapter, remains mysterious. Among the dictionary definitions of intelligence are "the capacity to acquire and apply knowledge" and "the quality, exercise, or product of intellect." Not surprisingly, the definitions vary with the cultures that contrive them, even when the cultures are as similar as the British and the American. British dictionaries typically refer, as Block and Dworkin (1976) have pointed out, to "mental agility" or "quickness of wit," but American dictionaries rarely include speed as an attribute of intelligence. All the definitions are fair enough for ordinary use but not much help to the psychologist. Binet decided intelligence was "the tendency to take and maintain a definite direction; the capacity to make adaptations for the purpose of attaining a desired end; and the power of autocriticism" (1916, p. 45).

* Data collected during the 1960 revision of the Stanford-Binet make it possible to use the test with students up to age eighteen.

How would you judge the worth of a definition of intelligence?

In 1921 the *Journal of Educational Psychology* invited recognized experts in intelligence to define the object of their interest. The experts could not agree, and E. G. Boring was prompted to conclude that "intelligence is what the tests test" (1923, p. 35). Allport was little more specific when he called intelligence "the capacity for solving the problems of life" (1924, p. 104). David Wechsler believes that IQ scores derived from his tests indicate "the aggregate or global capacity of the individual to act purposefully, think rationally and to deal effectively with his environment" (1958, p. 7).

So you can see that even the experts are unsure where the object to be measured begins or ends or what it is made of, and the major tool available to draw a picture of it is the very yardstick that is doing the measuring. If that seems like an unsatisfying and roundabout way to measure a trait of great social significance, it is.

Why is intelligence difficult to measure?

Even if everyone agreed fully on the meaning of intelligence, it is improbable that it could ever be measured directly. Illustrating the complications involved in using indirect evidence, Lloyd Humphreys (1976) offers the analogy of measuring height. If we could not measure height physically, we might collect such data as length of bones and size of palms. Given enough of those crude indices, we might pool them and approximate a person's height from the composite score. But, as Humphreys warns, pooling all the data still would not suffice. We would have to decide, somehow, on the *weight* or importance of each indicator. And, with intelligence tests, the weighting of test items is often a matter of conjecture or values. The heaviest weights in most intelligence tests are awarded to verbal components, and even measurement experts disagree about how much emphasis to place on verbal skills in the assessment of intelligence.

THEORIES OF INTELLIGENCE

With the help of various yardsticks, several versions of the structure of the intellect have evolved in this century. Binet, as you read earlier in this chapter, considered intelligence an entity rather than a bagful of separate faculties. But he realized that it was vastly complex and embodied many different abilities. Following Binet's suggestion that intelligence must include consideration of an individual's ability to adapt and survive in his or her environment, a whole chronology of theories surfaced. Here is a sampling, in order of their emergence.

Spearman's Theory. Working in England about the time that Binet was developing his test in France, psychologist Charles E. Spearman arrived at a two-factor theory of intelligence. One factor was general (dubbed g by Spearman) and was described as operating in tasks requiring reason and judgment. It might be likened to the entire mechanical system of an automobile. The other factor was named s, for special, since Spearman thought it related to special abilities or functions, such as those of a carburetor. (The analogy is ours.) The g factor explains the common enough phenomenon of the individual who scores high on a variety of tests. The s factor would explain, for example, why one may score high on a vocabulary test and less high on a math test.

Thurstone's Theory. By the 1930s, Americans were entering the scene with some theories of intelligence. An early contribution came from Louis Thurstone, who divided Spearman's original two factors into what came to be called Primary Mental Abilities (PMAs). Rather than Spearman's two factors, Thurstone argued, numerous and varied abilities—the PMAs—contributed to total intelligence. The PMAs included reasoning, word fluency, perception, spatial visualization, and memory. Thurstone's interpretation of intelligence would later be applied to diagnostic testing for identifying functions in which a child shows below average, average, or superior ability.

Cattell's Theory. Thurstone's theory was not destined to remain unmodified for long on the quickly changing scene of American psychology. By 1940, Raymond B. Cattell proposed that two forms of intelligence acted to influence the PMAs that Thurstone hypothesized. Cattell christened the two forms *fluid* and *crystallized*. Fluid intelligence embraces one's adaptability, the capacity to perceive things and integrate them mentally, and appears independent of formal education and experience. For example, some adults have childrearing skills that seem intuitive. With no training, they are able to nurture, transmit expectations, and disipline fairly.

By comparison, schooling and environmental enrichment determine an individual's crystallized intelligence, which relates to the skills, abilities, and understanding gained through instruction and observation. Crystallized childrearing skills may be developed through intentional education. Here, practices might be built on principles of reinforcement, knowledge of developmental stages, and so on. When an individual of high fluid intelligence is restricted in experience or education, he or she will show less crystallized intelligence.

Guilford's Theory. More recently, J. P. Guilford has drawn a *structure of intellect* in the shape of a cube divided into 120 cells, each cell for one element of intelligence. Eighty occupants have been assigned cells thus far (see Figure 3.1). In each cell, three major dimensions interact: operations, content, and product. By operations, Guilford means the ways in which people think; content is what they think about, and product is the result of the other two.

Multifaceted theories of intelligence—a necessary complexity?

Guilford's theory is similar to Thurstone's in implying that rather than having a general intelligence—as Binet and Spearman suggest—an individual may be "intelligent" in a variety of ways. For example, a person might have a good memory (operations) for math (symbolic content); or one might make quick decisions about the adequacy of knowledge (operations-evaluation) of systems (products).

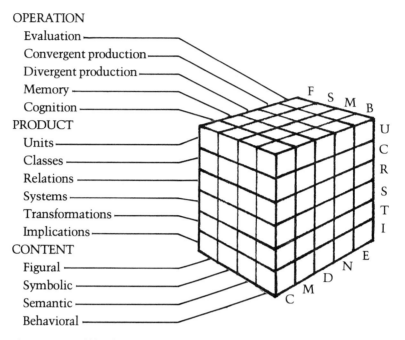

OPERATION
  Evaluation
  Convergent production
  Divergent production
  Memory
  Cognition
PRODUCT
  Units
  Classes
  Relations
  Systems
  Transformations
  Implications
CONTENT
  Figural
  Symbolic
  Semantic
  Behavioral

Figure 3.1. Guilford's Structure of the Intellect Model

Although Guilford proposes many more cells than Thurstone did PMAs, the cells are more carefully ordered and linked by the three dimensions than were Thurstone's mixed bag of abilities. Thurstone introduced the multifaceted theory and Guilford has taken the approach to an extreme. The single entity envisioned by Binet has somehow grown to a complex structure with more than a hundred parts.

The dimension of operations has attracted considerable attention, particularly the distinction that Guilford makes between convergent and divergent thinking. Thinking *convergently*, an individual seeks a single right answer to a question or a single right solution to a problem. The *divergent* thinker looks for a variety of possible answers or solutions. Many situations require only convergent thinking—adding the check in a restaurant, for example. But deciding on the best buy among three used cars demands some divergent thinking. We shall return to divergent and convergent thinking in Chapter 9.

Information Processing Theories. The most recent theories of intelligence diverge from their predecessors, many of which were constructed with measurement in mind: intelligence was defined so that it could be measured, and so that, in turn, people could be ranked by contrasting their mental capacities with those of others. Even within Guilford's structure-of-the-intellect theory, people sought to fix the dimensions in such a way that they could be measured.

Some cognitive psychologists, among them Earl Hunt (1976) and Robert

Sternberg (1979), place less emphasis on measurement—i.e., the IQ score—and address their theorizing to the understanding of whatever machinery works in the brain to produce thinking. Their theories seek to explain what we do with information once we encounter it.

Hunt's theory rests on the *distributed memory model,* which represents an adaptation of computer technology directed at solving problems. It has been called the "box in the head" approach because of the computer diagrams used to depict information storage and transformation. The model involves three stages: *preconscious thought, conscious thought,* and *long-term memory.* The mental processing of information is depicted in Figure 3.2. At various steps in the flow of information we decide whether to ignore, store, or actively operate

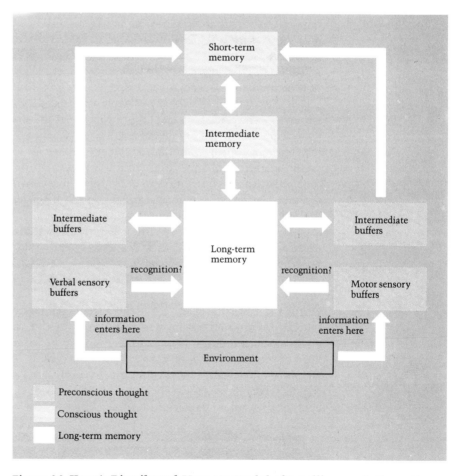

Figure 3.2. Hunt's Distributed Memory Model of Intelligence. Information is perceived by the sensory buffers, which instantaneously reject some and accept some. Accepted information is compared to long-term memory storage. If it is recognized, it is funnelled to short term and intermediate term memory to be used in solving a problem at hand.

on the data provided by the environment. Although Hunt's description of the system takes many minutes to read (and even longer to understand), Hunt reminds us that the parts of the system operate in fractions of seconds. He also points out that the speed at which the system operates differs slightly for each of us. Individual differences are thought to exist at each step in the model and help explain why some of us are quicker than others at problem-solving.

Robert Sternberg's somewhat different explanation of information processing identifies two levels of mental activity which are initiated by the sensing of a problem. The first level, which Sternberg believes to be the more important, is that of the *metacomponents:* at this level, we select potential approaches to the problem. At the second level, termed *components*, we implement the selected methods of attack and try to solve the problem.

Is information processing the same as intelligence?

Both information-processing approaches, Hunt's and Sternberg's, provide important insights about performance on intelligence tests. For example, they indicate that success in problem-solving may not depend entirely on speed at each level. Sometimes, the best problem-solvers prove to be those who spend more time *preparing* for the attack. In Sternberg's theory in particular, selection of strategies is crucial: time spent on it can pay off in faster and more accurate execution than that of people who speed through the metacomponent level. (The notion of mental preparation at the metacomponent level is a historically important one. As you will see in Chapter 9, other theorists use the idea in their analysis of human problem-solving.) Hunt's more detailed model provides additional opportunities for individual differences to appear, and each opportunity contributes to that mysterious construct called intelligence.

Besides giving us a new way to look at intelligence by identifying steps in the processing of information, these theories may help to make the teaching-learning process more successful. The information-processing framework lets us break problem-solving into parts; then specific weaknesses in any part can be pinpointed, and as Sternberg suggests, particular methods or shortcuts might be taught to problem-solvers with problems.

Piaget's Theory. Jean Piaget too speculated about the internal processes that govern our mental abilities. But although Hunt and Sternberg theorize in terms of the computer, Piaget's background in biological sciences directed his view of intelligence. Human beings, as Piaget saw it, are endlessly engaged in adapting, biologically and psychologically, to the environment. For example, if the body becomes excessively hot, it sends blood flowing closer to the skin to cool itself; similar adaptation, Piaget held, occurs on the mental or cognitive level.

Piaget (1952) maintained that *adaptation*, which involves the assimilation and accommodation of which we read in Chapter 2, and *organization*, which is what we have previously referred to as cognitive structure or schemas, are two invariant (ever-present) functions in living organisms. He said that "every intellectual operation is always related to all others. . . . Every schema is thus coordinated with all the other schemata and itself constitutes a totality with differential parts. Every act of intelligence presupposes a system of mutual implications and interconnected meanings" (p. 7).

Intelligence, then, in Piaget's view, is a process of cognitive development that involves many operations; and intellectual growth, from the same point of view, represents progress through the developmental periods discussed in Chapter 2, influenced by the operations involved in those two constants, organization and adaptation.

HOW THEORY RELATES TO THE TESTS

One of the most remarkable and intriguing research efforts of this century focuses on the relationship of the brain itself to intelligent behavior. The research could, among other things, explain why some people are better at

This English class (shown earlier) also demonstrated dramatically the complementary use of verbal and visual (language and nonlanguage) techniques for enhancing learning. The first frame shows the students acting out a scene from a script (a spatial, visual experience); the second frame shows the same student actors, with the addition of a student simulating the part of cameraman (expanding the spatial, visual experience); the third frame shows the students focusing in on the actual scene (another visual consideration).

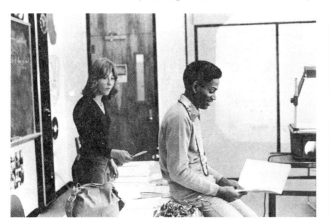

convergent (or divergent) thinking than other people—and the answer would have, of course, significance for intelligence testing. Most conventional intelligence tests are convergent, seeking a single right answer to each question. Some critics say this penalizes the divergent thinker, although it can be argued that the intelligence test doesn't penalize anyone. It simply measures one's convergent reasoning power. A good many educators suggest that schools currently overemphasize convergent thinking at the expense of the divergent variety. The suggestion raises an unanswered question: Should the student who tends to convergent thinking be taught differently from a student with an identical IQ who tends to think divergently? The answer may be provided by what is called split-brain research.

Split-Brain Research. Neurologists and medical practitioners have long known that the two halves—hemispheres—of the human brain appear to control different human responses. More than a century ago, speech functions were found to be located in the left hemisphere in most people. Because language was generally believed to be the highest function of human intelligence, most theorists concluded that the left hemisphere of the brain was considerably more important than the right. More recent evidence, however, has eroded that theory. Indeed, the right hemisphere is now believed to be responsible for such talents as understanding and using spatial relationships, recognizing aspects and areas of our environment, and engaging in mental imagery (Bogen, 1977). In short, the nonlanguage chunk of grey matter on the right side of our heads performs important perceptual functions.

What is hemispheric specialization?

Many of the findings about hemispheric specialization have come about through surgery that severs the two hemispheres. Experimentally, the surgery was first performed in the 1950s on cats and apes, and later on human patients with epileptic disorders. Researchers felt the surgery was justified in humans because splitting the brain seemed to impede epileptic seizures. The complicated split-brain research has confirmed the idea that the human brain is responsible for two very different specialties in intelligent behavior. The research has also developed another crucial fact: the two general types of intellectual behavior—language and nonlanguage—do not compete but complement one another. In a sense, each side of the brain helps its counterpart.

Recent research (Kershner, 1977) links reading difficulties in students of otherwise average ability to faulty cooperation by the two halves of the brain. For most of us, the left hemisphere takes charge when we read, perceiving the symbols we call letters. When the right hemisphere competes rather than cooperates with the left hemisphere in responding to those symbols, the brain is forced to work at less than full capacity. The confusion in the complementary roles of the two sides of the brain may provide the key to understanding why some bright children have trouble with even the simplest printed words.

There are, however, powerful individual differences in hemispheric domination of behavior and those differences are healthy and normal. Although some of us are rational, verbal, and mathematically oriented, others are artistic and intuitive. So what does a dual-function brain imply for teachers? If intelligence really has its origins in the physical structure of the hemispheres, can teachers have much effect on their student's intelligent behavior? From most split-brain researchers, the answer is a resounding yes.

Does the split brain have meaning for educators?

Michael Gazzaniga (1977) has highlighted the significance of split-brain research for educators:

> Superiority in the verbal area might not necessarily mean superiority in the visual-spatial area—while the reverse may also hold true. If this proves correct, it may well follow that a particular child might be able to solve a problem using verbal symbols with greater ease than using visual-spatial ones [and vice versa]. . . . When a child's talents lie in visual-spatial relations and he or she is being forced into a curriculum that emphasizes the verbal articulatory modes of solving a conceptual problem, this child will encounter enormous frustration and difficulty which may well result in hostility toward the teacher and, worse, toward the learning process itself. If the teacher were to be made aware that the child is specialized in visual-spatial skills . . . the discouragement and the subsequent hostility might be avoided if the child is allowed to use his special talents (p. 94).

Gazzaniga and other researchers believe that educational practices have shortchanged nonverbal abilities by stressing and overvaluing verbal skills. J. E. Bogen (1977), an early split-brain theorist, believes that learning in virtually any area is likely to improve if teaching methods employ both language and nonlanguage techniques. Wittrock (1977) reviews several studies that seem to support the simultaneous use of both modes of intelligence. For example, he reports studies that show that when students use vivid imagery—mental pictures—verbal information is better recalled.

The implications of the split-brain findings are fairly direct: we need more diversification of curriculum and methods in order to capitalize on the untapped potential of the right hemisphere. These suggestions are not meant to minimize the importance of language skills; the use of language is surely a masterwork of intelligence. Rather, we propose that increased attention to nonlanguage abilities should enhance and complement language skills, and broaden intelligent behaviors.

The Meaning of IQ Scores

Whatever intelligence is, intelligence tests do not measure it perfectly or directly. Some of the criticism and misunderstanding of the tests, especially among nonprofessionals, results from their name, which implies that they *can* measure intelligence perfectly. Another misconception about the tests is that each item in a test is supposed to reflect the whole intelligence. Thus, any individual item can be cited as unfair to someone whose cultural background or experience does not facilitate an appropriate answer. If a test item required seven-year-olds, for example, to identify an ear of corn, a farmer's son could reply as a matter of course. The equally bright son of a New York subway

"IQ scores have a strong correlation with reading skills. That's not surprising, because reading is a big part of group IQ tests. A low IQ is a challenge to develop better reading skills than the IQ score predicts."

What are some limitations of and misconceptions about IQ?

motorman probably would be baffled. Such items are described as "culturally loaded." Representatives of minority groups complain vehemently that IQ tests are culturally loaded.

What intelligence tests do best is measure and predict academic performance. For that reason, Lee J. Cronbach (1970, p. 3) proposes that "test of general scholastic ability" might be a better name than "intelligence test." When used to *assess* school-related skills, the tests work equally well for all groups. When they are used to *predict* school achievement, they have not been found biased against any subgroup, (Messé, Crano, Messé, and Rice, 1979). With any segment of the school population, the tests serve to identify students who are not likely to interact well with standard schoolroom fare. Generally, these are exceptional students—those who are especially full of, or deficient in, intellectual abilities. Exceptional students, their characteristics, and instructional suggestions are discussed in Chapter 11.

WHAT'S THE SCORE?

IQ, or intelligence quotient, is as misleading a designation as intelligence test because it reflects *performance on a given test*, more than an individual's acuity in relationship to his or her heritage, environment, and experience. In order to understand the IQ score's relation to intelligence, let us return to an idea presented at the beginning of this chapter. Intelligence is a *construct*. Remember that a construct is something unobservable and not directly measurable, such as motivation, ideas, and even time. Despite progress from the sundial and the hourglass to the quartz watch, we still cannot measure the passage of time with absolute accuracy. We have the same problem with intelligence.

Not only are we unable to measure either time or intelligence perfectly, we can't measure them directly. We observe indications of time passing, such as seconds ticking off on a clock, and we observe behaviors performed or problems solved as indications of the invisible intelligence. Our measures of both—time and intelligence—are expressed in symbols we have devised to represent the constructs. A minute or a second is not time, but a *symbol* for time. An IQ score is not intelligence, but a way to express one interpretation of it. Unfortunately, the symbols are often confused with the construct they are meant to represent. Confusion leads to errors, for seconds and IQ scores are only as accurate and useful as the instruments used to gauge them. A malfunctioning watch may make you late for an appointment; a misinterpreted IQ score may affect a child's future career.

In any case, the IQ score tells little about an individual's relative strengths and weaknesses. Two students with the same IQ may well have quite different capabilities: one did better on one kind of test component and the other did better on another kind. One of them may later design automobiles and the other practice medicine. Clearly, the IQ score is limited in the amount of information it can convey; to be useful, it must be supplemented by our own good judgments and observations.

TYPES OF SCORES

Now that you understand that much, you may ask how an IQ score is calculated. Originally, the score was determined by comparing a child's mental and chronological ages. Chronological age is age in years and months at the time the intelligence test is administered. Mental age is identified by the number of correct answers. Thus, the following formula was used to arrive at the *ratio IQ:*

$$\frac{\text{Mental Age}}{\text{Chronological Age}} \times 100 = \text{IQ}$$

A child of seven with a mental age of seven thus would have an IQ of 100, a six-year-old with a mental age of nine would have an IQ of 150, and an eight-year-old with a mental age of six would have an IQ of 75. The ratio supposedly indicated that a child whose achievement on a test was 25 percent above average would continue to develop 25 percent faster than average children of the same age until they all reached fifteen.

Why was the ratio IQ abandoned?

But as children underwent repeated tests at different ages, it became evident that they did not grow mentally at a steady, predictable rate any more than vegetables did physically. In addition, psychologists were at a loss concerning adults. They recognized that people did not continue to grow smarter all of their lives and that a sixty-year-old did not necessarily have twice the intelligence of a thirty-year-old. But where and when and why did intellectual growth stop?

So the ratio IQ has been replaced by a *deviation* IQ. The term *deviation* refers to how much the IQ scores differ from the average at any given age. Somewhat more complicated to calculate than the ratio IQ, the deviation IQ has the advantage of taking into account the different rates of mental development at different ages. In the deviation IQ, the varying rates of growth are standardized so that an IQ of 90 at age seven is the same as an IQ of 90 at age fourteen.

An Average of What? Intelligence tests and IQs would signify nothing if tests were not designed to reflect a nationwide average of intelligence. An IQ of 130 assigned on the basis of a test developed in, say, the wealthy suburban New York village of Scarsdale would not be comparable to an IQ of 130 calculated on the basis of another test developed in, say, an impoverished village in Mississippi.

Like opinion pollsters, test developers attempt to cut an exact cross-section of the country's children on which to base their average score of 100, and thus achieve standardization. For practical reasons, they seek their samples among schoolchildren. But not all children of a given age are in school. If their parents are migrant workers, the children may be helping in the apple orchards or the orange groves, no matter how the law reads. Furthermore, as children grow older, the duller ones tend to quit school: those who remain will have a higher average intelligence. So Johnny, who demonstrated an IQ of 130 in the first grade, may come up with an IQ of 120 when he is a high school senior respectfully called John. He has not become less intelligent; the competition has become tougher.

These are quibbles, we know, for John as an adult will probably not be meeting many migrant workers' children among his associates, and he will be competing for promotion with other persons pretty much like himself. The point is that the IQ is neither a precise index of one's mental stature in relation to all other Americans nor an unchanging figure suitable for tattooing on one's arm.

The Mental Timepiece. To return to our analogy with time, the intelligence test can be considered a mental timepiece and the IQ as a reading of an individual's mental time at a given point and under particular circumstances. On two different tests, such as the Stanford-Binet and the Wechsler Scale, the same student is likely to emerge with somewhat differing scores. On similar tests administered a few days apart, a student may register different—though not too different—readings, depending on how much sleep he or she has had the night before, how a date behaved at the class dance, what minute variations appear in test questions, or simply whether the student is running fast or slow that day. The phenomonon may be compared to two watches running at ever so slightly different rates and giving different readings by the end of a day.

When the Tests Goof. On occasion, for whatever reason, the results of a test may wander far off base. The psychologist Robert L. Williams (1974) writes that when he took an intelligence test at the age of fifteen in Little Rock, Arkansas, his IQ was recorded as 82, and his counselor suggested that he become a bricklayer. "My low IQ, however, did not allow me to see that as desirable," Williams says, so he went on to obtain his Ph.D. at Washington University in St. Louis, to become a professor of psychology there, and to serve as national chairman of the Association of Black Psychologists.

Are IQ scores reliable?

The point here is that, despite the expertise, time, and effort that have been dedicated to the preparation of intelligence tests, the tests are not perfect. They relate to and will help predict performance in school for *most* people. But when an individual's performance and IQ score differ as Williams's did, skepticism about the test, or the way it was administered, is in order.

Group versus Individual Tests. Not all intelligence tests are intended to be administered the same way. The most obvious difference is whether they are given to a group of students or to one student at a time. The Stanford-Binet and the Wechsler tests are given individually; others to, say, a whole grade. Each testing method has its merits. Group tests cost much less. They signal the presence of *exceptional* children (see Chapter 11) who may require special instruction. Individual tests permit a trained examiner, by questioning and observation, to detect abilities and disabilities that a group test would miss. Individual tests can also produce a more accurate IQ score than group tests, because a child who gets a chance to explain an answer may reveal reasoning power or knowledge that initially was obscured.

Another important difference between the two kinds of test is that, in testing an individual, the examiner does all the reading and records all the answers. In a group test, the students read the items, so the group test may measure reading skills more than general mental capacity. Group test directions are read to the whole class, so each student receives only limited attention. For the average youngster, this may not matter much, but for those with impaired hearing or other physical problems, and those who speak English as a second language, it does matter. A misunderstood or unheard direction may lead to errors that are not due to ignorance.

Why use a group test?

Group testing may also penalize the elderly. When the WAIS (the adult version of the Wechsler intelligence tests) was being standardized, it was administered individually to a collection of people over sixty who served as guinea pigs, so to speak. Their scores would provide the average that would set the standards for that age group. But the human guinea pigs used to fall asleep on the job (Wesman, 1955). If that happened on a group test, the IQ score derived from that test would be invalid.

Other problems associated with testing adults pertain to motivation and interest. Schaie and Willis (1979) have concluded that IQ tests for adults produce valid scores only if the tests include tasks that adults consider relevant and important. In individual tests, the administrator can more easily note whether or not the respondent is interested and working on the questions. In a group, an adult who turns off on a test may go unnoticed. So, although they are less expensive, group tests are not preferable when we wish to get as valid as possible an assessment of intelligence.

The Absolutely Fair Test. IQ tests for adults have been criticized as unrelated to the daily tasks faced by people past school age (Schaie and Willis, 1979). More vehement criticism of IQ tests in general has come from those who charge the tests are not relevant for nonwhite, non-middle-class folk. Statistical evidence that black children *average* somewhat lower than white children on intelligence tests has evoked the criticism mentioned earlier in this chapter that the tests are *culturally biased.* That is, the questions they ask relate to the experience and upbringing of white middle-class youngsters, rather than to those of, say, black, Hispanic, and American Indian children.

Statements by "persons in responsible positions" who feel that way were gathered by Anne Anastasi:

> "The use of Test *X* is discriminatory because members of a minority group score lower on it than do members of the majority culture."
>
> "If an intellectual or emotional difficulty can be attributed to environmental handicaps in the individual's background, it should be discounted and over looked because it is not part of his real nature."
>
> "Specially developed culture-fair tests are needed to rule out the effects of prior cultural deprivation in assessing a child's educational readiness or an applicant's job qualifications" (1973, p. 346).

Accordingly, a number of educational researchers attempted to devise intelligence tests that were free of cultural bias. The notion was doomed from birth, because everything we know or can do is influenced by cultural, that is, environmental, circumstances. Consider as innocent-looking a question as "Who discovered America?" The answer "Columbus" reflects cultural bias (Zach, 1972). A Scandinavian might well insist that the correct reply was "Leif Ericson," an Irishman, "St. Brendan," and a Lebanese, the dozen Phoenician seafarers said to have landed in Brazil before the birth of Jesus. An American Indian might consider the whole question to be culturally biased. (Insistence on any single answer as "correct" would also demonstrate convergent thinking, by the way.)

Must intelligence tests be culture bound?

Because the IQ and cultural influences seemed inseparable, researchers then turned to devising "culture-fair" tests that employed material common to many cultures and that challenged reasoning power rather than knowledge. But few such tests have yielded results different from those of the "biased" tests. Ethnic groups continued to rank, on the basis of *average* scores, in the same order on both kinds of tests. In one series of "culture-fair" tests, Chinese children recently arrived from Hong Kong and Taiwan with little English outperformed the white American norm. Eskimo children equaled the white American norm. Black children did better on some "biased" tests than they did on the "culture-fair" tests (Jensen, 1973). So "culture-fair" tests thus far have added little if anything to what traditional intelligence tests can do.

The most recent avenue of investigation in the search for fairness has been named *neurometrics*. A neurometric assessment eliminates all verbal questions. Instead, electrodes are taped to a person's temples to record brain responses and activity on an electroencephalograph, or EEG. The result is a "fingerprint of the brain" that evidences the speed and manner in which the brain responds to sensory stimuli or changes in stimulus patterns. For example, a sensory pattern may consist of a series of two clicks followed by a buzz. The brain adjusts to the pattern with repeated exposure. The adaptation is indicated by the amount of specific electrical activity in the brain, as measured by the EEG. If the pattern is changed, say by the addition of a soft click to the series, the amount of electrical activity changes. The change, technically called the "evoked potential," can be measured for its speed and amount.

Neurometrics was originally explored to help identify brain damage or retardation in children. The EEG patterns for brain-damaged or retarded children were unusual and tended to correspond with results from Stanford-Binet or Wechsler IQ tests given later (Rice, 1979). Neurometrics is currently viewed as a possibly promising way to test students who have language or hearing problems that interfere with regular IQ testing. If it proves useful with them, neurometrics will most likely be applied to preschool youngsters and to those who have different cultural backgrounds.

Nature versus Nurture

Every ethnic group, of course, encompasses superior, average, and inferior individuals. But when tests yield different mean scores for different ethnic groups, they inevitably raise this question: How much of intelligence is hereditary and how much results from environment?

Supporters of the fixed, inherited intelligence theory often cite three points as evidence:

1. Although IQs vary widely in any given population, IQs change little in any individual from year to year.
2. Youngsters with initially high IQs stay well ahead of the average academically and socially, whereas individuals with initially low IQs lag farther and farther behind in achievement as they grow.
3. Twins' IQs generally are similar, indicating that genetic material governs mental as well as physical characteristics.

The controversy over nature versus nurture has flared repeatedly ever since Darwin's cousin, Galton, concluded in 1869 that distinguished men ran in distinguished families. Galton failed, at least at first, to consider that in England's class society, it was easier to attain distinction if one were rich and aristocratic. The issue was raised in the United States by Goddard, as we mentioned earlier in this chapter, and led to the shocking immigration law of 1924.

Shown here is a group of children receiving a test that evaluates a specific skill, such as reading. This is a standardized test on a prerecorded tape which instructs the children on each question. However, note that the teacher also explains the test and monitors the children to check whether they have understood the instructions. Many things tend to interfere with testing, such as inattention or lack of familiarity with this kind of test. In this case a ten-minute test took thirty: the children were new to this school and had never been exposed to this kind of test. Because of this unfamiliarity, time on the test was ignored. The children's scores will determine the level of type of reading group, from advanced to remedial, to which they are assigned.

For a while after that, in a changed national mood, many people believed that it was unthinkable to ask whether or not intelligence was inherited. But in the late 1960s it was suggested that the matter merited further investigation. That suggestion evoked charges of racism and fueled disruptions in several colleges. The controversy centered on Arthur Jensen.

Jensen (1969) claimed that data collected in more than thirty years of intelligence testing indicated that blacks scored consistently lower than whites on intelligence tests. The lower scores, in Jensen's thinking, are due in large part to inheritance. Jensen supported his claims by citing that, as a group, blacks score about 15 points lower than do whites on standard IQ tests and that on no valid test yet constructed do blacks score as well as whites.

Jensen's statements elicited a variety of responses, some of them printable. Sowell (1977) points out that the lower IQ scores of blacks as a group are similar to the score patterns of European immigrant groups in the 1920s. The Europeans' initial problems seemed to stem from differences of language and culture. Once the immigrants and their children came to understand American culture and the English language and to fit into the national mainstream, they scored as high as or higher than the average. Sowell and others hold that the economic, cultural, and language problems that blacks continue to face are much like those which the immigrants encountered.

For the following ten years, no major flareups occurred in the nature-nurture controversy. But late in 1979 Jensen rekindled the debate with his book *Bias in Mental Testing*. In it, he concludes that a verbal advantage of whites over blacks does not explain the IQ differences on standard tests. To support his conclusion, he cites these facts: Blacks appear to do slightly better on tests emphasizing verbal skills than they do on performance tests. Whites score better on IQ tests written in black ghetto slang than do most blacks. Among black and white children of equivalent socioeconomic backgrounds, the whites score about 12 points higher than their black peers.

Ironically, both Jensen and his critics propose abandonment of IQ tests in elementary schools. The critics contend that the differences in IQ scores can be traced to bias in the tests. Jensen is willing to discontinue the tests in lower grades because they may serve merely to identify gifted or dull students. However, the debate between Jensen and his critics over the inheritance of intelligence continues.

Clearly, both heredity and environment influence intelligence. There is not as yet—and there may never be—firm evidence that one or the other is dominant. Neither is there evidence that heredity operates on a racial, rather than an individual, basis. Psychologists generally assume that heredity sets the upper limits of intelligence but that environment determines whether or not those limits will be attained. Between heredity and environment there is constant interaction. But the results of the interaction are unpredictable. That is because a single environmental factor will have differing effects on the different hereditary components of different individuals. Similarly, a heredity factor will have different effects on differing environmental factors. Further-

What is the evidence that intelligence is inherited?

. . . learned?

. . . and why does it matter?

more, some inherited characteristics are not immutable, but can be changed by environment (Anastasi, 1973).

IN THE CLASSROOM

Whether nature or nurture is dominant remains a fascinating question, but the answer—whatever it may be—should not concern you too much as a teacher. A good many authorities believe that even if it were proven that heredity is more important to intelligence than environment is, teachers still would have to teach as though environment were the controlling factor.

One reason is that some hereditary characteristics can be changed by environment, as we noted just above. Another is that, even if heredity accounts for as much as 80 percent of intelligence, as Jensen proposes, the remaining 20 percent represents a considerable area of intellectual functioning. A teacher's concentration on that 20 percent, it is argued, might produce some impressive results in the form of higher school achievement.

The Development of Language

LANGUAGE AND INTELLIGENCE

A relationship between language and intellectual growth was indicated in the third of Bruner's benchmarks, set down in Chapter 2. That benchmark bears repetition here: "Intellectual growth involves an increased capacity to say to oneself and others, by means of words or symbols, what one has done or what one will do." We often get our first impressions about a person's intelligence from the way he or she speaks. When we listen to others express their thoughts, we are swayed not only by what they say but by the way they say it. Our subjective assessments of the intelligence of those around us are built on the verbal abilities we hear demonstrated. Intelligence tests from Binet's on have had, not surprisingly, a strong verbal component. But recently there has been strong, renewed interest in a connection between the way youngsters acquire fluency in language and the construct that we call intelligence.

How are language and intelligence related?

It has long been realized that a high correlation exists between verbal skills and scores on intelligence tests. People adept at using words tend to score high; the less adept score low. That indisputable fact raises some questions: Do verbal skills indicate intelligence? Do they help foster the growth of intelligence or aid us in storing information? Or do intelligence tests simply overemphasize verbal skills and so favor people high in those skills? Some critics of intelligence tests say no, verbal skills do not necessarily indicate intelligence and yes, intelligence tests certainly overemphasize verbal skills. Those critics contend that the tests favor individuals thoroughly at home with standard English and discriminate against those who deviate from it.

It is difficult to determine whether or not the critics are right. The answer to the second question, however, that of the relationship between verbal skills and thinking, is clearer. Much of thinking involves the manipulation of abstract symbols, and we appear to depend greatly on language to provide those symbols. But before we go too far into that interesting psychological issue, let's look at language from a somewhat broader perspective.

An average adult commands some 50,000 verbal symbols to convey thoughts, ideas, wishes. But how people acquire language remains a puzzling question that evokes other questions: How is it that we are able to understand words? How does one string together words to express a vague shadow of thought? Why do such vast differences exist in individuals' ability to use and comprehend language?

Most of us take it for granted that young children's speech is inept, clumsy, and immature. But if we listen carefully to youngsters, we find a rich and impressive array of patterns and developmental differences—as well as considerable deviation from standard American English. There are grammatical aberrations, one-word sentences, unique words. A small child, seeing a tree buffeted by wind, may remark, "That tree sure is being winded." Young children are "hitted," and complain that one "gots" more chocolate milk than the other. Have they heard others speak so, and are they merely imitating others' speech? Or do they use some internal system of rules and invent words and phrases? These are some of the issues one confronts in studying language development and usage.

WHAT IS LANGUAGE?

Language, like most other aspects of complex human behavior, is difficult to define. For one thing, it is not synonymous with communication. There are many ways to communicate without language, although they are often less precise than language. Raising an eyebrow to someone may signal a message, but the message may be vague, unnoticed, or meaningless. And if the eyebrow twitched unintentionally, should a message be read? And how?

It is also important to remember that each time we use language we are not necessarily limited to audible speech. Language includes both the communications we can *hear*, such as *speech*, as well as those which we can *watch*, such as American Sign Language (ASL). The language of the deaf, ASL, is visual rather than audible and parallels our spoken forms of language quite nicely. Like any other language, ASL has a distinctive grammar and structure. Children learn to speak it in much the same way they learn standard English (Pines, 1979).

Formal language, be it manual ASL or oral speech, provides us with a set of symbols that can be referenced and defined, and it gives us a structure, or grammar, for organizing the symbols. The use of language is more intentional, more purposeful, more goal-directed than communication without language.

Table 3.1. The Sequence of Emerging Language Behaviors

Birth to 6 months	*The infant period.* The child produces such sounds as grunts, cries, gasps, shrieks, chuckling, and cooing (at 4 months).
6 months to 9 months	*The babbling period.* The child produces units of utterances called babbling that differ from one situation to another. These units begin to be acoustically similar to adult utterances because the child sloughs off the irrelevant phonemes rather than acquiring new phonemes.
9 months	*The jargon period.* Stresses and intonation patterns in strings of utterance units clearly correspond to those of the adult. Some imitation of general language-like patterns can be identified. Specific morphemes cannot be distinguished easily by the listener.
9 months to 1 year	*The quiet period.* The decrease in vocalization during this period of development is interesting. Language habits continue to develop but changes are not immediately apparent to the observer. One reason for this period of relative quiet may be the discontinuity in language development between the previous stage and next stages; a transition occurs from the use of jargon to the use of words as the adult knows them.
1year to 2 years	*The holophrastic stage.* The child uses single words to indicate whole phrases. He can use base structure, but transformational rules to produce the surface structure have not been acquired. The single word is the start of the child's vocabulary. Preconventional "words" are considered words by the parent because a given sound pattern is used consistently in similar situations (for example, using "muk" for milk). These vocalizations sound like words and may be considered words by the prideful parents. The child understands much of what he is told. He demonstrates his comprehension by responding in a way that is meaningful to the adult—he may obey a command or point to an object. At the end of this period, the child produces from 20 words (at about 18 months) to 200 words (at about 21 months).
2 years	*The spurt in word development.* Many conventional words appear in the child's vocabulary, which increases from 300 to 400 words at 24 to 27 months to 1000 words at 36 months. He produces two- and three-word utterances, phrases, and sentences in which the pivot-open structure is well established. A given word can be used with a number of intonations: specifically, declarative ("doll."); emphatic ("doll!"); and interrogative ("doll?").
3 years	*The sentence period.* At 36 to 39 months, the child can use 1000 words; he uses sentences containing grammatical features that anticipate the adult's use of language rules. He uses functionally complete sentences—that is, sentences that clearly designate an idea as in the sentence, "This one riding horse."—that are grammatically incomplete.
3 to 5 years	The child uses sentences of all types: non-understandable sentences, functionally complete but grammatically incomplete

sentences, simple sentences, simple sentences with phrases, compound sentences, complex sentences, and compound-complex sentences.

5 years to maturity — The individual's language system shows more frequent use of sentences with complex structure, increases in the variety of types of sentences, and increases in the length of sentences.

From Di Vesta (1974), pp. 47–48.

But how do humans acquire symbols, grammar, and meaning? Let's start by considering the typical order of language development.

THE SEQUENCE OF LANGUAGE DEVELOPMENT

The emergence of language is surprisingly orderly. Although the rate at which children learn to speak varies considerably, the sequence is relatively sturdy. Table 3.1 summarizes the major steps in the acquisition of language.

From birth until about six months of age, an infant produces sounds such as grunts and cries that are genetically organized; these sounds appear to represent states of need, and the child has little or no choice about making them. He or she merely responds to the internal and external environment. At around six months, psychologists believe, children enter the babbling stage. Now many of the child's sounds more nearly resemble parts of adults' words; the child has discarded many sounds not heard in the environment. When a child is about a year old, eager parents detect—often prematurely—single words that seem to approximate adults' words. Soon some of these utterances are heard more frequently and regularly. When frequency and regularity increase, we can be fairly sure that the child is beginning to attach some meaning to the symbols, as with the word *Mama*.

Mama is important to speech's development. It has become increasingly evident that the conversations between mothers and their babies, even before the babe has uttered a single understandable word, constitute the first steps in learning to talk.

The Holophrastic Stage. From one to about two years of age, children talk increasingly with one-word sentences. These one-word segments of information are meant to represent whole phrases, hence the term *holophrastic*. One-word, holophrastic speech may utterly confuse a listener who does not appreciate the word's context. Little Joan's "Go!" may mean "I want to go outside" or "You go" or "Let's go together" or "The car goes" or dozens of other ideas. To understand Joan's meaning, it is necessary to observe what she is doing. Even then it may take some practice, because Joan may use other cues along with the word. A loud, high-pitched "Go!" may indicate that she is ready to go eat, whereas the same "Go!" accompanied by a tug of the hearer's hand could mean that she wants to play a game.

In what sequence does language develop?

Onward and Upward. In the second year of a child's life, vocabulary increases at least threefold, from 300 or 400 words to a thousand or more. At the same time, the child begins to string together two- and three-word phrases that convey more specific meaning than the single-word utterances and are not used in so wide a variety of situations.

These rudimentary sentences are sometimes referred to as "telegraphic speech," because they omit nonessential information. "Want ball" sounds like the classic student telegram home: "Send money." In recent years, psychologists have wondered, do two and three year olds use a simplified grammar to build telegraphic sentences? A series of studies has shown that young children do pattern their words according to a grammatical structure (R. Brown, 1973), although the rules are not clear, because they seem to differ from those of adult grammar. But children at this stage can obviously understand adult grammar. If parents can decipher the one- and two-word sentences, and respond to them in adult language, the child will be stimulated to speak more (Pines, 1979). And, in speaking more, children get additional practice in the rules of language that they will eventually follow unconsciously. By increasing use of even the simplest of these rules, children heighten their language capabilities immeasurably and create their own sentences according to the grammar. They still omit unnecessary information, but most of the novel and sketchy sentences are readily understandable. Braine (1963) cites some examples: "more

"Yes, I think that education boosts intelligence. If you turn the question around, it becomes more obvious: Without formal schooling, how many of these children would be able to do math, reading, writing? Well, if no schooling lowers intellectual performance, then schooling must raise it. Actually, I'm not very interested in intelligence as an abstract potential. It's much easier to deal with if we refer to intellectual behaviors."

page" (read some more, please); "more car" (drive around some more); "all-gone sticky" (I washed my hands).

Rules and Regularization. From here on, children gradually elaborate their language, gathering a broader vocabulary and approximating complex and sophisticated adult grammar. But it will be years before they master adult speech patterns, partly because of a peculiar deviation in language development.

It seems reasonable to think that children will learn certain rules for words—such as creating a plural noun, or changing a verb to past tense—and that they mistakenly apply the rules to irregular words. If a child has learned that adding *ed* to a regular verb will convert it to past tense, then we would expect that child also to apply that rule to irregular verbs. And, indeed, children say "goed," and "comed," and "beed." However, Slobin (1971) reports that this commonsense sequence is probably the reverse of the way children learn and use adult grammar. He observes that the irregular words are often learned first, and correctly. Then a child learns, say, the past tense for several regular verbs, and suddenly applies the new rule to the earlier correct words. Children will thus learn the proper forms "He ate it," "I found it," and "I saw you" *before* they try to regularize the verbs as "he eated it," "I finded it," and "I seed you." Slobin hypothesizes that forms of the irregular words are learned independently, and that the child may see no connection between "eat" and "ate" or between "do" and "did." "Eated" and "ate" are merely different words, not contradictions of one another. Slobin reports that the phenomenon occurs in many languages, and is not peculiar to Western culture.

HOW IS LANGUAGE ACQUIRED?

The general progression of early language development tells little about *how* and *why* language develops. There are two major and conflicting theories about that. One theory, the *behaviorist* position, uses only external, observable events to support its hypotheses. The competing theory, a *psycholinguistic* position, speculates about the events that occur inside the learner's head.

Behaviorism and Operant Conditioning of Language. Behaviorism, discussed at length in Chapter 5, is well represented by B. F. Skinner, who devoted a book to the analysis of language learning (Skinner, 1957). His position, echoed by behavioral philosophy, is that speculation about unobservable events—such as those which occur inside the head—is not scientific. If we confine our analysis to external, measurable phenomena, he says, we will be on firmer ground.

In Skinner's view, verbal behavior is learned from what happens after one talks. If one is punished or ignored for making a particular sound or saying a certain word, then one will decrease the use of that sound or word. Similarly, if one is rewarded for saying something, one will tend to repeat whatever was said to gain another reward. If imitation plays a role in language acquisition, Skinner says it is because the child has been rewarded for imitating speech. This simplified version of language development is based on *operant* conditioning, because the environment (consequences) teaches a person to *operate* on the environment with words. The child is praised and cuddled and given a drink for uttering something like "water." These consequences teach children that they can operate on the environment (actually on Mommy or Daddy!) by saying "water."

Does conditioned language permit creative thought?

Although the behaviorists originally looked at the more obvious consequences of children's speech—praise, a hug, and a drink following the word "water"—others took note of the more subtle consequences that also encourage the child. Bruner (1978) closely studied mothers talking to their infants; in recording the mothers' speech on tape, Bruner noticed that the mothers used, apparently unconsciously, a system of successive approximations to encourage their children to employ well-formed speech. For example, they would frequently ask their children to name something, such as a picture in a book. When the child didn't know the name, Mom would supply it—the first time. But once the mother thought that the child knew the name, she no longer spoke it. She might ask again for it, or offer an additional cue, but she tended to hold out for the right, well-formed word. For a more detailed description of this procedure, called *shaping* or *successive approximation*, and the larger process of operant conditioning, see Chapter 5.

Transformational Grammar. Noam Chomsky, the inventor of the theory of transformational grammar, works at the Massachusetts Institute of Technology, only a few miles from Skinner's Harvard. But the distance between their theories seems interstellar. Chomsky (1959) has criticized Skinner's views as overly simplistic because Skinner refuses to consider internal events. For Chomsky, Skinner's learner is little more than a robot, responding automatically to stimuli. Learners do more than respond to stimuli, Chomsky says. They *transform* stimuli according to rules of grammar stored in their heads. The transformation consists of sequencing words to invent sentences and of generalizing grammatical rules to apply them to new vocabulary. In sum, learners use their own bags of tricks to confront language and manipulate it to suit their needs (Chomsky, 1965).

How does transformational grammar differ from operant conditioning of language?

For Chomsky, all humans everywhere have the inborn inclination to learn and master language. All humans capable of learning a language do so, he points out, and they do it in the same sequence and at about the same time. Skinner, by contrast, counts on the environment, not some inherent predisposition, to cause words to be associated with other words.

The issues have never been settled, but many theorists feel uncomfortable about Skinner's radical behaviorism and his dismissal of internal events. Yet Chomsky's dependence on internal mechanisms as an explanation for language development also seems unsatisfying. Just hearing language and listening to others speak is not enough to trigger those innate structures to produce words. For example, the deaf parents of a normal child exposed him to several hours of TV a day in the hope that he would learn to speak and understand standard English. They were sorely disappointed. Although the child had acquired fluency in sign language by the age of three, he could not understand or speak English. The voices on TV could not, of course, respond to the child's babble, so there was no spoken *interaction* with the child. Responses to the child's attempts at speech were needed for the child to learn to talk (Pines, 1979).

One possible resolution to the conflict in the two theories, Skinner's and Chomsky's, lies in acknowledging that parts of each are probably valid. Reward or punishment, practice and imitation do indeed influence language development, *and* learners do use innate tendencies to learn and create language. Environment's effects and the innate capacity for language are both evidenced by the facts that there are many different languages and that even within a culture there are varied speech patterns or dialects.

CULTURE, LANGUAGE, AND THE CLASSROOM

The language we speak and the culture in which we live are closely related, but *how* they relate to one another is debated as vehemently as the differences between Skinner and Chomsky. For you as a teacher, the issue is likely to have more than theoretical importance: would you, perhaps subconsciously, expect less from a youngster who spoke black English vernacular (BEV) on the ground that the youngster came from an inferior culture? Or would you accept that the youngster's speech merely reflected a *different* culture?

Before you answer the questions for yourself, let's consider some diverse approaches to the language-culture relationship. It is more than tempting to think that cultural influences shape and change language. Cultural interests, attitudes, and needs appear to determine at least *some* of language, Di Vesta (1974) points out, and we expand and elaborate our vocabularies in accordance with those interests, attitudes, and needs. Eskimos understandably have invented at least a hundred terms for snow. The Trobrianders, a primitive South Pacific tribe, have many names for each type of fruit they eat, one name for each stage of growth. A future engineer should be able to distinguish, as Roger Brown (1965) suggests, among the ninety-odd varieties of engineering listed in the Massachusetts Institute of Technology's catalogue. Even socially, lots of us find it necessary to increase our store of words, to wit: *hip, far out, cool, bad, with it, funky, heavy, jazzy, premium.*

Language and culture: Which shapes the other?

Whorf's Hypothesis. But not everyone agrees that cultures build vocabularies to reflect their needs and interests. In the view of linguistics expert Benjamin Whorf (Carroll, 1956), language *causes* needs, beliefs, and perceptions of the world, and the way we talk about and categorize the world determines how we perceive and respond to that world. If thought resembles inner language, then one can comprehend only that part of the environment for which one has linguistic symbols. If your neighbor speaks—and thinks—with words different from yours, then that person's reality also is different.

Most current theorists doubt that language *causes* a particular view of the world. Rather, they acknowledge the *influence* of language on thought, and stress the interdependence of the two (Kess, 1976).

There seem to be three ways to look at the relationship between language and thought (Di Vesta and Palermo, 1974). Two of them correspond roughly to views of the larger process of cognitive development, discussed in Chapter 2.

Language and Thought Are Synonymous. Because thought is internal and unobservable, it is unworthy of scientific analysis, Skinner asserts. Language, its external counterpart, is measurable, manipulable, and controlled by the environment. That interpretation of the relationship between language and thought and of the influence of environmental experiences on both reflects some of Bruner's developmental theories. You will recall that Bruner suggests that cognitive development can be speeded by appropriate arrangement of the environment (See Chapter 2). He says also that language is our only means of representing thought. So the behaviorist may look at difficulties in learning to speak as indicating problems in learning to think; Bruner may see those same difficulties as an indication of environmental interference with cognitive development.

Thought Precedes Language. The view popularized by Piaget through his theories of cognitive development says, in summary, that language development accompanies but lags a bit behind cognitive development. Children first develop meanings and mental structures (Piaget calls these structures "schemas," as you saw in Chapter 2) and then seek to express these thoughts. Before a child can say, "More dolly," he or she must be able to think about the possibility of continuing to play with Raggedy Ann.

Does thought require language?

Language Precedes Thought. The view that language precedes thought is most like the Whorfian hypothesis that language causes need. When applied to thought, the theory suggests that the language and words we use direct our mental processes. The Soviet linguist L. S. Vygotsky, in support of this view, concluded that "the use of the sign, or word, is the means by which we direct our mental operations, control their course, and channel them toward solution of the problem confronting us" (1962, p. 58).

Which view is correct? As with theories of language development, no one can say for sure. The speculation and debate continue, because the question of the relationship between language and thought is an important one. In a Whorfian world, it would seem nearly impossible to comprehend and empathize with someone from a different culture who spoke another language or even another dialect. The same would be true if Piaget's interpretation is correct. If thought precedes language, it may be that our cultural attitudes and personal values are established before we ever express them verbally. The position voiced by the behaviorists and Bruner, however, tempers the determinism implicit in the other two views. If the environment and its arrangement have an effect on our language and thought, then the possibility of understanding among different cultural groups increases.

Different or Deficient? Regardless of which view of the language-thought relationship appeals to you, there is no denying that difficulties among cultures (and subcultures) result from existing differences in languages. Not the least of the problems is the issue of black English vernacular. For many years, psychologists and laymen alike believed that BEV represented an inferior means of communication, and Bernstein's (1961) thesis about language differences among social classes lent scholarly credibility to the idea. Bernstein suggested that there were two general types of language, one roughly that of the lower social class and the other of the middle social class. The first, a *restricted code*, which does not closely follow standard English grammar, is simple, rigid, and easily predictable; the second, an *elaborated code*, is more flexible, offers more alternatives, and is less predictable. But like Eliza Doolittle in Shaw's *Pygmalion*, no one is forever bound to either code, Bernstein (1972) says; an individual, a family, or a whole subculture simply *prefers* one code or the other. Much like Whorf, Bernstein maintains that "every time the child speaks or listens, the social structure is reinforced in him or his social identity shaped. . . . Thus, children who have access to different speech systems or codes . . . may adopt quite different social and intellectual orientations and procedures despite a common potential" (1972, pp. 473–74).

Developing an intensive preschool program to help lower-class youngsters succeed in school, Carl Bereiter and Sigfried Engelmann (1966) fitted in Bernstein's hypothesis. Bernstein avoided an outright evaluation of the restricted code, but Bereiter and Engelmann did not, and they evidently consider BEV lacking as a language:

> Culturally deprived children do not just think at an immature level: many of them do not think at all. . . . They cannot hold to questions while searching for an answer. They cannot compare perceptions in any reliable fashion. . . . They do not just give bad explanations. They cannot give explanations at all, nor do they seem to have any idea of what it is to explain an event. The question and answer process which is the core of orderly thinking is completely foreign to them (1966, p. 107).

The view that BEV is deficient as a language has encountered some strong opposition in recent years. One prominent opposition spokesman, William Labov, suggests that that view is simply racism in academic clothing; Labov (1972) argues that black dialect is neither inferior to standard English nor a product of cultural deprivation: it is just different.

In the Classroom. The Bereiter-Engelmann view, Labov warns, may be adopted all too easily in the classroom. Teachers seeking to explain poor

A teacher on BEV: "The kids have just come from home—their neighborhoods where it's just that way. 'Ain't' is just part of almost every child's vocabulary. It takes me a year and you have to work at it, but eventually I'll get it out of them. That's the one thing I think they resent most of all—their language being corrected, even though you're doing it for their own good. But for them it's just a natural thing to say. Like Spanish with some of them. It's just a language difference, and like any foreign language it can cause some problems when you're trying to teach. You have to work with it that way—including being interested in their culture where that language comes from. I've been fortunate over the years; this is the third year of busing we've had, and we've never had a fight in the classroom. I treat it just like any other foreign language, and it works."

achievement on the part of disadvantaged youngsters may find it convenient to hold BEV's alleged lacks responsible. Instead of trying to understand cultural heritage and instead of recognizing the equivalence of differing dialects, Labov says, teachers may lower their expectations of the disadvantaged learner and lose interest in helping him or her.

Should nonstandard dialects be permitted in school?

What do we do about it? you may ask. The question is a tough one, for the problem is complicated and thorny, and emotions often outshout possible solutions. Conflicts similar to those over BEV arise elsewhere. In the Western United States, the growth of the Mexican-American population has increased the number of nonstandard dialects in use. Comparable problems have developed in Canada around the French and English languages. California and Canada have undertaken experimental programs called "total immersion," in which elementary school students are instructed almost entirely in a language other than their native tongue. A California youngster may be addressed in formal Spanish by his math teacher; a French-speaking second grader in Canada may get and copy down her homework assignment in English. The programs are still in their infancy, but participating students appear to learn to speak the second language quickly after immersion, and some students show indications of thinking in it. Youngsters unconsciously and spontaneously address their parents in the second language and use it to order ice cream at the soda fountain.

Other programs aimed at assaulting the language problem propose to fit instruction to each student's needs, abilities, and interests. Baratz and Baratz (1970) urge that standard English be formally taught as a foreign language to those black children who speak BEV; in such teaching, instructors themselves would use BEV predominantly. The proposal—not yet suitably tested or widely adopted—is intended to achieve the same end result as the language immersion programs, to produce citizens who would be at home in both the majority and minority cultures. (England provides an example of how that would work: people who live in Yorkshire usually communicate among themselves in the Yorkshire dialect, which baffles outsiders, but employ the Queen's English in talking to non-Yorkshiremen.)

But even if all teachers and theorists suddenly come to believe that BEV, like other languages, is merely different rather than deficient, racial or cultural problems are hardly likely to disappear automatically. Classrooms are not games of checkers, from which one can withdraw when things do not go well. Scores of societal rules operate in the schools, and students who communicate differently from their fellows may unintentionally violate those rules. So, as you read at the start of this section, the relationship of language and culture is of more than theoretical interest, but we have a long way to go in coping with the difficulties it engenders.

Summary

Although intelligence is a major component of students' entry characteristics, its precise nature remains undetermined. It seems to be defined differently in different cultures and to be made up of several behaviors or skills. Yet, many people have attempted to measure something that they call intelligence.

The first modern test to measure intelligence was devised by Alfred Binet in Paris, introduced in the United States in 1908, and revised as the *Stanford-Binet Test* by Lewis M. Terman in 1916. The test was administered to one individual at a time. The first mass test, the *Army Alpha*, was employed by the United States Army in World War I, and gave great impetus to intelligence testing in schools and industry. Because the Stanford-Binet Test was designed for children and adolescents, David Wechsler of Bellevue Hospital, a clinical psychologist whose patients were adults, devised the *Wechsler Scale* in 1944. He subsequently produced Wechsler scales for preschool children and for youngsters between the ages of six and sixteen. The Stanford-Binet and Wechsler scales are the most widely used tests.

Part of the difficulty in creating a measure of intelligence lies in the disagreement about how intelligence functions. Alfred Binet concluded that intelligence increased with age, that its development could be accelerated by training, instruction, and mental exercise. J. P. Guilford, who has drawn a *structure of intellect* as a box containing 120 cells, stresses *convergent* and *divergent thinking*. Convergent thinkers seek a single answer to a question or problem; divergent thinkers weigh the possibility of several answers. Piaget believes that ascertaining the *quality* of a child's thinking is more meaningful than attempting to describe how much intelligence is present. The reasoning behind a child's responses allows an estimate of the child's current level of cognitive development, and instructional programming, Piaget claimed, should be built on that basis.

Split-brain research has produced new theoretical developments about the brain's role in intelligent behavior. The two hemispheres of the brain apparently originate quite different but complementary processes of intelligence. The left hemisphere is responsible for verbal, mathematical, and analytic behaviors, whereas the right produces spatial, perceptual, and recognition skills. Although each half of the brain has its own duties, it is becoming increasingly clear that no brain can operate at maximum efficiency unless both sides communicate and cooperate. Researchers of hemispheric specialization have called for increased classroom emphasis on nonlanguage activities, which should help to fulfill the potential of the right half of the brain.

Because of this diversity of theories on what intelligence is and how it functions, attempts to measure it have encountered considerable criticism. Part of this criticism is a result of misunderstanding. Intelligence tests do not measure intelligence precisely, and the IQs they yield do not represent a fixed quantity or quality of intellect. The tests serve best to predict performance in school or in a job. The IQ reflects the score on a given test, and an individual's IQ may vary somewhat on different tests at different times.

One complaint about intelligence tests is that they are *weighted* in favor of white middle-class youngsters because the questions are based on a white middle-class culture. But tests designed to eliminate possible bias usually produce the same results as the supposedly unfair tests. That fact has rekindled the debate about the influence of heredity on intelligence. Most psychologists believe that both heredity and environment contribute to intelligence, but the relative weight of each remains unknown.

For teachers, the answer may not be too important. Some hereditary characteristics may be changed by environment. Furthermore, even if heredity accounted for as much as 80 percent of intelligence, the remaining 20 percent would represent a considerable area in which a teacher could work to improve student performance.

As language is the most evident sign of intelligence, its development is an important consideration. Generally, a language is made meaningful through a grammar that organizes its arbitrary symbols. At birth, infants start up the long ladder of communication, although their excited noises bear little resemblance to adult speech. At about twelve months, children are using one-word, *holophrastic* "sentences" to communicate a variety of meanings. Their vocabulary begins to grow immensely, and they quite systematically apply rules of grammar to their language.

Mothers appear to be the earliest and perhaps the most important language teachers their children have. They provide the stimulation and give-and-take conversations that children need to learn the essentials and etiquette of speech.

There is little consensus about why language develops. Two major theories involve *behaviorism*, which focuses on the effects of the environment, and *transformational grammar*, which emphasizes an inherited and universal ability to acquire language.

Similar disagreement abounds regarding the relationship between thought and speech. Just which comes first, thought or speech, or if they are inseparable, remains a puzzle.

Culture surely is related to one's language, although the direction of the influence is not entirely clear. Whorf proposed that language causes culture; a modified view is that culture and language influence one another.

Subcultures with dialect differences have often been viewed as intellectually and socially inferior, on the basis of their mode of communication. Recent attacks have been made, however, on the idea that language differences constitute deficiencies.

Chapter Study Guide

CHAPTER REVIEW

1. Intelligence must be measured indirectly because

   a. it is a construct based on an assortment of intangible qualities and behaviors.
   b. attempts to measure it directly have been criticized as racist.
   c. a direct measure would require evaluation of the electrical potential of the brain.
   d. a direct test would have to rely exclusively on verbal components, and the relation of language to intelligence is in dispute.

2. Which of the brain's hemispheres would be principally engaged in performing each of the following activities, which are used in various contexts to test intelligence?

   a. making patterns from colored blocks
   b. tracking a pencil through a maze
   c. making verbal analogies
   d. drawing inferences from pictures
   e. identifying synonyms of a word

3. Both the Binet and Wechsler scales

   a. were used to limit the number of immigrants entering the United States.
   b. were used to devise the Army Alpha tests of intelligence.
   c. can be used to determine the IQ of children.
   d. focus primarily on verbal abilities.
   e. all of the above.

4. Theories of intelligence

   a. have generally become more complex in recent years.
   b. have never been successfully tied to intelligence testing.

    c. rely heavily on computers for interpretation.

    d. show slight differences in wording, but all seem to share the same underlying theme.

    e. are basically elaborate explanations of verbal problem-solving.

5. The deviation IQ

    a. has been replaced by the use of the ratio IQ.

    b. assumes a steady rate of intellectual growth.

    c. allows comparison of IQ scores across different age groups.

    d. averages IQ scores across different age groups.

6. Individual IQ tests

    a. are usually used only when children speak English as a second language.

    b. do not require reading by the examinee.

    c. eliminate the problems of trying to motivate children to do well on tests.

    d. do not require the examinee to follow directions.

    e. rather than group tests are used in most schools.

7. Language

    a. like cognitive thought appears to develop in stages.

    b. generally precedes communication.

    c. may incorporate the use of symbols but does not necessarily do so.

    d. is often less goal-directed than communication.

8. For what purpose was Binet's intelligence test originally intended? For what purpose was Wechsler's? In what way do the Binet and Wechsler scales indicate different conceptions of intelligence? For what purpose is each of these tests principally used today?

9. How does the *deviation IQ* differ from the *ratio IQ*? What limitation in the ratio IQ was the deviation IQ designed to counteract? Why is an individual intelligence test more reliable than a group test?

10. How do the behaviorist and transformational grammar positions differ in explaining language acquisition? Which side do you think has the better argument? Which seems to make people more "intelligent"? Are the two viewpoints mutually exclusive?

FOR FURTHER THOUGHT

1. Which limitations or drawbacks of intelligence tests do you find most serious? In view of their limitations, would you use the tests at all? Under particular circumstances? For specific purposes? Explain.

2. "[There is no] evidence that heredity operates on a racial, rather than an individual basis. Psychologists generally assume that heredity sets the upper limits of intelligence but that environment determines whether or not those limits will be attained." From these statements what can you infer about the teacher's responsibility to help individual students improve their intelligence?

3. Recent research shows that in humans the left and right brains are specialized for quite different purposes: the left brain, verbal and mathematical, using symbols to

perform sequential logic; the right, perceiving sensory imagery and patterns and spatial relationships. Generally, schools have emphasized the verbal and mathematical to the neglect of the sensory-visual-imaginative. What implications can be found here for the importance of the arts to the curriculum? Which of the arts do you think would utilize the right brain most fully?

4. Language, thought, and intelligence are closely tied. Can you think of some advantages of being bilingual or multilingual? Are there any disadvantages to speaking and thinking in more than one language? Do you think that speaking a second language may increase one's intellectual capabilities?

5. If a person could be taught a method to increase his or her vocabulary and subsequently his or her verbal abilities, do you think that intellectual abilities would also increase? Consider the same question about physical abilities.

IMPORTANT TERMS

intelligence	ratio IQ
construct	deviation IQ
mental age	group test
Army Alpha test	individual test
Wechsler tests	culture bias
Stanford-Binet test	neurometrics
fluid intelligence	nature-nurture
crystallized intelligence	language
structure of intellect	holophrastic stage
convergent thinking	operant conditioning
divergent thinking	behaviorism
information processing	transformational grammar
distributed memory	black English vernacular
metacomponents	restricted code
components	elaborated code
split-brain	total immersion
IQ score	

SUGGESTED READINGS

BLOCK, N. J., AND DWORKIN, G. (eds.). *The IQ controversy.* New York: Pantheon Books, 1976. An unbalanced presentation of the nature/nurture argument. The editors make no bones about which side they take (nurture), and do provide a fairly representative view of the environmentalist position.

BLUM, J. M. *Pseudoscience and mental ability: The origins and fallacies of the IQ controversy.* N.Y.: Monthly Review Press, 1978. Remarkable mostly in his negativism, Blum attacks all aspects of mental ability testing. Even creativity comes under fire.

FINCHER, J. *Human Intelligence.* New York: G. P. Putnam's Sons, 1976. Fascinating discussion by a journalist of what makes us run. Polished writing and intriguing insights.

FISHBEIN, J., and EMANS, R. *A question of competence: Language, intelligence, and learning to read.* Chicago: Science Research Associates, 1972. A theoretical but highly readable account of the relationship between language and reading. Includes a Piagetian perspective of language.

FOSS, D. J., and HAKES, D. T. *Psycholinguistics.* Englewood Cliffs, NJ: Prentice-Hall, 1978. Introductory text on language acquisition and production.

JENSEN, A. R., et al. *Environment, heredity, and intelligence.* Compiled from the *Harvard Educational Review.* Cambridge, MA: Harvard Educational Review, 1969. Includes the now famous and provocative essay by Jensen which raised a storm of controversy about the inheritance of intelligence. Seven responses, ranging from technical to emotional, and Jensen's rebuttal complete the book of readings.

RESNICK, L. B. (ed.). *The nature of intelligence.* Hillside, NJ: Lawrence Erlbaum Associates, 1976. Advanced and wide-ranging articles on realities and fallacies about intelligence and its measurement.

SATTLER, J. M. *Assessment of children's intelligence* (rev. ed.). Philadelphia: W. B. Saunders, 1974. An extremely comprehensive discussion of the nature of intelligence, intelligence testing, and diagnosis of intellectual deficit.

SMITH, F. *Comprehension and learning: A conceptual framework for teachers.* New York: Holt, Rinehart and Winston, 1975. Introduction to language and concept formation, with emphasis on classroom applications.

THOMSON, D. S., and the EDITORS OF TIME-LIFE BOOKS. *Language.* New York: Time-Life Books, 1975. A lay approach to language development and usage. High in human interest, the book blends research, theory, common sense, and marvelous examples.

ANSWER KEY

1. a; 2.a. right, b. right, c. left, d. right, e. left; 3. c; 4. a; 5. c; 6. b; 7. a

4

Personality and Affective and Moral Development

Understanding of development is, of course, essential to teaching. But teaching—whether your students are children, adolescents, or adults—requires something more. Whenever someone is teaching and someone else is learning, the personality characteristics of both become involved.

You have probably exclaimed more than once, "What a personality!" You may have been expressing admiration for a television performer, a statesman, a friend, a new acquaintance, even a professor. But everyone has a personality—a unique set of characteristics.

How are affect and personality related?

Many of your own characteristics, which reveal themselves in actions, reflect what you know—your cognition. Knowledge alone, though, does not govern all your behavior, or your pupils' or anyone else's. The other major influence is how one *feels*. Educational psychologists describe feelings as *affective variables*. The word *affect* means feelings and values and emotions. As a teacher, you will find affective variables important because they interact with cognitive processes in the acquisition of knowledge—in short, in learning. But an understanding and awareness of the variables will enable you to do more for your students than teach them to read, write, and calculate. It will help you to understand them, and yourself, as human beings—as individuals who not only think but feel.

Theories of Personality Development

As you have discovered thus far, educational psychology is rife with positions and counterpositions, theories and countertheories. So there are many theories about personality, all attempting to identify the experiences that weigh most heavily on evolution of personality. The ideas of Erik H. Erikson may prove the most useful to you. Erikson, unlike most other theorists, considers that personality develops throughout one's life, rather than only when one is growing up.

ERIKSON'S THEORY

Erikson took Sigmund Freud's theory of child development as a base, broadened and expanded it, and added his own unique ideas. Personality develops, Erikson proposes, in eight stages, each marked by conflict. Successful development in any of these stages produces traits and characteristics that permit one to cope with life with little difficulty; unsuccessful development virtually guarantees trouble. Let's consider those eight stages:

What are Erikson's eight stages of psychosocial development?

1. *Basic trust versus basic mistrust.* (First year of life.) The first broad set of characteristics an infant acquires embodies trust or mistrust toward others and self. Whether trust or mistrust dominates is largely determined by the kind of care the infant receives in the early months. When those who

nurture an infant are consistent, dependable, and benevolent, the baby learns that he or she can rely on them; such infants learn also that they can trust themselves and their capacity to cope with their own urges. A baby demonstrates trust by relaxed sleeping, feeding, elimination, and contact with others.

Most parents can tell, of course, when their baby is hungry, tired, cold, in pain, frightened, or angry, and they respond accordingly. When a parent or caretaker is insensitive to the child's needs or habitually responds angrily or erratically, the baby learns not to count on the world for comfort. Mistrust, which Erikson defines as "a readiness for danger and an anticipation of discomfort" (Evans, 1967, p. 15), results. Erikson sees trust as the foundation of a healthy personality. But no one is totally trustful or mistrustful. Consider, for example, the infant who is tossed in the air by a loving sister or father. Flying upward, the baby feels mistrust. Caught safely, the baby feels trust. But mistrust recurs the next time the infant soars ceilingward. Nevertheless, a person who develops normally will reflect a sense of trust of the world and of self. One who encounters problems in the first year of life—a baby, for instance, who has been accidentally dropped when tossed around—may tend toward mistrust.

2. *Autonomy versus shame and doubt.* (Second and third years.) The child now possesses voluntary muscle control, and cognitive as well as physical abilities are increasing rapidly. In this period, the major developmental conflict involves autonomy. The child reaches toward independence and a kind of dignity; he or she wants to do things unassisted and to choose and decide.

When allowed to loosen some of the bonds of complete dependence, to make choices within their capabilities, children create the framework for self-direction. At the same time, they must be able to rely on firm and reassuring parental or other adult control when necessary. Erikson says that this stage is decisive for attaining a healthy balance between self-expression and self-control—i.e., when to speak out and when to shut up.

It is at this stage also that children develop the ability to feel pride in their accomplishment. Three-year-old Chris, for example, was delighted to be allowed to wield a small shovel and "help" his grandfather plant the family's live Christmas tree out-of-doors in January. The hole had been dug long before, but Chris—along with Grandpa—pushed in and tamped down the loose soil to cover the tree's ball of roots. Not long afterward, Grandpa unexpectedly sold the house. Chris heard the news with dismay. "But how," he asked, "will I be able to watch my tree grow?" Don't worry: the buyers of the house assured Chris that he could visit his tree anytime he wished for the rest of his life.

But if, when children are developing a sense of accomplishment, overprotective, overcritical, or impatient parents stifle their kids' growth, the youngsters become ashamed of their efforts and filled with self-doubt. Such children are likely as adults to prove straightlaced, to observe the letter rather than the spirit of the law, and to have "a lasting propensity for doubt and shame" (Erikson, 1963, p. 254).

3. *Initiative versus guilt.* (Third through fifth years.) Erikson defines initiative as "the quality of undertaking, planning, and 'attacking' a task for the sake of being active" (1963, p. 255). By ages three to five, children move around more independently and easily. Their ability to use language is expanding furiously. They are energetic and curious. They are also capable of attack and conquest; they enjoy fighting with other children for toys or adult attention. But the child is now developing a conscience and will feel guilt about aggression, fantasies of aggression, and failures. Parents should help children learn to control aggression, and should also allow them to initiate action and to ask questions without encountering derision. If initiative is too restricted, Erikson believes, the child's conscience becomes cruel and oppressive, and adults with that kind of background judge both themselves and others too harshly.

4. *Industry versus inferiority.* (Sixth through twelfth years.) Beginning at about age five or six, children want to learn to do things, to build, to master skills, and thereby to win recognition for industriousness, for being competently productive. A sense of inferiority, on the other hand, is born of the feeling that one cannot and never will be able to produce. This is the major

---

Erik H. Erikson

Erik Homburger Erikson was born in 1902 in Germany. His Danish parents separated before he was born, and his mother later married a pediatrician.

The young Erikson was not a good student. His formal education ended with his graduation from secondary school. During his late teens and early twenties, he wandered about Europe, reading, writing, briefly studying art, and working at woodcuts. He felt alienated from his middle-class family and described himself as a bohemian. One can recognize at that point in Erikson's development the roots of an important part of his theory—the identity crisis of youth and the need for a period between childhood and adulthood in which identity is established.

At age twenty-five, Erikson accepted a friend's offer of a teaching job in Vienna, at a school that today would be called progressive. It had been established by an American who had gone to Vienna to study with Sigmund Freud and had set up the school for her own and for other American and English children. Many of the pupils were undergoing psychoanalysis with Freud's daughter, Anna, and Erikson himself became one of her patients. Sigmund Freud then chose him as a candidate for psychoanalytic training. Erikson remained in Vienna from 1927 to 1933, becoming a member of Freud's inner circle, teaching, and studying the Montessori method of education as well as child and adult psychoanalysis.

As fascism burgeoned in Europe, Erikson went to Denmark and then came to America, settling in Boston, where he was the first child psychoanalyst. Though his only academic degree was his high school diploma, he was offered, and accepted, a post at the Harvard Medical School; in 1936 he moved to the Yale University Institute of Human Relations to conduct research on children's growth and development.

Erikson was particularly interested in soci-

developmental conflict of the early school years. School experiences prove important in determining how successfully a child develops a sense of industry.

During these years, most children learn not only specific skills but how to work with others. Those who cannot will be poorly equipped for progress toward adulthood.

What theme underlies all eight stages?

5. *Identity versus role confusion.* (Puberty and adolescence.) The identity stage marks childhood's end. During adolescence, rapid body growth and the changes accompanying puberty challenge the sense of continuity and stability. For Erikson, a sense of ego identity represents confidence in one's ability to maintain internal sameness and continuity. The sense of identity has its roots in the first experiences of self-recognition in infancy, and in the development of independence, dignity, self-worth, and competence in children. In adolescence, the young person must integrate his or her physical attributes, aptitudes, abilities, ways of adapting, and social roles into a solid sense of self. Identity evolves through a process of self-observation and judgment. At its best, a sense of identity is experienced as a feeling of well-being; it includes acceptance of one's body as it is, confidence in "where one is going," and assurance that people important in one's life will bestow recognition.

ety's effect on personality development. In 1938 he traveled with an anthropologist to a Sioux reservation in South Dakota to observe Indian culture and childrearing practices, and later studied the Yurok tribe in Northern California. In California, where he lived from 1939 to 1949, he participated in a long-term study of child development at the Institute of Child Welfare at the University of California. At a rehabilitation center for emotionally disturbed World War II veterans, Erikson became aware of problems of identity as he observed them in the center's patients.

His first book, *Childhood and Society* (1950), has become a classic text on human development. In it, Erikson proposed stages of psychosocial development from infancy to old age, the first such life-span developmental theory. Erikson's later writings include essays and books on the lives of Hitler, George Bernard Shaw, Maxim Gorky, Martin Luther, and Mahatma Gandhi. He put each into social and historical perspective, indicating how their in-

dividual efforts to resolve inner struggles coincided with their times in history. ■

Source
Coles, R. *Erik H. Erikson: The growth of his work.* Boston: Little, Brown, 1970.

"Some kids that come in are so shy, or so afraid, that you have to begin to prove to them they can do it. There's a lot of anxiety that holds them back at the beginning. In the first week or two or three, depending—I'll give them work I know they can do. I don't care if it's writing the alphabet, just to free them from that anxiety. And I'll be liberal with As and 100s. Once they start feeling good about themselves, once that happens, I'll go a step higher, progress from there."

The danger in adolescence is the feeling of not knowing who one is or where one is headed. To avoid such confusion of roles, young people identify with heroes, cliques, and crowds, and conform to what others of their age are doing.

Erikson introduced the term *identity crisis*, meaning a turning point at which development may progress or falter. An identity crisis is particularly likely to occur during adolescence; further development depends on its resolution. Whether the crisis is resolved relatively smoothly or presents great difficulty depends in turn, Erikson believes, on what society offers. During this period, the adolescent needs adult models other than parents, strong bonds with peers, an ideology, and diverse experiences with individuals and groups.

Adolescence should provide a moratorium, a time relatively free of other demands, during which a pattern of identity can be designed and attained. A firm sense of identity is necessary for the tasks of adulthood, and identity is both preserved and modified in all subsequent stages.

6. *Intimacy versus isolation.* (Young adulthood.) The next stage begins in the twenties. Only after a real sense of identity has been established can one achieve intimacy with another. Intimacy involves caring about someone else—someone special—and sharing activities, thoughts, and feelings. For Erikson, intimacy requires commitment even though it necessitates sacrifices and compromises. Sexual intimacy is only one aspect of a more general capacity for human relationships. Failure at this stage results in isolation, a state of self-absorption in which real intimacy is avoided.

7. *Generativity versus stagnation.* (Middle adulthood.) Experienced in the forties and fifties, generativity focuses on the next generation. It may manifest itself in parenthood, in guidance for others than one's offspring, or in creative and humanitarian efforts that will affect the yet unborn. Individuals in whom generativity is lacking care only about themselves.

8. *Ego integrity versus despair.* (Old age.) The final stage of life, which begins in the sixties, confronts the final task—development of what Erikson calls integrity, or the acceptance of one's life as one has lived it. One comes to believe that how it has been lived is one's own responsibility, and that it is futile to wish that things had been different. Without that sense of integrity, there are only despair and fear of death.

Implications. Erikson's theory evolved from his rich experiences with people of diverse cultures, ages, and social circumstances. At each stage, the society in which one lives has an important effect. Each stage involves a crisis, a turning point, requiring changed behavior. Since no crisis is ever totally and finally resolved, the individual must also face up to and integrate disappointing aspects—mistrust, shame and doubt, guilt, a sense of inferiority, some identity confusion, self-absorption, stagnation, and despair.

Particularly relevant to teachers is Erikson's point that the different personal concerns of people at different ages are crucial to their continuing development.

In the preschool years, when children struggle with autonomy, wise teachers will allow them to do for themselves all that they can and will provide opportunities to try things out. Teachers should also guide students away from tasks too hard for them, while assuring them that soon they will be able to accomplish more such sensitive activities. Teachers should not attempt, of course, to control preschoolers by ever holding them up to public derision, saying, for example, "Shame on you, Jennifer. You know better than to do that."

In kindergarten, with developing initiative, children still will benefit from a learning environment that fosters autonomy, but because they are vulnerable to fear of failure, they should not be compared unfavorably with peers or older siblings. They should be urged to try to surpass their own performance, not that of others.

For elementary school children, a teacher can be concerned with encouraging special abilities and fostering cooperative work and play. Children should take pleasure in their work, but a child at this age may become too work-oriented: Erikson fears that "workaholics" are formed in this stage, if they get the notion that others regard work as the most significant aspect of life. Children should feel that although they are rewarded for what they can produce, they are also valued for such personal attributes as gentleness, courage, humor, kindness, playfulness.

Do Erikson's stages have implications for educators?

In adolescence, the search for identity and the concomitant confusion may lead to difficulties. Choice of career looms as a frightening and complex decision. A teacher may offer support by saying, "I know that this is a hard time for you, that you are having to try to get yourself together and make some tough decisions. Can I help?" A teacher can also assist by conveying a sense of regard for each student, whatever his or her personal flaws and gifts. Competent career counseling is important at this time for high school youths about to begin their college years.

As young adults work to establish intimacy with others, they may need opportunities to discuss interpersonal relations. Their concerns about marriage, living together, divorce, and choices about childbearing and childrearing can be addressed specifically in college or adult education courses in psychology, sociology, education, and other relevant areas. For adults in midlife, concerned with generativity, classes can foster their creative and humanitarian interests. For older adults, educational settings can provide opportunities not only to continue to develop knowledge and skills, but to review their lives positively, to see themselves in the perspective of their time and place.

Erikson's theory, though widely respected, has stimulated thinking but not a great deal of research, because it is difficult to test Erikson's complex formulations, and because the last stages, in particular, are described only briefly and broadly.

It will be useful to examine another theory of adult development, one that examines in greater detail the issues that arise for individuals between the ages of about twenty to about fifty. Presented as work-in-progress, the theory is a result of ongoing research conducted by psychologist Daniel J. Levinson and his colleagues at Yale University.

LEVINSON'S THEORY

Childhood and adolescence are formative times, and educators know that it is important to integrate educational theory and methods with an understanding of young people's development. But what about the rest of the life cycle? How can one understand adult learners and one's own changes in adulthood? Developmental psychology is expanding to include developmental processes continuing through adulthood into old age. This new area of social science is called life-span developmental psychology. A broad-based view of the life span is useful in preparing young people for adulthood as well as in working with college students and fully mature people in adult education.

Levinson and his associates ask, "Is there an underlying order in the progression of our lives over the adult years, as there is in childhood and adolescence?" (1978, p. ix). Their current long-term research project is designed to acquire information about possible developmental sequences, and they are constructing a theory of adult development from the age of about twenty.

The data for their first study, reported in *The Seasons of a Man's Life* (1978), were collected through extensive biographical interviews with forty men between the ages of thirty-five and forty-five. There were ten novelists, ten biologists, ten business executives, and ten industrial workers. It remains to be seen whether the theory is applicable beyond so special an assortment of people, and in particular whether or not it applies to women. But it is one of the few theories of development that focuses on adults.

What is the life structure?

The theory centers around the concept of life structure—the pattern or design of an individual's life at a given time. The life structure includes a concept of the self, a concept of the external world, and the relationships one builds with other people and social systems. The course of a life can be seen as an invariant series of transitions and stable periods. During a transition, one is changing one's life structure on the basis of choices necessary at that time in life. During a stable period, one lives within the life structure one has created, built also on crucial choices.

"Adult learners are usually a little rusty in school skills . . . you know, some of them don't remember how to take tests, organize their notes. But are they ever motivated! This is not a big social event for them. They're here by choice, expecting hard work."

Before considering the developmental periods, let us look at what Levinson calls the *eras* of life, its broad underlying structure.

1. *Preadulthood.* (Birth to about twenty-two.) The preadult era is a time of rapid growth and learning, during which the individual makes the change from helpless infancy to readiness for responsible adulthood. Most research on human development has focused on this era.
2. *Early adulthood.* (Ages seventeen to forty-five.) The early adult era includes the time of choosing and engaging in an occupation, raising a family, and developing a way of life. At this age, a person experiences energy, a passion for life, ambition. He or she also experiences great stress, making decisions that can bring costs as well as rewards.
3. *Middle adulthood.* (Ages forty-five to sixty-five.) Linked to the immediately preceding era by an important transition period, middle adulthood is the time in which people become the seniors of society. Biological capacities begin to wane, but accumulated knowledge, experience, and wisdom make people of this era valuable leaders and contributors. They are responsible now for guiding, teaching, and counseling the new generation of young adults.
4. *Late adulthood.* (Beyond age sixty-five.) In late adulthood, there is an increasing sense of bodily decline, a greater frequency of serious illness. The responsibilities of middle adulthood are reduced, and there is opportunity to pursue other interests. It can be a time of using more of one's inner resources and of taking the widest view of one's world and its important issues. In this era one prepares for the end of one's life.

Evolution of Life Structure in Early and Middle Adulthood.

Concentrating on early and middle adulthood, Levinson's research team has formulated a framework of age-related developmental periods. The end of preadulthood is marked by the *early adult transition*, which takes place between the ages of seventeen and twenty-two and serves as a bridge between adolescence and early adulthood. The life structure built in adolescence is abandoned, and choices involved in setting up a new structure are made. The individual develops a sense of self as junior adult and establishes new relationships with people and institutions. This is a period of testing and exploring possibilities, a preliminary step toward adulthood.

How are transitions and eras related?

This transition leads into a more stable period, called *entering the adult world*, for the years between twenty-two and twenty-eight. One now lives with one's transitional choices and tries to build a new life structure, working toward a vision of the future, building a pattern of roles and identity, interests, goals, and relationships.

Then comes the *age thirty transition*, which occurs between twenty-eight and thirty-three. There are always flaws in the first adult structure for one's life; now the individual reassesses that structure. The process for most of us is accompanied by turmoil, confusion, and a sense of urgency at being "over thirty." Everything comes under scrutiny; new, sometimes painful, choices are made, along with some recommitments to earlier choices.

Settling down takes place from the early thirties to about age forty. The person builds and lives within a second adult life structure and works toward fulfilling aspirations. This is a period of investment and commitment to family, work, and other interests. There is an increasing sense of order, plus the ambitious planning and pursuit of long-range goals.

Between about forty and forty-five comes another turning point, the *midlife transition*. It is a bridge between early and middle adulthood, and is usually a time of struggle. As in all transitions, it begins with a reappraisal of one's life, thinking about what one has attained and questioning the life structure one has designed. Time is now more limited: "What do I want to do with the rest of my life?" The self becomes redefined and integrated; relationships with the external world are renegotiated. The new, and third, adult life structure differs markedly from earlier ones.

The next stable period, *entering middle adulthood*, involves building and maintaining the new structure. Another reassessment, the *age fifty transition*, lasts from fifty to fifty-five or so. This seems to be less dramatic, involving minor changes but fewer major choices. For those who did not reexamine their lives and make changes at forty, the upheaval may come now.

Less is known about the remainder of life, in terms of Levinson's theory. There appears to be another stable period, called the *culmination of middle adulthood*, from fifty-five to sixty, and then a late adult transition, from sixty to sixty-five, after which the era of late adulthood begins. Figure 4.1 summarizes the eras and transitions of Levinson's theory.

Implications. Is Levinson's theory universally applicable? Does it apply to women as well as men, to different socioeconomic groups? We don't know. Intensive study of adult lives is just beginning. What are the advantages of thinking in terms of this newly formed and relatively untested theory? Levinson says,

> The perspective of the evolution of the life structure enables us to conceive of adulthood not as a static state nor as a random flux of events but as a sequence that evolves in accord with its own developmental principles. . . . At the level of personality, we change in different ways. Yet, I believe that everyone lives through the same developmental periods in adulthood, just as in childhood, though people go through them in their own ways. Each individual life has its own unique character. Our theory of life structure does not specify a single, "normal" course that everyone must follow. Its function, instead, is to indicate the developmental tasks that everyone must work on in successive periods, and the infinitely varied forms that such work can take in different individuals living under different conditions (1979, pp. 38–39).

Whether you as a teacher are working with preadult or adult students, it is useful to have a framework for thinking about the entire life span. It will allow you to see developmental issues at all ages, not only in childhood and adolescence. If you work with young people, you will have a concept of the choices

Figure 4.1. Levinson's Theory of Adult Development

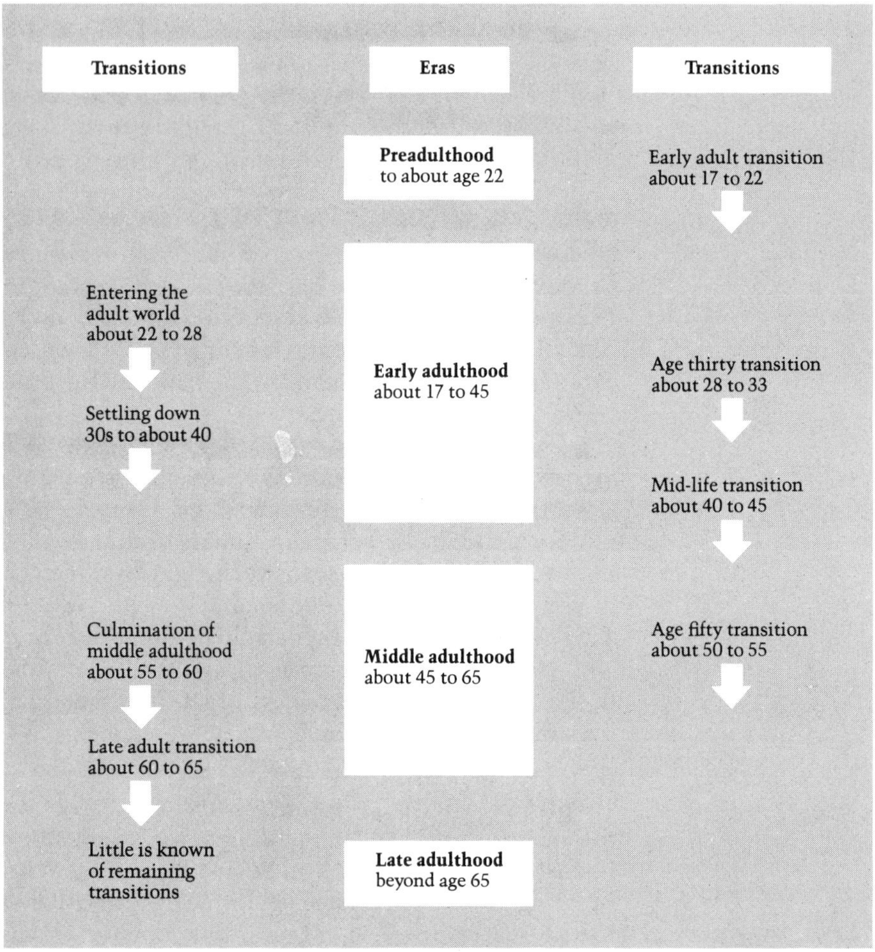

Transitions	Eras	Transitions
	Preadulthood to about age 22	Early adult transition about 17 to 22
Entering the adult world about 22 to 28		
Settling down 30s to about 40	**Early adulthood** about 17 to 45	Age thirty transition about 28 to 33
		Mid-life transition about 40 to 45
Culmination of middle adulthood about 55 to 60	**Middle adulthood** about 45 to 65	Age fifty transition about 50 to 55
Late adult transition about 60 to 65		
Little is known of remaining transitions	**Late adulthood** beyond age 65	

that lie ahead for them, and you can help to prepare them for the building of satisfying life structures. If you work with adults, you will be aware of the struggles unique to different periods of the life cycle.

Self-Concept

Now that you have thought about development through the life course, let us focus on an affective variable often mentioned in Erikson's and Levinson's theories, the self-concept—the individual's view of him- or herself. It is an important component of life structure and has been shown to be related to how well students at all levels do in school or in any learning situation. To underscore a point we made at the beginning of this chapter, an understanding of the self-concept—along with other affective and developmental variables—will help you not only to teach cognitive skills more easily but to do a better job of teaching your students to appreciate and value themselves realistically.

THE EFFECTS OF SELF-CONCEPT

Donald Felker (1974) has defined self-concept as the total view one has of one's self, a unique set of perceptions, ideas, and attitudes that differ to varying degrees from the view that other people have of the individual.

What are the ingredients of self-concept?

Self-concept is shaped by experience—in youngsters by scoldings, praise, parental expectations and demands, a missed fly ball, a spilled glass of milk, a neat jackknife dive at the pool. ("I'm clumsy. . . . I guess I'm kinda stupid. . . . Hey, I'm a pretty good athlete!") The resulting beliefs help to make one what one *is*, *does*, *can do*, and *wants to do*. They are perceptions of self. Every child has a self-concept before entering first grade. The self-concept, Felker suggests, serves three purposes: it maintains inner consistency, determines the interpretations of experiences, and provides expectations.

Inner Consistency. Physiologists maintain that the body constantly strives for equilibrium, or balance, technically termed *homeostasis*. For example, if the body becomes too hot, it sends blood coursing closer to the skin's surface to cool it. Similarly, some psychologists argue that people attempt to keep psychological balance, or consistency. If you're bored, you try to increase your activity. If you're burdened by overactivity, you try to cut down on what you're doing.

"What an individual thinks about himself is a vital part of internal consistency," says Felker. Furthermore, "the child or adult will act in ways which he thinks are consistent with the way he sees himself. If he feels he cannot do a task and that he is dumb, then he is likely to act and behave in such a way as to come out looking dumb" (p. 7). Felker is saying that, even if one's self-concept is negative, one tends to maintain and protect it by behaving in accord with it.

How does self-concept affect learning?

Interpretation of Experiences. Similarly, our views of ourselves govern our judgments of events that affect us. People with poor self-concepts often look sourly even on agreeable experiences, and see the worm as dwarfing the lovely rose. That is why, Felker contends, it can be difficult to improve one's view of oneself.

Expectations. How we feel about ourselves also influences our decisions to do or not do certain things, and how we carry out our decisions. For example, a sixth grader who considers him- or herself a good student, expects to go to college, and has confidence in future success is likely to do whatever is required to succeed. According to Felker,

> every individual carries with him a . . . set of expectancies which operate to determine how he is going to act. If he expects good experiences, he acts in ways which bring them about. If he expects bad experiences, he acts in ways which make these expectations come true and then says to himself, "See, I was right" (p. 19).

Self-Concept in the Classroom. If you as a teacher are to do the best possible job of helping your students to grow, it is essential to realize that a youngster's self-concept is one of the most important aspects of personality, and that it relates strongly to the desire to learn. Students who take a dim view of themselves are likely to reflect that view in their attitudes toward school and in their academic achievements.

Every teacher discovers this sooner or later, but a study by Wattenberg and Clifford (1964) demonstrated it rather strikingly. They examined a group of kindergartners for self-concepts and returned two and a half years later to see

Opposite page: This fifth-grade teacher in a very traditional school has based his class methods, his own theory of teaching, on improving and strengthening, on making use of the student's self-concept and the student's desire for a positive self-concept. Behavior is visibly rewarded with badges. Names are recorded from week to week on the charts that match the badges. Independence is fostered—the students are allowed to leave their seats whenever they want to get water or go to the bathroom. Each student periodically gives a talk in front of the whole class.

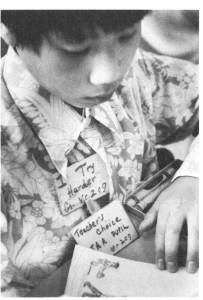

how the children were doing at reading. The youngsters with poor self-concepts lagged behind those with good self-concepts, no matter what they scored on IQ tests. Other researchers, among them Coopersmith (1959) and Hill and Sarason (1966) found similar patterns in higher grades. A good self-concept may not *cause* reading skill, but it is apparent that they accompany one another.

CHANGING SELF-CONCEPTS

Does self-concept relate to behavior?

Because human beings are such complex creatures, self-concept manifests itself in many contradictions. In defending our self-concepts, we may put out of mind, or blame others for, behavior we consider unbecoming of us. The process may be unconscious, yet many people consciously disapprove of their own actions and have difficulty accepting them. Though we cherish our self-concepts, many of us see ourselves as something less than what we would like to be, and we all strive toward our ideal selves.

Teachers and parents can take advantage of that psychological phenome-

Students are responsible for keeping track of their own reward tabs and "conduct" cards. A different student each day is made "teacher's aide" to perform special tasks helpful to the teacher. And each student is recognized in special ways as an individual (like "Happy Birthday!") throughout the year. The teacher's comment: "It works. I've done it for nineteen years. Just for example—I got a note from her [pointing out a child who has had a reputation as an extreme behavior problem] mother this morning, thanking me for what I've done so far—like it was a miracle."

non in trying to improve youngsters' self-concepts. Felker offers some suggestions toward that end:

1. Adults should praise themselves, serving as models to demonstrate that they value themselves.
2. Children should be taught to praise themselves and others.
3. Children should be guided and helped to evaluate themselves realistically.
4. Children should be instructed in how to set reasonable, realistic goals.

Because, potentially, almost any student can shine at *something*, Ringness (1975) argues that teachers can do much to improve students' self-concepts by helping youngsters to find *their* something. He cites some examples from his own experience as a high school teacher:

A bright student with almost no friends gained self-confidence and acceptance by schoolmates by becoming expert at chess and teaching others to play. A similar student proved adept at gathering and tending frogs, snakes, and other creatures for the biology class collection. A boy with little musical talent developed leadership and initiative as the band's drum major.
An unattractive girl worked to improve her appearance and became the respected make-up artist for school plays.
A long, skinny youth too light for football won esteem as a cross-country runner.
Four troublesome students grew interested in electronics and did so well that they were made junior teaching assistants in physics (p. 141).

The youngster who cannot make the baseball team, Ringness suggests, may become the team's manager or the school newspaper's baseball reporter. The student who cannot quite fill a role in the school play may prove a good stage manager. The possibilities are many, and success in a field related to a student's original goals enhances self-concept.

SELF-CONCEPT IN ADULTHOOD

You will recall that Erikson considers the revision and consolidation of identity, another term for self-concept, the crucial developmental issue of adolescence. This does not mean that self-concept remains unchanged during a lifetime. Adolescence is a significant period in the evolution of the self-concept, but changes occur throughout adulthood.

In young adulthood, changes in self-concept can come about through changes in social roles. Adults assume new, private roles as wife, husband, parent, and new public roles as architect, cabinetmaker, bus driver, teacher. Occupational roles are central to the sense of self; we often say who we are by announcing what we do: "I'm a teacher." Self-esteem is influenced by how society views an occupation, and by our own and others' evaluation of how competent we are at our jobs.

As Levinson and his colleagues have observed, there are cardinal times of self-assessment throughout the adult years. Often one is troubled by a feeling of disparity between what one wanted to be and what one is, not only in terms of social status or material possessions, but in a sense of not having satisfied inner needs and wishes. From midlife on, the individual becomes aware of physical decline, minor at first but increasingly noticeable, which requires modification of one's view of the physical aspects of self.

Why would the self-concept continue to change through adulthood?

Psychoanalyst Carl G. Jung (1964) was the first to point out that a process he called *individuation* takes place in middle adulthood; a person incorporates more of the previously unconscious aspects of the self and feels freer from social constraints and demands. This is consistent with research findings of psychologist Bernice Neugarten and her associates. In one study of 100 men and women between the ages of forty-five and fifty-five, this time of life was described as a time when they felt able to differentiate the self more fully (Neugarten, 1968).

In late adulthood, however, the self-concept may become less positive. With retirement, previous occupational roles contribute much less to self-esteem. In addition, our society does not value the elderly in the way older cultures do, or did. As a group, elderly people seem to have more negative self-concepts than do younger people (e.g., Mason, 1954). There are, however, great individual differences; not all elderly people see themselves negatively.

As you work with adult students of various ages, it is important to keep in mind that self-concept will influence their ability to learn. Adults who return for further education often do so in a period of transition when they are experiencing earthquake-like shifts and tremors in the foundation of personality, the self-concept. A teacher's sensitivity will have far-reaching consequences for adult learners who are moving along developmentally without quite being able to articulate what is taking place. They may now develop latent talents and capacities and discover new inner resources of wisdom and creativity.

Also, of course, your own self-concept will strongly influence your work as an educator. You will convey your view of yourself, your appreciation of your own occupational skills and personal attributes, to students in numerous ways, and you will serve as a model for many students.

Sex Differences

Thus far, we have talked mostly about people in general, male and female alike. But we cannot discuss affective and developmental variables without considering that one's sex is a significant aspect of personality. An individual's identity as female or male has meaning for the person and for the surrounding world.

When four-year-old Andy was asked, "Are boys different from girls?" he replied with emphasis, "Yes!" His mother pursued the matter: "How are they different?'' Andy pondered; this was harder. Finally he explained, "Because boys aren't girls and girls aren't boys."

Many of us older than four can't do much better than Andy at answering that question. Certainly we can specify anatomical differences, which Andy must know but chooses not to discuss. Beyond that, what differences can we cite with certainty? Do males and females really differ in terms of cognitive and affective variables? And if so, how much? And why? What differences are determined by biology, and what by the culture in which we live?

ARE THERE REAL SEX DIFFERENCES?

In an exhaustive review of the research on sex differences, Maccoby and Jacklin (1974) attempted to distinguish myth from reality and then summarized their findings:

Unfounded Beliefs
1. *Girls are more "social" than boys.* "Any differences . . . are more of kind than of degree. Boys are highly oriented toward a peer group and congregate in larger groups; girls associate in pairs or small groups of agemates, and may be somewhat more oriented toward adults, although the evidence for this is weak" (p. 349).
2. *Girls are more "suggestible" than boys.* The findings indicate that boys and girls are equally influenced by their peer groups.
3. *Girls have lower self-esteem.* Girls' self-concepts do not seem to be lower or less positive than those of boys. The only real difference found was of kind, not quality. Girls consider themselves more self-confident, boys consider themselves strong and dominant.
4. *Girls are better at rote learning and simple repetitive tasks, boys at tasks that require higher-level cognitive processing and the inhibition of previously learned responses.* No evidence suggests that either sex is better or worse at learning on any cognitive level.

What are popular myths of sex-related differences?

5. *Boys are more "analytic."* No evidence bears this out.
6. *Girls are more affected by heredity, boys by environment.* This is a complex matter, but Maccoby and Jacklin conclude that both sexes are influenced equally by environmental factors.
7. *Girls lack achievement motivation.* Most of the research reveals no differences between males and females, but in some cases girls were found to have greater motivation than boys.
8. *Girls are auditory, boys visual.* "The majority of studies report no differences in response to sounds by infants of the two sexes. At most ages, boys and girls are equally adept at discriminating speech sounds. No sex difference is found in memory for sounds previously heard" (p. 351).

Well-founded Beliefs
1. *Girls have greater verbal ability than boys.* Until early adolescence, no

differences between the sexes exist, but at about age eleven girls begin to demonstrate a superiority that increases through high school and possibly beyond. Girls are more fluent and score higher on tasks that involve analogies, comprehension of difficult written material, and creative writing.

2. *Boys excel in visual-spatial ability.* Again there are no differences until adolescence, but from then on males are more skilled in such things as perception of depth, map reading, and visualizing how an object will look if it is rotated.

3. *Boys excel in mathematical ability.* Beginning at about ages twelve and thirteen, boys increase their skills faster than do girls.

4. *Males are more aggressive.* Numerous studies indicate that boys at all age levels, in several different cultures, demonstrate more aggressiveness than do girls. (Aggressiveness is defined as intent to harm others.)

Are there any valid sex-related learning differences?

If you are a young woman who always got the best marks in the math class, or a young man who commands the language superbly, do not be tempted to picket Maccoby and Jacklin, or even to dismiss their findings. What their study shows is that females *as a group* are superior in verbal ability and that males *as a group* excel in math. Not all girls surpass boys in verbal ability; not all boys surpass girls in math. The exceptions exist as well as the rules, and the exceptions apply to all the psychological differences between the sexes; they apply too to some of the physiological differences.

Other differences between the sexes may (or may not) exist; the research yields contradictory results, Maccoby and Jacklin have found, about tactile sensitivity, fear, timidity and anxiety, level of activity, competitiveness, dominance, compliance and nurturance, and "maternal" behavior.

In short, the evidence is strong that males and females differ in some characteristics; the evidence also indicates that, in some areas where males and females were believed to differ, few or no differences actually exist. For still other characteristics, there is insufficient evidence to permit conclusions.

WHENCE THE DIFFERENCES?

There are two major explanations of how sex differences in behavior and skills originate. One is that they are determined by biology. The other is that society establishes roles for each sex, and that parents and teachers groom children for these roles.

Evidence in support of the biological explanation is not clear and is accompanied by a great deal of speculation. Currently, many researchers are looking for differences, if any, between the male and the female brain. The researchers have found none in size and structure, but there may be some diversities, as yet undiscovered, in certain control processes. For example, the differences in verbal and spatial capabilities could stem from variations in the organization and function of the left hemisphere, which, you recall, usually controls language, and the right hemisphere, which usually controls spatial abilities. One speculation is that male and female hormones diversely affect brain functions

Even today some people tend to be a little surprised—at least our photographer was—when they suddenly discover themselves face-to-face with a group of young girls playing loudly, roughly, and "aggressively"; or when they find themselves in a coed home economics class (bottom) where, according to the teacher, "the boys are more interested than the girls." We asked one boy in class, "Do you think sewing and cooking and stuff like this is mostly for girls?" "No," was all he said, more interested in picking his yarn out than talking to us. We got similar treatment from the girls when we asked whether they were playing a "boy's game."

(McGuinness and Pribram, 1978). Such research is just beginning; at this point we must consider biological differences in the brain as an interesting hypothesis, but we should not jump to conclusions.

What are the origins of sex-related differences?

The second explanation—that training produces differing behavior in the sexes—is supported by substantial evidence. Our society has established norms and beliefs about how males and females should conduct themselves: Boys must not cry or play with dolls; men should be dominant; girls should not fight; women should be nurturant. We are all familiar with the prescribed roles and with the ways in which children and adults are encouraged to conform to them.

Parents respond differently to boy babies or girl babies from the first hours of life (Rubin, Provenzane, and Luria, 1974), and from then on teach their children the behavior expected of their sex. In several studies of childrearing practices, Block (1973) has found that, with boys, parents emphasize achievement, competition, and control of feelings; with their daughters, they emphasize skills in interpersonal relationships and encourage expression of feelings. Apart from such intentional teaching, parents unconsciously treat boys and girls differently. In one study, for example, mothers were observed to be more responsive to male infants, and both parents spoke differently to girl babies, using more baby talk and expending more effort to get them to smile and say something (Moss, 1974).

Teachers often act quite differently toward boys and girls. In a study of fifteen preschool classrooms, Serbin and O'Leary (1975) found that teachers paid a great deal more attention—a rewarding circumstance—to aggressive and disruptive boys than to girls of identical behavior, and were more likely to respond to girls when they were passive and dependent. In addition, the researchers report,

> Teachers, we found, actually teach boys more than they teach girls. . . . All 15 of the teachers gave more attention to boys who kept their noses to the academic grindstone. They got both physical and verbal rewards. Boys also received more directions from the teacher, and were twice as likely as the girls to get individual instructions on how to do things. . . . We found one exception to the general pattern. When the class engaged in an explicitly feminine, sex-typed activity such as cooking, the teachers did tend to pay more attention to the girls. Even so, they still offered brief conversation, praise and assistance, while the boys got detailed instructions (p. 102).

Walter Mischel (1966) points out that actually many individual differences exist within each sex, and that the behavior of the sexes overlaps in numerous ways. Traits that have been stereotyped as masculine or feminine can in fact appear in either sex, and traditional sex roles act to prevent the integration of various personality qualities within the individual. Evidence from studies of diverse cultures strongly suggests that sex differences in behavior result primarily from the dictates of a particular society, transmitted through the process of social learning (which will be discussed later in this chapter).

READING AND SEX DIFFERENCES

One difference that you will encounter as a teacher is that girls read better than do boys—a fact implicit in girls' greater verbal skills generally. Researcher Carol Dwyer (1973) has examined the reasons for this. "There seems to be little doubt," she says, "that reading is generally seen as a feminine activity, and that this classification has the effect of lessening boys' motivation to excel in reading, probably since there are very strong taboos against males participating in any part of the feminine role (although the converse is not necessarily true)" (p. 463).

Significantly, what is true of American boys and reading is not true of German boys. Dwyer cites research by Preston (1962), who studied both American and German fourth and sixth graders. American girls, Preston found, did indeed read better than American boys, but in Germany the boys surpassed the girls. Dwyer's explanation: "Elementary school teachers in Germany are predominantly male and . . . the German culture regards reading and learning as activities well-suited to the male role" (p. 465). So German boys, unlike their American counterparts, see no conflict between the demands of schooling and the demands of the sex roles their society imposes.

THE IMPLICATIONS FOR TEACHING

What, then, should educators do about all this? Should girls be taught differently from boys? Should curricula emphasize math for boys and English and literature for girls? There are no clear implications that the answers ought to be yes. But we do have to realize, and to keep in mind, that there are differences between the sexes; there are sex roles; and sex roles appear to be part, expecially among elementary school youngsters, of an individual's cognitive structure and psychological makeup.

How can teachers help overcome sex-role stereotyping?

Recognition of those facts of life does not mean, though, that you as a teacher must sit back and do nothing. You can remain constantly watchful for, and avoid, sex-role stereotyping that assigns some activities exclusively to boys and others to girls, or attributes certain characteristics to one sex or the other. ("Boys are strong and brave. Girls are weak and timid.") Such stereotyping probably has been all too common. In a booklet, *Dick and Jane as Victims* (Women on Words and Images, 1975), the twenty-five authors examined eighty-three elementary-aged reading books for signs of stereotyping. They found that girls and women appeared in these books much less often than boys and men.

	Ratio
Boy-centered stories to girl-centered stories	7:2
Male illustrations to female illustrations	2:1
Male occupations to female occupations	3:1
Male biographies to female biographies	2:1

In earlier research (1972), reported in the the same booklet, the authors found that girls were depicted as docile, weak, and foolish and boys as active, strong, clever, and humorous. Since 1972, however, beginning reading books have changed—though some problems remain. "Some females were found who were clever, competent, and initiating, as well as a few males who did not have to hold back their tears, and who were able to honestly express emotions" (1975, p. 66).

Of course there are differences, physiological and psychological, between males and females. But as teachers we must not let sex-role stereotypes inhibit us from helping students of either sex to develop a broad range of goals for their lives.

Moral Development

We have been tracing several of the strands of human experience that come together to form the pattern of individual personality. Now we shall turn to still another aspect of our lives that changes over time, our moral values and beliefs.

The handiest dictionary defines morality as the doctrine of right and wrong in human conduct. This is simple enough. But views of right and wrong vary with time, place, and even family. In ancient Sparta, you probably recall, a council of elders examined each newborn child to decide whether it should live or die. But contemporary Athens considered the Spartan practice immoral. Incest is taboo in most societies, but in the African Wateita tribe brothers marry sisters when they cannot afford enough cows to buy another bride (Westermarck, 1922); nineteenth-century French peasants often kept their daughters as concubines. Disapproval of murder antedates the Ten Commandments, but among the Thugs of India the strangling of travelers persisted as a religious rite into the twentieth century. In short, as everybody knows, one people's morality is another's sin.

But surely most people in the United States today agree on the value of such qualities as honesty, truthfulness, and regard for the rights of others, don't they? Then shouldn't those qualities be taught in school? Teachers once thought that they could easily pass on such values to their students. Beginning in the 1830s, William Holmes McGuffey's textbooks (known as McGuffey readers) warned generations of American children against such evils as lying, cheating, and disobedience. In the 1930s, though, efforts to implant specific virtues in pupils were largely abandoned for several reasons.

One was the Freudian theory that a child's character was pretty much formed by age five, making moral education a responsibility of the parents rather than of the teacher. Another was the finding that the efforts were wasted: all children disapproved of cheating, but most of them cheated when circumstances made cheating sufficiently tempting (Hartshorne and May, 1928). A third factor in the passing of the "this is good, that is bad" style of teaching morality was the inability of parents, school boards, and teachers to agree on what, beyond such fundamentals as honesty, constituted desirable principles. One family's patriotism was another family's chauvinism, one's godliness was another's superstition, one's respect for authority was another's apathy.

HOW MORAL SENSE DEVELOPS

Yet, as every teacher knows, children *do* acquire moral values in school from both classmates and instructors. What—if anything—a teacher should do to influence those values remains a touchy issue. An understanding of how children develop a sense of morality should help you to determine your own course. There are currently two dominant theories about moral development.

One is the cognitive developmental approach that originated with Jean Piaget in 1932 and has been advanced by Lawrence Kohlberg of Harvard since the late 1950s. The other is Albert Bandura's social learning approach. The Piaget-Kohlberg theory, in essence, is that a sense of morality develops by stages.

Among the tools that Piaget used in the studies that led to his conclusion were little two-part stories. Piaget (1932, p. 118) presented them to children between the ages of four and thirteen, and one story involving boys named John and Henry is typical:

1. John, who is in his room, is called to dinner. He goes down and pushes open the dining-room door. Behind the door is a chair and on the chair is a tray on which are fifteen cups. John does not know that. He opens the door. The door hits the tray. Crash go the cups. All of them break.
2. Henry's mother is out and Henry tries to get some cookies in the cupboard. He climbs on a chair and while reaching for the cookie jar he knocks down a cup, which breaks.
   Who was naughtier, John or Henry?

What is the meaning of a cognitive developmental approach to morality?

Younger children judged John to be the guiltier because he had done more damage. They disregarded the innocence of his intention in opening the door and his ignorance that the cup-laden tray was behind the door. Children of about seven or more held Henry guiltier because he had broken the cup while reaching for the cookies, which presumably he should not have in his mother's absence. But the older children took into account that neither John nor Henry had meant to break the cups.

Piaget's Two Stages. On the basis of countless such experiments, Piaget concluded that children's views of good and bad changed as the children grew and that their moral development progressed with their cognitive development. He decided that moral development occurred in two general stages.

In the first stage, morality is imposed from without. A young child views good and bad solely in terms of what adults, and notably parents and teachers, allow or do not allow. Rules, in this stage, are sacred and unchangeable.

In the second stage, which begins to emerge at age seven or eight, the sense of right and wrong develops from within as a result of social contact, chiefly with the child's fellows. The view of morality now responds to the need to get along with others, and reflects the child's newly acquired capacity for putting him- or herself in someone else's place. Rules are no longer handed down from on high and can be revised or abandoned by agreement.

Kohlberg's Six Stages. Building on Piaget's foundations, but reaching into higher age levels than Piaget did, Kohlberg reported finding six stages of moral development. Kohlberg places the two lowest stages on the level of *preconventional* moral judgments, the middle two on the *conventional* level and the top two on the *postconventional* level (see Table 4.1, p. 127).

On the preconventional level, the child in Stage 1 distinguishes between good and bad by two criteria: (1) Will I be praised or punished for doing it?

(The result to the child, not the nature of the behavior, is what counts.) (2) Can they make me do it? (The child defers as a matter of course to authority and superior firepower.)

In Stage 2 of the preconventional level, an action is right if it satisfies the child's needs and desires and, on occasion, those of others. Human relations in this stage have a businesslike, give-and-take aspect: "All right, I'll watch TV with you at your house if you let me use your walkie-talkie." Warmth and friendship are present but pragmatism dominates.

On the conventional level, the standards are those of most American adults. In Stage 3, the guideline is "Will this please other people and make them like me?" In Stage 4, a sense of duty becomes more important than personal preference. "Why, I *have* to do *that*," for family, or team, or hometown, or country. Or "It's the law! If everybody did just what they wanted, can you imagine what the world would be like?"

What are Kohlberg's stages of moral development?

Kohlberg (1973) believes that the postconventional level, Stages 5 and 6, is attained as a consistent style of moral thinking only in adulthood, usually not before the late twenties. In Stage 5, an individual acknowledges and abides by society's rules, not so much from a sense of duty as because the rules represent a consensus. Unlike Stage 4 people, the Stage 5 individual realizes that what seems just and right today to a majority may be considered unjust and wrong next year. He or she is prepared to accept and even work for change, provided it is brought about by legal procedure. A Stage 5 attitude toward marijuana would be, "Smoking pot is against the law, so it is wrong. If scientists some day find that pot does not hurt anybody, the law can be repealed and pot smoking no longer will be morally wrong because it won't be illegal. But that would be up to the people we elect—and if they don't do what the majority of voters believes is right, we won't reelect them." (Stage 5 has been called the "official morality" of the American government.)

Only a minority of people ever reaches Stage 6. Here one's conscience guides one's behavior in accordance with self-chosen ethical principles. The Golden Rule exemplifies such principles. So does the definition of goodness as the greatest personal liberty that is compatible with equal liberty for everyone else. The principles must be logical, consistent, broad enough to cope with most moral dilemmas, and applicable to everyone.

Kohlberg's Test Case. Like Piaget, Kohlberg arrived at his theory by presenting his subjects with little stories, the best known of which is this:

> Heinz's wife lay dying of cancer and her doctors believed that the only treatment that might save her life involved a form of radium newly discovered by a druggist who lived in the same town as Heinz and Mrs. Heinz. The radium cost the druggist $200 but he charged $2000 for a dose. Heinz scraped together $1000—all he could raise—by borrowing from friends. He asked the druggist to cut his price to that or let Heinz pay the other $1000 later. The druggist refused. So Heinz in desperation broke into the drugstore to steal the radium. Should he have done that? (Kohlberg, 1963).

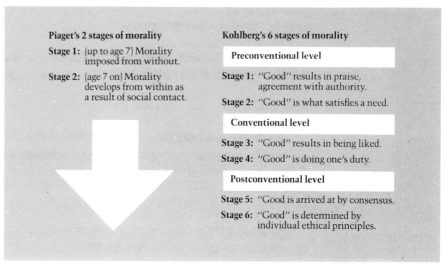

Figure 4.2. Piaget's and Kohlberg's Stages of Moral Development

A yes or no answer does not suffice. Anyone in any of the six stages could give that kind of answer without disclosing anything about his or her level of moral development. Kohlberg was searching for the reasoning behind the answers. So he asked additional probing questions: Did the druggist have the right to charge so much? Would it be all right to put the druggist in the electric chair for murder? Should the punishment be greater if Heinz's wife is an important person?

The answers that follow to the basic question "Should he have done that?" exemplify the six stages. They do not constitute verbatim responses by Kohlberg's subjects, but were synthesized by Kohlberg's associate Elliot Turiel (1966) as representative of yes and no thinking at every stage.

Stage 1:

> *Pro (or Yes):* It isn't really bad to take it—he did ask to pay for it first. He wouldn't do any other damage or take anything else and the drug he'd take is only worth $200, he's not really taking a $2000 drug.
>
> *Con (or No):* Heinz doesn't have any permission to take the drug. He can't just go and break through a window or break the door down. He'd be a bad criminal doing all that damage. That drug is worth a lot of money, and stealing anything so expensive would really be a big crime.
>
> (In this stage, the amount of damage is the chief concern of the subjects, most of whom thought Heinz was in the wrong. Intent is ignored.)

Stage 2:

> *Pro:* Heinz isn't really doing any harm to the druggist, and he can always pay him back. If he doesn't want to lose his wife, he should take the drug because it's the only thing that will work.

Table 4.1. Summary of Kohlberg's Stages of Moral Development

Levels	*Stages*

I. Preconventional level.
    Cultural labels of right and wrong are responded to but are interpreted in terms of either physical or hedonistic consequences of action.
	1. Punishment and obedience orientation.
	    Avoidance of punishment and unquestioning deference to power determine action and are valued implicitly rather than in terms of their support of an underlying moral order.
	2. Instrumental relativist orientation.
	    Action is determined by the instrumental satisfaction of one's own needs and occasionally of the needs of others. Reciprocity may be present but is more a matter of *quid pro quo* exchanges than of gratitude, loyalty, or justice.

II. Conventional level.
    Maintaining the expectations of the individual's family, group, or nation is perceived as intrinsically valuable. The attitude is not only one of conformity to expectations in social order, but of loyalty to it, largely maintaining it, justifying it, and identifying with the persons involved in it.
	3. Interpersonal concordance (good-boy) orientation.
	    Action is determined by what pleases or helps others, with much conformity to stereotypical images of majority behavior. Behavior is judged by intentions for the first time.
	4. Authority and social-order-maintaining orientation.
	    Action governed by duty, respect for authority, fixed rules, and concern for maintaining the social order.

III. Postconventional level.
    There is a clear effort to define moral values and principles that have validity apart from the authority of the groups of persons holding these principles and apart from the individual's own identification with these groups.
	5. Social-contract legalistic orientation.
	    Action is defined in terms of general individual rights and standards that have been critically examined and agreed upon by the whole society. There is a clear awareness of the relativism of values and opinions and a corresponding emphasis upon procedural rules for reaching consensus. Emphasis is upon the possibility of changing law in terms of rational considerations or social utility rather than maintaining it rigidly, as in the previous stage. Outside the legal realm, free agreement and contract are the binding elements of obligation.
	6. Universal ethical principle orientation.
	    Action is defined by a decision of conscience in accord with self-chosen ethical principles that appeal to logical comprehensiveness, universality, and consistency. These are universal principles of justice, of the reciprocity and equality of human rights, and of respect for the dignity of human beings as individual persons.

Con: The druggist isn't wrong or bad, he just wants to make a profit like everyone else. That's what you're in business for, to make money. Business is business.

(Intent and pragmatism pop up here: business is business.)

Stage 3:

Pro: Stealing is bad but this is a bad situation. Heinz isn't doing wrong in trying to save his wife; he has no choice but to take the drug. He is only doing something that is natural for a good husband to do. You can't blame him for doing something out of love for his wife. You'd blame him if he didn't love his wife enough to save her.

Con: If Heinz's wife dies he can't be blamed in these circumstances. You can't say he is a heartless husband just because he won't commit a crime. The druggist is the selfish and heartless one in this situation. Heinz tried to do everything he really could.

(In both answers, avoidance of blame is the dominant motive. "What would people think?" is implicit.)

Stage 4:

Pro: The druggist is leading a wrong kind of life if he just lets someone die. You can't let somebody die like that, so it's Heinz's duty to save her. But Heinz can't just go around breaking laws and let it go at that—he must pay the druggist back and he must take his punishment for stealing.

Con: It's a natural thing for Heinz to want to save his wife, but it's still always wrong to steal. You have to follow the rules regardless of how you feel or regardless of the special circumstances.

(A sense of duty and regard for law and order impelled these answers.)

Stage 5:

Pro: Before you say stealing is wrong you've got to really think about this whole situation. Of course the laws are quite clear about breaking into a store. And even worse, Heinz would know there were no legal grounds for his actions. Yet I can see why it would be reasonable for anybody in this kind of situation to steal the drug.

Con: I can see the good that would come from illegally taking the drug, but the ends don't justify the means. You can often find a good action behind illegal action. You can't say that Heinz would be completely wrong to steal the drug, but even these circumstances don't make it right.

(The "official morality" evidences itself here: the law is the law, but perhaps the law is wrong in this case and ought to be changed.)

Stage 6:

Pro: Where the choice must be made between disobeying a law and saving a human life, the higher principle of preserving life makes it morally right—to steal the drug.

Con: There are so many cases of cancer today that with any new drug cure, I'd assume that the drug would be scarce and that there wouldn't be enough to go around for everybody. The right course of action can only be one that is consistent to all people concerned. Heinz ought to act, not according to his particular feelings to his wife, nor according to what is legal in this case, but according to what he conceives an ideally just person would do in this situation.

(Let conscience be your guide—with the rights and needs of others ever in mind.)

Kohlberg put Heinz's dilemma in various forms to youngsters living in cities in the United States, Taiwan, and Mexico and to youthful villagers in Turkey and Mexico's Yucatan peninsula. The results were similar everywhere, although the villagers provided nobody in stages 5 and 6. Kohlberg has concluded that moral development takes place everywhere in the same way, stage by stage, each stage evolving from the stage immediately below. Thus, there can be no backsliding, no reversion from Stage 4, say, to Stage 3; and no skipped stages. (Richard Kramer in 1968 and Kohlberg and Kramer in 1969 found that some students did seem to have retrogressed between their high school and their college sophomore days but Kohlberg later reinterpreted that evidence to support his theory.)

CRITICISM OF KOHLBERG'S THEORY

What problems stem from Kohlberg's theory?

In the past few years there has been considerable criticism (e.g., Aron, 1977) of Kohlberg's research, of the theoretical model, and of other studies based on the Moral Judgment Scale, the series of problems developed by Kohlberg to measure moral reasoning. One criticism is that the basic research was done only with males; is it appropriate to generalize the findings to females? Another is that different studies have used different versions of the Moral Judgment Scale and different methods of scoring and reporting results. Therefore we cannot be sure they are measuring the same variables. A third criticism is that the Moral Judgment Scale measures moral reasoning, not behavior. Some studies show that people who score at different levels behave identically in actuality (Haan et al., 1968). Conversely, people who behave in morally different ways—those who have broken the law and those who have not—often score at the same level of moral judgment (Fodor, 1971).

A fourth criticism is that very few people score at Stage 5 or 6 in any of the studies. Are these real stages, or ideals? Do they represent a set of liberal political beliefs rather than politically unbiased moral judgments? And, finally, there remains the question of whether people actually attain the stages in order rather than move directly, for example, from Stage 2 to Stage 4. Research has provided insufficient data for certainty about the developmental sequence of moral behavior.

SOCIAL LEARNING

Albert Bandura, the leading spokesman for the social learning approach, holds quite different views of moral development from those of Piaget and Kohlberg. The premise of social learning is that children acquire their moral

"Adolescents are going through quick changes, and now is a good time to change some unproductive personality traits. I try to play down the boys' machismo—show them it's OK to be soft or to cry—and I try to make the girls open up—be more assertive, things like that." This comment comes from a male teacher in a bilingual program serving students from Spanish-dominant cultural backgrounds in which sexual stereotyping tends to be strong. In the schools we visited we found girls taking shop and drafting, majoring in agriculture (which included servicing and running the school lawnmowers); and boys in design, horticulture and home economics. These courses still tended to be male- or female-dominant in actual numbers, but neither male nor female expressed discomfort at being there or at being a minority.

standards, as well as most other learning, by observation and imitation. They do what they see other people doing, provided that what other people do does not lead to punishment. Children imitate almost everyone—Mommy, Daddy, older brothers and sisters, family friends, playmates, television characters, Goldilocks, and even the Three Bears. Playing house, playing doctor, playing cops and robbers, dressing up like Mommy or Daddy, all are forms of imitation, born of observation of reality and fiction.

When children imitate, they do not limit themselves to actions. They adopt the standards of behavior and the emotional characteristics of people whom they admire and want to be like, that is, people with whom they identify. As youngsters grow, and especially in the later stages of adolescence, they identify increasingly with people other than their parents—with the boys in their bunch, or the belle of the senior class; with the star quarterback or the captain of the girl's field hockey team; with famous athletes and musicians; even with teachers, if they are resentful of Mom's and Dad's preachments. Conflicts arise in their moral standards.

Standards versus Behavior. What people believe is right or wrong and what they actually do are, of course, often contradictory. Even young children often refrain from acting as they see others act because reward and punishment influence behavior. In an experiment, Bandura, Ross, and Ross (1963a) showed three groups of small, similar children a three-version movie in which the sole character pummeled a plastic doll. Each group saw only one version. In the first version, the character was punished for mistreating the doll. In the second version, the character was rewarded with praise and goodies. In the third version, nothing at all happened to him. Then the experimenters turned all the children loose on a doll like the one in the film. Children who had seen the character punished behaved far less aggressively than did children from the other two groups. But when the experimenters promised all the children rewards for beating the doll, all of them attacked it. The three groups alike had learned the behavior from the film character, but the carrying out of the behavior depended a good deal on punishment and reward.

As a teacher, though, do not expect to predict accurately what your pupils' behavior will be in a given situation simply because you think you know their state of moral development. As the Hartshorne and May studies mentioned earlier in this section demonstrated, children may disapprove of cheating, lying, and stealing but will cheat and lie and steal under certain circumstances. So will adults. Psychologists argue furiously over whether to judge a person's moral development by beliefs or by actions. It seems to us that both must be taken into account. But why do youngsters and people generally act on occasion contrary to their professed moral standards?

Children respond to "Do as I do" more than to "Do as I say." A child whose parents forbid it to cuss will not use bad language if the parents do not. But if Daddy hits his thumb with a hammer and explodes with a "god-damn-it" the child will learn to use the phrase too, from observation. Children behave as

Does observational learning of moral behavior contradict cognitive developmental theory?

Cluster School Flunks Formality

Michael K. Frisby

It was five minutes before the bell was to ring signaling the beginning of another school day at the Cambridge High and Latin School.

Many teachers stood, arms folded, in the corridors, oblivious to the confusion that surrounded them as students danced to the latest hit record blaring from their radios and tape players.

But in two rooms on the second floor, the scene was different. About 50 students were talking casually—often on a first-name basis—with several teachers.

The students and their teachers were preparing for the school day at the "Cluster School," an alternative public high school which operates inside the larger Cambridge High and Latin School.

The school's unique approach is based on Harvard Professor Lawrence Kohlberg's concept of a "Just Community School" where moral education is a basic part of the curriculum.

The bell rings, signaling the beginning of the first class of the day. In one classroom, 12 students take seats in a circle with their creative writing teacher. The teacher is not sitting at her own desk; a student is there. No one seems to mind.

At Cluster, the relationship between teachers and students is less formal than at ordinary schools.

"I get to know the students better and I get to give them attention in a small classroom setting," said Diane Tabor, the creative writing teacher.

One student at Cluster said: "We have more freedom in this school and the teachers care if you are learning or not. The public school I went to was like a jail. The teacher treated us like animals and babies."

The school's curriculum is based on the premise that treating real-life situations as matters for democratic decision by students, teachers and parents will stimulate the students' moral reasoning and moral actions. So the school offers a unique program of moral decision-making along with the basic high school courses.

The Cluster School was founded in the summer of 1974 by a group of parents, teachers and students. The students volunteered for the school. The 65 who now attend were selected from among the volunteers by random lottery within categories of neighborhood, race, year in school and sex to reflect the larger high school population.

In another class, teacher and students are discussing an incident during a recent basketball

most of their peers do. The more children they see breaking a rule, as experiments by Hill and Liebert (1968) have shown, the more likely they are to break the rule themselves. Children will cheat—on a test, for example—if the need is compelling and the likelihood of getting caught is small.

Among adults too, thought does not necessarily govern action. In one famous series of experiments that involved more than a thousand individuals, Stanley Milgram (1974) at Yale amassed depressing evidence of that. Milgram directed each of the thousand or so subjects—who did not know they were being studied themselves—to administer increasingly severe electric shocks to a "victim" who was actually a collaborator of Milgram. The shocks, Milgram explained, were to punish the "victim" for mistakes in the course of an exgame when two team members, both Cluster students, showed "disrespect" to each other.

One member of the team is saying the argument was an "isolated incident," the result of the pressure of the game, and should not be taken out of context. But the majority of the 12 students in the class begin discussing particular incidents in which they felt students had shown disrespect toward them.

By the end of the class, many students are resolving to be more careful to respect their fellow students.

The class is a Cluster advisory group meeting—a regular feature of the Cluster program in which students and teachers discuss any personal or academic problems that they want to discuss.

During these classes, teachers encourage role playing, consideration of fairness and morality, and active participation in group decisions in order to develop a sense of moral responsibility in the students.

Every Friday, the school holds community meetings which involve parents as well as students and teachers.

Together, the school community makes decisions on rules for the school and sometimes applies sanctions.

Once, during the school's first year, students dealt with the theft of $10 by an unknown student. The students decided to repay the money by taxing each student equally. Peer pressure from the community prompted the culprit to confess and he was required to make restitution.

The cumulative effect of the school's combination of conventional and moral education is evident in the comments of the students.

One student said that his lifestyle has changed drastically during his first year at the school. "I used to waste a lot of time at my old school," he said, "but I feel that the Cluster School has helped me find constructive things to do with my time."

He said that at his old school he hung around with students who skipped school a lot, cheated and got high often. "But now I feel that I have matured. I have confidence in myself."

"This school is a real pleasure," said one 17-year-old who last year attended a conventional high school. "Last year I used to skip school, but not this year, because classes are not a drag. Students can sit down and talk to teachers about anything. They are our friends." ∎

From Boston *Globe*, April 21, 1977, p. 4.

periment in learning. Although the "victim" screamed and pleaded and warned that the shocks (which were faked) might kill him, 65 percent of the subjects delivered "shocks" up to 450 volts, which might indeed have been fatal. The subjects were not thugs, but ordinary folk. They had no animosity toward their "victim," whom they had never met before. They agonized over what they were doing, and they were relieved and delighted when they discovered they had been hoaxed. But like a lot of other people past and present, they had followed orders.

So, you may well ask, if that is the way people behave, what is the point of concerning yourself about your students' stages of moral development?

Kohlberg (1969) found at least a partial answer to that. He studied some of the people who obeyed and some who disobeyed Milgram's orders. He discovered that, of the subjects who ranked in his Stage 6, some 75 percent had resisted Milgram's commands. But of the subjects who ranked in lower stages, only 13 percent had disobeyed Milgram. Still, 25 percent of the Stage 6 subjects *had* followed orders. How would you account for that? The fact is, people in the same stage of moral development do not necessarily judge the same situation in the same way. After all, remember there were Stage 6 people on both sides of the question: "Should Heinz have stolen the radium?"

A DILEMMA FOR TEACHERS

If Kohlberg is correct, then it might be possible for teachers to stimulate their pupils' moral development. The procedure would involve:

Presenting dilemmas such as Heinz's.
Encouraging pupils to think such problems through and to discover flaws in their reasoning.
Exposing them to the attitudes that would be expressed, pro and con, at the stage immediately above their own. (If you talk about Stage 5 to Stage 3 children, you will baffle them, but Stage 4 would prove both comprehensible and provocative.)

All this presupposes that you can identify your pupils' present stages. The distinctions that Kohlberg draws between the various stages may seem unnecessarily fine to you but you have to be able to tell them apart if you want to use them.

If teachers *can* raise their pupils' levels of reasoning, a major question arises: Should they try? The basic issue in poor Heinz's case was: Should he steal the radium? The answers yes and no can be given at any stage. Does it matter in a practical sense how the answers are arrived at? Does an individual benefit by progressing, say, from Stage 4 to Stage 5? Does society benefit by the individual's progress? Do the benefits—if there are any—to the individual and to society conflict? May not an individual in a higher stage suffer, or even fail to survive, in situations where lower stages dominate? Consider a Stage 6 infantryman in a Stage 4 army where duty and obedience are the supreme virtues. Does he follow orders when he considers the orders immoral? If he refuses, we may applaud him. But suppose a whole division were made up of Stage 6 soldiers—an unlikely circumstance—and their sense of morality led to the nation's defeat in a defensive war.

Should morality be taught intentionally in the schools?

The arguments for and against "teaching" moral development in school are located, like moral development itself, in the affective domain. That is, they are based on one's values and attitudes about moral development, rather than on facts and evidence. A typical argument *for* teaching moral behavior would be this:

> I believe that it's important for kids to have some sense of morals and ethics. Because the schools are an important force in children's lives, it's logical that they be partly responsible for all aspects of children's growth, including moral development.

An argument *against* teaching moral behavior might go something like this:

> For most of history, the responsibility for moral development has rested with the family and the church, or neighborhood groups. Let's keep it that way. Schools have no business meddling with such affairs. If the responsibility is placed in the schools, they will try to push certain values or beliefs on people who don't need or want them.

As a teacher, you will never be able to control completely your pupils' behavior and, we think, it would be wrong for you to try. But in assisting their moral development, you will be equipping them better to choose their behavior. For teachers there are several simple rules:

1. Be consistent in what you say and in saying and doing.
2. Remember that children learn things incidentally; much of their behavior has been developed through observation, not through formal instruction.
3. Reinforce the development of higher levels of moral thinking and behavior.
4. Think about your own behavior and behave yourself!

Summary

According to the theories of Erikson and Levinson, human development takes place through a series of age-related periods. In each period, certain key issues must be addressed. How well an individual deals with these issues determines the nature of further personal development.

By school age, children have acquired individual affective characteristics. An understanding of those characteristics will enable you to teach them better, because those characteristics affect their learning. Among the important characteristics is *self-concept*, or what students think of themselves. Children with poor self-concepts do less well in school, even if they possess high IQs. Self-concepts may be improved, and continue to be reassessed and modified throughout adulthood.

Sex differences also have their effect on learning and the development of personality. Some of the differences, besides the obviously biological, may be inherent; others emerge as the result of parental training and the adoption by youngsters of what they consider appropriate sex roles. And some supposed differences have proven nonexistent. Although each sex *as a group* surpasses the other at certain kinds of learning, there is no indication that they should be taught differently. What should concern teachers is the avoidance of sex-role stereotyping.

Youngsters go to school with certain moral standards, which change as the children grow. Whether or not schools should become involved in teaching morality is a sensitive issue, and in the 1930s schools largely abandoned efforts to do so. But the schools can assist moral *development* without setting specific standards.

That development, Piaget concluded, occurs in two stages. In the first stage, children differentiate good and bad solely in terms of what adults permit; in the second stage, which children enter when they are seven or eight years old, a sense of right and wrong generates within them as a result of the youngsters' need to get along with others.

Expanding on Piaget's work, Kohlberg suggests that there are six stages, which he divides into three levels: the *preconventional*, the *conventional*, and the *postconventional*. In the first preconventional stage, the child's guidelines are (1) will an action earn praise or punishment? and (2) can they make me do it? In the second stage, good and bad are defined by needs: an action is good if it satisfies the child's needs or, perhaps, someone else's. The morality of most American adults is at the conventional level. At the third stage one asks, "Will this please other people and make them like me?" At the fourth stage one feels an obligation to society rather than to one's self. Persons who reach the fifth stage, at the postconventional level, accept a societal consensus of right and wrong. If one disagrees with that consensus, one may work to change it, but only by using accepted means. In the sixth stage, conscience guides behavior in accordance with ethical principles such as the Golden Rule.

Bandura views moral development quite differently from Piaget and Kohlberg: his premise is that children acquire their moral standards, as well as other learning, by observing and imitating others, so long as the resultant actions do not lead to punishment.

Children and people generally do not always act in accord with their beliefs in what is right and what is wrong. So you as a teacher may never be able to control completely your pupils' behavior. But you can serve as a model for them and, by assisting their moral development, heighten the chances that the behavior they most often choose will be good.

Chapter Study Guide

CHAPTER REVIEW

1. Although most sex-related learning differences have been proved to be unfounded, research indicates that

   a. boys are more analytic.
   b. girls are more auditory.
   c. girls have lower self-esteem.
   d. boys excel at high-level cognitive operations.
   e. girls show superior verbal performance.

2. At each of Erikson's stages of personality development,

   a. a crisis is encountered.

   b. a decision is made to stay or progress.

   c. evidence is based on people's behavior.

   d. people choose between higher or lower moral thinking.

3. The several eras of Levinson's developmental theory are linked together by

   a. identity crises.

   b. commitments.

   c. philosophical questions.

   d. transitions.

Answer questions 4–11 True or False:

4. Although affective learning is important, it has no observable influence on cognitive development.

5. One difference between Piaget's theory of cognitive development and Erik Erikson's theory of personality development is that Erikson's stages of personal growth can be mastered in more than one order.

6. Experimental evidence shows that a good self-concept causes high academic achievement.

7. According to Felker, one way to improve a child's self-concept is to encourage the child to praise him- or herself.

8. The self-concept is a cluster of beliefs.

9. The self-concept becomes increasingly rigid as adults age.

10. Most sex-related behaviors have biological origins.

11. Sex-role stereotyping is not particularly harmful.

12. Kohlberg's theory of moral development resembles Piaget's thought in that both men view moral development as essentially a _____ process. But Kohlberg posits _____ stages whereas Piaget posits only _____ . People whose actions are governed by self-chosen ethical principles are in Kohlberg's _____ stage.

13. The premise of Albert Bandura's "social learning" is that children acquire their moral standards by _____ . They adopt the standards of behavior and emotional characteristics of people whom they _____ .

14. How did the experiment by Bandura, Ross, and Ross suggest that people do not always act in accordance with their beliefs? Was their theory confirmed or contradicted by the experiments of Stanley Milgram?

FOR FURTHER THOUGHT

1. Which of Erikson's first five stages of personality development has potentially the greatest influence on a student's self-concept? In what ways can school experience affect self-concept? Taking into account your own personality and way of relating to people, how could you most effectively act to strengthen a student's self-concept?

2. According to Felker, people will interpret things that happen to them and will act in ways consistent with the way they see themselves (whether their self-concepts be positive or negative). In turn, the way people see themselves often depends on the expectations that others seem to project toward them (in accordance with the self-fulfilling prophecy). From this perspective, speculate about the probable consequences of implying that a student is untrustworthy or incapable of learning. In your experience, is it true, conversely, that expecting the best from a person helps him or her to become a better person?

3. Some teachers are reluctant to teach morality in class for fear of imposing their own values on children; others believe that it is important to teach values and that, in any case, the teacher constantly reveals his or her values indirectly or unconsciously. (Even the decision to avoid values entirely represents a value judgment that is communicated to students.) Where do you stand now on this controversial issue? Could you defend your position?

4. In his book *Development through Drama* (1967) Brian Way makes the point that the arts develop personality by strengthening imagination and intuition, and by helping to fulfill student aspirations. How would the strengthening of imagination facilitate moral development? How would fulfillment of personal aspirations help a child avoid some of the pitfalls in Erikson's stages of personal development? Both imagination and intuition tend to be personal and immeasurable. Should they, for that reason, receive less attention than the cognitive goals of the curriculum? Explain.

IMPORTANT TERMS

personality	individuation
affect	verbal ability
Erikson's stages	visual-spatial ability
identity crisis	sex-role stereotype
eras of life	moral development
transitions	Kohlberg's stages and levels
self-concept	social learning
inner consistency	

SUGGESTED READINGS

BROWN, R., and HERRNSTEIN, R. J. Moral reasoning and conduct. In Brown, R., and Herrnstein, R. J., *Psychology*. Boston: Little, Brown and Co., 1975, pp. 287–340. One of the most comprehensive accounts of moral development available. Weaves together research, theory, and actual incidents into a cohesive and highly interesting position.

COVINGTON, M. V., and BEERY, R. G. *Self-worth and school learning*. New York: Holt, Rinehart and Winston, 1976. An interesting combination of theory in self-concept and classroom strategies intended to maximize success and enhance the self-concept.

ERIKSON, E. H. *Childhood and society* (2nd ed.). New York: W. W. Norton, 1963. In a psychoanalytic framework, Erikson lays out his famous eight stages of human development.

ERIKSON, E. H. *Identity: Youth and crisis.* New York: W. W. Norton, 1968. An extension of Erikson's *Childhood and society,* directed toward an understanding of adolescent development.

FELKER, D. W. *Building positive self-concepts.* Minneapolis: Burgess, 1974. Short on theory and strong on practical techniques for teachers, the book stresses applications for elementary-age youngsters.

HAMACHEK, D. W. *Encounters with the self.* New York: Holt, Rinehart and Winston, 1971. A fairly comprehensive account of a theoretical and historical perspective on self-concept, finishing with teaching tips and ideas about enhancing one's own image of self.

HERSH, R. H., MILLER, J. P., and FIELDING, G. D. *Models of moral education: An appraisal.* New York: Longman, 1980. (See Hersh et al. below.)

HERSH, R. H., PAOLITTO, D. P., and REIMER, J. *Promoting moral growth: From Piaget to Kohlberg.* New York: Longman, 1979. These two volumes by Hersh and colleagues form companion pieces. The first introduces and compares six approaches to moral education, with an emphasis on an eclectic model. The second is an extensive review and uncritical exploration of Kohlberg's ideas applied to the classroom.

LICKONA, T. (ed.). *Moral development and behavior.* New York: Holt, Rinehart and Winston, 1976. Variety of viewpoints on moral development, including research, theory, and practical issues in the classroom.

SPENCE, J. T., and HELMREICH, R. L. *Masculinity and femininity: Their psychological dimensions, correlates, and antecedents.* Austin, TX: University of Texas Press, 1978. Recent research on gender development.

TOBIAS, S., and WEISSBROD, C. Anxiety and mathematics: An update. *Harvard Educational Review,* 1980, *50* (1), 63–70. This article reviews sex differences in mathematics and suggests directions for the future.

ANSWER KEY

1. e; 2. a; 3. d; 4. F; 5. F; 6. F; 7. T; 8. T; 9. F; 10. F; 11. F; 12. cognitive . . . six . . . two . . . sixth; 13. observation and imitation . . . admire

The Tasks of Instruction: Learning and Teaching

Thus far in this book we have concerned ourselves with what students carry to school with them along with their schoolbooks, i.e., their "entry characteristics." In Part II, which you are about to begin reading and which incorporates chapters 5 through 13, we shall turn our attention to the psychology of learning and teaching and, in effect, to what *teachers* should carry to school with them. We shall consider, chiefly, methods of instruction, which must vary because children vary. If all children had the same characteristics, they would all come up with pretty much the same marks, and every teacher would teach every class every year in pretty much the same way. Teaching, then, would be a dull way indeed to make a living. On the other hand, even the most dedicated, psychologically astute, and versatile teacher cannot know fully all the characteristics that will influence a pupil's learning, or how much of a pupil's bundle of characteristics to take into account in preparing and executing a course of instruction. The best the teacher can hope for is a general understanding of the differences among learners and of the fundamentals of learning theory, and a mastery of the procedures and processes that make for expert teaching. In addition to a repertoire of teaching procedures, we emphasize flexibility and an attitude of experimentation. Competent teaching requires a willingness to plan carefully, try out, and evaluate various teaching approaches.

This part of this book is intended to help you toward those ends. Its first two chapters, 5 and 6, are devoted to the psychological processes involved in learning. In Chapter 5 we shall consider those processes in the behavioral framework (i.e., observable behavior and what controls it), and in Chapter 6 we shall look at the cognitive framework (i.e., the mental operations required in learning and remembering). But the major portion of Part II focuses on the practical applications of that knowledge in the classroom. Among the questions discussed in chapters 7 through 13 will be:

Should teachers set objectives for classes and individuals and, if so, how should they go about it?

What are concepts, and how are they transmitted to students?

How do you teach students to solve problems?

What can a teacher do to inspire creativity?

How do you handle "exceptional" children who suffer from so-called learning disorders, who are emotionally disturbed, or who have far-below-average IQs? And what can you do about gifted students who tower above their classmates intellectually?

Can a teacher aim student energy toward classroom objectives?

How do you deal with chronic misbehavers and keep a classroom peaceful and at work?

We hope that Part II will provide answers or help you to find your own.

The Behavioral Framework of Learning

Learning, according to behaviorists, is the process of changing behavior more or less permanently. It often results from repeated experience. If ten-month-old Eric is scratched by the family cat every time he pulls the cat's tail, he learns eventually that he had better not pull the cat's tail unless he is prepared to be scratched again. When Eric stops pulling the cat's tail, he demonstrates by his changed behavior what he has learned. Some learning occurs after a single experience: When Molly wins a prize in the state lottery, the odds are strong that—though she has won only once—she will buy more lottery tickets. Both instances exemplify the influence of the *consequences* of behavior in changing behavior.

A good deal of learning comes about less dramatically, from observation of others. In a broad sense, observation is a form of experience, although the experience takes place only inside the head. The change of behavior then manifests itself in imitation of what others have been seen to do. This kind of learning, usually known as observational or social learning, will be considered in detail later in the chapter.

But not all changes of behavior result from learning. Some, such as development of the ability to walk, come with growth, or maturation. In a classic study, Dennis and Dennis (1940) observed the infants of two Hopi Indian tribes. One tribe bound babies to cradleboards for most of the waking day; the other left them free to crawl and try to stand. Youngsters of both tribes began walking, on the average, at the same ages. So the natural processes of biological growth too cause behavioral changes. Whether a change in behavior reflects maturation or learning or both working in tandem is often difficult to determine. Would the cradlebound little Hopis have learned to walk if no one with whom they had contact ever walked? The scant available evidence indicates that the answer is no. But except under extreme deprivation, physical maturation proceeds to the timing of a still-mysterious clock until its influence becomes less obvious in adolescence.

The Invisible Process

Unfortunately for psychologists, teachers, pupils, and everybody else, learning cannot be watched at work. In its functioning, it apparently involves many and varied physiological and chemical activities among the cells busy inside the brain. Because those activities elude observation and measurement at first hand, their existence can only be inferred. Psychologists therefore describe learning as a *construct*. A construct is a concept based on indirect evidence; that is, it is built of inferences drawn from observed results. (Review the box on page 17 for more information about constructs.)

THE VISIBLE EVIDENCE

The only way to determine whether or not someone has learned something is to observe his or her behavior, or performance. A relatively permanent change of behavior, demonstrated by repeated performance, implies learning: if a first grader is told that c-a-t spells *cat* and immediately repeats *c-a-t*, the youngster has not necessarily learned to spell the word; she could merely be using the short-term memory storage, which is discussed in Chapter 6. But if the child spells *cat* correctly the next day and the next week, the performance indicates that she has learned.

How are learning and performance related?

As a yardstick of learning, performance is a less-than-perfect tool. For one thing, learning often does not get a chance to perform. A common, and loud, complaint of students runs, "I knew *all* that stuff, but they left most of it out of the test." Another weakness of performance derives from the circumstance that individuals evidence learning in a variety of ways and in some of them more effectively than in others. Certain students talk better than they write; others write better than they talk. Some tackle multiple-choice questions with ease and fumble when they have to produce long written answers; others have the skills reversed. In everyone, the quality of performance varies, but students face the necessity not only of learning a subject but of learning how to perform in that subject to the teacher's satisfaction.

If all the pupils in a class know certain material equally well—an unlikely situation indeed but a necessary assumption here—how can a teacher judge *who* has learned *what* if performances prove unequal? And how does a teacher determine that a student has learned the subject if the student has not learned the teacher's standards of performance? There are no single best answers to such questions, though you may find several for yourself after you have read chapters 14 and 15.

Using performance as a yardstick of learning, though, may not be so unfair as it seems. All over the world, people are guided by societal standards of behavior, or performance. If you cannot or will not perform to cultural expectations—well, society does not award grades, but it does hand out consequences.

PERFORMANCE AND PRACTICE

There is another good reason why performance is important. When we perform an act, we are also practicing it. Some teachers, remembering from their own days as pupils having had to practice to the point of boredom or fatigue, disdain practice as part of the learning process. But, short of boredom or fatigue, practice is fundamental to much of learning. (That unfortunately holds true even when what has been learned is wrong—as any duffer on a golf course could tell you.) Some students may require more practice than others, the differences depending on who they are and how much they already know about a given subject or about material related to it.

Why is performance important?

Practice is so common a word and represents so familiar an idea that you may never have given a thought to how and why it affects us. In the language of psychology, practice is the repetition of a *response* to a *stimulus*. Response and stimulus constitute basic elements of the psychological theory called behaviorism, which influences many American educators and provides the foundation for the techniques of behavior modification. In reading about behaviorism, to which most of this chapter will be devoted, you will find theoretical explanations not only for the effects of practice but for the whole process of learning.

Behaviorism

Behaviorism's premise is that every human and animal action constitutes a response to a stimulus. To behaviorists, nothing happens without a stimulus, a cause. A leaf trembles only when a breeze whispers through the tree and the breeze stirs only because the air is warmer elsewhere and the air is warmer elsewhere because.... A pigeon interrupts its pecking in the middle of the street only because a car is coming and the car is coming because.... The cause-and-effect or stimulus-and-response rule applies, in the behaviorist view, to human beings as it does to everything else.

What are the rules of behaviorism?

Determinism—the idea that every event is caused by other events—is a fundamental principle of behaviorism, but several other tenets also set behaviorism apart among theories of learning. Strict behaviorists confine their studies to *external, observable* events. Few behaviorists would insist that internal events such as thinking and feeling do not occur, but most would argue that those events do not lend themselves to scientific analysis because they cannot be observed or measured. Their concentration on observable data leads behaviorists to avoid subjective impressions in analyzing and describing the learning process. Behaviorism is distinguished also by its efforts to put its principles of learning into practice, and it has affected business and industry as well as the fields of education, childrearing, and mental health.

THE GESTATION OF BEHAVIORISM: PAVLOV'S EXPERIMENTS

As a theory of psychology, behaviorism was born in the United States early in this century. But it was conceived—in the biological sense—in nineteenth-century Russia with the discovery of *classical conditioning*.

Classical conditioning sounds forbidding, but the experiments that established its existence have been described irreverently as "teaching a dog to spit on cue." Its principles were determined by Ivan Petrovich Pavlov (1849–1936), a Russian physician and physiologist who chanced on them while exploring how the body digests food and drink. Pavlov won the Nobel Prize in 1904 for advances in physiology, but it was classical conditioning that made his name part of the language in the phrase "Pavlov's dogs."

Philosophers as far back as Aristotle had noted that if things were contiguous, occurring together frequently, they tended to become mentally associated. In his discussion of memory, Aristotle incorporated mental associ-

"Students must do something with whatever they're learning. I don't mean that a skill should be functional in society right this second; some skills won't be useful until much later. What I mean is that they have to actively practice and demonstrate that they are learning something. I don't take for granted that students will absorb everything on their own. The proof is in the performance."

ation into his law of contiguity, but he could not explain the phenomenon. Pavlov investigated how mental association came about, how it strengthened and weakened, and a great deal more that is related in one way or another to learning.

Although Pavlov's work on learning dealt primarily with dogs, and although Aristotle lived some twenty-three centuries ago, classical conditioning is not so remote from the classroom as you might think. In Chapter 10 you will find illustrations of its applications there. But first let's consider what Pavlov was up to.

For his studies of the digestive system, Pavlov implanted a tube in a dog's salivary gland so that he could measure the amounts of saliva the dog secreted under different conditions. As Pavlov approached the dog one day with a tray of powdered meat, the dog salivated, although previously the saliva had flowed only when the dog had begun to eat. The food constituted an *unconditioned stimulus*, a natural, uncontrived, external event. The salivation was an *unconditioned response*, an unlearned response elicited by the environment. An unconditioned response simply represents doing what comes naturally, the way a just-born baby yowls when the doctor slaps it to start it breathing. (The terms are usually abbreviated to US, for unconditioned stimulus and UR for unconditioned response.)

The oftener Pavlov showed the dog the food, the more the dog salivated in advance. After a time, Pavlov began ringing a bell immediately before he delivered the powdered meat. Until then, the ringing of the bell would have had no particular effect on the dog—except perhaps to wake it from a nap: it was a *neutral* stimulus. But the dog soon associated the sound of the bell with food and salivated whenever the bell rang. The bell had become a learned or *conditioned stimulus* (CS) rather than a neutral stimulus and the salivation a *conditioned response* (CR). Aristotle's law of contiguity was in operation.

Contiguity here refers to the joining of two stimuli, an unconditioned one and a conditioned one. So what gets changed in classical conditioning is a stimulus; thus a formerly neutral stimulus becomes able to evoke a response because of its association with another stimulus. Figure 5.1 summarizes the procedure.

How does classical conditioning operate?

Extinction. If Pavlov rang the bell repeatedly in a single session and did not come up with food, the dog eventually caught on and ceased "to spit on cue." This phenomenon is called extinction. The following day, though, when Pavlov took the dog to the laboratory and rang the bell but did not provide the meat, the dog salivated again, demonstrating that a response that had been temporarily extinguished might *recover spontaneously*.

Generalization. Pavlov found too that after a time the dog responded to other sounds, such as that of a whistle, as though Pavlov had rung the bell, and the more bell-like the noise, the greater the dog's reaction. That was generalization, a response to one stimulus because the stimulus was similar to another that already produced a conditioned response.

Discrimination. To eliminate generalization, Pavlov produced food only after he had rung the bell and never after any of the other sounds. The dog thus learned to distinguish one sound from another by discrimination.

Higher-Order Conditioning. When Pavlov accompanied the sound of the bell with a black square shown on a screen, the dog came to associate the square with the sound of the bell, and the sight of the square induced salivation. Once a neutral stimulus, the square became a new conditioned stimulus and the bell continued to serve as the original conitioned stimulus. The process of linking a CS to a new CS is called higher-order conditioning. Figure 5.1 outlines the basic classical and higher-order conditioning model.

Variety of Response. Pavlov's dog, as we have called it, actually was a whole kennelful of dogs, each with its individual characteristics and tempera-

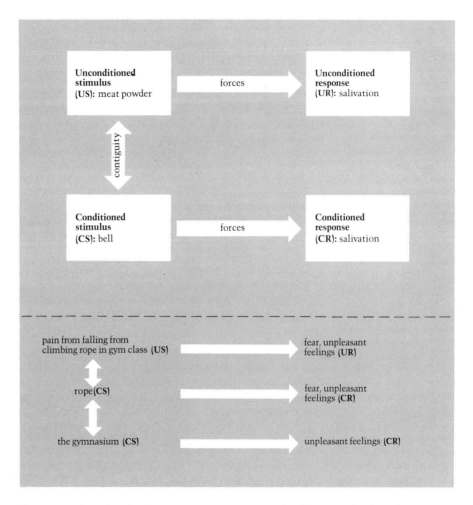

Figure 5.1. The Classical Conditioning Model. **The diagram depicts both classical and higher-order conditioning in operation. A student falling from a climbing rope in the gym automatically experiences unpleasant feelings from the unconditioned stimulus of pain. The rope, orginally a neutral stimulus, becomes associated with the pain and thereafter evokes a similar emotional response. Higher-order conditioning–the linking of two or more conditioned stimuli–occurs when the gym itself becomes paired, or associated, with the rope. With such a dramatic event, practice may not be required!**

ment. Accordingly, the dogs differed in the intensity of their responses to Pavlov's experiments. Some became conditioned easily, others with difficulty, not unlike people. For that reason, Pavlov could never be certain that a conditioned stimulus would produce an expected response. The implications for teaching are clear: students do not respond identically to stimuli any more than Pavlov's dogs did, and their differences have to be taken into account.

Adding It Up. Classical conditioning, then, consists of presenting together or pairing—in obedience to Aristotle's law of contiguity—an unconditioned stimulus and a conditioned stimulus and repeating the pairing a number of times. The more repetition, the stronger the response, as evidenced by the dog's increasing salivation each time Pavlov appeared with food. Eventually, the conditioned stimulus alone will evoke the response that the unconditioned stimulus used to evoke on its own: the CS substitutes for the US. If two conditioned stimuli are repeatedly paired, one of them may act as an unconditioned stimulus in a phenomenon called higher-order conditioning.

A response disappears (extinction is said to occur) if the conditioned stimulus is applied too often without the unconditioned stimulus. The dog, you remember, stopped salivating after Pavlov had repeatedly rung the bell without providing the food. But the response may recur later spontaneously, and the recurrence is termed spontaneous recovery.

A conditioned stimulus need not always be precisely the same. If it is similar, as the whistle and the bell were for the dog, generalization will enable the stimulus to elicit the expected response, and the greater the similarity, the stronger the response. Generalization, which is essential to learning, is useful only to a point: too much generalization in classical conditioning may lead to superstitious emotional reactions. Consider the fellow who lies in bed awake, anxious because he has just seen *The Night of the Living Creepies*. A little discrimination would lead him to realize that Creepies are harmless figments of imagination. But classical conditioning deals with involuntary responses, doesn't it? (Can you explain why fear of Creepies will probably fade after a time? The definitions we gave of *extinction*, will help.)

CLASSICAL CONDITIONING AND LEARNING

Pavlov considered conditioning and learning to be the same and to represent establishment of some kind of connection in the central nervous system between a stimulus and a response. Reflexive behavior, of which salivation is an example, is of no great concern to the teacher: unless the subject is home economics and the class is baking a cake, no pupil is likely to water at the mouth at the prospect of a new lesson. But some contemporary psychologists see classical conditioning as explaining emotional, or affective, development. The emotional responses of pupils to their teacher and to what they are being taught will be determined by the conditioned and unconditioned stimuli to which the pupils are subjected.

CONDITIONING AND EMOTION

How is classical conditioning related to affective behavior?

How conditioning may operate on human emotion was demonstrated in a series of experiments described by Vernon (1972). The experiments involved an electric shock device that was hooked to the fingers of a group of collegians. When the gadget delivered a mild, two-second shock accompanied by the whine of a buzzer, the students' hearts began to beat faster, a sign of emotion. Several minutes apart, to allow the hearts to slow down to normal in the interim, the shocks were repeated twenty times, always to the sound of the buzzer. Always the heartbeats accelerated. Then the experimenter sounded the buzzer to portend a shock. But the experimenter disconnected the shock device, put it away in view of the students, and asked them to try *not* to react when he next sounded the buzzer. They failed: at the buzz, their hearts accelerated. The students had involuntarily responded emotionally to the conditioned stimulus—the buzzer—even though they knew no shock would follow.

The Case of the Three Leonards. If phenomena like that occurred only in psychological laboratories, they might be of no more than scientific interest. But they appear frequently in the world outside the labs, though they may not be recognized for what they are—Pavlovian principles at work. We know a man who used to detest a certain given name, which we shall say was Leonard, and who disliked immediately anyone who bore it. He had known in childhood a raucous adult named Leonard and in youth he had worked with another Leonard whom he considered incompetent and quarrelsome. He thereafter generalized that all men named Leonard would prove disagreeable. Some years later, he was thrown together inescapably—in the army—with a third Leonard who proved to be engaging, quiet-spoken, and dependable when survival demanded dependability. Our acquaintance's distaste for him at the start slowly gave way to discrimination among Leonards and eventually to extinction of his phobia about the name and its bearers. The behaviorists' technical explanation for what happened is this: in classical conditioning, of which the case is an example, the unconditioned or conditioned stimulus *reinforces* an involuntary response. The first two Leonards' unpleasant behavior represented the conditioned stimuli that reinforced our acquaintance's dislike of the name. But when the decent Leonard came along, the reinforcement was withheld and our acquaintance's conditioned response—dislike—was gradually extinguished.

Is math anxiety inherited?

Fear of Figures. Skill in mathematics is sex-related. During adolescence, boys begin to outdistance girls in math achievement; through college, the gap widens. It is not simply that girls take fewer math courses or that they do less homework. Girls often show a negative emotion toward mathematics, popularly called "math anxiety."

According to Sheila Tobias (1978), math anxiety is a learned response, and is largely responsible for females' poor performance. Tobias does not use classical conditioning theory to support her position, but it does offer an explanation. Because of sex-role expectations, girls often reject attributes generally connected to boys: logical, oriented toward math or science careers, persistent in problem-solving. These attributes are conditioned stimuli (CSs) that evoke negative feelings in a person striving to be "feminine." As students grow older, mathematics itself becomes part of the cluster of CSs associated with the masculine role.

A similar case can be made for males who suffer from home economics anxiety or sewing anxiety. So classical and higher order conditioning help to maintain stereotyped sex roles. Not only do we imitate live models, but our own emotions add motivation to continue or avoid certain roles. As we implied in Chapter 4, it is possible to diminish sex-role attitudes, including math anxiety, by nurturing and reinforcing new opportunities for both sexes.

Hope and Fear. Among the theorists who link classical conditioning and emotional development, one of the most important, O. Hobart Mowrer, agreed with Pavlov that classical conditioning and learning were the same thing. But Mowrer (1960) argued that Pavlov unknowingly was conditioning not his dogs' salivary glands but their emotions. Mowrer reduced these emotions to hope and fear. Learning, he held, consists of developing responses that inspire

"Some kids come in here and they've been to three or four different schools a year. So who's interested in them? They're used to being a problem. You get stuck in the back of the room and that's it. They're really used to that kind of treatment, and they come in here very turned off and way behind grade level. So the first thing I

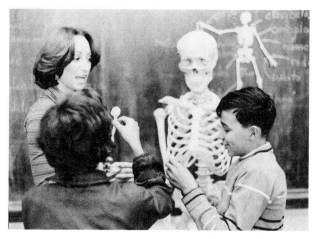

hope, that is, that make one "feel good," and of restraining responses that instill fear, that is, that make one "feel bad." As an example, Mowrer cited a parrot's speech. The parrot is born with the ability to make speech-like sounds. That appears obvious, but it is an important point in Mowrer's system because he believes, as do certain other psychologists, that we can learn only what we already have the potential to do. Though the parrot is equipped to "talk," it learns best how to do it if its owner speaks to it when he or she feeds it. Eating makes the bird "feel good." When human speech accompanies eating repeatedly, the parrot comes to associate eating and talking. After a time, human speech *alone* makes the parrot feel good. Because the bird can emit more or less similar sounds itself, its own speech also makes it feel good and the better it feels the more it will talk. The bird has not been induced to talk by any external reward; it would presumably be fed in any case. The bird merely does what it is capable of doing because it has associated the good feeling of eating with making sounds.

In Mowrer's view, human beings behave similarly. Babies learn to talk because feeding and fondling make them feel good and they associate the feeling with the pleasant sounds their parents produce. The closer a baby comes to duplicating those sounds, the better he or she feels. If the parents were to scold and yell when attending the infant—as, unfortunately, some parents do—the infant would come to associate speech with fear, that is, with feeling bad. He or she then might be inhibited in learning to talk.

The crucial factor in classical conditioning, though, is Aristotle's law of contiguity. If the stimuli—US and CS or CS and CS—do not occur together, the conditioning is unlikely to take effect.

have to do as a teacher is get them to want to learn. They begin to feel that this is a good place to be, that I'm interested in them, that they can *do the work—and suddenly they're crazy about school. They love it."*

THE BIRTH OF BEHAVIORISM

Pavlov's findings represented behaviorism's period of gestation as we indicated some pages back. Behaviorism's delivery coincided with a rebellion against the traditional psychology of the time. For several decades after Wilhelm Wundt established the first experimental psychological laboratory in Leipzig in 1879, studies in psychology confined themselves to the literal meaning of the word. (*Psycho-*, as you may know, is a prefix denoting mind and -*logy* a suffix for science.) Wundt had been a physician and a physiologist and he had a strong philosophical bent, so he attempted to analyze the working of the mind bit by bit in the manner of a physician-physiologist-philosopher. Because he could not look at the mind through a microscope to watch it think, he trained people to peer into their own minds and report to him everything that they felt or sensed or thought (Wundt, 1910). This process of looking inward, of pondering every flash in the brain-pan, struck an increasing number of psychologists—especially Americans—as missing the forest for the trees. What did it objectively reveal about the whole person? Would it not be more rewarding to observe, measure, and analyze what people actually did, how they *behaved?*

One man to whom the questions occurred was John Broadus Watson (1878–1958), who for his doctoral thesis was observing rats exploring a maze. His work and Pavlov's findings, with which he was familiar, fostered his belief that all human and animal activity constituted responses to external stimuli. Watson did not deny that things went on in people's heads. But he postulated that feelings did not determine behavior, so it served no purpose to consider them in discussing the causes of behavior or in attempting to change it. Anyway, feelings could not be observed or measured or weighed, and therefore did not merit scientific study. Only what people did—their performance— counted. And Pavlov had made a remarkable contribution by showing how precisely responses to stimuli could be measured.

In 1913, five years after he had become professor of experimental and comparative psychology at Johns Hopkins University, Watson published his manifesto, "Psychology as the Behaviorist Views It." The article was to swerve the direction of American psychology and set off a still-persisting ruckus. The word *behaviorist* was Watson's invention.

Watson's theory echoes, of course, one side of the centuries-long debate about free will and determinism—the doctrine that events control human courses of action. What Watson added to determinism was the concept that behavior could be changed if one could systematically change external events. That concept has come to be called behavior modification.

The Conditioning of Albert. Behavior modification had important roots in a series of experiments, in the most famous of which Watson brought together a borrowed infant named Albert and a white rat. Albert and the rat became friends, and one day as Albert was reaching toward his pal, Watson banged a steel bar with a hammer. The noise, naturally, terrified Albert. Thereafter, whenever Albert tried to clutch the rat, Watson banged. Soon Albert whimpered or yowled at the mere sight of the rat—and of furry toys— even when Watson refrained from wielding the hammer. Albert had been conditioned to associate the rat with noise, whether or not there was any noise (Watson and Rayner, 1920).

What was Watson's role in founding behaviorism?

Watson was not primarily interested in education, and he was by no means a learning theorist, but Albert's reactions convinced Watson that by conditioning he could control human learning and behavior in general. He proclaimed:

> Give me a dozen healthy infants, well formed, and my own special world to bring them up in, and I'll guarantee to take any one at random and train him to become any type of specialist I might select—doctor, lawyer, artist, merchantchief and, yes, even beggarman and thief, regardless of his talents, penchants, tendencies, abilities, vocations or race of his ancestry (Watson, 1925, p. 82).

Few behaviorists today would endorse such an extreme pronouncement. But Watson's focus on the environment is an important legacy for many contemporary psychologists.

THE ADVENT OF B. F. SKINNER

Watson ceased writing about his theories several years after he abandoned the academic life for the advertising business, and the banner of behaviorism was snatched up in the 1930s by Burrhus Frederick Skinner (1904–), whom the American Psychological Association has voted the most influential psychologist, alive or dead. (Outside the academic world, Skinner is one of those rare scholars who rank in popular consciousness only a little below professional football players, golfing champions, rock stars, and television doctors. *Time* magazine for September 20, 1971, devoted its cover and a seven-page article to him.)

To Skinner, there is no soul or mind; people are simply organisms. Men and women are products of what they have learned and experienced and of their individual genetic codes, which interact with the environment. Skinner finds the products unsatisfactory: human beings fight wars, murder, riot, pollute, exploit their fellows and the Earth, overpopulate, and covet their neighbors' wives or husbands. But behavior can be changed, in Skinner's view, because he holds that all behavior is controlled by its *consequences*, that is, by what happens to you *after* you have done something. He proposes that if certain consequences are provided and others withheld, undesirable activities will be replaced by those that society claims to value.

For Skinner, the most important consequence of a response is *reinforcement*, which is any stimulus event that will strengthen or maintain the behavior that produced it. For most of us, the term *reinforcement* seems synonymous with reward, which produces pleasurable feelings. For Skinner,

B. F. Skinner

B. F. Skinner's philosophy of determinism and his nonchalance about the inner workings of a human have been the source of much criticism. In an interview, he once remarked, "As far as I'm concerned, the organism is irrelevant either as the site of physiological activities or as the locus of mentalistic activities" (Evans, 1968, p. 2). His notions of determinism center, of course, on the impact of the environment on human learning. It is the environment, and not the "inner person," which directs behavior. Thus, to control the environment is to control behavior.

It was his sense of environmental control, reinforced by success in pigeon experiments, which led Skinner to propose—and build—a controlled environment for babies. He called his invention the "air crib" and published a description of it in *Ladies' Home Journal* in October 1945. (Notice the timing: World War

however, reinforcers do not work because they make us feel good. Strict behaviorists, remember, avoid using internal events such as good feelings to explain observable phenomena. A reinforcer is defined by the effect it produces—the increase or maintenance of a response—and not by any feelings associated with it. Skinner's philosophy and principles are elaborated in his book, *About Behaviorism* (1974).

OPERANT CONDITIONING

For applying his principles, Skinner has devised *operant conditioning*, originally based on experiments he undertook after having read Pavlov and some articles by the philosopher Bertrand Russell on Watson's behaviorism. Unlike classical conditioning, which deals with *involuntary* responses to stimuli, operant conditioning concerns *voluntary* responses or *operants*, which constitute most of human behavior. Even a smile, a stroking of one's beard or hair, a shift in one's seat, are operants. They are called so because they represent willful operations on the environment rather than passive reactions to it.* Operant conditioning involves encouragement by reinforcement of desirable voluntary behavior and discouragement of undesirable voluntary behavior.

---

* *Operations*, in a behaviorist sense, refers to obvious, external movements. Compare this to Piaget's definition of *operations*, noted in Chapter 2, as internal mental manipulation.

II had just ended, and the baby boom began.) The air crib is a solid, glass-walled enclosure with sound proofing and controlled temperature and humidity. With this air conditioning, an infant needs no clothes. As a substitute for diapers, a long sheet is rolled onto a spool as it is soiled. Filtered air protects the infant from germs. Outlandish? Skinner's younger daughter, Deborah, spent over two years in an air crib. Although skeptics rumored that she was permanently disturbed by the event, Deborah is happy and healthy.

Despite his reliance on environmental causes of behavior, Skinner must take some personal credit for a creative prank he pulled as a Hamilton College student. Bored with student life, Skinner and a friend had bright orange posters printed up with the announcement that the very next day, Charlie Chaplin would deliver a lecture in the college chapel. In the wee hours, the two jokers pasted the posters about town, and then called the local newspaper to make sure the announcement would appear on the front page. By noon, the college administration had posted police to stop traffic and advise drivers of the hoax. Still, some 400 cars managed to get through and most mistook a pep rally in the gym for the Chaplin gathering. Perhaps it was for lack of reinforcement that Skinner sought other activities for more serious study. ■

Sources
Evans, R. I. *B. F. Skinner: The man and his ideas.* New York: E. P. Dutton, 1968.
Skinner, B. F. *Particulars of my life.* New York: Alfred A. Knopf, 1976.
"Skinner's Utopia: Panacea, or Path to Hell?" *Time,* September 20, 1971, pp. 47–53.

Skinner, however, strongly opposes punishment as a means of changing behavior, for reasons to be elaborated in Chapter 10.

Skinner's Box. For the experiments that led to the development of operant conditioning, Skinner used a soundproof box with a transparent top and side and a food dispenser that a rat could operate by pressing a lever.

What is the effect of delayed reinforcement?

Skinner put a rat in the box and just watched and waited. The rat, after sniffing around the box for a while without finding much of interest, finally pressed the lever—an example of operant behavior. A pellet of food immediately dropped into a cup that was part of the dispenser. The rat devoured the pellet. Because the pellet had appeared *immediately*, it reinforced the operant, and the rat soon was working the lever as fast as it could chew the pellets. Had the pellet's drop been delayed a minute or two, the food would have reinforced whatever other operant behavior the rat was engaging in at the time—scratching itself, twitching, or waving its tail, perhaps. The point is that operant behavior is encouraged by *immediate* reinforcement. Delayed reinforcement may miss the target.

One of Skinner's most important contributions involves the delivery of reinforcers to the learner. *Reinforcement schedules* describe when and how often reinforcers may be applied. It can be seen that altering the schedule will also change the rate of learning and its permanence. We will summarize the most important reinforcement schedules in Chapter 10.

From Rats to Pigeons to People. Using reinforcement, Skinner has taught pigeons to walk figure eights, play Ping-Pong, and, in World War II, to guide missiles. Describing the figure eight experiment, Skinner has said:

> I watch a hungry pigeon carefully. When he makes a slight clockwise turn [an operant], he's instantly rewarded for it [by food provided from outside the box]. After he eats, he immediately tries it again. Then I wait for more of a turn and reinforce again. Within two or three minutes, I can get any pigeon to make a full circle. Next I reinforce only when he moves in the other direction. Then I wait until he does both and reinforce him again and again until it becomes a kind of drill. Within ten to 15 minutes, the pigeon will be doing a perfect figure eight ("Skinner's Utopia," 1971, p. 50).

The pigeon has learned by successive approximations of the desired behavior, a technique called *shaping*, which is a fundamental principle of operant conditioning.

What is shaping?

Skinner realized that learners do not usually leap from no skill to perfect accomplishment. Learning is much more gradual. The instructional question that fits this idea is: How can we most effectively move a learner toward a particular goal? Skinner's reply is that we must arrange the learner's task in small steps, where each step moves closer to the goal, is easily attainable, and is rewarded. Typical teaching, Skinner complains, allows students to find their own route to the goal (and many do not), and provides reinforcers only when the goal is reached. The system of successive approximations helps to ensure repeated success and keeps learners aimed in the right direction.

In training pigeons to guide missiles, Skinner conditioned several birds to peck for four or five minutes steadily at a target depicted on a screen. Then the birds were harnessed in the nose of a mock-up missile, facing a similar screen on which the target would appear while a real missile was on its way. Pecking at the target's moving image, the pigeons unwittingly controlled the missile's fins and held the missile on course. By now, no reinforcement was necessary to keep the pigeons pecking. As part of their operant conditioning, they had been taught that you can't win 'em all, but like slot machine gamblers at Las Vegas, they had been reinforced occasionally enough to maintain their interest in the game.

Skinner's pigeons never saw combat because the equipment that they necessitated proved too bulky for the missile and because, as Skinner wryly explains: "No one would take us seriously" ("Skinner's Utopia," 1971, p. 50). Skinner is taken a great deal more seriously nowadays, especially by educators, when he argues that students as well as rats and pigeons are taught by operant conditioning techniques.

Operant Conditioning in the Classroom. Practical application of operant conditioning to teaching is considered in detail in Chapter 10, but Skinner merits quotation here on that point:

> Unfortunately, a student does not learn simply when he is shown or told. Something essential to his natural curiosity or wish to learn is missing from the classroom. That something is positive reinforcement. In daily life he looks,

listens, and remembers because certain consequences are contingent upon his doing so. He responds to the things he sees and hears, and when his responses are reinforced, he acts in the same way again. He also learns to look and listen in special ways which encourage remembering because he is reinforced for recalling what he has seen and heard, just as a newspaper reporter knows and remembers things he sees because he is paid for reporting them. Consequences of this sort are lacking when a teacher simply shows a student something or tells him something. . . . Positive reinforcers occur in nature, but they are not well used in simple telling and showing (1965, p. 99).

The Mysterious Process. For all its seeming simplicity, operant conditioning remains an often puzzling phenomenon. Responses to it may be obvious and even measurable, but to determine what stimuli caused the responses frequently proves difficult: the stimuli usually are numerous, subtle, and unobservable. You smile—operant. Why did you smile? If someone smiled at you and prompted your smile in return, the stimulus and the response are obvious. But if no one smiled at you and you smiled anyway, what inspired the smile? A fleeting recollection of a pleasant conversation? Anticipation of a date? A sense of well-being because the sun shines? Or some inner command of which you yourself are unaware? A rookie baseball player, stepping up to the plate in the big leagues for the first time in his life, may hitch his belt and tug at his cap, but never be able to explain why. But if he hits a homer that first time up, there is a high probability that for the rest of his career he will hitch his belt and tug at his cap. (Lots of superstitions originate like that.)

The Discriminative Stimulus. Because operant stimuli are so difficult to identify, some teachers conclude that the sole purpose of operant condi-

Living by Operant Conditioning

A whole way of life controlled by operant conditioning is described by Skinner in his novel *Walden Two* (1948), of which more than a million copies have been sold. Skinner's idea of Utopia, Walden Two is a self-sufficient rural commune directed by a Skinner-like benevolent despot and operated by Planners and Managers for the benefit of the less exalted residents. Members of the community cheerfully engage in a few hours' work a day for which they are allotted points that buy them room, board, clothes, and a modicum of luxuries; off duty, which is most of the time, they devote themselves to music, art, and literature and live without economic concerns, conflicts, jealousies—or freedom. But freedom is an illusion anyway, Skinner contends in *Beyond Freedom and Dignity* (1971), a nonfiction extension of *Walden Two*; if civilization is to survive, he says, it will have to employ either repression, which would be unpleasant, or operant conditioning, which could be agreeable. ∎

tioning is to control responses by altering consequences, that is, reinforcement. That is indeed *one* purpose. But another and major job for the school is to control *stimuli*. A stimulus can be viewed as a cue or prompt, and acceptable behavior often depends on sensing a cue and responding the right way at the right time.

How does a discriminative stimulus work?

When you teach someone to respond to a particular stimulus or set of stimuli in a particular way, you are said, in the language of psychology, to build a discriminative stimulus, which is symbolized as S_d. An S_d is a stimulus that prompts a certain response, and it is built by repeated reinforcement of a response in the presence of the S_d.

Figure 5.2 depicts this sequence. The S_d signals the learner that if the appro-

Figure 5.2. The Operant Conditioning Model. In each of the examples, you will note, the discriminative stimulus (S_d) serves as a prompt or cue for the behavior that follows. Each behavior then has a consequence: here the consequences all are meant to be reinforcers, but punishment is a possible consequence. Both types of consequence have an influence on whatever behaviors produce them.

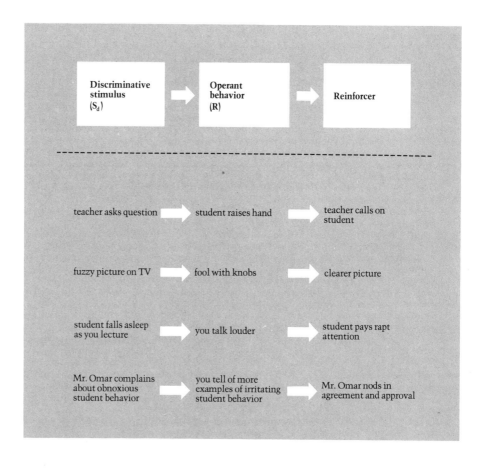

priate response is made, reinforcement may follow. As a result, the learner is more likely to respond correctly; he or she discriminates among stimuli to react to one that makes the biggest promise of reinforcement (Schwartz, 1978). For example, Ralph, who is in the first grade, has a speech difficulty and is also slow in reading. His teacher wants him to recognize the printed word *butter*. If the teacher reinforces Ralph with praise each time he gets closer to reading *butter* aloud correctly, then the word *butter* that has been lettered on the blackboard will eventually become an S_d that cues Ralph's proper response when he sees *butter* lettered again or comes on it in his book.

Discriminative stimuli are not merely interesting aspects of the learning process, they are essential to living and surviving. Imagine a motorist for whom a STOP sign is not an S_d! Or a student who cannot discriminate between the time to talk and the time not to talk in class. (What would you suggest as an appropriate S_d for such a student?)

In sum, the discriminative stimulus is a cue that begins the whole operant conditioning sequence. It derives its cueing property from what happens after a response. If reinforcement follows the response, the S_d likely will become more potent; if punishment follows the response, the S_d will probably become a signal that that particular response should not be repeated. Figure 5.2 depicts the whole operant conditioning model and provides several examples of this type of learning (see also Figure 5.3).

Classical versus Operant Conditioning

Classical and operant conditioning differ in several important ways. The fundamental distinction is this: in operant conditioning, the consequence of a voluntary response leads to an increase—or decrease—in the frequency of the response; in classical conditioning, a formerly neutral stimulus becomes capable of evoking an automatic, involuntary response.

Among other differences:

In operant conditioning, the reinforcement *follows* the response; in classical conditioning, the reinforcement *precedes* the response.

In operant conditioning, delivery of the reinforcer depends on what the learner does; certain behaviors bring reinforcement, others do not. In classical conditioning, reinforcement does not depend on the learner's response: rather, the reinforcement produces the response and the learner receives the reinforcement no matter how he or she behaves.

How do operant and classical conditioning differ?

In operant conditioning, the reinforcer—money or praise, for example—can be used to reinforce thousands of different responses in thousands of situations. Therefore the reinforcer is described as transsituational. In classical conditioning, the reinforcer generally will maintain or strengthen only a single, particular response, and the reinforcer is described as situation-specific. Let's say that, because of the tight fit of the furniture in your dorm

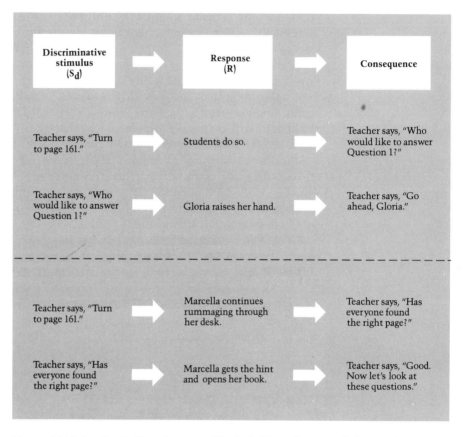

Figure 5.3. Behavior Is Continuous. **The labeling of parts of the environment and of behavioral responses helps to examine the relationship of behavior and environment, but the labels are not permanent, static fixtures. In the examples above, the consequences do follow certain behaviors, but they immediately become discriminative stimuli for other responses.**

room, you frequently bang your knee against the corner of your desk. The pain almost certainly will make you feel bad every time; you'd be an odd character indeed if it made you feel good on occasion. In classical conditioning, in short, you have no choice of responses: by its very nature, classical conditioning is involuntary.

In operant conditioning, what becomes associated or paired is a stimulus and a response; in classical conditioning, two stimuli become associated. To put it another way, in operant conditioning a stimulus becomes linked to a new response; in classical conditioning, a stimulus becomes linked to a new stimulus.

In describing operant conditioning, most behaviorists avoid speculating about internal, mental events. Classical conditioning, by comparison, cannot be discussed without reference to the organism's inner workings. This posed little problem to Pavlov (1955), who often wrote about complex mental processes.

HOW THE TWO TYPES OF CONDITIONING MERGE

Despite the distinctions between them, classical and operant conditioning do not represent two entirely different ways of learning. They overlap, and the overlap is important. The link between them is that reinforcement in operant conditioning is identical with the conditioned or unconditioned stimulus in classical conditioning, as Figure 5.4 illustrates. Furthermore, when operant conditioning occurs, so does classical or higher-order conditioning. As Figure 5.4 indicates, the consequence of behavior in operant conditioning need not be a reinforcer in the sense of reward; it may be punishment or something else to be avoided. But a punisher in the operant scheme is still a reinforcer in the classical scheme: because a reinforcer helps to maintain a response associated with it, a bad consequence will maintain bad feelings.

How do operant and classical conditioning overlap?

Because the overlap occurs at the point of reinforcement, let's recall the nature of reinforcement. A reinforcer is a stimulus that increases or maintains the strength of a response that is associated with it. In operant conditioning, the voluntary response that is strengthened precedes the reinforcement; in classical conditioning, the involuntary response follows reinforcement. The reinforcing stimulus therefore works on two responses: the operant response that produced it and the emotional or reflexive response that follows it.

The Importance of the Link. So what? you may ask. In the classroom, the major implication of the link between operant and classical conditioning is the importance of consequences to a behavior. The teacher who frowns, scolds, and employs sarcasm—that is, provides aversive consequences—must expect reinforcement of "bad feeling" in the classical sense. Contrarily, pleasant or positive consequences not only increase the likelihood of good behavior but will probably lead to the development of "good feeling" about the behavior. This is discussed in detail in Chapter 10.

THE PROS AND CONS OF BEHAVIORISM

Behaviorism, despite its broad influence, remains controversial. When Watson, its founder, abandoned teaching to go into the advertising business, he became a highly successful executive by applying his theories. When you buy an advertised product rather than a similar one with whose name you are unfamiliar, or whose advertising or packaging is less impelling, you evidence your conditioning. But because Skinner and other "pure" behaviorists refuse to speculate about what goes on in the mind, a great many people, including students of education, reject his methods. They *know* that their minds work, and they find it inconceivable that serious, rigorous scientists should ignore mental processes. Skinner and other pure behaviorists appear to their critics as manipulators attempting to control mindless automatons. The psychologist Herbert O. Kelman, like Skinner a professor at Harvard, says, for example, "For

Figure 5.4. The Merger of Operant and Classical Conditioning. The link between operant and classical conditioning is the reinforcement. Notice that an operant reinforcer is identical to an unconditioned or conditioned stimulus. In both models of learning, the reinforcement performs the same task: it maintains or strengthens the response associated with it. When the models are visualized, as in this figure, the operant reinforcer can be imagined to work *backward* on the response that preceded it, whereas the classical reinforcer works *forward* on the emotional or reflexive response that follows. Thus, a reinforcer simultaneously affects two very different types of responses. If punishment follows the operant response, as in two of the examples, the operant response would be expected to decrease, but the emotional response would still be strengthened.

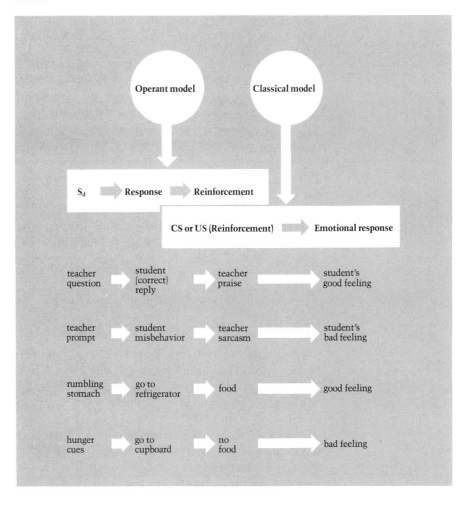

those of us who hold the enhancement of man's freedom of choice as a fundamental value, any manipulation of the behavior of others constitutes a violation of their essential humanity, regardless of the 'goodness' of the cause that this manipulation is designed to serve" ("Skinner's Utopia," 1971, p. 52).

Can the mind play a role in conditioning?

Skinner replies that he changes the environment, not the people, and that human beings, including schoolchildren, then respond to the altered environment.

The New Behaviorism

Skinner's orthodox behavioral psychology has undergone some reinterpretation in recent years by scholars who accept some but not all of Skinner's ideas. A number of behaviorists no longer insist that what goes on in human minds should be ignored. Though they stress the importance of stimuli and responses, they speculate that the mind intervenes between stimulus and response. To those theorists, an organism confronted by a stimulus does not act like an automaton. Rather, it considers the stimulus in the light of its own needs and characteristics and devises a fitting response.

SOCIAL LEARNING

This *neobehaviorist* approach is exemplified by the *social learning* theory of Albert Bandura and his late colleague Richard Walters. (We described social learning briefly in Chapter 4. See pages 130–131.) Social learning is described as neobehaviorist because Bandura builds on operant conditioning's principles. It is called social learning because it concerns itself chiefly with the ways children and other people acquire behavior appropriate to their social context and to the immediate circumstances. In a fashionable New York restaurant, one is expected to tip the waiter 20 percent of the bill; in a Moscow restaurant, one does not tip the waiter—at least openly—because Soviet Russia officially frowns on the practice. At a heavyweight boxing match, the contestants batter one another bloody and receive cheers and rich rewards; the same men fighting on a city street might be hauled off to jail for disorderly conduct.

Social learning, then, involves knowing *what* to do *when* and *where*, and what *not* to do. Social learning comes about, usually, by observation rather than by direct instruction—a major point in Bandura's theory. It matters to teachers, if you are wondering, because teachers serve as important models for observation and imitation.

LEARNING BY OBSERVATION AND IMITATION

How does mediation alter behaviorism's philosophy?

Reinforcement and other behavioral principles are important in social learning. But Bandura finds that simple operant conditioning alone does not explain some of the manifestations of learning by observation and imitation. Frequently, behavior is not demonstrated for a long time after it has been or should have been learned, making it appear that operant conditioning is not at work. The learning is there, though. It is stored in the learner's head. For that reason, Bandura incorporates in his theory the idea of *mediation*, which means that processes occurring in the brain come between the stimulus and the response. For Bandura, external reinforcement is not absolutely necessary for learning, but it helps to *maintain* whatever has been learned by observation and imitation.

So operant conditioning explains social learning if we accept mediation, which requires that the learner remember the behavior and envision the reinforcement. Bandura (1974) adds one more vital assumption: humans are active and self-regulatory, and initiate many behaviors. Although this idea may seem commonsensical, compare it to Skinner's assertion: "A person does not act on the world, the world acts upon him" (1971, p. 211). The importance of Bandura's conception of the active learner is further discussed in Chapter 10, under the topic *self-control.*

Six-year-old Barbara provides an example of learning by observation and imitation. Barbara has just had her first ride in her uncle's new power boat. At the ride's end, she sees her uncle tie the boat to the dock with some deft knots. In the afternoon, Barbara and her uncle go for another ride. The trip over, Barbara leaps from the boat and ties it to the dock with creditable knots. "Very good," says her uncle, making Barbara feel warm inside and eager to tie up the boat in the future. Barbara and her uncle have demonstrated, in a commonplace incident, social learning in action.

VICARIOUS REINFORCEMENT

What moved Barbara to observe and imitate her uncle in the first place? In Bandura's theory, Barbara was motivated by *vicarious* reinforcement. That is, we see someone doing something and we either see or expect to see that someone being reinforced for having done it. So we imitate the action in order to win reinforcement for ourselves.

How does vicarious reinforcement work?

Actually, vicarious reinforcement (and vicarious punishment) usually operates more complexly. Bandura (1971) outlines several features of vicarious reinforcement that make it an effective incentive. When we watch a good movie or read a good novel, much of what we feel is what the screenwriter or author intended us to feel. By giving characters emotion, and by connecting their actions to emotional responses, the author somehow moves those emotions from the printed page or the screen into our heads. In psychological terms, vicarious reinforcement *is arousing* to the observer. This emotional conditioning increases or decreases the likelihood of imitation.

Because vicarious reinforcement is emotionally important to the observer, it *directs attention* to a model's behavior. This helps the observer to understand the social situation in which the behavior is displayed; it shows how the model fits in, and interacts with, his or her environment.

Seeing a model reinforced for a certain behavior *conveys information*. From watching a single model many times, or by watching many models, a learner constructs hypotheses about what behaviors are connected to what outcomes, and the hypotheses guide the learner's attempts to imitate.

The Importance of Imitative Learning. Social learning begins in early childhood. Little girls and boys practice it when they dress up in their parents' clothes or sit at the wheel of the family car. Other mammals do it. A chimpanzee raised among human beings learns to eat with a spoon and sit at the table. Cats learn tricks faster when they see other cats doing them (Herbert and Harsh, 1944, pp. 81–95).

Observational learning, i.e., learning by imitation, does not always result in the copying of a model's action. For example, imagine entering a post office on the French-speaking island of Guadeloupe. The person ahead of you in line asks the clerk, "Do you speak English?" and the clerk replies, "*Non.*" Rather than repeat the query, as you were going to, you shift into your high school French. So observation may inhibit rather than evoke imitation.

Does imitation learning generalize?

Anything and everything that people can learn from experience, Bandura holds, can be learned by observation (1967). Other researchers (including Brown and Herrnstein, 1975) wonder whether Bandura stretches the evidence. They argue that most research into imitation has dealt with fairly specific behavior, such as hitting a Bobo doll, imitating spelling, and saying "please" and "thank you" at the dinner table. Little evidence has been gathered to show that people learn broader *classes* of behavior—such as aggressiveness, fluent speech, or good manners—by observation.

But people somehow do learn general classes of behaviors, and most of the skills involved are not taught directly at home or in school. There is growing evidence too that most of us have *learned to learn* through observation (Gewirtz, 1971; Zimmerman and Rosenthal, 1974). Such generalizable imitation itself represents an extremely broad and complex array of behavior. There are no sturdy alternative theories about how such social learning occurs, and social learning theory has a great deal of uncharted territory, but it offers a revealing view of much human learning.

The setting of an example for observation and imitation can induce desirable new behavior, discourage old, undesirable behavior, and encourage the repetition of old, desirable behavior. (Unfortunately, bad examples may induce bad behavior: youngsters being cruel to their peers, or children learning to steal by watching television.)

Why is learning by imitation efficient?

An important characteristic of learning by observation is efficiency. In Skinner's operant conditioning, in which the reinforcer is delivered after the response, we sometimes have to wait a good while for the response to appear. In the operant technique called shaping, the process usually takes even longer, because several responses—each approximating desired behavior better than its predecessor—must be reinforced. Observational learning, however, occurs internally, with no one standing around waiting to hand out reinforcers. And, as Bandura and his colleagues have shown, overt, obvious practice is not neces-

"There's no way around memorization, huge amounts of memorization. It's hard, and most kids don't like it. Sometimes I find a game to make it easier, but even the game gets boring. Warning them that, say, they can't get in college without memorizing doesn't help—college is too far away. I give them more immediate

sary for imitation. Almost anyone can observe a simple action and imitate it pretty well immediately. With more complicated behaviors, there may be overt practice that serves to sharpen the imitation. In any case, learning by observation is extremely common as well as efficient.

Incentives. When six-year-old Barbara tied her neat mariner's knots, she probably did so, we explained, out of a sense of vicarious reinforcement, which is not something we can see. The influence of *visible* incentives in encouraging and inhibiting imitative behavior is much easier to establish, as the Bandura experiment described in Chapter 4 demonstrated.

Identification. Along with rewards and punishments, a major incentive to behavior is identification. Children and young people tend to imitate the behavior of others whom they admire and want to be like, or, as psychologists say, with whom they *identify*. The objects of admiration may be people with whom they have contact, as Barbara does with her uncle, or characters in the movies and on television, or the heroes or heroines in books, or Superman or Mickey Mouse.

Imitation is enhanced, first, if the observer perceives similarities between her- or himself and the model (Rosekrans, 1967). This helps to explain why boys most frequently imitate other boys and girls other girls. The perceived similarities, though, embrace not only physical characteristics but intelligence, attitudes, and behavior.

Imitation increases, too, if the learner endows the model with high status or prestige (Bandura, Ross, and Ross, 1963b). Prestige itself may serve as an important vicarious reinforcement, promising the learner extra status for emulation of the idol's behavior.

What is the value of behavioral models?

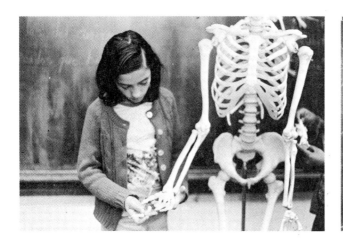

consequences they can relate to, like frequent quizzes. Or I split them up into small groups to compete for who can learn these five definitions the fastest. But they've got to memorize—here's a stimulus, there's the response. Without those stimulus-response links, they haven't got a chance."

Attention. Oral instructions are usually effective in gaining student attention and readying them for imitation. But instructions, like other stimuli, influence different students differently. You say, "Watch this," and Bill snaps to attention, whereas Dick continues to fiddle with his fingernails. One important reason for such variation is the two boys' reinforcement history (Whitehurst, 1978). Bill has been rewarded for "watching this"; Dick has not. You can deal with Dick in either of two ways: you can pair reinforcement with "Watch this," to make that command more effective in the future, or you can seek out a discriminative stimulus that already works for him.

Types of Models. In recent years, the public has become increasingly aware that television does more than entertain; it influences. What and how much influence TV exercises is much debated. But there is no question that it presents symbolic models of behavior, and the plethora of violence it depicts makes many educators and theorists worry that viewers tend to accept aggression as a reasonable means of solving social problems (Ervon, Huesmann, Lefkowitz, and Walder, 1972).

Are symbolic models effective?

Spokesmen for television argue that tube criminals are usually punished, so if learning by observation occurs, vicarious punishment should teach that crime doesn't pay. The argument weakens when one tallies vicarious reinforcements and punishments on an hour-long cops-and-robbers program. Consider a hypothetical criminal depicted as possessing power, influence, and money, and as living in luxury. He (male criminals predominate) is also articulate, cunning, and intelligent. His escapades constitute most of the program and only in the last moment is he caught. The comeuppance? "Book 'im, Duke!"

Repeated viewing of TV violence tends to lessen vicarious punishment by

Mark Twain on Imitative Behavior

In an essay entitled *Corn-Pone Opinions*, Mark Twain derided the human tendency to do as others do. (The title came from an aphorism of an old friend of Twain in Missouri: "You tell me whar a man gits his corn-pone, en I'll tell you what his 'pinions is.")

Twain wrote, in this brief excerpt:

I am persuaded that a coldly-thought-out and independent verdict upon a fashion in clothes, or manners, or literature, or politics, or religion, or any other matter that is projected into the field of our notice and interest, is a most rare thing—if it has indeed ever existed.

A new thing in costume appears—the flaring hoopskirt, for example—and the passers-by are shocked, and the irreverent laugh. Six months later everybody is reconciled; the fashion has established itself; it is admired, now, and no one laughs. Public opinion resented it before, public opinion accepts it now, and is happy in it. Why? Was the resentment reasoned out? Was the acceptance reasoned out? No. The instinct that moves to conformity did the work. It is our nature to conform; it is a force which not many can successfully resist (Geismar, 1973, p. 215). ■

desensitization. If the emotional impact of violence is blunted by frequent exposure, viewers feel less sting of conscience about committing mayhem in their own environment (Cline, Croft, and Courrier, 1973).

Schools generally have little or no control over pupils' television habits at home, but some school systems recruit parents to monitor their children's viewing habits. And parents sign contracts with the schools promising to provide a quiet environment each evening for study; contracts also encourage parents to limit children's TV time.

Among people with whom children have direct contact, those whose influence is most obvious include parents, big brother and big sister, one of the kids down the block, and schoolmates. For seven-year-old Stevie, the most enviable of creatures, apart from his father, is seven-year-old Alan, who can skim a pebble over the park lake farther than anyone else in the neighborhood. For scrawny, fourteen-year-old Guy, a high school freshman, the admired model is Tony, a senior and the school's star quarterback. For thirteen-year-old Anne, it is sixteen-year-old Maria, the best player on their basketball team.

The influence of teachers is sometimes much less *apparent*, and many a teacher despairs after a hard day that the example he or she has tried to set will ever be followed. This happens more often in secondary school than in elementary school: elementary school youngsters emulate their teachers as they emulate their parents, but junior and senior high school adolescents *seem* to imitate their peers much more than they do their teachers. But it is one of the subtler aspects of learning by imitation that the model's behavior may be stored inside the imitators' heads as though it were in cold storage, to incubate and emerge years later. So the secondary school teacher who treats his or her class courteously, shows enthusiasm, and speaks grammatically is not presenting an ignored example. Imitation may be merely deferred.

Take the case of Ms. Roberts, a high school math teacher, and a youth named Mark. Mark always arrived in class unwashed, never had his homework ready, and fluttered around the room throughout the period like a sparrow that had come through an open window and could not find its way out. Six years later, just graduated from college, a clean and courteous Mark appeared in Ms. Roberts's classroom at the end of a school day.

When is imitation deferred?

"I have come to apologize," he said. "I behaved dreadfully when I was in your class. But I want to let you know that I learned a great deal from you, even though I almost flunked math. I did not realize it at the time, but you set a splendid example for me, and I've been trying to follow it ever since my junior year in college."

Of course, a single example such as this does not establish that imitative responses may be stored in an observer's head for years before they are demonstrated. (The science of human behavior tries to avoid single examples in establishing *any* principles.) Many events in Mark's life might have influenced his change of behavior. But the anecdote does have a moral: the eyes of the classroom are upon you!

Summary

Learning consists of changing one's behavior as the result of experience or observation. Because learning takes place inside the mind and cannot be watched at work, the only way to tell whether or not a person has learned something is to see how well he or she does it. Performance, to most learning theorists, is synonymous with practice; the longer the practice, the more enduring the learning. Psychologists define practice as the repetition of a *response* to a *stimulus*. Both response and stimulus are basic elements of the psychological theory called behaviorism. The theory's premise is that all human and animal actions constitute responses to stimuli. A natural, uncontrived event or object will elicit a natural response; at the sight of food, Pavlov's dog's mouth watered. Such events or objects are designated *unconditioned stimuli* and the actions they evoke are called *unconditioned responses*. If a contrived stimulus—the ringing of a bell, in the case of Pavlov's dog—is repeatedly associated with a natural, or unconditioned stimulus, it will bring about the same response as the unconditioned stimulus did. The artificial stimulus is known as a *conditioned stimulus*, and the response it elicits is a *conditioned response*. The responses are involuntary, and the phenomenon of which they are part is called *classical conditioning*.

B. F. Skinner, the leading spokesman and theorist of behaviorism, has gone beyond classical conditioning and propounded what he calls *operant condi-*

"The sequence is mostly like this: I make sure a task is the right size, so they will probably succeed; then I cue or guide them as necessary. When they get it, I lavish praise. I've learned about twenty ways to give praise. Some children are embarrassed if you do it publicly, so it has to be private. Some only respond to certain words; some love any form of attention."

tioning, which deals with voluntary responses or *operants*. Most human behavior consists of operants, which may be of no more significance than a smile, or a stroking of one's beard or hair. Skinner believes that all behavior is controlled by its *consequences*, and that a change of consequences will change behavior. For changing consequences, Skinner employs a *reinforcer*, which is something that will increase or maintain whatever behavior produces it. Skinner prefers not to use a *punisher*, which will decrease or suppress the behavior that produces it. Other theorists, beginning with Thorndike, have suggested that reinforcement and punishment alter behavior because of feelings they produce: gratification or displeasure.

Neobehaviorist scholars accept some but not all of Skinner's ideas. They grant the importance of stimuli and responses, but they contend that organisms do not react automatically to stimuli: they respond as their own needs and characteristics require. The neobehaviorist approach is exemplified by the social learning theory of Albert Bandura, who argues that much learning is acquired by observation rather than instruction. The primary vehicle for observational learning is *vicarious reinforcement.* The relevance of social learning to teaching lies in the fact that teachers are closely observed and imitated by their students.

Chapter Study Guide

CHAPTER REVIEW

1. Learning in any organism, including a human one,
   a. must be inferred from the organism's observable performance.
   b. must be reinforced by an overt external reinforcer to be maintained.
   c. can generally be observed directly by watching the organism as it responds to its environment.
   d. usually can be observed directly (for example, operant conditioning), but must be inferred on a few occasions (for example, language acquisition).
   e. requires some form of instruction and overt rehearsal.

2. Mr. Shoo, pointing out that Freddie only got 55 percent right on his last exam, insists that Freddie did not learn the material. Mr. Shoo may be failing to
   a. remember the theory of "formal discipline."
   b. follow good behaviorist principles of learning.
   c. take into account Freddie's entry characteristics.
   d. distinguish between learning and performance.
   e. distinguish between operant and classical conditioning.

3. In the Pavlovian experiments with classical conditioning,
   a. dogs were trained to salivate after the presentation of meat.
   b. dogs were trained to salivate following the presentation of a formerly neutral stimulus.
   c. behaviors rather than reflexes were conditioned.
   d. salivation increased when the dogs became tense.
   e. meat was paired with salivation in order to condition a response to a black square.

4. A child was playing in the kitchen when the tea kettle on the stove began to whistle. The child reached to the top of the stove to pull the tea kettle closer, and burned his hand. Now the child starts crying whenever he hears the whistle. The whistle sound is a
   a. CS for fear.
   b. US for fear.
   c. CS for reaching to the top of the stove.
   d. US for reaching to the top of the stove.
   e. US to stop playing in the kitchen.

5. In higher-order conditioning
   a. a CS will evoke either of two distinct responses.
   b. two CSs are paired simultaneously with a single US.
   c. a new stimulus comes to evoke responses after being paired with a US.
   d. a new stimulus comes to evoke responses after being paired with an established CS.
   e. none of the above happens.

6. Is it ever possible in classical conditioning for the reinforcement to be withheld?
   a. Yes, because the reinforcement occurs in classical conditioning in the same manner that it occurs in operant conditioning.
   b. It depends on whether the response is voluntary or involuntary.
   c. No, because reinforcement occurs in every trial in classical conditioning, no matter what response is reinforced.
   d. Yes, because if the reinforcement is occasionally withheld, the behavior will be less likely to become extinguished.
   e. Yes, in classical conditioning, but it is not possible in higher-order conditioning.

7. From what we know about the relationship between a person's sex and attitudes, it is likely that
   a. a female who has an aversion to mathematics and numbers will never be comfortable in a job requiring arithmetic calculations.
   b. likes and dislikes are often an outcome of societal expectations based on one's sex.
   c. males will be more able to overcome fears than will most females.
   d. females will continue to show anxiety to analytically oriented subjects.
   e. an increase in militant feminism will have little influence on the affective development of females.

8. For behavior modifiers, the primary task in changing a child's behavior is to
   a. talk to the child.
   b. control the consequences of the behavior.
   c. discuss behavior change with the parents.
   d. research the background of the child.
   e. study the family tree.

9. You have taught Fido to chase his tail whenever he sees you point your thumb upward. Today, however, Fido began tail-chasing when he saw you make an obscene gesture to someone. What process of learning best explains Fido's confusion?
   a. spontaneous recovery
   b. stimulus generalization
   c. higher-order conditioning
   d. classical conditioning
   e. positive reinforcement

10. An educational psychology student regularly slept from the beginning of class straight through to the bell. In one class, however, he abruptly sat up, grabbed his

books, and headed for the door because an alarm clock had been set off beneath his chair. The student _____ when he should have _____ .

a. discriminated; generalized
b. generalized; discriminated
c. learned a conditioned response; shown an unconditioned response
d. developed a motor chain; been classically conditioned
e. was classically conditioned; developed an operant behavior

11. An effective reinforcer will always
    a. increase the frequency or strength of a response.
    b. reduce deviant behavior.
    c. be reinforcing for all children.
    d. arouse us vicariously.
    e. increase voluntary behavior and decrease involuntary behavior.

12. A puppy has been taught to come when Master calls. Master finds a big hole dug in the yard, calls the puppy over to the hole, and smacks the pup hard. What behavior is *most probably* being reduced here?
    a. hole-digging
    b. listening
    c. going to Master when called
    d. finding a hole in the yard
    e. calling the puppy

13. At first, Mary kissed John only after they had begun discussing his problems. Later, Mary kissed John only after a quarrel. Finally, she kissed him only after a terrible, screaming fight. Strange as these behaviors may seem, what process *best* accounts for the increasing severity of John and Mary's fights?
    a. punishment
    b. shaping
    c. avoidance learning
    d. delaying reinforcement
    e. generalization

14. Most of us have learned to close the windows in our house or dorm when we hear the rumble of thunder. The sound of thunder serves as a(n)
    a. reinforcer.
    b. unconditioned stimulus.
    c. conditioned stimulus.
    d. discriminative stimulus.
    e. aversive stimulus.

15. Vicarious reinforcement and learning through imitation are important notions to supplement Skinner's ideas of behaviorism because they help explain
    a. why reinforcers do not always increase behaviors.
    b. how direct reinforcement and punishment act on behaviors.
    c. the need for shaping of complex behaviors.
    d. why structured contingencies are needed for learning.
    e. learning in the absence of direct reward.

16. Certain things can be identified that enhance learning through imitation. In particular,

    a. oral instructions are necessary to ensure modeling.

    b. perceived similarities between the model and learner encourage imitation.

    c. the model and the learner in instructional situations should be the same sex.

    d. active rehearsal of behaviors to be imitated seems crucial.

    e. modeling of attitudes increases vicarious reinforcement.

FOR FURTHER THOUGHT

1. Tell how useful you think either practice or operant conditioning would be in the following learning situations: learning routine tasks; approaching problems that can be reduced to separate, familiar parts; approaching novel problems for which creative thinking may be necessary; learning sensibilities and appreciation; teaching people to fear or avoid certain harmful things; teaching people to hate and fear other people (as some dictators have done).

2. What implications—pro or con—can you find in Milgram's experiment (described in Chapter 4) for the behavioral theory of learning?

3. The German poet Goethe once said, "We learn from what we love." Do these words imply any more than Mowrer's view that babies learn to talk because feeding and fondling make them feel good and they associate the feeling with the pleasant sounds their parents produce? What implications has Mowrer's view of learning for establishing the right classroom atmosphere?

4. Suppose an intelligent, sensitive student resented being "manipulated" to learn by means of external rewards. Would it be possible to explain the student's resentment in terms of conditioned learning? Can conditioning explain the pleasure mature scholars find in pursuing learning?

5. Define a discriminative stimulus that seems to you important to be able to teach. Describe an adequate response to the stimulus. Now describe the reinforcement you would use to teach the S_d. Why did you choose the particular form of reinforcement you did?

6. A philosophical problem for the practitioners of behavior modification is this: If all of us learn our values only through conditioning, who should have the right to determine which values and behavior are desirable and worthy to be perpetuated in others through further conditioning; and on what grounds could the choice of values be made? [Interested students may pursue these questions by reading Skinner's *Walden Two* (1948) and *Beyond Freedom and Dignity* (1971).]

7. How could you use imitation learning to reduce unproductive sexual stereotypes or sex roles found in the classroom? How could students serve as models to help reduce sexual stereotypes? How could professionals in the community help?

8. If we assume that many antisocial behaviors are learned through imitation, would it be best to censor examples of those behaviors from mass media such as newspapers and television? How could models of destructive or criminal behaviors be used to teach appropriate behaviors?

IMPORTANT TERMS

performance
behaviorism
classical conditioning
contiguity
unconditioned stimulus (US)
conditioned stimulus (CS)
unconditioned response (UR)
conditioned response (CR)
extinction
generalization
discrimination
higher-order conditioning
math anxiety
behavior modification
operant conditioning
shaping

successive approximations
reinforcement schedule
reinforcement
discriminative stimulus (S_d)
transsituational reinforcer
situation-specific reinforcer
neobehaviorism
social learning
mediation
vicarious reinforcement
observational learning
imitation learning
identification
desensitization
modeling

SUGGESTED READINGS

Because there are dozens of well-written recent books on behaviorism and behavior modification, any list like this will necessarily omit a number of good ones. Here, then, are some arbitrary recommendations of books that you should find useful. (Several that deal more with practical application are suggested at the end of Chapter 10.)

BIJOU, S., AND RUIZ, R. (eds.). *Contribution of behavior modification to education.* Hillsdale, NJ: L. Erlbaum, 1980. Wide variety of articles describing behavioral applications from preschool to college.

CRAIGHEAD, W. H., KAZDIN, A. E., and MAHONEY, M. J. *Behavior modification: Principles, issues and applications.* Boston: Houghton Mifflin, 1976. A full-fledged textbook on behaviorism's development and meaning, and the ethical issues involved, plus a broad range of applications.

KAZDIN, A. E. *History of behavior modification: Experimental foundations of contemporary research.* Baltimore: University Park Press, 1978. Despite its ponderous title, this is a readable and accurate review of the evolution of behavior theory. Most interesting is an account of the bursting of a unified theory into several splinter groups. Focus is on treatment of deviant behavior.

MALOTT, R. W. et al., *An introduction to behavior modification.* Kalamazoo, Mich.: Behaviordelia, 1975. Far-ranging and highly interesting, it treats topics as diverse as the philosophy of behaviorism and the changing of behavior of a candy addict.

SKINNER, B. F. *About behaviorism.* New York: Alfred A. Knopf, 1974. Skinner, the guru of behaviorism, applies that philosophy to all human endeavors in this readable treatise.

SKINNER, B. F. *Beyond freedom and dignity.* New York: Alfred A. Knopf, 1971. Skinner brings together arguments for avoiding traditional but "incorrect" beliefs about human affairs. Whether or not you agree with his reasoning, this short book should stimulate a lot of thought.

SKINNER, B. F. *The technology of teaching.* New York: Appleton-Century-Crofts,

1968. Essays on operant approaches to teaching and learning by one of the most important psychologists of all time.

WILLIS, J., AND GILES, D. (eds.). *Great experiments in behavior modification.* Indianapolis: Hackett Publishing Company, 1976. Survey of creative, original experiments grounded in behavioral philosophy. The editors selected 116 studies from some 2000 possibilities, then condensed them into two-page abstracts for a quick overview.

ANSWER KEY

1. a; 2. d; 3. b; 4. a; 5. d; 6. c; 7. b; 8. b; 9. b; 10. b; 11. a; 12. c; 13. b; 14. d; 15. e; 16. b

6

The Cognitive Framework of Learning

In chapters 2 and 3 you encountered references to cognition. The term, you may remember, in ordinary language means knowing. But in psychology it encompasses the processes of thinking and learning, that is, how human beings and other organisms acquire, organize, store, and use information. *Cognitive* psychologists hold views of those processes that differ from the theories of the orthodox behaviorists of whom you read in Chapter 5.

Back in 1890, William James published his famous *Principles of Psychology*, in which he asserted that psychological data consist of "(1) *thoughts* and feelings, and (2) *a physical world* in time and space with which they coexist and which (3) *they know*" (p. xiii). A behaviorist, you recall, is unimpressed by thinking and knowing, because they cannot be observed or directly measured. Although behaviorism has dominated psychology for much of this century, it has fallen short in explaining logical thought and language (Murray, 1978). So interest in cognitive psychology has surged in recent years. Since thinking and knowing continue to be unobservable and difficult to measure, cognitive research must make inferences about mental processes by studying external evidence.

What about James's physical world? Cognitive theorists agree that environmental consequences have powerful effects on human behavior. But they add that the brain can think systematically—constructing rules and plans, and storing important information—and can cooperate with the environment in guiding behavior. In short, there is a constant interplay between an active, information-processing being and a changing environment.

If Pavlov's dogs and Skinner's rats and pigeons demonstrate the principles of behaviorism, Wolfgang Köhler's chimpanzees (1925) exemplify some aspects of early *cognitivism*. Köhler, a psychologist at work on an island off Africa, hung a bunch of bananas from the top of a chimpanzee's cage out of the beast's reach. Then Köhler put two old crates in the cage. After puzzling over the situation for a moment or two, the ape stacked one crate atop the other and climbed to the bananas. Another of Köhler's experiments required his chimps, of whom he had several, to reach food placed outside their cages, near which Köhler had left a scattering of sticks. After a brief period of frustration, during which the apes threw some of the sticks at the food, the creatures began to use the sticks to rake in their snacks. One particularly shrewd fellow named Sultan even employed a short stick to bring a longer one within his grasp.

How did the behav-
ior of Köhler's apes
strengthen Gestalt
theory?

The chimps, in Köhler's view, had perceived all the elements of their situation—crate, sticks, and food—as related to each other, and had an *insight*—a sudden recognition—of the solution to the problem. Köhler believed that insight was an important tool of learning and a key to problem-solving, a major purpose of learning. One sized up a situation as a whole and applied insight to deal with it.

Köhler's theories reflected the divisions among psychologists. Köhler was a disciple of Max Wertheimer of the University of Frankfurt. Wertheimer had been trained in the traditional psychology of Wilhelm Wundt, had broken with it, and had founded *Gestalt* psychology (see box). Gestalt is a word used in psychology to mean configuration, or pattern, or the "whole picture." Wertheimer considered Gestalt principles essential to good teaching. Teachers should organize material, he argued, so that students can see a subject as a whole and thus come to understand it rather than learn it piecemeal by rote. Indeed, learning is not a jigsaw puzzle, where the pieces fit together into a finished pattern. Bits of learning add up to more than a predictable pattern. Gestalt psychologists expressed this idea with their credo: The whole is greater than the sum of its parts.

Wertheimer's and Köhler's ideas differed not only from Wundt's but from those of many British psychologists and of the American Thorndike. The British and Thorndike believed that learning resulted primarily from trial and error. (Thorndike based his views on his experiments with cats. He had put hungry cats in cages with food outside. He left it to the cats to discover by trial and error that they could get out of their boxes if they pulled a chain in the box.)

The Cognitive Position

Wertheimer and Köhler were among the forerunners of those who take the present-day cognitive position and study the processes involved in the acquisition, organization, and storage, and use of information. There are many possible approaches to each aspect of cognition and many interpretations of research data.

POINTS OF AGREEMENT

Certain tenets of cognition, however, are widely shared, and are winning ever-increasing acceptance. New findings may require their amendment, but as they stand, these tenets offer a good deal of enlightenment on the complexities of cognition. The apparently fundamental factors are:

1. External stimuli, flowing incessantly to our eyes, ears, and skin, engulf us in information about our environment and often communicate the same thing in several different ways. If you chat with someone face to face, for example, you both *hear* and *see* the other person, and it has been established that hearing and seeing make for more accurate perception of speech than does hearing alone. (That is why, as you may have noticed, a person who hears poorly will look intently at a speaker's face.) On the other hand, a single stimulus may provide several kinds of information about an individual or an object. When someone speaks, for example, the sound waves of speech tell you not only what the speaker is saying but where he or she is and, to lesser degrees, his or her mood, state of health, and education. (If you have a sharp ear for accents, you may even be able to determine where

the speaker lives. We know a traveled New Yorker who told a new acquaintance at a party: "Hmmm. I'd say you come from the border of North and South Carolina, about seven miles inland." She missed by only a mile.) In short, the *message* of a communication—the printed word, the spoken word, and the gesture—is wrapped in the *style* of the communication. This is a complex package, and humans are surprisingly swift in unwrapping it.

2. People are equipped in a variety of ways to pick and choose from the information that external stimuli supply in quantity. Besides the obvious options of looking or not looking and listening or not listening, they may mobilize the processes of attention. By attention to cues, they may detect in a voice nuances of meaning, inflection, and emotion that may reveal more about the speaker than the speaker intends to disclose. With practice, people get better and better at that kind of selectivity.

What are the major tenets of cognitive theory?

3. People are equipped also to deal in a variety of ways with the information they have chosen. When you have heard someone speak, you can build from what he or she has said by associating it with other things you already know. You can commit it to memory, if it seems worthwhile, or you can dismiss it immediately. You can translate the words into mental images.

Gestalt Psychology

At about the same time that behaviorism was sinking its roots into American soil, the seeds were being sown for the Gestalt school of psychology in Germany. Three men—Max Wertheimer, Wolfgang Köhler, and Kurt Koffka—are recognized as the fathers of Gestalt psychology. In 1911, while riding a train during his vacation, Wertheimer glanced out the window and was impressed by the illusion that stationary, flashing lights a certain distance apart gave the appearance of light moving from one point to the other. When he reached his destination, Wertheimer stopped in a toy store and bought a child's stroboscope (a device which presents light at different rates). Wertheimer used this toy in the first of two years of experiments directed at determining why motion can be perceived in stationary objects. He named the illusion the *phi phenomenon.*

Two of Wertheimer's subjects in his experiments were Koffka and Köhler. They were so influenced by Wertheimer's ideas that they, in effect, became his publicity agents. In sum-

4. When people apply particular processes to information repeatedly, they develop lasting systems for dealing with it. These systems are referred to usually as cognitive structures, or, in the term preferred by Piaget (Chapter 2), as schemas.

5. Cognitive structures develop and change. Piaget, you recall, labeled this *accommodation*. People constantly reorganize their ways of looking at themselves, at others, and at the world by relating and fitting new information to their own complex needs, desires, personalities, and cultures.

What the Five Points Suggest. Human beings, in the view of cognitive psychology, seek information, interpret it, file it in memory, and act on the basis of it and of other data already sorted in their heads. If human behavior is not controlled by stimuli but by how people interpret and react to stimuli, then psychologists cannot precisely predict behavior and "there is no way to be sure of the outcome when you intervene in anyone's life"(Neisser, 1975, p. 162). The real aim of psychology, then, Neisser argues, is the understanding of human nature rather than its control.

Despite its focus on unobservable mental processes, cognitive psychology

---

marizing his experiments, Koffka and Köhler claimed that a perceived whole is greater than just the parts added together, that the mind actively uses stimuli to form meaningful patterns. Gestalt psychology had been launched. By 1920, Koffka and Köhler had referred to Wertheimer's work so frequently in their own writing that Gestalt theory was well known in Germany. Köhler experimented with animals to extend the principles of the theory, while Koffka became the vocal evangelist spreading

The mind actively combines stimuli so that you can perceive a "whole" even when the picture is incomplete.

the news of Gestalt theory. It was time to conquer American psychology.

In an early visit to the United States in 1924, Koffka vigorously attacked American theories of behaviorism and trial-and-error learning. Back home, Köhler's ape studies suggested the notion of insight, which supported the attack on behaviorism. Eventually, with World War II on the horizon, all three psychologists sought intellectual asylum in the United States and remained until their deaths. Their early Gestalt ideas developed into cognitive principles of learning. However, behaviorism's hold on American psychology has been so ·strong that only recently has cognitivism—with the legacy of Wertheimer, Koffka, and Köhler—gained widespread acceptability. ∎

Sources

Boring, E. G. *A history of experimental psychology* (2nd ed.). New York: Appleton-Century-Crofts, 1950.

Hilgard, E. R. and Bower, G. H. *Theories of learning* (3rd ed.). New York: Appleton-Century-Crofts, 1966.

"I always begin a lesson with an explanation of what we're going to be doing and why. I usually also include a kind of pretest: 'Do you know this? . . . or that? What do you think happens when . . .?' And I include some questions to find out what they're interested in—curious about—so that I can use that as I'm going through the lesson. Then I go through all the parts—straight through without stopping—everything I'm doing in this lesson. I don't expect them to remember much now, but the point is that they've heard it and seen it. Next time they hear it, it'll ring a bell."

has made rapid progress in recent years. Much of this growth has emerged from basic laboratory research. The contrived conditions of a laboratory may seem quite a distance from the classroom, but fairly specific tips for teachers have begun to emerge. And many of these tips have been supported by field research in schools. The contributions of cognitive psychology are thus increasingly important, and, coupled with behavioral principles, should improve teacher effectiveness. Even where cognitive mysteries have not been solved, an examination of the general area should heighten your respect for the complexity of human beings and whet your appetite to understand more about them. One of the most remarkable manifestations of human complexity is memory, and cognitive psychologists have given much thought to its operation.

Memory

What are memory's limits?

Without memory, we could not learn. We could not even qualify as intelligent animals, much less civilized human beings. Each time we reached into a tree to pluck a banana, we would have to discover anew that we had to peel the fruit before we could munch it. Each time we roved a shore in search of dinner, we would have to discover anew that oysters are edible and stones are not. So, in effect, we are largely what we remember.

Memory's capacity is awesome. Ordinary folk, in a lifetime, store billions of items of information in their memories, including some 50,000 words and a greater number of images—of scenes, of objects, of faces. Extraordinary folk may perform even more impressive feats of memory, at least in special ways. Napoleon needed only to glance at a map to remember every village, road, watercourse, and hill his troops would encounter in battle. Leonardo da Vinci needed to see someone only once to draw a perfect, telling likeness. The conductor Arturo Toscanini could set down accurately the score of a symphony that he had not heard in forty years. The philosophy professor Irwin Edman could recount with precision the content of almost every book he had ever read. A one-time Russian newpaper reporter known to psychologists only as S. indicated that the *potential* of memory might be virtually boundless. Given a list of seventy unrelated objects, S. could repeat it flawlessly, top to bottom or bottom to top, years later. S. quit journalism for the stage, where in three shows a night he invited audiences to pepper him with nonsense syllables. After an audience ran out of nonsense, S. would write every syllable on a blackboard. The blackboard was soon scrubbed, but S.'s memory was not. Many performances later, he still could come up with the three lists of syllables of any earlier night. S. ascribed much of his curious ability to the phenomenon that he "tasted" and "saw" oral sounds and musical tones. Every voice, for him, had its distinctive color. A musical tone of a certain pitch and loudness felt, he said, like borsch on his tongue and appeared like a brown strip edged with red tongues in his mind. If the pitch and the volume changed, the taste and the image changed too. "Tasting" and "seeing" made it easier for him to remember everything he heard, S. explained (Luria, 1968).

THREE SYSTEMS OF MEMORY STORAGE

S. was almost certainly unique, but everyone of normal mental health is equipped, psychologists believe, with three distinctive memory storage systems—sensory, short-term, and long-term. Although it is convenient to think of these systems as separate, it is more probable that they are related levels of a single memory system (Atkinson et al., 1974). (See Figure 6.1.) As an example of their possible interrelationship, Shiffrin (1975) proposes that attention to an interesting stimulus not only helps orient the sensory storage but also alerts long-term storage for the receipt of new material.

Sensory Storage. Information in the form of environmental stimuli bombards us in great quantity and enters the sensory storage system. Evidence suggests that sensory storage holds accurate images of incoming stimuli while the brain searches for recognizable patterns or features. When familiarity is established—this all takes less than a second—information is passed to short-term storage. The irrelevant stuff decays immediately, and the sensory storage busily attends to new stimuli.

Short-Term Storage.   The function of short-term storage, psychologists hypothesize, is to hold information just long enough to sort it out and determine whether or not it merits keeping. If you remembered *everything* that happened to you, day after day, including every inane conversation along with the significant ones, your head would soon be unbearably cluttered with trivia. In short-term storage, which is known also as primary memory and short-term memory, we dismiss the trivia and pass on the worthwhile data to long-term storage. Separating the trivial from the significant is an important function of

How does information travel through memory?

Figure 6.1. The Three Systems of Memory Storage

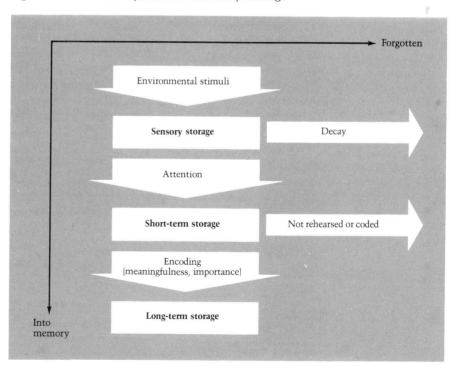

short-term storage. It does this by *encoding*, or interpreting, the images of stimuli sent from the sensory register. If you were asked what you have just now read, you could not reproduce each word; that image has already decayed. But you could give the general meaning of the words, thanks to the encoding processes of short-term memory.

There is a great body of psychological evidence that the capacity of the short-term storage part of our memory systems is limited in space as well as in time-span. In a classic article entitled "The Magical Number Seven, Plus or Minus Two," G. A. Miller (1956) argued that we have room in short-term storage for from five to nine bits of information at a time or, on average, seven. Many demonstrations have borne out Miller's contention.

If, for example, you give someone—other than the remarkable Russian S.—a list of twenty words or numbers and ask him or her to recall as many as possible, your test subject will probably come up with about seven. They will not necessarily be the first seven or the last seven; they may have been anywhere in the list. If you group the words in phrases or sentences, the subject will remember more words, but the number of bits—phrases or sentences—probably will still not exceed seven. That is why telephone companies restrict phone numbers to seven digits. The apparent limitations of space in short-term storage also require that, when you are introduced to someone, you process the name into long-term storage right off; short-term storage won't have the room to keep it for you, because incoming information will boot it out of the way.

Long-term Storage. On the other hand, the capacity of long-term memory, as we remarked earlier, is awesome. Yet most of us tend to think of it as rather limited and believe that if we do not use fairly often what we have learned we forget it and lose it forever. Psychologists studying memory currently believe, though—with some qualifications—that anything stored in long-term memory remains there forever.

Sturdy evidence for the durability of long-term memory comes from hypnosis, under which people recall events that elude them during normal conditions. Evidence comes also from electrical stimulation of the brain. In the 1940s, the Canadian neurosurgeon Wilder Penfield tried to locate in the brain the sites of epileptic seizures. Prodding with an electrode in a memory area, he found that patients, still awake, remembered long-faded occurrences. Moving the electrode released memories of different occasions. Despite this discovery, the physical structure of long-term memory remains a mystery, although speculation increases that chemical substances are responsible. The psychological structure—what activates long term memory, how images are coded and stored, and how information is retrieved—is unknown.

One of the simplest ideas about the operation of long-term memory was developed by Aristotle, who compared it to a library. Cognitive researcher David Rumelhart (1977) reviews the analogy:

> For a data storage system like a library, storage itself poses no problem; a new book *can* be added to a library just by putting it on the shelf. If this were always

done, however, the library would be useless. No one would ever know whether or not the library had a particular book. Even if one were certain that the book was there, the probability of ever finding it among the many thousands of volumes on the shelves would be very small. Therefore, libraries spend considerable effort preparing books to be put on the shelf. Each book is carefully cross listed in the card catalog. It is listed according to author, title, and any subject to which it seems pertinent. Moreover, to insure that a book can be located even when neither its exact title nor author are known, books on similar topics are located near one another on the shelves. If information is desired on a certain topic, sometimes only one book on that topic need be found in the card catalog. Once the appropriate area of the library is located, a leisurely search through the books in that vicinity will often lead to most of the books in the library on that topic (p. 203).

How are memories retrieved?

Rumelhart's analogy implies two important dimensions of the memory system: (1) organizing information in storage; (2) retrieving information from storage. There are thought to be two general retrieval routes, *association* and *recognition*. To illustrate: You are trying to find a book on cognition that you have used before but whose author you have forgotten. You may go to the card catalog, looking for sensible connections. Aha! Here are twenty cards on cognition. You breeze through them until you find the one you want. Or you could go to the stacks of books related to learning, and—Aha again!—you suddenly see a book with a bright orange cover. Without even reading the title, you recognize it as the object of your search. Here are those two routes again: In one, you seek among the connecting links (association), and in the other, you recognize a particular pattern (recognition) which leads to the same goal (Simon, 1979).

Is memory retrieval an active or a passive process?

These two options may be a little fuzzy (and actually both may operate simultaneously inside long-term memory), so let's consider another example. You are asked, "Who was the guy who composed several symphonies as he grew deaf?" There are several associations here to help search your mental list of composers, and presently you reply, "Beethoven." But without the question and its clues, you can bring forth the same little mental schema by listening to one of Beethoven's symphonies or by seeing his picture.

Memory works much more automatically and rapidly than these examples imply; and as particular portions of memory are used and rehearsed, the retrieval process requires even less time and less conscious effort.

THE ROLE OF THE SCHEMA

Although memory involves the storage of information, remembering is more than a matter of retrieval, in the cognitive view. An essential component of memory is the schema, or cognitive structure, which we mentioned briefly earlier in this chapter.

The term *schema* for a cognitive structure sounds Piagetian (see Chapter 2), and it should come as no surprise that Piaget had some thoughts about the role of schemas in the functioning of memory. He proposed (1968) that there are

How Long Do People Remember?

In a study of long-term memory, Harry P. and Phyllis O. Bahrick and Roy P. Wittlinger (1974) gave six tests to 392 high school graduates ranging in age from seventeen to seventy-four. The tests related to other members of their high school graduating classes, which had varied in size from 90 to 1100 students. The tests and the results:

Test 1: The subjects were asked to write, within eight minutes, the names of as many classmates as they could remember.

Result: Recent graduates recalled about forty-seven names each, whether their classes had been large or small. People who had been out of school forty or more years averaged nineteen names. Recall diminished steadily with age, but the amount of decline each year also diminished.

Test 2: The subjects were shown ten cards with five pictures on each. One picture on each card was a classmate, the other pictures came from yearbooks of other graduating classes. The subjects were allowed eight seconds to look at each card and point out the classmate.

Result: Only those who had been out of high school more than forty years failed to identify at least 90 percent of the pictures. The score for those elders averaged 75 percent.

Test 3: The subjects were shown ten cards similar to those in Test 2, but names were substituted for pictures, and the subjects were asked to pick out the classmate's name on each card.

Result: People who had been graduated within fifteen years of the test identified 90 percent of the names; people in their late thirties or beyond got 70 to 80 percent right.

Test 4: Each of ten cards had a name typed at the top and the subjects were asked to match the name with one of five pictures below. All pictures were of classmates.

Results: People graduated within fifteen years of the test matched 90 percent; those out of school twenty to twenty-nine years did less well and the oldest subjects averaged 60 percent.

Test 5: Each of ten cards had a picture at the top, to be matched to one of five names below.

Result: People graduated as long as thirty-five years before the test matched 90 percent of pictures and names.

Test 6: The subjects were shown ten pictures from their yearbook and asked to give the full names of the classmates the pictures represented.

Results: Younger graduates got almost 70 percent right but performance declined with age and the oldest graduates were able to put names to less than two out of ten faces.

The study confirmed that people recognize what they have learned better than they can recall it and that they retain visual information longer than verbal information. The researchers found also that women outperformed men, except for men who had been out of school for forty or more years; the older men bested the women on all but the first test, which involved free recall. The researchers suggested that women may learn more than men initially, but the men may retain longer what they have learned. ■

two sorts of schemas to hold ideas. One type stores images or events and, predictably, is subject to forgetting. The other type is used to store *operations*, the mental manipulations of logical thought. This second type, called operative memory, is thought to improve over time. Little evidence supports that idea. In tests of the two sorts of memory, both deteriorate sooner or later (Maurer et al., 1979).

Another line of research provides an alternate view of the schema's role in memory. Everyone knows that we sometimes compose memories based on events that occurred at different times. For example, you may recall having met Winfred in the summer of 1976 at a party. In fact you met Winfred in 1975, in between classes. It was Chris you met in 1976. If you become aware of your confusion, you could say that your schemas got mixed up, and that you *reconstructed* the event by unintentionally distorting some of the information.

Why are memories imperfect?

Back in 1932, Frederick Bartlett reported on a series of experiments that seemed to show how memories became reconstructed. He had hundreds of students read, several times, a bizarre passage called "The War of the Ghosts." After reading, the students were asked to retell the story as accurately as they could. Bartlett found that as time increased between reading and recall, students invented, distorted, and omitted more and more. To Bartlett, the results indicated that what we remember is determined not only by what we see and hear but by the shape of our already formed schemas. To put it another way, our memories are controlled by our points of view, that is, what we know, feel, and believe.

Replications of Bartlett's experiments have not always produced the same outcomes, and some evidence shows little of the reconstruction that Bartlett found. There is indeed distortion of past events, but Bartlett assumed the distortion occurred at the time of recall. A competing hypothesis is that events are reshaped as they enter memory rather than when they emerge. The issue is not resolved, and it is possible that reconstruction occurs both at the entry and exit of stored information.

"I try to cover only as much as they can absorb at one time. It's just something I sense in them; of course, after a few weeks I do get to know them pretty well. So then we break up into groups, and I have them take some time going over the same things themselves. The lab exercises make them really focus in. It brings out

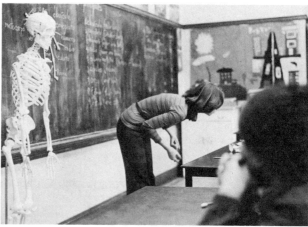

In a much more recent experiment than Bartlett's, Loftus and Palmer (1974) showed their subjects a film of an automobile accident, then gave them questionnaires about it. But the questionnaires differed slightly. Half the subjects were asked, "About how fast were the cars going when they *smashed into* each other?" The other half were asked, "About how fast were the cars going when they *hit* each other?" (The italics are ours.) A week later, the subjects were asked, "Did you see any broken glass?" Of the subjects whose first question had used the word *smashed*, 32 percent said they had seen shattered glass; of those whose question had read *hit*, only 14 percent reported having seen broken glass. No glass had been broken in the mishap. And the subjects who had been given the "smashed" question estimated the cars' speed at about 30 percent greater than did those who had had the "hit" question.

The Loftus and Palmer study indicates how we pull together information from several sources to construct a "memory" or schema of an event and may employ, in retrieving from memory, information beyond our actual experience. The study also demonstrates that memory as a process is highly active: we reorganize our schemas as we gain more information, even if the information is incompatible with our experience.

LEARNING AND THE SCHEMA

Building on the idea of schemas, David P. Ausubel (1963) has constructed a theory of *meaningful verbal learning*. That theory holds that—other than by rote—we learn and remember what we have learned only to the extent that the information is subsumed by existing cognitive structures, or schemas. By *sub-*

a lot of questions that they have to answer. It also brings out their curiosity. As they start working and talking they start remembering, or wanting to remember by themselves. On their own. I can tell how they're doing just by walking around and listening."

sumed, Ausubel means that a piece of information is included in, or attached to, an existing schema and then categorized (see Figure 6.2). New information that cannot be attached to cognitive structures must be learned by rote; that is, it must be practiced over and over, until it has its own little schema. So meaningfulness depends on how easily information is subsumed.

Early in a child's life, many events and objects are stored in memory with little connection to other schemas. And sometimes faulty connections are made; it is easy to do when words have multiple meanings. Consider the five-year-old who was asked to repeat the digits 2-5-4 backward. He turned his back to the questioner and said confidently, "Two, five, four."

As children experience more of their environment, they can correct and modify much of the faulty mental wiring and add new circuits. This vast circuitry, built by the environment, has broad implications for childrearing and schooling. An impoverished environment almost necessarily will result in fewer schemas, and weak connections among those schemas present. If thinking, problem-solving, and communication are diminished as a result, then the environment has contributed to a reduction in intelligent behavior.

Why are entry characteristics important for schema development?

Ever since formal schooling began, probably, students have complained that much of their lessons consists of dry, dull facts that must be committed to memory for no good reason. Considering their relatively immature cognitive structure, their complaint makes some sense. Much of what they are being taught *is* meaningless to them. It follows that teachers should try to show, within reason, associations among facts, events, principles, and theories presented in the classroom. This is hard work, for it suggests that we must take into consideration what is already meaningful to the learner and exploit it by connecting new material to it. This idea is supported by Benjamin Bloom's

Figure 6.2. Cross-indexing and Subsumption of Schemas. The schema *leather object* is connected to many other schemas, and the number and strength of these connections depend on experience and practice. Information without connections to existing schemas must be learned through rote memorization.

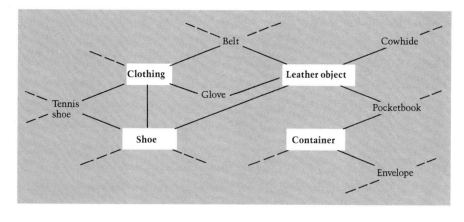

suggestions about *student entry characteristics* (Chapter 1). If we ignore them, we may as well put our lectures on videotape and head for the teachers' lounge.

For meaningful learning to occur, the learner's cognitive structure must include the requisite mental ability, store of ideas, and background of experience. The potential meaningfulness of information therefore varies with the age, intelligence, occupation, and culture of the learner. For example, if you were trying to teach a two-year-old not to poke a safety pin into an electrical outlet, it would do no good to mention electricity and the danger of shock.

REMEMBERING AS RETRIEVING

Now let's return to the two dimensions of memory that we mentioned earlier, the storage and retrieval of information. Although information once placed in long-term storage remains there forever—in the current view of psychologists—digging it out on demand is another matter. Everyone has experienced the frustration of being unable to recall a name, a word, a fact that is "on the tip of my tongue." Nearly everyone has drawn a blank on a question in an exam and remembered the correct answer only on the way back to the dorm.

Why? Many psychologists think that we fail to use our filing systems effectively. Let's consider those explanations.

Forgetting. Among laymen, the commonest view is that we remember what we use frequently and forget what we do not use. Psychologists call this explanation of forgetting the *disuse theory.* Yet all of us occasionally recall incidents that we have not thought about since they occurred, perhaps many years before. In experiments, adults under hypnosis have come up with the names of their second-grade teachers and of their classmates, facts that eluded them in their waking state. A writer whom we know once had had to acquire fluency in Portuguese. But since then he had not spoken or read the language for decades, and as his plane approached Portugal on a vacation trip he complained to his wife, "I can't remember a word of Portuguese." When they boarded a taxicab at the Lisbon airport, though, he engaged in rapid-fire conversation with the driver—in Portuguese. So the disuse theory of forgetting is, at best, vulnerable.

Why does forget-
ting occur?

Another theory of forgetting, borrowed from psychoanalysts, holds that we intentionally forget what we do not want to remember. This is referred to as *intentional* or *motivated forgetting.* It is probably true that we try not to think about unpleasant or emotionally painful experiences. But much that we forget is neither unpleasant nor emotionally painful, so the repression theory hardly accounts for all forgetting.

A more acceptable explanation of forgetting is that of *interference*, that is, that new information erects a roadblock to the recall of old information, and vice versa. Imagine a lawyer with an acute memory who has just completed writing a contract for a client and can recount its complex details without even glancing at the document. He then turns to another contract for another client. He is interrupted by a telephone call from the first client, who wants to know the precise provisions of a specific clause in the first contract. The lawyer has to look it up—concentration on the second contract constituted interference.

When new learning blots out old learning, the phenomenon is described as *retroactive inhibition*. When old learning impedes new learning, the term used is *proactive inhibition* (see Figure 6.3). As with the theory of reconstruction, there is debate about *where* inhibition occurs: Is it during the storing of information into memory, or during the retrieval from memory? Here, too, it seems likely that the answer is "In both" (Peterson, 1977).

Retroactive Inhibition. In a typical experiment illlustrating retroactive inhibition, a group of subjects is asked to memorize a string of words or nonsense syllables designated List *A*. Then half the subjects are asked to memorize a second set of words and syllables called List *B* while the other half rests or sleeps. Hours later, all the subjects are requested to write down as much of List *A* as they can remember. Those who rested or slept invariably do far better than those who had had to learn both lists. List *B* had run interference against List *A*.

How does interference operate?

Proactive Inhibition. In a similar experiment illustrating proactive inhibition, half the subjects are requested to memorize list *A* and the other half is permitted to loaf or sleep. Then all the subjects are given List *B* to learn. When all are asked, later, to repeat List *B*, the half who first learned List *A* do far worse than those who learned only List *B*. In this case, the earlier learning—List *A*—impeded recall of List *B*.

Imagine that you are working on a list of French words, and you come to *place*. If you are like the rest of us, you should have a tough time remembering its English equivalent, town square. Why? Because the word looks exactly like the English word *place*, meaning location, your earlier learning may continue to surface.

Figure 6.3. The Two Types of Inhibition

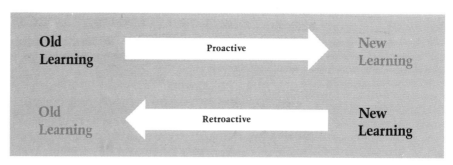

Another example of proactive inhibition, common to all of us, manifests itself with every new year. On January 3, when you write a check or a letter, you are likely to discover that you have dated it for the previous year.

The Scope of Interference. There is more to interference than a clash between new and old learning. Sleep is one factor that affects it: if you sleep after having learned something new, you are likely to remember it better than if you do not sleep. Apparently during sleep potential interference from previous learning is reduced. Normal activities are another factor: incidents that occur between learning and having to remember produce interference. A similarity between two subjects being studied more or less simultaneously also heightens interference: a student who has just completed homework in French will find the French interferes with the assignment in Spanish. If you have talked with a number of people during the day, you may not be able to recall just who told you that good story. If you are a baseball fan, you may have trouble remembering who won the World Series in . . . uh. . . .

The forgetting that we do as a result of interference—and it happens to us all—seems to constitute a two-fold problem. It can result from poor initial storage (perhaps because material was not meaningfully connected to existing structures), or from a malfunction of our retrieval systems. If retrieval is at fault, the information is on file, but at least for the moment we cannot get to it (Peterson, 1977).

Remember S., the Russian journalist (page 185)? Even he ran into trouble with interference. At one point in his career, he could not control the trivia that cluttered his head. During his stage show, material memorized at an earlier performance would suddenly emerge and mix with new material (Luria, 1968). S.'s dramatic situation would baffle any teacher attempting to reduce his interference but, for the rest of us, several means exist for lessening interference and improving retrieval.

REMEMBERING BETTER

In everyone, even that phenomenal Russian, some forgetting is inevitable. But certain factors or conditions facilitate the remembering of verbal information in learning. Among them are:

1. *The degree of original learning.* The better something is learned, the easier it becomes to remember. In any course of study, students reach a point—one hopes—where they can recall the subject matter and thus demonstrate learning, to a degree. The pupil who continues to study beyond that point and who constantly retrieves the material and practices recalling it achieves *overlearning.* With overlearning, the student (a) makes forgetting less likely; (b) greatly increases the possibility of using the information in new situations; and (c) fortifies resistance to interference by material already learned or still to be learned. Teachers for the most part cannot control the amount of study in which students engage. But expanded explanation in

"I first of all make sure I have their attention. After that, I wish I could just pour information into their heads. But every word I say is colored by their personal backgrounds. If we start talking about how a new science fiction movie has distorted certain laws of physics, three kids are lost because they don't know what

the classroom, augmented with additional explanations and followed by review, enhances learning in the way that independent review and practice at recall do. A demonstration was provided by Wilson (1948). She expanded a 300-word passage, by adding explanations and examples, to 600 words and then to 1200 words. Her students' achievements improved with the size of the passage. Explanations, examples, and demonstrations have special value when an instructor presents information by lecture.

2. *The similarity of learning and recall conditions.* Recall is greater when it occurs under conditions similar to those that existed at the time of learning. For the teacher, this means that the learning situation should include experiences that will resemble as closely as possible those of the testing situation. A high school physics student, for example, who has merely heard an experiment described will perform it on a test less well than a student who has seen it demonstrated or who previously has undertaken it.

3. *Reduction of interference.* Interference may be lessened in a number of ways. In the experiments that require remembering List *A* after learning List *B*, for example, it has been established that, up to a point, the longer the time that elapses between the two tasks, the better the performance. Psychologists theorize that the memory uses the interim to consolidate the recollection of List *A*, fortifying it against interference by List *B*. Sleep may work in the same way; an alternative explanation is that when we sleep we engage in no activities that produce interference. An elapse of time is particularly useful when two subjects being learned are similar. The pupil

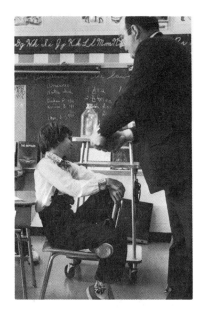

science fiction is. Another three haven't seen the movie. Even if every single student hears and understands exactly *the same idea, they'll reorganize it in their memories so it comes out different. I remember one kid who was positive that David Copperfield was the author of* Charles Dickens!"

studying both French and Spanish will have less trouble with homework if he or she tackles math or physics or chemistry between the two language assignments.

Much interference results from confusion of the attributes of similar material. It is important, then, for teachers to eliminate the confusion by (a) pointing out the attributes that two concepts share; (b) emphasizing the attributes that are dissimilar; (c) indicating the attributes present in one concept and not in the other.

What learning conditions enhance retention?

4. *Meaningfulness.* We have mentioned meaningfulness in considering Ausubel's theory; it is also the paramount influence on recall. As used by psychologists, meaningfulness often means association rather than meaning. Demonstrating meaningfulness, psychologists present a list of words to a group of subjects and ask the subjects to write down as many other words as possible that each word on the list brings to mind. The original words that elicit the largest numbers of associated words are those that, it turns out, are also the best remembered. The reason is simple enough. The number of associated words correlates with the experience the subject has had with the listed word; that is, the greater the experience with a word, the greater the number of associations it will produce. In short, the more one knows about a word, the easier it is to remember.

From a teacher's point of view, that phenomenon is not particularly relevant. What is relevant is the concept of meaningfulness as it relates to the meaning of the word, sentence, or passage. Every word has a *denotative* and a *connotative* meaning. The denotative is the dictionary's definition of the word. The connotative is the meaning we may give to a word as a result of our attitudes and emotions. "He [or she] is a pig" is a sentence with both denotative and connotative meanings. So it can be—and is—argued that the meaning of a word, a phrase, a sentence is the meaning the hearer brings to it. That is, one's knowledge determines how much a word, a phrase, a sentence means to one.

5. *Organization.* Students do not necessarily organize information—as you may know from your own experience in studying—in the manner that it is presented. But the better organized the presentation, the more likely students are to duplicate the presentation's structure. The benefits should be obvious: students need spend less time on organizing the material themselves, and enjoy more time for the memory-processing that will facilitate recall.

A well-organized presentation, fundamentally, (a) tells students where the instruction will take them; (b) reminds them, by topic headings, where they are at any point; (c) goes over the ground again, by intermittent and final reviews, to show them where they have been.

6. *Rehearsal.* Familiar or meaningful information is transferred easily into long-term memory, and little practice is needed to speed its passage. Brand new material requires more rehearsal, so teachers should provide opportunity for practicing with it (Kumar, 1971).

7. *Rate of presentation.* The purpose of rehearsal, thus, is to help move information into long-term storage. Rehearsal occurs when the material is still in short-term memory. But, you remember, short-term storage has room for only about seven chunks of information. When a teacher presents new material at a furious pace, students cannot rehearse, and not much of the material will go to rest in long-term memory.

AGING AND FORGETTING

Do memories age well?

Some of you who do not plan to work with school-age youngsters may reasonably ask whether these instructional ideas apply to adults. During adulthood, don't we begin a downward slide that makes learning and memory functions less powerful? Most of us have the idea that certain phenomena automatically accompany aging—loss of muscle tone, dulling of hearing, lessening of sexual capacity, and weakening of memory, to name a few. Even medical practitioners help to spread the belief that in general, human abilities begin to decline after the age of eighteen. But recent findings dispute, and in some cases dispel, such notions. (Chapter 3 addresses the issue of decline in mental abilities during adulthood.)

Some researchers wonder whether mature adults show *maximum* performance on given tasks, or only *typical* performance. If a forty-year-old does poorly on a memory task, for example, is it because he *cannot* do better, or because he

Meaningfulness through Organization

Students endlessly demand relevance in school learning. But making materials relevant is difficult for a teacher, because meaningfulness is subjective and tied to personal experiences and interests. One important tool for enhancing meaningfulness is the use of *structure*. Do you remember Jerome Bruner's remarks about the structure of knowledge (p. 53)? He asserted that bodies of knowledge have certain structures that must be exploited by a teacher. Relationships among facts, ideas, concepts, and principles should be explored and arranged so that students can see the "big picture" as well as the parts.

The importance of structure is widely accepted by cognitive theorists and receives much support in the research literature. Here is one example of the use of structure to help learners organize a batch of terms relating to minerals:

Gordon Bower (1970) provided four cards with structured arrangements like this one to a group of students. To another group he gave four cards with the same number of words (121 in all), but the words were placed randomly within each box and were, therefore, unrelated. The students who saw the organized diagram with related words remembered three times as many words as the second group.

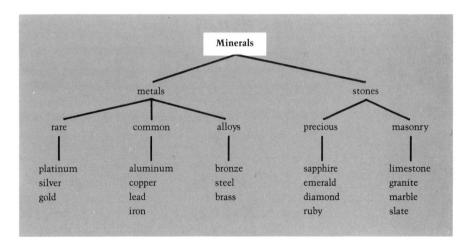

While students are learning, they often form their own structures—categorizing, sequencing, and making associations between bits of material. Bower's experiment shows that learning may be improved when the teacher provides clear structure by showing how material can be organized. ∎

did not do better? New research has shown that adults, even the elderly, can greatly improve memory performance when they are coached to be less cautious in responding, when tasks are particularly interesting, and when they practice regularly (Carroll and Maxwell, 1979). These studies cast new light on aging and memory. There is little doubt that memory falters with increasing age, but age is not alone responsible; other factors, modifiable by the environment, also contribute to forgetting.

MEASURING MEMORY

Teachers and psychologists often want to measure what someone remembers. There are three ways to measure learning and remembering.

The Savings Method. In this system, used chiefly by experimental psychologists, the testing is based on the fact that people *relearn* faster than they *learn*. If you learned to knit as a child, have never knitted since, and believe that you have completely forgotten how to do it, you might be surprised to discover how soon you "pick it up" again with a little instruction. Some learning, apparently, is always "saved"—hence the name of the testing method. Harold Burtt (1941), a university psychologist, demonstrated the phenomenon in an experiment with his son. Beginning when the child was fifteen months old and continuing until he was three, Burtt read the same three passages of Greek poetry daily to him. The little boy did not understand a word. When the boy was eight years old, Burtt gave him the same three passages to memorize, and three new passages. The boy performed much better on the passages he had heard earlier than on the new ones.

Measuring memory by the savings method, psychologists set a task for a subject—memorizing a list of words, say—and note the number of trials the subject requires to attain perfection. After a period of time, they assign the same task again to the same subject and count the necessary trials again. The second count is subtracted from the first to produce the *savings* score. The method is useful scientifically to determine the degree to which learning is retained, but because it is restricted pretty much to materials that can be readily memorized, it is rarely if ever employed in the classroom.

The Recall Method. Recall is what you do when you dial a friend's telephone number without looking it up, or remember your kid sister's birthday, or recount in an essay examination the essential points of a chapter in a textbook. Recall comes in two varieties, free and aided. Free recall pops up with the information without need for a cue: you don't have to look at your dorm building to remember your room number. Aided recall demands some external stimulus: you may not be able to remember in what movie you last saw Robert Redford until you go to the movies and see him again.

The recall method of measuring learning and memory is employed by both psychologists and teachers. It simply requires students to demonstrate that they have learned what they have been taught by performing an assigned task or by coming up with correct responses to questions. (The questions often contain cues that aid recall, although not always by design.)

How can memory be measured?

In psychologists' experiments, a student may be given a list of words and asked to recall as many as possible; or the student may be allowed to read a prose passage one or more times and then asked to recall its content or to repeat it verbatim. Or the student may be shown a geometric figure or a design and, some time later, be asked to reproduce it graphically.

In the classroom, the recall method requires the filling in of a blank in a sentence, or the completion of an unfinished sentence, or the giving of a short answer to a question, or the writing of a long essay. In teaching, the most effective application of the recall method is the essay examination. Although essay examinations usually go beyond mere recall and may require that students synthesize the subject matter, the process of synthesis itself necessitates recall. That is, you cannot explain what something is about unless you remember the something's essential components.

The method has a flaw as a yardstick of learning. Recall places a heavy demand on memory, storage, and retrieval, and sometimes, as you know, our retrieval system does not retrieve stored information. You may not be able to recall, when asked, all the chemical formulas you learned in high school, for example, but you almost certainly would recognize them if you saw them. So you *have* learned them, though you might not be able to prove it on a recall test.

The Recognition Method. By testing for recognition, teachers and psychologists attempt to get around the recall method's pitfall. Experimenters using recognition generally work like this: the individual being tested is assigned something to learn and later is shown new material along with the old material that was to be learned. The individual then is asked to distinguish between them. In teaching, multiple-choice questions constitute the most common type of test. In a variation, the individual may be shown a number of items, one at a time, and asked to say "old" or "new" or "yes" to old material and "no" to new material. The basis of the recognition method, of course, is the assumption that when a person has learned or seen something, he or she will recognize it later and be able to tell it apart from unfamiliar items.

Two Methods, Two Memories? Is one method generally better than the other? Does each have its merits for specific purposes? Do they measure different things? A number of such questions arise, and a good many of the answers are incomplete. Some psychologists maintain not only that the two methods measure different things but that there are two kinds of memory, recall and recognition. Others argue that the memory is the same, but that the two methods influence retrieval differently. For example, multiple-choice tests in the recognition method provide more cues than do the essay examinations of the recall method. The more cues you are given, the more likely you are to remember, so a student studying for a recognition test does not worry much about retrieval. But for a recall test, one not only has to learn the information but be prepared to retrieve it. An instance: one of the authors of this text says, "I know the fifty states and would do well on a recognition test. But on a recall test, I might have a hard time because I have never devised a systematic way to retrieve them."

What we can conclude is that recognition tests are more sensitive to memory than are recall tests and provide a more nearly complete picture of what has been learned and stored in the mind's file. But a teacher's objectives may be better served on occasion by an essay-type examination of the recall method.

Verbatim Memory. Frequently, students complain that they have to spend too much time regurgitating what teachers have told them, when they ought to be devoting the time to solving problems and thinking. Education *is* much more than mere regurgitation, but however distasteful memorization may be, we know that a certain amount of it is unavoidable. There are times when verbatim recall is essential. Furthermore, no one can think in a vacuum: one must have the basic building blocks of facts and rules for constructing solutions to problems. Fortunately for students and teachers, there are at least three methods for easing the pains of memorizing. As a teacher, you may want to pass them on directly to your students, or to apply them yourself in instruction. Although these memorization tips may seem a little gimmicky, research supports their superiority over sheer repetition of material (Paivio and Yuille, 1969).

All three methods involve the forming of associations among ideas, and the creation of mental images—the more bizarre the images the better. In *The Night Thoreau Spent in Jail*, there is a splendid example of the use of those techniques. The passage that follows, a conversation between Thoreau and a fellow prisoner named Bailey, embodies the example:

> BAILEY: I wish I was a writer. If I could write my name, I'd die happy.
> THOREAU: Then you'd do better than most writers. *Bailey's* not a hard name.
> BAILEY: I know the start of it. It's the start of the alphabet backward.
> THOREAU: *(Stooping to the floor.)*: I'll teach you the rest. B. . . A. . .
> BAILEY: That's as far as I know.
> THOREAU: Who's Bailey?
> BAILEY: *I* am.
> THOREAU: That's your next letter. I! I am I.
> BAILEY: How do you write it?
> THOREAU: *(Making a stroke in the dust.)*: Simple as a beanpole. Straight up and down. B-A-I—there, you're halfway through your name already. So you *turn the corner*—like this:
> *(He draws an "L.")*
> That's an "L"—B-A-I-"turn the corner." Now. Here's a rough one.
> *(He squints up at the goggle-eyed* BAILEY.*)*
> How much hair have you got?
> BAILEY: Enough to comb.
> THOREAU: That's it. Bailey needs a comb to comb his hair!

(Drawing in the dust.)
There it is: "E"! And when you're all through, you want a nice tree to sit under.
  So you make a beanpole with branches on the top: that's "Y"!
(He draws it.)
And there's your name.
BAILEY: Jehosophat! You make it simple!
(As he traces the letters on the dirt floor, turning to HENRY *for approval.)*
"B-A-Beanpole-Turn the Corner-Comb-Tree."
THOREAU: You've got it! Now you can write your name! "Bailey"! (From the
  play *The Night Thoreau Spent in Jail* by Jerome Lawrence and Robert E. Lee,
  © 1970 Lawrence and Lee, Inc.)

Now, suppose you want to remember Piaget's terms *accommodate* and *assimilate.* You can create a mental image of a young swain sitting in his date's living room waiting for her to come downstairs, while she calmly delays upstairs to be a few minutes late. With that picture in mind, you think "a-calm-date (for *accommodate*) and sim-ply late (for *assimilate*)."

One of the three methods that employs those techniques goes back to the ancient Greeks. It is called the *loci method, loci* of course being the Latin for *places,* and it was devised to help orators go on at length without notes. A speaker associated various points of his speech with the rooms and furniture and statuary of some building he knew well, such as his home. He opened with a mental image of the foyer, then mentally strolled from room to room, with each room reminding him what he wanted to say next. The scheme is attributed to the poet Simonides of Ceos and had a strange and tragic genesis. Simonides, the story goes, attended a great banquet, and while he was out of the room briefly, the roof fell in, killing all the seated guests and crushing them beyond recognition. But Simonides identified the bodies by recalling where each of the diners had been sitting. After that he went into the memory-training business, and the Greeks thought so well of his system that they supposedly put up special buildings designed just for oratorical practice. The loci method, which continues to be highly regarded by memory experts, may be applied to any material that lends itself to organization in the form of an outline.

Are there useful memory aids?

A second technique, called the *link method,* has proven effective in remembering words and names. It involves associating a word or name with a mental image. You want to remember *rhinoceros.* You picture the river Rhine in zero weather, filled with ice floes. *Chimpanzee?* You picture a sprouting pansy. (Why sprouting? Because *chimp* means a sprout on an old potato.) You want to remember *behavior modification?* Picture a pretty *model* graciously *thanking* a cocktail party hostess. Henry Thoreau's advice to his cellmate, Bailey, was an example of the link method.

The *peg* method, a third technique, also works with words and images, and is used to remember a list in sequence. It requires two steps. The first is to memorize a series of numbers and rhyming words: one, bun; two, shoe; three, tree; four, door; five, hive; six, sticks; seven, heaven; eight, gate; nine, line; ten, hen. Once this sequence is mastered, the second step can begin. This involves forming a vivid image associated with the *objects* in the rhymes (not the numbers). Here is an example of its use: You are going shopping and intend to go to four stores in a particular order. First, you will go to the florist's, then to the second-hand store, then the hardware store, and finally to the grocery. You imaging a flower stalk with a bun perched on top, and then a beat-up, second-hand shoe, and so on. To review the original shopping plan, you bring forth the zany images, which are now connected to a numerical order because of the "peg" list of rhymes.

MEMORY AND PERCEPTION

Near the beginning of this chapter, we listed some widely accepted tenets of cognitivism and noted that "external stimuli, flowing incessantly to our eyes, ears, and skin, engulf us in information about our environment." The quantity of that information is vastly greater than we can possibly use. For example, we can glance at a landscape and record it as a whole in memory, but nobody could take in the position of every leaf on every tree, the precise location of every blade of grass, the siting of every bird's nest or anthill. And sight, of course, is only one of our senses. The psychologist Edward Bradford Titchener, a student of Wundt, calculated that the elementary sensations that bombarded the human mind exceeded 46,708. His table of them (1910) looks like this:

Elementary sensations	Number
Color	Roughly 35,000
White to black range	600 to 700
Tones	About 11,000
Tastes	4 (sweet, sour, bitter, salty)
From the skin	4 (pressure, pain, warmth, and cold)
From the internal organs	4 (pressure, pain, warmth, and cold)
Smells	9 classes, possibly including thousands of elements
Total	46,708 plus the uncounted smells

How does perception screen information?

We shield ourselves from this cloudburst by using one of the processes of *perception*. Strictly defined, perception is the interpretation of the sensations received by the sensory organs; more broadly, it is the interpretation of experiences. The perceptual process we employ to bounce off the flood of sensations is *selective attention;* we pay attention to some sensations and ignore others. Most of our learning and remembering—intentional learning—results from selective attention. Perception in general and selective attention in particular are influenced by our existing cognitive structures, that is, by our memory. We pay attention to and seek out information that supports what we already know and believe, and sometimes discard the rest. But without memory, we could not determine what sensations and experiences to accept and what to ignore, so memory and perception interlock.

Here is an example of memory's influence on perception. Read the following passage and determine what is going on.

> Rocky slowly got up from the mat, planning his escape. He hesitated a moment and thought. Things were not going well. What bothered him most was being held, especially since the charge against him had been weak. He considered his present situation. The lock that held him was strong but he thought he could break it. He knew, however, that his timing would have to be perfect. Rocky was aware that it was because of his early roughness that he had been penalized so severely—much too severely from his point of view. The situation was becoming frustrating; the pressure had been grinding on him for too long. He was being ridden unmercifully. Rocky was getting angry now. He felt he was ready to make his move. He knew that his success or failure would depend on what he did in the next few seconds. (Anderson et al., 1977, p. 372).

Most folk might say that the passage depicts an impending jail break. Richard Anderson and his colleagues (1977) found that college wrestlers thought it described a wrestling match. Clearly, one's experience influences perception and, in turn, colors the information that migrates into long-term storage. In Anderson's view, "high-level schema can influence a person to impose one framework on a message" (p. 377). Sjogren and Timson (1979) repeated the study but gave some of the students the passage with a title that clearly interpreted the story. Nevertheless, 20 percent of the college students given titles chose an interpretation that contradicted the meaning of the title.

As another example, consider the case of Albert Bandura, whose views on learning by imitation are discussed in chapters 4 and 5. Cognitive psychologists have claimed that Bandura is one of their own (Wittrock, 1978); behaviorists also view him as kin (Goodall, 1972).*

How do perception and memory interact?

In summary, here is the reciprocal relationship between perception and memory: (1) the schemas or memory structures affect how events are perceived, and (2) the perception influences how information is stored in memory and recalled.

Aside from memory, our perceptions govern all sorts of behavior—from how we vote in an election to where we sit in class. We choose candidates by our perception of them. We apparently choose seats on the left or right side of a classroom, on the basis of two factors (Gur, Gur, and Marshalek, 1975, pp. 151–53):

1. *Which side of our brain is more easily triggered into action.* The left cerebral hemisphere deals with the verbal and the analytic; the right hemisphere with the sensual and perceptual. Individuals in whom the left hemisphere is more active tend to move their eyes to the right in conversa-

---

* What does Bandura have to say about this? He's squarely in the middle: "[The theory I prefer] includes within its framework both the processes internal to the organism as well as performance-related determinants" (1974, p. 865).

tion and under questioning in experiments; when the right hemisphere is the more active, eyes move more frequently to the left. People whose eyes shift to the left frequently choose to sit on the right side of the class, and "right movers" on the left.

2. *What kind of topic is under study.* Whether one is a "left mover" or a "right mover," the nature of the subject may impel one to change one's seat. If the class is tackling mathematics or another of the exact sciences, at least some students who ordinarily prefer the right side of the class will shift to the left. The findings imply that the direction in which one moves one's eyes and the choice of a seat indicate a preference for the exact sciences or for such subjects as art. But whether or not the changing of seat arrangements for students will facilitate their learning of a given subject remains to be determined.

It is clear that we all perceive and internally store features of the environment according to our own experience. The important remaining question is, Why? For ages, we have known that subjective impressions differ from person to person. More than a hundred years ago, in an astronomy lab in England, trained observers were startled to discover that even in the "objective" measurement of star speed, they perceived the same event differently. Eleanor Gibson (1969), a noted cognitive theorist, offers an explanation. She proposes that we all have an inborn need to reduce uncertainty. Our environment is complex, with millions of stimuli, mostly irrelevant, bombarding us. We automatically seek to make order of this chaos, to discover structure, and to reduce our uncertainty. When we locate distinctive, recognizable features, we reduce uncertainty, and that is automatically reinforcing. (Compare this idea to a behaviorist formulation of reinforcement.) From Gibson's explanation, the answer to why perception influences memory is that it must! It happens automatically, there seems to be a developmental sequence behind it, and it appears inborn.

One line of evidence that supports Gibson's theory deals with how beginning readers differ from more experienced readers. Apparently, young children attend to more irrelevant stimuli in their search for order; older children focus more rigorously on relevant features. Young readers therefore learn more *incidental* material and fewer central concepts, whereas the situation is reversed for older students. Ross (1976) remarks that this is an important developmental trend, because attention to irrelevant stimuli (and the resulting incidental learning) does not pay off in the long run.

Cognition and Reading

Students in school base much of their learning on material they read and are frequently engaged, as you are now, in reading. Students are often given a reading assignment with the faith that they will mysteriously absorb some of the material. Some absorb it pretty well, but many students struggle to com-

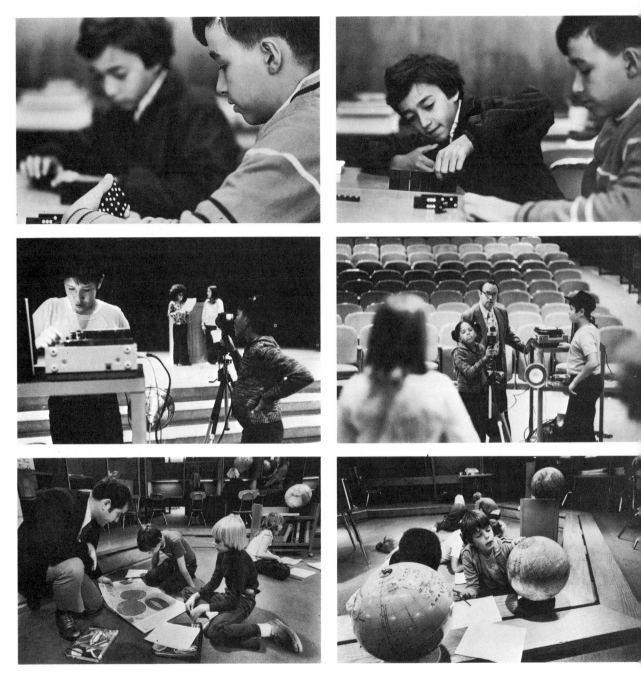

"There's so much going on inside kids' heads and so many new things, it's a wonder that they can sort it out and store it for later use. Sometimes I catch myself bombarding them with too many facts or concepts. Then I will try to arrange an activity that's related and relaxing. I think this gives them a chance to work with the new materials, and it helps it soak in before I give them a new batch of facts."

prehend the printed word. Perhaps because of this struggle, many students—and adults—avoid reading once school is over. Cognitive psychologists would like to unravel some of the mysteries of reading, and extensive research has asked, "Can written discourse be structured so that it is more comprehensible?"

Robert Gagné (1978) has recently summarized a body of reading research, and offers these tips to help students profit from textual material:

1. **Remind the learner of previously learned, related material.** This should alert students' existing schemas so that new material can be subsumed more easily. It may also increase the relevance of the assignment.
2. **Ask questions that can be answered by the material to be read.** If students are actively involved in thinking about their reading, it should improve comprehension. Also, answering questions during reading requires that new information be rehearsed. The practice will help commit material to long-term memory.
3. **Provide objectives or goals for reading.** This will orient students to important points in the material.

What advice does cognitive psychology offer for improving reading?

When a teacher develops his or her own material for students to read, there is somewhat more flexibility than when material prepared by a publisher is used. For example, you can insert questions in a passage or group them at the end, list objectives at the beginning or space them throughout, and put the summary at the beginning or at the end (or both!). Word difficulty, examples, and organization are under your control. With these choices, what makes the most sense? Research offers some direction but no certainties, so be prepared to experiment.

Ellen Gagné (1978) finds that written material is more easily stored in memory when it stimulates the reader's imagery. Vivid words, interesting and relevant pictures, and concrete examples all help to evoke mental images. Questions or objectives spaced throughout the reading passage usually improve recall. Finally, presenting a concept more frequently in a passage will help retention (Kintsch et al., 1975). Unanswered questions must depend on your best judgment. Close attention to student performance will help to determine the worth of new tactics that you try. Student opinions should not be neglected, a point understood by some publishers today.

Language and Thinking

Early in our discussion of the workings of memory, we said that the most important variety of memory, from the standpoint of learning, is *verbal memory*, which, we hope we have made evident, is related to thinking. But whether language and thinking are interdependent—that is, whether thinking cannot occur without words—has long been a matter of debate among psychologists. The pioneer behaviorist Watson considered thinking to be merely subvocal speech—speech that was not emitted. A totally contradictory position is taken by the Russian psychologist Lev Vygotsky, who holds that "thought is not merely expressed words, it comes into existence through them" (1962).

Are words simply a vehicle for thought?

Except for the most orthodox of behaviorists, few psychologists would contend that we never think in words or sentences. Yet we do seem to be able to think in images, wordlessly, in certain circumstances. For example, if you are asked to think about your house, you do not need words. If, however, you are asked to explain how you feel about your house, you will have to put your thoughts into words. The crucial question is, Did you need words to formulate your thoughts about the house, or is there some preword cognitive process called thought that needs words only for expression? Is that the reason we sometimes know what we want to say, but cannot find the words with which to say it?

Slobin considered the issue and concluded; "Clearly, one cannot *equate* thought with either speech or language. But, still language must play an important role in some cognitive processes" (1971, p. 102). One way in which language influences the cognitive processes was suggested by Whorf (Carroll, 1956), who concluded that the language one speaks determines how one thinks and what one thinks about. Research since Whorf indicates that, although language makes us sensitive to stimuli and influences how we think about things, language does not *determine absolutely* how or what we think. We may not have a word or a phrase or a sentence for a concept, yet the concept may well exist for us.

EDUCATIONAL IMPLICATIONS

This chapter has acquainted you with the framework of cognitive theory. But how does all of this relate to you as a teacher? What are the educational implications?

As teachers, we are interested in our students' mental—or cognitive—processes: how they organize knowledge mentally, how they interpret new knowledge in terms of existing knowledge (the cognitive structure), and how they relate new knowledge and experience to the old. To a degree, we are again raising questions about assimilation and accommodation. But beyond the cognitive processes themselves, we as teachers are interested in how instructional techniques influence the cognitive processes. We do not want to use a method of instruction that makes cognitive processing too difficult for the student; neither do we want to teach in a way that will lead the student to organize and use the knowledge inappropriately.

The cognitive framework suggests a number of implications for designing instruction. In Chapter 8, we shall discuss ways of doing so for the teaching of concepts, which develop from the organizing, classifying, and categorizing of information. In Chapter 9 we shall explore problem-solving and creativity from a cognitive perspective, and in Chapter 12 we shall discuss motivation and how perception influences behavior.

Summary

Cognitive psychologists concern themselves with the processes by which we acquire, organize, store, and use information, rather than with how we acquire overt behaviors. Though differing in their approaches and in their interpretation of researchers' findings, cognitivists widely share—on the basis of current knowledge—certain tenets:

We receive information from external stimuli in several ways, using sight, hearing, and other senses.

We are equipped in several ways to choose the information to which we will attend.

We are equipped also to deal with that information in several ways, associating it with what we already know, memorizing it, translating it into mental images, or dismissing it.

When we apply particular processes repeatedly to information received, we develop *cognitive structures* or *schemas.* Our cognitive structures or schemas develop and change, both when information enters memory and when it is retrieved.

One important process we employ is memory, which, psychologists believe, takes three forms: *sensory storage, short-term storage,* and *long-term storage.* Information remains in sensory storage only fractions of a second; it either decays or goes on to short-term storage, where it is dismissed promptly or sent to long-term storage, to join billions of other items.

Information stored in long-term memory is sometimes difficult or impossible to retrieve. The most persuasive explanation for such forgetfulness is that of *interference,* in which new information blocks the recall of old information, or vice versa. In learning, interference may be reduced by *overlearning;* by logical organization of the material as it is presented; by the separation in time of subjects that may be confused, such as French and Spanish; and by testing under conditions similar to those in which the material was taught. Other important factors are the meaningfulness of the material and opportunity for rehearsal. If retrieval is the major hurdle in remembering, then memory may not deteriorate with age. Retrieval can improve with practice.

Memory may be measured by the *savings method,* used chiefly by experimental psychologists; by the *recall method,* which requires students to demonstrate learning by performing tasks or answering questions; and by the *recognition method,* in which students must distinguish what has been taught previously from new material. Recognition tests seem to surpass recall tests in measuring what has been learned, but recall tests on occasion may better serve a teacher's objectives.

For *verbatim* recall, which is essential to some kinds of learning, three methods that involve the forming of associations among ideas prove helpful. One of them, the *loci method* employed by the ancient Greeks, mentally connects ideas and locations. A second technique, the *link method,* associates words or ideas with mental images. A third, the *peg method*, involves the rhyming of words and numbers, plus mental images.

Interlocked with memory in cognition is *perception*, which by broad definition is the interpretation of experience; without memory, of course, such interpretation would be impossible. Our perceptions govern our behavior, even, it appears, where we choose to sit in a classroom. The search for perceptually distinct and stable features of our environment may result from a need to reduce uncertainty.

Reduction of uncertainty is also important in enhancing reading skills; locating distinct features of letters and words improves speed and comprehension. The teacher can foster reading comprehension by careful use of questions, objectives and stimulating passages, and by drawing relationships to previous learning.

Whether the brain can think without words is vehemently debated by psychologists. Research indicates, however, that although language does not *absolutely* determine how we think, it exerts considerable influence.

For teachers, an understanding of the cognitive processes discussed has many practical applications in the classroom.

Chapter Study Guide

CHAPTER REVIEW

Answer questions 1–11 True or False:

1. Verbal memory may be the most important for school learning, but it has been shown that people retain visual information longer than verbal information.

2. There is a one-to-one relationship between each stimulus and the bit of information it provides.

3. A crucial difference between human perception and that of lower animals is that whereas the animals must select a limited number of items for attention, humans can absorb all stimuli simultaneously.

4. Recognition tests are more sensitive to memory than recall tests.

5. On the average, a person can retain seven bits of information in short-term storage.

6. In proactive inhibition, something learned earlier impedes the recall of something studied later.

7. The disuse theory holds that we tend to disuse, or forget, things that threaten our self-concept.

8. In overlearning, needless additional time is spent on a subject that could more profitably be spent on another.

9. When two learning tasks are similar, leaving a lapse of time between them will improve recall of both.

10. Because it permits accurate measurement of the degree of learning, the savings method is the most frequently used kind of memory test in the classroom.

11. Gestalt psychologists believed that the pieces of a problem could be added together to form the whole problem.

12. *Association* and *recognition* are terms for the memory processes of _____ .

13. The loci method of aiding memory can be applied to any material that lends itself to _____ .

14. Memory arranges bodies of information in patterns called _____ .

15. There are _____ memory storage systems, or stages. The function of the second stage is to _____ .

16. According to the authors, the most persuasive explanation of forgetting is _____ .

17. When new information is attached to existing memory schemas, Ausubel calls the process _____ .

18. If memorizing names of new students causes a teacher to forget last semester's students' names, _____ inhibition has occurred.

19. _____ information requires more rehearsal and a slower rate of presentation.

20. The use of occasional questions and vivid imagery in reading material may _____ recall.

FOR FURTHER THOUGHT

1. On the basis of Köhler's experiment with apes, Wertheimer concluded that teachers should organize material so that students can see a subject as a whole and thus come to understand it, rather than learn it piecemeal by rote. Would an equally valid conclusion be that the most effective learning takes place when students are motivated to discover by themselves the interrelation of things?

2. Thorndike concluded from his experiments with cats that "learning resulted from trial and error." Are there dangers in generalizing from the results of animal experiments? As described in the text, did Thorndike's experiment with cats offer the same opportunity for the exercises of insight that Köhler's did?

3. Research shows that most of our experience remains on file in memory—to be surprisingly evoked, at times, by hearing an old tune or by the taste of food. Creative writers also use dreams to gain access to memories buried in the subconcious. Do you think this kind of information retrieval ought to be a regular part of the curriculum? Why?

4. From your understanding of Ausubel's theory of meaningful verbal learning and the general idea of meaningfulness, explain why sequence is important in the

development of curriculum. Would a knowledge of individual students' backgrounds be equally important, for the same reasons?

5. One of the key elements in cognitive theory is the relation between memory and cognitive structures or schemas. Try to recall (without looking at your text) important points you have learned in this chapter. Then review the text. Can you explain your recall performance in this instance by reference to the discoveries of Bartlett and Ausubel?

IMPORTANT TERMS

cognition	subsume
Gestalt psychology	disuse theory
cognitive structure	intentional forgetting
schema	interference
memory	retroactive inhibition
sensory storage	proactive inhibition
short-term storage	overlearning
long-term storage	savings
encoding	recall
association	recognition
recognition	link method
operation	loci method
reconstruction	peg method
meaningful verbal learning	selective attention
rote learning	reduction of uncertainty

SUGGESTED READINGS

BLUMENTHAL, A. L. *The process of cognition.* Englewood Cliffs, NJ: Prentice-Hall, 1977. Up-to-date information and research about perception and memory storage. Moderately difficult; for the student who is serious about cognitive psychology.

BOURNE, L. E., DOMINOWSKI, R. L., and LOFTUS, E. F. *Cognitive processes.* Englewood Cliffs, NJ: Prentice-Hall, 1979. Excellent introductory text on the major areas of cognitive psychology.

BOWER, G. H. How to . . . uh . . . remember! *Psychology Today,* 1973, 7(5), 62–70. The author of dozens of research articles on memory, Bower gives a chatty and informative account of some of his research and of the use of memory aids.

GLASS, A. L., HOLYOAK, K. J., and SANTA, J. L. *Cognition.* Reading, MA: Addison-Wesley, 1979. Arguing that short-term and long-term memory models are obsolete, Glass and colleagues reorganize the cognitive area around types of information processing.

LINDSAY, P. H., and NORMAN, D. A. *Human information processing: An introduction to psychology* (2nd ed.). New York: Academic Press, 1977. Only three chapters of this general psychology text focus specifically on memory, but the entire book is worth reading because of its witty, informal style.

LOFTUS, G. R., and LOFTUS, E. F. *Human memory: The processing of information.* Hillsdale, NJ: L. Erlbaum, 1976. Entertaining introductory account of memory function, concluding with a chapter on semipractical applications.

MAYER, R. E. *Thinking and problem solving: An introduction to human cognition and learning*. Glenview, IL: Scott, Foresman, 1977. A good introductory primer on issues in cognitive psychology. Each chapter presents cognition from a different point of view (e.g., thinking as hypothesis testing).

NORMAN, D. A. *Memory and attention*. New York: John Wiley, (2nd ed.), 1977. Short book with honest coverage of important cognitive principles. The unusual and appealing format uses pieces of original research and theory, with Norman "translating" the more difficult portions. Introductory level.

POSNER, M. I. *Cognition: An introduction*. Glenview, IL: Scott, Foresman, 1973. A short but comprehensive treatment of memory systems and mental functioning.

ANSWER KEY

1. T; 2. F; 3. F; 4. T; 5. T; 6. T; 7. F; 8. F; 9. T; 10. F; 11. F; 12. retrieval; 13. organization in the form of an outline; 14. cognitive structures or schemas; 15. three. . .sort out information to see whether or not it is worth keeping; 16. interference; 17. subsumption or subsuming; 18. retroactive; 19. unfamiliar or meaningless; 20. improve.

7

Setting Learning Tasks

One major reason that you may have chosen teaching as a career went unmentioned by design in Chapter 1. It is your belief, which you perhaps never have felt it necessary to put into words, in the value of education.

But what *is* education's value? What *are* its purposes? If you asked a hundred people in your hometown those ancient questions, most of them would probably say, "So you can get a better job and make more money." A sizable minority might reply, "So you can be a good citizen and contribute to society." Fewer might answer, "So you can learn to think better," or "So you can enjoy a more satisfying life."

When we asked the questions among ourselves, one of us said, "To learn to solve problems and make decisions. We have to solve problems and make decisions every waking minute of our lives, whether we're choosing among brands of cereal in a supermarket or, say, sitting on the town council." Another of us said, "To learn to question. We ought to be questioning everything we do and do not do, as individuals and as members of society." The third said, "To prepare young people for life, liberty, and the pursuit of happiness." All the answers reflect the broad purpose of education. The last one, though, about life, liberty, etc., falls in the category of *word magic* (Dyer, 1967, pp. 14–15); it sounds fine, it covers everything, and it specifies nothing.

Goals and Objectives

If the goals of education are to be achieved, many school administrators and teachers believe, they must set specific objectives rather than indulge in word magic. Right now, let's clarify the distinctions between goals and objectives. *Educational goals* are broad and abstract and are exemplified by such statements as "Students will be competent in reading and mathematics." They are important in planning general curricula, but they are of little help to a teacher. Objectives—or, rather, *behavioral objectives*—are precise and measurable. They are designed for individual classrooms and even individual students, and tell a teacher what to teach and what has been learned (but they do not dictate *how* to teach). Because behavioral objectives are specific, they are much narrower in focus than educational goals, and a single goal may include dozens—even hundreds—of behavioral objectives.

Educational goals and objectives—how are they related?

For example, educational goals are often stated like this: "By the end of the term the class will appreciate the art of the Renaissance" or "Students will possess a thorough understanding of American history" or "Students will be familiar with the major plays of Shakespeare." Toward goals like those, there are no milestones or road maps. It is easy to lose the way and, if you arrive, to remain unsure that you are in the right place. The goals sound good, but they tell little if anything about what to teach and how to determine whether or not students have learned what you have taught. How do you measure appreciation? How do you evaluate a thorough understanding? How much familiarity does a student need to be familiar with Shakespeare's plays?

Table 7.1. Differences between Goals and Objectives

Characteristic	Educational Goal	Behavioral Objective
Specificity	quite general	highly concrete; precise
Durability	enduring	temporary
Importance	to society	to the individual
Direction in overall curriculum development	much	little
Direction in teacher planning	little	much
Aid to students in learning	little	much

BEHAVIORAL OBJECTIVES

The fuzziness of educational goals such as those has led many educational psychologists and educators to advocate the setting of behavioral objectives, which fit precisely into Bloom's Theory of School Learning (Chapter 1). A behavioral objective is what a student or a class will be expected to do in an observable and measurable way after you have taught. Educational goals and behavioral objectives differ, in brief, like this:

Educational goal: Students will speak Russian fluently.

Behavioral objective: Asked in Russian about the place where they live, students will respond in Russian without hesitation or help from a dictionary, framing at least five sentences with no more than two errors in Russian grammar.

Other differences between educational goals and behavioral objectives are shown in Table 7.1. Their advantages and disadvantages, and how to state them and use them if you decide to do so, will be discussed later in this chapter. Behavioral objectives represent only one of the many approaches to teaching that have developed since World War II.

THE EDUCATIONAL SHAKEUP

Until the late 1950s, education ranked in public esteem with Motherhood and the Constitution. Except for a few oddball educators and some campus theorists, hardly anybody asked embarrassing questions about it and hardly anybody thought that better ways of education might be needed. If, in places, education showed signs of ailing, it was assumed there was nothing wrong with it that money could not cure. The more money a school system spent on school buildings, textbooks, athletic fields, and teachers' salaries, the more confident citizens were that their children were getting the best possible education.

Americans were shocked out of their smugness about their schools when the Soviet Union rather than the United States launched the first space satel-

Task Analysis: Learning to Tell Time

Performing a task analysis—breaking a large task into smaller components and sequencing them—sounds like a fairly routine job. Beneath the surface, however, the procedure can become complicated. The difficulty increases in the affective domain, where it is sometimes impossible to put subtasks into logical or necessary order.

Glaser and Reynolds (cited in DeCecco and Crawford, 1974) spent a considerable amount of time developing a task analysis for a seemingly straightforward lesson: learning to tell time. To give you a sense of how complex a task may actually be, less than half of Glaser and Reynolds's task analysis is reproduced here (pp. 36–37).

Subtask A: For writing the hour and minute in sequence (Example: 7:35)

1. Reading the number on the clock face to which the little hand is pointing.
2. Reading the number on the clock face which the little hand has just passed.
3. Determining the number indicated by the little hand.
4. Writing the number of hours the little hand indicates.

Subtask B: Same purpose as A but focusing on the big hand

1. Writing "00" when the big hand points to top center of clock.
2. Associating the word *o'clock* with 00 and top center of clock. . . .
3. Counting clockwise by ones every single mark from the zero point to determine number indicated by the big hand.
4. Counting clockwise by fives every fifth mark from the zero point to determine the number indicated by the big hand.
5. Counting clockwise by fives from zero point and then by ones to determine the number indicated by the big hand.
6. Determining the number indicated by the big hand.
7. Then, writing the number of minutes the big hand indicates.

The point of this example isn't to make you happy that you already know how to tell time. The difficulty of devising good task analyses will have to be weighed against their benefits. And there are some benefits that go beyond merely discovering a proper order to present lessons. For example, the task analysis is a tremendous help as a diagnostic tool. It helps to pinpoint where along the learning path the student may be faltering. If a larger task involves certain prerequisite skills, then the task analysis can help the teacher evaluate quickly whether the student has the skills or not. In short, a task analysis can serve as an aid in evaluating student entry characteristics, in planning lessons, and in measuring learning outcomes. ■

The teacher of this English class has a set of goals for her students which, in one period, includes objectives in each of the three domains. In the affective domain the goals for this period were: (1) awareness of the link between names and self-images and (2) arousing interest in and excitement about the process of play and scriptwriting. In the psychomotor domain the goals for this period were manipulation of tools and manual improvisation to achieve the self-expression in the first affective goal. In the cognitive domain the goals were: (1) to describe the basic terms and techniques of play and scriptwriting, (2) to review and critique a written work, and (3) to develop a completed work suitable for submission to journals and magazines.

lite, Sputnik, in October 1957. What was wrong with our schools? Couldn't they turn out brighter minds and better scientists than Russian communist schools did? The Cold War was in one of its frostier periods, and the answers seemed to involve the nation's survival. Jerome S. Bruner wrote, "What may be emerging as a mark of our generation is a widespread renewal of concern for the quality and intellectual aims of education ... accentuated by what is almost certain to be a long-range crisis in national security" (1960, p. 1).

The Changes. As a result, curricula and teaching methods as well as American smugness were shaken up. Some of the innovations and reforms had been stewing since World War II. In that war, the government had employed psychologists to set up training programs for such military occupational specialties as piloting combat planes and firing machine guns. The psychologists soon found that traditional methods—instruction, examination, and grading on the curve—did not work well. A student pilot might achieve the highest mark in his class and still flunk fatally if he had not mastered every single one of the multiple skills required to fly in combat.

How did attitudes toward education change after World War II?

So the psychologists undertook what is now called *task analysis*: it consists of breaking down the job of flying a plane or firing a machine gun or cooking for a company of infantrymen—who are with good reason always hungry—into its essential components. Then they devised courses of instruction for each component, followed by tests for mastery of that component, practice on the job, and, finally, evaluation of total performance. The method worked. (We won the war.)

After the war, several former military psychologists determined to try to apply to general education what they had learned in the services: they became educational psychologists. In the next two decades, developments followed apace. John B. Carroll (1963) suggested that because some students learned more slowly than others, schools should allot time for a given subject on the basis of the individual student's aptitude, rather than by a rigid schedule. Allowed enough time, Carroll argued, even the slowest students would catch on to most of what their teacher was telling them. (The argument assumed that, beyond slowness, there were no serious impediments to learning. Carroll's model of instruction has several components, but "time spent" is one of the most important elements.)

Can mastery be achieved without explicit objectives?

Bloom's Contribution. Taking off from Carroll, Benjamin Bloom (1968) published an article that, though it appeared in an obscure newsletter, achieved wide influence. Students should be taught, Bloom proposed, until they have mastered a subject or a segment of a subject, no matter how long it takes. This is called *mastery learning*. Furthermore, he said, the whole system of grades and marks based on the normal curve was wrong and unfair. If Tom needed five times as long as Jane to learn to add six and twelve, but came out right in the end, then Tom was as much entitled to an A as Jane was. After all, the primary objective was to learn, not to set a speed record.

Bloom believes that precise statements of goals are necessary to discover whether students are mastering their coursework. He has continued to sharpen his conception of mastery learning, and his extensive review of literature on the topic shows that the mastery model has bridged the distance between theory and practice (Bloom, 1976). A fuller discussion of mastery learning appears in Chapter 16.

Mager's Contribution. In the same decade of ferment in education, the 1960s, Robert F. Mager wrote a book, *Preparing Instructional Objectives* (1962), that changed a lot of teachers' thinking about what they were doing. Mager devoted his book's brief preface (p. vii) entirely to a fable in which a Sea Horse sets out with seven pieces of eight to seek a fortune. Presently the Sea Horse meets an Eel. The Eel talks the Sea Horse into parting with four pieces of eight for one of the Eel's flippers, to enable the Sea Horse to travel faster. Then the Sea Horse encounters a Sponge, which sells the Sea Horse a jet-propelled scooter for even faster progress. (That takes the last of the pieces of eight.) Racing along, the Sea Horse comes upon a Shark. When the Shark asks the Sea Horse where he is going, the Sea Horse explains that he is on his way to find a fortune. The Shark suggests that if the Sea Horse will take a short cut through the Shark's open mouth, he will save himself a lot of time. The Sea Horse accepts the offer. The moral, says Mager, is that when one is not sure where one is going, it is possible to end up someplace else and never know it.

What did Mager's Sea Horse teach?

Mager's purpose is to help teachers and students know where they are going and whether or not they have got there. In Mager's view, a statement of goals must focus on learners' behavior after the learners have been instructed. Hence, what he calls "instructional objectives" are often termed "behavioral objectives." They have to be precise and concrete. A student's *understanding* of a subject would not qualify as precise and concrete because understanding takes place in the head. You cannot see it. You cannot measure it directly. And in any case two people—a teacher and a department head, say—might disagree on whether or not the student understood. Notice that behavioral objectives aim at the outcomes, the end products, of instruction. For this reason, they are often associated with the behaviorist philosophy (although you certainly do not have to espouse behaviorism to make use of objectives).

Writing Behavioral Objectives

At first, you will find the writing of objectives to be hard work. Changing familiar old fuzzies into more precise terms takes practice, but we think the effort will be well spent. Let's consider how to do it.

THE THREE ELEMENTS OF A BEHAVIORAL OBJECTIVE

Mager (1962) suggests that a complete behavioral objective should contain three separate components, each of which increases the precision and concreteness of the statement. The components are as follows:

What are the components of a complete objective?

Terminal Behavior. The term means observable, measurable behavior to be displayed when instruction ends. In specifying a desired terminal behavior, it is important to state what the student—not the teacher—should do, and it is important that its presence or absence be easy to determine.

Terminal behaviors comprise *acts*, such as listing, stating, describing, or even jumping. In the writing of an objective, *acts* should not be confused with *abstractions* (Mager, 1972). Abstractions—exemplified by appreciating, knowing, listening, sympathizing—go on in the head and can only be inferred. Acts are fine for terminal behaviors; abstractions are used for stating educational goals.

Level of Performance. Once a desired terminal behavior has been described, the next step is to stipulate a minimum level of acceptable performance—for example, "80 percent correct" or "within ten minutes"—that indicates *how well* or *how much* or *how fast* the terminal behavior should be displayed.

If one level is set for an entire class, it will probably be fixed to accom-

"You really need to love kids. That's the most important part. Everything you hear about—busing, integration, slow learners—fast learners, should you teach this way or that—what it boils down to is what happens in your class. There's a lot of work to it! What am I trying to give as a teacher? I'll turn that right around—it's not what I'm trying to give to a child, it's what I'm trying to get out of each of them."

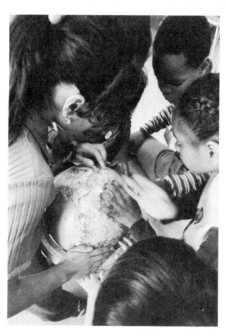

modate the students of least ability. (Setting it higher may guarantee their failure.) But a low level for all won't motivate the brighter youngsters. The solution lies in individualizing required performance levels: on the weekly vocabulary list, 90 percent correct may be a reasonable goal for William, and 70 percent a challenge for Alison. Even experienced teachers occasionally demonstrate bad aim in setting performance levels, but the levels aren't immovable targets and can be changed instantly and at will if the situation warrants.

What difficulties may be encountered in setting performance levels?

Some educators eschew performance standards on the grounds that the standards are arbitrary and give a false sense of precision. But acceptable levels of performance must be established, of course, for grading. There are two issues here: should standards be developed before or after instruction, and should the teacher share those standards with students? There is little evidence on which to base answers, so experiment.

Special Conditions. Sometimes, students may be expected—or permitted—to perform with special equipment or under unusual conditions—working a calculator, using a dictionary, or consulting cue cards for a speech. Any such conditions for demonstrating a terminal behavior should be included in the objective. So should special restrictions, such as "the student will translate a 400-word passage from Portuguese to English *without the use of a dictionary.*"

THE THREE DOMAINS

In setting down behavioral objectives, you should determine too whether you will be dealing chiefly, in a particular course, with imparting knowledge, or developing personality, or enhancing physical skills. Those three broad goals fall into what educational psychologists call *domains*. The domains often overlap, but each has its own emphasis.

The Cognitive Domain. The area that involves imparting knowledge is called the cognitive domain.

The Affective Domain. Emotional development lies within the affective domain, which embraces feelings, interests, attitudes, and values; in fact, the domain has so many noncognitive aspects that it covers much of what we call "personality." In the affective domain, a teacher might wish to lead an overly shy pupil who never raises a hand in class to acquire self-confidence and to join actively in classwork.

The Psychomotor Domain. In the psychomotor domain, the goal is the development of physical skills: the psychomotor domain refers to movement or action—everything from the blink of an eye to handwriting or to shooting a basket. An example of teaching in the psychomotor domain: Showing a first grader how to grasp a crayon.

In preparing behavioral objectives, you should keep in mind what domain you are working in. Teachers have their enthusiasms and interests like everybody else, and it is all too possible for an enthusiasm or an interest to engross a teacher in one domain when the goal and behavioral objectives are in another. An English teacher, for example, may want to inspire a class with a love for Shakespeare. That is clearly in the affective domain. But on a test the teacher asks, "From what play is the line *'How has the ass broken the wall, that thou art out of the city?'* "* The question is clearly in the cognitive domain.

The moral: If you want students to become addicted to poetry, an affective goal, do not expect to be able to measure their addiction precisely in terms of cognitive behavioral objectives. In short, keep your eyes on the goal, and don't mix up goals.

Cognitive Goals and Objectives. Most classroom instruction takes place in the cognitive domain, so let us consider first how to set educational goals and behavioral objectives in that domain. Assume that you are going to be teaching second graders reading, writing, and arithmetic. At the start of the term, by means of tests, talks with your pupils, and a look at their first-grade report cards, you find out how much your pupils know; what they know is part of their entry characteristics in terms of Bloom's Theory of School Learning. Your broad educational goals for your pupils are fixed by the curriculum, which is devised by administrators and textbook publishers. But classes and teachers differ. On the basis of the pupils' entry characteristics and of your own judgment of your skill as a teacher, you decide how far you will be able to advance the class. Then you prepare your behavioral objectives. They should be stated briefly and clearly, thus:

For arithmetic: Without the use of a calculator, pupils will correctly add six single digits.
For reading: Pupils will read aloud two paragraphs from the textbook, without stumbling, and will explain the passage in their own words.
For writing: Using the weekly vocabulary list, pupils will write four sentences of at least five words each, legibly and with no more than two errors in spelling.

What is the connection between the teacher's objectives and the student's?

In writing behavioral objectives, it is important to remember that they represent not what you want to teach, which is a lesson plan, but what you want the students to be able to accomplish as a result of your instruction. If you are teaching, say, a fifth-grade class and you write, "I will teach the causes of the Civil War," you are preparing a goal for yourself. If you write, "Pupils will be able to list at least two economic causes of the Civil War," you are preparing a behavioral objective for the class. Although teacher goals and precise objectives focus on different aspects of instruction, they obviously should be consistent with each other.

If you are using behavioral objectives for the first time, you may find it practical to lay out broad goals for the whole course, on the basis of what the

* If you are wondering about the answer, the line is from *Timon of Athens* (act 4, sc. 3, line 357).

Table 7.2. The Cognitive Domain Taxonomy

1.0 *Knowledge*
    1.1 Knowledge of specifics
    1.2 Knowledge of ways and means of dealing with specifics
    1.3 Knowledge of the universals and abstractions in a field

2.0 *Comprehension*
    2.1 Translation
    2.2 Interpretation
    2.3 Extrapolation

3.0 *Application*

4.0 *Analysis*
    4.1 Analysis of elements
    4.2 Analysis of relationships
    4.3 Analysis of organizational principles

5.0 *Synthesis*
    5.1 Production of a unique communication
    5.2 Production of a plan, or proposed set of operations
    5.3 Derivation of a set of abstract relations

6.0 *Evaluation*
    6.1 Judgments in terms of internal evidence
    6.2 Judgments in terms of external criteria

Adapted from Bloom, B. S. (ed.). *Taxonomy of educational objectives: Cognitive domain.* New York: David McKay, 1956.

class already knows. For the first unit of the course, set specific and precise objectives. At the completion of the unit, analyze the results and apply them in setting objectives for the next unit. Continue the procedure, unit by unit, until the objectives for the course as a whole have been attained. If you have succeeded beyond your expectations, note how much more the class achieved than you had specified. Your notes will help in preparing next year's objectives.

Bloom and his colleagues (1956) have prepared a taxonomy of the cognitive domain, which many have found useful in developing behavioral objectives. A *taxonomy*, as you may know from biology or zoology, is a system for classifying objects or events, and Bloom has applied the system to education. His taxonomy, shown in Table 7.2, establishes a sequence of complexity, or *hierarchy*, for the various aspects of the cognitive domain. The most elementary level is at the top and the most advanced at the bottom. You may want to refer to the taxonomy when you are writing behavioral objectives in the cognitive domain. It can be particularly helpful to ensure suitable coverage of a particular topic. For instance, although analyzing and synthesizing material are admirable goals, they may be inappropriate for an introductory course, even at the college level. If a course focuses on acquiring specialized vocabulary, then perhaps the first two levels of the cognitive taxonomy—knowledge and comprehension—should be stressed.

How may taxonomies assist in developing objectives?

The cognitive taxonomy, as well as the affective and psychomotor taxonomies discussed next, provides guidance for the measurement of student growth. The taxonomy offers illustrations of what behaviors fit each level of the cognitive hierarchy; it also provides sample test items for each of the levels. In Chapter 15 we will show how the taxonomies may be used to help develop achievement tests.

Affective Goals and Objectives. In the affective domain, there are two general goals. One is the development of student interest in subject matter. The other is the development of positive self-regard. Because the affective domain encompasses such intangibles as emotions, attitudes, interests, and everything else that make up "personality," behavioral objectives are less easy to specify than cognitive objectives are.

Emotions, interests, and attitudes cannot be measured directly; they can only be inferred from behavior. A high school junior who is studying French and who takes a French classic novel out of the school library has *probably* become imbued—as the teacher hoped—with a love for French. A hasty judgment on the teacher's part, though, is inadvisable. Does the student make sure the teacher notices the book? And if so, is the student merely conning the teacher into giving a higher grade? Or does the school librarian report to the teacher that the student takes French books home frequently and chats about them enthusiastically on returning them?

What makes affective behavioral objectives elusive?

It takes a good deal of observation, direct and indirect, to permit a decision on whether or not an affective goal has been attained. Direct observation, of course, is what the teacher personally sees. Indirect observation is what other people—the student's classmates, the librarian, the guidance counselor—tell the teacher.

"In our system, each teacher has to write out goal statements and pass them to the principal. Then all the principals send them to the superintendent's office. I know some teachers who turn in lists of vague objectives that can be interpreted a dozen different ways. They complain that it's busywork. Of course it is! Vague

Table 7.3. The Affective Domain Taxonomy

1.0 *Receiving (attending)*
    1.1 Awareness
    1.2 Willingness to receive
    1.3 Controlled or selected attention

2.0 *Responding*
    2.1 Acquiescence in responding
    2.2 Willingness to respond
    2.3 Satisfaction in response

3.0 *Valuing*
    3.1 Acceptance of a value
    3.2 Preference for a value
    3.3 Commitment

4.0 *Organization*
    4.1 Conceptualization of a value
    4.2 Organization of a value system

5.0 *Characterization by a value or value complex*
    5.1 Generalized set
    5.2 Characterization

Adapted from Krathwohl, D. R., Bloom, B. S., and Masia, B. B. *Taxonomy of educational objectives: Affective domain.* New York: David McKay, 1964.

Lee and Merrill (1972) have written a book devoted to the writing of affective behavioral objectives, and Krathwohl and his associates (1964) have developed a taxonomy for the affective domain (see Table 7.3). These resources are particularly useful because affective objectives are so hard to prepare.

statements aren't worth bothering with. When I think back, before I learned how to write specific objectives, I wonder how I organized my teaching. Maybe I didn't."

Psychomotor Objectives.   Goals and objectives in the psychomotor domain, which embraces physical activity in all its variety, concern elementary school teachers more than they do teachers in the secondary schools. In the lower grades, merely teaching a youngster to hold a pencil or a crayon correctly can constitute a goal, and using the pencil or crayon properly can constitute the behavioral objective. In the higher grades and the secondary schools, the psychomotor domain is the territory chiefly of physical education teachers and athletic coaches.

A number of sample objectives for various grades are suggested by Kibler, Barker, and Miles (1970). Among them are:

For arm and shoulder movements:
   Throw a baseball 35 feet.
   Do 10 chin ups.
For lower limbs:
   Run the 100-yard dash in 15 seconds.
   Raise and lower the right leg 10 times in succession from a prone position to
      a 45-degree angle.
For hands and fingers:
   Distinguish between a quarter and a nickel by touch (pp. 68–70).

A taxonomy for the psychomotor domain has been prepared by E. J. Simpson (1972; see Table 7.4). Gronlund (1978) credits this taxonomy with having wide application to many motor skills. An alternative psychomotor taxonomy geared toward physical education has also been developed by Anita Harrow (1972).

The Overlapping Domains. Most of the time you are in the classroom, you will be operating in several domains at once. A youngster reciting Lincoln's Gettysburg Address is demonstrating cognition, affect (if the student feels anxious about reciting), and psychomotor skills (by standing, gesturing, and speaking). Cognitive instruction in the principles of good citizenship extends into the affective domain. Discipline, which is considered in detail in Chapter 13, lies in both the affective and psychomotor domains and influences cognition.

Are the three domains really separable?

As a teacher, just remember which domain is most important to you at the moment and set your behavioral objectives accordingly.

MOVING FROM EDUCATIONAL GOALS TO BEHAVIORAL OBJECTIVES

Behavioral objectives and educational goals do not constitute simple substitutes for each other. Table 7.1 showed several important distinctions between the two types of goal statements; it should be clear, after consideration of the table, that one type is not inherently better than the other: they have different

Table 7.4. A Psychomotor Domain Taxonomy

1.0 *Perception*
    1.1 Sensory stimulation
    1.2 Cue selection
    1.3 Translation (from idea to movement)

2.0 *Set (preparedness)*
    2.1 Mental set
    2.2 Physical set
    2.3 Emotional set

3.0 *Guided response*
    3.1 Imitation
    3.2 Trial and error

4.0 *Mechanism (proficiency)*

5.0 *Complex overt response*
    5.1 Resolution of uncertainty
    5.2 Automatic performance

6.0 *Adaptation (to new situation)*

7.0 *Origination (of new psychomotor skills)*

Adapted from Simpson, E. J. The classification of educational objectives in the psychomotor domain. In Ely, D. J., and others, *The psychomotor domain.* Washington, D. C.: Gryphon House, 1972, pp. 43–56.

purposes and meanings. In our view, the statements are complementary and should be used together.

Educational goals without related behavioral objectives lack clarity and direction. But explicit objectives unconnected to broad educational goals may seem to represent only random skills. Educational goals help to coordinate and justify the smaller behavioral objectives. In a sense, an educational goal is a whole, comprised of its representative parts, the behavioral objectives.

Behavioral objectives become more difficult to write in the higher grades because of the increased complexity of the subject matter and because the teaching goals more frequently involve *understanding* and *appreciation* (see Figure 7.1). Understanding and appreciation can be vague concepts. But along with knowledge, they are essential to education, and behavioral objectives can be set for them to transform them from vagueness to clarity. Gronlund illustrates how this can be done. He starts with a list of behavioral objectives which we shall call List *A:*

1. Defines each technical term in his own words.
2. Identifies the meaning of each technical term when used in context.
3. Distinguishes between technical terms that are similar in meaning.

Then Gronlund offers a second list, which we shall call List *B:*

1. Understands the meaning of technical terms.
    1.1 Defines the terms in his own words.

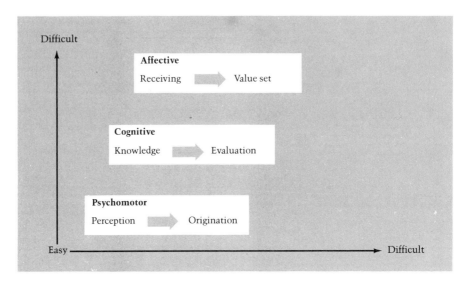

Figure 7.1. Relative Difficulty in Writing Objectives in the Three Domains. In general, the psychomotor domain allows the most straightforward development of objectives, because its concerns are already stated in terms of observable behaviors. Cognitive skills require more translation into representative behaviors, whereas affective outcomes are often very difficult to convert to overt behavior. Within each domain, objectives become harder to write as levels increase in complexity.

1.2 Identifies the meaning of the term when used in context.

1.3 Distinguishes between terms that are similar in meaning (1978, p. 4).

Can educational goals be translated entirely into objectives?

The lists look almost identical, but they are not. The addition of the top line to List *B* is crucial. It "makes clear," says Gronlund, "that the [broad goal] is *understanding* and not *defining, identifying* or *distinguishing between*. These latter types of behavior are *simply samples of the types of performance that represent understanding*" (p. 5).

So if you are writing behavioral objectives for subject matter to which understanding and appreciation are essential, you may want to apply Gronlund's technique: it involves stating the overall goal, such as understanding or appreciation, and then listing representative samples of the behavior that describes the goal. The samples have to be merely representative because so many kinds of behavior demonstrate understanding or appreciation that you could not cite them all.

Goal Analysis. Converting educational goals into selected behavioral objectives can be difficult. Suppose you begin with an affective goal, say, increasing appreciation for Impressionist art. How would you translate the goal into representative action verbs and objectives? Mager (1972) has suggested a method he calls *goal analysis*, which means determining some of the parts that comprise a fuzzy whole. Here is an example. Imagine two people who differ in their tastes. One is fond of Impressionist art; the other considers it old hat. How would you expect them to *behave* differently with respect to Impressionist art? The fan probably would talk enthusiastically about works recently seen in museum shows, buy coffee-table books on the Impressionists, and, perhaps, even try some Sunday painting. The other person would hardly do any of those things. Their differences in behavior represent so-called approach responses and avoidance responses (Mager, 1968), and provide a good start toward locating representative action verbs for the goal of appreciating Impressionism.

Why analyze a goal? In analyzing a goal, small, seemingly inconsequential facets of behavior can prove significant. Mager (1972) relates an anecdote about hotel managers who wanted their bartenders to have "good personality," and who were then asked to specify what distinguished bartenders with good personality from those without. On the plus side some included "handles glasses without spilling," and "smiles visibly when serving customers." But, a number of managers objected, surely those attributes were too trivial to represent personality. All right, they were asked, what they would do with a bartender who was surly, or slopped drinks. They responded, "Fire him!" Mager suggests the following simple test for triviality: What is the consequence of *not* displaying the behavior? The point is that in analyzing a goal, small behaviors can be significant.

"We don't do much with psychomotor or affective objectives. It's crazy. If a student has trouble operating equipment, we blame it on cognitive problems. If a student is really turned off or has no friends, we ask whether he's mastered science objectives 13 and 14. I'm not saying cognitive skills aren't important; it's just that they overlap with other areas that shouldn't be ignored."

UNFINISHED BUSINESS

Let us assume that, having read the discussion of their pros and cons that follows, you will give behavioral objectives a trial. How do you determine them? They are not ends in themselves, as you have seen, but means of achieving the broader, long-range goals of education. Some goals, such as the shaping of good citizens, are primarily for the benefit of society as a whole. Others, such as teaching youngsters to read, write, and manage arithmetic, primarily benefit individuals. But they benefit *all* individuals and thus indirectly serve society. Still other goals will have their value for only a few individuals: not everyone, obviously, should be expected to conquer calculus, acquire fluency in French, or master the bass viol.

An obvious consideration, then, is, For whom are you setting the objectives? Another, perhaps less obvious, is, How much learning do you want to demand? Should you accept only adequate performance in, say, Spanish from a youth who wants to become an automobile mechanic and require near-perfection from another who aspires to the foreign service?

THE PROS AND CONS

However effective and practical the writing of behavioral objectives may prove to be for you, it will not solve all the problems of the classroom. But advocates cite these advantages:

1. Setting behavioral objectives helps a teacher's planning. One of us once spent about 200 hours with five graduate students developing behavioral objectives for an educational psychology course in the expectation that the objectives would help the undergraduates. To the surprise of everyone, the behavioral objectives turned out to be as useful to the instructors as they were to the students. Having written the objectives, instructors knew precisely what they were responsible for teaching and were left free to concentrate on developing lesson plans and procedures aimed at the objectives. None of the instructors ever again—at least that year—went to class in near-panic, wondering "What the devil am I going to teach today?" Their teaching became more effective—and more fun.
2. Written objectives make evaluation easier. The teacher does not have to puzzle over what the next test should cover: it will cover the objectives of the unit under study. The simplest way to grade such tests is pass/fail: if a student fails, he or she simply needs more work. The last point will be expanded on in Chapter 15.
3. Objectives arm the teacher for Parents' Night questions and for administrators' visits to observe teachers in action. Ever since the onset of inflation, parents have been concerned about just what their school taxes are buying, and administrators have been sensitive about accountability. A teacher

What do the advocates claim about behavioral objectives?

who has prepared objectives can answer parents' and administrators' questions specifically: "Yes, Leslie has just mastered this and this and is now working on such-and-such."

4. Objectives reduce student bewilderment and guessing games about what the teacher wants. If the teacher tells the class at the start of instruction what the objectives are, the students can stop worrying ("Will that be on the test?") and can concentrate on learning. Suppose you are teaching social studies, and the immediate topic is the Treaty of Versailles. If you have defined your objectives to the class, the students will know that what you are after is not a recitation from memory of a list of the statesmen who attended the peace conference or a statement of how long the discussions went on, but a written, 2000-word essay on the connection between the terms of the treaty and the rise of Adolf Hitler.

Critics of the use of behavioral objectives are numerous, and their complaints embrace the practical and the philosophical. We begin with the practical; the last two criticisms are philosophical:

1. Behavioral objectives for individual students, which are most effective because students differ so much, are difficult to write. They may be feasible for elementary school teachers with 30 or so pupils, but for secondary school teachers whose pupils may number between 90 and 130 there isn't time.

What do the critics say?

2. Behavioral objectives may be suitable for simpler subject matter in the lower grades but are too difficult to prepare successfully for complex courses and impossible to write for art and music classes and others where teachers' judgments must be subjective.

3. The best grading system for behavioral objectives is pass/fail, but most schools do not use it. So how do you mark?

4. Gifted students, eager to learn a lot fast, may find objectives that are set for a whole class to be too restrictive, holding them back. But individualized objectives are often not feasible because of the time they demand to prepare.

5. Adherence to behavioral objectives prevents teachers from seizing unforeseen opportunities for instruction. A morning newspaper's headline about a presidential veto of a welfare funding bill, say, might lead to an enthusiastic discussion in a class in government. But the teacher may have to ignore it because it would require a detour on the road to the finish line.

6. When behavioral objectives apply to a student's emotional development, for the purpose of eliminating what the teacher considers a bad habit and instilling what the teacher considers a good habit, the objectives infringe on the student's rights; it is not the teacher's business to change people's personalities.

7. Education is not salami. It should not be sliced, weighed, and neatly wrapped as though it were.

TO USE OR NOT TO USE?

Are behavioral objectives really worthwhile in terms of bettering student achievement? Some research indicates that they do improve learning; other research indicates that they do not. But Melton (1978) has shown that the research often oversimplified the problem by asking, "Do objectives work or not?" More pointed and more pertinent is this question: Under what conditions are behavioral objectives useful? Research would be more fruitful, Melton says, if it addressed such issues as student interest in employing the objectives, what kinds of subject matter are best served by objectives, and how closely objectives are tied to evaluation.

Are objectives worth the effort?

Some research, though, has helped us to understand objectives more clearly. Increasing evidence shows that objectives may influence learning because they aim students in the right direction and help alert them to materials that might otherwise be ignored (Melton, 1978; Duchastel, 1979). However, when lessons are already tightly and clearly structured, objectives may not be much help (Hartley and Davies, 1976). Finally, and underscoring the purpose of this chapter, it has been noted that the training of teachers in the construction and use of objectives *can* enhance student learning (Piatt, 1969).

One of us once asked hundreds of students who had been given behavioral objectives what they thought: most of them replied that they believed they had been helped by knowing the objectives. Behavioral objectives probably do improve relationships between teachers and students, who can work as a team instead of wasting time trying to outguess each other.

A decision to use or not to use behavioral objectives is one you will have to make for yourself. We recommend that you base your decision on experience with them. Try them to see how they work for you. Give them time—perhaps a couple of school years—for it takes a while for students and teachers to feel comfortable with a new system. After a fair trial, consider the results: were they worth the effort?

Summary

Education has many purposes. Some are for the benefit of society, some for the benefit of the individual. They usually are stated in broad terms. It is the business of educators to translate the broad terms into more precise statements.

As a means of measuring how much students have learned or otherwise gained from their schooling, many educators advocate setting *behavioral objectives*. A behavioral objective is what a teacher expects a student to be able to do after having been taught. Behavioral objectives provide evidence about whether or not the general goals of education are being achieved.

Behavioral objectives, along with several other changes in teaching methods, were developed after World War II, in which a number of psychologists

"I hardly ever write my own behavioral objectives. Our school bought one of those giant published collections, so I just sift through and choose the ones relevant for my class. It gives me a lot more time to plan instruction and to individualize. I individualize by either assigning special objectives to brighter children, or by setting their performance levels higher."

working for the government found that traditional methods of instruction did not work well in training combat pilots and other military men. Learning improved, the psychologists discovered, when what had to be mastered was submitted to *task analysis*. Students tackled one unit at a time and had to be thoroughly skilled in the current unit before they went on to the next one. Soviet Russian success in launching the first space satellite in 1957 accelerated the application of such methods of teaching to the public schools.

Complete behavioral objectives contain three separate parts: a terminal behavior, a level of acceptable performance, and any special conditions surrounding the performance.

Behavioral objectives may be set in any of the three domains of teaching and learning. The *cognitive domain* involves the imparting of knowledge. The *affective domain* embraces emotions and attitudes about oneself and others. The *psychomotor domain* covers all physical skills. The three domains overlap, and a single performance, or behavior, by a student may extend into all three domains. It is advisable for a teacher to determine which domain is most important to the lesson at hand and, for the long run, it is important to avoid confusion about which domain the teacher is working in.

Whether or not the setting of behavioral objectives greatly improves teaching and learning remains debatable. Teachers may settle the argument for themselves by experimenting with behavioral objectives and determining whether the results justify the effort involved.

Chapter Study Guide

CHAPTER REVIEW

1. Behavioral objectives, as compared to educational goals,
   a. tend to be less specific and to cover large areas of content.
   b. are less worthwhile.
   c. are less general and state what to look for in students' behavior as the outcome of instruction.
   d. have been used in the schools for many years and have generally met with teacher satisfaction.

2. Task analysis serves to
   a. state behavioral objectives.
   b. help identify the separate skills needed to perform a desired task.
   c. describe the educational goals that need to be taught.
   d. prepare the youth of America for military service.
   e. shift the emphasis in learning from time spent on a task to the nature of the task being learned.

3. Benjamin Bloom and Robert Mager would probably agree that
   a. desired outcomes of teaching should be specifically stated before instruction is to begin.
   b. educational objectives have little value for education and should be abandoned.
   c. through correct use of task analysis most students will be able to master a skill within a predetermined amount of time.
   d. unless objectives are stated, learning will be unlikely to occur.

4. Psychomotor objectives are
   a. aimed at developing the use of muscles, coordination, balance, and even sight.
   b. used in the primary schools, and replaced by cognitive and affective objectives in the secondary schools.
   c. the concern of the gym teacher, whereas cognitive objectives are the concern of the classroom teacher and affective objectives of the school counselor or psychologist.
   d. used when a teacher wishes to help a student change his or her attitude toward a particular subject area.
   e. used for describing learning tasks; affective and cognitive objectives are used to determine the nature of instruction.

5. The different domains in which behavioral objectives may be written

   a. are essentially separate and the concern of different personnel within the school environment.

   b. encompass a small part of the learning that occurs in schools and must be supplemented with educational objectives.

   c. include only the skills of learning of specific facts and bits of information, and of learning of attitudes.

   d. have been stated and described in the literature devoted to education, but still present some problems in implementation.

   e. have been made completely separate and identifiable through the development and use of taxonomies.

6. Task analysis and behavioral objectives grew out of a need to improve

   a. conduct.

   b. performance.

   c. self-awareness.

   d. motivation.

   e. psychology.

7. Besides precision and concreteness, Mager urged that behavioral objectives set the _____ under which a student demonstrates behavior and stipulate a _____ level of performance.

8. Behavioral objectives are not _____ in themselves, but _____ of achieving the broader long-range goals of education.

9. A maxim for using behavioral objectives successfully is "Keep your eyes on the _____ and don't _____ goals."

10. Behavioral objectives are formulated on the basis of what the class already _____ and of your general _____ .

11. *Without rereading this chapter,* you will be able to identify the italicized portion of this objective as a _____ .

12. Emotion, interests, and attitudes cannot be measured directly; they can only be inferred from _____ .

FOR FURTHER THOUGHT

1. Do a task analysis for any not-too-involved operation; e.g., draw a square, make change, hang a picture at the proper height. Try out its effectiveness on a young brother, sister, or child of your acquaintance. (Be ready to revise your analysis if it doesn't promote learning.)

2. One of the common frustrations of teaching is that after painstaking preparation of material and goal-setting, the students turn out to be uninterested. Often, "lack of student motivation" is blamed for this state of affairs. A more productive approach might be to give more attention to what Bloom calls the student's *entry characteristics*—past experiences, present interests, and psychological needs—on the theory that nothing is ever taught, only learned.

Select a skill, understanding, or appreciation that you might teach to a child of your acquaintance. Develop an approach to the subject that would be likely to engage *this child's* interest, along with behavioral objectives suited to *this child's* development. If possible, try it out. Keep a log of the experience.

3. The authors rejected their broad educational goal, "To prepare young people for life, liberty, and the pursuit of happiness" as an example of word magic—"specifying nothing." While conceding that the statement is extremely general, let's reexamine some of its possible implications. It suggests, first, that education should be for living; that is, that it should deal with life concerns and not with knowledge for its own sake. Second, to educate for liberty requires developing autonomous persons who can make independent choices and assume responsibility for their own behavior. Third, to educate for "happiness" would certainly include cultivating artistic tastes and sensitizing students to questions of value. The crucial questions for behavioral objectivists are: Is it possible to write useful behavioral objectives for such important educational goals? If not, should one therefore dispense with the goals? What is your answer to the first question? What advice would you give the authors on the second?

4. Consider the pros and cons of behavioral objectives given at the end of this chapter. Ask the opinion of teachers who have had experience with their use. Do you see any patterns emerging, by subject area? by temperament? by philosophy?

IMPORTANT TERMS

educational goal
behavioral objective
task analysis
goal analysis
terminal behavior

level of performance
special conditions
cognitive domain
affective domain
psychomotor domain

SUGGESTED READINGS

There are dozens of how-to-do-it books in print about setting goals in the classroom. In general, these books are short, readable paperbacks with a tremendous variety of examples. The listing here is admittedly incomplete.

BROOKS, P., BENEDICT, L. G., HUTCHINSON, T. E., and COFFING, R. T. *Defining educational objectives from goals: Breaking down fuzzy concepts.* Amherst, Massachusetts: National Evaluation Systems, 1974.

BURNS, R. W. *New approaches to behavioral objectives* (2nd ed.). Dubuque, Iowa: Wm. C. Brown, 1977.

EISS, A. F., and HARBECK, M. B. *Behavioral objectives in the affective domain.* Washington, D. C.: National Science Supervisors Association, 1969.

GRONLUND, N. E. *Stating objectives for classroom instruction* (2nd ed.). New York: Macmillan, 1978.

HANNAH, L. S., and MICHEALIS, J. U. *A comprehensive framework for instructional objectives.* Reading, Mass.: Addison-Wesley, 1977.

KRYSPIN, W. J., and FELDHUSEN, J. F. *Writing behavioral objectives: A guide to planning instruction.* Minneapolis: Burgess, 1974.

MAGER, R. F. *Goal analysis.* Belmont, Calif.: Fearon, 1972.

MAGER, R. F. *Preparing instructional objectives.* Belmont, Calif.: Fearon, 1962.

VARGAS, J. S. *Writing worthwhile behavioral objectives.* New York: Harper & Row, 1972.

The following three books provide comprehensive hierarchies of objectives in each of the three domains; the hierarchies proceed from simple to complex educational behaviors. The books are extremely useful in helping to organize objectives according to the broader purposes of education.

BLOOM, B. S. (ed.). *Taxonomy of educational objectives: Cognitive domain.* New York: David McKay, 1956.

HARROW, A. J. *A taxonomy of the psychomotor domain.* New York: David McKay, 1972.

KRATHWOHL, D. R., BLOOM, B. S., and MASIA, B. B. *Taxonomy of educational objectives: Affective domain.* New York: David McKay, 1964.

ANSWER KEY

1. c; 2. b; 3. a; 4. a; 5. d; 6. b; 7. conditions...minimum; 8. ends...means; 9. goal...mix; 10. knows...goals; 11. special condition; 12. behavior

Cognitive Approaches to Teaching and Learning Concepts

In discussing memory early in Chapter 6, we pointed out that if people lacked memory, they would have to learn anew each time they ate a banana or an oyster. If we asked you now what a banana and an oyster have in common, you would say that both are food. Your answer would demonstrate a *concept*. What concepts are, why they are important to learning, and how they may be taught constitute the content of this chapter.

For a beginning, let us consider the following doodles. These are glugs.

These are nonglugs.

Which of these are glugs?

Is *glug* a concept?

If you are as sharp as you think you are, and sharp enough to become a teacher, you have quickly determined that 2, 3, and 4 are glugs and the rest nonglugs. To figure that out you probably did three things:

1. You looked for a characteristic or characteristics that glugs shared and nonglugs did not.
2. You perceived that glugs consist only of curved lines and nonglugs only of straight lines. So you formed two concepts, one of glugs and one of non-glugs.
3. You applied the two concepts, as a principle, to solving the problem. (The principle is that the shape of a doodle's lines distinguishes glugs from non-glugs.)

What Is a Concept?

A concept, in the language you learned in elementary school arithmetic, represents a *set* in your mind. More formally, a concept is a grouping of objects, events, ideas, or people that share one or more major attributes that set them apart. *Automobile* is a concept because cars, whether they are decrepit VW Bugs or glistening Rolls-Royce Silver Clouds, possess in common these attributes: they are private, passenger-carrying, self-propelled, road-traveling vehicles. *Dog* is a concept because dogs, whether they are Great Danes or Chihuahuas, all belong to the genus *Canis familiaris*. (No, barking is not an essential dog characteristic; at least one breed does not bark.) *Democracy* is a concept; *dictatorship* is a concept. So is *love*. Because a concept represents an abstract grouping, it takes at least two of anything to constitute a concept. You can't have a one-man democracy, a dictator must have someone to dictate to, and a lover someone to love.

WHAT CONCEPTS DO FOR US

A concept is made, not born. Two-year-old Tommy calls the big, round, red-and-white plastic object that rolls around the living room floor "ball!" but it may be several years before he forms a concept that Mommy's tennis balls and brother Joey's football—which of course is not even round—also exemplify *ball*. As Tommy grows, his concept of ball broadens: eventually it embraces the ball in the pinball machine, the great ball of fire that is the sun, and myriad round objects in between.

But why do we bother to form concepts or write a chapter in a textbook about them? Aren't they just an added complication to life in general and educational psychology courses in particular?

Could we survive without concepts?

Quite the contrary. Concepts reduce the complexities of life, learning, and teaching. We are endlessly bombarded, you remember from Chapter 6, by external stimuli, and if we had to deal with each one individually we should soon be overwhelmed. So, as we said, the mind classifies stimuli, grouping them by their similarities, to cut down the number of objects, events, and ideas that it must store for handy reference. The process produces concepts.

Relationships between concepts establish principles. For example: (1) winged animals fly; (2) studying helps grades; (3) reinforcement increases behavior. Each word in these principles is a concept. Putting the concepts together gives us principles, and principles permit us to solve problems. We shall consider problem-solving in the next chapter. So concepts are the building blocks of mental activity; without them we would have a difficult time constructing thoughts, plans, and ideas.

Some concepts, such as *squares* (consisting of four equal sides and four right angles), are so simple that we pick them up early in life. More complex and abstract concepts generally have to be taught, unless, of course, the learner is another Sir Isaac Newton and arrives without instruction at a concept like that of gravity. But that demands *creativity*, which also will be considered in the next chapter.

For Newtons and us non-Newtons alike, the formation of concepts is—in the view of cognitive psychologists—one of the major ways in which we respond to and attempt to collaborate with our environment. Formation of

Teacher: *Can you tell me what shape this is?*
Child: *Jay-jay!*
Teacher: *A jay-jay shape? What shape is a jay-jay shape? Is it square?*
Child: *Yea!*
Teacher: *It's a circle! It doesn't have any edges. See, it goes right over your head. Here's another circle. It goes* round *and* round, *just like that! What do we call that, Tracy? A circle? Why don't you feel the circle. Hold it in your hand and feel* around *it. Hold it in your hand and feel how* round *it is. See how round it is? Round doesn't have any corners. How about these? Are these the same?*
Child: *Yea!*
Teacher: *They are?*
Child: *Yes.*
Teacher: *How come they're the same?*
Child: *Round.*
Teacher: *They're* not *the same! One's a circle. What's this one Sharon?*
Child: *Triangle.*
Teacher: *Triangle! It has* edges *and* points. *Can you say* triangle, *Michael? Feel the shape of your triangle . . . Now, let's not put the circles and triangles and squares together! Because they're* different. *Let's put the circles inside this . . . and the triangles inside this . . . and the squares inside this. Can you do that?*
Child: *I can!*
Teacher: *OK. Is that what goes in, Michael?*
Child: *Yep!*
Teacher: *What is it?*
Child: *A* square!

concepts organizes our thinking about the world, enhances our ability to understand it, and makes it easier for us to live in it.

ATTRIBUTES OF CONCEPTS

Every object, person, and event is made up of characteristics, which are called attributes. You can form a concept on the basis of a single attribute shared by two or more objects, events, or ideas. The attributes may be as fundamental as size, or shape, or height, or weight, or color. All blue objects could constitute a concept. So could all objects that are, say, ten feet high. More complex concepts may involve many attributes—the number is virtually infinite.

But in the mind of the individual forming the concept, the attribute or attributes must be *relevant*. If the relevant attributes are not present in an object, event, or idea, that object, event, or idea does not fit the concept. A relevant attribute in the concept of democracy is the choice of governors by the governed. Whether the nation is as large as the United States or as small as San Marino, and whether the chief of state is a president or a king are irrelevant to the concept of democracy.

What is a defining attribute?

Relevant attributes are often referred to as *defining* attributes because they determine the definition of a category. An attribute that is not essential to the definition is dubbed an *irrelevant* attribute. Irrelevant attributes are not necessarily useless. They can help in categorizing, as the straight lines of nonglugs helped you to categorize glugs.

If something possesses all the relevant attributes of a category, it is described as a *positive instance* or *example*. In the absence of one or more defining attributes, it becomes a *negative instance* or *nonexample*. You will come across all four terms again.

Changing Roles and Shifting Meanings. Relevant and irrelevant attributes often swap places, because relevance and irrelevance reflect circumstances and the needs at the moment of the individual forming the concept. For example, to a turnpike toll collector who generally categorizes vehicles by the toll they must pay, the relevant attribute of a blue, ten-foot-high, twenty-ton truck ordinarily would not be its color or its height but its weight, which on that turnpike determines the toll. But if the state police sent out an alarm along the turnpike for a blue, ten-foot-high, twenty-ton truck, all three attributes would become relevant.

All of our lives we continue reshaping our concepts that way. "My concept of a 'gene' or a 'seductress' or of President Eisenhower is certainly not the same as it was ten years ago," Arthur Koestler has written, "though the verbal label attached to each of these concepts has remained the same" (1966). Not only do our concepts change but, at any time, they differ from those of other people using the same verbal labels. (Even the meaning of the labels themselves alters. As Koestler has pointed out, "electron once meant a piece of amber and Homer's cosmos a flat disc covered by a vault.")

Why do people arrive at different concepts despite the identical labels? Because concepts are created and expanded by experiences; our experiences differ and our memory systems, discussed in Chapter 6, broaden the differences in screening and reshaping the experiences. We avoid chaos because, fortunately, people of a given place and time usually agree on the *general* meaning of concepts and their attributes.

Learning about Concepts

How do concepts evolve?

In studying concepts, youngsters learn to classify objects, events, and ideas by their common attributes. Almost every student's entry characteristics at any level include some experience in that area. Any first grader can distinguish among dogs, cats, and rabbits, a feat that he or she probably found difficult or impossible at, say, age two. (Two-year-olds usually identify any four-footed creature smaller than a horse as a dog, which itself is a concept, albeit a mistaken one that eventually is revised. When a learner can identify both relevant and irrelevant attributes of a concept, he becomes more exact in its use and the concept becomes more useful in formal, abstract thought.) The first grader will have to develop a somewhat higher skill at concept formation to tell a dog from a wolf or a fox or a jackal seen at the zoo. Of course, it will be a rare modern youngster who ever encounters a wolf or a fox or a jackal on the loose, so you may be moved to ask, Then why does it matter? It matters because youngsters who do not form concepts at low levels will have serious problems in forming concepts at higher levels.

Many concepts develop naturally from easy to difficult or from concrete to abstract, according to a belief that has gained in acceptance in recent years. Piaget's theory of the sequence of periods in cognitive development has been extended by other researchers to concept development: Klausmeier (1976) proposes, with strong experimental evidence, that in concept development children move through several hierarchical levels roughly associated with age and experience; the levels are attained in unchanging sequence, and each level must be developed before the learner moves up to the next one. (Klausmeier and Piaget are not, however, in perfect agreement. Klausmeier and Hooper [1974] explore substantial differences between their work and Piaget's.)

MENTAL SHORTCUTS AND BUILDING BLOCKS

How do concepts simplify learning?

Concepts simplify learning and eliminate the necessity for learning related things over and over. For example, once a youngster has formed the concept of corn, wheat, rye, barley, and oats as *grain*, the concept of grain serves as a kind of shorthand in such fields as social studies, botany, nutrition, and agriculture. (But be careful! Concepts vary from place to place: in England, wheat, barley, rye, and oats constitute the concept of *corn* and what we Americans refer to as corn the English call maize.) Similarly, the concept of oysters, clams, and mussels as *bivalves* helps in zoology to distinguish them from some 20,000 other kinds of mollusks.

Language underlies most concepts, and we use words or symbols to form new concepts. That becomes especially important in acquiring abstract concepts for which there are no tangible examples: teaching the concept *expectation* would prove difficult indeed without using words—which are concepts. Thus, concepts can help to build new, more complex concepts.

Concepts simplify teaching, especially on the higher levels. If you had not come to college already equipped with a great many concepts, it is likely that none of your instructors and professors could every get through to you, because what they are telling you can be comprehended only in terms of the concepts you possess.

But perhaps the most important reason of all for learning about concepts is that, as we mentioned earlier in this chapter, the relationship between concepts establishes principles. On the basis of principles, we can apply concepts to problem-solving and decision-making. When an individual has categorized an object, an event, an idea, or another person and relates it, or him, or her, to a principle, the course of action to be taken becomes clearer.

As Klausmeier (1976) has pointed out, sturdy principles allow cause-and-effect hypotheses testing, understanding of concepts' relationships with each other, and transfer to novel situations. And principles permit explanation and prediction of events. Since concepts are the foundation of principles, they truly provide the material for much of what we call intelligent behavior.

Teaching about Concepts

The heading of this section reads the way it does, instead of "Teaching Concepts," because for the most part you will not be teaching concepts; you will be teaching students how to recognize whether or not an object, an event, an idea, or an individual fits into a particular category. Nevertheless, we may use the term *teaching concepts* for convenience.

"We use nonexamples a lot. If we use only examples, the kids con us—and themselves—about what they're learning. We find out what they don't *know by using nonexamples . . . whether they can distinguish between this concept and that concept."*

Several factors influence the teaching and learning of concepts, as Klausmeier, Ghatala, and Frayer (1974) point out. Those factors are (1) the learner's entry characteristics, in terms of age, level of achievement, and cognitive style; (2) the methods of instruction, which we shall get around to shortly; (3) the concept being taught.

HARD ONES AND EASY ONES

Some concepts are much more difficult to teach than others and more difficult to grasp. The more defining attributes a concept possesses, the tougher you and your students will find it. Consider Saponite, a "hydrous magnesium aluminum silicate occurring in soft, soapy, amorphous masses and filling veins and cavities (as a serpentine or diabase)." Because of its many defining attributes, each of which has its own set of defining attributes, Saponite as a concept obviously is more difficult to teach and learn than another mineral, gold. Gold is merely a "metallic element having a characteristic yellow color, is heavy, is soft, and is the most ductile and the most malleable of metals."

What makes certain concepts more difficult than others?

Abstract concepts are more difficult than concrete concepts. You can create a clear mental image of a house, a grain, a bivalve, but you cannot create a mental image for abstractions such as democracy, dictatorship, or love, and in some cases the concepts are so abstract that it is hardly possible even to state their defining attributes. Take *love*. What would you say were its defining attributes? See what we mean? But most concepts are easier to deal with.

TECHNIQUES FOR TEACHING CONCEPTS

For a start at teaching concepts, you will need to keep the three essential components in mind: (1) defining attributes; (2) examples and nonexamples, which are also called, you remember, positive instances and negative instances; (3) feedback, which means informing students whether they are right or wrong.

Rule-eg and Eg-rule. The two commonest and most important methods of presenting concepts to students are:

1. Stating the defining attributes and following them with examples. Here a teacher is explaining *fish*: "A fish is a vertebrate animal that spends its life in water. It breathes through gills. It usually has fins, which it uses in somewhat the way that land animals use limbs. Now, in this slide you see a trout, which is one of many thousands of kinds of fish. You can see its gills *here* and its fins *here*. Now in *this* slide, you are looking at a trout's skeleton. The skeletal structure is what leads us to classify fish as vertebrate animals." This procedure—attributes followed by examples—is handily dubbed *rule-eg* by educators. (The *eg* part, if you're wondering, derives from the abbreviation e.g., which of course translates to "for example.")

How do the rule-eg and eg-rule procedures differ?

2. Giving the examples of the concept first and following them with their defining attributes, a reversal of the procedure we just described. This method is called *eg-rule* and works thus: To teach the concept of *topography* (making maps that show the physical features of land), a teacher handed out dittoed maps of the United States and asked students to study them. The maps had the proper topographical markings, but no explanation of the markings' meanings. The students quickly recognized the country's outline, and then developed a fairly accurate legend for reading the map. Their legend explained the defining attributes of the map: land of various altitudes, major rivers, and other bodies of water. Using the *eg-rule* procedure, the teacher had guided the class to an understanding of *topographical map*, first using an example, then helping students to discover the defining attributes.

Variations on a Theme. Teachers sometimes present the defining attributes and then ask students to propose examples. In still another approach, a teacher may provide both examples and nonexamples of a concept, and then come up with new examples and nonexamples and ask students to say which are which. That is what we did when we confronted you with glugs and nonglugs at the beginning of this chapter. In that approach, students may be asked also to specify the defining attributes.

What does it mean to "learn" a concept?

Choosing the Approach. Which procedure works best? It all depends. No one method proves most effective for every concept and for all students all the time. In deciding what to do when, you will find it helps to keep in mind exactly what you intend students to *do* with the concepts. Are they merely to provide a definition of a new concept? Give relevant and irrelevant attributes? Distinguish between examples and nonexamples? Show links between a new concept and previously learned ones? Use the new concept to develop a principle? Give a novel example of the concept? Do several or all of these things?

Obviously there are many ways a student can be asked to demonstrate "learning" of a concept. But detailing exactly what sort of performance you expect will help you decide what sort of instruction to provide. For instance, guiding learners to discriminate between examples and nonexamples is easier than helping them to state the defining attributes involved in their discrimination. Yet, a clear understanding of relevant attributes appears to help in the learning of more complex, abstract concepts (Francis, 1975).

Let's assume that you want your students to do everything listed above. That will demand rigorous preparation on your part. Fortunately, Herbert Klausmeier and his colleagues at the Wisconsin Research and Development Center for Cognitive Learning have been working for years to develop general rules for teaching about concepts. Here are some resultant guidelines (Klausmeier and Allen, 1978):

Before teaching, perform a "concept analysis." This involves looking for the

"I test constantly when we're working with new concepts. I don't mean formal testing, but things like recitation or even brief discussions. The point is to let me know whether the kids are understanding the concepts. I need to know right now, not at the end of the week."

connection between the new concept and others, defining the concept, listing its relevant and some of its irrelevant attributes, locating representative examples and nonexamples, relating the concept to relevant principles, and inventing problem-solving exercises in which the concept (and related principles) must be used.

Don't teach above the kids' heads. Children on the earlier periods of cognitive development may be unable to comprehend fully the concept of *music;* for them, it may be enough to focus only on the definition and recognition of examples of music. More advanced learners might be expected to distinguish examples and nonexamples of music and mathematical aspects of music. Classes made up of students of widely diverse abilities present an ever-recurring problem. The answer: individualize as best you can.

In teaching, balance examples and nonexamples (Klausmeier and Goodwin, 1975). If examples are too similar, or if too few nonexamples are given, students will develop bizarre personal definitions of a concept. Where a student persists in a mistaken concept, the teacher must question: Does the student know the defining attributes and can he or she distinguish examples and nonexamples? One of us watched an instructor present several examples of *assimilation* in a school situation; he then defined *accommodation,* but gave no examples. On a subsequent quiz, most students could not answer a question about *assimilation* in the home. They may have thought mistakenly that the school environment was a defining attribute of *assimilation,* as no nonschool illustrations had been given. Neither could they clearly distinguish *assimilation* and *accommodation.* A

"You've got to use concrete, tangible examples with students or they won't learn the concepts. I know that most of them are capable of abstract thinking, but it's a fairly new skill for them and they prefer seeing something right in front of them. The tradeoff, of course, is that if you use only one or two concrete examples, some students will form weird concepts. Abstract examples are more difficult, but they're more generalizable."

simple compare-and-contrast routine would have provided important examples and nonexamples of both *assimilation* and *accommodation*.

How Many Examples? By now, an important question has probably occurred to you: How many examples and nonexamples should a teacher offer to get a concept across? Again, it depends. With some concepts, it is necessary only to present the defining attributes. With others, a couple of examples and nonexamples will suffice. Still others will require a lot of examples and nonexamples. The more complex the concept, the greater the number and variety of examples and nonexamples it is advisable to provide.

But remember, a concept that may seem simple to you as a teacher may not seem simple to a class. You presumably found the concept of glugs absurdly easy, but a first grader would consider it a tough one. The complexity of a concept has to be considered in terms of students' entry characteristics—their age, their stage of development, the amount of knowledge they possess. So, you will have to decide for yourself how many examples and nonexamples your subject and your particular class will need.

Pitfalls. Among the mistakes your pupils commonly will make in classifying objects, events, ideas, and people are two called *undergeneralizing* and *overgeneralizing*.

In undergeneralizing, they will dismiss an example as a nonexample. A middle-class suburban second grader, for example, may easily classify a pictured one-family dwelling like his or her own as a house, but rule out a thirty-story apartment tower in a nearby city as also being a house. The youngster fails to consider the relevant attribute that both buildings are dwellings.

In *overgeneralizing*, they mistake an irrelevant attribute for a relevant attribute. It is easy to assume that whales and dolphins exemplify the concept *fish*. They have the general shape of fish, and they live in water. But those are irrelevant attributes. Some relevant attributes of fish—cold-blooded, water-breathing—are not so obvious. But they are important to forming an accurate concept of fish and to distinguishing fish from such mammals as whales and dolphins.

The Moral. When you are teaching a concept, consider your examples carefully to make sure that irrelevant attributes will not look to your students like relevant attributes. When you yourself understand a concept, it is very easy to present confusing attributes.

Let us suppose that you and your educational psychology professors have exchanged places and that you are trying to teach them the concept of positive reinforcement for use in modifying behavior. (We discussed the theory of reinforcement in earlier chapters, you remember, and we shall get to its practical applications in Chapter 10.) If you are like most educational psychology instructors, you will define positive reinforcement as "a stimulus that increases the probability of the recurrence of the response that preceded it," or words to that effect. You will follow that definition with some examples of stimuli that will serve as reinforcers. Most of your examples are likely to resemble what people generally consider rewards—a small gift, a smile, a pat on the back, or praise that the whole class hears. Rewards may constitute reinforcers, of course, but being rewarding is not a defining attribute of a reinforcer. So, still in your role as instructor, you would do well to include among your examples of positive reinforcement some in which the stimuli are not rewards. Here is an example: a teacher sharply rebukes a student for tossing paper airplanes around the classroom during an arithmetic lesson. The student, happy to have provoked the teacher, launches even more paper airplanes. The rebuke has reinforced the behavior, but it certainly has not been a reward as we understand rewards. As instructor, you would do well also to include some nonexamples of positive reinforcement, in which the stimuli are rewarding but not reinforcing. An instance of that: a parent gives a chocolate

Pitfalls — is it possible to anticipate them?

How can examples be used for optimum effect?

bar to a youngster who has just cleaned up his room. The chocolate represents a reward. But the following week the youngster fails to clean up his room. The chocolate of the week before served as a reward, all right, but it failed to serve as a reinforcer. A defining attribute of a reinforcer is that it works; if it doesn't work, it is not a reinforcer.

Matching and Divergent Pairing. A couple of rules for selecting examples and nonexamples are suggested by Klausmeier et al. (1974):

1. *Matching,* in which the teacher presents an example and a nonexample that have the same irrelevant attributes and differ only in one relevant attribute. Let us suppose you are teaching botany and you want students to learn to identify a red oak. You show them that the red oak's relevant attributes are alternating buds, a cluster of buds at the end of each twig, and leaves edged with points. For a nonexample of the red oak, you turn to the white oak, which is very similar to the red oak and has the alternating buds, and the cluster of buds at the twigs' ends. But the white oak's leaves are rounded rather than pointed. In distinguishing between the matched trees, you point out, you dismiss the position of the buds as irrelevant attributes and concentrate on the shape of the leaves, the relevant attribute.
2. *Divergent pairing,* in which the teacher presents two examples of the same concept that differ greatly in their irrelevant attributes. Let's use the red oak example again. You may show pictures of red oaks in spring, with just budding leaves; in summer, in full growth; in autumn, with leaves turning color; and in winter, leafless. The shape of the leaf remains the relevant attribute. Whether the leaves are budding, falling, or absent is irrelevant.

"The way I present concepts depends on the type of activity, mostly. If it's straightforward factual material, lecturing, I give the concept definition, then

In helping students to distinguish between relevant and irrelevant attributes, you may not have to match and pair, for most concepts, as much as those rules imply. But with some complex concepts, matching and pairing will prove helpful, and probably essential.

Identifying Attributes. Another useful procedure suggested by Klausmeier et al. (1974) consists of presenting examples of a concept and pointing out the defining attributes. Suppose you are teaching the concept *personification*, the defining attribute of which, you say, is "giving human characteristics to animals, ideas, and inanimate objects." You offer an example: "Pussy said to the Owl: 'You elegant fowl, how charmingly sweet you sing.'" Then you point out, "In this case, the cat (an animal) has been given the ability to talk, which is a human characteristic, and the owl (another animal) has been endowed with a singing voice, which is also a human characteristic."

You may follow the same procedure for nonexamples. Here is one for personification: "The very hungry old man finally found a few slices of bread, but they were so stale that they were as hard as rocks." You could then explain, "The bread, an inanimate object—except for the yeast in it—is being compared to rocks, which are also inanimate. Personification requires that you give human characteristics to something nonhuman, but the attribute 'as hard as rocks' does not involve a human characteristic."

How should relevant attributes be emphasized?

The important point is this: defining attributes must be emphasized in discussion of a new concept. One straightforward method for focusing students' attention on them is to list the defining attributes as single words and ask students to explain each word (Klausmeier, 1978). For a sixth-grade class, the list of defining attributes for the concept *experiment* might read:

examples. If we're working at a more relaxed pace, where kids might be exploring things, then I try to give concept definitions at the end, like a summary.''

demonstration
validity
hypothesis
scientific data
observation
comparison
outcome

Students are virtually certain to digest the defining attributes if they have to *use* them, and once they have acquired a concept, they will retain it better and be able to generalize with it if they are required to employ the concept in solving relevant problems.

Practice. In Chapter 6, we pointed out that new material needs prompt rehearsal in order to move from short-term memory storage into long-term storage. Two problems often arise in this connection. One is that students may be given too many new concepts at once. Short-term storage cannot hold all of them and they interfere with each other and evaporate. The other is that teachers frequently say, "Read these pages," or "Study this list of terms for tomorrow," and trust that the students will arrange on their own to practice. Most students, of course, wait until the last moment to cram, and the outcome is the same as that of the first problem: too many concepts at once.

Is more practice better?

Teachers can ease both problems. In teaching, don't pack a lesson too full of new concepts, and do provide opportunity for practice in class. In an experiment, Anderson and Kulhavy (1972) had a group of students invent sentences that contained newly learned concepts. This group retained the concepts far better than a second group which had only repeated the concept definitions. As the type of practice is varied, student will be better able to transfer or generalize the concepts to new situations.

Feedback. When students are practicing the concept as part of their instruction, feedback — telling them when they are right and when they are wrong — facilitates their learning. It makes sense to provide feedback as soon as possible. Long delays in feedback permit interference, confusion, and even forgetfulness of the whole circumstance. You may limit feedback, of course, to "correct" or "incorrect," but feedback in which "correct" or "incorrect" is accompanied by an explanation of the relevant attribute or attributes can be particularly important in the early stages of concept mastery. With after-the-fact explanation, it becomes a lot easier for students to tell glugs from nonglugs.

Now, let's sample some elementary and high school textbooks and how they deal with concepts. Their methods sometimes diverge a bit from those we have suggested, but the intent is the same: to teach students to classify information and to recognize new examples of a concept.

We'll start with a page from a high school history text (Bartlett, Fenton, Fowler, and Mandelbaum, 1969). (See Figure 8.1.) The purpose of the text and

Figure 8.1

I. How the Historian Classifies Information

A historian who collects information from newspapers or other sources must arrange the data in his notes for his readers. Usually a historian tries to answer a particular question, for example: "What caused the Civil War?" In a book or article, he gives the evidence on which his answer is based. If he does not arrange evidence to answer a question, he can only list facts helter-skelter. No one would waste his time reading such an account. But what determines the evidence the historian takes down in his notes in the first place? Will all historians doing research on the same subject take the same notes?

Historians often select and arrange facts on the basis of categories. Suppose a historian had uncovered two facts: first, that King John signed the Magna Carta in 1215 and second, that Eli Whitney invented the cotton gin in 1793. He might classify each fact according to historical periods, placing King John in the Middle Ages and Eli Whitney in the modern period. Or, he might categorize them according to aspects of human life, classifying the Magna Carta as a political event, and the cotton gin as a contribution to economic development.

Your study of history begins with the problems of selecting and arranging data. In order to concentrate on these problems without becoming involved in a true historical subject, data have been chosen that would not usually be considered historical at all. In class, however, you will be able to examine the implications of your conclusions for the study of history.

Below you will find a list of eighteen words. You are to arrange in groups those words that seem to belong together for some reason. For example, if you had been given the words *tiger, pine tree,* and *iron ore,* you might classify them as animal, vegetable, and mineral. You can probably think of a number of additional ways to classify these three terms. Think of as many classifications of the following eighteen terms as you can. Come to class prepared to discuss your classifications.

shark	tuna	pike
turkey	condor	eagle
rabbit	ostrich	sheep
cat	lion	pheasant
grouse	black bass	collie dog
rainbow trout	elephant	barracuda

2

accompanying exercise is to show high school students that historical facts can be categorized like objects or events. The authors recommend that students study history in the same scientific way historians do: by selecting and arranging data.

As we said, you can examine an object to determine whether it possesses all the relevant attributes of a certain category. Our definition of a concept, you will remember, is a class of objects or events that have one or more characteristics in common. Certainly, historical facts are events and can be grouped into categories on the basis of their shared characteristics or attributes. The categories might be historical periods, because we tend to think of history as a chronological sequence of events. But there are other ways to view it, and the categories might be aspects of human life. As a teacher, you might pick a category such as aggression or political manipulation and ask your students to think of historical events that fit into those classifications. The point is that, as the historians in Figure 8.1 suggest, you can use a conceptual approach to teach history by the rule-eg or the eg-rule methods.

In Figure 8.2, an example from an elementary science book (Smith, Blecha, Pless, 1974), the objective is to teach the concept *solid*. The approach here is that of eg-rule. The students are shown several examples of solids. Notice how the objects vary in their irrelevant attributes. Size, shape, color, degree of hardness, texture, and other characteristics differ, following the rules of matching and divergent pairing found on pages 252–253 of this chapter. The teacher using this display could ask the students for a definition of solid, or could give one. Because the page asks also for additional examples of solids, the teacher can evaluate how well the students have learned the concept and can provide additional feedback to eliminate confusion between the relevant, or defining, attributes and the irrelevant attributes.

The next example of teaching concepts is taken from a high school English text, *Encounters* (Carlsen, Tovatt, Alm, and Carlsen, 1967). The concept *restlessness* is presented through poetry. (See Figure 8.3.) The authors first give a general description of restlessness, without listing specific, relevant attributes. The relevant characteristics of abstract concepts such as restlessness are often difficult to specify, but the more specific you can be in identifying the relevant attributes, the more successful you will be in classifying examples of the concept. (Can you give a couple of defining attributes of *restlessness?* Does the following dictionary definition help? "The inability to remain at rest; . . . perpetually agitated or in motion" [*Random House Dictionary of the English Language, Unabridged Edition,* 1966]. Would a vocabulary list help students with this concept?)

The authors follow a brief introduction with several poems, including Edna St. Vincent Millay's poem "Travel." The last stanza of "Travel" conveys the theme of restlessness, and, as the authors of the book intended, teaches the concept of restlessness. If you were teaching from this or a similar book you could employ several strategies based on the rule-eg and eg-rule approaches to teaching concepts. As with other examples, you could ask the students to

Figure 8.2

1. What are solids?

Which of these have you seen?
Are they hard or soft?
Do they keep their shape?
Are these things solids?

102 Can you add examples of solids to those pictured above?
What things are best known by their shape: A ball?
A kite? A brick?

identify the relevant attributes of restlessness on the basis of the poems they read. You might compare a dictionary definition of restlessness with the definitions the students provide, and that could initiate a provocative and productive class discussion. For an assignment, you might ask the students to

Figure 8.3

RESTLESSNESS No one is ever quite content. The worlds beyond the horizons always seem to promise something strange, new, exotic. Jet streams across the sky lead the imagination. Magazine pictures of foreign countries suggest a more exciting life than one knows. Even maps lure the mind and make one discontent with his present state. Restlessness is a confusing, cloudy emotion that one is never really without.

Have you ever yearned to be free
from cares, duties, and social restrictions
and yet could not follow the restless urgings of your heart?
If you have, perhaps you too know
"what the caged bird feels."

Sympathy

I know what the caged bird feels, alas!
  When the sun is bright on the upland slopes;
When the wind stirs soft through the springing grass,
And the river flows like a stream of glass;
  When the first bird sings and the first bud opes,   5
And the faint perfume from its chalice steals—
I know what the caged bird feels!

I know why the caged bird beats his wing
  Till its blood is red on the cruel bars;
For he must fly back to his perch and cling   10
When he fain would be on the bough a-swing;
  And a pain still throbs in the old, old scars
And they pulse again with a keener sting—
I know why he beats his wing!

I know why the caged bird sings, ah me,   15
  When his wing is bruised and his bosom sore,—
When he beats his bars and he would be free;
  It is not a carol of joy or glee,
But a prayer that he sends from his heart's deep core,
  But a plea, that upward to Heaven he flings—   20
I know why the caged bird sings!

PAUL LAURENCE DUNBAR

Restlessness begins with a sickness of the heart,
  a yearning to break with the old patterns.

Spring

I said in my heart, "I am sick of four walls and a ceiling.
I have need of the sky.
I have business with the grass.
I will up and get me away where the hawk is wheeling,
Lone and high,
And the slow clouds go by . . ."

RICHARD HOVEY

The restless heart often turns to travel
  as the best means for easing its discontent.

Travel

The railroad track is miles away,
  And the day is loud with voices speaking,
Yet there isn't a train goes by all day
  But I hear its whistle shrieking.

All night there isn't a train goes by,   5
  Though the night is still for sleep and dreaming,
But I see its cinders red on the sky,
  And hear its engine steaming.[1]

My heart is warm with the friends I made,
  And better friends I'll not be knowing,   10
Yet there isn't a train I wouldn't take,
  No matter where: it's going.

EDNA ST. VINCENT MILLAY

1. The reference is to the old coal-burning, steam-driven locomotive.

find several examples of poems that relate to the concept restlessness. To aid in evaluation, either for instructional or grading purposes, you might select several poems or passages from poems that bespeak restlessness, and others that do not, and require students to identify those which exemplify the concept.

Now look at the display in Figure 8.4 taken from an elementary level social science textbook (Senesh, 1973). The concepts *job* and *busy* have been defined for the students (in an accompanying long-playing record). The students' task is to identify the circumstances of "being busy."

Basically, the authors followed the rule-eg approach, but in this case they require the student to use the definition in order to identify the concepts exhibited in the pictures. Frequently instructors will include an intermediate step of providing examples that are identified, then following with unidentified examples, so that the students can test their knowledge. Here the students go directly from the definition, or rule, to situations that require identification and classification. The use of this approach depends, as we said earlier, on the level of the students and the difficulty of the concept. As with the other examples, the teacher can go further than the book's exercise with activities that expand on the textbook learning.

Figure 8.4

Mother Has a Job

Mother is busy all day.

Figure 8.5

Connotation

We all know what a fox is. But if a friend says to you, "You old fox!" is your friend trying to tell you that you've grown a long bushy tail? More likely, your friend doesn't mean that you are exactly like a fox, but that you have some of a fox's characteristics. Foxes are famous for their cunning in outwitting hunters. Your friend has complimented you, not told you that your tail is showing.

The connotation of a word is an extra meaning the word has gained. Connotations often come from an attitude toward something that many people share. For instance, a cat will play with a mouse before killing it. It will pretend to let the mouse go, then pounce on it again. The mouse is too small to fight back. The cat seems cruel to us, so we say that a catty person is someone who gossips about you when you're not there. Like the mouse, you can't fight back.

To tell the difference betweeen the connotations and the denotations of a word, just remember that the denotations of a word do not change. "Draw" always means (1) to sketch, (2) a gunfighter, (3) to pull out, and (4) to close, etc. The exact meaning will depend on the context in which the word is used. But the connotations of a word depend on the person using it, the situation, and other factors. Two sentences may be exactly the same, yet say different things. If your mother and father say, "Your room is cool," they are probably talking about the temperature. But if your best friend says, "Your room is cool," your friend may mean that he or she likes it very much. The word "cool" has different connotations when used by different people.

Exercise 4

These words have connotations that most people recognize. For each word write a connotation.

	word	denotation	connotation
1.	lemon	yellow fruit	_____
2.	pain	unpleasant sensation	_____
3.	chicken	fowl	_____
4.	dodo	an extinct bird	_____
5.	nut	hard-shelled fruit	_____
6.	tiger	striped jungle animal	_____
7.	dumbbell	bodybuilding weight	_____
8.	peach	a fruit	_____

A Model for Concept Teaching

Objective: Given examples and nonexamples of Concept *X*, the student will identify the examples.

Teaching Procedure:

1. Present the concept label and the concept's defining attributes.
2. Present positive examples of the concept, emphasizing the defining attributes.
3. Present negative examples of the concept which help distinguish defining attributes from irrelevant attributes.
4. Present positive and negative examples of the concept. Ask the student to identify the positive examples. Then ask why the negative examples are not examples of the concept.
5. Pose realistic problems to give students opportunity to apply the concept.
6. Encourage active, overt practice with new concepts.
7. Give feedback at all points where students actively participate. ∎

The last example is from a junior high literature text (Weiss et al., 1977). This is an exercise designed to teach two concepts about meaning: *denotation* and *connotation* (denotation has already been discussed). The authors begin with an example, give the rule, and then give examples that contrast the two concepts. Finally, the student is asked to complete the remaining examples. This is a variation on the eg-rule procedure. Note that only one example begins the sequence, so students consider a single brief episode before reading the rule. (See Figure 8.5.)

These five examples have shown you ways that concepts are taught in student textbooks that you may use. We hope also that they helped to reinforce some of the things that we have presented in the chapter.

Summary

Concepts constitute groupings of objects, events, ideas, or people that share one or more major *attributes* that set them apart. Formation of concepts reduces the complexities of life because it involves classification of external stimuli that otherwise would overwhelm us. The relationship between concepts establishes principles, which permit problem-solving.

Instruction in the formation and recognition of concepts simplifies learning and teaching. Three steps are important in teaching about concepts: (1) definition of the *relevant attributes;* (2) provision of *examples* and *nonexamples* of the concept; (3) *feedback* to the students, that is, telling them whether they are right or wrong.

"I usually use word lists . . . terms related to important ideas. The kids look up the definitions of each word, use the word in a sentence, and hand them in. They grunt and groan when I pass out the word lists, but you should see their faces later when they all—every one of them—score well on a quiz. They complain because it's the thing to do at that age. I ignore it as long as they get their work done."

x

262

Whether the examples are presented before or after the attributes depends on circumstances. When the examples are given first, the technique is known as *eg-rule*; when the examples are offered after the attributes, the technique is called *rule-eg*. Because students' recognition of a concept is related to how well they know the concept's defining attributes, many teachers prefer to use rule-eg. The number of examples the teacher should present varies with the difficulty of the concept; the harder the concept is to acquire, the more examples it is advisable to give.

Students often encounter difficulties with concepts because they tend to *undergeneralize* and to *overgeneralize*. In undergeneralizing, they fail to recognize a relevant attribute; in overgeneralizing, they mistake an irrelevant attribute for a relevant one. Teachers may overcome such errors by (1) *matching*, in which the teacher presents an example and a nonexample that have the same *irrelevant* attributes and differ only in one relevant attribute; (2) *divergent pairing*, in which the teacher presents two examples of the same concept that differ greatly in their irrelevant attributes.

Another useful procedure consists of presenting examples of a concept and stressing its *defining* attributes, coupled with the offering of nonexamples and explaining why they are nonexamples.

Although feedback to students may consist merely of "correct" or "incorrect," feedback accompanied by explanation usually proves more helpful, especially in the early stages of instruction.

Chapter Study Guide

CHAPTER REVIEW

1. A concept is approximately the same thing as a

    a. theorem.
    b. principle.
    c. hypothesis.
    d. set.

2. Relevant and irrelevant attributes often reflect

    a. a difficult concept.
    b. the momentary needs of the person forming the concept.
    c. a fuzzy conception.
    d. the difference between rule-eg and eg-rule.

3. Concepts eliminate the need for

    a. forming hypotheses.
    b. thinking.
    c. abstract ideas.
    d. learning related things over and over.

4. Children who do not form concepts at low levels of thought

    a. will have difficulty forming concepts at higher levels.

    b. should be taught concepts by the rule-eg method.

    c. should be given extra reinforcement.

    d. have been taught improperly.

5. The more complex a concept, the more helpful it is to

    a. use the eg-rule approach.

    b. give numerous positive instances.

    c. state the defining attributes first.

    d. give numerous negative instances first.

6. If a child fails to recognize that a whale is a mammal after the concept of *mammal* has been taught, he or she is

    a. overgeneralizing.

    b. undergeneralizing.

    c. a slow learner.

    d. failing to recognize a gestalt.

7. _____ express relationships between concepts.

8. In order to fit a concept, a person, thing, or event must possess the _____ attributes.

9. When teaching a concept, consider your examples carefully to make sure that irrelevant attributes will not look like _____ attributes.

10. If a white kitten and a black panther are both given as examples of the concept *cat*, that is called _____ pairing.

11. In teaching concepts, long delays in _____ permit interference, confusion, and forgetfulness.

12. In teaching the concept of *dangling participle*, an English teacher first gives several examples, then asks students what the examples have in common. This approach sounds like the _____ method of teaching concepts.

13. Teaching many concepts at once will promote _____.

FOR FURTHER THOUGHT

1. Comment on the effectiveness of the teaching of the concept of *solids*, as illustrated in the page from the elementary textbook (page 257). The technique used is the eg-rule. Are any nonexamples shown? How well are the irrelevant attributes taught? the defining attributes? (Is it potentially confusing to ask the question about hardness and softness within the context of this lesson as designed? Why or why not?)

2. Although the authors refrain from recommending any particular presentation of concepts, their examples tend to indicate that the rule-eg (deductive) approach usually is more reliable than the eg-rule (inductive or discovery) approach. Which approach would seem to you more involving or stimulating to the learner? Which would probably promote more independent learning? Which would be more useful in original research? Is there any reason to believe that the suitability of the approach may depend at least in part on the age or ability of the learner?

3. Many basic concepts are learned by children experientially before they arrive at school. For example, by moving they intuit, *through awareness of their own bodies*, the meaning of concepts such as inertia, gravity, balance, momentum, stress, and torque. Similarly, practice in the arts can teach experientially such concepts as similarity, contrast, proportion, and rhythm. As an experiment, when you are alone, try any free and large-scale movements, keeping tuned to the kinesthetic sensations of your body. Or try some random doodling or drumming, with your fingers or a stick. What concepts might be taught from scratch in these ways? How could you capitalize on children's natural pleasure in such activities to help reinforce concepts being developed in more academic contexts?

4. Make some notes for teaching a particular concept at a particular level. Take into account the entry characteristics of your (hypothetical?) audience and the nature of the concept itself. Decide on a method of presentation: oral, written, audiovisual, an activity, or some combination of these. Keep in mind the suggestions provided by the authors for presenting examples. If possible, try out your model on a live group of learners.

IMPORTANT TERMS

concept	eg-rule
principle	concept analysis
concept attribute	undergeneralize
defining attribute	overgeneralize
irrelevant attribute	example matching
concept example	divergent pairing
concept nonexample	overt practice
rule-eg	

SUGGESTED READINGS

ELLIS, H. C. *Fundamentals of human learning and cognition.* Dubuque, Iowa: Wm. C. Brown, 1972. While providing a comprehensive background for cognitive issues, Ellis keeps classroom applications flowing throughout this readable text.

KLAUSMEIER, H. J. Instructional design and the teaching of concepts. In Levin, J. R., and Allen, V. L. (eds.), *Cognitive learning in children.* New York: Academic Press, 1976, pp. 191–217. Klausmeier, widely known for his research in concept formation, lays out a clear, step-by-step model for teaching concepts in the classroom.

KLAUSMEIER, H. J., and ALLEN, P. S. *Cognitive development of children and youth: A longitudinal study.* New York: Academic Press, 1978. Detailed description of research and emerging theory of the building blocks of thought, concepts. Notable for its comprehensiveness—covering children in grades one through twelve—the research provides clear instructional tips.

KOLESNIK, W. B. *Learning: Educational applications.* Boston: Allyn & Bacon, 1976. Although only a portion of this introductory book is about cognitive learning, the emphasis is clearly on helping a teacher understand the practical applications of the theories.

LEVIN, J. R. What have we learned about maximizing what children learn? In Levin, J. R., and Allen, V. L. (eds.), *Cognitive learning in children.* New York: Academic

Press, 1976, pp. 105–134. Summarizes relevant research on the use of visual imagery—pictures—in teaching cognitive skills.

SMITH, F. *Comprehension and learning: A conceptual framework for teachers.* New York: Holt, Rinehart and Winston, 1975. Although this entire book is a good resource, two chapters in particular are of relevance: Chapter 5—Meaningfulness and Memorization—discusses strategies for teaching concepts and verbal material. Chapter 8—Instruction and Instructors—provides a more general discussion about teaching within a cognitive framework.

ANSWER KEY

1. d; 2. b; 3. d; 4. a; 5. c; 6. b; 7. Principles; 8. defining *or* relevant; 9. relevant *or* defining; 10. divergent; 11. feedback; 12. eg-rule; 13. interference *or* forgetting

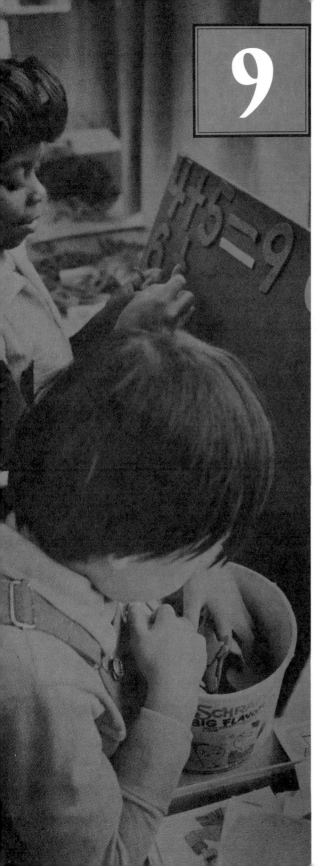

9

Problem-Solving and Creative Behavior

You have just solved a problem, albeit a minute one. You opened this textbook to this page, which is your next required reading. You may have solved your problem in any one of a number of ways. You may have looked for the page's number in the list of chapter headings at the front of the book. You may have riffled the pages until you came to this one. You may even have foreseen the problem and left a bookmark in place or have turned down the corner of the page, when you last put the book down.

All of our days, from birth to decrepitude, human beings and other animals confront problems, small or great. Learning to solve them is a major purpose of education, and solving them has been described as the highest level of intellectual activity. Concepts, about which you read in the preceding chapter, form an essential element in that activity. But if human beings restricted themselves only to solving the problems that confront them, we would not be writing these words, you would not be reading them, and all of us would still be living in African trees. For human progress—if that is the right word— depends not only on solving self-evident problems but on detecting problems that are not self-evident and on thinking creatively to solve them. Anyone over the age of six knows that if a living room lamp goes dark, the solution to the problem is to put in a new light bulb. One does not have to be much older than that to realize that if all the living room lamps go out, the solution is to install a new fuse. But inventing the system of lighting by electricity represented recognition of a problem that was not self-evident, and the application to it of creative thinking. This chapter will survey what psychologists believe they know about solving problems, self-evident or not, and creative thinking.

What is a problem?   For the record, a *problem* consists of a situation requiring a solution in

"Well, now, some of the kids in this class want to become vets. To become a veterinarian is extremely difficult. It's almost harder to become a vet than it is a doctor. So I keep pushing them—you know, like how are they going to handle this gerbil? She's diabetic and pregnant. Are they going to save her, or her babies? I want them to save both. OK, now—how? I try to get them to think about it as an

which one does not have a ready, immediate answer. (That definition might *seem* to exclude a blown-out light bulb from the category of problems, but the only ready, immediate answer would be to flick the switch to try the bulb again.) Some psychologists would add to the definition "and in which the person or animal involved is motivated to find a solution." In short, if a solution is not demanded, no problem exists.

In addition to providing an answer, what does problem-solving do?

Instructional psychologist Robert Gagné (1977) takes the definition of problem-solving further. He notes that solution of one problem promotes the learning of a strategy for tackling similar problems. This idea can be linked to Robert Sternberg's (1979) information-processing view of intelligence, discussed in Chapter 3. You will recall that the *metacomponent* level of intelligence involves the selection or invention of problem-solving strategies. The *component* level refers to the application of the strategies. The learning that results from successful problem-solving should improve both the metacomponents and the components, and thus intelligence itself.

How Do We Solve Problems?

The all-important question, of course, concerns how we solve problems. Is problem-solving a process of trial and error? Or does it involve sudden insight, in which we put two and two together? For teachers, some additional questions arise:

When students solve a problem, do they remember what they have learned better than if they had been *given* the solution?

original problem—forget what's been done before. Think of as many different approaches to the problem first—no matter how crazy. Then we talk it through. Some of these kids are better at it than others. Some of them come up with zany stuff too—but I'll tell you, toward the end of the year some of these kids are starting to come up with really good ideas."

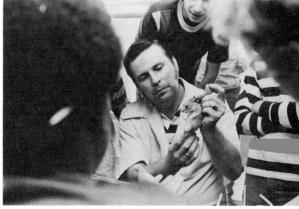

When information is essential to the solution of a problem, do students acquire the information more eagerly than they would if there were no problem?

Why are some students—or people generally—more creative than others in solving problems?

If creativity is unevenly distributed among us, can it be instilled by training, as skills in math or automobile maintenance or carpentry can be taught?

Behaviorist and cognitivist psychologists answer differently.

THE BEHAVIORIST VIEW

E. L. Thorndike, whom you have met before in this book, held that problem-solving was essentially a process of trial and error. He based his belief on the behavior of the hungry cats that he placed in boxes, with food in full view but out of reach. At first, the cats made only unsystematic efforts to escape the boxes. They pawed, they scratched, they attempted to squeeze through openings too small even for skinny cats. Finally, by accident, they yanked a rope that opened a door in the box. Each time Thorndike put the cats back in the boxes, they took less time to get around to yanking the rope. So, Thorndike concluded, his cats learned the solutions by trial and error: no insight was involved.

Skinner offers another behaviorist explanation: "A person has a problem when some condition will be reinforcing but he lacks a response that will produce it. He will solve the problem when he emits such a response" (1974, p. 111). And how does he emit the response? By changing the environment, which provides the stimuli that control behavior.

How does the habit-family hierarchy operate?

A comprehensive theory of learning that relates to problem-solving was developed by Clark Hull, an earlier behaviorist. One of Hull's principles was what he called the *habit-family hierarchy*. For any given drive or need, Hull believed, every individual has a behavior *repertoire* of possible responses. For example, as this section is being written, the light in the room goes out. Besides flicking the switch, replacing the bulb, and checking the fuse box, I could telephone the power company, sit in darkness and wait to see if the bulb lights again, rig up a flashlight pointed toward the typewriter, or go and buy a gasoline-powered generator. There are, then, a whole family of possible responses. But in Hull's system, the responses are not of equal strength, to be exercised at random. They are arranged in a hierarchy, with the one at the top most likely to occur, and the one at the bottom least likely. What fixes their order? The response at the top is the response that has provided the greatest reinforcement in encounters with similar problems. In this case, replacement of the light bulb has the greatest probability of success.

The relationship of the habit-family hierarchy to problem-solving is this: When you have a problem, your first response will be from the top of the relevant hierarchy. But that may not solve the problem. So you work your way down the hierarchical ladder until you find a response that does solve the problem.

Hull's theory, you may already have detected, includes three important factors:

1. Stimulus and response.
2. Association, the relationship of two ideas born of experience.
3. Trial and error.

All three factors are emphasized in the various theories of problem-solving that can be categorized as behavioristic.

THE COGNITIVIST VIEW

Early cognitivist theories of problem-solving emphasized the concept of *insight*, which manifests itself in sudden, internal revelation of a solution when one looks at the problem in a new way. Gestalt psychologists, the fore-runners of present-day cognitivists, would say that a problem exists when a person's perception of the world does not provide a solution, and that to find the solution the person must reorganize his or her perceptual field. Remember Sultan, one of the chimpanzees with which the Gestalt psychologist Wolfgang Köhler did research (Chapter 6)? Sultan's problem was that he was inside the cage and the bananas were outside, beyond his reach. As Sultan perceived his world at first, the short stick that he had was useless for snagging the bananas. So he sulked a while. Then he reorganized his perceptual field. With an apparent flash of insight, he realized that the short stick could be used to pull in a longer stick that would reach the bananas.

Sultan and Archimedes—how might their insights differ?

It was a similar flash of insight, no doubt, that inspired Archimedes to run naked from his bath and race through the streets of his native Syracuse in Sicily yelling "Eureka, eureka!" ("I have found it.") "It" was the solution to the problem put to him by his friend King Hieron, who suspected that the royal crown was not pure gold, but had some silver in it. Could Archimedes determine the truth? Stepping into his bath one day and seeing the tub over-flow, Archimedes suddenly arrived at the answer. If he put the crown, and equal weights of silver and gold into a tub of water separately, the rate of the water's overflow would reveal whether or not the crown was all gold. (At least, that's the way the story has come down to us. Even if it isn't true, it exemplifies insight.)

Are we sophisti-cated computers?

Problem-Solving as Information-Processing. Modern cognitive psychologists believe that it takes more than reorganization of the perceptual field to explain problem-solving, and they are interested in how people acquire, store, and transform information to arrive at answers. Programming of elec-tronic computers has shaped the recent offshoot of cognitive theory termed *information-processing*. Just as the computer manipulates sets of data, the human brain transforms information to solve problems. The brain, of course, does more. It is already active and does not need an operator to turn it on or to instruct it. It fashions new, original ways of processing information. Its plans are not so rigid as the programs of a computer. It is flexible and insightful, and it makes errors.

The simplest information explanation of problem-solving involves several logical stages. First, you perceive a problem and realize that its solution is a goal to be attained. Then you assess where you are and gauge how distant the goal is. You systematically consider possible plans for closing the distance, choose one, and try it. If the plan gets you to the goal, you have solved the problem. If the plan does not bridge the gap, you revise it or discard it and develop another plan.

Actually, unless the problem is small and easily solved, you will probably take small steps, using a series of plans and testing each for progress toward the goal. On larger problems with no ready solutions, it is rare that a single master plan will sweep you to the goal.

The information-processing theory differs, obviously, from Hull's. His theory of the habit-family hierarchy assumes, in accord with the behaviorist credo, the problem-solver's control by the environment. Testing of plans is based on the problem-solver's collection of information and the information's application to the situation. Jerome Bruner and two colleagues, who did research on how people develop and test hypotheses, report that some of the individuals they studied took a cautious approach in examining and revising their hypotheses, whereas others behaved dramatically and daringly, accepting the risks (Bruner, Goodnow, and Austin, 1956). The cautious approach has been dubbed *conservative focus*, and the bold approach *focus gambling*.

"Every day when I come in I put a general question on the board for the kids to work on during the day. It's always something they have to go to various books and do some research on in order to answer. It's strictly optional—not all the kids do it, but you'd be surprised at how many do. . . . I also put up a word for them to

BEHAVIORIST VERSUS COGNITIVIST VIEWS

Neither behaviorists nor cognitivists have all the answers to the questions that problem-solving poses. But both positions have increased our understanding. As Bourne, Ekstrand, and Dominowski have put it:

Who's right?

> [The] viewpoints are not necessarily contradictory, and a researcher need not choose one to the total exclusion of the others. However, each investigator must decide how he will think and talk about problem-solving, and the different emphases of these viewpoints probably reflect different conceptions of what is important in solving problems. It is also possible that a particular view is most advantageous for studying a certain type of problem (1971, p. 47).

Those comments were directed at researchers in psychology, but they have significance for teachers. The type of problem presented, the kind of solution required, and the purpose of both all will influence what a teacher does about problem-solving in the classroom, and how he or she does it.

OBSTACLES TO PROBLEM-SOLVING

Are you a creature of habit? Are you given to conformity? If your answers are yes you may have more trouble solving problems than people who can truly answer no. Habit and conformity work against effective problem-solving, Davis (1973) asserts, and their effects have been demonstrated in various experiments, of which one of the most famous involves *Luchins' Water-Jar Problems*. In the table that follows, there are seven such problems:

unscramble, and we have an informal "pre-breakfast quiz" that they can turn in any time during the day. I like a busy class—full of brain teasers that the kids enjoy."

Capacity of empty jars

Problem	A	B	C	Required capacity
1	21	127	3	100
2	14	163	25	99
3	18	43	10	15
4	9	42	6	21
5	20	59	4	31
6	23	49	3	20
7	15	39	3	18

In each of the seven problems, you have three empty jars of differing capacity. How would you use them to measure out the amount of water under *required capacity* in the last column? Don't read on until you have written the answers.

You have the answers? And in every case you came up with the formula $B - A - 2C$? Too bad. Your answers are correct, of course, but you could have solved Problem 6 more simply by $A - C$ and Problem 7 by $A + C$. You took the longer route out of habit, which you formed in doing problems 1 through 5. If you did that, you have lots of company. Most people fall into the same trap, a state of fixation sometimes called *response set*. In that situation, an individual responds to all similar problems in the same way, grouping them as a set. Normally, that's good, as the discussion of concepts in Chapter 8 indicated. But on occasion, as in the water jars problems, such responses prove inefficient. And sometimes they may be totally ineffective.

Are problem-solving obstacles preventable?

The Pliers and the Pendulum. In another famous demonstration (Maier, 1930), two strings hang from a ceiling and a pair of pliers lies on the floor. The problem involves tying the loose ends of the strings together, although the strings are so far apart that the subject cannot grasp both at once. The solution, as many a subject quickly perceives, is to tie a weight to one string and swing it, pendulum fashion, so that it comes within reach. But because of the apparent absence of a weight, few people actually execute the solution. Most fail to realize that the pliers can serve as the weight: they are too used to thinking of pliers only in terms of their primary purpose. This phenomenon, called *functional fixedness*, is an aspect of conformity: it keeps us from realizing that objects may serve other uses than their conventional ones and that there's more than one way to skin a cat. (Nikita Khrushchev may have been suffering from bad manners, but he certainly was not suffering from functional fixedness when, in one of the more famous episodes of modern history, he banged the top of a United Nations desk with the heel of his shoe to express the Soviet Union's disapproval. A more inhibited statesman, or a more conforming one, would have borrowed a gavel or remained quiet—and gone unnoticed.)

For adeptness in solving problems, then, it is essential to break the bonds of habit and conformity, and to look at situations in new and different lights.

IMPROVING PROBLEM-SOLVING

Some people, obviously, are better at solving problems than are other people. (If you demand evidence, try the water-jars and strings-and-pliers challenges on your friends.) Problems of one kind or another beset everyone every day and are tackled with varying degrees of skill, and in varying ways. Sometimes we refuse to recognize them as problems. Sometimes we recognize them and just hope they will go away. Sometimes we evade them and then claim we have solved them. Sometimes we dump them on other people to solve. And sometimes we tackle them head-on.

For example, a husband and wife, both of whom have jobs, take turns at shopping on Saturday. Almost incredibly, on successive weekends, each of them misplaced the automobile keys at the supermarket. The husband, to whom it happened first, retraced his steps from checkout counter to each aisle he had walked, searching shelves and scanning the floor. Unsuccessful, he asked the store manager to announce his plight over the loudspeaker, on the chance that someone had found the keys. Still no keys. Reasoning then that the keys almost certainly had to be outside the supermarket, he searched the parking lot and then the area around and under the car. No luck. Hmmmm . . . One possibility remained, though it was an unlikely one. He emptied the bags of groceries onto the floor of the car's trunk. The keys were in the third bag, where he had dropped them unknowingly while paying at the checkout counter. When his wife lost her keys the following week, she solved her problem differently. She phoned her husband to bring the other set. (The lost keys, by the way, were later found under the driver's seat.)

Another example, also about keys: The news editor of an evening newspaper arrived at the office at 6 A.M. to find the small night staff in a tizzy. Half an hour earlier, the door to the teletype room had slammed shut and locked, and the keys to it were inside. The teletypes were spewing out news for the paper's first edition, which was due to go to press in an hour, but the staff could not get to the dispatches. They awaited the news editor's permission to break the door's glass window. The editor shook his head. "Give me your hammer and screwdriver," he told the teletypes' attendant, who kept the tools in his apron. With a couple of taps by hammer and screwdriver, the editor lifted the pins in the door's hinges and the door came loose. (Cheers.)

Because there are different ways of approaching problems, and because some people prove better than others at reaching solutions, many educational psychologists believe that students would benefit by training and experience in problem-solving.

Bloom's Problem. Benjamin Bloom, whom you met in chapters 1 and 7, has argued that most research on problem-solving has improperly stressed the solution instead of the mental processes leading to the outcome (Bloom and Broder, 1950). If research can discover a successful problem-solving style, then perhaps that style can be taught to others. Of course, one must know how problems are solved before devising a training program.

Following the style of developmentalist Jean Piaget, Bloom asked college students to "think aloud" as they solved written problems. When the transcripts of successful and unsuccessful solvers were compared, several important differences emerged:

What distinguishes good and poor problem solvers?

1. Poor students had trouble at the very beginning of a problem. Sometimes they impulsively skipped over directions. Or they read and immediately ignored an instruction.
2. Although they seemed to have just as large a storehouse of information in their heads, poor students were often unable to use relevant knowledge to solve their problems.
3. Good students would construct and logically test hypotheses, whereas poor students took a helter-skelter approach, often choosing a solution intuitively, or giving up if none came to mind.
4. Poor students had a negative attitude toward problem-solving. They believed that reasoning was not important in solving problems, and that "you either know the solution or you don't." Predictably, such students had little confidence in their own problem-solving ability.

On the basis of the strategies used by successful students, Bloom developed a program to enhance problem-solving skills. College students carefully examined their own strategies, compared them with a successful, written-out one, and noted differences in the methods. Over weeks, students gradually improved by thinking aloud through their problems and by attempting to imitate successful strategies.

Discovery Learning. A more common method meant to develop problem-solving skills is called *discovery learning*, which means helping students themselves find a solution, rather than handing it to them. Although placing more responsibility on the students would seem to make teaching easier, the discovery method actually requires a good deal of planning and guidance. On the route to discovery, some students need continual attention and some may require considerable steering, whereas others may zip along on their own. The instructional rules for discovery learning are few but important:

1. Students must have previously learned the concepts and principles required for the solution of the problem.
2. The teacher must ensure that students understand the nature of the problem and the objective of the activity. The solution must be recognizable when it is discovered.
3. Prompts and cues may be provided to help students recall requisite concepts and principles.

"When I started teaching, I was really keen on pure discovery learning . . . you know, set them off with a problem and let them wander until they find some solution. What a mess! Only a couple kids would be able to work through the problems. Some would come to wrong solutions and it would break their hearts. Today we still do lots of discovery work, but there's much more structure and guidance."

If teaching for discovery takes all this forethought, is it worth it? Advocates of discovery learning cite these advantages:

1. *Students learn to learn.* Everyone needs to know certain basic facts, which should be taught. But human knowledge burgeons so fast that many supposed facts are outdated even before a student leaves school, so teachers and students have wasted time. Besides, a teaching program that just stuffs students with information fosters the idea in them that by graduation time they know all they need to know and can stop learning. But learning should go on all of one's life. So the greatest service the school can perform is to prepare young people for lives filled with learning, and exposing them to the discovery method is among the best ways to do it.

What is the case for discovery learning?

2. *Students become better motivated.* Many people enjoy puzzles, as the popularity of crossword puzzles, Scrabble, and hundreds of other brain-teasers attests. So students find the unraveling of a problem's components and the reweaving of a solution can be far more interesting than traditional ways of learning. Motivation is born of interest.

3. *Students remember and transfer more.* Because they are interested, students retain more of the information they acquire on their own than they do of force-fed data from the teacher. If metacomponents of intelligence are strengthened through discovery, then the learner can generalize new strategies to a whole class of related problems.

4. *Students become active rather than passive.* Students *seek* the information they think will solve a problem, rather than wait for the teacher to provide it. In doing so, they learn how to acquire knowledge and how to judge the usefulness and relevance of facts—necessary elements in learning to learn.

The Other Side of the Coin. A somewhat different view of discovery learning is that of David P. Ausubel, whom you met in Chapter 6. Ausubel, you recall, has a theory of *meaningful verbal learning*, and he distinguishes between *rote learning* and meaningful learning. Rote learning occurs when what you learn has no significance to you, even though you understand the individual words. Meaningful learning takes place when you can connect new information with what you already know.

Here is an example of the distinction between rote and meaningful: Clark Hull, the behaviorist mentioned earlier in this chapter, labeled a certain phenomenon *reactive inhibition*. He expounded on it like this: "The evocation of any reaction generates reactive inhibition. Reactive inhibition is spontaneously dissipated in time" (1943, p. 300). If your educational psychology professor warned you to be prepared to explain reactive inhibition on the next test, you probably would memorize Hull's prose, but it is unlikely that you would know what Hull meant. That, in Ausubel's view, represents rote learning. But suppose your professor said: "Reactive inhibition is somewhat like fatigue. If you perform a task for a while, fatigue sets in. But if you take a break and rest, fatigue dissipates." Your professor's explanation would provide a foundation or cognitive structure to which you could attach reactive inhibition, and the concept would become meaningful.

To Ausubel and other cognitive psychologists, the important aspect of learning is: How readily can the new information be attached to the existing cognitive structure? The way the knowledge is acquired is of much less significance; i.e., information and knowledge are not necessarily more or less meaningful because they came from discovery or from a teacher's lecture. As Ausubel puts it, the issue is

> not whether learning by discovery enhances learning, retention, and transferability, but whether: (1) it does so *sufficiently*, for learners who are capable of learning concepts and principles meaningfully *without* it, to warrant the vastly increased expenditure of time it requires; and (2) in view of this time-cost consideration, the discovery method is a feasible technique for transmitting the substantive content of an intellectual or scientific discipline to cognitively mature students who have already mastered its rudiments and basic vocabulary (Ausubel, Novak, and Hanesian, 1978, p. 529).

In fairness, it must be said that discovery learning methods, as well as Bloom's training program, focus on fairly restricted problems. As Ausubel and his colleagues point out, there is little research evidence that a training program will improve the solution of real-life problems, or that the skills will transfer to problems of a different sort. But there may be times and circumstances when the discovery learning approach is not only acceptable but advisable.

When To Use Discovery. The discovery learning technique may prove appropriate, Ausubel indicates, when you are introducing new and difficult concepts to pupils who are in the concrete operations stage or formal operations stage of cognitive development (Chapter 2). Such children may lack the cognitive structure that would enable them to grasp the concept, or rule, you want to teach them. So you provide the structure by giving them examples of the concept, and then let them discover, or attempt to discover, the rule. In such instances, the discovery method may work better than explanation by the teacher. The method is useful also in:

When is the discovery method effective?

1. Determining whether or not students have learned something you have taught. For example: You want to know how well a student understands a certain concept. You give the student examples and nonexamples and ask him or her to discover the examples.
2. Teaching problem-solving techniques. For example: You present a problem and instruct the students to apply discovery by visualizing the problem in a different way. The problem initially might be to suggest methods of building a better mousetrap. Looking at it in a different way, students might discover that the real problem was to banish mice, and come up with varied proposals for doing so.
3. Engendering facility in using the scientific method. Here the discovery would involve the teacher's description of a situation. The students then would be expected to define the problem they saw, form hypotheses, collect data, and draw conclusions.

Problem-Finding and Creativity

In school or out, most of the problems we confront daily are not of our own contriving. They are *presented* to us. Such problems are often sharply defined and easily recognizable. Your room is too cold. You have a chemistry examination next Wednesday. You have run out of cash and may not be able to get home for the holidays. The solutions to such problems also are sharply defined and easily recognizable: they lie at the end of straightforward paths. For the cold room, you put on a sweater. For the chemistry examination, you read your textbook and try to decipher your notes. For cash to get home, you write to Dad. A presented problem may be as simple as calculating the area of a rectangle or as complex as bridging the Hudson River at its widest point, but the problem and the goal always remain clear, and there is a standard way—or ways—to solve it.

Discovered problems are something else again. They are neither sharply defined nor easily recognizable—in fact, they may be as shapeless, when first discovered, as ghosts—and there is no routine, established system for dealing with them. They are not presented to us. Like beauty, they are in the eye of the beholder. But it takes a rare eye and a rare beholder: the discovered problem is one that most people do not see.

Why should we learn to discover problems?

Teaching concerns itself generally with presented problems. In any subject of study, the problems are time-tested, the answers are known, at least to the teacher, and for each problem there is one "best" solution. Don't knock it.

That is how, of course, each generation passes on to the next what is already known about the world and its creatures, including ourselves.

Discovered problems are those which someone has sought out. But why bother? Don't we have enough problems? Should teachers inspire students to look for problems and instruct them in how to find them? The answers are implicit in the words of Einstein: "The formulation of a problem is often more essential than its solution, which may be merely a matter of mathematical or experimental skill. To raise new questions, new possibilities, to regard old problems from a new angle, requires creative imagination and marks real advance in science" (Einstein and Infeld, 1938, p. 92). In his dictum, Einstein confined himself to science, but his concept applies to virtually everything in which we engage, from architecture to zoology. Railroad trains, automobiles, airplanes, printing, penicillin, jazz, modern dance, credit cards, hybrid corn and "miracle" rice, educational psychology—among hundreds of examples that may occur to you—derive from discovered problems. So, in fact, did the wheel.

Undiscovered problems, on the other hand, prove costly and even tragic. Many square miles of the Atlantic not far from New York Harbor are devoid of life because no one discovered in time the danger of dumping sludge—treated sewage—in the sea. The Sahara Desert marches steadily north, turning fertile land to sand, because no one saw the danger in allowing nomads' goats to devour all vegetation. Hundreds of square miles of Central Russia have become uninhabitable and dangerous even to travel through, Soviet scientists in exile report, because no one saw the danger of explosion from buried atomic waste (Tumerman and Medvedev, 1976). The last passenger pigeon, whose billions of kin used to darken America's skies in annual migrations, died in 1914 because no one had seen the problem in unrestricted shooting. So it seems to make good sense to teach students how to discover problems.

THE LITTLE-TILLED FIELD

Among the least studied areas in all of psychology is that of problem-finding. A good many books and hundreds of articles consider problem-*solving*. Few deal with problem-*finding*. But the research of Getzels and Csikszentmihalyi (1975) suggests some approaches that warrant experimentation. In one study, the researchers observed thirty-one art students at the Art Institute of Chicago. They asked the students, one at a time, to draw a still-life using any or all of thirty objects the researchers supplied. Some of the students chose only two of the objects, some as many as nineteen. Some just looked at their chosen objects, some smelled them, bit them, tossed them in the air, and rolled them in their hands. Many of the artists chose the same objects—a leather-bound book, a bunch of grapes, a white wooden ball. Others chose objects that hardly anyone else bothered with. The researchers' presumption was that the more objects an artist used, the more he examined their characteristics, and the more uncommon they were, the more original the final work.

The presumption was confirmed by a jury of art experts. Seven years later, the researchers checked up on the thirty-one students. Fifteen had abandoned art, seven remained marginally involved, and nine had achieved some eminence: the work of one of the nine had been bought by a great museum. The success of the nine reflected their sensitivity to numerous stimuli (the greater number of objects they chose to draw), to the texture and characteristics of the stimuli, and to the uncommonness of the stimuli. In short, they had discovered problems instead of solving presented problems.

Hints for Teachers. Most of your students probably will not become artists. But the results of the research suggest that, to encourage problem-finding in the classroom, it might be useful to: (1) encourage youngsters to explore their environment more carefully; (2) develop a sensitivity to a youngster's momentary curiosity; (3) include in the classroom environment stimuli that are unique, original, or slightly disturbing.

Much of the school environment, of course, already seems designed to increase youngsters' awareness, but that awareness usually relates to what already is known. That is why sensitivity to curiosity becomes important. When a student poses a question or a problem that sounds irrelevant or peripheral, we might ponder the question or problem instead of reminding the student of the business at hand. But teachers cannot afford to accommodate every whimsical idea that pops into youngsters' heads, so a teacher may have to walk a tightrope between squelching curiosity and maintaining sequence and structure in the classroom. The introduction of provocative stimuli also is a bit tricky. Because students, like other people, differ so greatly, stimuli that appear original and unique to some of your pupils will just evoke yawns from others. What will slightly disturb some may overwhelm others. The solution lies in variety: when you introduce discordant stimuli, try to offer something for everyone.

Can curiosity be cultivated?

Finding problems, as Einstein said, may be more important than solving them. For the teacher, having students find problems can prove a good way to give students experience in problem-solving. One approach to this involves asking students to identify problems and then to solve them. But it is essential to point out to them that how the problem is stated or defined will determine how it is answered: the narrower the definition, the narrower the solution. For example, if the problem is put as "What can police do to reduce violent crime in big cities?" the answer might be "Put more people on patrol." But if the question is asked as "What can society do to reduce violent crimes in big cities?" the answers might encompass jobs for the jobless, elimination of slums, longer sentences for offenders, and the like.

Problem-finding is probably related to question-asking. Frequently, students are given a fact or an episode to practice and retain until they are tested on it. Because the new information may have little meaning other than being related to a test and a grade, students may partition it off in their heads, not even trying to relate it to information already stored there. What need is there to inquire further about an episode? In fact, questioning students may be punished by goal-directed teachers who want to avoid being sidetracked. If the educational environment will not nurture question-asking, then students cannot be expected to know that questions will further their understanding, or even whether questions *should* be asked.

A Lesson for the Professor

Divergent thinking is exemplified in the following account by Dr. Alexander Calandra of Washington University:

Some time ago I received a call from a colleague who asked if I would referee the grading of an examination question. He was about to give the student a zero for his answer to a physics question, while the student claimed he should receive a perfect score and would do so if the system were not set up against the student.

The question was "Show how it is possible to determine the height of a tall building with the aid of a barometer." The student's answer was: "Take the barometer to the top of the building, attach a long rope to it, lower it to the street and then bring it up, measuring the length of the rope. The length of the rope is the height of the building."

Now this is a very interesting answer, but should the student get credit for it? I pointed out that the student really had a strong case for full credit, since he had answered completely and correctly. On the other hand, if full credit were given, it could contribute to a high grade, which is supposed to certify that the student knows some physics, but the answer did not confirm this. I suggested that the student have another try at answering the question. I was not surprised that my colleague agreed, but I was surprised that the student did.

I gave the student six minutes, with the warning that the answer should show some knowledge of physics. At the end of five minutes he had not written anything. I asked if he wished to give up, but he said no, he had many answers; he was just thinking of the best one. In the next minute he dashed off his an-

swer: "Take the barometer to the top of the building and lean over the edge of the roof. Drop the barometer, timing its fall with a stopwatch. Then using the formula $S = \frac{1}{2}at$, calculate the height of the building."

At this point I asked my colleague if he would give up. He conceded and I gave the student almost full credit, but I recalled that he had said he had other answers to the problem, so I asked him what they were.

"There are many ways of getting the height of a tall building with the aid of a barometer," said the student. "For example, you could take the barometer out on a sunny day and measure the height of the barometer, the length of the shadow of the building and by the use of simple proportion determine the height of the building."

"Fine," I said, "And the others?"

"If you want a more sophisticated method you can tie the barometer to the end of a string, swing it as a pendulum, and determine the value of g at the street level and at the top of the building. From the difference between the two values of g, the height of the building can, in principle, be calculated."

"If you don't limit me to physics solutions, there are many other answers, such as saying to the superintendent of the building, 'If you will tell me the height of this building, I will give you this barometer.' "

At this point the student was asked if he really didn't know the answer. He admitted that he *did*, but that he was fed up with teachers trying to lead him to think that there was a *single* answer to every question. He suggested, and rightfully so, that "critical thinking" ought to include the notion that *divergent* answers are possible for almost any problem. ∎

PROBLEM-SOLVING AND CREATIVITY

Problem-solving and creativity are complex, little-understood processes, and any conclusions we draw from what is known are subject to cancellation without notice. Guilford, whom you encountered in Chapter 3, sees problem-solving as the result of *convergent* or *divergent production.* Convergent production, you may recall, means coming up with a *single best* answer to a problem. Divergent production involves the generation of *many* possible answers. (See the box for an example of divergent thinking.) Although single best answers may be the most common method of solving problems in American

"He just saw something in that book and had to experiment with it. I'd say he's always into something—trying it out and going back and trying it some other way. I try not to shake him loose unless I have to—like when the bell rings and the class is over. Sometimes he comes up with really clever designs—other times, absolutely zero. I don't know where he picked up his persistence, but it's really paid off.

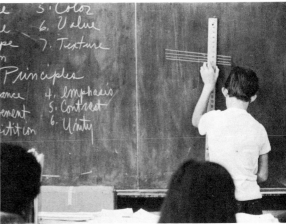

classrooms, many psychologists believe that divergent production—multiple answers—represents a valuable and largely untapped resource. Those psychologists generally equate divergent production (i.e., divergent thinking) and creativity. In the sense in which the psychologists use *creativity* here, the term refers to a special kind of problem-solving: when problems have no clear-cut answer, several alternative answers may be appropriate.

What kinds of problems call for creativity?

A high school mathematics teacher whom we know was asked by a colleague to talk to his social studies class about her problems as $1-a-year mayor of her village. She outlined this situation: The village has 100 families, spread out for almost two miles along a single road paralleling the Hudson River. To pay for police and fire protection and maintain the road and the water supply, taxes are high. Some of the land on the river side of the road is vacant, and if more houses were built there, there would be more taxpayers and taxes for each family could be cut. But the village has a zoning law requiring that any house site must be at least 10,000 square feet in area. Most of the vacant sites were not quite that size. When she took office as mayor, the teacher explained, that did not matter much because all the sites had ancient land grants giving them rights to "enjoy" the river's underwater land and anybody who wanted to build could fill in enough of the river to produce a 10,000-square-foot plot. But the village, the county, and the state all had recently passed laws forbidding the filling of the riverbank.

Could the class see the implications? Yes, people had to pay taxes on land they could not use or sell: nobody would buy a useless plot. That was unfair. Also, the village would not be able to raise more money by having more taxpayers. At the guest teacher's suggestion, the class then defined the problem: To find a way to allow more houses to be built without violating any law, or to eliminate the unfairness of having to pay taxes on useless land.

Students proposed these solutions: "Have the village buy the useless land and turn it into a park." "Have the village stop charging taxes to people who cannot build on their land." "Change the zoning law." The first two suggestions were economically impossible; the village could not afford either way out. The third was politically impractical; the villagers would not permit a change in the zoning law.

Well, the class asked, what had the mayor done? "I proposed that the underwater land covered by the old land grants be counted as part of the property, so that technically anybody who had, say, 7900 square feet of dry land would be considered to have more than the required 10,000 square feet. That way, nobody has to fill the river, and the village gets more taxpayers. I checked the proposal with the state's environmental protection agency and they said that it was the most creative solution to the problem that they had heard of."

Two weeks after her visit to the social studies class, the math teacher was still getting suggestions from students for other possible solutions.

Why is it difficult to define creativity?

Who's Creative? A creative person, as defined by some theorists, is one who makes or invents things that are useful to a society or a culture. That definition limits the field to such people as Picasso, Einstein, and Edison.

(Edison might not have agreed with the definition. He said: "Genius is 1 percent inspiration and 99 percent perspiration.") Another, more liberal point of view is that creativity is distributed in the population much the way money is. Some of us have a lot, most of us have a fair-to-middlin' amount, and the rest of us have very little. This point of view gives everyone credit for at least some creativity, and it implies that to be creative one does not have to produce something unique and valuable to society. It is enough if the product is novel to its creator. An insurance broker, for example, may find little inspiration and excitement in his work, but if he paints in his spare time, it doesn't matter that his paintings are terrible: his hobby brightens his life.

Probably we should not rigidly adopt either of the definitions, then, but rather agree that both types of creativity are worthwhile.

Product, Process, and Person. If we knew more about the processes of creativity, psychologists speculate, perhaps more of us could become much more creative. In examining those processes, psychologists have taken several different approaches. The most obvious, called the *product approach*, judges people as creative by what they produce—an original idea, a tale, a machine, a picture. But this approach leaves unexplained why and how such people are creative, so some theorists concentrate on what is called the *process approach*: these theorists try to investigate the inner workings of the mind that manifest themselves in creativity. One widely known analysis (Wallas, 1921) indicates a four-step sequence:

1. *Preparation.* In this stage, knowledge is acquired, ideas are vaguely sensed as fitting together, and the existence of a problem is recognized.
2. *Incubation.* Consciously or unconsciously, the mind mulls over the ideas and categorizes them.
3. *Illumination.* Everything suddenly falls into place, and the solution becomes apparent (as with Archimedes, and Sultan the chimp).
4. *Verification.* The solution is tested.

Should creativity be judged only by its outcome?

Fair enough. But one might go through the whole process and still come up with nothing. So the process approach alone seems too limited to describe the whole of creativity. For that reason, still other researchers prefer to study the creative *person*. Usually, they do this by seeking out a group of people known to be highly creative—outstanding scientists or architects, for example—and examining their backgrounds, development, and characteristics. From the results, obtained by tests and a variety of measurements, the investigators contrive a profile of a creative person. The trouble is that some people match the profile but demonstrate no creativity.

Obviously, no one approach provides all the answers to the puzzle of creativity, but all three contribute to our understanding.

Creativity and Intelligence. One important point about which we still lack clear understanding is the relationship, if any, between creativity and intelligence. That is, do you have to be smart to be creative? The studies that

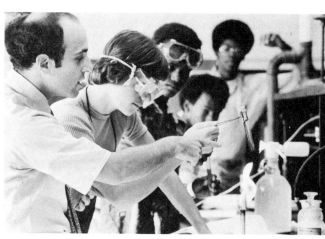
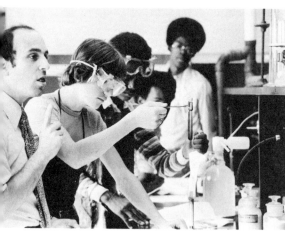
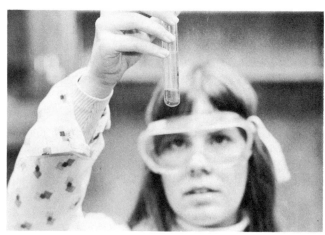

"No. No. You only have 1 plus 2, 1 plus 3, 1 plus 4, 1 plus 5, 1 plus 6. That's five different combinations. So you should only have five test tubes—you don't need the sixth. I would take this formula back here .. you mixed the same thing twice? You're going to have to record observation and conclusion. Once you dump that out you'll never remember what's what. OK, now go back and try it again. Use your notes—we went over it step by step in class, all you have to do is follow that and think. Think each step through! Think about what you're doing. Think about why you're doing it. Got that? OK, get to it!"

have attacked that problem have produced ambiguous answers. But the studies strongly suggest that creativity demands at least an average degree of intelligence, an IQ of 100 or so. Below that level, creativity seems rare or nonexistent. Above that level, creativity and intelligence do not appear to be interdependent. One can have an IQ of 150 and yet be devoid of creativity, or one can have an IQ of 150 and be tremendously creative.

Stimulating Creativity. Whether or not creativity can be acquired, or taught, also remains unclear. But several techniques that are intended to *stimulate* creativity have been applied in the classroom. One method, widely used in business and industry in recent years, is *brainstorming*. Participants are encouraged to voice any ideas that pop into their heads, no matter how bizarre the ideas may seem, and no criticism is permitted while responses emerge. Sample question: How can a group of commuters from the same suburb reduce costs and fuel consumption? Sample answer: Harness a V formation of wild geese to haul a glider. When the flow of responses wanes, then systematic evaluation of the ideas may begin.

How does brainstorming stimulate creativity?

In setting up a brainstorming session for a class of twenty-five or thirty, it probably will prove useful to have students work in groups of half a dozen. Each group may then present its zaniest—or its best—schemes to the whole class, which may discover that two or more ideas can be combined. Even when brainstorming yields no practicable suggestions, it spurs original thinking.

Another technique, devised by Osborn (1963, pp. 286–287), applies seventy-three "idea-spurring" questions to common objects such as can-openers. Here they are:

Put to other uses? New ways to use as is? Other uses if modified?

Adapt? What else is like this? What other idea does this suggest? Does past offer parallel? What could I copy? Whom could I emulate?

Modify? New twist? Change meaning, color, motion, sound, odor, form, shape? Other things?

Magnify? What to add? More time? Greater frequency? Stronger? Higher? Longer? Thicker? Extra value? Plus ingredient? Duplicate? Multiply? Exaggerate?

Minify? What to subtract? Smaller? Condensed? Miniature? Lower? Shorter? Lighter? Omit? Streamline? Split up? Understate?

Substitute? Who else instead? What else instead? Other ingredient? Other material? Other process? Other power? Other place? Other approach? Other tone of voice?

Rearrange? Interchange components? Other pattern? Other layout? Other sequence? Transpose cause and effect? Change pace? Change schedule?

Reverse? Transpose positive and negative? How about opposites? Turn it backward? Turn it upside down? Reverse roles? Change shoes? Turn tables? Turn other cheek?

Combine? How about a blend, an alloy, an assortment, an ensemble? Combine units? Combine purposes? Combine appeals? Combine ideas?

The Osborn approach, if not the specific questions, may be applied to a considerable number of human activities, from football formations to world politics. Checklists of this kind abound, and offer a good way to set pupils thinking creatively.

Two techniques that complement checklists have been proposed by Davis (1973). In the first, each attribute of an object or situation is listed and considered separately to determine how, if at all, it can be improved. In the second technique, which is an extension of the first, the object's or event's dimensions are identified, ways of varying each attribute are listed, and then all possible combinations are evaluated.

For example, you ask your students to come up with a new and better bookmark. First, they would consider a bookmark's major attribute: its use to identify a page in a book. Then they would consider the various objects suitable—a slip of paper, a piece of string or ribbon, a paper clip—and examine each in terms of size, shape, color, material, tendency to skid and get lost. The next step would involve combining the best attributes of each. A truly sharp class might come up with a two-inch-wide, six-inch-long strip of translucent red plastic with a clip at the top to hold it in place, and a sliding indicator at the side to show how far down the page the reader had gotten before closing the book. For optional equipment, the class might propose a spring that would open the book at the right place when the book is picked up. The possibilities are boundless, and your class may decide to go into production of super-bookmarks, get rich, and hire other people to finish their schooling for them.

Still another technique for stimulating creativity sets students to considering how animals, insects, and plants solve problems and whether or not the solutions might be adaptable by human beings. For example, discussion of how bees store honey in a honeycomb might suggest a more compact and efficient way to park automobiles (Arnold, 1962).

Is creativity training effective? Ausubel et al. (1978) assert that creativity training programs have not been shown to assist real-life creative problem-solving. Rather, the programs enhance conditions *associated with* creativity, such as the ability to defer critical judgment, the development of multiple possible solutions to problems, and the appreciation of ambiguity. Genuine creativity is demonstrated, Ausubel says, not when someone appreciates ambiguity, but when he or she produces something original, useful, and of high quality. Even so, if training exercises improve the conditions surrounding creative behavior, and if students enjoy them, then the likelihood increases that students will make creative contributions to society.

Measuring Creativity. Because the concept of creativity remains as yet elusive, precise measurement of it is thus far impossible. Many researchers believe, however, that creativity has four essential components, the presence of which may at least be demonstrated and observed. These components are:

1. *Fluency*, which is the capacity to come up with ideas, possibilities, consequences, and objects in a fast and steadily flowing stream.
2. *Flexibility*, which is the ability to approach a problem from several directions, and to change approaches readily when a shift seems advisable.
3. *Originality*, which is manifested by unique or surprising proposals or responses.
4. *Elaboration*, a facility for expanding and embellishing ideas.

Several methods have been devised for detecting and measuring these components, the most widely used is a system called the *Torrance Tests of Creative Thinking*. One such test, for example, provides a student with a colored piece of paper shaped like a cocktail frankfurter. The student then is asked to place the piece of paper, which has an adhesive base, on a page of the test pamphlet, use the frankfurter shape as a basis for the most original drawing the child can contrive, and then given the drawing an apt but provocative name. A child who produced a dachshund and labelled it *Dog* would rate low but one who drew lips and teeth around the colored paper and labelled the result *Cookie Eater* would rate high.

Tests designed to measure creative behavior usually have time limits. Of course, creative problem-solving cannot be turned off and on like a faucet, and the use of timed tests has provoked much skepticism. The evidence, however, shows that reasonable time constraints are usually harmless, and sometimes even improve creativity test scores (Hattie, 1980). Other criticisms are not so easily answered.

What attempts have been made to measure creativity? Such tests have led to some success in distinguishing between people who are otherwise judged to be creative and those judged to be noncreative. But several questions about the tests linger. Do they measure *potential* or merely *present* creative functioning? Do the responses that the tests demand bear on reality or do they represent fun and games? Can the tests predict with accuracy who among the tested will make important and creative contributions to society? In short, how would Einstein have scored?

Perhaps time will provide the answers. After all, serious efforts to measure creativity by modern psychological standards began less than three decades ago. Then again, time may yield no answers. Is creativity so nebulous, so unpredictable that attempts to measure it are folly?

Creativity and Adolescents. One of the most widely shared characterisitics of adolescents is a tendency to conformity, which many psychologists agree derives from the desire to be accepted by the adolescents' peers. But creativity and conformity are less compatible than cats and dogs; *some* cats and *some* dogs do get along together, whereas the traits of the creative, such as unconventionality, self-assertiveness, and confidence in one's own judgment, are by their very nature absent in the conformist.

It would *seem*, then, useless to expect creativity in most adolescents. Some theorists suggest, in fact, that creativity begins to taper off in the third or fourth grade, and that it might happen even earlier. One example involves little Barbara, who was three when she went along with her grandparents one October day for a walk in a nearby wood. On her return to her grandparents' home, she painted a picture that she called *The Leaves Falling* and that creditably captured the autumn atmosphere. To encourage her, her grandparents had the picture framed and hung it among their works by somewhat better known artists. Three years later, Barbara accompanied some visitors on a tour of her grandparents' house, and one visitor, pointing to Barbara's masterpiece, asked, "Who did that?" Barbara said gravely, "I did. But, you know, I couldn't do that now."

Some research indicates, though, that despite the anxiety to conform, adolescents are *capable* of creativity. A program for stimulating creativity in sixth, seventh, and eighth graders has been prepared by Gary A. Davis (1971): in a pilot test, twenty-three upper-middle-class seventh-grade students produced 65 percent more ideas considered creative than did thirty-two control subjects, who had not received the training. For older adolescents, tried and tested methods still are lacking.

But program or no program, teachers of adolescents can inhibit or stimulate creativity. The teacher who insists on convergent thinking and demands the one best answer to a problem will have a class of noncreative, conforming students. The teacher who encourages divergent thinking, and who employs such techniques as attribute-listing and brainstorming, will find that even older adolescents may respond creatively.

Summary

Problems great or small confront all of us all of our days, and a major purpose of education is to teach us to cope with them. Many problems are self-evident; others are recognized only by creative minds. Psychologists disagree on how human beings go about solving problems. Thorndike saw the process as one of trial and error. Skinner explains it as a matter of response to a change in environment. Clark Hull proposed that everyone has a *repertoire* of possible responses to a problem, arranged in what he called a *habit-family hierarchy*; the first response applied is the one that has proved most reinforcing in the past. In opposition to those behaviorist views, cognitivists emphasize *insight*, a new way of looking at the immediate problem, but to insight they add information-processing, which computer programmers have tried to mimic on their machines. This approach stresses the perception, storage, and transformation of data from a problem, and the systematic testing of possible solutions. Neither behaviorists nor cognitivists have all the answers, but both contribute to understanding.

One common technique for providing students with experience in problem-solving is *discovery learning*, which lets them find things out for themselves; although it has its merits, Ausubel questions whether it generally justifies the time and cost it involves. He argues that more important than the

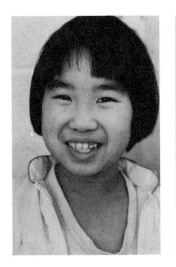   

We asked these students what problems they thought about in or out of school. Some of their answers: "Building bridges. I'd like to build a sky bridge between my house and my best friend." "I sell newspapers after school. I'd like to figure out a way to sell more." "How to keep from getting wet in the rain without a raincoat or boots or umbrella." "When we first came here all the kids made fun of us, calling us awful names and stuff, and telling us to go home. That was a big problem."

methods employed is whether learning is *meaningful*; i.e., whether new information can be connected to what the student already knows.

Although much study has been done on problem-*solving*, little has been devoted to problem-*finding*, which involves creativity. *Divergent thinking*—the suggestion of several or many possible solutions to a problem—is considered by many psychologists to require creativity.

Creativity appears to demand an IQ of at least 100, but much higher IQs are not necessarily accompanied by creativity: one may have an IQ of 150 and still lack creativity. Whether or not creativity can be taught or acquired remains unclear. But techniques intended to stimulate creativity are available for classroom use; they include *brainstorming* and Osborn's seventy-three idea-spurring questions. Creativity cannot be measured with precision, but four components that researchers consider essential to it may be detected by such methods as the *Torrance Tests of Creative Thinking*.

Chapter Study Guide

CHAPTER REVIEW

1. Behaviorist views of problem-solving tend to emphasize
   a. classical conditioning.
   b. reorganization of ideas through insight.
   c. reinforcement of trial-and-error behavior.
   d. information processing.

2. The essential idea in Hull's theory of problem-solving is the

   a. repertoire of responses.
   b. stimulus and response.
   c. hierarchy of responses.
   d. association of opposites.

3. The crucial difference between Hull's theory of problem-solving and the cognitivists' theory is that the latter stresses the learner's

   a. control over the environment.
   b. reliance on focus gambling.
   c. use of brainstorming.
   d. process approach.

4. Information processing theory likens problem-solving to

   a. inventing a new memory.
   b. computer operations.
   c. acquiring insight.
   d. the several approaches to creativity.

5. According to cognitive psychologists, more important to problem-solving than the way knowledge is acquired is whether or not

   a. the problem-solver is intelligent.
   b. insight is present.
   c. accommodation takes place.
   d. the new information can be attached to the existing cognitive structure.

6. Gestaltists believed that problem-solving depended on reorganizing one's _____ field.

7. _____ and _____ work against effective problem-solving.

8. _____ keeps us from recognizing that objects may serve other than their conventional uses.

9. According to Albert Einstein, "The _____ of a problem is often more essential than its solution."

10. Guilford and many other other psychologists see the key to creative problem-solving in _____ production.

11. Three approaches to measuring creativity are the product, _____ , and person approaches.

12. Bloom found that poor problem-solvers have a _____ attitude toward reasoning during problem-solving.

13. For discovery learning to be effective, students first must have learned the _____ required to solve the problem.

14. In a brainstorming session, evaluation of responses occurs _____ .

15. In an art show, first, second, and third place awards may be given. This illustrates the _____ approach to measuring creativity.

FOR FURTHER THOUGHT

1. Consider the pros and cons of the discovery method of learning versus verbal learning, using your own experience for evidence. By and large, has the discovery or inquiry approach tended to make you more interested in what you were learning? more capable of learning on your own? Has it improved your retention later? Would you yourself use the method in a teaching situation? In what kind of situation and for what purpose?

2. The authors suggest three ways to nurture curiosity and problem-seeking in children: encourage them to explore their environment; develop sensitivity to a child's momentary curiosity; and provide classroom stimuli that are unique, original, or slightly disturbing. Specify some concrete ways for carrying out each of these suggestions.

3. Suppose you are a researcher interested in developing a new test of creativity. How would you show that the test measures what it is supposed to?

4. Howard Gardner, brain-researcher and author of *The Arts and Human Development: A Psychological Study of the Artistic Process* (1973), suggests that the observed decline in children's creativity at about age six to seven can be attributed to the child's natural tendency to form concepts at that age and to the tendency of the schools to emphasize cognitive learning through verbal means. (All of this tends to organize the child's original percepts into society's ready-made concepts.) Exercise your own creativity by brainstorming with others for some ways in which the schools might cultivate the creative traits of fluency, flexibility, originality, and confidence in one's own judgment.

IMPORTANT TERMS

problem
information-processing
habit-family hierarchy
insight
response set
functional fixedness
discovery learning
divergent thinking
problem-finding

product approach
process approach
person approach
brainstorming
fluency
flexibility
originality
elaboration

SUGGESTED READINGS

ADAMS, J. L. *Conceptual blockbusting.* San Francisco: W. H. Freeman, 1980. Written by an engineering professor, this slim volume offers dozens of exercises in creative thinking. Although the emphasis is on personal development of creativity, most exercises could be applied to the secondary level classroom.

BARRON, F. *Creative person and creative process.* New York: Holt, Rinehart and Winston, 1969. A detailed description of Barron's work at the Institute of Personality Assessment and Research, ranging from measurement of creativity to discussion of creative processes in scientists, women, and writers.

DAVIS, G. A. *Psychology of problem solving.* New York: Basic Books, 1973. Thorough and readable review of problem-solving theory and applications. Contains many suggestions for enhancing problem-solving and creative skills.

DAVIS, G. A., and SCOTT, J. A. (eds.). *Training creative thinking.* New York: Holt, Rinehart and Winston, 1971. A compendium of training programs and ideas, all adaptable to the classroom.

FELDHUSEN, J. F., and TREFFINGER, D. J. *Creative thinking and problem solving in gifted education.* Dubuque, IA: Kendall/Hunt, 1980. This uncritical volume presents a large assortment of teaching tips for enhancing creativity. Over half of the book is devoted to resource materials: description, purpose, how to order, and so on.

MANSFIELD, R. S., BUSSE, T. V., and KREPELKA, E. J. The effectiveness of creativity training. *Review of Educational Research,* 1978, 48 (4), 517–536. Thorough and critical review of research literature devoted to commercially produced creativity training programs.

MORINE, H., and MORINE, G. *Discovery: A challenge to teachers.* Englewood Cliffs, NJ: Prentice-Hall, 1973. For practitioners with little background in the behavioral sciences, this manual describes a variety of techniques for applying discovery learning in the classroom.

OSBORN, A. F. *Applied imagination* (3rd rev. ed.). New York: Chas. Scribner's Sons, 1963. This classic book addresses imaginative talent: what it is, what it's worth, and how to develop it.

ROSNER, S., and ABT, L. E. (eds). *The creative experience.* New York: Dell Publishing Co., 1970. Fascinating interviews with twenty-three artists and scientists about their own conceptions of the creative act.

ROTHENBERG, A., and HAUSMAN, C. R. (eds.). *The creativity question.* Durham, NC: Duke University Press, 1976. Perhaps the best available book of readings on the many faces of creativity. Ranges from ancient musings to current research, with some emphasis on unusual aspects (e.g., creativity and the split brain).

STEIN, M. I. *Stimulating creativity: Individual procedures.* Vol. 1. New York: Academic Press, 1974. Excellent review of techniques and suggestions for developing creative talent.

TORRANCE, E. P. *Encouraging creativity in the classroom.* Dubuque, IA: Wm. C. Brown, 1970. A nuts-and-bolts approach to enhancing creativity, focusing on the elementary-level child.

WICKELGREN, W. A. *How to solve problems.* San Francisco: Freeman, 1974. Geared to well-defined problems in math and science, the book is filled with strategies and examples.

ANSWER KEY

1. c; 2. c; 3. a; 4. b; 5. d; 6. perceptual; 7. Habit. . .conformity; 8. Functional fixedness; 9. formulation; 10. divergent; 11. process; 12. negative *or* poor; 13. concepts or principles; 14. after responses are finished; 15. product

10

Behavioral Approaches to Instruction

Behavior modification, the subject of this chapter, sounds awesome and forbidding. Because it represents the application of the principles of behaviorism (Chapter 5), the very term *behavior modification* may evoke in you a grim mental image of schoolboys and schoolgirls pressing or pecking levers like Skinner's rats and pigeons or "spitting on cue" like Pavlov's dogs.

Advocates and practitioners of behavior modification, whose numbers have increased vastly in recent years, argue that it is not like that at all. On the contrary, they contend, behavior modification engenders self-respect, independence, and a desire to learn in students, and nurtures mutual respect among pupils and teachers. The results, its proponents hold, are that learning becomes easier and pleasanter for students, and teaching easier and pleasanter for their instructors.

Before interest in behavior modification surged in the past two decades, educators could explain students' failure quite simply. If Eddie was not catching on to his third-grade work, it was because "he just isn't very bright." If Scott was forever kicking and punching his fourth-grade classmates, it was because "he's an aggressive child." If Debbie never paid attention to her sixth-grade teacher, it was because "she has emotional problems." How did we know she had emotional problems? Because she never paid attention!

Behavior modification takes a different approach. It looks for external conditions that may be related to the youngster's behavior and attempts to modify them. And for all youngsters, whether or not they have particular problems, it seeks to create conditions conducive to learning.

The rationale of behavior modification is this: All behavior is affected by what happens *before* or *after* it. For example:

Before   You are driving too fast and you spot a police patrol car in your rearview mirror.

Behavior   You slow down.

After   Police car whizzes by to chase someone else.

What is behavior modification

There is no way, in the behaviorist view, to change behavior directly. It can be changed only by changing the conditions that precede it or follow it. What happens *before* a behavior may serve as a stimulus to prompt the behavior. What happens *after* a behavior may encourage a more frequent recurrence of the behavior, it may discourage a recurrence, or it may serve to maintain the current rate of the behavior's occurrence. For example, after the police car whizzes by you, you may resume speeding because the cop has gone on, or you may continue to drive slowly because you might have been caught.

Teachers encounter hundreds of opportunities daily to shape and arrange *before* and *after* conditions systematically; i.e., to alter the environment and thus change students' responses to the environment. "Befores" and "afters" happen whether or not a teacher plans them. So the question is not *whether* to permit their occurrence, but how much time and energy to spend in considering and directing them. Like all teaching, behavior modification is an art as well as a science. Its practice is not suited to everyone. Teachers with average or above-average organizational ability do best with it, especially if they are mildly compulsive and teachers who are "very nondirective, highly intuitive, or very existentially oriented generally" do not do well at it (Abidin, 1971, p. 38).

Beginning a Behavior Modification Program

If you determine to undertake a behavior modification program in school, you would be wise to consult the school psychologist and to prepare for careful training and planning. For a program outside school, you may require a considerable amount of self-study (see Suggested Readings), although many private behavioral consultants offer assistance for a fee. In the sections of this chapter that follow, you will find helpful guidance on how to proceed and what to expect.

TARGETING A BEHAVIOR

How is a behavior targeted?

David presents a discipline problem in your eighth-grade class. Your first step toward modifying his behavior will be to *define the problem*. It will not do simply to say that he is unruly: that can only be your subjective judgment. You are going to have to specify *observable, measurable* activities. So you target David's undesirable behavior thus: "David is out of his seat much of the time, talks to his buddies all over the room during lessons, and pays no attention to instructions."

You cannot tackle all David's sins at once. So you decide to try to keep him seated, on the logical ground that he will have to cut down on his roving conversations and therefore may listen more to you. But your goal remains vaguely stated: it is still a wish, not a deed. So, again, you become specific: "Within two weeks, David will not leave his seat without permission more than five times a day." (You know you are not going to make David a model pupil immediately or possibly ever; you just want to reduce the nuisance to manageable proportions.) You may not achieve your objective, but any progress will prove encouraging.

How does the baseline function in teaching?

To ensure that you recognize progress when you see it, establish a *baseline*, or starting point. You do it thus: Before you begin any remedial procedures, keep a record for a few days of how many times David wanders each day. Penciled checks on a memo pad will serve. The daily average will constitute your baseline, telling you what David's behavior is before you have done anything about it. Some teachers skip the baseline procedure, arguing that they will *know* when behavior has changed. But it is easy to go wrong. We know an elementary school teacher who began a behavior modification program with a student like David and for the same purpose—to reduce his movements in class. One day she reported that she was about to abandon the

"I would call this child overly independent. She comes from a very large family and attends school only once or twice a week. When she is in class, she's withdrawn and has great difficulty communicating. I try not to call attention to her—I just let her be. But whenever she comes over to me I give her everything I have. I want her to come to me. Right now I'm trying to reinforce that one thing—her effort to make contact with me—before I worry about anything else."

program because it had proven "completely ineffective." She had not drawn a baseline, but observers of her program had. When the observers compared their baseline with the student's current behavior, they found that his unnecessary movement had been reduced by 18 percent. The teacher's annoyance at the youth, it seems, had clouded her judgment of the results.

Now, with baseline fixed, how to change David's behavior? You have two alternative courses: You can tackle the undesirable behavior itself, using reinforcement and other modifying techniques described later in this chapter. Or, you can approach the problem *indirectly*, substituting what educational psychologists call an *incompatible behavior* for an undesirable behavior. In David's case, this simply means giving him something to do that he wants to do and is able to do, but that cannot be done unless he is in his seat. That is where the description *incompatible* comes from. The assigned incompatible behavior could be a crossword puzzle, the updating of class records for the teacher, or the auditing of the class bankbook, among dozens of possibilities. But it must be something that cannot be accomplished when David is roaming.

The incompatible behavior approach lends itself to at least partial elimination of a diversity of problems. For example: Suppose that Kevin, who is in junior high school and is something of a showoff, is prone to a kind of vandalism. When other students are around, he delights in leaping at the corridor ceiling to yank down the noise-reducing panels. Appointment as an assistant to the teacher's aide who keeps order in the corridor—or tries to—should replace Kevin's undesirable behavior with an incompatible behavior. He can hardly tear down the ceiling while helping to police the halls, and his urge to show off to his peers should help him take his assignment seriously.

In an actual fifth-grade application, Ayllon and Roberts (1974) focused on several seemingly uncontrollable youngsters who wandered about and disrupted other students' work. The researchers arranged to award points, later exchangeable for privileges, for correct responses in the troublesome kids' workbooks. The goof-offs increased their efforts, and their disruptive behavior simultaneously decreased.

What are the criteria for incompatible behaviors?

Incompatible behaviors have to be chosen with care, and there are two criteria for selecting them:

1. They must be truly incompatible with the undesirable behavior.
2. They must appeal to the youngsters involved and should be something that the youngsters already know how to do at least in rudimentary fashion.

TASK ANALYSIS

Any modification of behavior, whether it involves teaching a first grader to recognize the word *man* on the blackboard or improving the self-concept of a junior high school freshman, requires the setting of an objective. Task analysis makes it easier to attain the objective. You might build a log cabin in a forest or a sod house on a prairie with a very simple task analysis, but you would be foolish to try to build a modern house without a careful one. Task analysis consists simply of looking at each of a job's many steps and recognizing their essential sequence: choosing the site, deciding on the house's size and design, acquiring the materials, digging the hole, constructing the foundation, and so on. You cannot put the roof on until you have the supporting walls up.

In teaching and behavior modification, task analysis involves: *breaking down an overall subject* or behavior into its components, which can be dealt with one at a time; and *determining their essential sequence,* if any. You cannot teach multiplication and division until your pupils have mastered addition and subtraction. In a cooking class, it probably does not matter whether students learn first to bake a cake, or concoct an Irish stew. But it *is* important that they *first* know how to read a list of ingredients, how to measure them, and how to operate a stove.

Teachers have always used task analysis, of course, after a fashion. But like pioneer aviators, they often have flown by the seat of their pants. As a teacher, you are likely to find a systematic approach employing careful task analysis more effective.

What are the steps in task analysis?

Neither we nor anybody else can tell you how to undertake a specific task analysis for every situation, but we can offer some guidelines:

1. Determine your objective and write it down, stating explicitly what you want your students to achieve and how you want them to demonstrate their achievement. In behavior modification especially, be sure your objective is realistic. You cannot expect to solve all the world's—or all your

students'—problems. The more grandiose your objective, the more likely you are to fail. Teachers lack the time, energy, and resources to achieve major transformations of the school environment, and students lack the necessary attention span. So tackle one or a few small problems at at time.

2. Establish a baseline, as in targeting a behavior. From it you can measure the results. Progress will reinforce *you*. (Reinforcement is discussed below.) Lack of progress will signal a need to reconsider your approach.

3. Notice and write down what individual skills, segments of knowledge, or modifications of behavior are necessary for attaining your overall objective and how you want your students to manifest them.

4. When one skill, etc., flows from another—as multiplication and division flow from addition and subtraction—write down their sequence.

What tasks are most difficult to analyze?

Those guidelines sound easy enough to follow, don't they? But it can prove difficult to define and even more difficult to sequence some tasks. The difficulty is greatest in the affective domain. Suppose your objective is to improve Fred's self-concept. You find the following behaviors that indicate Fred does not think much of himself:

1. Poor posture: Fred slumps in his seat, as though he wants to hide, and he does not stand up straight when answering questions.

2. Self-disparagement: Fred frequently shrugs off his wrong answers and says: "I know I'm dumb" or "Okay, so I'm a dope."

3. Lack of poise: Fred never looks teachers or classmates in the eye.

4. Lack of confidence: Fred invariably reacts to new lessons by saying: "I can't do it" or "I don't know how to do it" or "Help me. I don't get it."

Undertaking a task analysis on poor Fred's behalf, how would you put his behaviors in sequence for eliminating them? Does any one behavior seem to depend on another? Not really. So you might start work on any one of Fred's less admirable characteristics. Perhaps, though, in line with the advice to keep your objective realistic, you will want to begin with Fred's posture, which may be the easiest to change.

In short, some task analyses will not indicate a sequence. In other cases, a proper sequence may be highly important. That is why we are able to offer only guidelines: successful task analysis will be up to you.

Reinforcement

In Chapter 5 you encountered the general concept of reinforcement as it applies to both classical and operant conditioning. In this section we will look at the several varieties of reinforcement and how they may serve in the classroom. The processes of reinforcement are shown in Table 10.1.

But before we go any further, we want to emphasize one point: a reinforcement is a reinforcement only when it works; i.e., when it increases or maintains a behavior as it is intended to do. The only way you can determine

Table 10.1. Behavior Change Summary

	Increase or maintain a behavior	Decrease a behavior
Add to environment	Positive reinforcement	Punishment
Remove from environment	Negative reinforcement	Extinction

whether or not you have hit on a reinforcement is to observe the effects. You may believe, for example, that patting Valerie on the back for turning in a neater-than-usual arithmetic paper will reinforce neatness in Valerie. But Valerie may dislike being touched by adults, and your intended reinforcement may seem to her a kind of punishment.

Reinforcers fall into two broad categories, positive and negative.

POSITIVE REINFORCERS

If you grant Heather fifteen minutes of free time to spend on her embroidery because her handwriting is improving so much, you are applying *positive reinforcement*. Positive reinforcement is a matter of *presenting* something to increase a behavior, and you are presenting Heather with free time to encourage her efforts to write more neatly. Positive reinforcers may be either *primary* or *conditioned*.

Primary Reinforcers. Such basic human needs as food and drink and other things that human beings find naturally rewarding are primary reinforcers. A liking for cookies or candies, for example, does not have to be learned: cookies and candies are unconditioned stimuli (USs).

An experiment described by Vernon (1972, p. 21) exemplifies the use of a primary reinforcer in teaching. The experiment involved Charlie, an almost-five-year-old in a Headstart program who, despite weeks of effort by his teacher, could not count to ten. The experimenter rigged up a board with ten small light bulbs, any number of which could be lit simultaneously. The experimenter turned on one light and Charlie said "One." The experimenter gave Charlie a piece of chocolate. After a thirty-second pause which left Charlie time to develop a craving for a second piece, the experimenter turned on two lights. You may guess the rest. Charlie made a few mistakes on the way to ten and when he did err, he received only the right answer, not the candy. But within eighteen minutes he was counting to ten and correctly identifying the number of bulbs in any group lit at random, out of numerical sequence. Having only ten bulbs to light, the experimenter on the spur of the moment cut up a sheet of colored paper into many segments and within a few minutes more Charlie was counting slips of paper up to twenty. Until the experiment, Charlie simply had seen no reason to bother to learn to count. The candy had supplied a reason.

Teachers who use primary reinforcement of that kind often encounter the objection that children should not have to be bribed to learn. The answer is that they are not being bribed, which implies an inducement to wrongdoing. They are being paid to do something worthwhile, and virtually no one will work hard for long without some kind of payment. Children who are highly motivated to learn and who *appear* to need no reinforcers almost always have received reinforcement at home. It is also often objected that rewarding a class laggard is unfair to the laggard's classmates. Evidence is clear, however, that classmates do not appear jealous when reinforcement is bestowed (Christie, 1975).

The uses of primary reinforcers such as candies and cookies, however, are limited. Primary reinforcers, because they are tangible, concrete objects, cannot be used at a high frequency for a long time. We get satiated—stuffed—too quickly. Imagine Charlie's taste for chocolate if the experiment has taken two hours and ninety-five pieces of candy. Primary reinforcers are most effective with young children and retarded children. A class of ninth graders may enjoy an occasional box of candy at their teacher's expense, but it isn't likely to transform them into little Charlies within eighteen minutes. Besides, conditioned reinforcers are cheaper and more versatile than chocolate.

Reinforcers and Social Status

Do candy and cookies and other tangible rewards prove more effective as reinforcers among poor children than among middle-class youngsters? Are middle-class children more susceptible than their less fortunate schoolmates to praise, smiles, and pats on the back? The assumption long has been that the answers are yes. But it could be wrong and it may have derived, Schultz and Sherman (1976) suggest, from the fact that behavior modification researchers have often employed tangible reinforcers among lower-class children and observed changes in behavior. Schultz and Sherman reviewed sixty-two studies that compared the effectiveness of particular reinforcers at various socioeconomic levels. They concluded that:

1. Differences among social classes in their preferences of reinforcers *cannot* be assumed;
2. Claims that the findings of such differences are consistent are unfounded and misleading (p. 39).

The safest way to determine what a child prefers as a reward is to present a wide choice. ■

How are primary
and conditioned
reinforcers dif-
ferent?

Conditioned Reinforcers. Unlike primary reinforcers, the need for which is present from birth, conditioned reinforcers consist of things we have *learned* to like or value. In the classroom, they are often represented by smiles or praise, games, a session of listening to music or stories, small gifts such as crayons, gold stars, tickets, or points that count toward higher marks, a field trip, free time for play or a class party, or just plain teacher attention!

Conditioned reinforcers presumably gain their power to influence behavior from the process of classical conditioning. A conditioned reinforcer is a once-neutral stimulus that has been paired frequently with a primary reinforcer or a potent conditioned reinforcer and thus has acquired reinforcing qualities of its own, like Pavlov's bell (Chapter 5).

A smile becomes a conditioned reinforcer early in a child's life. At first, a smile means nothing to a baby; it is a neutral stimulus. But a smile usually accompanies a warm milk bottle or a pleasant bath or some other desirable attention, and shortly the smile will become a conditioned reinforcer, engendering a feeling of well-being even in the absence of bottle or bath. So the baby will gurgle cheerfully, a desirable behavior.

Money is a conditioned reinforcer. To a young child it is at first a neutral stimulus. But by the time the child enters first grade and has been to the supermarket repeatedly with Mommy or Daddy, money has become a conditioned reinforcer because money buys gum and popcorn and comic books.

NEGATIVE REINFORCERS

Negative reinforcement should not be confused, as it frequently is, with punishment. Like positive reinforcement, it is a procedure or action that increases a behavior. But rather than *presenting* something desirable, it *removes* something undesirable or aversive.

How are positive
and negative rein-
forcement alike?
Different?

Tony's mother nags him to bring in the garbage can from the curb. Tony finds nagging aversive, so he begins to bring in the garbage can regularly. Rain-soaked clothes are disagreeable, so they increase the likelihood that you will don a raincoat or carry an umbrella in wet weather. Parents frown on poor report cards, so more homework gets done. In the classroom, the condition that is removed in negative reinforcement often takes the form of threats, sarcasm, humiliation before fellow students, or an order to go to the office of the vice principal in charge of discipline.

Negative reinforcement is a common process, and it occurs naturally in life. But the intentional, planned use of negative reinforcement is a delicate matter. It can have unintended side effects, such as those described later in the discussion of punishment. Another problem is that negative reinforcement often leads to escape behavior (Zeiler, 1978). That is, a person increases some behavior in order to escape an aversive stimulus. (Consider for a moment how any aversive stimulus can give rise to a new behavior.) If a teacher or parent can control all possible escape routes, negative reinforcement may work. Too often, though, escape routes go unguarded, and the wrong behavior gets reinforced.

Think of your state legislator, Harlan Houdini, who hasn't been voting to your liking lately. You send him a strongly worded letter intended to induce him to change his ways. If your letter proves an effective aversive stimulus, Houdini indeed may. But Houdini could choose other escape routes: he may increase his use of his wastebasket; he may dictate a "Thank you for your concern" note and continue to vote as he pleases; and he may avoid reading all mail bearing your return address. Alas, Houdini has many possible escapes, and negative reinforcement may fail to change his voting behavior.

A more commonplace example: Charles, a ninth grader, studies regularly but for the past year he has been getting poor marks. Grades of D and F are aversive to him, because they evoke criticism from his teachers and parents, who think he can do better. The traditional escape—"try harder"—provides no relief. So Charles discovers escape routes that reinforce more quickly. He begins cheating on exams, and cutting classes or skipping school altogether.

Why is negative reinforcement a sensitive matter?

Aiming to improve some behavior, teaches, parents, and peers often present aversive stimuli. Sometimes they work, sometimes not. Is there no way to predict accurately when a negative reinforcement scheme will help change the targeted behavior? Because individuals differ so much, we cannot make infallible, precise suggestions. But here are some general guidelines:

1. Think in advance of the possible escape routes. Can you control them, or make unacceptable routes less appealing?
2. Don't threaten—a lower mark, no car, no dessert—unless you are prepared to follow through.
3. Couple the procedure with positive reinforcement for desired behavior. When a start is made along the correct escape route, give acknowledgement and support.

CHOOSING AND USING REINFORCERS

Both positive and negative reinforcers achieve the same ends, increasing or maintaining behavior. (If they do not, of course, they are not reinforcers.) But they are not magic wands that bring about miracles. They must be chosen and applied with care and forethought, and in accordance with a few basic rules:

1. A reinforcer should be associated in the student's mind with the behavior that the teacher wants to reinforce. A teacher may smile dozens of times a day, but a smile will work as a reinforcer most effectively when it accompanies a "Good work, Joe" or "That's a fine paper, Eileen." The reinforcement should be delivered during or immediately after desirable behavior if possible. If it must be delayed to the end of the period or the day, the teacher should make it clear why the student has won approval.
2. A reinforcer must be something the student values, not what the teacher believes the student values. For example, the school principal is often

stereotyped as a negative reinforcer, but several studies show that the principal's attention can be a powerful positive reinforcer (Darch and Thorpe, 1977).

Remember Valerie, whom we mentioned at the start of this discussion of reinforcement? Valerie does *not like* to be patted on the back. Student preferences may be determined by observation. Or, if it is a matter of considering what pupils want to do in free time that is being offered as a reward, by asking them. (This can prove tricky, though: what they want to do on Monday may not be what they want to do on Tuesday.)

What are some guidelines for applying reinforcers?

3. At the start of a reinforcement program, a reinforcer should be provided *every time* the behavior occurs. But as the behavior strengthens, reinforcement should come sporadically and unpredictably; it will produce more lasting results than reinforcement that arrives on schedule.

4. Provide reinforcement only for behavior that represents genuine achievement, however small. Rewards in *advance* of progress are unlikely to work, and may even reinforce the wrong behavior (i.e., whatever preceded the reinforcer).

"I'm trying to get every one of these kids involved in the class—that's why I use the reward system. A 'tab' system. See the box there? It's a number box they use in the lower grades. Well, I use it up here and we give out credits [tabs] for language, geography. . . . When they read they get a credit. They get credits for kindness—helping others—for conduct. . . . And I keep accurate records. They come up at the end of a day and say, 'I have so-and-so many tabs.' And that gets put down in a book. This eliminates guesswork. I never have to say, 'Gee, ah, Pamela—she's a cute looker. I think I'll give her a B in oral reading.' So I have a very accurate record to reinforce the fact that everybody gets the same treatment, good-looking or not. And anything they can do that is an improvement, I want to recognize—that's why I give credits—tabs."

5. **Be honest**. Rather than offer undeserved praise, devise a compliment your conscience can live with (for instance, "I'm glad to see you're trying harder, Robin," or "That's certainly an improvement, Chris").

What is the Premack Principle?

The Premack Principle. Though students differ considerably in their responses to intended reinforcers, most of them enthusiastically approve the idea of free time—for reading comic books, playing tic-tac-toe, or just talking. The concept derives from the Premack Principle, arrived at by the experimental psychologist David Premack (1959). In sum, the Premack Principle states that the more preferred of two behaviors can be used to strengthen the less preferred. In practical terms, that means that if a boy prefers playing poker to studying French irregular verbs, his enjoyment of poker can be employed to the benefit of his knowledge of French grammar. The procedure is simple: "Arnold, when you have conjugated these three verbs correctly, you may have twenty minutes of free time to play poker." Salzberg (1972) reports that free time as a reinforcer has doubled or tripled the rate at which students work.

In one example of free time as a reinforcer, a junior high teacher awarded stars on accurate completion of math problems (Page and Edwards, 1978). Fifteen minutes before the end of the class period, anyone with a star earned free time. The procedure dramatically reduced classroom disruptions and increased performance in math. It was discovered, incidentally, that a teacher needs no previous training in behavioral principles to carry out such procedures.

Free time isn't the only reinforcer to make the Premack Principle work. Careful observation will suggest many activities that tempt students. Youngsters in Sudbury, Massachusetts, for instance, are allowed to operate the computer after completing class assignments, and Taffel and O'Leary (1976) have even used math activities as rather surprising Premack reinforcers.

Some Cautions. The care and forethought with which reinforcers should be applied assume particular importance when the reinforcers are negative ones. Should we knowingly or unknowingly intensify behaviors of avoidance in students? Is nagging the best way to get Tony to bring in the garbage can? Is the teacher's best approach to a student doing poorly in mathematics to say: "If you don't show more effort, Becky, I'm going to have to flunk you"?

It can be, and is, argued that the world is like that, and that teachers who practice negative reinforcement are preparing youngsters for the world. But it can also be argued that negative reinforcement in the schools, which is all too common, may be partly responsible for what is wrong in the world.

Is it appropriate to introduce aversive stimuli such as threats, sarcasm, and humiliation before the class so that they can be removed after behavior becomes more desirable? Such stimuli may well have some of the potential side effects of punishment that are discussed later in this chapter.

Finally, remember that it is problem behavior that requires systematic behavioral intervention. If students already demonstrate high achievement and present no management problems, leave well enough alone: there is a chance that if you externally reinforce behaviors that have already been learned, students will become less responsive to those reinforcers in the future (Bates, 1979).

EMOTIONS AND LEARNING

Two weeks before the summer vacation ends, Kurt, who is in the fifth grade, says, "Gee, I wish vacation was over. I can hardly wait for school to start." His cousin Larry, a seventh grader who has been visiting Kurt's family and who attends another school, says, "Ugh! Not me!" Kurt's last report card came with As and a few B + s. Larry's marks ran to Cs, a D, and an F. As any teacher knows, students who enjoy school tend to do well, and those who dislike school usually do poorly. On first encounter, that fact may bring to mind the old question "Which came first, the chicken or the egg?" Does Kurt do well because he likes school or does he like school because he does well? Like most youngsters, Kurt and Larry entered first grade eagerly and both had IQs that hovered around 105. A good deal of the difference in their attitudes and achievements since then, it is reasonable to suspect, derives from their emotional experiences in school. For effective teaching and for facilitating youngsters' emotional (affective) development, it is imperative to bear in mind the processes of classical and operant conditioning (Chapter 5). In classical conditioning, conditioned stimuli (CS) evoke conditioned, emotional responses (CR), thus:

A birthday present (CS) makes Larry feel good (CR).
His teacher's sarcasm when he muffs an answer (CS) makes Larry feel bad (CR).

What role do emotions play in learning?

When a conditioned stimulus repeatedly accompanies a neutral stimulus, the neutral stimulus begins to evoke an emotional response. Larry's teacher's sarcasm is at its most biting during lessons in arithmetic, which originally was a neutral stimulus. So Larry begins to loathe arithmetic and eventually all lessons, and school. And because his teacher has red hair, Larry has generalized his dislike for her to a dislike for all people with red hair. Kurt's teacher, on the other hand, avoids sarcasm, nurtures his progress, and helps him to get the right answers in arithmetic, at which, in the beginning, he was no better than Larry. So Kurt likes arithmetic, lessons, teachers, and school.

The classical conditioning of emotions also occurs within the framework of operant conditioning. There is a link between classical and operant conditioning, as we pointed out in Chapter 5, because reinforcement in operant conditioning is identical with the conditioned or unconditioned stimuli of classical conditioning. Suppose you have just solved a problem in physics and your professor has reinforced you by saying "Excellent work!" You are likely to feel good about the reinforcement, a conditioned stimulus, and you are likely also to feel good about problem-solving, and to undertake more problems on your own.

In 1967, Vernon (1972, p. 18) asked some 300 university students, mostly freshmen, three questions:

1. What is the name of your best teacher in high school?
2. What was that teacher's subject?
3. What is your major subject at this university?

Forty-one percent of the students were majoring in their best teacher's subject, a remarkable figure in the light of the facts that many students had not yet chosen their majors and that many subjects taught at the university were not in high school curricula.

The implications for teachers are clear. If you want your pupils to become enthusiastic about what you teach, and to have positive feelings about themselves and about you, you must create the proper emotional environment, and reinforce them frequently along the path of learning.

TO PUNISH OR NOT TO PUNISH

Punishment offers another way of modifying behavior, and inevitably virtually every teacher faces this dilemma: To punish or not to punish? You may already have strong opinions on the issue. Most educators, most parents, and most students do. But let us approach the subject with open minds and consider these questions:

What do we mean by punishment?
How effectively does punishment modify behavior?
When if ever is punishment justified?

Any discussion of punishment is complicated by the fact that laymen and psychologists usually define the word differently. Our dictionary describes punishment as "retributive suffering, pain, or loss; a penalty inflicted on an offender through judicial procedure; severe, rough, or disastrous treatment."

Most of us believe that all punishment involves aversion, although the behaviorist says nothing about pain or penalty. From a behaviorist perspective, any stimulus that *decreases* behavior is considered punishment. (Reinforcing stimuli, you remember, including negative reinforcement, maintain or increase behavior.) If a stimulus fails to reduce the response, it cannot be punishment. For example, detention after school represents a punishment to most pupils. But Angela, who is frequently sentenced to detention for failing to do her arithmetic homework, *likes* to be kept after school. She finds her teacher's after-hours activities interesting to observe and much more fun than going home to help her family with the chores. Perhaps the individual attention gained after school actually reinforces her misbehavior. So detention is no punishment to Angela, and she continues to skip her homework.

Although Skinner and other behaviorists feel that punishment is generally

Is negative reinforcement the same as punishment?

ineffective in changing behavior, punishment is a practice older than education and its supporters can quote potent authority for its use, the Bible: "Foolishness is bound up in the heart of a child, but the rod of correction shall drive it from him" (Proverbs 22:15).

The Pros and Cons. Among educators and psychologists, punishment remains hotly controversial. Some arguments against it are:

1. If it induces stress, it will interfere with thought processes. The overlap between the affective and cognitive domains is most apparent when high anxiety muddles thinking.
2. Classical conditioning theory holds that bad feelings develop as an automatic result of aversive stimuli. The theory also holds that those feelings generalize, or spread, to other parts of the immediate environment. So the teacher, the subject, and even the school may become disliked because the student associates them with punishment.
3. Mild punishment produces only temporary results; once forgotten or its threat removed, the undesirable behavior will probably recur.
4. Punishment may incite aggression; the bad feelings produced through classical conditioning can sustain and intensify aggression.
5. The use of punishment presents an antisocial model for students; it teaches that punishment is an acceptable and useful tool for getting one's way.

Defenders of punishment, whose numbers grow as school violence increases, argue:

1. Prohibition of punishment is a sentimental fantasy, based mostly on utopian dreams.
2. Evidence that punishment shows limited effectiveness is scant, and usually obtained in work with laboratory animals.
3. There are occasions, in and out of school, when positive reinforcement cannot be counted on to work.
4. Even when its effect is temporary, punishment quickly removes a source of annoyance, and restores the right of other students to freedom from disruption.
5. Punishment of a single student can powerfully influence others who might be tempted to misbehave; learning by imitation is involved here.

Do you use punishment with others? Effectively?

These are the major arguments. You will hear them repeatedly, because they are often points of contention among teachers, administrators, and parents. Despite the debate, punishment occurs frequently in our society. If you intend to work within the schools, investigate local policy toward punishment. Besides official, written rules, there are unwritten policies guiding or limiting the use of punishment.

How Punishment May Be Used. Punishment, unless it is extreme, does not eliminate a behavior, it merely suppresses it for a time. In the period in which the behavior remains suppressed, the teacher can work to remove the source of the behavior. Good procedure, if you find punishment essential, is:

1. Make it clear why the punishment is being administered. Punishment is notably more effective when the reason for it is provided (LaVoie, 1974; Parke, 1977). The rationale must be understandable to the offender: It will not help to discuss abstract ethical issues with a first grader. Pressley (1979) has found that younger children are impressed by rationales that stress the physical consequences of behavior, whereas emphasis on property rights and the feelings of others is more effective as children grow older. This finding is consistent with Piaget's theories of cognitive and moral development (chapters 2 and 4). Before concrete operations, youngsters are strongly egocentric and have trouble analyzing multiple aspects of a situation. Their sense of *moral realism* focuses on the immediate consequences of an action.

2. Explain not only what the student must *not* do, but what is expected of him or her. "Stop that, John, and do what you are supposed to do" probably fails as a corrective because John may not know what he is supposed to be doing. A tactful reminder should help redirect John's attention: "Remember that we're trying to measure the cricket's chirping. We have trouble counting when you are talking, John."

3. Accompany punishment with positive reinforcers designed to reinforce an incompatible behavior. If you have just criticized Gail's poor volleyball serve, be sure to praise her better efforts.

4. Administer punishment as cool, professional therapy rather than as a form of revenge born of anger. In those ancient words of parents, "I'm having to do this for your own good" and "This hurts me as much as it hurts you."

5. Punishment should be applied with maximum intensity from the onset of serious misbehavior (Zeiler, 1978). If punishment slowly builds from mild to severe, the recipient grows accustomed to it, and the punishment may have little or no control over behavior.

6. Apply punishment as soon as possible after a misbehavior. If you delay the punishment, it may decrease the wrong behavior; theoretically, the behavior closest to the consequence (punisher *or* reinforcer) is the one most influenced.

How are punishment and extinction similar? Different?

Extinction: A Special Case of Punishment. Although we usually imagine punishment to involve the presentation of something aversive, such as a swat or a dressing down, there is another type of punishment that creates much less controversy. Called *extinction,* it *takes away* some reinforcing stimulus, such as a privilege. (Table 10.1 summarizes the procedures.)

One common extinction technique is *time out,* which resembles expulsion from society (the classroom) for a fixed period and confinement in solitary. Teachers have been using time out, of course, for centuries—standing youngsters in a corner, face to the wall, or sending them from the room. But time out is most effective when the teacher understands the psychological processes involved and adheres to all the requirements. Time out represents the separation of the offender from the environment in which he or she receives reinforcement of misbehavior, and its purpose is to reduce the behavior.

Research has shown that brief time outs—even those only a minute long—can work as well as longer periods (White, Nielson, and Johnson, 1972), and that students themselves can determine the length of effective time out (Pease and Tyler, 1979). Hall and his colleagues (1972) demonstrated an effective extinction program by having parents ignore their child's shouting and whining. After a short time, the withdrawal of the parents' attention (the reinforcer) reduced the child's obnoxious behaviors.

Although removing a reinforcer may seem less offensive than its counterpart, the presenting of a punisher, it creates its own problems. The major difficulty is that as soon as reinforcement ceases, the unwanted behavior usually increases in frequency. Also, aggression can result (Kelley and Hake, 1970). During extinction, pigeons and people alike evidently puzzle over the reinforcer's disappearance, and increase the behavior in an attempt to bring it back. The increase is temporary, lasting only until it is understood that the behavior is no longer related to the reinforcer. The increase, though, may dishearten you, because it signals an opposite effect from what was intended. Be patient and wait for the behavior to fade.

What problems occur with extinction?

A second problem lies in choosing the correct reinforcer to withdraw. It can be difficult, sometimes, to identify precisely what is maintaining a certain behavior. If you withdraw the wrong stimulus, extinction cannot occur. Or several reinforcers may be working; withdrawing a single one may have no effect. If you discover that there are too many reinforcers for you to withdraw, or that you are not in control of the reinforcers, you will have to try alternatives discussed in this chapter.

SHAPING

A behavior modification technique more agreeable than punishment is shaping. It is called that because it is not unlike what a sculptor does, starting with a block of granite and, bit by bit, chiseling closer and closer approximations of what he or she has in mind. In the classroom, though, you will be dealing not with blocks of granite—no matter what you may think on a bad teaching day—but with human beings, so your tools will not be chisels, but reinforcers. Shaping consists of reinforcing each closer approximation of a desired behavior and of withholding reinforcement when the approximation does not represent progress. Skinner employed shaping when he taught his pigeons to walk figure eights (Chapter 5).

What are the essentials of a shaping program?

For a teacher, the essential steps in beginning a shaping program are:

1. Targeting a desired behavior.
2. Fixing a baseline.

3. Selecting appropriate reinforcers.
4. Analyzing the task, and sequencing the segments.
5. Applying the reinforcers systematically.

An example on an elementary level:

You want Matthew to learn to write the figure 4 (a target).

You have found that Matthew cannot draw a straight line (a baseline).

You know that Matthew likes jelly beans (reinforcers).

You realize that writing 4 requires drawing two vertical lines and a horizontal line (task analysis).

You decide to concentrate first on having Matthew achieve one straight vertical line (a sequence).

Putting shaping into practice, you draw a vertical line for Matthew and ask him to produce one like it. His line emerges rather shaky, and its top is a good deal off due north. You say "Well, that's pretty good" and you give him a jelly bean. But you add "Now let's see if you can draw the line so that it doesn't lean over, as though it were going to fall." For a more nearly vertical line, another jelly bean. The process of getting the squiggles out of Matthew's lines, of adding a horizontal line to the vertical line to make an L, and of adding

Teacher: *Now, we know we've had trouble in the past, right? What have we had trouble on? Working . . . and getting our work what? Done. All right. Would you read this contract to yourself and see if you understand it? You let me know if there's anything on here that you don't understand, OK? Now, read it out loud.*
Student: *Contract by. . . .*
Teacher: *Want to write your name in here? OK, go ahead. . . .*
Student: *I agree to . . . to . . . concentrate on each of my assignments, and to do a reasonable amount of work at one time without leaving my desk and to complete a single day contract in reading and math and one other area every day. After doing this five days in a row I will receive. . . .*
Teacher: *OK, now we're going to talk about what you want as a reward after we talk about the contract. Do you understand what "concentrate" means?*

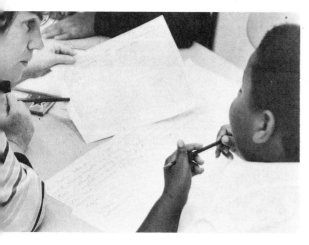 

another vertical line to make a 4 involves similar steps, including jelly beans.

But let us leap to the high school level. Samantha writes legibly, spells and punctuates properly, uses good grammar, and turns in terrible term papers, which could get her flunked out of college. You analyze, break down, and put in sequence the major steps in writing a term paper:

1. Introductory paragraph stating the essay's theme and purpose.
2. Body of the paper, which offers evidence and argument.
3. Conclusion, suggesting the inferences that may be drawn from the evidence and argument.
4. Summary (optional).

Most English teachers, we suspect, expect students to encompass all those steps in an essay's first draft and to improve the essay progressively in second, third, and perhaps fourth drafts. That, of course, is a form of shaping. But each time, the student's efforts and capability stretch thin. A better way, we suggest, is for the teacher to help the student learn to perform one task well before proceeding to the next one.

Shaping requires some careful orchestration on the teacher's part. If the

Student: *Keeping your mind on one thing.*
Teacher: *That's right. So we want to keep our mind on what one thing?*
Student: *Work.*
Teacher: *OK. Have you had trouble with this in the past? What does something like this contract help you do?*
Student: *Work.*
Teacher: *Do you think that this is a good idea? Do you agree to do this? All right, let's go over this a little more.*
     . . .

Teacher: *OK? Now, would you like to sign it, Owen? Are you sure you understand it all? Is it acceptable to you? Do you think the reward we've put in here is enough? OK. Now I'll sign it . . . and we'll get Miss Sherman to sign it.*

steps forward are too short, students become bored and inattentive. If the steps are too long, students stumble and become discouraged. Shaping, like any other form of teaching, is an art as well as a science, and must be practiced accordingly.

How Often Should You Reinforce? When you introduce a subject or a desired behavior that is new to your students, they will learn it or acquire it fastest if you reinforce every correct response. Reinforcement at that rate is known technically as a *continuous* or *FR:1* schedule. The FR stands for *fixed ratio* and the 1 means that the ratio of reinforcement to appropriate response is one-to-one. The problem with the FR:1 schedule is that, in a normal class of twenty-five students, it is virtually impossible to maintain. An effective reinforcement for every student every time would leave little time for teaching. So simply do the best you can, aiming for an FR:1 but keeping the ratio within practical bounds.

What is a reinforcement schedule?

Once a subject or a behavior has become familiar to students, the ratio of reinforcement to response may be thinned to, say, FR:5, or one reinforcer for each five responses. Laboratory rats on an FR:50 schedule quickly discover that they must press a lever fifty times (do they know how to count?) to earn a snack, and they work the lever fast and vigorously. They work even harder and more steadily when the experimenter shifts them to *VR*, or *variable ratio*, schedules in which they never know when their next meal is coming. VR schedules mean that appropriate behaviors are reinforced essentially at random.

Case History: A Treatment for Rorey

The following case history concerns a four-and-a-half-year-old boy who was a pupil in a nursery school. His time out was administered at home, but much of the procedure may be applied to older children by teachers.

Rorey fought with his peers, threw tantrums, and refused to obey instructions (Zeilberger, Sampen, and Sloane, 1968, p. 49). The school psychologist recommended to Rorey's parents, who had sought advice:

1. Immediately after Rorey acts aggressively or disobediently, take him to the time out (TO) room. (A bedroom in Rorey's house was stripped bare to serve: time out rooms should have no reinforcing stimuli present.)
2. If Rorey is taken to the TO room for ag- gressive behavior, say "You cannot stay here if you fight." As Rorey is taken to the TO room for disobedient behavior, say "You cannot stay here if you do not do what you are told." Make no other comments.
3. Place Rorey in the TO room swiftly and without conversation other than the above. Place him inside and shut and hook the door.
4. Leave Rorey in the TO room for two minutes. If he throws tantrums or cries, time the two minutes from the end of the last tantrum or cry.
5. When the time is up, take Rorey out of the TO room and back to his regular activities without further comment on the episode, i.e., in a matter-of-fact manner.
6. Do not give Rorey explanations of the program, of what you do, of his behavior, or

POKER CHIPS AND PAYOFFS

"There's no praise to beat the sort you put in your pocket," said the seventeenth-century French playwright Molière. His aphorism succinctly sums up the reasoning behind what educators and educational psychologists call a *token economy.* A token is simply something a child can put in his or her pocket—a poker or tiddlywink chip, a brightly colored pebble, a gold star, a ticket like a movie ticket, or just a slip of paper. The economy part of the phrase signifies that the token is a medium of exchange, like money, to be used to buy a possession or a privilege. In short, a token is a payoff, handed out for a desirable behavior. Token programs initially were used in classes for retarded or emotionally disturbed youngsters. But in the last decade, they have been adopted in regular classes, and their increased use concerns some skeptical observers.

Is a token economy for kids like a government economy for adults?

An important problem, the critics argue, is that such blatant external reinforcement will create a more external locus of control among participants (see Chapter 4). That is, students will have less sense of personal control over the environment. However, research evidence suggests just the opposite (Deiker and Matson, 1979), that a token procedure may promote an internal sense of control. Perhaps this is because tokens give quite clear reminders of behavioral consequences: "If I do this, then that will happen."

As reinforcers, tokens have proved highly effective when used with discretion and with understanding of their limitations. They will not solve all

---

engage in discussions of these topics with him. If you desire to do this, have such discussions at times when the undesired behaviors have not occurred, such as later in the evening. Keep these brief and at a minimum.

7. Ignore undesirable behavior that does not merit going to the TO room. "Ignore" means you should not comment on such behavior, or attend to it by suddenly looking around when it occurs.
8. Ignore aggressive or disobedient behavior that you find out about in retrospect. If you are present, treat disobedient behavior to other adults the same as disobedient behavior to you.
9. Reinforce desirable cooperative play frequently (at least once every five minutes) without interrupting it. Comments such as "My, you're all having a good time" are

sufficient, although direct praise that does not interrupt the play is acceptable.
10. Always reward Rorey when he obeys.
11. Special treats, such as cold drinks, cookies, or new toys or activities should be brought out after periods of desirable play. It is always tempting to introduce such activities when they will interrupt undesirable play, but in the long run this strengthens the undesired behavior.
12. Follow the program 24 hours a day (obviously impossible in school, but practicable with parents' cooperation).

Rorey's behavior under that regimen improved. You may have noticed, though, that the program did not depend entirely on time out. Rules 7 and 8 represented extinction and 9, 10, and 11 constituted reinforcement. ∎

classroom problems. They may not work for all teachers. They may not work for all students. Their employment is controversial. Many parents, teachers, and administrators object to them on such grounds as:

1. Virtue should be its own reward. One should not demand or expect payment for doing what one ought to be doing anyway (learning, studying, and behaving properly).
2. Payment to one youngster for being good provides an incentive to others to be bad, so that they can get a cut of the loot. (Evidence does not support this fear; see Christie, 1975.)
3. Teachers in a token economy tend to rely on tangible reinforcers to the exclusion of more desirable "social" reinforcers such as praise.

Advocates of the token system reply to the first cavil that the objectors rarely refuse to accept their own paychecks and to the others that, yes, a token economy does necessitate care in its implementation. Further, they insist that tangible reinforcement is only a means of initially motivating students, and that the long-range goal of any token system is to help students learn to work for *intangible* goals (O'Leary, 1978). They add that a great deal of research indicates its efficacy in a wide range of applications, from decreasing stuttering and relieving depression to improving reading accuracy. Tokens have even been used to teach fifth graders about the workings of historical and current economic systems (Krasner and Krasner, 1973). Among the advantages of a token economy, its supporters cite the following:

What are the pros and cons of a token economy?

1. It works well with youngsters who do not respond to smiles, praise, or the bait of better marks on report cards.
2. It is flexible enough to permit its use among students of any social and economic grouping, age, or IQ. Tokens may be offered for virtually any desired modification of behavior. The rate of payment can be set to suit the student's wants and level of sophistication. What the tokens will buy can be widely varied, conforming to student tastes.
3. Tokens do not pall, as other reinforcers may, because they are like money. (Few people tire of money.)
4. Tokens minimize disruption of study. When a youngster gets a piece of candy or a cookie as a reinforcer, he or she almost always pauses to consume it. A token may be placed on a youngster's desk with a brief "For sitting still five minutes" and the youngster can carry on, undistracted.
5. Tokens provide immediate and frequent reinforcement of the behavior that earns them. (In contrast, a good mark may not show up in a report card for weeks.) But because there is an inevitable time lag between receipt of a token and its expenditure for something desirable, the system incidentally teaches students to accept delay in gratification.
6. Tokens often inspire youngsters to behavior that they previously avoided, and so may broaden their interests.

Setting up a Token Economy. A teacher who wants to adopt a token system will be wise to seek the help of the school psychologist, if there is one. A token system may involve a single student, a few students, or an entire class. If the system is restricted to one or a few pupils, it is essential to explain to the nonparticipants that they do not need such special attention and that improved behavior by those who do need it will benefit all. (The explanation should reduce the chances that good students will turn themselves into bad students to become eligible for payoffs.) A step-by-step procedure toward a token economy might be this:

1. Specify to the students involved what kinds of behavior will earn tokens.
2. Choose, perhaps by vote of the students, subject to the teacher's veto, a wide variety of objects purchasable for tokens. (Some teachers establish little stores, open at recess and at the end of the day, stocked with candies, cookies, crayons, picture books, spinning tops, and other toys. The cost will not be prohibitive and the PTA and local merchants may be induced to contribute to it.) Also purchasable, and especially appealing to older students, can be free time to play basketball or a field trip to a historic site. If you veto a preference, explain why.
3. Agree with students on rates of payment and prices of purchasable items; keep both realistic. Items may not be purchased on credit.
4. Assign each student involved, if possible, tokens easily identified as his or her property—blue chips for one, red chips for another, green pebbles for a third—to reduce the possibility of youthful fraud. (Shrewd students may try gambling for tokens, or sell services such as doing someone else's homework.) If you use paper slips as tokens, write a student's name on his or her slips. Explain that tokens are not transferable.

How would you develop and operate a token economy?

Running a Token Economy. When the ground rules have been made clear, the token system can start operating. Here are some suggested guidelines:

1. Distribute tokens freely in the first few days, and try to see that every student involved gets as many as fifty or seventy-five each day. A first-grade teacher who wants Mark to learn to put on his own boots, jacket, coat, hat, and muffler might award Mark five tokens for going to the coatroom, five more for each article he takes from the hook, and five for each one he dons by himself.
2. Grant tokens immediately after every desirable action, so that students will know what they did to earn them. (Delay of even a few minutes may reinforce the wrong behavior.)
3. Once students understand the system, cut down on the number of tokens bestowed, and accompany each bestowal with praise, smiles, or thanks.
4. If fines are levied for undesirable behavior, they should probably not apply to tokens already bestowed; rather, assess penalties against tokens yet to be

earned. In any case, the use of fines is a sensitive matter, and O'Leary (1978) cautions that it may create an expectancy of bad behavior.

5. Keep records of each student's earnings. The chore may be burdensome at the start, but when the system is well underway, the time it saves by reducing behavior problems and accelerating learning will make up for the effort it demands.

6. Plan ways to maintain behavior change. In efforts to that end, researchers have involved students' peers (Walker and Buckley, 1972) and parents (Fairchild, 1976). In Fairchild's ingenious study, teachers awarded the tokens, but parents provided the reinforcers that the tokens bought. One second grader in that experiment increased his reading from three to twenty-two pages a day while tokens were awarded. After tangible reinforcers were withdrawn, he continued to improve, reading upward of seventy pages a day!

7. From the beginning of the token economy program and throughout its operation, prepare to *phase it out*. The token economy is one of the more revolutionary ideas to emerge from the theory of and research into behavior modification. It has great merit as a temporary measure. But a doctor does not keep dosing a patient with penicillin after the patient has fully recovered from pneumonia. A token economy creates an artifical environment that should be replaced opportunely by a more nearly natural environment. In a more nearly natural environment, effort and achievement are followed sometimes by smiles and praise and sometimes by nothing at all. Thoughtful planning, perhaps with the aid of the school psychologist, can help the transition from the contrived token economy to the less certain social system of the school.

CONTINGENCY CONTRACTING

Like the token economy, *contingency contracting* borrows from the work-day world. Its formidable name simply means agreement between two people or two groups that when one has completed a specified amount of work, the other will pay a specified price. In short, reward is contingent on performance. Contingency contracting embodies Grandma's Law: "When you finish the broccoli, I will bring you your ice cream, not before." Contingency contracting applies the Premack Principle (page 306). The principle states, in effect, that people and other animals will do what they prefer not to do if it will entitle them to do something else that they want to do ("Arnold, when you have finished with the questions for Chapter 10, you may have twenty minutes of free time to play poker.")

By now, you are probably muttering, "Everybody knows that. What's the big deal?" True, parents, grandparents, teachers, and administrators have been contracting with children informally for perhaps centuries. But laymen's contracts often do not stand up in court. (Neither do they change behavior very much.) So here are some guidelines that should help your contingency contracting stand up:

Under what circumstances can learning be contracted?

1. Try contingency contracting when:
   a. A pupil and a teacher are not getting along well together.
   b. Several pupils are not getting along among themselves.
   c. Pupils are not clear about what they are supposed to be learning or doing.

Contracting may be used among students of any IQ and of any grade level through graduate school. One of our doctoral candidates devised a contract that helped him meet deadlines for his dissertation research. At the beginning of the research, he gave his faculty advisor a sum of money. Each time a thesis chapter was completed on time, a portion of the money was returned. If a deadline were missed, that portion of the money was to be sent to the student's *least* favorite political organization. (The student regained all his money and is now on the faculty of another university.)

2. Contract for the performance of:
   a. Behaviors that can be observed.
   b. Behaviors that are simple to attain.
   c. Behaviors that pupil and teacher agree are reasonable goals.
   d. Behaviors that are incompatible with the behaviors it is desirable to eliminate.
   e. Behaviors that the pupil will be able to maintain beyond the contract's expiration.

Make sure that the terms are fair to both sides and that you will be able to carry out your part. Do not promise a youngster tickets for a circus unless you know that the circus will show up this year and that seats will be available. Make sure that the pupil really wants what you promise and is unlikely to be able to get it from another source such as Grandma.

3. In carrying out your part of the contract:
   a. Keep steps toward the goal small, and take them one at a time. If you are working toward John's getting a passing grade in fifth-grade arithmetic by the term's end, for example, start with one problem in, say, multiplication that you are confident he can do. Tell him: "When you have done the problem correctly, you may read your comic book"—which he has been trying to hide—"for five minutes." Giving John a problem too difficult for him in the beginning will discourage him, and he will forgo the comic book privilege. If you are attempting to instill neatness in a second grader, do not say, "Matthew, put your things away" but instruct him, "Matthew, take your mittens to the clothes closet," and when he gets there say, "Now put them in your coat pocket." With a high school sophomore who never brings in homework, be satisfied initially with one assignment a week.

Would contracting encourage stiff, formal relationships?

b. Provide a small reinforcer for every step, and bestow it immediately. At the start, reinforce even an approximation of the desired behavior. Later, reward *only* perfect performance.

c. Never provide reinforcement for refraining from undesirable behavior. Do not say, "Adam, I will give you a chocolate bar if you stop running round the room." Make a deal this way: "Adam, if you sit quietly in your seat for the next fifteen minutes, you will get a chocolate bar." Notice that the emphasis has shifted to a desirable behavior.

Like everything else in education—and life—contracting does not always work smoothly. Some students will fail day after day to fulfill the contract terms. When that occurs, the contract should be reviewed. The tasks may be simplified, or gradually reduced in number, or both. If those steps prove ineffective, reconsider the reinforcers you have employed. Perhaps they do not appeal strongly enough to the student, and other reinforcers should be substituted.

On the other hand, sometimes a contract may go too well. If a student completes assigned work way ahead of time, the contract underestimates the student's potential. The first day that that happens, let the student enjoy the free time. Thereafter, stiffen the contract's terms. You are unlikely to create hard feelings on the student's part. He or she more probably will take pride in getting more work, and the pride will serve as a reinforcer.

THE PROBLEM OF ADOLESCENTS

Why are adolescents a challenge to behavior modifiers?

Educational psychologists have concerned themselves chiefly with preadolescent youngsters, and most of the research in the field has centered around that age group. So high school teachers often feel understandably frustrated: the most important reinforcers for their students are sex, money, and the approval of their peers, none of which, obviously, teachers can provide or control. But, if you are going to teach in high school, do not despair. One potent reinforcer for high school students is free time, under the Premack Principle. It may seem illogical to reward the most disruptive or the most sluggish youngster in the class with an hour off on Friday afternoon because he or she has accomplished something that other students take for granted. But if you set a baseline for that student, make a contract, pay off, and then compare results with the baseline, you may be happily surprised by the progress made.

Contingency contracting of that kind is of course useful to the high school teacher, but contingency contracting in general is also highly useful to the students. Youngsters who work their way through Homme's five levels to full control of their own behavior acquire valuable training for college and for the world outside the classroom (see box, p. 323). In the typical high school senior class, the teacher remains the directing force, setting the tasks and making the judgments. But after graduation, students are on their own. Those who have learned to direct their own behavior have a long leg up on the rest.

Much writing on behavioral techniques has focused on children, because the bulk of research has involved elementary-age youngsters as subjects. But behavioral methods have been used extensively with adults, too; references such as the *Journal of Applied Behavior Analysis* give many examples of success in changing adult behavior. Below is a list of adult situations and behaviors that have been tackled and reported in the literature. The list is by no means complete, and, frankly, was compiled by a random search of the relevant literature.

sleep disorders	overeating
excessive anxiety or fear	self-regulation of asthma
depression	sharing
drug and alcohol abuse	listening
nail biting	marital problem-solving
stuttering	emotional outbursts
developing assertiveness	suicide attempts
increasing dating	inaudible speaking
sexual difficulties and deviations	lack of eye contact
urinary retention	complaining

Changes in behavior are not always permanent; some unwanted habits unfortunately return after a journal goes to press!

Some behaviorists, including B. F. Skinner, have looked beyond the individual to ponder enduring societal challenges, such as racial integration, mass transit, pollution control, and unemployment (Herson, Eisler, and Miller, 1975; Kazdin, 1978). Large-scale, planned intervention, they claim, will benefit the culture more than will selective changes in individuals. A step in that direction occurred when an entire elementary school was put on a token economy (Boegli and Wasik, 1978). This operation, involving more than 450 students, appeared to result in less classroom disruption, less negative teacher behavior, improved student achievement, and fewer teacher resignations. ■

Even the potent influence of peers among adolescents can be harnessed by contingency contracting, with impressive success. For example, West and Axelrod (1975) saw a previously successful system flop when kids rejected as "baby stuff" the earning of dimes for reductions in disruptive behavior. The researchers then recruited George, a popular thirteen-year-old class leader, as a "student consultant." George's behavior suddenly improved and the class speedily imitated it.

Even the token economy, childish as it seems on the surface, may be employed with success among high school students. We know an English teacher who resorted to gold stars, of all things, as reinforcers for a class of lackadaisical, uninterested juniors. No behavior modification expert, she told

"Phony praise? Never. My job is to see that these kids learn, and when they show that, the praise just flows naturally. Most kids know when you don't mean it. They get a sour attitude, you lose their trust. If you overdo praise, you'll have a tough time bringing their feelings around."

us she had been astonished by the change that came over them: abruptly, they began to concentrate on their studies, manifested a high degree of motivation, and replaced opposition to her with cooperation.

So, future high school teachers, take heart!

SELF-CONTROL

Heaven helps those who help themselves! The time-worn maxim is gaining credibility among those behaviorists who are willing to speculate about what happens between stimulus and response, and who are dissatisfied with the image of the human being as a passive organism that merely responds to external happenstance. The traditional behaviorist view of an all-controlling environment has derived from evidence obtained in the laboratory, where the environment changes mostly as a function of the experimenter, not the learner. Outside the lab, however, the learner does fiddle with his world, and there is constant reciprocal interplay between individual and environment. The point seems obvious, but radical behaviorists still insist that the external environment is in charge (see, for example, Rachlin, 1978; Skinner, 1971). Nevertheless, interest in the learner as a source of self-control is growing.

Is self-control a scientific concept?

It is surprising that the view of humans as active, initiating creatures has been resisted for so long in the philosophy of behaviorism. Perhaps reluctance to study internal events is to blame. But behaviorists have been using those internal events—thinking, planning, inventing—ever since Watson put the

---

Responsibility in Contracting

As you and your pupils gain experience with contracting, you and they will find that students can assume increasing responsibility in managing the system. Five levels of procedure have been fixed by Lloyd Homme and his associates (1973):

Level 1: *Full control by teacher*
   Step 1. Teacher determines amount of reinforcement.
   Step 2. Teacher determines size of task.
   Step 3. Teacher presents contract to student.
   Step 4. Student accepts contract and performs task.
   Step 5. Teacher pays off.

Level 2: *Partial control by student*
   Teacher determines size of task, but student and teacher jointly control amount of reinforcement.
                    or
   Student determines size of task, and teacher determines amount of reinforcement.

Level 3: *Equal control by teacher and student*
   Teacher and student jointly determine size of task and amount of reinforcement.
   Student fixes reinforcement, teacher sets task.
   Teacher and student reverse roles described immediately above.

Level 4: *Part control by teacher*
   Student fully controls amount of reinforcement and partly controls amount of work.
   Student fully controls amount of work and partly controls amount of reinforcement.

Level 5: *Full control by student*
   Student sets the size of the task and the amount of reinforcement, writes the contract, does the job, and pays him- or herself off.

   At each level, all methods should be practiced before moving to the next higher level. ∎

fear of fur into little Albert. It is a logical extension to turn the planning inward to control of oneself. The idea is especially appropriate for adolescents soon to shed the protection of school and home.

Self-control, Brigham (1978) suggests, involves a decision between immediate, probable consequences and distant, less probable consequences. For instance, Joe has the option of studying (with a distant, possible consequence of a good mark) or going to a bull session down the hall (an immediately reinforcing event). If he chooses to study, and accepts delay of his reward, he is said to have self-control. But if we can delay rewards, doesn't that contradict the behavioral rule of immediacy, which states that consequences prove the most effective when delivered quickly after a response? Not necessarily, if we admit that cognitive processes are responsible for coding and storing information, and that such processes can bridge the distance between present and future. Cognition thus mediates between stimulus and response. The idea is not far-fetched to cognitive psychologists, and even neobehaviorists have used cognitive processes to help explain learning by imitation (see Chapter 5).

Mahoney and Thoreson (1974) give three general strategies for self-control:

What methods will enhance self-control?

1. *Self-observation* refers to specifying problem behavior and carefully recording its frequency. Its purpose is to establish a baseline, or starting point. Such *self-monitoring* sometimes changes behavior by itself (Kazdin, 1974; Piersel and Kratochwill, 1979). In those cases, the observed data apparently indicate how present behavior differs from hoped-for behavior. If that feedback alters behavior, other steps are, of course, unnecessary, but there is no way to determine the effects of self-monitoring unless it is tried!

2. If self-monitoring does not alter behavior, then *environmental planning* becomes necessary. That means, for the most part, changing aspects of the environment that seem to prompt problem behavior. In the vocabulary of Chapter 5, it involves identifying and changing discriminative stimuli. For example, self-observation may reveal to Jayne that she does not study after her radio emits a favorite tune: at that point, her imagination takes off like a balloon, and she drifts into activities more appealing than study. So the radio evidently serves as an S_d for inappropriate behavior. Jayne's environmental planning could indeed be simple—it would require only that she not turn on the radio until she has studied.

3. *Behavioral programming*, the third procedure, may be used in conjunction with the first two methods. It basically involves self-delivery of consequences for behaviors. The consequences may be overt, such as allowing oneself special activities ("After I have written 500 words, I will watch TV for an hour."), or providing tangible reinforcers or punishers. Or consequences may be covert; that is, silent and private ("I did it!" "I'm really pleased at the progress I'm making" [Meichenbaum and Cameron, 1974, p. 286]).

A considerable amount of research has studied the use of self-verbalizations as a method of self-control. Unfortunately, self-verbalizations used alone usually fail to improve classroom behaviors (Pressley, 1979). On the other hand, Pressley reports that when children are asked to *model* self-verbalization behavior for other youngsters, their own self-control improves.

A student who is to be taught methods of self-control must first agree, without coercion, that a problem needs to be solved, and that he or she is willing to commit time and energy to the solution. When control can be transferred at least in part from parents or teacher to the youngster himself—that is, transformed from external to internal—two important things happen. First, the child moves nearer to a major goal of schooling: self-regulation. Second, the teacher's or parents' time is freed for other things.

As in many experimental programs, first attempts may not work. Then it is useful to recall the behavioral principle of *shaping*. Are there aspects of self-control that *did* work, and can be merged into new approaches? Instead of shifting control abruptly to a student (or to yourself), can you find compromises for sharing control? O'Leary (1978) proposes that peer prompting, peer reinforcement, and competition can help a self-control program.

Much research has yet to be done on self-control. For example, it is not clear whether children in different cognitive developmental periods (say, concrete operations versus formal operations) are able to manage self-control schemes equally well, although there is speculation that older children learn these skills more readily (Parke, 1977). If you decide that Julie's poor study habits cannot await published research, experiment yourself. Start small, make no extravagant promises, inform her parents, and seek out resources to help get started. The Suggested Readings at the end of this chapter give a couple of good references to begin with.

AFTER SCHOOL LETS OUT

Summer comes, and teachers tired from months of teaching understandably assume that their responsibilities to their students are ended, at least for the time. But students end the school year with strong impressions and behaviors, many of them implanted by their teachers. So teachers do have some responsibility for what students do in their free months. If you have instituted a behavioral program, you must plan how to keep it effective in your absence. Here are some guidelines.

How can behavior change be maintained?

1. A couple of months, at least, before the school year's end, pair reinforcers such as tokens or gold stars with natural reinforcers like praise and smiles, and then phase out the tokens and stars.
2. Cut down the whole reinforcement schedule. There are fewer reinforcers in the world outside than, perhaps, there ought to be, and students should become used to the fact.
3. Do not begin a major behavior modification program late in the year; it won't have time to get off the ground before the semester's end. We have seen teachers organize a complex token economy scheme two weeks before

school was to let out. The effects were just becoming evident when the school year ended, and the students were left feeling as though they had bought counterfeit lottery tickets.

4. Interest and involve parents in your activities and discuss with them ways of maintaining good results during vacations. Home-based extensions of school programs can be quite simple, as demonstrated by Dougherty and Dougherty (1977). Those researchers wished to improve completion of homework and to reduce talking out in class of fourth graders. Daily report cards, with marks for "behavior," "schoolwork," and "homework" were sent home with each student. Parents were asked merely to discuss the marks with their children, and to save the cards so that progress could be reviewed easily. Both targeted behaviors quickly and markedly changed.

A Final Word on Behavior Modification

Superficially, behavior modification appears as simple and straightforward as sliding a coin into a vending machine and getting a plastic bag of salted peanuts in return. It is not. Human organisms, including teachers and students, are enormously complicated. People have an awesome capacity to learn, and we grow up stimulated, reinforced, punished, and guided by an infinite number of learning situations. Sometimes we are reinforced and sometimes we are punished for the same behavior—for example, killing another person in wartime and in peacetime. Sometimes a stimulus inspires good feeling; at other times, the same stimulus inspires bad feeling: snow delights us if we plan a weekend of skiing, and depresses us if we have to make our way through it to the doctor.

The behavior modification procedures we have outlined will not make you a magician overnight; skill in their use takes much time and practice. Neither will the procedures work instantaneous changes in your students; you will need a good deal of patience, dedication, and flexibility if the changes are to become longlasting. Your students are under your control (more or less) for only part of their day. What you do and say *does* influence them, but they are subjected to thousands of other influences as well. You may be most effective in perpetuating *your* influence if you keep three guidelines in mind:

1. Think small, achieve big (Malott, 1972). You cannot solve all the world's problems or change all the behaviors of your students. Choose the behaviors that appear most important to amend and work on them systematically: you will better the odds for success that way.

2. Keep your behavior modification plan simple and consistent. There are perhaps a hundred approaches to any behavior you target. Select one or two and adhere to them. Too complex a scheme will leave you no time for teaching.

3. Teach behaviors that can be maintained by the environment. Ayllon and Azrin (1968) term this the "Relevance of Behavior" rule. It makes no sense

to develop behaviors that may lead to punishment by next year's teacher, or be unacceptable outside of school.

How can you make sure a behavioral program is reasonable?

In any program for changing behavior, important ethical questions arise and the use of behavioral techniques does cause considerable concern. (Perhaps if the techniques were less effective, there would be less concern.) Behavior modifiers are sometimes portrayed as insensitive, totalitarian folk and children as their powerless puppets: obviously, teachers and other shapers of behavior are usually bigger than their subjects, and can reinforce and punish. Some theorists worry that behavior modification, especially in schools, helps those in authority to create docile youngsters (Winett and Winkler, 1972). Appropriate use of the techniques can do much to allay the fears.

The More Things Change . . .

It wasn't called behavior modification in those days. But the two notes that follow, reproduced from The Teacher's Gazette *of November 1908, indicate that teachers knew a thing or two about educational psychology.*

To Obtain Good Behavior

There are so many trifling annoyances in school that it would keep a teacher on the alert most of the time if she were to take notice of them all. A plan which has been tried and has proven an incentive to the children to make the order in the room as nearly perfect as possible, is as follows: Divide the room into two, three, or four divisions, whichever is suitable. Divide a corner of the board into as many squares as there are divisions in the room. In each square draw five stars. The division whose deportment is best from morning until recess receives a mark in its star. The one showing the best behavior from recess until noon gets a mark in its star. This is continued until the close of school at night. When a division has received the greatest number of stars in a limited space of time, it has its stars erased, and a crescent put in each place. This causes a pleasant rivalry between the several divisions to see which one can keep the best order. The unpleasantness of keeping an eye on the children is taken out of the teacher's hands, leaving it almost entirely with the pupils themselves, and this is always a fortunate thing.

To Insure Punctuality

For two years and a half I have been teaching and substituting in ungraded schools. In all of them I have found the same trouble to secure promptness. I have tried several plans and found these the most satisfactory: Have an "Honor Roll" placed on the wall upon which the name of every child is written.

Every child that does not miss a day or come late for a week receives a star at his name. The one having the greatest number of stars at the end of the term receives a prize. The stars may be bought at any stationery store for ten cents a box. The little gilt stars are bright and will please the children wonderfully.

I also read one chapter every morning from some interesting book. In this way many books may be read during the year and the children become so interested in the story that they will be sure to be at school in time to hear the chapter read. Some of the books I have found most successful are "Black Beauty," "Alice's Adventures in Wonderland," "Five Little Peppers," "Little Men," "Little Women," etc. I hope this plan may prove as successful for some other teacher as it has for me. — Clara E. Buchanan, in *Normal Instructor*. ∎

"Mandy has been practicing self-control for, oh, two months. She's keeping track of her outbursts. We gave her little dittoed graph paper, she's charting her behavior, and it's clear that she's slowing down a bit. One of the biggest problems is to get other kids to ignore her."

Behavior modifiers should center on the *purposes* of changing youngsters' ways and must examine their own personal motives (see Malott, Tillema, and Glenn, 1978).

Consider Ben and yourself. Ben makes several trips daily from his desk to yours, usually to ask about something simple. He doesn't disturb classmates, and he times his visits to moments when you seem to be free. But his chattering wears on your nerves. If you can reduce his question-asking, has Ben profited, or have you? Ben might benefit from encouragement to do more independent work, and you would suffer fewer interruptions. There is no clear answer, but there is a guideline: If the planned behavior change will help the learner contribute to or get along better in society, then it is probably a good idea. If it is intended merely to ease your day, it needs stronger justification.

Summary

Behavior modification's proponents hold that learning and teaching may be made easier and pleasanter by applying the principles that govern conditioning; i.e., responses to environmental stimuli. Teachers have hundreds of opportunities daily to alter the classroom environment and change behavior.

Essential preliminary steps in a behavior modification program:

1. Define the problem specifically.
2. Target the aspect of behavior to be changed.
3. Set an objective and a time limit for attaining it.
4. Undertake a task analysis.

Behavior may be modified by reinforcement, a direct approach, or by substitution of an incompatible behavior for an undesirable behavior, an indirect approach.

Reinforcers have two forms, positive and negative, both of which are intended to increase a behavior. *Positive reinforcers* consist of tangible or intangible rewards; *negative reinforcers* represent removal of an aversive condition. In either case, they are reinforcers only if they work, and not all reinforcers prove effective with all students. One reinforcer that is popular with many different kinds of students is free time, a concept based on the *Premack Principle* (a more preferred behavior can be used to strengthen a less preferred one).

Another technique for modifying behavior involves *punishment*, which is not to be confused with negative reinforcement. Though punishment is widely applied, it remains highly controversial among educators and the public; the relative effectiveness of physical and psychological punishments also is debated.

The ways in which behavior modification techniques may be applied are numerous. One of them is called *shaping*, in which the teacher reinforces each closer approximation of a desired behavior. Another is the *token economy*, which involves distribution of simulated currency, such as poker chips or gold stars, for desirable behavior; the tokens may be used by students to purchase tangibles such as candy, toys, and books, or intangibles like free time. A wide selection based on students' expressed preferences and teachers' suggestions is recommended. Still another technique is designated *contingency contracting:* in this approach, students contract to perform in certain ways for agreed on compensation.

Self-control has gained favor among behaviorists who speculate about cognitive processes that help delay gratification. Self-control methods are similar to other behavioral procedures; they involve careful observation of behavior and the changing of the behavior's antecedents and consequences.

Whatever the method, the use of reinforcement creates an artificial situation and should be phased out gradually, so that the modified behavior becomes a matter of habit without expectation of payment.

Chapter Study Guide

CHAPTER REVIEW

Answer questions 1-9 True or False:

1. Behaviorists believe there is no way to change behavior directly.

2. Any behavior targeted for change must be observable and measurable, according to behaviorists.

3. To increase a behavior, something must be added to the environment, while a decrease in behavior calls for removing something from the environment.

4. A primary criterion for a successful reinforcer is that it be something the teacher believes the student values.

5. It is important, for purposes of encouragement, to reinforce at first for genuine effort, even though achievement may be lacking.

6. A difference between punishment and negative reinforcement is that the first tends to decrease a behavior whereas the second tends to increase a behavior.

7. Negative reinforcement tends to develop escape or avoidance responses.

8. An advantage of a shaping program is that it rewards a student for gradual improvement.

9. From the beginning of a token economy program and throughout its operation, the teacher should prepare to phase it out.

10. Behavior modification looks for _____ conditions related to behavior and attempts to modify them.

11. Before attempting to measure progress in behavior modification programs, it is first necessary to establish a starting point or _____ .

12. Sometimes it is possible to substitute a(n) _____ behavior, an approved activity the student likes to do, for an undesirable behavior.

13. Sequencing skills for task analysis is most difficult in the _____ domain.

14. The only way you can determine whether or not you have hit on a reinforcement is to observe the _____ .

15. A _____ reinforcer is a once-neutral stimulus that has been paired frequently with a primary reinforcer.

16. Premack's principle states that the more _____ of two behaviors can be used to strengthen the less _____ .

17. By the behaviorist definition, punishment is not punishment unless it _____ .

18. Shaping consists of reinforcing each closer _____ of a desired behavior and of withholding reinforcement when the _____ does not represent progress.

19. VR schedule means that appropriate behaviors are reinforced essentially at _____ .

20. At the beginning of an extinction procedure, the targeted behavior usually _____ .

21. A written agreement that specifies student and teacher responsibilities is termed a _____ .

22. In discussing self-control, behaviorists must be willing to make assumptions about _____ .

23. In simple terms, self-control involves a decision about _____ .

FOR FURTHER THOUGHT

1. As the authors indicate, the practice of payment for work done in school is often defended on the grounds that "it is realistic preparation for the world outside." What is your attitude toward this view? Is it the principal function of the schools to prepare students for "the world as it is," or to equip them with a vision of what the world might be like?

2. Of the various kinds of reinforcers discussed in this chapter—primary, conditioned, negative—which do you think would generally be most effective? Why? Which agrees best with your sense of values? Which do you think would build the best personal relationship between teacher and student?

3. Develop a model program for changing the behavior, or learning, of either an actual or a hypothetical student. In either case, be sure to define the problem in observable terms and target the desired behavior in measurable terms. Then select any of the direct behavioral modification techniques described in this chapter and outline a suitable program. In setting up the program, be sure to take into account both the nature of the desired learning and the personality of the student.

4. Why is self-control apparently so hard for most of us? What contingencies of your own environment would have to be changed to make self-control more attractive to you? Are you in control of those contingencies?

IMPORTANT TERMS

behavior modification
baseline
incompatible behavior
task analysis
positive reinforcers
negative reinforcers
primary reinforcers
conditioned reinforcers
reinforcement
Premack Principle
conditioned stimulus
conditioned response

punishment
extinction
time out
shaping
reinforcement schedule
token economy
contingency contracting
self-control
self-observation
environmental planning
behavioral programming
discriminative stimulus

SUGGESTED READINGS

The following group of books are all characterized by their presentation of standard behavioral techniques (i.e., conditioning, reinforcement, shaping, imitation, and so on). The emphasis is on classroom application, and each book provides dozens of illustrative examples of behavior modification in action.

AXELROD, S. *Behavior modification for the classroom teacher.* New York: McGraw-Hill, 1977.

BLACKHAM, G. J., and SILBERMAN, A. *Modification of child and adolescent behavior* (3rd ed.). Belmont, CA: Wadsworth, 1980.

GIVNER, A., and GRAUBARD, P. S. *A handbook of behavior modification for the classroom.* New York: Holt, Rinehart and Winston, 1974.

KAZDIN, A. E. *Behavior modification in applied settings* (rev. ed.). Homewood, IL: Dorsey Press, 1980.

MARTIN, G., and PEAR, J. *Behavior modification: What it is and how to do it.* Englewood Cliffs, NJ: Prentice-Hall, 1978.

MIKULAS, W. L. *Behavior modification.* New York: Harper and Row, 1978.

MILLER, L. K. *Principles of everyday behavior analysis.* Monterey, CA: Brooks/Cole, 1975.

SULZER-AZAROFF, B., and MAYER, G. R. *Applying behavior analysis procedures with children and youth.* New York: Holt, Rinehart and Winston, 1977.

THORESON, C. E. (ed.). *Behavior modification in education.* The 72nd Yearbook of the Society for the Study of Education (Part 1). Chicago: University of Chicago Press, 1973.

WALKER, J. E., and SHEA, T. M. *Behavior modification.* St. Louis: C. V. Mosby, 1976.

The next books are more restricted in focus but, like the previous books, are directed toward classroom application with myriad examples.

DARDIG, J. C., and HEWARD, W. L. *Sign here: A contracting book for children and their parents.* Kalamazoo, MI: Behaviordelia, 1976.

DeRISI, W. J., and BUTZ, G. *Writing behavioral contracts.* Champaign, IL: Research Press, 1975.

FOSTER, C. *Developing self-control.* Kalamazoo, MI: Behaviordelia, 1974.

HOMME, L., CSANYI, A. P., GONZALES, M. A., and RECHS, J. R. *How to use contingency contracting in the classroom* (rev. ed.). Champaign, IL: Research Press, 1973.

KAZDIN, A. E. *The token economy: A review and evaluation.* New York: Plenum Press, 1977.

STAINBACK, W. C., PAYNE, J. S., STAINBACK, S. B., and PAYNE, R. A. *Establishing a token economy in the classroom.* Columbus, OH: C. E. Merrill, 1973.

WILLIAMS, R. L. and LONG, J. D. *Toward a self-managed life style.* Boston: Houghton Mifflin, 1975.

ANSWER KEY

1. T; 2. T; 3. F; 4. F; 5. F; 6. T; 7. T; 8. T; 9. T; 10. external; 11. baseline; 12. incompatible; 13. affective; 14. effects or change in behavior; 15. conditioned; 16. preferred. . .preferred; 17. works or decreases a behavior; 18. approximation. . .approximation; 19. random; 20. increases; 21. contingency contract; 22. internal events or thought processes; 23. delaying rewards or immediate versus delayed reward.

11

Teaching Exceptional Children

A friend of ours tells us that when he was going to elementary school early in this century, the principal remarked to our friend's parents, one Back-to-School Night, that our friend and his brother were "exceptional children." The parents beamed, thanked the principal, and raised the boys' weekly allowance from a dime each to fifteen cents. *Exceptional* had, in the language of educators, only one meaning: the boys were pupils of far-above-average achievement and classroom manners.

What does *exceptional* mean?

The meaning has changed. Exceptional now embraces all youngsters whose entry characteristics deviate from the norm mentally, physically, or emotionally to a degree that they demand special attention to help them develop to their maximum.

Among them may be:

- Pupils of apparently normal intelligence who suffer from an inability to master one or more subjects—even such basics as reading, writing, or arithmetic.
- Compulsively overactive youngsters (usually boys) who often disrupt classwork.
- Youngsters who have trouble speaking.
- Students with emotional or behavioral disorders.
- Youngsters with physical problems—poor vision, or poor hearing, or impairments that limit their mobility.
- Pupils with a combination of problems. Physically impaired children, for example, may develop emotional disturbances, and some physically sound children who are emotionally disturbed may develop speech difficulties.
- Mentally retarded children like those with whom Binet worked.

Those examples do not exhaust the long list. Just how many youngsters fall into each of the various categories designated as handicapped no one knows for sure. For *learning disabilities* alone—the inability of some mentally normal children to cope with certain subjects—estimates have exceeded 20 percent of the school population and up to 70 percent in urban slums (Swanson and Reinert, 1979); but the figures vary widely because they depend on how the compilers define learning disorders. How many individuals need special education services is difficult to determine precisely. One reason is that children may have more than one problem, so they fit more than one category. Another is that not all those requiring special services have been identified, but authorities estimate that between 10 and 15 percent of school-age young people are eligible for such services.

In 1976 the Bureau of Education for the Handicapped in the United States Office of Education conducted a survey to ascertain the number of handicapped individuals in each category. Table 11.1 summarizes the findings. In the same age brackets, it is also estimated, there are approximately 1.5 million gifted children. The country thus has nearly 10 million exceptional children.

When people talk about exceptional children, they use several key terms. *Impairment* refers to diseased or defective tissue, exemplified by brain dam-

334

Table 11.1. Estimated Number of Handicapped Children Served and Unserved by Type of Handicap

	1975–76 Served (projected)	1975–76 unserved	Total served and unserved	Percent-age served	Percent-age unserved
Total: Age 0–5	450,000	737,000	1,187,000	38	62
Total: Age 6–19	3,860,000	2,840,000	6,700,000	58	42
Total: Age 0–19	4,310,000	3,577,000	7,887,000	55	45
Speech impaired	2,020,000	273,000	2,293,000	88	12
Mentally retarded	1,350,000	157,000	1,507,000	90	10
Learning disabilities	260,000	1,706,000	1,966,000	13	87
Emotionally disturbed	255,000	1,055,000	1,310,000	19	81
Crippled and other health impaired	255,000	73,000	328,000	78	22
Deaf	45,000	4,000	49,000	92	8
Hard of hearing	66,000	262,000	328,000	20	80
Visually handicapped	43,000	23,000	66,000	65	35
Deaf-blind and other multihandicapped	16,000	24,000	40,000	40	60

From the annual report of the National Advisory Committee on the Handicapped, abstracted in *American Education,* June 1976.

age, which may be caused by a lack of oxygen at birth. *Disability* has to do with the imperfect functioning of a part of the body; one who cannot control the muscles required for speech has a communication disability. We commonly hear the terms *disorder* and *dysfunction* used as synonyms for that kind of disability. The term *disability* applies also to the somewhat rarer absence of an organ or limb, as in the case of a child born without arms. *Handicap* refers to the problems that impaired or disabled people confront in their environment. A college student confined to a wheelchair said, "Yeah, I have a disability; but I am not handicapped—until I try to get into a building that has a revolving door as its only entrance."

A Bill of Rights for the Handicapped

What led to Public Law 94–142?

Exceptional individuals have been around for a long time. It was not, however, until fairly recently that society developed major concern about the education of exceptional children. One major advance occurred in 1971 when the Pennsylvania Association for Retarded Children sued the Commonwealth of Pennsylvania for failure to provide free and appropriate public education for all the state's mentally retarded citizens. The state then entered into a court-approved consent agreement establishing the rights of the retarded to suitable education and giving parents the right to participate in placement decisions for their children. A year later, as a result of *Mills* vs. *The Board of Education*

Shown here is a mainstreamed class containing several handicapped and special needs children. One child, Frankie, is on the floor with the other children during a general class lesson, following which he moves to a corner of the room where the special needs children are preparing for a vocabulary session using art for language development. "Frankie is feeling a little upset about what some of the kids have said to him about his legs. Some of the kids didn't know him and they said, 'What's the matter with your legs?' and he said, 'I'm crippled.' They didn't know what that meant and I felt he needed to—for a little while at least—handle that on his own, and that was hard for him. So the first big job we have in this kind of class is just to help the kids relate to each other. I've had special needs children in my class every year for the last two years, and this year is no different. I enjoy it. I look forward to these kids. We always have a great class."

in the District of Columbia (1972), rights to equal educational opportunities were extended to *all* handicapped children. After several years of litigation on local and state levels, Congress in 1975 passed the Education for All Handicapped Children Act. That legislation, commonly known as *Public Law 94–142*, became the most comprehensive, far-reaching federal mandate for special services to children between the ages of three to twenty-one years. Its most important objectives are:

1. To provide equality of opportunity for education for all American children.
2. To provide free public instruction amid the *least restrictive environment* that is practical for the individual. This means that though some children still will require special classes or special schools, most handicapped children will join the mainstream and may receive supplementary instruction designed to keep them there. Expenditures that eventually may total $4 billion have been authorized for that purpose.

The act embodies, in effect, a bill of rights for the handicapped, the provisions of which include:

Comprehensive and nondiscriminatory testing and evaluation. No single test may be used to determine the least restrictive placement of a pupil: several tests, as nearly free as possible of cultural or racial discrimination, must be employed. (Under that provision, the psychologist Dr. Williams on pp. 78–79 probably would not have been advised to become a bricklayer.)

Individualized education programs (IEP) for the handicapped and the gifted. Schools may assign students to specially tailored instruction, and parents may request such instruction. The plan for each program must state goals, define specific objectives, outline teaching methods suited to the student's entry characteristics, and establish criteria for evaluating whether or not the goals of the program are being reached. (The box provides examples.)

Extension to education of the due process clauses that govern America's legal system. (*Due process* means, of course, that no one may be imprisoned or fined without a trial.) Under Public Law 94-142, parents are entitled to participate in the development of IEPs, to challenge a student's placement in an IEP, and to review school records concerning the student.

There are many more such provisions in the act; we have cited only a few important samples. The act has no expiration date, so mainstreaming presumably will be a fact of educational life for years to come.

<aside>What are the major provisions of the Education for All Handicapped Children Act?</aside>

MAINSTREAMING: PRO AND CON

Whether exceptional children benefit or suffer by being integrated with average children has long been debated—and is still debated—by educators.

The Arguments for Mainstreaming. Proponents of mainstreaming, some of whom filed the lawsuits that brought about passage of Public Law 94-142, contend:

- Special classes and special schools for the handicapped are merely convenient sidetracks for shunting children who have been wrongly diagnosed as hopelessly stupid, but whose learning problems originate in their cultural or economic background (Jones, 1976).
- Assignment to a special class or school labels children as different and the labeling may damage them more than their original problems ever could (see box on p. 340).
- Special classes and schools aren't much good anyway. They deprive children of the incentive to compete that they would find in regular classes. Pupils in special classes do worse, or at least no better, than similarly handicapped children in regular classes (Baroff, 1974). (Actually, studies of these points yield equivocal evidence. The issue cannot be considered settled.)
- Special classes and special schools deny *in*equality of opportunity for education, which the United States Supreme Court required in 1954, in *Brown* v. *Board of Education.* That landmark decision abolished the practice of providing "separate and equal" facilities for minority groups, and held that segregation led to *in*equality of opportunity.

What arguments support main-streaming? oppose mainstreaming?

The Arguments against Mainstreaming. Opponents of main-streaming, some of whose contentions have been summarized as follows by Bruininks and Rynders (1971), argue:

- Handicapped children cannot possibly compete with average children, and their self-esteem suffers when they are placed in regular classes. Assignment to special classes usually has had a humanitarian motivation, to protect the handicapped from ridicule and the frustration inherent in failure (Mac-Millan, 1977).
- Criticisms of special classes are often based on poorly designed programs and inept research.
- Mistakes in diagnosis and placement may indeed be made, but they should not be attributed to the existence of special classes.

Though the debate continues, the current mood in the field is perhaps best summarized by Chaffin: "Although the present mainstreaming programs do not offer proof that they are an improvement over traditional delivery systems, they are certainly no worse and hold the promise of much more" (1974, p. 17). But fulfillment of that promise will depend on you as a teacher. Mere inclu-

Individual Educational Programs

Perhaps no two specialists in the field will ever agree on the precise meaning of the term *appropriate education* mentioned in the Education for All Handicapped Children Act. But the law has provisions designed to guarantee that each child's needs are met, and one important provision is for Individual Educational Programming (IEP).

The IEP is meant to link the assessment of a child's entry characteristics with instructional objectives, methods and evaluation—that is, to provide *appropriate education*. It resembles Bloom's Theory of School Learning mentioned in Chapter 1 of this book. The two IEP plans show that the IEP works simultaneously at two levels. The *total service plan* represents a scheme for general, long-range goals. An *individual plan* is developed for each general goal. The overall IEP contains elements discussed in this book:

Entry characteristics: chapters 1, 2, 3, 4

Sample IEP Total Service Plan

Student's Name _____
School _____
Date of Program Entry _____
Annual Goals: (Rank from most to least important if possible.) _____

Summary of Entry Characteristics
_____
_____
_____
_____
_____

Short-Term Specific Objectives	Specific Educational and/or Support Services	Person(s) Responsible	Percent of Time	Beginning and Ending Date	Review Date

Percent of Time in Regular Classroom

Placement Recommendation

Planning and Placement Committee Members
Present _____
_____
_____
_____
Meeting Date(s) _____

Committee Recommendations for Specific Procedures, Techniques, Materials, etc.

Objective Evaluation Standards for each Annual Goal Statement, and Timetable for Evaluation Procedures

Behavioral objectives and task analysis: Chapter 7

sion in a regular class will not eliminate a handicapped child's difficulties. Even though they will receive additional help, handicapped children need special attention in the classroom and teachers need special understanding of them.

COPING WITH NEW DEMANDS

Is the law too idealistic?

Regular classroom teachers often feel anxiety about mainstreaming, and many find it difficult to show enthusiasm and positive attitudes toward it (Alexander and Strain, 1978). Like most new legislation, PL 94–142 raises some problems and requires some adjustments by those whom it affects. Dixon et al. (1980) attest to teacher "burnout" as a result of increased stress in trying to comply with the law. Burnout is aggravated, they say, because many school districts have not yet developed effective retraining programs for their staffs. The difficulty in coping with the demands of PL 94–142 has even earlier origins, though. Most states do not require prospective regular teachers to take a single course in special education. So it is little wonder that school administrators hope for miracles to solve a range of frustrations:

Strategies and techniques: chapters 8, 9, 10
Objective evaluation standards: chapters 14 and 15

The IEP thus is simply a compilation of good educational practices, rather than of innovations. But importantly, it should help to reduce dependence on and misuse of labels; it views students in noncategorical fashion, a point underscored by the word *individual* in its title. (The term *noncategorical* means that labels or categories of exceptionality, such as *learning disabled*, are not used.)

Each student is unique, with his or her own needs, interests, and capabilities, and the different degrees of handicap will influence the types of objectives and methods specified in the IEP.

In this noncategorical view of handicapped children, you may detect a paradox. On one hand, a uniform set of guidelines is presented for dealing with all such youngsters, no matter what type or degree of dysfunction is apparent. On the other hand, there are general characteristics of certain *types* of handicaps, and it would seem unwise to ignore what is known.

Sample IEP Individual Plan

(Complete one of these for each goal statement specified on Total Service Plan; use reverse side if more space is needed.)

Student's Name _____ Goal Statement _____
School _____
Person(s) Completing Form _____

Behavioral Objectives	Task Analysis of Objectives	Strategies and/or Techniques	Materials and/or Resources	Projected Starting Date	Projected Ending Date	Comments

The most effective approach, probably, would be to use what *is* known about a category such as emotionally disturbed to decide broadly what behavior or competency might be expected of a given child. Then, push the label into the background and employ the IEP for specific direction about educational planning. Remember: in the long run, the only overall purpose of labeling is to help the student. ■

Poor attitudes of teachers and students.

Inadequate and uneven skills of professional staff.

Vast amounts of time spent on student evaluation, conferences, planning and paperwork.

Parents who cannot or will not participate in cooperative planning.

But the picture is not so bleak as it may seem to you. Much of the mainstreaming squabble is overly simplistic. The dramatic "either regular class or special class" conflict rarely occurs. Mainstreaming has many variations, and exceptional students often spend only part of a day in the regular class. And schools provide plenty of support services: resource room teachers, remedial reading teachers, school psychologists, speech therapists. In addition to the skills these people can offer exceptional children, they also have free advice to help you cope with new challenges. So let us look at the characteristics of the kinds of exceptional children that you are likely to encounter.

Children with Sensorimotor Impairments

Any child who has a disability affecting speech, hearing, seeing, or moving is said to have a sensorimotor impairment. Such children are usually easier to spot than other exceptional children. Their impairments are often quickly measurable: it is no problem to determine the extent, for example, of hearing

The Perils of Labeling

When teachers label exceptional children as emotionally disturbed or educable mentally retarded and the like, the labels are likely to stick to the children for the rest of their lives —unless the children grow up to be Einsteins or Churchills. In teachers, the labels often induce negative stereotypes: teachers maintain their prejudices, Foster and Ysseldyke (1976) have shown, even in the face of evidence that the labels are wrong. Teachers then may translate their attitudes into behavior: they expect certain things of children they have branded exceptional and show their expectations in their approaches, whereupon the children meet the teachers' expectations. So you have the self-fulfilling prophecy manifesting itself in what psychologists call *teacher expectancy.*

Another result of labeling is the sense of satisfaction that derives from categorizing a student. Labels tell us nothing about what to do with the labeled child, but the more satisfied we feel with our diagnosis, the less likely we are to get off our category and do something about it.

Labels, like insurance rates, are based on group rather than individual behavior. (You may have a perfect driving record, for example, but if you are a male under twenty-five years of age and live in a big city, you will have to pay a high premium for car insurance because people in your category are considered highly risky customers.) But children are individuals, not statistics. The categorizations we suggest in this book provide only general guidelines for understanding them. As teachers, never let labels obscure the genuine individual differences within a category. ■

loss or deviation from twenty-twenty vision. Intellectual or emotional characteristics are far more difficult to appraise.

The physically impaired child *may* or *may not* be impaired intellectually: it is wrong to assume that because a child speaks, sees, or hears with difficulty—or not at all—or suffers some other physical disorder, he or she possesses lessened mental abilities. Many children troubled by sensorimotor problems show normal cognitive and affective development. In others, emotional and academic problems overlap the physical ones. And some children with specific learning problems develop symptoms of physical impairment in response to their learning disorders. In short, children with the same physical impairment may display vastly different intellectual and social characteristics.

What sensorimotor impairments will you find among students?

Each of the four major types of sensorimotor impairment—speech, hearing, and sight disorders, and physical disabilities—will be discussed independently in the following pages, but you should keep in mind that children may be beset by more than one of them. For example, a partly deaf child may also experience difficulty in communicating, either because of the hearing loss or because of another physical impairment, such as a cleft palate.

COMMUNICATION DISORDERS

Children who have trouble speaking or understanding the spoken word are said to suffer from communication disorders. This form of sensorimotor impairment affects more school-age children than any other. Speech and language problems are often found in children with other types of learning difficulties, either because of or in addition to them. However, what appears to

"You'd be surprised at the variation in our EMR kids—enormous individual differences. They don't look alike, think alike, speak alike, or learn alike. But, yes, they do have things in common. They need reinforcement and they love attention. Just like 'normal' kids."

be a language problem may not be one at all; if a mentally retarded ten-year-old shows the cognitive skills of a three-year-old, it is normal for the child to speak like a three-year-old.

There are three types of language problems. One is *receptive*, which involves difficulty in taking in and interpreting information from the environment. A second is *expressive*, and describes inability to communicate information adequately to others. And *expressive and receptive difficulties* combine the two. Each type is a continuing problem. All of us have had trouble on occasion understanding others and sometimes have read and understood a word we cannot pronounce or define. Victims of communication disorders encounter these frustrations all the time.

Speech and language problems may originate in a number of different sources. Physical problems can hinder hearing or speaking. Deafness and impaired motor functioning interrupt receptive and expressive abilities respectively. Aside from obvious physical limitations, identifiable perceptual or neurological processes contribute to expressive and receptive language difficulties. Auditory perception, the ability to associate a sound or word with a concept, may be the source of a language problem. Auditory discrimination (distinguishing between sounds), auditory analysis (giving meanings to strings of words by applying the rules of grammar), and retrieval skills (summoning words and meanings from our memory banks) are all physical and perceptual skills needed for normal communication. Weakness in any of them may result in a communication disorder.

Are communication disorders easy to detect?

Emotional problems also may lead to difficulties in communication, exemplified by children who stutter. Most language specialists believe that stuttering, or language *disfluency*—as it is now being called—is a learned disorder. Disfluency is typically found in children rather than adults, and usually begins between the ages of two and seven. Children during this time are learning the rules of grammar, sentence construction, and adult speech, and most of them exhibit some disfluency; pausing or editing while speaking is to be expected in young children. But a fuzzy boundary separates normal development and communication problems. When a child continually repeats words, phrases, or parts of words, or appears anxious, hurried, or uncomfortable when stuck at some point in communication, the boundary has been crossed. These unusual speech patterns are believed to develop in response to environmental rewards: the child can gain attention by stuttering, or can express hostility or manipulate others, such as parents or teachers, by requiring them to respond differently from the way they respond to other children.

HEARING DISORDERS

Any significant loss or distortion of hearing is considered a disorder. The source may be prenatal—a mother's illness, or drugs taken or a trauma suffered during pregnancy—or the disorder may be hereditary or result from a childhood ailment. About 14 million Americans suffer some hearing loss. Many children with other learning disabilities, particularly those which are organically based, have a hearing problem too.

Hearing impairment affects three important aspects of life. On the physical level, danger signals such as an approaching automobile's horn or a train's whistle may go unheard. On the cognitive level, learning becomes difficult because of limited communication. And affectively, hearing loss cuts natural ties to the environment; the absence of common sounds may result in a sense of isolation and in psychological strain. All three consequences of hearing loss—physical, cognitive, and affective—should be considered by teachers when planning instruction for students whose hearing is impaired.

Depending on its cause, hearing loss can be treated with drugs or surgically, or through auditory rehabilitation programs that include the use of hearing aids and instruction in lip reading. Psychological or educational counseling may be provided when social, emotional, or learning problems occur.

VISUAL IMPAIRMENT

Visual impairment may be as minor as the need for corrective lenses or as severe as total blindness. In many less extreme cases, the teacher will be the first person to recognize that a child needs glasses. But as many as 1.5 million

---

What to Do If Johnny Can't Talk

Communication disorders may be the commonest sensorimotor impairment affecting school children. Approximately 10 percent of all Americans have a disorder that interferes with communication. Sometimes these disorders go unrecognized in the home. Parents may consider a lisp cute, or continued "baby talk" by a six-year-old as innocent and endearing. Unfortunately, such parental reactions thwart early identification and remediation procedures essential to helping children with speech and language problems, and you, the teacher, may be the first knowledgeable person a child encounters who can help.

What signals a possible problem? Culatta and Culatta (1981) suggest some simple questions you might keep in mind as you listen to your students.

Can I understand this student easily or is it a chore to interpret what he or she says?

Is the voice I hear what I would expect, or does it sound like that of a much older person, a younger person, or one of the opposite sex?

Does he or she look odd when talking? Do facial or body movements detract from the message? Does the child appear to be suffering during speech?

Are consonants dropped from words? Are mostly vowel sounds used?

Is sentence structure obviously faulty?

Is the student embarrassed by his or her speech or reluctant to talk?

Does the child show unusual confusions or reversals in speech?

If the answer to any of these questions is yes, a call to the school speech pathologist or speech teacher is in order. Consultation with a professional will help identify the source of the problem. More important, the speech professional can work with you and the child to improve language or speech abilities. ∎

Americans will never see well enough to read, despite glasses. In most such cases, the visually impaired student is described as needing a specially trained teacher, a specially designed or adapted curriculum or materials, and specific educational aids.

Problems with vision are best attacked when they are identified early. In some cases, sight can be improved; in others, deterioration can be halted. That is why many schools require a yearly eye examination for each student.

Until recently, remediation of impaired vision and educational materials for partially sighted or blind students were limited. Corrective lenses, seeing-eye dogs, instruction in Braille, and hired readers were all that could be offered. Scientific advances in the 1970s have changed that. New medical procedures allow correction or improvement of previously untreatable visual impairments. Development of the laser cane greatly increases the mobility of the blind; the cane uses a light beam to probe the environment ahead, and sends off auditory and tactile signals to warn of obstacles, stairs, or curbs that interrupt the beam. The Kurzweil Reading Machine for the Blind, a sophisticated application of computer technology that translates written words into spoken language, allows the blind to "read" almost any book. Although the visually impaired certainly face social, emotional, and educational problems not faced by people with good eyesight, great strides are being made to help them lead almost normal lives.

PHYSICAL DISABILITIES

The loss of a limb, the lack of control of a muscle, neurological abnormalities such as cerebral palsy, or impairments with unidentifiable sources, like epilepsy, are all physical disabilities. Educational programs for victims of each of these disabilities are as varied as the impairments. The most common educational barrier faced by physically disabled students is the architectural one presented by the school itself. Under PL 94–142, many of the environmental hurdles in school buildings are being eliminated.

The Learning-Disabled Student

Among handicapped pupils, those with learning problems—often called *learning disabilities* or another of some three dozen such phrases (see Table 11.2)—seem to be by far the most numerous. They appear easy enough to describe. They are youngsters of normal intelligence, without apparent physical, sensory, or cultural handicaps, who find it almost impossible to learn one or more subjects. In the particular fields where they mire down, they lag several years behind their peers and they achieve a great deal less than might be expected of them on the basis of their performance in other areas.

They constitute one of the more baffling phenomena of education: among both experts and laymen the dimensions of learning disabilities are often almost comically misunderstood. Cruickshank has remarked:

> Parents in their concept of learning disability have talked with me about nail biting, poor eating habits, failure of the child to keep his room neat, unwillingness to take a bath, failure to brush teeth. Teachers have questioned me about disrespectful children, children who will not listen to the adult, children who are sexually precocious, children who are aggressive—all in the belief that these are learning disability children. One parent asked me if the fact that his college-student son wore long hair and, he "suspected," lived with a girl outside his dormitory was a result of learning disability! (1972, p. 382).

What causes learning disabilities?

Even among specialists, learning disability means different things to different people. For example, there is little known and even less agreed on about the causes of various learning disorders. Specialists once blamed "minimal brain dysfunction." When it became apparent that minimal brain dysfunction is exceedingly hard—or impossible—to detect, many specialists wondered whether they had been using a label as a cover-up for unknown causes.

If causes remain uncertain, can we still produce an acceptable definition of learning disablties? The most generally accepted definition, now incorporated into PL 94–142, appears to be that devised by the National Advisory Committee on Handicapped Children:

Table 11.2

In 1966, a government task force on "minimal brain dysfunction" (an earlier term for learning disabilities) located thirty-eight terms used to describe learning disordered youth. The terms follow (Clements, 1966).

Association deficit pathology	Character impulse disorder
Organic brain disease	Hyperkinetic impulse disorder
Organic brain damage	Aggressive behavior disorder
Organic brain dysfunction	Psychoneurological learning disorders
Minimal brain damage	Hyperkinetic syndrome
Diffuse brain damage	Dyslexia
Neurophrenia	Hyperexcitability syndrome
Organic drivenness	Perceptual cripple
Cerebral dysfunction	Primary reading retardation
Organic behavior disorder	Specific reading disability
Choreiform syndrome	Clumsy child syndrome
Minor brain damage	Hypokinetic syndrome
Minimal brain injury	Perceptually handicapped
Minimal cerebral injury	Aphasoid syndrome
Minimal chronic brain syndromes	Learning disabilities
Minimal cerebral damage	Conceptually handicapped
Minimal cerebral palsy	Attention disorders
Cerebral dys-synchronization syndrome	Interjacent child
Hyperkinetic behavior syndrome	

Children with special learning disabilities exhibit a disorder in one or more of the basic psychological processes involved in understanding or in using spoken or written languages. These may be manifested in disorders of listening, thinking, talking, reading, writing, spelling or arithmetic. They include conditions which have been referred to as perceptual handicaps, brain injury, minimal brain dysfunction, dyslexia, developmental aphasia, etc. They do not include learning problems which are due primarily to visual, hearing or motor handicaps, to mental retardation, emotional disturbance or to environmental disadvantage (1968, p. 34).

But, what are the "basic psychological processes"? There are so many interpretations of psychological processes that a clear understanding of the phrase is unlikely. Even if certain processes could be described precisely, it may not be known whether a disorder results from genuine impairment or from slow development (Turnbull and Schultz, 1979). What are "perceptual handicaps, brain injury, minimal brain dysfunction, dyslexia, developmental aphasia, etc."? The terms produce no agreement among teachers, pediatricians, or theorists.

What does *learning disability* mean?

Public Law 94–142 attempts to make the definition of learning disabilities mean more by translating it into terms of school achievement. Given instruction suitable to his or her age and overall ability, a "learning disabled" child is one who lags significantly in one or more of these areas: speaking, reading comprehension, basic reading skills, writing, spelling, listening, mathematics, math calculation, and math reasoning (Federal Register, 1976, p. 52407).

Thus, there must be evidence that a child's achievements do not reflect his or her potential; and the extension of the definition places great importance on accurate assessment of potential and achievement. Predictably, educators have become less concerned with the origins of learning disabilities and more with valid assessment and teaching approaches.

An acceptable definition should lead to precise assessment of various learning disorders. But even with the emphasis on educational achievement, parts of the definition are open to interpretation. For instance, "potential" may be measured with an intelligence test, the IQ scores of which are controversial (see Chapter 3). Now, if the definition of learning disabilities is poorly understood, everything that follows—assessment, placement, setting of goals, educational programming—may be improperly designed.

Researchers and measurement specialists are working hard to improve precision in defining and measuring learning disabilities, and the field is changing rapidly. We recommend that you review new developments from time to time; the Selected Readings at the end of the chapter give sources that provide current information on everything from definitions to discriminative stimuli.

Meanwhile, the causes of learning disorders remain mysterious, and their careful definition, measurement, and treatment have not been accomplished. So the situation that seemed simple in the first paragraph of this section—a mentally normal child's inability to learn one or more subjects—is, as researchers and scholars in the field admit, "a mess" (Freeman, 1976).

SPOTTING THE SYMPTOMS

If you intend to teach, you will be chiefly concerned not with the causes of learning disorder but with behavior in class that manifests the most obvious symptoms among the hundred that a government task force has listed (Clements, 1966).

Many learning problems go undetected until a child enters school. Some mildly learning-disabled youngsters plod along undiagnosed until junior or senior high school. So classroom teachers are crucial for uncovering disorders. Simple observation of behavior, or *informal assessment* (Fremont et al., 1977) usually sets the stage for a more extensive formal assessment by a specialist. Here are a couple of questions to help you spot symptoms by routine observation.

1. Compared to peers of the same age and grade level, does the child show a particular behavior with much greater frequency or intensity?
2. Does the behavior actually interfere with the child's thinking, academic progress, or emotional and social performance?

With these questions in mind, let's examine some of the symptoms of learning disabilities.

The Pupil Who Cannot Sit Still. The most frequent manifestation of learning disorder is *hyperkinesis*, or *hyperactivity*. That may be what is wrong with your future pupil who bounces around the class a great deal, squirms and wriggles constantly while sitting, pays no attention to what you are teaching, chatters away to a friend across the aisle, and has difficulty following instructions. Overactive youngsters, particularly boys, are often regarded as classroom management problems, and may be given drugs to calm them down. This issue is discussed more fully in Chapter 13.

The Pupil Who Sits Too Still. A less frequent symptom of learning disorder—and one that may go unrecognized because it causes teachers no overt bother—is *hypoactivity*, the opposite of hyperactivity. That may be what is wrong with the pupil who sits still and stays quieter than you might expect a child to be.

The Pupil with Social Difficulties. Some students are regularly disobedient or disruptive. A single overly aggressive child in a classroom can be a chronic source of irritation and shadow a teacher's success with the remaining students.

The Pupils with Other Symptoms. Excessively clumsy children who walk awkwardly and write and draw poorly—indications of faulty coordination—also may be found among the learning disordered. So may youngsters suffering from *perseveration*. That term means automatic or involuntary repetition of behavior. Reading aloud, perseverative pupils often have to voice words, phrases, or sentences several times before they are able to proceed. Emotional instability, faulty memory, distractibility, and poor perception—of which tone deafness is one aspect—also may appear in learning-disordered students. Rarely, though, does any child suffer from all or even most of those problems.

A CASE HISTORY

Learning disorders take so many shapes and appear to have such diverse origins that no case can be pointed to as typical. So Walter is not typical. But you may be teaching a youngster at least somewhat like him. Ten years old, Walter is the third of four children of highly educated, upper-income, professional people. Walter is extraordinarily good-looking and can be very charming when he feels like it. His physical health is excellent. His height and weight are normal for his age. On the *verbal absurdities* segment of one intelligence test, he scored on the twelve-year-old level. On another intelligence test that used only pictures, he demonstrated an IQ of 109. But Walter reads at second-grade level. Walter is learning disabled.

Like may other learning-disabled youngsters, Walter is hyperkinetic, or compulsively overactive. A brain specialist has found no indication of dysfunction. Walter's hyperkinesis has persisted despite medication.

In school, Walter has been kept in a regular class. Two years ago, struggling at the bottom of the slowest reading group, he began to show certain symptoms that underscored his reading problems. Most obvious, of course, were his hyperactivity and very short attention span. Paying careful attention to his attempts at reading aloud, Walter's teacher noticed that he sometimes substituted words or phrases of his own invention. For example, the written sentence, "Jim did not want to go to the store after school" became the spoken "Jim didn't want to go to the store . . . with his mother."

Although not trained in remedial reading, the teacher realized that Walter needed specialized help as well as concentrated, individual attention that was impossible in a class of twenty-three youngsters. Walter was referred to a reading specialist, who administered a short battery of diagnostic tests. (The specialist judged that a comprehensive clinical evaluation, taking two or three days, was unnecessary if Walter's problem could be pinpointed with the brief testing.) Walter was found to have difficulty with three specific areas: letter confusion (d and p; b and d), substitution (reading "when" for "what"), and "medial vowel confusion" (reading "step" for "stop"). The specialist and the school's resource reading teacher, using an individual education program (IEP), laid out precise objectives, teaching strategies, materials, and assessment procedures. The IEP also specified the regular teacher's and the resource teacher's responsibilities. For thirty minutes a day, Walter meets with the resource teacher, who also assigns brief homework activities.

To address the hyperactivity problem, the school psychologist sketched out a behavior modification plan that involved some self-control exercises for Walter and the use of shaping and positive reinforcement by his teachers and parents.

His hyperkinesis, now reduced, is expected to disappear naturally as he approaches adolescence; it generally does. The reading disorder? On standardized achievement tests, Walter's reading comprehension and vocabulary are still below average. But there is noticeable improvement. The gap between his ability (defined by his high-average IQ) and his achievement has narrowed. Once a subject to be avoided, reading is now tolerable and sometimes fun for him. In Walter's words, "Yeah, I can read lots better than when I was a little kid."

COPING WITH THE PROBLEM

Although it is widely accepted that high school students and even adults suffer from learning disabilities, most research and training programs have focused on children. Attempts are under way to continue such programming through college (Goodman and Mann, 1976).

For learning disorders in general, several supposedly remedial programs have been devised and training materials have been marketed. None of the programs and materials we have examined has produced results that can yet be called impressive.

Meanwhile, what do you do with little Tommy when his performance in class in some subjects is considerably less than what you might rightly expect of him? A kind of rule of thumb is suggested by Myers and Hammill (1976). Though they discourage adherence to any rigid formula, they propose that in the first three grades, a child whose performance is *more than a grade level* behind his apparent ability may be a candidate for special educational programming. Above the third grade, the yardstick would be a disparity of two or more years between performance and expectation.

Reynolds and Birch (1977) list the general corrective approaches used to treat learning disabilities:

What treatments are used with learning disabilities?

Metabolic: Foods presumed to interfere with learning or appropriate behavior, especially those containing certain dyes, are removed from the diet.

Psychoanalytic: The child's early family history is seen as the culprit, and intervention seeks to help the child cope with that history and to boost his or her "ego strength."

Nondirective counseling: A therapeutic program is loosely structured and permissive and emotional warmth and caring are stressed. The procedure aims to help the child solve his or her own problems. Adolescent peers sometimes have been used as counselors (Jacks and Keller, 1978).

Psychophysiological: The psychophysiological group of programs is based on the idea that a learning disabled child is developmentally slow in one of the

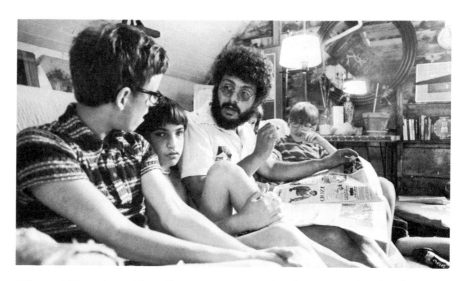

"These children depend heavily upon concrete, visual imagery. They hardly ever seem able to use abstractions or to generalize. But that's OK—we have plenty of other things to concentrate on. Social skills and self-help skills take a lot of our time."

basic psychological processes (attending, memory, sequencing, etc.). The approach pinpoints deficiencies and matches teaching strategies with them.

Participatory responsibility: As in nondirective counseling, the overall goal is to have students solve their own problems. The programs are usually applied in a group, democratic setting. Personal decision-making is stressed.

Applied behavior analysis: This is a scholarly term for behavior modification. As chapters 5 and 10 show, the method alters behavior by contolling its consequences. No speculation about internal correlates or causes of disability is necessary. If an inappropriate behavior appears, change it.

Remedial education: Whatever works may be used, including parts of the other methods described. Stress is placed on proper teaching (rather than on inadequate children), early detection, and cooperation of specialists with the regular classroom teacher.

Reynolds and Birch admit that the various approaches have fuzzy boundaries and overlap occasionally. Which method is best? It is impossible to say. Certainly, remedial education, borrowing heavily from behavior modification and from the psychophysiological area, is the most widespread practice. But like the vague definition of learning disabilities itself, remedial education means many different things. The other programs, perhaps more clearly defined, have not proven universally effective or even moderately good.

Why can't learning disabilities be promptly treated and cured?

We do not mean to suggest that structured techniques for helping learning-disordered youngsters are worthless; what we do mean is that too many methods are as yet poorly evaluated, or require knowledge and preparation greater than most teachers have and beyond the scope of most educational psychology courses. Still, regular classroom teachers cannot shrug off the responsibility for dealing with learning-disordered children. Possible sources of help to you in meeting that responsibility include the Suggested Readings at the end of this chapter, courses in your college that consider the nature and nurture of exceptional students, and your peers who have been trained in special education.

The Emotionally Disturbed or Behavior-Disordered Student

The terms *emotional disturbance* and *behavior disorder* are often used interchangeably, although it is supposed that inclement behavior merely reflects internal emotional storms. We will make no distinction between the terms, as both are used widely to describe the same observable disability.

Emotional disturbance seems to be an occupational hazard of childhood and adolescence. Most children suffer from emotional difficulty sporadically. The symptoms—oversensitivity, moodiness, fearfulness, irritability, tantrums, destructiveness, and hyperactivity—are familiar to parents and teachers. Usually the indisposition is no worse than a mild cold and quickly passes, causing neither parents nor teachers much concern. When the symptoms are moderate and infrequent and do not recur repeatedly in the same form, a youngster is not categorized as emotionally disturbed. To how many young people the label does apply is uncertain. The American Psychiatric Association (1964), considering only children in the elementary schools, put the incidence at 7 to 12 percent. Teachers consider about one out of five children to have behavior disorders, with the majority of such students showing only mild problems (Kelly et al., 1977). Investigators do agree that until late adolescence, emotionally disturbed boys outnumbered girls by ratios ranging between two to one and four to one. After adolescence, the rate for boys drops and the rate for girls rises (Hewett and Blake, 1973).

What characterizes an emotionally disturbed student?

A major reason for the uncertainty about the prevalence of emotional disturbance in the young is that behavior disordered children are difficult to define. Such children have been classified as psychiatric cases, as neurological cases in which there has been brain damage, or as cases of blocked emotional growth, which makes children antisocial or unsociable. In still another approach, they have been viewed as youngsters who have learned undesirable behavior and can be helped to unlearn it (Deno, 1978). The last approach may interest you most as a teacher, because pupils who do not adjust to the requirements of classroom order neither learn nor let others learn.

Behavior-disordered youngsters do not necessarily have lower IQs than normal children. Because of the stress under which they labor, they often score low on intelligence tests, but when and if their disturbance eases, many do impressively better. Though they are difficult to define, they are fairly easy to identify. Teachers' judgments usually prove accurate when youngsters later are screened scientifically for emotional disturbance.

A CASE HISTORY

Nine years old, Glenn was easy to single out as emotionally disturbed. The only child of a divorced mother, who evidences affection and concern for him but who frequently leaves him alone in the evening when she goes out on dates, Glenn rampages through the midwestern suburb in which he lives. He tramples neighbors' gardens, kicks the spokes of other children's tricycles and bicycles, delights in deflating tires of parked cars, and torments smaller children when a nearby playground is unattended by adults. In school, he jeers at his fourth-grade classmates when they answer the teacher's questions, and he tries to trip them on their way to the blackboard. Glenn's physical health is good. His IQ on a Wechsler Intelligence Scale for Children is 95. He reads at second-grade level but he handles arithmetic at fourth-grade level. Despite his lag in reading, he does not appear to be learning-disordered.

Glenn has been kept in a regular fourth-grade class. But he gets thirty minutes of help daily in the school's resource center, and he receives instruction in a corrective reading program and occasional after-school attention from his teacher. He is taken weekly to a mental health center for counseling, and he gets medication for hyperkinesis. Glenn's emotional state thus far has shown no improvement. But he has begun to make some academic progress, which became noticeable after he was assigned to help another student who was slow at arithmetic, Glenn's best subject. That seems to bear out the idea that every child is good at *something*, and profits by emphasis on that something.

COPING WITH THE PROBLEM

Because behavior disorder, like learning disorder, remains a good deal of a mystery, specialists disagree on how to deal with it. You remember that emotional problems are often thought to be at the root of severely disruptive behavior. Some therapists therefore aim for the child's affective domain instead of the overt behavior.

Some theorists of this orientation, notably Carl Rogers (1951), argue for total permissiveness toward emotionally disturbed children in the belief that it will promote emotional growth, with which should come stability. But a major defect of total permissiveness, Whelan (1966) counters, is that it gives such children no guidance in how to tell acceptable from unacceptable behavior. The mental world of disturbed children is chaotic. If the children are to draw order out of chaos, they must have adult help. So a middle course between permissiveness and rigorous discipline, with grownups serving as both warm friends and tough top sergeants, has been proposed as a useful approach.

For that reason, among others, behavior modification is now being widely applied to emotionally disturbed children (Wallace and Kauffman, 1978). The techniques, discussed in Chapter 10, clarify for them the distinctions between what they are expected to do and what they are expected *not* to do. That is a manifestation of discipline. At the same time, the technique makes acceptable behavior attractive, so that the children tend to choose it themselves. That is where the permissiveness comes in. And by training children to comprehend that effort and good behavior do not always win immediate reward, the technique stimulates emotional growth.

Why use behavior modification methods to treat the emotionally disturbed?

Returning Teachers to Teaching. The behavior modification approach recognizes the reality of the central nervous system (in which emotional disturbances originate) and of cognition and thought (which are essential to learning). But their effects can only be inferred: you cannot see the central nervous system at work or put a yardstick on cognition and thought. So, the behavior modification argument goes, teaching should concentrate on behavior you can see and measure. If that view is adopted, teachers stop considering disturbed children as mental patients and treat them as pupils. The emphasis shifts from why the children have problems to what they are ready to learn and how to teach them. Teachers teach, instead of trying to practice psychiatry.

KEEPING PEACE IN THE CLASSROOM

To most teachers, emotionally disturbed children do pose problems of conduct as well as of learning. The need to maintain order in the classroom is ever present, at least in conventional schools. One way to deal with particularly unruly children is the procedure called "time out," which we have explained in Chapter 10.

The Engineered Classroom. A nine-point program for dealing with disturbed children who cannot function in class has been devised by Hewett, Taylor, and Artuso (1969) who designed an "engineered" classroom geared to the behavior modification approach. The room's facilities provide areas for learning and activity that are intended to strengthen pupils on six levels in which they are deemed deficient. The levels are designated *attention, response, order, exploratory, social,* and *mastery.*

An *Order Center,* one of the room's facilities, contains puzzles and games: their purpose is to teach pupils to pay attention, respond, and follow directions.

An *Exploratory Center* invites arts and crafts activities and simple scientific investigations.

A *Communication Center* permits two or more children to engage in social behavior.

A *Mastery Center* provides study booths and individual work tables.

How does an "engineered" classroom operate?

The centers are put to use in connection with the nine-point program when children fail to function successfully in class. The program's first point constitutes its least restrictive procedure. The remaining eight increase in restrictiveness step by step. The steps of the program are:

1. Send the pupil to a study booth to work on the failed assignment. (For *mastery.*)
2. Modify the assignment. (Also for *mastery.*)
3. Restate firmly what the teacher expects of pupils (For *social behavior.*)
4. Send the pupil to the Exploratory Center. (For *exploration.*)
5. Send the pupil to the Order Center. (For improving *order.*)
6. Take the pupil from the room and agree with the child on a task, such as walloping a punching bag or running around the building. (For improving *response.*)
7. Provide individual tutoring. (For improving *attention.*)
8. Order "time out."
9. Send the pupil home.

A completely "engineered" classroom is still a rarity, but much of the procedure can be applied in any school. The general concept of successively restrictive educational treatments is important in any classroom that has mainstreamed youngsters. The point is that the first strategy attempted should be as close to normal as possible. If that works, fine. If it is only partly successful, or fails, move to the next stage, which is somewhat more restrictive. The final steps are used only as last resorts.

Life Space Interviewing. A nonbehavioral approach to dealing with emotionally disturbed youngsters has been proposed by Redl and Wattenberg (1959). Called *Life Space Interviewing* (LSI), it broadly resembles psychotherapy, but a teacher does not need extensive professional training to understand and employ its basic features. And though it was designed for use in crises, its techniques can be applied in a day-to-day program. It works thus:

1. Initially, the teacher tries to get an impression of the troubled student's perceptions of a specific incident or of school in general.
2. The teacher hypothesizes: are Carol's perceptions at the root of her problem or problems, or do they represent something deeper and more complex?
3. After Carol has explained how she feels, the teacher chats with her about what she can do about her difficulties. The teacher carefully refrains at this stage from moralizing about what she *ought* to do.
4. If Carol fails to acknowledge all the realities of the situation, the teacher then tries to clarify it: "If you do *this, that* consequence is likely; if you do something else, then this may happen."

Can a disturbed person be reached by a person-to-person approach?

In each step, the teacher's attitude should be sensitive, supportive and objective; the teacher maintains neutrality and avoids suggestion of punishment. The teacher may be able also to provide the student with additional facts about her behavior and thus help her to understand the contradictions between her perceptions and the real world.

The LSI procedure may help teachers as much as students, Redl and Wattenberg believe, by providing them with comprehension of how students view their world and by helping them assume a neutral posture and avoid outright punishment. But like most other approaches, LSI presents its problems. When twenty-four other children are clamoring for attention, it is not easy to find time to apply LSI to one. And where undesirable behavior is involved, it can be almost impossible for a teacher to remain cool: neutrality usually takes lots of practice.

What Becomes of the Children?   Whether or not psychotherapy proves useful for disturbed youngsters remains debatable. One study concluded that two-thirds of the cases improved with or without therapy (Lewis, 1965). Another study found that children designated as disturbed early in their schooling were not so labeled by the time they reached fifth grade (McCaffrey and Cumming, 1967). It appears impossible to predict which children will get over their emotional disturbances and which will not. A related question concerns the value of placement in special classes for emotionally disturbed youngsters. Twenty-one such children were followed for nearly six years by Vacc (1972); he compared those in special classes with those in regular classes and found no differences in terms of achievement, peer rejection, or behavior ratings. Thus it appears that regular classroom teachers, with support and advice from specially trained colleagues, may be able to handle moderate levels of emotional disturbance in some of their students.

Educable Mentally Retarded Children

The educable mentally retarded (EMR) are youngsters whose IQs range roughly between 50 and 70 and who thus possess only half to two-thirds or so of the average child's intelligence. They are also known as "mildly" mentally retarded. (Severely and profoundly retarded complete the below-average portion of the intelligence continuum.) Their designation as educable mentally retarded children implies that they are regarded as capable of (1) acquiring at least a minimum of academic education; (2) living more or less normal lives as citizens; (3) holding jobs.

Some 700,000 EMRs attend the public schools, according to the federal Bureau of Education for the Handicapped (1970), but as MacMillan (1977) points out, the incidence of retardation is enormously difficult to pin down because definitions of it may differ from place to place. The most recent definition developed by the American Association of Mental Deficiency, which has offered several in the past, says: "Mental retardation refers to significantly subaverage general intellectual functioning existing concurrently with deficits in adaptive behavior, and manifested during the developmental period" (Grossman, 1973, p. 5).

Let's analyze that. "Significantly subaverage intellectual functioning" here means an IQ score below 70. "Adaptive behavior" refers to skills dependent on age: in early childhood, they include speech, language development, and self-help; in adolescence, they embrace basic academic abilities and participation in group activities (Grossman, 1973). The "developmental period" runs from infancy to age eighteen.

The chief difference between the AAMD's latest definition and earlier ones is that the new definition specifies impairment of *both* intelligence and adaptive behavior. Table 11.3 depicts the two-dimensional structure of the AAMD's definition: a youngster may have an IQ of, say, 60 and not be classified as mentally retarded in the absence of evidence of dysfunctional adaptive behavior. Fair enough, in theory. But, as skeptics point out, reliable measures of adaptive behavior do not exist, and MacMillan (1977) predicts that most educators will continue to use the IQ as the sole criterion.

Physically, most EMRs approximate the normal in height, weight, and appearance. Defects of vision, hearing, speech, or coordination appear in them more frequently than they do in average children, but are still not typical (Kirk, 1972). In motor skills and physical fitness, they lag behind the average, and the deficiencies broaden as the youngsters grow older (Dunn, 1973).

Socially, the adjustment of EMRs is a matter of dispute. Some researchers contend that they blend without much difficulty into everyday life (Goldstein, 1964). But intensive follow-up studies have found that many adult EMRs live impoverished and unhappy lives (Heber and Dever, 1970). Most of those studies involved EMRs who had attended special classes or had been institutionalized; it remains to be seen whether or not mainstreaming will make a difference.

What are the characteristics of EMRs?

In regular classes, EMRs are likely to manifest several characteristics that distinguish them from other students. They may demonstrate short attention spans, lack of concentration, and unwillingness to participate in class activities. Some of this behavior results from insensitive teaching, in which teachers talk over their heads and then ask them to respond to material that they do not understand. Because they experience failure repeatedly, they succumb easily to feelings of frustration, compounding their academic difficulties with behavioral problems. Of course, these same behaviors may characterize the learning-disabled or emotionally disturbed child. The important difference lies in mental potential: the EMR child is not so called unless he shows a below-average IQ.

Academically, EMRs can be expected to acquire basic skills—reading and arithmetic—more slowly than do their peers. Usually, progress in those areas seems to parallel advance in mental age, which is about a quarter to a third below normal. But individuals vary greatly: when a curriculum emphasizes reading, an EMR may learn faster to read. Little research has been done on *comprehension* of what is read (MacMillan, 1977), so there is little convincing evidence that understanding of the printed word accompanies speedy recognition of it. A similar difficulty may exist in arithmetic: EMRs may catch on to how it's done, but *reasoning* about it is much tougher for them (MacMillan, 1977).

Table 11.3. Rationale of AAMD Definition of Mental Retardation with Dual Criteria of Retarded Intellectual Functioning and Adaptive Behavior

	INTELLECTUAL FUNCTIONING	
	IQ below 70	*IQ 70 or above*
Deficient	Mentally retarded	Not mentally retarded
Not Deficient	Not mentally retarded	Not mentally retarded

SPOTTING THE SYMPTOMS

Mild retardation usually goes undetected below the age of six, and special programs for EMRs in kindergarten have been rare. Early discovery is difficult. Slow cognitive growth, such as late learning to speak, may reflect either mental retardation or developmental lag. Few communities have established programs to screen children before entry into public school. Even when screening programs are organized, the tests used have questionable validity.

When preschool youngsters have seemed backward, they have simply been kept in kindergarten for another year. Samuel A. Kirk (1972) has suggested that EMRs and the community both would benefit if such children were identified early in the kindergarten term by individual intelligence tests. They could then be helped by special teachers, in preparaton for regular schooling. On the other hand, individual tests are expensive and few schools can afford them.

Generally, few children are designated EMRs in their first three years of school because teachers and administrators quite rightly hesitate to take so serious a step without long observation of pupils. By the time the youngsters are nine or ten years old, however, their academic grades and their IQ scores usually pinpoint them as needing special instruction.

A CASE HISTORY

Guillermo is thirteen years old, but unlike most other EMRs he is so undersized that he appears to be no more than eight. He stands four feet four inches high and weighs seventy-two pounds. He is quite handsome, though. He is the third of four children and is extremely close to his mother but not to his stepfather, a New York sanitation department laborer. Guillermo's two brothers, who are older than he is, are doing extremely well in school, and his sister is a slightly better than average pupil. But Guillermo reads, writes, and does arithmetic only on the first-grade level, and on the Wechsler Intelligence Scale for Children (Revised) he demonstrated an IQ of 64. Guillermo has been arrested twice for breaking into parked cars, and there is evidence of emotional disturbance, possibly related to resentment at his mother's remarriage. But his basic problem is mental retardation, which may have been caused by a long illness in infancy. In school, he spends part of his time in regular class and part in a special class for the EMRs.

COPING WITH THE PROBLEM

The EMR child is not simply slower to learn than other children. The problem is more complicated than that. Educable mentally retarded children do not easily pick up knowledge and information without instruction, as normal children do. They have difficulty generalizing, or transferring what they have learned to new situations, as normal children do. Itard's Wild Boy of Aveyron, for example, could pick out one certain knife from a collection of objects when Itard wrote the word *knife*. But when Itard substituted a knife of somewhat different shape and wrote the word, the boy could not *generalize* that a knife was a knife, whatever its shape (Davis and Ecob, 1959).

For teaching EMR children, behavior modification has been widely adopted in recent years. Behavior modification is implicit or explicit in most of the principles that Kirk recommends for instructing EMRs (1972, p. 214).

1. *Try not to let the children fail.* Lead them to the right answer: provide clues if necessary, reword the question, simplify the problem, narrow the choices among possible repsonses. But do not let them fail; success is a reward, or "reinforcer" in terms of behavior modification.
2. *Provide immediate feedback.* If a child's answer is correct, say so at once. If the answer is wrong, say so only in terms that will lead the child to the right answer.
3. *Reward correct responses immediately.* Reinforcement can be tangible or intangible: candy is dandy, but praise will serve. As children progress, their own successes will generally provide enough reinforcement, so your rewards may not be necessary.
4. *Find the level at which the children work best.* Too easy a task will not challenge them to maximum effort. Too difficult a task will invite failure and frustration.
5. *Proceed systematically, step by step.* Basic essential knowledge must be taught before more difficult material.
6. *Take small steps.* Minimal advances from lesson to lesson will facilitate learning and will help to ensure success on each step.
7. *Provide for positive transfer of knowledge from one situation to another.* Help the children to *generalize* by presenting the same concept in a variety of settings and relationships: if children are taught that a diesel engine can power an automobile, a truck, or a boat, they should comprehend, by

transfer, the meaning of "diesel locomotive." (Negative transfer is something else: it is what happens when, water-skiing for the first time, you lean forward as you do on snow skis.)

What can be done to help EMR students?

8. *Repeat instruction sufficiently to develop overlearning*, which means learning *beyond* the point of mastery. Without overlearning, children may forget tomorrow what they have learned today, and retarded children seem to require more repetition than do normal children.

9. *Space the repetitions, rather than cram them into one or two lessons.* After you have presented a new concept, return to it now and then, varying the settings. That will not only drive it home, but will help the children exercise transfer.

10. *Limit the number of concepts presented in one period.* Do not tell children, "This letter is sometimes pronounced *ay* and sometimes *ah.*" Teach one sound at a time until it has been overlearned. Then teach the other sound in a different setting. If you present both sounds at the same time, children may become confused. Introduce new material only after older material has become familiar.

11. *Highlight what is important in each subject presented.* Direct the children's attention to the relevant points and emphasize those points. That should help the children to acquire the ability to discard the irrelevant.

12. *Organize daily lesson plans to provide pupils with experience in success.* That is implied in Point 1 but it is so important that it bears restatement. Because EMRs have usually known only failure and thus fall easy victims to frustration, their success is essential to their learning. The best way to cope with their necessity is to arrange day-to-day programs presenting them with short-range as well as long-range tasks at which they will succeed. The principle applies to all youngsters, but especially to the retarded, to whom failure has become a way of life. Teachers dealing with the retarded must see to it that children not only avoid failure, but actually savor success.

Can EMRs handle basic school subjects?

What Can EMR Children Learn? Retarded children cannot absorb everything that normal children do, so they pose the question: What and when should they be taught? Because few children are designated retarded in the first three grades—a point mentioned earlier—special instruction for them usually begins when they are nine and, nowadays, may continue through high school. Throughout their school careers, improvement of their reading, writing, arithmetic and communication skills is emphasized. (The box on p. 360 shows an instructional package meant to help teachers provide math instruction to EMR children. Its components parallel the requirements of the individualized educational program set forth in Public Law 94–142.) In secondary schools EMRs are also taught:

Home building skills, among them home economics and household mechanics.

LEVEL 2   **G29**

PROJECT MATH INSTRUCTIONAL GUIDE

STRAND	Geometry
AREA	Shape
CONCEPT	2-Dimensional

	INPUT	OUTPUT

		LEARNER
BEHAVIORAL OBJECTIVE	States the names of 2-dimensional geometric shapes.	Identifies examples of 2-dimensional geometric shapes.

ACTIVITIES

1. **Identifying the Shapes.** Give the learner several attribute pieces. Hold up a picture of a circle, and state, "This is a circle." Point to one of your shapes that is a circle. Introduce the words *triangle, square,* and *rectangle* in the same way. For the triangle, say, "This shape has three sides. It is a triangle." For the square, state, "This shape has four sides, all of which are equal. It also has corners like the corners of a sheet of paper. This is a square." For the rectangle, state, "This shape has four sides: two sides may be longer than the other two. It also has corners like the corners of a sheet of paper. This is a rectangle." Randomly ask the learners to point to each of the four shapes. State only the shape name.

2. **Shapes in Pictures.** Show the learner the pictures on activity sheets G29.1 and G29.2. Ask the learner to point to the circular shapes in the pictures. Repeat for square, triangular and rectangular shapes. Each time, give only a description of the shape. You might also use magazine pictures for this activity. If you wish, have the learner color the shapes with different colored crayons: "Color all the shapes with three sides with a blue crayon, color all the shapes with four equal sides with a red crayon," and so forth.

3. **Shapes in the Classroom.** Name a geometric shape. Ask the learner to point to an object in the room having that shape. If the learner has difficulty, demonstrate by saying, "Rectangular shape," then pointing to the door. Vary the activity by using characteristics of the shapes instead of shape names.

4. **Touching Shapes.** In a non-transparent bag, place at least two shapes. Ask the learner to close his eyes and to reach into the bag for a shape. State that you want him to find a circle (square, rectangle, triangle). Repeat the activity until the learner is able to find all of the shapes using only his sense of touch.

MATERIALS

Attribute pieces, paper bag, activity sheets G29.1 and G29.2.

SUPPLEMENTAL ACTIVITIES   G29: a, b, c, d.

EVALUATION

Give the learner magazine pictures featuring objects of different shapes. Ask the learner to mark all objects that do not contain or are not a rectangular shape.

Social skills, including how to follow directions, how to dress, how to behave, how to choose careers, and how to get along generally in society.

Physical and mental health care, which embraces personal hygiene and appearance, self-acceptance, establishment of values, wise use of leisure, and pride in accomplishment.

Along with normal students, they may be introduced to art and music. Educable retarded students are generally considered to lack special talents for those fields, but there are exceptions, which led Lindsley to argue that more effort should be made to find and develop unsuspected skills (1965, p. 35).

The Effort and the Reward. As a teacher you may wonder, when your pupils include EMR children, whether the results of instruction will prove worth the trouble. Baller (1936) studied 206 pupils in classes for the mentally deficient in Lincoln, Nebraska, and fifteen years later Charles (1953) tracked down most of them to determine how they were doing. Eighty percent were married; and 80 percent of those married had children. The IQs of the seventy-three children whom Charles tested ranged from 50 to 138, with a group average of 95. Eighty-three percent of all the adults whom Charles located were self-supporting. Some lived in shacks, but some had expensive houses. Most of the men worked as laborers and most of the women were housekeepers, but a few of the group had risen to managerial positions. Charles administered Wechsler-Bellevue tests to twenty-four of the adults, and the scores proved considerably higher than the Binet scores attained back in the school for defectives fifteen years before. A second follow-up study, about thirty years after Baller's original research, found a majority of the subjects still self-supporting (Baller et al., 1967).

What becomes of EMRs? But the picture may be considerably less rosy currently. In a 1970 study, Heber and Dever found that most adult EMRs had jobs, but on the lower rungs

---

Living Statues and Brimming Bowls

In working with retarded children, Alfred Binet (1909; cited in Torrance and White, 1975, pp. 78–79) invented a number of techniques, two of which are described by him below:

Having children who did not know how to listen, nor to regard, nor to be quiet we discovered that the first duty was not to teach them the idea which seemed to us most useful to them, but that, first of all, they must learn to learn; therefore . . . we devised what were called exercises in mental orthopedics. . . . Just as physical orthopedy straightens a crooked spine, so mental orthopedy straightens, cultivates, and strengthens the attention, memory, perception, judgment and will. We did not seek to teach the children an idea, a memory, but we put their mental faculties in order.

We began with exercises in immobility. It was arranged that once a day, in each class, the teacher would ask all his pupils to strike an attitude and keep it, like a statue, for several seconds at first, then a whole minute; the attitude was to be taken instantly, at a signal, then abandoned instantly, at a second signal. In the first trial, they accomplished nothing; the en-

tire class was convulsed with foolish laughter. Then, little by little, they were calmed; the exercise lost its novelty, the children grew accustomed to it. Their self-respect became involved. The honor was to the one who could hold the attitude the longest time. I have seen children who had been turbulent, noisy, disobedient, the despair of their teachers—I have seen, I say, these children for the first time make a serious effort and bring into play all their vanity in order to remain immobile; they were, then, capable of attention, will, and self-control. What was called the *game of statues* became so popular that the children demanded it. . . .

I will cite also . . . the exercises for motor skill. . . . We began by carrying bowls full of water; it was necessary to carry them from one table to another without spilling the least drop in the saucer; and it was very difficult, for the distance was long and the bowls were full to the brim.

. . . These games are nothing but lessons for training the will; modest lessons which are appropriate to the capacities of the child, but which actually force the will into activity. . . . All this is . . . as valuable as lessons in history and arithmetic! ∎

of the pay and status ladders. In the more recent days of rising inflation, increasing automation, and a tight job market, EMRs may have more difficulty than ever before in supporting themselves and their families.

Payne et al. (1977) speculate that three important factors create vocational problems for EMRs. First, employers hesitate to hire them and, if they do get jobs, fellow workers may make their lives even more difficult by negative attitudes. Second, if a job is distasteful, the mildly retarded worker may be more inclined to quit than to search for ways to make the job more tolerable, perhaps because he lacks the ability to explore abstract hypotheses; i.e., possibilities. Third, vocational education for the EMR is sometimes inadequate. He or she must acquire and practice skills demanding physical dexterity, and know how to fill out an application for a job. Schools also should emphasize the "work personality," Brolin (1976) suggests. The EMR has to be taught explicitly what students of normal intelligence learn naturally: that he must arrive at work on time, follow directions, complete a job, clean up after it, and cooperate with fellow workers.

It is impossible to determine precisely, MacMillan (1977) warns, whether placement in regular or special classes proves more beneficial to EMRs in later life. So a more significant question is: What *level* of educational placement is most appropriate?

If you read further on the subject, you may come on studies that report:

- Retarded children in regular classes full time are rejected by their normal classmates. They are also not fully accepted by other retarded children who attend full-time special classes.
- Children in full-time special classes seem to enjoy better self-concepts and to be better adjusted generally than their retarded fellows in regular classes full time. But children who spend half a day in regular classes and half in special classes feel even better about themselves than do those who are in special classes all day.
- Youngsters whose IQs are in the upper range of the EMR category and who attend regular classes full time do as well as or better than similar pupils in full-time special classes. Youngsters with lower IQs may progress faster in special classes full time.
- In the split-day program, youngsters who attend both regular and special classes, each part time, have been found to score higher than those in all-day special classes.

What is the meaning of *least restrictive environment*?

MacMillan (1977) thoroughly reviews such studies, but cautions against firm conclusions on EMR social, emotional, and academic adjustment. Some of the studies are seriously flawed. Even in properly conducted studies, the results refer to EMRs as a group, and it is reckless to assume that each child fits a mold. In determining where to place EMRs, social, emotional, and practical considerations have to be balanced. Maynard C. Reynolds (1962) has drawn a pyramidal ladder (see Figure 11.1) that suggests ways of dealing with various

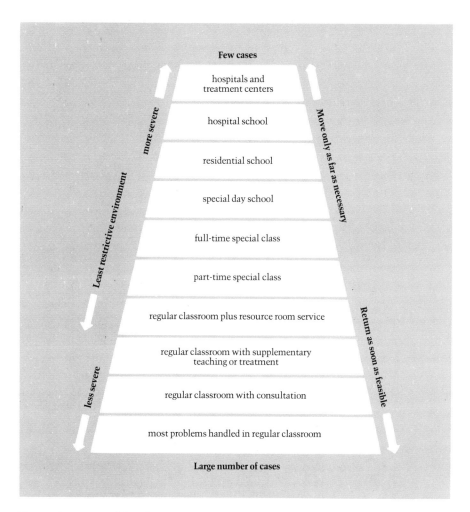

Figure 11.1. Reynolds Hierarchy of Services

degrees of retardation; the ladder aptly meets the *least restrictive environment* clause of the Education for All Handicapped Children Act.

But recently, Reynolds and Birch (1977) have modified the pyramid (see Figure 11.2) because the original model, they say, emphasized places over instructional needs. The newer version explicitly includes educational strategies for all types of handicap and shows that they do not demand special places for their application. The new model is not yet in operation, and its use will take time to evolve. In practice, it will pose a challenge to regular classroom teachers who will face more diverse learners and strategies.

The final decision on placement and teaching strategies will depend on the student's degree of retardation or other handicap, the makeup and attitudes of

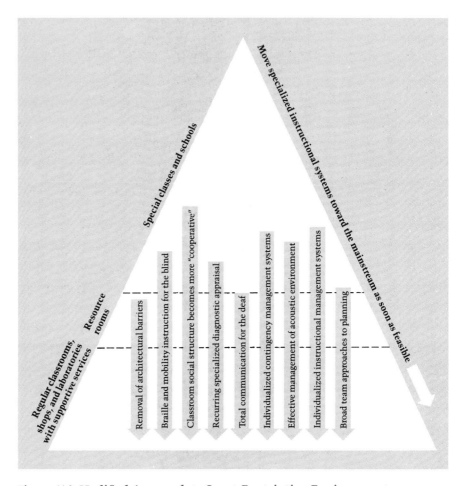

Figure 11.2. Modified Approach to Least Restrictive Environment

the regular class to which the youngster might be assigned, and the characteristics of the available teachers.

The Gifted or Talented Student

Gifted people constitute a precious natural resource (Gardner, 1961) and represent a major asset in the wealth of any nation. They too are "exceptional." But in the schools they may be neglected because they are deemed to need no help. Or they may go unrecognized. (See the box on p. 368.)

Like "exceptional," the term *gifted* used to have a single meaning, *high intelligence*. As late as 1931, the White House Conference on Children cautioned that "gifted" meant "merely the child with exceptional intelligence."

Since then the implications of "gifted" have broadened greatly. The gifted student may be described as one endowed with well-above-average intellectual capacity (an IQ, say, of 120 or more) or with a superior talent for something worth doing.

The former United States Office of Education (now Department of Education) produced a more explicit definition that is favored by most states and school systems:

What qualities are included in giftedness?

> Gifted and talented children . . . are those who have demonstrated any of the following abilities or aptitudes, singly or in combination: (1) general intellectual ability, (2) specific academic aptitude, (3) creative or productive thinking, (4) leadership ability, (5) visual and performing arts aptitude, (6) psychomotor ability (Marland, 1972).

Although some theorists argue with the definition (see Renzulli, 1978), it has at least drawn attention to the multiple facets of giftedness. Nevertheless, schools continue to favor the first portion of the definition, intelligence and academic aptitude, perhaps because those qualities may be more readily measured. Let us first examine the time-honored criterion of high intelligence.

Intelligence is "the capacity to know or understand," but the more of it there is, the more suspicious human beings seem to be of it. The idea was already ancient when the seventeenth-century poet John Dryden wrote that "Great wits are sure to madness near allied" and the belief persists: if you are extraordinarily acute intellectually, you have to be at least a little wacky, and largely unfit to cope with life.

Should you as a teacher, then, expect your brightest pupils to be bespectacled, undersized, emotionally unstable oddballs? The evidence is to the contrary. Lewis M. Terman, who translated Binet and adapted the Binet intelligence tests for American use, began in the 1920s to study 1500 youngsters whose Stanford-Binet IQs averaged 150 (1925). The research was designed to follow them through adulthood and to be carried on to the year 2010.

In school, Terman's 1500 ranked two to four grades ahead of other children of their age and excelled in virtually all subjects—a blow to the belief that smart children have to be one-sided. The 1500 were also superior physically, emotionally, morally, and socially. As adults, most of them remained that way. "So far," as Terman put it, "no one has developed post-adolescent stupidity," and they continued to enjoy better than average physical and mental health (1954, p. 214).

It was their accomplishments, though, that demonstrated they were "a precious natural resource." Of the 800 males—fewer women went to college or entered professions in those days—the professionals numbered seventy-eight with Ph.D.s, forty-eight with medical degrees, and eighty-five with law degrees. There were seventy-four college and university professors, and forty-seven of those who became scientists were named in *American Men of Science* for 1949. Nearly all the numbers were ten to thirty times greater, as Getzels and Dillon (1973) point out, than would have been found among 800 men of the same age chosen at random. By the time the 800 were forty years old, in 1950, they had produced 93 books, 2000 scientific, technical, and professional articles, 275 miscellaneous articles, some 375 plays, novellettes, and short stories, and had acquired more than 230 patents (Terman and Oden, 1959). Follow-up studies of the Terman group continue, the most recent focusing on whether these gifted people have been satisfied with their lives* (Sears, 1977; Sears and Barbee, 1977).

Do gifted youngsters burn out as adults?

In efforts to ensure that these precious natural resources are utilized to their full potential, schools have adopted a variety of programs for the intellectually gifted, and the State of Pennsylvania has passed a law requiring that the gifted be allotted as much money for education as the handicapped. In fact, several states now require that IEPs be developed for gifted students (Karnes and Collins, 1978).

As you might guess, there is no agreement on whether IQ scores should be used to identify giftedness. Viewpoints range from raging antagonism (Alvino and Wieler, 1979) to support (Laycock, 1979). Most school systems with structured programs for the gifted continue to use tests of mental ability *in concert with other measures*, such as teacher ratings.

One problem with the use of IQ scores as indicators of giftedness is that minority groups tend to be under represented. This fact fuels the already hot

* They have been.

"This program is for the bright kids. It's strictly enrichment. They come out here to the learning center to work with atlases, globes, encyclopedias, different reference books. Ordinarily I'll give them a packet of papers to work on. They'll work individually or in groups of two page by page. They'll jump around—grab a book as soon as it's available, then go back to another spot. We have to watch out that they don't just buzz around doing whatever they're momentarily interested in.

debate about the cultural fairness of mental ability tests (see Chapter 3). Torrance (1977) urges that nonintellectual facets of giftedness be examined carefully among disadvantaged, minority students. He suggests looking for such characteristics as skill in visual arts, creativity, motivation, and persistence in problem-solving. Disadvantaged students of high potential may need special remedial work in cognitive areas and Torrance observes that peer tutoring may serve when other resources are limited (see Chapter 13).

THE SPECIAL PROGRAMS

Programs for the gifted fall roughly into three categories: enrichment, grouping, and acceleration.

Enrichment in its broadest sense embraces all special provisions for the intellectually gifted, including college-level courses in high school, advanced classes, seminars, independent study, and a score or more of others. In practice, enrichment means extra opportunities and facilities for such youngsters *in regular classrooms.*

What programs have been tried with gifted students?

Grouping involves placement of pupils in a class in which all of them have similar capacities, i.e., the brightest in one class, the average in another, the least bright in a third.

Acceleration includes any method that shortens the time it takes for a student

They're supposed to be working on long term, real-life problems. We use contracts—that seems to give them a stronger sense of commitment. Sometimes there are payoffs for their projects, and that helps build commitment, too. For example, two kids have had articles published in a local newspaper. They're really turned on to journalism.

to be graduated—skipping grades, combining two years work in one, summer courses, and the like.

Are the Programs Worthwhile? Study of enrichment has been limited, but research by Ziehl (1962) at the elementary level and by Arends and Ford (1964) at the junior xigh level indicated that intellectually gifted children thrived on enrichment. Often, however, enrichment is not highly regarded. Of course, enrichment, like remedial education, encompasses many different practices. Julian Stanley (1977), who supports acceleration, has found most enrichment practices to be busywork, irrelevant, and just plain boring. Teachers, he believes, are not sufficiently trained to develop worthwhile enrichment activities, and often seem to observe the motto "more is better." Those who favor enrichment today are alert to its weak record, and are careful to outline conditions that favor its use (Renzulli, 1977).

A good deal more work has been done on acceleration. The studies have produced evidence in its favor at all levels from first grade to college (Laycock, 1979). Children admitted early to elementary school did better than their classmates all the way to graduation and had fewer emotional problems (Worcester, 1956). Research on ninety-five high school students with IQs of 150 or higher showed that the accelerated pupils surpassed their peers in mathematics, science, and social studies (Justman, 1953). Accelerated students apparently retain their lead in adulthood. Twenty-five years later, in a follow-up study of Terman's 1500 bright children, Terman and Oden (1947)

Cautions for Career Counselors

Talented people and even geniuses do not always win early recognition, even from their teachers. Milton E. Larson (1973) has compiled the following examples of cases that might give pause to guidance counselors:

Einstein was four years old before he could speak and seven before he could read. Isaac Newton did poorly in grade school, and Beethoven's music teacher once said of him, "As a composer he is hopeless." When Thomas Edison was a boy, his teachers told him he was too stupid to learn anything. F. W. Woolworth got a job in a dry goods store when he was twenty-one, but his employers would not let him wait on a customer because he "didn't have enough sense." A newspaper editor fired Walt Disney because he had "no good ideas."

Caruso's music teacher told him, "You can't sing. You have no voice at all." The director of the Imperial Opera in Vienna told Madam Schumann-Heink that she would never be a singer and advised her to buy a sewing machine. Leo Tolstoy flunked out of college; Wernher von Braun flunked ninth-grade algebra. Admiral Richard E. Byrd had been retired from the Navy as "unfit for service" until he flew over both Poles. Louis Pasteur was rated as "mediocre" in chemistry when he attended the Royal College. Abraham Lincoln entered the Black Hawk War as captain and came out as a private. Louisa May Alcott was told by an editor that she could never write anything that had popular appeal. Fred Waring was once rejected for high school chorus. Winston Churchill failed the sixth form (secondary school grade). ■

found that those who had been accelerated had done better than those who had not been accelerated, in such areas as jobs, education, marital happiness, and physical health. More recently, Julian Stanley (1980) of Johns Hopkins University has been helping mathematically talented youngsters to move through school at an awesome pace. The box describes his program.

So neither enrichment nor acceleration is particularly controversial. But grouping stirs passionate rows among educators and laymen. For one thing, research into its efficacy has yielded contradictory results. For another, it has become a philosophical issue involving "elitism" and "equality." Critics of grouping charge that it is unfair to poor children and to youngsters from a few ethnic minorities. Summarizing a report by the Findley Task Force on ability grouping, Esposito asserts:

> Among the studies showing significant effects, the slight gains favoring high ability students scholastically is more than offset by evidence of unfavorable effects on the learning of students of average and below average ability, particularly in the latter. Whatever the practice does to build or inflate the self-esteem of children in the high ability groups is counter-balanced by evidence of unfavorable effects of stigmatizing those placed in average and below average ability groups as inferior and incapable of learning. . . . Homogeneous ability grouping, by design, is a separative educational policy, ostensibly according to students' test performance ability, but practically, according to students' socio-economic status and, to a lesser but observable degree according to students' ethnic status [1973, p. 170].

Is it fair to give special attention to gifted students?

Now consider the argument of Gowan (1977), who uses the analogy of athletics:

> There a coach knows what he is looking for: athletic performance. He recruits likely candidates and stimulates whatever abilities they present. . . . He has a qualitatively different curriculum, which is practiced intensively, and no one regards him as an elitist for insisting that his charges have special and extra training. For him physical education is the stimulation, to their ultimate maximum, of the talents presented by his students. And when he does this, we honor him, pay him a large salary, and brag that he has produced an All-American player or an Olympic star (pp. 21–22).

It should be noted that special programs for gifted students do not have to be an all-or-none proposition. One clever compromise was adopted in 1977 in Pittsburgh. Its "scholars' program" groups gifted kids from all over the city one day per week. The remaining days are spent in regular classrooms with careful enrichment.

THE TALENTED

To be *talented*, one need not be intellectually distinguished, though it is of course possible to be both. The talented rank among the exceptional. The term talent covers a vast diversity of human attributes: it has been suggested that for *any* conceivable human activity, there is a special talent and at least one individual who possesses it.

But not all talents pay off equally, because not all activities are valued equally. Human society rewards the talented not for how good they are at what they do, but for how *useful* society considers whatever it is they do. And society changes its mind about that, from time to time. In early Rome, a few talented folk earned upper-bracket incomes by foretelling the future from slaughtered chickens' livers and gizzards. Alive today, the same folk might be hard put to pay the rent for a storefront in a slum. Fortune-telling has not gone quite out of fashion, but faith in chicken entrails has. Recognition and reward of a talent often depend on where the talent is displayed, under what circumstances, and by whom. A talent for showmanship is demanded of a TV master of ceremonies but is considered unseemly in a heart transplant surgeon. A talent for oratory is highly regarded in a statesman such as Sir Winston Churchill but is disapproved of in a barber. A talent for killing may earn a gangster a jail term in peacetime, and medals in wartime.

Smorgasbord for an IQ of 150

Paul Dietz, a slender youth in wire-rimmed glasses, loves war games of all kinds—from World War II platoon fights to dungeons and dragons. Says he: "I like to look at the mistakes commanders made in the past, as an intellectual exercise." Colin Camerer has a more direct interest in combat, since he lists as his main concerns "business and power." He adds: "Someone's going to be making decisions, and frankly I want to be there." Eugene Stark, by contrast, has a more modest policy: "I try to appear as normal as possible. If you go around broadcasting that you're a weirdo, then people look at you like you're a weirdo."

Testing Feat. The reason why some people might look on the three students as a little odd is that they graduated last week from Johns Hopkins University at the age of 17. All have IQs of more than 150. And all three— along with five other precocious seniors—were found at the early age of 12 or 13 to be mathematical wizards, capable of feats such as scoring well on algebra tests without ever having taken the subject.

Their graduation is a milestone in a unique program at Johns Hopkins, the Study of Mathematically Precocious Youth. It was begun in 1971 by psychology Professor Julian Stanley, 58, who remembered his boredom in Georgia public schools and decided "to save these kids from the same experience." Stanley, a statistician, sought out 12- and 13-year-old children in the Baltimore area who had already shown promise in math. He asked them to take the Scholastic Aptitude Test normally given to college-bound high school students. The result: a group of seven boys scored well over 700 (out of a possible 800), a feat matched by only 5% of 18-year-old males. Besides Dietz, Camerer and Stark, the test also identified two other youngsters who are graduating from Johns Hopkins this year—Michael Kotschenreuther, 18, and Robert Addison, 19—as mathematically gifted. Stanley also helped other youthful math wizards, whom his testing turned up, get into other colleges. Among them: Eric Jablow, 15, who this year became the youngest boy ever to graduate from New York's Brooklyn College.

As Stanley's program has become increasingly well-known, hundreds of seventh-graders have been pouring in from a wider and wider area to take his tests and sample what Stanley calls a "smorgasbord of educationally accelerated opportunities." Some, who live near by, are ferried by their parents to special two-hour Saturday tutorial classes at John Hopkins. Tutored by other prodigies just a few years older than they, these gifted students now race

Talents that are certain of general approval—for athletics, for writing, for the graphic or performing arts, among the many possible examples—all share the quality of marketability. But

> other talents which are readily and universally recognized in everyday life are almost wholly overlooked [when scholars make lists of talents]. . . . The talent to love, to understand, to empathize, to be compassionate, to be of service; the talent of coping, of surviving, of getting through and getting along with grace and authenticity. These, it would seem, are indisputably talents. . . . Why then are they neglected in conventional conceptions of talent and educational objectives? . . . they need as much as any other to be discovered and encouraged in our children in and out of school [Getzels and Dillon, 1973, p. 705].

How to Discover Talent. In some students, some talents—for leadership, for music and drama, for the graphic arts—are irrepressibly self-evident. Students who spend their spare time drawing, painting, and perhaps sculpting are

through advanced algebra and geometry. Others leapfrog over grades, and some will attend a special summer session at Johns Hopkins.

"We don't have any particular program," says Stanley, whose recruits now total about 500. "If you're gifted and motivated, we'll help you do anything that fits you." The purpose of this speedup, says Stanley, is "so that mathematically talented youths can devote their most productive years to research." He adds: "Lots of people in this world worry mostly about those who have low ability. Somebody has to worry about the gifted."

Stable Introverts. One of Stanley's main disappointments is that for still disputed reasons, few girls test well on math (TIME, March 14). Those who do qualify for the special tutorials tend to drop out, and their feeling for the boys in the program is "almost one of revulsion," he says, because the girls view their male counterparts as socially immature. So far, he maintains, the boys seem to have few emotional problems. "Scientists are stable introverts," says Stanley. "They are not highly impulsive and tend to act rationally." Furthermore, he adds, it has been "demonstrated empirically" that mathematically gifted boys become interested in girls much later in life. "This has been a great asset in the early-en-

trance program because it gives them more time to study," he says approvingly.

Stanley's five Johns Hopkins protégés seem almost too dedicated to their calling. Spare-time reading tends toward math and science books, with a little science fiction thrown in for leavening. Favorite hobbies include, not surprisingly, chess and bridge. Stark and Camerer, however, seem drawn to non-scientific pastimes—Stark to softball and ragtime music on the trombone, Camerer to journalism. He has been writing stories about fashions and fishing for the *Beachcomber*, a free weekly published in Ocean City, Md.

For the future, most of the Johns Hopkins prodigies envision high-powered research careers following Ph.D. studies at—variously—the University of Chicago, Cornell, M.I.T. and Princeton. Three—Dietz, Stark and Kotschenreuther—have received National Science Foundation fellowships, prestigious grants awarded each year for advanced research. And Stanley is willing to bet on them all—using probability theory, of course—for "original contributions." ∎

From *Time* magazine, June 6, 1977, p. 64.

pretty likely to have artistic talents, and pupils who work in the science lab after school and read scientific literature are likely to have a talent for science. But because schools by their very nature concentrate on academic achievement, a lot of talent may get lost in the shuffle. High marks in curricular subjects do not guarantee talent's discovery. (See box.)

Tests for detecting potential but undemonstrated talent exist for your use as a teacher. Among them are:

In music, the Seashore Measures of Musical Talents.
In the graphic arts, the Meier Art Tests.
In architecture, mechanics, leadership, and a good many other fields, seventh and eighth *Mental Measurements Yearbooks* (Buros, 1972, 1978) describe measures.

Your school counselor or school psychologist can help you to select, administer, and interpret the tests.

Another van Gogh of Japan

Yoshihiko Yamamoto, a mentally retarded artist, has been called "another van Gogh of Japan" (Morishima, 1974). Yamamoto is multiply handicapped

Nagoya Castle (produced by Yamamoto in the seventh grade)

Nagoya Castle (produced by Yamamoto in the ninth grade)

How well talent may be predicted by such tests is the question that Project TALENT has undertaken to answer. By 1960, the project had tested 440,000 students in 1350 secondary schools all over the country (Flanagan, 1973) and it will continue to study the same people for twenty-five years to determine the relationship, if any, between their adolescent proclivities and their adult interests and success. So far, initial results show fairly clear links between high school interests, abilities, and later careers (Flanagan et al., 1973).

How can talents be identified and nurtured?

Fostering Talent. Discovering talent is one thing. Helping it to develop is quite another. And in this, the schools (for whatever reasons) are doing too little. Virtually alone, New York City provides high schools for the performing arts, for science, and for music and the graphic arts. The Portland, Oregon, schools have a program for identifying and developing talents. Countrywide, music and art classes have become more numerous, but make little special effort on behalf of the potentially great. That sums it up.

with an IQ of 40 and severe speech and hearing impairment. A dedicated teacher of the mentally retarded encouraged him to express himself artistically when attempts to work with his speech and hearing problems were not effective. Yamamoto's unusual ability suggests the importance of focusing educational programs on adaptive behavior. ■

Nagoya Castle (produced by Yamamoto at the age of twenty)

Kobe Harbor (produced by Yamamoto at the age of twenty)

Public Law 94–142 requires, you remember, *individual educational plans* for handicapped students. It does not mandate such attention to the gifted and talented, but it does encourage thought in that direction: special people need special attention. Some states agree, and now require individual educational plans for all types of exceptional youngsters. The responsibility for the programs rests with individual teachers. It is a responsibility that can be assumed with eagerness and pride. The talented, like the gifted, are a precious natural resource, and no nation can afford to risk overlooking a dormant Einstein—or a Paul McCartney.

PIAGET AND EXCEPTIONALITY

Over the past few years, researchers have shown increased interest in examining similarities and differences in the cognitive growth of normal and exceptional youngsters. If normal children are assumed to develop in orderly, successive cognitive stages (see Chapter 2), then interesting questions naturally emerge:

Do retarded children follow the same sequential pattern of cognitive growth, only more slowly?

Is the development of gifted children accelerated, or do they follow a different pattern of stages?

Do other forms of exceptionality—speech, hearing, visual deficits, emotional disturbance—indicate disruptions in the pattern of intellectual growth?

The bulk of such research has focused on retardation, but answers to the other questions are slowly beginning to emerge. With retarded children, it is clear that their cognitive development does, slowly, follow the ordered route that Piaget predicted (Schmid-Kitsikis, 1976). Also, the educable retarded—even as adults—find abstract thinking and hypothesis testing impossible. This suggests that their cognitive development does not enter the final, formal operational period. The moral reasoning of the retarded also develops slowly, and it too follows the same sequence predicted by Piaget (Moore and Stephens, 1974).

Do Piaget's predictions hold for exceptional people? Only a few studies have considered the mental development of learning disordered and emotionally disturbed students, but the general trend is that both groups lag in growth of cognitive operations (Reid, 1978). With emotional disturbance, logical thinking may be hampered because of distorted and highly subjective perceptions of reality. Schmid-Kitsikis (1973) observes that these children often "bounce" their reasoning between successive cognitive stages, and she speculates that such instability may be caused by a poor balance of cognitive and affective processes. Interestingly, Reid (1978) suggests that gifted youth do not necessarily advance through cognitive periods more rapidly, but instead show superior performance on tasks *within* a particular period. In summary, it is fair to say that the various forms of exceptionality confirm Piaget's theory on the sequence of stages in cognitive growth.

What are the implications of a Piagetian approach to the education of exceptional children? There are not many. Developmental researchers acknowledge that more study is needed to translate theory into clear practice. On the basis of what is known, however, Kim Reid (1978) suggests:

1. The learning of simple verbal rules (e.g., "The plus sign means 'add' ") should be minimized. They do not guarantee understanding, they do not enhance motivation, and they are static rather than dynamic aspects of knowledge.
2. A precise assessment of a child's mode of thinking should dictate particular teaching strategies. For instance, though children in formal operations can handle a short lecture, it will not suit the needs of preoperational students.
3. Because children are active learners, they should be allowed to explore, create, and focus on problems of interest. Learning tasks should not be prespecified, and teaching strategies should be altered according to the child's current interest.
4. Because of the importance of the equilibration process (see Chapter 2), any instructional activities should create mild conflict. Through contradictions and gaps in knowledge, the child will be motivated to seek a balance between the complementary processes of assimilation and accommodation. Without equilibration, knowledge becomes dry, dull, memorized facts.

Do cognitivists and behaviorists agree about anything?

Behaviorists, of course, are somewhat skeptical of an instructional routine that refuses to specify goals and that allows a child to judge what problems are worth facing. It is better, they say, to decide in advance what skills an exceptional student needs for adapting to society, find out which of those skills the child does or does not have, and teach toward the deficiencies. Since behavioral techniques have been far more extensively applied with exceptional students, it is tempting to present that approach as the "state of the art." But in fairness, a Piagetian analysis may prove to have worthwhile aspects, so it should not be shrugged off as an intellectual exercise. Perhaps the best strategy is to use tried and tested methods, and experiment now and then with alternative styles. Careful attention to your mini-experiments will help produce the most sensitive and productive mixture of techniques.

Summary

The term *exceptional*, in its educational sense, encompasses all students whose entry characteristics deviate from the norm to a degree that requires special attention in school. Exceptional pupils are estimated to number 8 million, and under the federal Education for All Handicapped Children Act they must receive instruction in regular classrooms whenever possible. Where that is not possible, the youngsters must be educated in the *least restrictive environment* that satisfies their needs. Further, the Act, Public Law 94–142, specifies that individual educational programs may be drawn up for each handicapped student, and that they contain long-range and short-term objectives, proposed methods, and evaluation techniques.

Mainstreaming, promoted by the Act, has been hotly debated for years and the argument continues, but mainstreaming is likely to become more widespread.

Among the handicapped, the most numerous are the *learning disabled*, children of apparently normal capacity who cannot master certain subjects such as reading, writing, and arithmetic. For one common symptom of learning disorder, *hyperkinesis*, or compulsive overactivity, amphetamines have frequently—and controversially—been administered. Drug treatment is beginning to give way to behavior modification. For other types of learning disabilities, several other approaches are used, but the most widespread practice is remedial education.

Less frequently found than learning disorder, but still rather widespread, is *emotional disturbance*, the incidence of which among elementary school pupils has been put at 7 to 12 percent. Emotional disturbance has diverse causes. Many cases receive psychiatric help, but it has been found that about two-thirds of the emotionally disturbed overcome their handicap with or without such treatment. Behavior modification is being applied for emotional disturbance in many schools, although alternative treatments such as *Life Space Interviewing* are available.

Some 700,000 handicapped children who attend regular schools are categorized as *educable mentally retarded* (EMR). They have IQs ranging between 50 and 70 and manifest poor adaptive behavior, but they are considered capable of acquiring at least a minimum of academic education, of living normal lives, and of holding jobs.

They do not learn in the way normal children do, however, and therefore need special teaching techniques, especially with respect to vocational training. The most important of those techniques is: try to avoid failure. Whether EMR pupils should be retained full time in regular classes, sent to special classes for half a day, or taught entirely in special classes is a matter of wide discussion. The answer, in any individual case, may depend on the degree of the pupil's retardation, and the characteristics of the regular classroom's teacher and the other students.

The term exceptional also includes the *gifted* and the *talented*. Gifted applies to students of well-above-average intelligence, an attribute that for centuries has been regarded with suspicion. Despite the persisting belief that the highly intelligent are likely to be odd, and that genius is akin to madness, long-term studies have found the opposite to be true. A group of 1500 individuals whose IQs averaged 150 was followed by Lewis M. Terman from childhood through adulthood. As children, they proved to be physically and emotionally superior to youngsters of lesser intellect, and their superiority continued in their years of maturity. The gifted have been described as a precious natural resource, and several programs are designed to help them fulfill their potential. Those programs are *enrichment, acceleration,* and *grouping.* Studies of enrichment and acceleration indicate they are useful. Grouping has been criticized on the ground that although it benefits the high IQ pupils to some extent, it labels average and below average students as inferior. Special care must be taken to locate gifted minority or disadvantaged students whose IQ scores may misrepresent their potential.

Talented students do not necessarily enjoy superior intelligence, but have a capacity for extraordinary performance in some field of endeavor. Some talents are manifested unmistakably, but *potential* talent may go unnoticed. For discovery of talent by teachers, various tests exist. For the development of talent, however, the country's school systems, with a couple of exceptions, do little. The responsibility for fostering talent thus seems to rest on the individual teacher.

Developmental theorists have recently shown that exceptional children generally follow the growth sequence predicted by Piaget. Their recommendations for instruction of exceptional students are meant to promote cognitive growth, but are yet untested.

Chapter Study Guide

CHAPTER REVIEW

1. Public Law 94–142 requires that
   a. all handicapped students will be eligible to receive an appropriate public supported education.
   b. special classes and special schools for handicapped students will be reduced in size.
   c. teachers will be specifically trained to diagnose handicapping conditions.
   d. most of the social and emotional problems of handicapped students will be solved.

2. If a child has a learning disability, then he or she
   a. is probably also mentally retarded.
   b. has an organic problem related to the functioning of his or her nervous system.
   c. is likely to have difficulty learning from regular classroom instruction.
   d. is easily identified through evaluation on an IQ test.
   e. will be treated medically until he or she is able to proceed at a normal rate within the classroom.

3. Informal assessment
   a. must be performed by trained professionals.
   b. has no place in the school.
   c. is based on simple legal steps.
   d. is often the beginning step in diagnosing disorders.

4. Educable mentally retarded students present problems in the regular classroom because

    a. they tend to be destructive and aggressive toward other students.

    b. it may be difficult for a teacher to hold their attention for an entire lesson.

    c. they are difficult to identify.

    d. they cannot learn regular academic skills such as reading and math.

    e. they exhibit severe social and emotional handicaps.

5. Gifted students

    a. make greater academic gains as a result of ability grouping than they do from enrichment.

    b. are easier to identify as a result of PL 94–142.

    c. show outstanding talent in some area.

    d. are likely to be shy and withdrawn in a regular classroom environment.

    e. show faster cognitive development than their normal peers, but mature physically at a slower rate.

6. Receptive communication disorder refers to

    a. a person's willingness to undergo therapy.

    b. difficulty in comprehending others' communication.

    c. the inability to speak intelligibly.

    d. stuttering.

7. IQ measures are probably *least* valid for identification of

    a. emotionally disturbed students, because they often respond poorly under stress and get easily frustrated.

    b. hyperkinetic children, because they have below-average verbal ability.

    c. retarded children, because they perform poorly on such measures.

    d. learning disabled children, because they have deficient psychomotor abilities.

    e. the gifted, because their high scores make it difficult to discriminate between levels of giftedness.

8. Tom is shy, withdrawn, and quiet to the point of being mute. Alex is boisterous, loud, and aggressive. Could both be emotionally disturbed?

    a. No, because emotionally disturbed children usually show evidence of brain damage, and neither of these boys does.

    b. No, because they are characterized as exact opposites.

    c. Alex *could* be emotionally disturbed, but it is more likely that Tom simply has a learning disability.

    d. Both *could* be emotionally disturbed, but we would have to know more about them.

    e. We cannot tell until we have an IQ estimate for each child.

Answer questions 9–22 True or False:

9. Studies show that of all the kinds of student handicap, learning disabilities are being least served under current conditions.

10. Conclusive evidence exists to show that special students do better when placed in regular classes.

11. The Education for All Handicapped Children Act has been called a bill of rights for the handicapped because it attempts to provide handicapped students with equal educational opportunity and entitles their parents to question the schools' treatment of their children.

12. Learning disorders are always accompanied by some degree of brain dysfunction.

13. Remedial materials based on understood learning disorders have been produced that yield impressive results.

14. People with sensorimotor impairment usually show a degree of retardation.

15. Until late adolescence, emotionally disturbed boys outnumber emotionally disturbed girls.

16. In using the LSI bpproach with emotionally disturbed children, the teacher uses depth psychology to help the student get to the roots of his or her problem.

17. The new definition of mental retardation provided by the American Association of Mental Deficiency specifies impairment of *both* intelligence and perception.

18. Evidence supports the conclusion that special classes are more beneficial to EMRs in their later-life adjustments than in present adjustment.

19. The psychoanalytic approach is used extensively to treat learning disabilities.

20. The engineered classroom fits the concept of the least restrictive environment.

21. IQ scores are now rarely used to identify giftedness.

22. Evidence suggests that Piaget's developmental theory generally holds for exceptional students.

FOR FURTHER THOUGHT

1. How can you tell whether a student has a temporary difficulty or a more permanent learning disorder?

2. Is Public Law 94–142 like many traffic laws—good in theory but not always practiced?

3. If we have little idea about what causes learning disorders (or emotional disturbance or some types of retardation), how can we possibly hope to cope with them effectively?

4. With so much attention being paid to exceptional students recently, is there some danger that the huge group of "normal" students will be forgotten?

IMPORTANT TERMS

exceptional	informal assessment
impairment	hyperactivity
disability	hypoactivity
handicap	perseveration
Public Law 94–142	emotional disturbance

individual educational program (IEP)
least restrictive environment
mainstreaming
sensorimotor impairment
communication disorder
expressive difficulty
receptive difficulty
language dysfluency
hearing impairment
visual impairment
physical disability
learning disability

behavior disorder
engineered classroom
life space interviewing
educable mental retardation
adaptive behavior
work personality
gifted
talented
enrichment
grouping
acceleration

SUGGESTED READINGS

BLACKHURST, A. E., and BERDINE, W. H. (eds.). *An introduction to special education.* Boston: Little, Brown, 1981.

GALLAGHER, J. J. *Teaching the gifted child* (2nd ed.). Boston: Allyn and Bacon, 1975. Broad approaches to all types of talented youth. Includes chapters on nature and characteristics of giftedness, and on gifted minority students.

GEORGE, W. C., COHN, S. J., and STANLEY, J. C. (eds.). *Educating the gifted: acceleration and enrichment.* Baltimore: Johns Hopkins Press, 1979. Proceedings from a symposium focusing on the acceleration-versus-enrichment controversy in education for the gifted.

Gifted Child Quarterly. A journal directed to school administrators, parents, and especially teachers. Focusing on educational programming for the gifted, it provides a blend of program descriptions, tips, and research articles.

HAMMILL, D. D., and BARTEL, N. R. (eds.). *Teaching children with learning and behavior problems.* Boston: Allyn and Bacon, 1975. Individual chapters about the characteristics and procedures for several types of handicapping conditions.

HEWETT, F. M. *The emotionally disturbed child in the classroom.* Boston: Allyn and Bacon, 1968. Hewett lays out his famous engineered classroom approach, blending behavioral practices with the design of the entire classroom.

INGALLS, R. P. *Mental retardation: The changing outlook.* New York: Wiley, 1978. A thorough, readable introduction to all forms of retardation.

JOHNSON, S. W., and MORASKY, R. L. *Learning disabilities* (2nd ed.). Boston: Allyn and Bacon, 1980. Recent developments in programs for treating learning disabilities.

LAUBENFELS, J. *The gifted student: An annotated bibliography.* Westport, CT: Greenwood Press, 1977. A huge compilation of written resources in giftedness, including areas of characteristics of the gifted, educational methods, and research. Annotations help sort through the entries.

MACMILLAN, D. L. *Mental retardation in school and society.* Boston: Little, Brown, 1977. A comprehensive, introductory text in retardation. MacMillan is known for his thoroughness and his willingness to go beyond what is known and provoke questions about what might be.

PETERSON, R. L. *Mainstreaming training systems, materials, and resources: A working list* (3rd ed.). Minneapolis: University of Minnesota (Leadership Training Institute, 253 Burton Hall, University of Minnesota, Minneapolis, MN 55455), 1976. An ongoing compilation of methods, materials, and innovations for helping handicapped students.

SEMMEL, M. I., GOTTLIEB, J., and ROBINSON, N. M. Mainstreaming: Perspectives on educating handicapped children in the public school. In Berliner, D. C. (ed.), *Review of research in education, vol. 7.* Washington, D.C.: American Educational Research Association, 1979, 223–279. Pros and cons and long review of research on mainstreaming.

TURNBULL, A. P., STRICKLAND, B. B. and BRANTLEY, J. C. *Developing and implementing individual educational programs.* Columbus, OH: Charles E. Merrill, 1978. Excellent workbook to speed compliance with Public Law 94–142.

WHALEN, C. K., and HENKER, B. (eds.). *Hyperactive children.* New York: Academic Press, 1980. Problems and progress in a prevalent form of exceptionality.

WIG, E. H., and SEMEL, E. M. *Language assessment and intervention for the learning disabled.* Columbus, OH: Charles E. Merrill, 1980. Broad treatment of communication disorders, with review of language development.

ANSWER KEY

1. a; 2. c; 3. d; 4. b; 5. c; 6. b; 7. a; 8. d; 9. T; 10. F; 11. T; 12. F; 13. F; 14. F; 15. T; 16. F; 17. F; 18. F; 19. F; 20. T; 21. F; 22. T

12

Motivation

It is your first day as a teacher. You are twenty minutes into your first lesson, in a tenth-grade class, when you become aware of two boys in the back of the room who appear to be paying no attention to your carefully planned lecture. One is staring out the window; the other dozes. Have you bored them already? Don't they want to learn? What do you do now? The questions and their answers concern motivation in the classroom, a topic that itself has motivated much research and generated a lot of theory but little agreement. So before we discuss what to do about inattentive pupils like the two boys in the back of the room, let's consider some theoretical points about motivation.

Theories of Motivation

What is motivation?

In approaching the topic of motivation, the first imperative step is to determine what motivation is. That sounds easy enough. Almost any teacher will tell you that a motivated student is one who enthusiastically tries to master whatever the teacher wants the student to learn. Thus an unmotivated student is one who does not enthusiastically engage in learning and who, indeed, may actively and enthusiastically *avoid* learning.

That seems to say it. But before we go any further, let's stop and think for a moment. Psychologists vary in their definitions of motivation, but almost all the definitions embody two components, *energy* and *direction*. So motivation includes the operations that energize behavior toward some goal. For example, the motivation behind any theory of motivation is the operation of describing and explaining *why* people, including students, behave in certain ways, persist in those ways, and change their ways. Of the relationship between motivation and learning, we can say, for a start, that when an act is performed "it is highly probable that this is because [an organism] . . . , has learned to do so . . . and is motivated to do so" (Hulse, Deese, and Egeth, 1975, p. 168). That is, one engages in activities that have succeeded in the past or appear likely to succeed now in achieving some goal.

The teachers' consensus, then, that eager students are motivated and unreceptive students are unmotivated is far off base. Both kinds of students are motivated, one kind to achieve a goal that requires study and the other kind to avoid study. The second kind may manifest motivation in a number of ways—by remaining passive, by actively resisting, by distracting the attention of the class, by being disruptive, to cite only a few.

We shall use the term motivation, though, as referring to desirable classroom behavior, and the motivating of students to mean the increasing or the sustaining of behavior toward a goal. To begin, we shall consider the important distinction between two factors in motivation, the *extrinsic* and the *intrinsic*.

EXTRINSIC MOTIVATION

How do intrinsic and extrinsic motivation differ?

To a behaviorist, as you know, human and other organisms are regulated by extrinsic—external—properties of the environment. We simply respond to the environment as it changes and, in a sense, appear passive rather than active initiators of our behaviors. In the absence of a clear consequence to a behavior, a behaviorist would probably say that the involved individual's "reinforcement history"—experience with a similar situation—helps to direct the behavior. (The strict behaviorist has trouble, though, explaining how a past event can influence present behavior without dependence on memory, an internal process of the kind that behaviorists decline to consider.)

Unlike strict behaviorists, neobehaviorists are willing to speculate about internal mechanisms that prompt action. For example, they hold that *expectation* of a reinforcer or punisher may serve as an incentive. But, to neobehaviorists, even expectation, which is internal, originates externally: what consequence followed similar behavior in the past? We examined external consequences to behavior in chapters 5 and 10. Operant conditioning, you recall, stresses the manipulation of consequences to build or strengthen (i.e., motivate) behavior. Classical conditioning helps to show why extrinsic stimuli work: they give rise to emotions. Because, in the behaviorist view, conditioning processes explain the development of action directed toward a goal, most behaviorists ignore motivation as a *construct*. Why, they ask, should one invent an unobservable process for what already can be seen and measured? Yet behaviorist philosophy, despite its demonstrable results, is far from perfect in describing and predicting changes in behavior.

INTRINSIC MOTIVATION

Extrinsic or intrinsic—is it important?

Other theorists assume that study of internal—intrinsic—variables can lead to better explanations of behavior. They object to the view that human beings are passive creatures given only to reacting. They take the position that we actively initiate and regulate our behavior, and that motivation is primarily internal. Intrinsic motivation may be inherited or learned, but nonbehavioral theorists usually do not distinguish between those origins—and that may be impossible anyway. For example, it is conceivable that at birth organisms have a built-in urge to explore. But the environment regulates the exploration: the infant quickly learns to avoid some things, such as a hot stove, and to approach others, such as a colorful toy. Both intrinsic sources thus interact inseparably. In any case, intrinsic variables are of course unobservable and must be inferred, and inference about human motivation has filled a veritable granary of hypothesized variables.

Around the turn of the century, instincts enjoyed great favor as sources of intrinsic motivation. The psychologist William McDougall (1908) insisted that virtually all human behavior, even the most complicated, reflected instinctive drives. Then the great interest in behaviorism caused psychologists to deny or ignore intrinsic explanations of behavior; only in recent years have theorists developed interest in them again. But cognitive and social psychologists today have turned from instincts to more persuasive explanations of intrinsic motivation. One such explanation, immediately following, deals with the beliefs that people have about the consequences of their behavior.

LOCUS OF CONTROL

If you assume that your careful attention to these words will help you to attain a high test score, you may be more motivated to read this than if you believe that there is no connection between study and grades. In other words, your beliefs influence your reading behavior. Julian Rotter (1966) and his colleagues have translated such beliefs into the widely studied motivational construct called *locus of control. Locus* being the Latin for place, locus of control may be defined as the place where—in your belief—a good many controls over your behavior are concentrated. Is it, in your opinion, within you or outside you? You can determine that in part by answering questions such as these:

Do you believe that you are reading this because you *choose* to or because you have to?

Do you believe that the results of whatever you do are determined by your own intelligence, abilities, and skills or by forces you cannot control, such as your parents' demands or the whims of a professor?

Internal and External Control. If you assume that you are the master of your fate and the captain of your soul, doing mainly what you *want* to do and achieving the results by your own efforts, you are said to have an *internal locus of control*. If you believe, on the other hand, that your ability and your skill won't make much difference, because luck and other people will govern the outcome of your efforts, you are said to have an *external locus of control*.

What is meant by internal and external locus of control?

Suppose we asked you, "Do you think you will be a good teacher?" And suppose you answer, "I don't know. It depends on what kind of class I get—whether the kids are well-behaved and want to learn. And I don't know whether or not I'll be able to motivate students. So much depends on whether I get a good principal and a decent school system and the proper facilities." That answer suggests that you weigh heavily on the external control side of the scale.

But suppose you answer, "I'm pretty sure I'll be a good teacher. I've always wanted to be a teacher and I usually do well at whatever I want to try." In that case, you would seem to lean toward the internal control side.

Do you perceive internal or external control? Does it matter?

No one, of course, is ever wholly on one side or the other, because all of us confront, from time to time, events beyond our control. You may be the best poker player in the dorm and consider yourself internally controlled, but if you are dealt a miserable hand. . . . All of us, on occasion, are in the right place at the right time, and in the wrong place at the wrong time. One of our graduate students was sitting in his car, waiting for the traffic light to turn green, when a stolen auto driven by a sixteen-year-old approached at high speed from the opposite direction, with the police close behind. As the young joy-rider roared into the intersection, against the light, a truck pulled out from the side street; the youngster swerved to avoid the truck and smashed into our student's car. Obviously, our student had had no control over that occurrence.

But what distinguishes internal from external locus of control is the way we interpret such happenings and whether or not we generalize that we are largely governed by such external forces. Everyone tends psychologically toward internal or external locus of control, and you will find that fact significant in your classroom for several reasons:

1. Students (and people generally) attach more importance to what they *want* to do than to what they *must* do.

"Every child in the room gets a different day to do an errand. Every week I change them, and I keep a record of who has done it when. See—when you're a new teacher you always pick the good ones to do the errands. Teachers always pick the nice-looking kids and the good kids in the room. They did the errands all the time—and the other kids don't get to do anything. So this is why I do this—develop a little bit of responsibility. And to motivate them. Every day someone else will be the Teacher's Aide. They're proud of it. I also give out chips and credits and things like Worker of the Week. I break the room up into clusters and assign a Captain in each group. When I started teaching I had the idea that kids should be intrinsically motivated, you know, from within. If I used extrinsic devices, I would destroy their inner desires. The problem was that almost none of the kids showed that great urge to learn and solve problems. So I've changed my tune about extrinsic devices. In fact, the extrinsic stuff—assigning errands, chips, and so on—helps to build what I'm looking for; curiosity, interest in material, good feelings about class. Sure, it takes time every week—but, hey, it's worth it!"

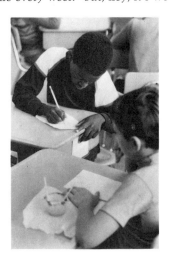

2. They are more likely to assume responsibility for voluntary behavior than for compulsory behavior.
3. They will work harder if they believe their efforts, rather than forces beyond their control, will determine their rewards.

Changing the Locus. One of us once participated in an experiment involving changes in the locus of control of school children in a New England city's black ghetto (Pratt and Owen, 1974). The experiment was undertaken in an effort to answer some questions. Why should students be expected to demonstrate responsible behavior when teachers and administrators take it on themselves alone to determine classroom relationships between teachers and students? In such situations, students become dependent on external control, often grow to resent it, and defy it by misbehavior. Then teachers respond to misbehavior by criticism and disapproval, increasing feelings of external control. Would it not help if some of the responsibility for classroom relationships were shifted to the students? Might that not work to change teacher behavior as well and eliminate or reduce some of the causes of conflict?

The experiment involved twenty-one third-, fourth-, fifth-, and sixth-grade classes. Teachers, who did not know the nature of the experiment, were asked to nominate the pupils they considered most disruptive. These youngsters were divided at random into two groups, one to receive special training, the other to serve as a control group. (Control here is not to be confused with the external and internal control we have been talking about. It is used in the scientific sense: a researcher feeds one batch of mice something suspected of causing cancer and does not feed the something to a second batch of mice, which serves as a control for judging the results.)

The experiment's immediate purpose was to determine whether the disruptive pupils could be trained to change their teachers' behavior by changing their own. The longer-range aim was to help teachers create a more supportive academic environment by smiling, praising, and encouraging students and accepting, when possible, their suggestions. In small groups, the students being trained met for an hour daily for two weeks, learning to influence their teachers. Among the ways they were told they could do it were:

Can the locus of control be shifted?

1. Sitting or standing, relaxed but alert, facing the teacher.
2. Looking the teacher in the eye frequently when the teacher is talking.
3. Nodding to indicate interest, attention, and approval.
4. Smiling, when a smile is appropriate, to denote appreciation of the teacher.
5. Asking the teacher whether the student has correctly interpreted what the teacher has said.
6. Telling the teacher that the student likes something the teacher is wearing or the way the lesson has been presented.
7. Offering to scrub the chalkboard, carry the movie projector, or otherwise help the teacher.

When the training ended, the results were not immediately visible. But about three weeks later, the atmosphere had changed in the classrooms the trained youngsters attended. The behavior of the entire class had improved: the training had rubbed off onto the *untrained* youngsters. The teachers were smiling more, approving more, and scolding less, and the pupils were learning. In the classrooms of the control group, nothing had changed.

To the researchers who conducted the experiment, at least, the study demonstrated that shifting the locus of control somewhat from external to internal—which was what seemed to have been accomplished—might make student-teacher relationships more profitable and more pleasant.

A major goal for teachers, the psychologist-educator Richard deCharms (1971) maintains, should be to help students learn to take control of their own lives. Obviously, youngsters will never assume responsibility for themselves if they remain constantly under external control. But it is important to distinguish between a structured learning environment and control—a distinction some teachers fail to make. A teacher may present a highly structured learning environment, but allow students great flexibility, responsibility, and freedom of choice; in another classroom, the learning environment may be devoid of structure yet rigidly dominated by a dictatorial instructor.

DeCharms, who designates internally controlled individuals as *origins* and the externally controlled as *pawns*, has some advice on how to turn a pawn into an origin:

> You teach him first to know his own strengths and weaknesses; second, to choose his goals realistically, taking careful note of his own capabilities and the realities of the situation he is in; third, to determine concrete action that he can take *now* that will help him to reach his goal; and fourth, to consider how he can tell whether he is approaching his goal, that is, whether his action is having the desired effect (p. 403).

For classroom use to those ends, deCharms has devised some helpful procedures. In one, called "My real self," the teacher posts a "Thought for the Week"—something like "The kind of person I want to be" or "My favorite daydream." The thoughts, which of course are designed to stimulate students to think about themselves and their feelings, are discussed in class during the week. One facet of the procedure that has proved highly successful is to have students, at the week's end, write a short essay on the week's thought, for inclusion in their private notebooks.

Another of deCharms's suggestions involves "stories of success and achievement." Designed to make students think in terms of success, the procedure presents them each week with a plot and a challenge. A typical plot: "A hero is trying to do something better than it has ever been done before." A typical challenge: "Tell how he actually works on it." Along with plot and challenge, the students are given ten words related to achievement, which they are to learn to spell, to define, and to use in their stories.

Another approach involves conferences between teachers and individual students. Such conferences are routine in most schools, but the reasons for them and the matters discussed vary considerably. In several studies, John Gaa

(1979) has shown that conferences to set goals enhance student achievement and help to internalize locus of control for both high school and elementary students. The most effective conferences, held weekly, begin with the teacher's report on the student's progress during the past week, and a brief preview of the coming week. Then, using a simple checklist of the assignments for the next week, the student ticks off his or her own goals for each assignment. Finally, student and teacher talk about what the student plans to do to attain the goals. These conferences may sound like lengthy negotiations for a union contract, but after a little practice they take only a few minutes per student.

Gaa's and deCharms's ideas, only briefly sampled here, may inspire you to contrive similar activities in your own classroom for tranforming pawns into origins.

Should instruction match students' control beliefs?

Matching the Locus. DeCharms's and Gaa's aproach seeks to change students' sense of control. An alternative approach involves leaving the locus of control where it is and devising instruction to match it. The latter raises questions like these: Will their learning and attitudes improve if externally oriented students are matched with a tightly structured situation? Will it help internally oriented students to give them more control over educational decisions, by such means as contingency contracts? (Contracting is discussed in Chapter 10.) The evidence is not clear, partly because of muddled research (cf. McMillan, 1980). But it is possible that most children, whatever their locus of control, can adapt to any reasonable instructional arrangement, and that there is little compelling reason to develop different methods to match their different perceptions.

ATTRIBUTION THEORY

A more comprehensive theory than Rotter's, incorporating locus of control but taking into consideration beliefs about causes *and* consequences of behavior, has been developed by Bernard Weiner (1974) and his colleagues. Weiner's ideas reflect what social psychologists call *attribution theory*, for reasons the following example should make clear:

> Danny got a C— on a test. He attributes his mediocre grade to the test's being too tough.
> Fred also got a C—. But he had not studied much in the week before the test, and figures he was lucky to get even what he did.
> Randy received an A. His ability earned it, he feels.
> Brian also got an A. He credits extra boning-up for several days before the test.

The boys' differing attributions for what they did on the test are not just useful explanations of past behavior; they help to establish expectations for future behavior. Expectations built on attributions, cognitive theorists hold, constitute important intrinsic influences on behavior. Weiner has devised a scheme for classifying attibutions that uses each of the four boys' explanations. The classification focuses, as Figure 12.1 shows, on two dimensions: *locus of control* and *stability*.

What does attribution theory add to locus of control?

"Hmmmm, interesting," you may be saying to yourself, "but what will I do with that in the classroom?" Adding the dimension of stability provides important clues to what turns students on and off in school and what teachers can do to help turn them on and off; and that is what motivation is about. Stable characteristics such as ability are enduring, as their name implies, and difficult to change; unstable characteristics such as effort can be quickly increased or decreased. From Figure 12.1, you can ascertain that beliefs about ability are personal and stable; beliefs about effort are also personal but susceptible to change. The difficulty of a task—test, recitation, or homework—is relatively stable but impersonal; someone else determines it. And luck, of course, is perceived to be unpredictable and dependent on events in the environment.

Attribution in the Classroom. All these aspects of attribution—ability, effort, task, difficulty, and luck—are *perceived*, it is important to remember,

Figure 12.1. Weiner's Scheme for Classifying Attributions

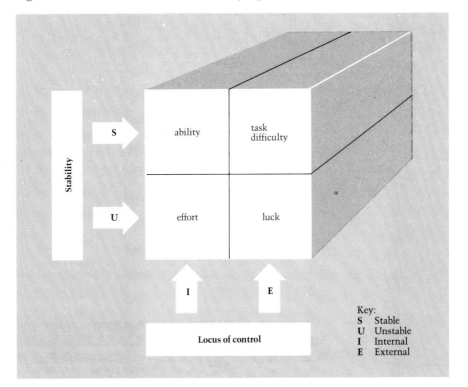

and not necessarily objectively real. Danny perceived the test as too tough, but Randy likely perceived it as fair enough. For a cognitive theorist, the subjectivity of perception—the fact that each of us has his or her own way of seeing things—is crucial, for our perceptions moderate between environmental stimuli and behavioral responses. The phenomenon helps also to explain why students behave so differently under the same conditions, that is, why their responses vary when their environment does not. For example, students demonstrate more persistence at a task when they ascribe success to their own efforts. And their attributions influence their preferences among tasks: Fyans and Maehr (1979) showed that students choose tasks that accord with their usual attributions. If students judge that ability achieved their past successes, they will seek out tasks that require competence rather than luck or special effort.

The attribution process occurs with our perceptions of others' behavior as well as our own, and teachers' perceptions of their students probably influence much of what goes on in the classroom. For example, in a series of studies of attribution and motivation summarized by Weiner (1972), teachers and student teachers were provided data about some imaginary pupils—how the students ranked in ability, how hard each tried on a test, what each achieved on the test. Then this question was asked: How much reward or punishment did the pupils merit?

The outcomes:

1. Regardless of how they performed on the exam, students who were believed to have tried harder were better rewarded than those who appeared not to have tried.
2. Regardless of effort, students of little ability were rewarded more generously than those of high ability.

Add up the two outcomes and you will find that students of little ability and high effort got the best deal. On that evidence, it appears clear that teachers value effort above ability, especially if a student has surmounted the obstacle of low ability by effort.

If, as evidence suggests, teachers' beliefs about the causes of students' achievements lead to the rewards and punishments given the students, then those attributions may affect teachers' choices of tasks for students and the intensity and persistence with which teachers approach instruction of each student. In that case, teachers influence students even more than has been taken for granted.

In their minds, teachers hold bright students more responsible for success, and blame the less able more for failure, Cooper and Lowe (1977) have found. Those impressions manifest themselves in overt behavior: bright kids reap more praise when they succeed, and the less able suffer more criticism when they fail (Cooper and Baron, 1977). The criticism grows sharper when failing students seem not to try (Medway, 1979).

How can attribution theory be used to advantage in the classroom?

Teachers cannot do anything directly about ability, because it is a stable characteristic. But they can ensure—or strive to ensure—that students understand that each of us controls the internal, unstable component of *effort.* Simple enough, right? Wrong. It is more complex than it sounds, because internal and external factors interact to produce students' beliefs about possible success or failure. For example, difficult tasks, set by the teacher and therefore externally controlled, require ability *and* effort for the student to succeed. With simple tasks, it is possible to succeed on the basis of *either* ability *or* effort.

The interaction of internal and external factors has direct implications for teaching. The teacher should set tasks that are *moderately* difficult, so that some ability and some effort will be required; but because ability varies considerably among students, teachers should individualize tasks as much as possible, i.e., tailor them to fit the student. Any task assigned to all students, you can be fairly certain, will produce a mix of successes and failures. And as failures occur and continue, you will encounter student misbehavior: misbehavior is the students' alternative means of motivation.

Does failure promote realistic attributions?

One problem in dealing with students who are prone to failure is that they may not react in the way that reinforcement theory holds they should; if they are rewarded for effort, they ought to try harder in the future. But Covington and Omelich (1979) have observed that some such students do not respond to reinforcement with increased effort, and others actually reduce effort. Why? Because they have become inured to failure and expect it. Covington and Omelich hypothesize that when students are confronted by a task they assume they cannot do, they turn to protecting their self-images. To that end, they attempt to appear capable-but-not-trying, which is the opposite of what impresses teachers, trying-but-not-capable. That image would be destroyed, of course, by increased effort after reinforcement. Even more obviously, and still in defense of their self-images, they take refuge in excuses. When such a student flunks a test, he does not quietly accept his mark: he explains with a straight face that he had not been able to study because his baby brother had eaten his notes, his reference books had been stolen by a burglar, and the electricity had gone off in his house for two days.

Can failure be reduced? Can teachers and students agree on reasons for failure? Covington and Omelich think so. They hold that the structure of most classrooms, in which students compete with each other, promotes excessive failure. They would change competition among students to self-competition, adopt the mastery technique (see Chapter 16), or shift to cooperative learning where no one need fail. Task analysis (chapters 7 and 10) can help to transform large assignments into a series of more manageable subgoals. Contingency contracting (Chapter 10), which explicitly details student tasks, can give students a less defensive sense of responsibility for schoolwork.

No matter what motivational device is used, the reduction of failure should help establish realistic and productive attributions. Remember, when students

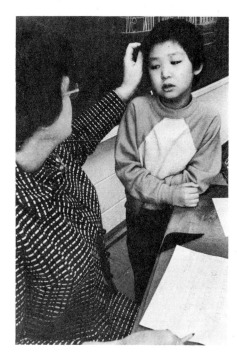

"As a teacher I've had to be just as concerned about the children's physical and emotional needs as their learning needs. If they come in here tired, or sick, or hurt—or hungry—how can I expect them to sit down and work as if nothing was wrong? I've had children come in here with raw bruises. . . . First I send them to the school nurse, then we can try to sit down and read. . . . Or if a child's lonely, first he has to feel that I'm a friend, that I'm interested in him, then we start getting interested in doing our work.

finish school, cognitive and affective behaviors become tools for coping with the rest of life.

ACHIEVEMENT MOTIVATION

Another theory about motivation, proposed by H. A. Murray (1938), is that all human beings have psychological as well as physiological needs. Murray listed twenty-eight such needs, but the one that has attracted the most attention is the *need to achieve*. That need is a drive to do well at something, not necessarily for praise, good marks in school, or a raise in pay, but simply for self-satisfaction. Though the drive is there, it is not always easy to detect, because challenge is required to activate it. How teachers can provide challenge will be discussed later in this chapter.

The person most concerned about developing programs to increase achievement and to measure it is David McClelland; for the last twenty-five years his name—which will become increasingly familiar to you as you teach—has been virtually synonymous with research and development of theory concerning the need for achievement. He has sought to link the striving for achievement to most human accomplishments, and in one of his boldest proposals he suggests that cultures advance and retreat with their entire society's motivation to achieve.

Does school success require a high achievement need?

It is hard to measure the need for achievement, as is true of most motivational constructs. Nevertheless, research has shown that individuals highly motivated to achieve tend toward an internal locus of control, and extrinsic rewards do not greatly influence their efforts (Vidler, 1977); they may exercise much self-control, postponing gratification until they have finished their work. Women have usually demonstrated less achievement motivation than have men; Horner (1972) argues that in women the motivation is repressed because of the fear that if they prove highly successful they may be penalized for overstepping traditional roles. Of course, if cultural values shape achievement motivation, increasing opportunities for women ought to reduce the fear of success and heighten their need for achievement.

Many programs have been designed to increase achievement motivation in schoolwork. Most such programs have not significantly increased study behavior, test scores, or grades. However, Alschuler (1973) suggests that the

Figure 12.2. Maslow's Hierarchy of Needs. Humans have a natural tendency to progress upward on the hierarchy, and each need must be generally satisfied before a new one is established. At any particular time, one need dominates and is termed *prepotent.* **Maslow proposed that a person would devote about 50 percent of his energy to fulfilling the prepotent need; the remaining 50 percent is split between adjacent needs. An abrupt change in the environment—landing in prison, or losing a job, for example—may cause regression to earlier stages. Although Maslow asserted that trhe hierarchy is universal, some critics feel that it reflects Western values and philosophy.**

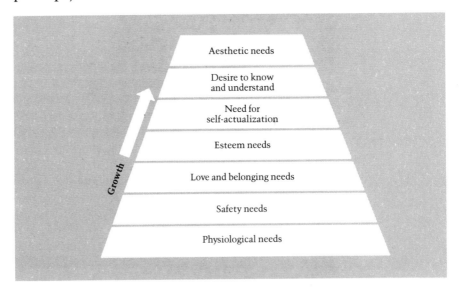

training programs may improve planning and self-control out of school, which perhaps is more important in the long run.

MASLOW'S NEED HIERARCHY

Abraham Maslow (1968), who wrote a great deal about motivation and personality development in general, theorizes that there is a hierarchy of needs, each of which must be met before the individual can progress to the next level of the hierarchy. The hierarchy is depicted in Figure 12.2.

Can success occur in lower levels of Maslow's hierarchy?

Maslow classifies the bottom four as *D* (for deficiency) needs; they represent physical and psychological survival, and they depend for satisfaction on external circumstances. Only when those needs have been met do the other three, which Maslow designates the *B* (for being) needs and which reflect intellectual development, have a chance to sprout from within. For example, a person who is starving is concerned primarily with finding food, and all other things, if they surface at all, are secondary until the food is found. You are wondering again, no doubt, what so obvious a fact has to do with teaching. But the student who is disliked, or thinks he or she is disliked, will behave in ways intended to fill the need to be liked. Too often, studying and learning do not represent one of those ways; even when they do, the student does the right thing for the wrong reason. So, Maslow holds, the student will never have the resources permitting progress up the hierarchy to the higher needs that, when fulfilled, ensure a well-adjusted, fully functioning individual—the kind of individual that schools maintain they are dedicated to turning out.

Motivation in Practice

What does *unmotivated* mean?

At the beginning of this chapter, we described the motivating of students as the increasing or the sustaining of behavior toward a goal. Setting goals is at the heart of motivation. But whose goals? When a teacher says that a particular student is motivated, all too often the teacher means that the student's goals are the same as those the teacher has set for the student—active engagement in an assigned task. But the so-called unmotivated student has a different set of goals from the teacher's. Motivation of the kind that teachers want can be stimulated by agreement between the teacher's expectations and the student's goals. This does not always require that the student change goals; it may mean that the teacher will have to modify his or her expectations of the student. But the specification of goals clearly understood by teacher and student can be highly motivating.

It is important to remember that every student has a goal, even if the goal, consciously or unconsciously, is to avoid doing schoolwork. The trick for the teacher is to arrange things so that the student's goals will be appropriate for the objectives of the class. Humanist educators, of whom Maslow is one, argue that students should be allowed to set their goals for learning and to choose activities that will help them achieve their goals. But whether you have an open class of the kind humanists advocate, or a highly structured class, the student's personal goals must accommodate the goals of the class; otherwise, you will have an uncooperative student, an "unmotivated" student, and perhaps a discipline problem.

TYPES OF MOTIVATORS

What can a teacher do to "energize" students toward pursuing appropriate educational goals? We have several suggestions for *motivators*, some of which you will find pretty obvious.

Attention. Most learning, of course, requires attention; one way for the teacher to gain and maintain attention is to banish distracting activities. A tic-tac-toe game going on during a lesson, it hardly needs to be pointed out, is a distracting activity. Because attention is internal, its control can be difficult. Saying "pay attention" may not suffice, especially when the task involves complex mental processes. For example, working with college students who were science majors, Wright (1979) found that they did better in solving logical problems if they jotted down possible cues, and then categorized them as relevant or irrelevant to the problem at hand.

Can learning occur without attention?

Attention from *others* is of course a potent motivator and can reinforce many different behaviors. A student who knows very well the answer to a problem will do even better in the future, in accord with reinforcement theory, if the teacher arranges to make him the center of attention in an audience of his peers. But where new learning is under way, an audience usually proves to be a hindrance. (Martens, 1972; Zajonc, 1965).

Expectations. How one feels about oneself—one's self-concept—profoundly influences *what* one does, and *how much* one does it, and you read in Chapter 4 that expectations constitute one aspect of self-concept. Students who expect to succeed in school generally work to succeed. You can motivate, or help to motivate, students by creating expectations of success in them. You may want to look again at Chapter 4 to refresh your memory about how to achieve that. The essential point is to encourage students to develop positive attitudes about themselves, so that they will be convinced they can do whatever is expected of them.

Whether a teacher's expectations concern appropriate pupil conduct or academic achievement, performance usually improves when expectations are expressed explicitly (Locke and Bryan, 1972). The advice, "Do your best," rarely motivates as effectively as the precise statement of goals.

Incentives. Everyone strives harder toward a goal when an incentive accompanies the striving. Often the incentive may be simply to reach the goal, as when you tackle a crossword puzzle; at other times, an actual reward may be associated with the goal. The use of reinforcement as reward or incentive is discussed at length in chapters 10 and 13.

Feedback. You have read about and know the importance of informing students how they are doing academically, and many teachers assume that only that kind of feedback really matters. Not so. It is equally important to take up classroom behavior with students. Unfortunately, teachers tend to do so only when provoked to anger, "correcting" students before the entire class; students who are the targets of such public criticism then become even less cooperative. Private conferences in which teachers tell students that they are pleased or displeased with the students' attitudes toward their studies, for example, work much better and can prove highly motivating.

Can learning occur without feedback?

Theoretically, feedback embodies two components: *information*, which delivers a cognitive message, and *affective value*, which stimulates the emotions and urges that a similar response be made or avoided in the future. Slavin (1978) suggests that theory can be applied practically in the classroom by giving two kinds of grades as feedback: one would tell the student how he is doing in relation to his classmates—the cognitive message—and the other kind of grade, performance feedback, would reinforce progress in relation to his own past work. But Slavin's proposal exemplifies the difficulty of matching theory and practice: feedback's components come in a tightly wrapped package, and it may not be so simple to untie and separate them.

Commitments. Much like setting goals, this motivational technique simply involves having students commit themselves to certain achievements. The many ways of inducing commitments from students include John Gaa's goal-setting conferences, use of explicit behavioral objectives, and contingency contracting. In terms of attribution theory, commitment increases when students believe that their own efforts and ability are involved. In practical terms, this suggests handing them part of the responsibility for developing plans, goals, and contracts.

What are some effective levers of motivation?

Challenge. In describing the need to achieve, a few pages back, we remarked that challenge was essential to activate the need to achieve. When students seem uninterested, they are not necessarily lacking in the need to achieve; it may be the challenge that they lack, and devising interesting challenges is up to the teacher. But children—and people generally—respond to challenge with either fear or confidence. The confident ones are motivated by expectation of success, the fearful ones by the desire to avoid failure. So the two groups tend to differ in tackling goals. Confident people prefer challenges tough enough to give a sense of special accomplishment but not so tough that they cannot be overcome. Fearful people select goals that are either very easy or very difficult to reach. Easy goals ensure that they will not suffer the humiliation of failure, but they do not provide the joy of success because "anybody could have done it." Difficult goals spare them the anguish of failure because "nobody could have done it." If you give a class a list of twenty-five words and ask your pupils

"There are some days, no matter how great you think class will go, no matter how many gimmicks you've got planned, you just don't connect with some kids. If you snoop a little, you can usually find out what the problem is. But some problems are really out of my hands. Mmm, it's hard to battle the big problems they bring from home. You know, last week she came in here very upset. I said, 'You get out of the wrong side of bed this morning?' And she said, 'Yes. Mother's been yelling at me all morning; besides, my dog's gonna have to go away. I can't keep him in the project.' It was on her mind! Good Lord! Her whole day! To think that when she got home that night he was going to be gone. So I said, 'Keep me informed. Because I like animals. Just let me know.' She really appreciated that—the fact that I allowed that day that she had that on her mind. That I was interested in this."

to predict the number of words each will spell correctly, the fearful students will come up with very low or very high figures. Confident students will offer realistic assessments of their chances. So in dealing with students who have poor self-concepts, remember this: everyone, as we have noted earlier in this book, delights in success. Therefore, balance the tasks you set for fearful students: choose both easy ones in which the students are sure to succeed, and more difficult ones that will provide real challenges. The successes should make the students less apprehensive about possible failures.

Discipline. If discipline is to serve as a motivator—and it can—you as a teacher must set firm rules and specify clearly the consequences of breaking those rules. That has two motivating results: it reduces or eliminates distracting behavior, and it helps students to discover that observance of the rules benefits everyone but breaking of the rules offers no gain to anyone. In Chapter 13 we will have more to say about the use of discipline to improve motivation and classroom management.

Curiosity. At first glance, curiosity is one of the simplest variables in the human repertoire, and it seems to be universally regarded as a positive attribute. Yet its precise definition, development, and measurement baffle researchers. One popular theory about its origins centers on the apparent need of all organisms to be aroused or stimulated. The scientific credibility of this idea was strengthened back in 1954 (Heron, 1961), when McGill University students volunteered to enter an environment in which they would do nothing but lie on a cot. (They had short breaks to eat and use the bathroom.) They were fitted with translucent goggles to dim vision, cuffs on the hands and arms to impede the sense of touch, and earphones that delivered a constant "white noise." They were paid twenty dollars a day, a hefty allowance at the time, but few students could take more than a couple of days of the experiment. They reported unmanageable stress, extreme boredom, hallucinations, and mental dullness, among other unpleasant effects. These findings, replicated in several experiments, seemed to show an inborn need for arousal.

But this research has been criticized on several counts. If a drive to be aroused exists, shouldn't stimulation reduce it by satisfying it temporarily? Other drives—hunger, sex, thirst—subside when appeased. But most research has provided evidence that we keep on seeking stimulation. And later experiments than those at McGill did not always produce the same traumas: Suedfield (1977) speculates that the early experiments simply frightened the students, and that their emotionality had little to do with sensory deprivation.

Must we have stimulation from the environment?

Other theories and research acknowledge the search for stimulation, but avoid talking about inborn drives to explain it. Kagan (1971), for instance, refers to motivation to resolve uncertainty. Confronted with the unfamiliar, unusual, discrepant, or incongruous, we concentrate on resolving our uncertainty. If we succeed, we are reinforced; if we do not succeed, we feel anxiety. Hunt (1977) takes a similar position but adds an information-processing rationale. When novel information does not accord with schema stored in the head, Hunt claims, the organism is stimulated to manipulate the information to attain a more comfortable match.

Kagan and Hunt agree on two other important points. One is that, although people vary, we often seek out incongruity or uncertainty in our environment—behavior that is probably what most of us know as curiosity. The second point is that too much incongruity, surprise, or dissonance is disconcerting as too little: neither extreme stimulates curiosity.

For decades, folk wisdom has charged schooling with squelching youngsters' curiosity and desire to explore. Not so fast! say Bereiter and Scardamalia (1977). They find evidence that curiosity and exploration decline not because teachers stifle them, but because of a natural developmental change. Early in life, exploration and discovery are the major routes to important social learning. But in late childhood, there is less and less payoff for exploring everything, for seeking every possible solution to every possible problem. In short, they become inefficient and troublesome ways to learn. On the other hand, curiosity is associated with creativity, positive self-concept, lessened anxiety, and general personal adjustment (Maw and Maw, 1970). So should we encourage it or not? The answer is yes, but moderately. Like the amount of stimulation humans seek, the Golden Mean is the aim.

Stimulating curiosity in young children is usually not difficult if the children feel comfortable in their surroundings. When you add too much stress, such as problems that are too difficult for them or overemphasis on high grades, they will spend their energy trying to reduce it, instead of letting curiosity direct them to worthwhile learning. With older children, a relaxed, friendly atmosphere is important too. Adolescents, though, may seem overly interested in conforming to the standards of their peers. They are curious, but their curiosity is often directed toward social behavior rather than academic work. Your ingenuity in teaching will be tested here. Try to harness curiosity: if students are fascinated with a dead owl found on the way to school, you may ask them to write stories or poetry about owls, draw or paint depictions of them, make feather arrangements, measure various feathers, mount and examine the skeleton, search for owl pellets to discover eating habits, and engage in a dozen other owl-connected activities.* On your part, it will take courage, spontaneity, creativity, and a willingness to set aside your objectives temporarily. If you are convinced that school is for students, and that a momentary interest of theirs is relevant and justifiable and can be usefully exploited, give it a try.

Competition and Cooperation. Undoubtedly, competition among students increases motivation, but its constant use in schools has engendered strong criticism. In Chapter 14 we shall discuss two approaches to testing and grading: in one, students compete against each other; in the second, they compete against themselves. There are times when you will want to use both kinds of competition. But the most important contest in which one can engage involves pitting one's own initiative against one's previous work; and you as a teacher would do well to emphasize that kind of competition.

Although much research has compared the classroom effects of competition and cooperation, some ambiguity persists in the findings. Studies have often used laboratory-like situations, with tasks rarely found in schoolwork. Nevertheless, the accumulated evidence points toward these conclusions:

1. Students, especially in high school, believe that as competitive pressure mounts, they learn more (Trickett and Moos, 1974). This belief has some support in fact: competitive classroom environments often do improve reading and math achievement (Michaels, 1977). On the affective side, competition may increase motivation to attempt and complete school tasks. However, students in competition place far more value on outperforming peers than on the quality of their own work (Ames and Felker, 1979).

---

* Vincent Rogers (personal communication, February 27, 1980) reports that such an owl study occurred in a school room he knows in a working-class, industrial city; the class is populated with enthusiastic, happy, achieving, curious kids—and no discipline problems.

2. Cooperation also produces strong affective outcomes, but of a different sort. Students show keener enjoyment of tasks, like each other more (Garibaldi, 1979), and are better satisfied with school in general (Wheeler and Ryan, 1973). Cooperative environments may also enhance cognitive skills. Even with first graders, Johnson et al. (1980) found that cooperative classrooms promote problem-solving and reasoning ability.

The apparent merits of cooperative activities have become increasingly important because of conflicts among students in integrated and main-streamed classrooms. At John Hopkins University, Robert Slavin (1979) and his colleagues have produced a variety of cooperative activities that promote acceptance between races. In one successful example, students were divided into small teams of mixed ability, sex, and race. Twice a week the team members met to help each other study for quizzes. Team quiz scores were based partly on each member's improvement, so everyone, regardless of ability, could contribute to the overall score. Similarly, Eliot Aronson's (1978) jigsaw

"Yes, ability is important. But it's interesting how much motivation can even things out. That's probably my biggest challenge: to see how much effort I can squeeze out of these kids. You know, even though competition gets a lot of bad press, it sure turns on the effort in some kids. But it turns off other kids, so I try to use it carefully."

"I've come to understand how interactive a classroom is. I know that I can influence students' motivation, and some of them change the way I perform. I find myself paying attention to the alert, excited kids. If I dwell on the kid who's falling asleep, then my mood changes and it's not much fun in here. The tricky part is that when I ignore the bored kid, he's certain to fall asleep."

methods, discussed in Chapter 13, use cooperative learning games to decrease racial tensions.

Roger and David Johnson, educational psychologists and proponents of a more humane school atmosphere, have discovered that cooperation may ease the trauma of mainstreaming. Earlier studies had shown that mere contact between handicapped and nonhandicapped students did not make them like each other better and sometimes even intensified rejection (Gottlieb, 1974). In a bowling class into which retarded youngsters had been mainstreamed, Johnson et al. (1979) arranged three different goal structures:

1. *Cooperative.* Teams of five students aimed to improve the previous week's total score by fifty points.
2. *Individual.* Without being placed on a team, each student tried to improve his previous score by ten points.
3. *Control group.* Instructions were "Just bowl," with no goal specified.

The cooperative teams developed far more friendliness, engaged in mutual reinforcement and apparently got better bowling scores.

Only recently has evidence begun to accumulate about the most important long-range question: can students generalize cooperative skills to new situations? That is, will the cooperative bowling team carry its new attitudes to the classroom and outside school? The answer depends on how cooperative skills are learned and practiced. If students merely play games together for half an hour a day, little change usually occurs. But if the entire classroom is made up of cooperative groups, the social expectations and desired norms are more likely to etch themselves into students' behavior (Hertz-Lazarowitz et al., 1980).

Should competition be eliminated?

A final word on competition: The fact that losing may be painful does not make competition responsible for all the ills of American society or schools. As Johnson (1979) suggests, a skillful teacher will know when to shift from cooperative to competitive to individual structures. Competitive activities can motivate students constructively when all participants share the rewards, and when grading is not stressed. Well-managed competition can also provide a stimulating change of pace for students ready to try out new learned skills.

Anxiety. Overanxiety about academic performance can interfere seriously with success, so you might conclude that decreasing anxiety would increase motivation. The conclusion would be wrong. Considerable research on the relationship between learning and anxiety has indicated that too little anxiety is as undesirable as too much. Anxiety is a form of arousal—of alertness, of awareness, of attention-paying. A teacher must evoke arousal to teach successfully, and it has been determined that there is an optimum level of anxiety which elicits maximum performance. As anxiety increases, so does performance—to a point. The trouble is that teachers often cannot identify that point. Neither does anyone know how to raise anxiety to the optimum level and then flick the switch so that anxiety will not rise higher.

Actually, the ways learning and anxiety work together are even more complicated than we have indicated. Denny (1966) found that students of high intelligence and high anxiety performed better on a complex learning task than did students of high intelligence and low anxiety. But the opposite proved true of students of less intelligence: in that group, students with low levels of anxiety surpassed those with high levels of anxiety.

During learning, where may anxiety occur?

Besides intelligence, other factors—distractions, the organization and difficulty of a task, the overloading of short-term memory—interact with anxiety to enhance or hinder learning. To make order of this complexity, Tobias (1979) suggests an information-processing approach to the problem. Recall that information-processing theorists liken learning to computer operations: information is screened, enters the brain, is coded into storage, and is transformed or manipulated to help solve a problem. Tobias hypothesizes that anxiety can interfere at any of three processing points:

1. *Preprocessing.* As information is read, seen or heard, anxiety may cause attention to irrelevent cues or meaningless details. The learner may be

preoccupied with personal problems (which themselves are augmented by anxiety), or be easily distracted. Any method that helps concentration should reduce anxiety at this stage. For example, elimination of known distractions, lengthened study time, or a videotape replay may improve attention to important information.

2. *Processing.* During memory storage and rehearsal, anxiety heightens when the information is difficult to absorb and poorly organized and when too much information burdens short-term storage. Memory aides, careful spacing and organization of material, and attention to difficulty may indirectly assist instruction by managing anxiety.

3. *Postprocessing.* Here, a student stumbles when asked to demonstrate learning, as on an exam. Lengthening exam times, shifting to criterion-referenced evaluation and a mastery model (see chapters 14 and 16), and presenting more short exams rather than one massive one may ease anxiety.

"I always feel a little guilty about not planning enough. I mean planning for motivating devices, not planning for content. There are few things more rewarding than inventing an activity that everyone loves to do. But who's got the time to plan outstanding activities every single day? I'm already putting in fifty or sixty hours a week. Maybe, if . . . I don't know."

The implication of Tobias's work is that methods of reducing anxiety work best if they are aimed at the processing stage in which most stress occurs. Because anxiety is related to much other evidence of poor learning—low grades, poor study skills, and insufficient study—it is vital that students and teachers work together to keep it within tolerable bounds (Culler and Holohan, 1980).

So what exactly should the teacher do to regulate levels of anxiety for bettering motivation? Educational psychologists do no yet know enough to permit precise recommendations. But, if you have a student who is obviously so highly anxious about an upcoming exam, say, that he or she is fumbling with the work, a private, encouraging talk with the student should help to reduce the anxiety. If the problem is chronic, though, and the student suffers from high anxiety most of the time, refer the student to the school psychologist, the counselor, or the principal.

Summary

Motivating students toward classroom goals is one of the most important roles of the teacher. Theories of motivation are useful tools to help you understand why behaviors occur and persist, and to direct you in finding practical tactics for energizing students. Behaviorists, concentrating on how the environment induces behavior, are generally more concerned with *extrinsic* motivation, whereas cognitive and humanist theorists place more importance on internal or *intrinsic* motivation.

One important aspect of intrinsic motivation is a student's belief about why consequences to his or her behavior occur, i.e., the student's *locus of control*. A youngster who feels largely *internally controlled* believes that success depends on his or her own intelligence and skill. An *externally controlled* student believes that other people and circumstances determine his or her fate. The differences between internally controlled and externally controlled students are significant because people attach more weight to what they want to do than to what they have to do. They are more likely to assume responsibility for voluntary behavior than for compulsory behavior. They will work harder if they believe their own efforts will bring reward. In many situations, shifting of the locus of control helps both teachers and students.

Locus of control has been incorporated into a broader theory of *attribution*. Attribution adds the important dimension of perception of *stability*, so that an event may be caused by something stable, as one's ability or one's job, or caused by something variable, as effort or luck. The teacher's reponsibility is to help students understand that effort is the most important motivational aspect under the students' control, and that a belief that failure results from low ability is self-defeating. The teacher must also strive to match task difficulty with the abilities of individual students. It is important, too, to realize that teachers' own attribution beliefs may influence their behavior toward students.

The *need to achieve* and *Maslow's hierachy of needs* offer alternative views of intrinsic motivation. Programs to build achievement motivation have not demonstrated much success in school. In Maslow's theory, a person must fulfill each need before moving to a more advanced psychological stage.

There are a variety of motivation techniques, ranging from the behaviorists' use of extrinsic reinforcers to the more subtle means of heightening curiosity. Competition has proven a powerful incentive, although it may have unintended side effects. Cooperative classroom structures may bring about both cognitive and affective gains, and help keep anxiety within tolerable limits. Other methods for reducing excessive anxiety depend on when anxiety occurs during the learning process.

Chapter Study Guide

CHAPTER REVIEW

Answer questions 1–13 True or False:

1. Evidence shows that most teachers in an achievement-oriented society value student ability above effort.

2. Students' beliefs about possible success or failure generally result from a mixture of internal and external factors.

3. A teacher who sets tasks that are only moderately difficult will fail to challenge students to do their best work.

4. A humanist view of motivation is that because everyone has a need to achieve, people work not for reward but simply for self-satisfaction.

5. Motivation-conscious teachers try to arrange things so that the student's goals will agree with the objectives of the class.

6. Intrinsic variables are unobservable and must be inferred from behavior.

7. Locus of control refers to the likelihood that a person will expend effort.

8. "Feeling good" about something is an important condition for learning about that thing.

9. Informed teachers deliberately arrange for all students to experience occasional failure.

10. *Origins* and *pawns* are deCharms's terms for motivated and unmotivated students.

11. Students whose control orientation is closely matched with type of instruction show greater achievement.

12. When students believe that chance or luck is responsible for success, they show less persistence at a task.

13. The need to achieve appears to be inborn, not learned.

14. In Maslow's hierarchy, each need must be _____ before a new one becomes prepotent.

15. The need to reduce uncertainty causes an organism to pay attention to _____.

16. Integration and mainstreaming have _____ attention to cooperative classroom structures.

17. When an actor suffers stage fright and cannot deliver a memorized speech, anxiety is said to occur at the _____ stage of information processing.

18. Almost all definitions of motivation embody two components, energy and _____ .

19. Weiner's attribution theory of motivation not only incorporates locus of control, but takes into consideration beliefs about causes and _____ of behavior.

20. _____ built on attributions constitute important intrinsic influences on behavior.

21. Any single task assigned to all students is bound to produce a mix of _____ and _____ .

FOR FURTHER THOUGHT

1. Some behaviorists have suggested that effective humanistic teachers are actually subtle behavior modifiers. What is your reaction to that assertion? Is it possible for a teacher to subscribe to both behaviorism and humanism?

2. Can a teacher be great at motivating students without knowing any of this chapter's theory? If so, then what is the relevance of theory?

3. Using students' curiosity to help structure their learning may alienate parents whose philosophy is that the teacher ought to dispense knowledge. How would you try to persuade those parents that curiosity behaviors might be worthwhile? What would you respond when you are accused of encouraging Reynold to be "nosy" or "snoopy"?

IMPORTANT TERMS

motivation
extrinsic motivation
intrinsic motivation
locus of control
external locus
internal locus
attribution theory

achievement motivation
need to achieve
Maslow's hierarchy of needs
prepotent need
sensory deprivation
information processing

SUGGESTED READINGS

ALSCHULER, A. S. *Developing achievement motivation in adolescents.* Englewood Cliffs, NJ: Educational Technology Publications, 1973. A lengthy review of Alschuler's many efforts to enhance achievement motivation, all built on principles of humanistic psychology.

BALL, S. (ed.). *Motivation in education.* New York: Academic Press, 1977. Introductory readings on various topics in motivation. Good overview, although some areas are dated (e.g., curiosity) with old references.

HARVEY, J. H., ICKES, W. J., and KIDD, R. F. (eds.). *New directions in attribution research. Vol. 1 and 2.* Hillsdale, NJ: Lawrence Erlbaum Associates, 1976, 1978. A high-level collection of readings on attribution approaches to motivation. Most articles do not report original research findings, but review related research and integrate those outcomes with theory.

WALLER, P., and GAA, J. Motivation in the classroom. In Coop, R. H., and White K., *Psychological concepts in the classroom.* New York: Harper and Row, 1974, pp. 151–191. Good introductory overview of motivational processes, stressing Maslow's humanistic model, and a cognitive viewpoint.

ANSWER KEY

1. F; 2. T; 3. F; 4. T; 5. T; 6. T; 7. F; 8. T; 9. F; 10. F; 11. F; 12. T; 13. F; 14. satisfied *or* fulfilled; 15. unusual *or* unfamiliar events; 16. increased; 17. postprocessing; 18. direction; 19. consequences; 20. Expectations *or* Beliefs; 21. successes . . . failures

Coping with Misbehavior

Misbehavior in school represents, as we remarked in the Chapter 12 discussion of Weiner's attribution theory, a student's creation of an alternative means of motivation. It may reflect either the failure of the teacher's efforts to motivate a student toward a desired goal, or the failure of the student to cope with academic demands. Because students vary in ability, we pointed out also, any task assigned to all students will produce a mix of successes and failures— a strong argument for individualized instruction.

But whatever the roots of misbehavior, as every experienced teacher knows and inexperienced teachers soon discover, maintaining discipline and a measure of decorum in class is vastly important. It can be as essential as instruction and as demanding on the teacher. In this chapter, then, we shall deal with the varieties of undesirable behavior that challenge teachers and with methods of countering them.

Does effective management occur before *and* after misbehavior?

The chapter, you should note, does not exhaust those methods. As Kounin (1970) has argued, successful classroom management involves far more than imposing discipline after misbehavior; it includes forethought and careful planning for instruction, which, with a willingness to experiment, help to prevent much disruption. In that sense, most of this book broadly addresses classroom management. More specifically, chapters 12 and 16 discuss management in a preventive, achievement-oriented sense. This chapter focuses on misbehavior.

Misbehavior

Concern about classroom discipline is widespread. In nearly every Gallup poll on education, adults rank it as the schools' most serious problem (Gallup, 1980). Students do too (Koch and Koch, 1980). Teachers vary widely in defining misbehavior—beginners object to more kinds of conduct than do hardened veterans—but teachers everywhere are preoccupied with it. The concern is not new; in the mid-1950s, nearly a third of urban teachers reported physical violence against them (Williams, 1979), and mayhem, especially in the junior high schools, supposedly has risen since then at a staggering rate (National Institute of Education, 1978). Do our perceptions match reality?

VIEWS OF CLASSROOM PROBLEMS

In a classic study, Wickman (1928) listed thirty-six characteristics or kinds of behavior that teachers generally frown on (see the box on p. 412). Then he asked several teachers and several psychologists and psychotherapists (then called "mental hygienists") to check off the ten manifestations that they considered most serious and the ten least serious.

How do teachers view misbehavior? How do psychologists?

Teachers and psychologists diverged sharply, as you already may have noted. The teachers were concerned about behavior that affronted their concepts of morality, or represented aggression, or otherwise impeded classwork. The psychologists shrugged off those behaviors as less important and concentrated on indications of emotional maladjustment such as unhappiness and shyness. The differences are understandable, of course, in the light of the distinct objectives of the two professions. The teacher's task is to impart knowledge and stimulate learning, *right now*. To the teacher, the youngster who misbehaves remains a *pupil*, albeit one with problems. The psychotherapist's task is to foster mental health, *for the long run*. To the psychotherapist, the teacher's misbehaving pupil is a *patient*, whose symptoms happen to manifest themselves in school as well as elsewhere.

Since Wickman's study, dozens of best sellers have made psychology pretty much a household word, most literate Americans believe that they know at least something about the science, and teachers accordingly appear to have drawn somewhat closer to the psychologists' point of view (Beilin, 1959). But teachers and psychotherapists remain a good distance apart (Brooks, 1978), because teachers still are dealing with pupils and psychotherapists still are dealing with patients. Certainly teachers have to be aware of undesirable characteristics in youngsters in their classes; certainly teachers, especially in the elementary grades, exert great influence on their pupils' emotional development. But the classroom would not be the place for individual therapy, even if teachers had the training and the time to administer it. Disruptive behavior, nevertheless, requires control, if for no other reason than that it infringes on the rights of the entire class. And misbehavior can be controlled.

THE CAUSES OF MISBEHAVIOR

Pertinent to the control of misbehavior, of course, is this question: What makes children that way? There are many competing hypotheses to explain school disruption. Some are ancient and built on casual observation. Others are fairly recent and emerge from learning theory. For the moment, we shall not attempt to evaluate any of them. Here is a representative sampling:

Why does misbehavior happen?

1. *Bad character.* This bit of folk wisdom took on a more scholarly appearance when Sigmund Freud and others set down some principles of personality. In general, an individual is thought to have relatively stable character whose seeds were planted in infancy, and whose roots grew deep in the first few years of life. Bad character thus develops in early childhood and primarily results from the misbehavior of parents. By the time a child enters school, he or she has a fairly fixed character (although it can be slowly altered by psychoanalysis).

2. *Deficient personality traits or motives.* Related to the Freudian explanation, this idea puts less stress on historical antecedents of personality traits,

and more on the interrelationships between traits and behavior. For example, chronically disruptive students are said to have weak self-concepts, external locus of control, and poor ego-strength. Need theory also fits this category, so obnoxious students may be characterized as having a need to dominate, a need for power, a need for authority, and so on.

How Teachers and Psychologists Differ on Misbehavior

Recent surveys indicate that teachers' views on student characteristics and behavior have changed little since 1928 when E. K. Wickman made his classic study. Wickman asked teachers and psychologists which ten of the thirty-six kinds of behavior listed below they considered to be the most serious signs of maladjustment in schoolchildren, and which considered to be the least serious.

1. carelessness
2. cheating
3. cruelty, bullying
4. destroying materials
5. disobedience
6. domineering
7. dreaminess
8. enuresis
9. fearfulness
10. heterosexual activity
11. imaginative lying
12. impertinence
13. inquisitiveness
14. interrupting
15. masturbation
16. profanity
17. obscene notes, talk
18. restlessness
19. shyness
20. silly, smartness
21. smoking
22. stealing
23. stubbornness
24. suggestible
25. sullenness
26. suspiciousness
27. tardiness
28. tattling
29. temper tantrums
30. thoughtlessness
31. truancy
32. unhappiness
33. unreliable
34. unsocial withdrawing
35. untruthfulness
36. whispering

PSYCHOLOGISTS' ANSWERS

10 most serious

1. unhappiness
2. fearfulness
3. unsocial withdrawing
4. cruelty, bullying
5. enuresis
6. shyness
7. suspiciousness
8. suggestible
9. temper tantrums
10. domineering

10 least serious

1. whispering
2. profanity
3. smoking
4. interrupting
5. tardiness
6. heterosexual activity
7. masturbation
8. carelessness
9. inquisitiveness
10. thoughtlessness

TEACHERS' ANSWERS

Note: The italicized answers were listed as *least* serious by the psychologists; those which are capitalized were listed as *most serious* by the psychologists.)

10 most serious

1. *heterosexual activity*
2. stealing
3. truancy
4. destroying materials
5. *masturbation*
6. untruthfulness
7. cheating
8. obscene notes, talk
9. impertinence
10. CRUELTY, BULLYING

10 least serious

1. *whispering*
2. imaginative lying
3. *inquisitiveness*
4. restlessness
5. silly, smartness
6. tattling
7. *thoughtlessness*
8. dreaminess
9. SHYNESS
10. stubbornness ∎

Wickman (1928)

3. *Poor moral development.* From theories of cognitive development have emerged theories of moral development, and these ideas share several principles. Development is universal, not peculiar to Western culture. Humans progress through a sequence of stages, where thought and behavior become progressively more sophisticated. The sequence is irreversible; we move forward, not backward. Just as a retarded student may be arrested at a low *cognitive* developmental stage, a delinquent may be fixed in a low *moral* developmental stage.

4. *Socioeconomic status.* This variable has been shown to relate to nearly everything, including disruptive classroom behavior. Although the relationships are sometimes powerful, the term *socioeconomic status* is woefully vague. For example, it includes ethnic heritage, parents' educational and occupational attainments, location of residence, income, status, parental attention to child behavior, number of books in the home, relative deprivation, and so on.

5. *Societal changes in general.* Because respect for adults and authority has decreased, and because the nuclear family unit has weakened, classroom disruption is a sign of the times.

6. *Boredom.* For a good many years, human motivation was assumed to be balance-seeking. If too many stimuli poured in from the environment, humans took shelter. Presumably, they wanted peace and quiet. In the mid-1950s, this theory was toppled by substantial evidence that humans are motivated to be active. As we noted in Chapter 12, we seek information from our changing environment, and we act on that environment. In this formulation, boredom is not a positive state but a negative one, and it can result from either of two related situations: repetition of similar stimuli (such as hearing the same song several thousand times), or inadequate stimuli (as when a person must face a plain wall for a long period). In either case, boredom results from sameness. Because of their need for arousal and a variety of stimuli, students may create their own stimulation. Usually, this response is at odds with the teacher's goals.

7. *Learning by imitation.* Children observe others aggressing, disobeying, and disrupting. Because of vicarious (imagined) reinforcement, such as improved status, power over others, and attention, they imitate undesirable conduct not only of their peers but of adults on the street, parents, and characters in comic books and, especially, on television.

8. *Teacher-initiated disruption.* Inescapable punishment creates aggression in the punished. Although this finding sounds more like what happens to rats standing on an electrified grid, it is easily generalized to a school setting. Teachers exude punishment in different guises: humiliation, sarcasm, inattention, and outright verbal and corporal attacks. Even well-intentioned teacher behavior may be interpreted by a student as aversive, and the classroom is a tight container, where students do not easily escape averse events. So the student aggresses back.

"He's sitting there, away from the others, because he seems to have trouble sitting near other children. He gets up; he starts verbal arguments; he complains that other children are bothering him. And he's very dependent; he's constantly coming over to us for attention—after every sentence! It's not a punishment. He understands why he's sitting there—that he's to finish one whole page in his workbook without getting up—then he can get up and show it to one of us. That contact, that reinforcement, is very important to him. You notice that he's still goofing off on the way back to his desk. We're ignoring that—just concentrating on getting him to sit still long enough to finish a whole page."

414

Can teachers promote student misbehavior?

Another version involves the frustration-aggression hypothesis. According to this notion, aggression occurs when goal-oriented behavior is thwarted or blocked. For example, if a student's unwitting and momentary goal is to daydream, and a teacher cuts the reverie short, the student is presumed to be frustrated and the likelihood of aggression increases.

9. *Teacher-contributed disruption.* In this situation, teachers unintentionally transmit a negative expectancy to students, who receive it and behave in a way that reinforces it. For instance, if a teacher expects a student to be a slow learner, the student may unwittingly be criticized more often, allowed less time to answer questions, and paid less attention to. With less opportunity to excel and less predicted payoff, the student's acheivement declines, and fulfills the teacher's expectancy. We shall explore expectancy effects further in Chapter 16.

10. *Teacher-reinforced disruption.* In this view, teachers are thought to shape and sustain undesirable behavior unintentionally, through teacher attention. If attention—even negative attention—is rewarding to a student, he or she will exploit ways to attain that reward. Since misbehavior gains attention much more effectively than does on-task effort, rewards can be acquired quickly.

11. *Student-reinforced disruption.* Here, the situation is similar to teacher-reinforced disruption, except that peers often know well that they help to promote misbehavior. Taunting, daring, egging on, laughing, and simple attention from other students can sustain misbehavior.

Which theory is right?

How can we summarize the several viewpoints about why disruption occurs in the schools? Because the topic of classroom management is important, much research and theory have been devoted to it, with little obvious resolution. Most camps of thought usually ignore competing theories. If they acknowledge them, it is to attack rather than incorporate. One must wonder about the objectivity of investigators, most of whom claim to have supportive evidence. But there are two possible interpretations to this. (1) Some of the evidence must be wrong, and we will have to look more closely to find the "real" theory. (2) The evidence is generally right, and there is no single cause to misbehavior. The theories do not conflict; actually, they complement one another.

We hold the second assumption, that the theories are complementary. If they seem to compete, it is because they differ in focus. Some revolve around the teacher, some around the broader environment. Some deal with historical causes; some seek to describe the inner workings of the student. We do not propose that all theories are equally good, because some explain better and predict better than others. Classroom misbehavior is complex and has multiple causes and consequences. So it makes sense to use several complementary practices to reduce it.

The practical application of theory demands a screening of ideas. Some of those we have listed cannot be put to work in school. The first five are interesting but societal or therapeutic in scope.* So we shall consider how to use the remaining six theories.

WHO MISBEHAVES?

Throughout school, boys cause far more trouble than do girls (Clarizio and McCoy, 1976). This fits the popular view of sex-related behavior: boys are more aggressive and active, girls more docile and compliant. As we remarked in Chapter 4, these differences seem more attributable to learning than biology. The behavioral differences persist in the classroom, however, regardless of their thoretical origin. There is one sex-linked behavior, though, the appearance and treatment of which have created much controversy.

Why are hyperkinetic youngsters labeled as misbehavers?

Some children—usually boys—cannot attend to instruction for more than a moment. Their flighty, fidgety behavior matches their short attention span. Often categorized as learning disabled, such youngsters are termed *hyperactive* or *hyperkinetic*. Their nonstop movement in class disturbs others, and teachers usually regard hyperactive youngsters as management problems. Hyperactivity in most children, fortunately, tapers off during adolescence. But that is little consolation to the elementary teacher who must cope here and now.

Drug Therapy. If a youngster has been diagnosed as hyperkinetic, it is likely that he receives daily medication, usually an amphetamine. In adults, amphetamines—which can be dangerous and occasionally fatal—serve as stimulants. In children who have not reached puberty and whose hormone content differs from that of adults, the drugs generally have a calming effect. Under careful administration, amphetamines prescribed for hyperkinetic children can increase attention span, decrease restlessness, and encourage the following of instructions. Such medication has sometimes been acclaimed as a magical cure-all and, indeed, Ritalin—the most commonly prescribed amphetamine—has wrought some dramatic changes in many youngsters' classroom behavior. And, its proponents argue, greater attention and less disruptive behavior should improve academic achievement. Unfortunately, research has failed to show academic gains attributable to medication (O'Leary, 1980).

Medication for hyperkinesis has been controversial since the *Washington Post* reported incorrectly in 1970 that between 5 and 10 percent of Omaha's school-age children were receiving doses of drugs to quiet them down. Critical articles appeared under such headings as "The Educator as Pusher: Drug Control in the Classroom" (Grinspoon and Singer, 1973), and the furor led to a congressional hearing. Many hyperkinetic children continue to receive medi-

---

* Issue 3—moral development—has received much attention in the last decade, and several values and morals curricula have been invented. Their effectiveness in managing disruption, however, is not supported by systematic evaluations (see Lockwood, 1978).

cation, however. How many? O'Leary (1980) estimates that 600,000 to 700,000 children receive medication in school. This works out to less than 3 percent of all children through the eighth grade, rather than the 20 percent sometimes cited.

Whatever the figure, public concern persists, not without reason. Among the problems accompanying medication, Sprague and Gadow (1976) cite:

Inadequate monitoring of the effects. Though teachers are sensitive to changes in behavior brought about by drugs, they often do not report such undesired effects as drowsiness to the child's family or physician.

Wrong levels of medication. Dosage is sometimes prescribed too high or too low, and can impede rather than improve learning. Parents may increase the amount of medication to "help" the child cope with special circumstances; or they may fail to provide the school consistently with the drug.

Other researchers mention additional difficulties:

How do drugs help to treat hyperkinesis? What are the potential problems?

Adverse side effects. The drugs cause diarrhea, temporary slowing of physical growth, sleeplessness, irritability, and depression in a small proportion of treated children (Roche et al., 1980; Johnson et al., 1976). Little is known about the long-term effects, and Eisenberg (1976) speculates that they may include interference with the functioning of the brain and with learning.

Dependence on drugs. Although amphetamines appear not to be habit-forming in children, they *may* imbue the children who receive them with the belief that drugs are quick and safe cure-alls, and so may lead to dangerous dependence on drugs in adulthood (Broudy, 1976).

Implications of inadequacy. Medication may induce children to think "Something's wrong with me. . . . I'm different." Renstrom quotes an eleven-year-old: "I have to take special pills to make me seem like everybody else" (1976, p. 106).

Because of the persisting doubts about drugs, some researchers prefer behavior modification as an alternative, and we recommend that behavioral techniques be applied first, and drugs be used only as a last resort. Behavioral research on hyperactivity is increasing rapidly, and much of it encourages reliance on that approach. Several methods discussed in Chapter 10 have been used successfully to contain hyperactive behavior; they include token economies in home and school, social reinforcement, self-control, and tangible rewards. Behavioral methods often improve achievement, an outcome that medication cannot claim (O'Leary, 1980).

TACKLING BAD BEHAVIOR

William, who is seven and in the second grade, is a tattler. His tattling has cost him any chance he had to make friends with classmates and has irritated his teacher, Ms. MacIlvaine. So Ms. MacIlvaine decides to apply one of the simplest techniques of behavior modification in an effort to change William's ways. Rather than chiding William when he comes to her to squeal on a fellow pupil, she ignores him. Rebuking him might reinforce William's behavior. Ignoring him, using *extinction*—the withdrawal of reinforcement—decreases his tattling. Additionally, she praises him on the rare occasions when he says something complimentary about another pupil, and, just for luck, she herself *models* appropriate behavior for him. So Ms. MacIlvaine's tactics work similtaneously to eliminate William's undesirable habit and to encourage a desirable habit.

Every one of the theories of conditioning about which you read in Chapter 5, every one of the methods of behavior modification that were discussed in

Crime in the Schools

VANDALS RANSACK SCHOOL IN MILFORD

Susan Mende

About 15 rooms, including the principal's office, were ransacked at John F. Kennedy School in Milford early Thursday in what police called the worst case of vandalism they had seen.

Although no damage estimate was available Thursday, one detective said he "never saw a job like this one."

Classes were conducted Thursday, some in the auditorium.

Vandals broke into the West Avenue elementary school sometime before 3:55 A.M. by smashing a large glass window in the rear doorway, police said.

An eight-page police report listed damage which included broken doors and windows of classrooms, health department, kitchen, and custodirooms; broken hallway water fountains, from which "water was all over everything"; and upturned teachers' and principal's desks which had been ransacked and emptied.

Police said acid burns on the science room floor were caused by chemical spills in the room. They said the fire department was called in to "take care of a smokey haze which came from the floor, and to be certain there was no threat of fire from the mixture of spilled chemicals."

Also, file cabinets and storage cabinets had been broken into and rifled; cartons of milk, taken from the kitchen, were later found in other parts of the school, partially consumed; and paints and inks had been thrown over the walls, police said.

In addition to some office, kitchen, and audio-visual equipment being thrown about the rooms, police later found assorted items outside the school, a short distance from nearby woods.

Police are processing blood samples found at the scene.

It has not yet been determined if anything was stolen, police said.

From the *Hartford Courant*, May 23, 1975.
Vandalism of the kind reported here costs the country's schools an estimated $600 million a year. How to reduce it? A Senate subcommittee that studied crime in the schools suggested that strict discipline alone would only increase the alienation of students from authority—an alienation responsible for much of the problem. Recommended is a program of firmness tempered with a demonstration of concern for individual students. In one school where such a program has been instituted, the principal couples disciplinary action with a show of interest in students' welfare, and encourages teachers to build close personal relationships with students, even to the point of entertaining them as weekend house guests. ■

Chapter 10, lends itself to application in the classroom. Because disruptive behavior—running around the room, fighting, tossing paper airplanes—bothers teachers most, a majority of the techniques will be employed to help a student *decrease* annoying activity. But all of the techniques can be used to *increase* a desirable behavior. And, like Ms. MacIlvaine, teachers can put two techniques to work at once, one of them to reduce an antisocial behavior and the other to encourage an incompatible, prosocial behavior.

Choosing a Technique. But, you may ask, which technique do I use when? How do I choose among positive reinforcement, negative reinforcement, extinction, shaping, punishment? A simple procedure discussed in Chapter 10 will help you answer your questions for yourself:

1. Target the behavior you want to change. (Be specific: don't describe the behavior as "disorderly during lessons" but as, for example, "fights with Billy in reading periods.")
2. Do a task analysis. What precedes and follows fighting? Can the fighting itself be broken into predictable parts that usually occur in the same sequence? Why does he start a fight only during reading lessons? Perhaps the assigned reading is too easy or too difficult (Bryen, 1975).
3. Establish a baseline. Keep a record of how often fighting occurs *before* you attempt to correct the situation, so that you will be able to determine later whether or not your approach works (Chapter 10).
4. Choose your goals and techniques on the basis of your task analysis. In this case, you may decide to take several steps, such as changing the seat of one of the combatants, providing reading material within the offender's capacity and praising him for success with it, and devising an assignment for him that is incompatible with fighting.

What are the general steps of a behavior change program?

Although reinforcement procedures are the most common method for changing behavior, they do not always work: for example, compared with girls, elementary-age boys are more responsive to peers' reinforcement than to teachers' (Henry et al., 1979). In high school, one measure of peers' importance as a source of reinforcement is that 35 percent of high schoolers consider their friends the "one best thing" about their school, compared to 4 percent who say that of their teachers (Benham et al., 1980). Unfortunately, it is misbehavior that peers sometimes reward, and you will have to harness peer influence creatively.

Help from Students. Ordinarily, teachers, parents, or professional therapists are used to help control deviant behavior. The use of peers, however, has sometimes proved effective. Besides, when peers can run a behavior change program or even help out, as in distributing tokens, they free a teacher's time for other responsibilities. Solomon and Wahler (1973) gave an example of peer control in a sixth-grade classroom. Five boys in the class of thirty were targeted as highly disruptive. Because peers should have high reinforcing value if they

Teacher: *OK, now we're going to do something different—I mean something that you've never done before, here.* (kids cheer) *All right! Quiet. Now, I want you all to guess who this is! This is a classmate of yours. I'm not making fun—we're just—this is called role playing: I'm trying to be another person. OK? You remember when Miss Hoye and I did this attitude thing?*

Students: *Yeah....*

Teacher: *OK, I want you to tell me—*

2nd Teacher: *What are you doing now? Are you rehearsing this?*

Teacher: *No. I'm trying to figure it out as I go along—it's coming to me—Who this person is. This is one of your classmates, OK? I'm not making fun! I'm just portraying some of the actions of this person—OK? Ready? Now, you think! A name—could be a boy, could be a girl. Right now I'm either, OK?* (begins to climb up on desk; (students giggle, makes noise by banging foot on desk; laughter) *OK? Who am I? Huh?* (student guesses) *No....*

2nd Student: *Elvin.*

Teacher: *Elvin! Was I close?*

Student: *You know, you looked just like him!* (laughter)

Teacher: *OK! Think of your classmates. Who has someone they'd like to role-play? Derrick? All right. Do you need a desk?*

Derrick: *No.* (sits and opens a book)

Teacher: *That's it? That's all? Come on Derrick! What else does this person do?*

2nd Teacher: *You have to do something and exaggerate a little so that——*

Teacher: *You have to act, Derrick! Doesn't everybody open a book? What else does this person do? Something that's unusual?* (student opens another book) *You're going to open your spelling book, too?* (noise from other students) *No! Now give Derrick a chance! This is not easy! This is not easy! And you're not supposed to give it away to who it is! But you should take on some of the characteristics of that person. His or her walk—if the person wears glasses, pretend you have glasses on. If a person's short, pretend that you're short. If the person is tall, act very tall. . . . Oh! that person has glasses!*

Several Students: (shouting) *I know! I know!*

Teacher: *Oh, wait a minute!* (holding students back) *Oh! I think I know what you're trying to do. . . . Do you need a piece of paper? No? Yes, you do—here. . . .*

Students: *I know. I know. . . .*

Teacher: *No, no! Shhh! Shhh! I don't know yet! Come on! All right, Teresa?*

Teresa: *Jeffrey*

Teacher: *It's Jeffrey. You know he was trying to show you that that was during the spelling test yesterday that Jeffrey took out his book! Jeffrey! Yes!* (laughter) *All right. Who thinks they can do a good role-play of Miss Sherman or me?* (eager laughter) *OK! Now, but remember you may sit at the desk, but not drink my lunch soda!* (laughter) *OK, now. . . .*

Must students be passive observers of misbehavior? are to help administer a program, Solomon and Wahler picked highly popular students to serve as "therapists." These students were taught a few simple behavior rules (ignoring misbehavior, praising appropriate behavior), and were asked to help the misbehavers. The procedure reduced disruption, and Solomon and Wahler wondered whether peers might be recruited to help treat more difficult behaviors, such as stealing and truancy.

Many other reported studies seem to involve peers as change agents. However, most studies concern exceptional—retarded, emotionally disturbed, etc.—students, and whether their findings can apply to the regular classroom may be questioned. McGee et al. (1977) note that researchers observe students' peers giving encouragement, prompting, and reminding about

421

appropriate behavior, but McGee has found few clear descriptions of how peers go about such incidental therapy. In sum, peer recruitment looks great when you read about it, but don't assume that it will automatically reduce classroom disruption.

Group Contingencies. In many studies demonstrating management methods, the teacher works with one child or a very few children. Such techniques often are effective, but because of their limited focus they can be extremely time-consuming and inefficient. There is some evidence that a teacher can work with a larger group—say, an entire class—without reducing effectiveness.

The term *group contingency* describes a procedure in which most or all of a class must exhibit a targeted behavior to earn a consequence. Hamblin et al. (1971) speculate that spontaneous peer tutoring and prompting occur during a group contingency, and they may help maintain behavior change (Rosenbaum et al., 1975).

Are group contin-
gencies fair?
In one study, Winett et al. (1975) compared three conditions, individualized instruction, architectural changes, and group contingencies, to improve social behavior in a sixth-grade classroom. The group contingency consisted of a simple rule: 90 percent of the students had to finish and hand in completed work before they could enjoy recess. The group contingency proved best at increasing quantity and quality of work and in improving social behavior.

Several studies have reported striking success with the "good behavior game." The game consists of posting simple rules that deal with only one or two disruptive behaviors. Then, students are split into teams and told that when a rule is violated, the offending team will be given a check. The team with the fewest checks wins extra privileges—special projects, going home ten minutes early, and so on. The game is thus a mixture of group competition and simple behavior modification. Harris and Sherman (1973) tried it with fifth and sixth graders, and it sharply reduced off-task behavior. But competition produced some negative side effects, such as harrassment, so they tried the game without teams. That also worked.*

When it becomes difficult to monitor an entire class, inventive educators sometimes employ special devices. Greenwood, et al. (1977) used simple apparatus to increase on-task behavior and academic achievement for fifty-four first, second, and third graders. They laid down several rules, such as "Look at the teacher when she/he is giving directions." Then, when all the kids in a class were following the rules, the teacher activated a wall clock and a light. At the end of each period, the good behavior time was computed and posted. If the class increased the time over the previous day's record, it was given extra recess or free time. In similar experiments, Packard (1970) reports that skeptical teachers (Hogwash!" one declared beforehand) became believers.

---

* Instead of detailing all possible responses, behaviorists often shortcut with the terms *on-task* and *off-task*. This simply indicates whether or not the learner is displaying appropriate behavior.

Aiming at reducing noise in seventh- and eighth-grade home economics classes, Wilson and Hopkins (1973) rigged a microphone to a sound level meter: whenever the noise level fell below a certain point, a radio, tuned to a popular music station, automatically turned on. After a few days, the radio was nearly always on. Schmidt and Ulrich (1969) used a sound meter for the same purpose in a fourth-grade class. The students were promised extra gym time for ten continuous minutes of "quiet," as measured by the meter. If during the ten minutes the meter ever moved above a certain level, a timer was reset, and the class started another ten minutes minus any reinforcement.

Token procedures, by definition, employ special apparatus—tokens—and sometimes additional equipment. Wolf et al. (1970) gave third- and fourth-grade teachers kitchen timers to help decrease out-of-seat wandering. The teachers set the timers for random periods averaging twenty minutes. Each student in his seat when the timer rang earned five points that could be redeemed for field trips, candy, clothes, and so on. The procedure is noteworthy because of its efficiency. Instead of having to pay a good deal of attention to particular behaviors, to particular children, and to delivering consequences, the teacher is freed to teach.

In a similar first-grade situation, Suratt et al. (1969) arranged for even less attention on the teacher's part. They rigged little remote-controlled lights on disruptive students' desks and appointed a fifth-grade student the "engineer" who switched the lights on or off according to whether or not students were on-task. When students compiled enough on-task time, they were awarded tickets exchangeable for favorite activities. Off-task behavior rapidly decreased, and Suratt gradually stretched out the time standard for earning the tickets.

These examples demonstrate the importance of ingenuity and experimentation in the classroom. In each case, behavior change was stressed, not feelings. You may wonder whether students *appreciate* or *want* such structured guidance. A recent Gallup poll (Koch and Koch, 1980) implies that they do, but we think it should not be taken for granted. In planning a classroom management program, students' affective responses should be carefully considered.

Changing Attitudes and Feelings. It is possible, of course, that the child who is belligerent in class fights with his fellows not because the reading material bores him as too easy or defeats him as too difficult: he may simply loathe reading, even though he can read at the class level. If that is true, it is likely that he associates reading with some unpleasant experience of school, as Larry did with math in Chapter 10, and does what comes most naturally to him—fight—to escape reading. The cognitive and affective domains are allies, not enemies. "Feeling good" about something—a condition in the affective domain—facilitates the learning of that something, in the cognitive domain. "Feeling bad" about it, on the other hand, impedes learning. So classical and higher-order conditioning—to which we devoted so much space in Chapter

5—can be harnessed to the benefit of pupils' mental health and of their learning. (And classical conditioning and operant conditioning share a link, you remember from chapters 5 and 10; the CS or US of classical conditioning is identical with the reinforcement of operant conditioning.) If a reinforcer makes a student feel good, he or she will probably associate feeling good with whatever behavior gained the reinforcement. And, similarly, feeling bad will be associated with whatever brought punishment.

How is classical conditioning related to classroom behavior?

An example of the practical use of classical conditioning to change student attitudes is cited by Roden and Hapkiewicz (1973), who believe that in the upper elementary grades, at least, most students have the necessary ability for subjects such as reading; if they lag, they lag for want of a reliable and practical stimulus to pair with the subject. The example derives from an experiment Roden conducted with seventh-grade inner-city students who read at third-grade level. He sent half the students, of whom there were well over a hundred, to remedial reading classes daily, to serve as controls. For the other half, he obtained several hundred library books ranging from kindergarten and first-grade level to Dickens. For thirty minutes of "reading time" each day, all students had to have their chosen books open on their desks. They did not have to read the books, but a student who finished a book went to a card file, pulled out his or her personal card, and wrote the name of the book on it. Each Friday, the instructor called for oral reports. Surprisingly, the better readers chose the easiest books first, breezed through them and reported on them with evident enjoyment before tackling the more difficult tomes. The poorer readers picked the toughest books—presumably on the theory that if one was going to fail, one should fail *big*—but did not read them. The urge to get a piece of the action grew too strong for them, though. The better readers were apparently having fun, and they were filling up their file cards and holding the class's attention while they reported what they had read. By the end of the eighth week, the last of the holdouts shoved aside *A Tale of Two Cities*, which he had not read, and picked up *The Bear That Wasn't*. Twenty minutes later, he noisily made his way to the card file: *he had read a book!* He was savoring success.

How can feelings be enlisted to spur learning?

Roden's control group advanced by a month for each month spent in remedial reading. But the experimental group gained more than two months for each month of the experiment. Even more impressive, they had learned to enjoy reading, and grumbled if "reading time" had to be skipped occasionally. By the end of the year, their parents reported they were reading more than they ever had, and had become highly optimistic about their academic futures.

In terms of higher-order conditioning, what had happened was this: A CS (reading) had been paired with another CS (success) often enough to engender a conditioned response (CR) of good feelings toward reading. But other interpretations are possible. For example, we could consider that the better readers, reading for fun and enjoying it, served as models for the poorer readers. Because there was no coercion to read and there was no extrinsic reward for reading, the students may have decided that reading was worth doing for its own sake; they may have attributed their success to each individual's efforts, in unknowing accord with attribution theory.

Because success evokes pleasant feelings in almost all of us, it should be an imperative of classroom management to provide experiences of success for every student. Most of us give lip service to that, but performance is something else again: any classroom you look into has its perpetual losers, who are the first to drop out of school because there are other places in which to experience success.

THE USE OF CORPORAL PUNISHMENT

In Chapter 10 we discussed the pros and cons of punishment for changing behavior, and noted that its use is hotly controversial. Corporal punishment is especially polarizing among educators and psychologists, although it is practiced widely. Here are some of the major arguments against it:

1. It fails to foster development of a sense of personal responsibility, as evidenced by the fact that high percentage of frequently punished delinquents do not change their ways. (In short, it doesn't work in the long run.)
2. It inhibits development of conscience, because to the youngster punishment represents the *might is right* level of morality, whereas affection, warmth, and praise, accompanied by reasoning, enhance the growth of conscience.
3. It often reflects the teacher's needs rather than the pupil's, and therefore appears retaliative rather than well intended.
4. It is not essential to keeping order in class, because in schools where it is forbidden, teachers and pupils manage well enough without it, and because there are alternatives that are effective.

What are the pros and cons of physical punishment?

Defenders of corporal punishment, who generally agree that it should be used only sparingly and as a last resort, argue:

1. Most youngsters recognize their own need for control and the justice of punishment for misbehavior. When punishment is meted out fairly, it strengthens the respect and affection children and adults feel for each other.
2. Psychological punishment does not always serve as well as corporal punishment, and neither should be used to the exclusion of the other. Their application depends on the circumstances. Some youngsters prefer moderate corporal punishment, the pain of which soon vanishes, to psychological penalties, the pain of which may long endure.
3. A teacher who devotes a great deal of time and energy to avoiding behavioral problems by other techniques may be short-changing students.

Educationally, fewer hours are available for lessons. Psychologically, students are deprived of experience: misbehavior is punished in the world outside the classroom, and the classroom is a good place in which to learn that fact of life.

4. Corporal punishment is almost never administered—at least in school—out of vengefulness. The rare teacher who abuses authority is as likely to misapply one kind of punishment as the other.

5. Though it should be rarely used, corporal punishment should not be forbidden. The *possibility* that it may be employed deters misbehavior.

Those are some of the arguments. Join them with the pros and cons listed in Chapter 10, and it becomes obvious that corporal punishment is a complex matter reflecting the diversity of philosophies that guide our schools and communities. You will encounter the arguments again and again, because the issue arises frequently. Teachers' associations bargain for corporal punishment in their contract negotiations with school boards. Civil liberties groups and some parents have sued to forbid it. Administrators often favor it, and conventions of educators debate it. Whether or not you apply corporal punishment will be up to you, unless your school district's rules prohibit it.*

Is Corporal Punishment Ever Justified? Outside the classroom, clinical psychologists sometimes administer painful punishment as a cure. June, for example, had been sneezing steadily for six months; neurologists, allergists, urologists, endocrinologists, psychiatrists, and hypnotists had been unable to help her. She continued to sneeze once every forty seconds. Then a psychologist decided on an unusual therapy. He devised a gadget that gave June, who was seventeen, an electric shock every time she sneezed. The sneezing stopped after four and a half hours of the treatment (Baer, 1971).

Is punishment in teaching ever justified?

Hardly anyone would argue that a small child should not be smacked for running out into a busy street, or sticking a finger into an electric lamp's socket, or reaching for a hot pot on a stove. The infliction of pain often may be the only means of saving a child from greater pain, because as Ausubel has written, "it is impossible for children to learn what is *not* approved and tolerated simply by generalizing in reverse from the approval they receive for the behavior that is acceptable" (1961, p. 29).

Public opinion gives some sense of justification. In a recent Connecticut survey, two-thirds of the adult respondents said yes when asked, "In general, do you think it is a good idea for parents to punish children by spanking them, or not?" (Institute for Social Inquiry, 1980). In Indiana, nearly all the junior high schools and three-fourths of the high schools use physical punishment (Elrod, 1979). And, after a five-year intermission, the Los Angeles public schools have reinstituted spanking in elementary and junior high schools (*Phi Delta Kappan*, 1980).

* Although the United States Supreme Court in April, 1977, upheld the use of corporal punishment in the schools, two states specifically prohibit it: Massachusetts and New Jersey.

"I've got a couple behavior management tricks that almost always work. A substitute teacher, believe it or not, showed me one of them. She invented this little baseball game with only one rule: three strikes against the class, and they all lose five minutes free time at the end of the period. The strikes are called whenever noise gets too high. I would have thought you'd need an objective standard for calling a strike, like anything above 90 decibels or something like that. But it works without it. I guess the kids sense when things are getting too rowdy. Also, once two strikes are called, it stays pretty quiet 'til the end of the period, I like the game—it's simple and it gives fair warning. The other thing I use is a kitchen timer to keep kids on-task during seatwork. I set it at random intervals, so they don't know when it will go off. When it dings, I scan the room, and anyone goofing off loses free time. Now I can spend time in student conferences instead of prowling around the room and nagging at them."

A school milieu that approves of aggressive treatment of misbehavers will promote punitiveness among its teachers (Haviland, 1979). There is compelling evidence that when teachers and schools are punitive, they engender similar behavior by children (Sloan, Young, and Marcusen, 1977). Since boys are more aggressive and more often punished for misbehavior, it is not surprising that boys hold stronger punitive feelings than do girls toward transgressors. As Haviland (1979) suggests, a morality founded on punishment reflects a social context larger than the school. Punitive schools are thus likely to receive justification from the community.

Must you punish in accord with community standards? If the community clearly opposes corporal punishment, it would be reckless to apply it in school. If the community favors it, you would be wise to use it sparingly anyway. So many alternatives exist for establishing classroom control that corporal punishment should not be necessary. If you must resort to it, remember that even if the United States Supreme Court and local law allow it, parents may sue if they believe the punishment excessive.

CHRONIC DEVIANCE: ARE WE STUCK?

Although we have not said so, this chapter focuses on the management of mild, occasional disruption. What about the student who is regularly antisocial or aggressive or who seems uncontrollable? You are not on your own, of course, in planning for students with serious adjustment problems, who show up in nearly every classroom (Feldhusen, 1979). From school to school, the resources differ, but school administrators—vice principals and principals—should always be ready to assist. Many school systems employ guidance counselors and school psychologists, who may be trained in the control of deviant behavior. The school psychologist may wish to use personality tests or observational measures before designing a program for a disruptive youngster. Finally, one of the most important resources is the experienced teacher. You will find colleagues whose classrooms are happy, smooth-running places. Enlist their aid.

But what will you do when all efforts fail and that kid continues to challenge your authority? The prognosis for chronic classroom disrupters, especially adolescents, is somewhat bleak for two reasons. First, chronic classroom disruption is usually one of a constellation of symptoms that regularly occur together, among them truancy, stealing, physical and mental aggression on peers—especially on "whipping boys"—and the like (Olweus, 1978). There are thus general patterns of antisocial activities, of which school behavior is only part. Groups of related behaviors seem to support each individual deviation. This stands to reason, because humans move toward consistency in behaviors: for example, aggressive traits usually do not appear in relationships with peers, and disappear in relationships with adults. The Jekyll-Hyde character who moves in and out of quite different traits is rare. The challenge of pervasive antisocial character traits is that they are difficult to alter; it would be much simpler if a single, situational behavior could be addressed.

Does antisocial behavior persist? When and why?

The second worrisome aspect of classroom disruption, as part of a constellation of behaviors, is durability. Robins (1966) followed several hundred males, for about thirty years, beginning when all were under eighteen years of age. All had been referred to child guidance clinics because of discipline problems in schools and truancy, aggression, and so on. In a large group of these boys, antisocial behavior could be traced to the beginning of school. Thirty years later, in their forties and fifties, the same group showed a high incidence of mental illness, alchoholism, criminal behavior, and social isolation. They perpetuate their own misbehavior by providing an environment that teaches their children the same misbehavior! This is not to suggest that deviant adults purposely lead their children into miserable lives. Social learning theory reveals how much social behavior is learned through observation alone, with no intent on the part of the model (Whitehurst, 1978).

In summary, easy cures with long-range results seem impossible, because individual behaviors are part of a complex package that is difficult to unwrap, sturdy, and lasting. In addition, you may have difficulty obtaining effective services for an extremely disruptive youngster, in part because mental health specialists disagree about *whether* the child needs treatment (Freemont and Wallbrown, 1979). These pessimistic notes do not mean we should shrug off classroom disruptions. Our culture pays an enormous psychic, physical, and economic price for antisocial behavior. Even if teacher and administrative interventions work only in the short run, they at least offer two important benefits. They make school life more pleasant for the time being, and they protect the rights of other students, teachers, and school staff.

In addition to the relatively specific strategies derived from research literature, several broader principles will prove worthwhile. Humans are active and require stimulation. If the classroom environment is unchanging and dull, students will create their own stimulation, of which inattention and daydreaming are merely variants. Preventively, teachers can stem disruption with assorted, planned alternatives intended to satisfy the students' need for arousal and curiosity. When plans fail and disruption occurs anyway, you will need to draw from a repertoire of intervention methods (Brophy and Putnam, 1979; McDaniel, 1980), including those discussed here and in Chapter 10.

On the basis of evidence and theory, it is likely that highly permissive environments encourage maladaptive behavior. *A clearly structured, friendly* environment seems to lessen antisocial activity. In brief, this suggests the use of a few simple rules that are relevant to learning, positively stated, and consistently applied. It also means the statement of precise academic goals, so there can be little ambiguity about what achievements are expected. It means careful consideration of unsupervised time, where peer pressure, reckless judgments, imitation of inappropriate models, and increased aggression may combine to result in mayhem.

The *friendly* aspect of the principle should not be forgotten. Being authentically friendly toward an obnoxious student may be exceedingly difficult. And it may even seem phony to act pleasant when a hateful kid is brooding with menacing eyes. Although it may be less phony to unleash a "natural" response to a surly child—by bellowing, threatening, scowling, physical aggression, and a variety of nonverbal behaviors—it almost certainly worsens the situation. Why? Because punishment looses a flood of instinctive behaviors known as aggression; that is, aggression is usually met with aggression. Also, social learning theory predicts that adult models who use aggression and hostility to solve problems will be imitated by observers.

What is your role in preventive management? For reasons even philosophers disagree about, humans need successful experiences. The youngster who fails routinely through his academic career is highly likely to show maladaptive behavior in the classroom. Successive failures damage the self-image, diminish aspiration and motivation, create hostility, and increase truancy and dropout incidence. Repeated failure is not good for building character, and it does not offer important lessons about real life (except the understanding that the environment can be exceedingly cruel). It teaches escape and avoidance behavior. Worse, when attendance is compulsory, a student may perceive regular failure as inescapable punishment, which may trigger aggression.

The answers to repeated failure are straightforward, known to all teachers, but sometimes poorly practiced. *Each child must be guaranteed success experiences.* This suggestion is not meant to erect a shield around incompetent kids. Every child can have genuine experiences of success under two manageable conditions:

1. If competitive activities regularly reward a certain few students, then they regularly punish certain others. Competition is frustrating for kids who rarely or never win. Use it cautiously, and arrange to spread rewards using handicaps or setting up competitions that recognize special, limited talents.

2. In a class whose students vary widely in cognitive abilities, the chronic loser is too often left to sink. When assessment comes due, he is given the same test as the rest of the class, is usually graded with some sort of implicit curve, and ends up toward the bottom. In other words, the child who starts off school slowly for whatever reason—developmental lag, emotional difficulty, poor motivation, less mental ability—has an ever-increasing distance over which to try to catch up. The distance translates to perceived or real failure. Ideally, individualization is the answer here, but it is an extremely difficult challenge to even the most experienced teacher. So let's focus on approximations, instead of Utopia. We *can* contrive more success experiences for failure-prone students, even if they are only a couple of words of genuine praise per day. For a student who has gone all day with no praise, no reinforcement, and no success, even the smallest encouragement may seem a powerful incentive.

When misbehavior does occur, your students' respect for you will increase if you handle it swiftly and fairly. Students expect classroom order and effective management (Callahan, 1980; Nash, 1976), and when they see it, the classroom is a happier place.

Facilitating Classroom Management

As we have suggested, there are two general means of dealing with misbehavior. One, using behavioral methods, is to target the behavior itself and design a plan to reduce it. The second involves indirect procedures that are usually aimed at prevention of misbehavior. Indirect procedures, the topic of this part of the chapter, are used to create a socially constructive atmosphere employing resources outside as well as inside the classroom.

HELP FROM OUTSIDE THE CLASSROOM

The hyphen in the name *Parent-Teachers Association* represents more than a nicety of punctuation. It emphasizes the link between formal education in school and informal education at home. They complement one another, and teachers can benefit their students and ease their own jobs by working with parents. Here are a few simple guidelines toward that end:

1. Keep in touch with pupils' parents. This is advisable at all levels but assumes particular importance in the lower grades, when parents are anxious to know how their children are adjusting to study. Don't rely entirely on report cards. Don't wait until a problem arises. Send an occasional note home about a youngster's progress. Incidentally, a note home about a successful learning experience may introduce even more reinforcement for a student; parents often praise their children for such messages.

2. Assure parents by notes that you are available to meet with them. (You can have the notes mimeographed to reduce the burden on you; your pupils can take them home, but make sure that they bring them back signed by their parents, as evidence of safe delivery.)

3. Put aside one afternoon a week for conferences with parents and include the information in your notes. But set up conferences by appointment only, or you may be overwhelmed by visiting parents one week and have none at all the next.

Help from outside school—how can it be obtained?

Several programs go far beyond those fundamentals and have had considerable success in involving parents and other adults in schoolwork. In Chicago, sixth graders at Grant Elementary on the tough West Side used to read, on average, two years below their grade level. Then the local school district superintendent, Albert Briggs, decreed that no students would be admitted to high school unless they could read at sixth-grade level. Toward that objective, Briggs established Operation Higher Achievement, which required participation of teachers, parents, and pupils. Virtually all parents of the school's 1350 students signed "contracts" in which they pledged, among other things, to encourage their children to read to them and to provide quiet, well-lit places for the youngsters to study. Teachers agreed to work with parents in promoting "reading festivals," pep rallies, and open houses. About one-third of the parents became intensely involved, and in one year their 400 youngsters recorded reading-score gains that averaged 1.1 years, a month above the national average. In a somewhat similar experiment at Martin Luther King school in New Haven, Connecticut, parents of almost all the 325 pupils go to monthly conferences and suppers with the school staff, and twenty-five of the parents serve as teachers' aides for ten hours a week (*Time*, November 8, 1976, p. 77).

An even broader program, launched in Ann Arbor, Michigan, reaches beyond pupils' parents and into the community at large. The experiment has recruited 125 elderly citizens, most of them in lonely retirement, as volunteer teachers of noncurricular subjects in sixteen schools: dubbed *grandpersons*, the volunteers pass on skills of tremendous variety, from puppetry and the construction of puzzles to knitting, gardening, and the writing of Chinese. Young and old get on famously together, and one ten-year-old boy, after a knitting lesson, confided to his aged instructor: "I just love learning" (Mehta, 1976).

CREATING A HEALTHFUL CLASSROOM CLIMATE

The child who said "I just love learning" almost certainly found the climate in his classroom ideal, whether or not he gave any conscious thought to it. And except for a few old-fashioned tyrants—we remember several curmudgeons who threw books, chalk, and chalkboard erasers at troublesome students—most teachers strive to create an agreeable classroom atmosphere. But the emotional thermostat does not always respond immediately to a teacher's touch. For one thing, traditional teaching methods foster competition rather than cooperation among students. The youngsters who know the answers wave their hands eagerly, hoping for a chance to show how smart they are and thus win the teacher's approval, and they are disappointed if not called on. Those who do not know the answers cringe in their seats and, often, resent those who do know. For another thing, mainstreaming and racial desegregation have not made all students love each other: white, black, oriental, and Hispanic pupils, especially in the higher grades, tend to associate only with others of similar characteristics, and tensions sometimes erupt in violence.

In an attempt to overcome racial animosities and to replace competition with cooperation, Elliot Aronson and a group of associates (1978) undertook an experiment in the schools of Austin, Texas, employing what has come to be known as the *jigsaw technique*.

The Jigsaw Technique. In a pilot study, Aronson and his colleagues divided a fifth-grade class into groups of six pupils each. The lesson chosen by the teacher happened to concern the life of the newspaper publisher Joseph

"A few years ago we began a more democratic system of school justice. Kids participated in developing a set of rules, sat as 'judges' when there were infractions, handed out penalties. It was amusing that the administration had to step in to lighten up the penalties. The kids were terribly harsh with each other."

Pulitzer, so Aronson prepared a six-paragraph biography of Pulitzer, each paragraph dealing with a different aspect of Pulitzer's life. Then Aronson cut the paragraphs apart, so that each pupil in a group got only one paragraph. To come up with a rounded—albeit brief—sketch of Pulitzer's life, the six pupils in a group had to collaborate rather than compete. Collaboration did not come easily at first: the youngsters had been conditioned to compete during their four and a half years of school. Furthermore, they were not all friends. One group, for example, included a Mexican American boy whose difficulty with English and resultant hesitancy to participate in classwork had led his classmates to consider him stupid and to make fun of him. When he had trouble explaining the content of his paragraph, a girl in his group berated him: "Aw, you don't know it. You're dumb, you don't know what you're doing." At that point, one of Aronson's co-workers intervened, "Okay," she said, "you can tease Carlos if you want to, but it's *not* going to help you learn about Joseph Pulitzer's middle years. The exam will take place in about an hour" (Aronson et al., 1975, pp. 47–48).

Can cooperation enhance motivation?

After several days of such experience, the youngsters in the group realized their interdependence, even with Carlos, and began taking pains to draw him out by probing questions. Carlos in turn relaxed, gained confidence, and became more fluent. Within a few weeks, the others in the group decided that they liked Carlos and that he wasn't so dumb, after all, and Carlos discovered that school could be enjoyable.

Aronson then undertook his study on a broader scale in classes that included 177 Anglos, 76 blacks, 41 Mexican Americans, and 1 Oriental; a control group consisted of 50 Anglos, 9 blacks, 20 Mexican Americans, and 2 Orientals.

After six weeks, Aronson found:

1. Grades of the study group improved significantly while those in the control group declined. Aronson views this result with caution, however, on the ground that it may merely reflect teachers' expectations.
2. Individuals in the groups felt friendlier toward students of other races with whom they had been working, but brotherly love did not extend beyond individuals. The experiment did not make *all* white youngsters admire *all* blacks or Mexican Americans, or vice versa.
3. Youngsters in the groups had developed stronger self-concepts than those in the control classes.
4. For the most part, pupils in the groups gained more positive feelings about school, whereas the control students gained more negative ones. Black youngsters proved to be exceptions: those in the groups and in the control classes alike had become more negative, but the degree of negativism was much less among those in the jigsaw groups.

Summing up his findings, Aronson concluded that the jigsaw technique had made the children happier, led them to feel better about themselves, and resulted in greater friendliness to classmates, without interfering with their learning. One participating teacher, discussing only her black students, said that although there had been no spectacular change in their grades, there had been dramatic changes in their self-esteem and in their acceptance by others. Another teacher was so impressed by her students' new attitudes and the improvement in classroom atmosphere that, she said, she planned to keep on teaching by the jigsaw technique forever. As for the failure to end racial animosities, Aronson suggests that six weeks may have been too short a time for effective results.

Clearer evidence of the effects of cooperative team methods on race relations emerges in a study by Slavin and Madden (1979). Analyzing desegregation practices in fifty-one high schools, they discovered that when students of different races were assigned to work together—in sports or in school activities—behavior and attitudes improved. In addition, they found that cross-racial activities bettered the social atmosphere far more effectively than multicultural textbooks, group relations workshops for teachers, class discussions about race, and minority culture courses. Slavin and Madden conclude that most traditional attempts to improve race relations represent wasted effort, and that more energy should be directed to promoting student interaction.

One objection to jigsaw and other cooperative techniques, raised by some teachers and many parents, is that if cooperation replaces competition, motivation to learn weakens. This objection, you remember, was refuted in Chapter 12. Aronson responds additionally that you do not have to beat someone else to achieve excellence yourself. In any case, the jigsaw technique appears to be another promising approach toward improving classroom atmosphere and thus facilitating classroom management.

ROLE-PLAYING

Role-playing in the classroom consists of the *acting out* by pupils of *situations and ideas*. A good many teachers consider it to be merely one more rabbit to pull out of the hat to liven a sleepy Monday morning or boring Friday afternoon. Not so, say its advocates: it has scores of applications, from dramatizing the working of the human digestive system to resolving moral dilemmas.

Role-playing, and humanist methods in general, do not have a solid research base. Recent evidence, however, gives tentative support to role-playing as a means of easing depression of fifth and sixth graders (Butler et al., 1980). Among other potential contributions of role-playing to pupils' development, Stanford and Roark (1974) list these:

1. Increased self-understanding and awareness of one's feelings and attitudes.
2. Development of empathy for and insight into other people.
3. Opportunity for experimentation with changes in behavior. (The passive child can assume assertiveness without fear of ridicule; the class clown can be serious for once and assess his classmates' reaction.)

Is acting a legiti-
mate tool of
learning?

4. Acquisition and practice of social skills. (Asking for a date, ordering a meal in a restaurant, applying for a job can be simulated in the haven of the classroom and classmates' suggestions can be considered, adopted, or rejected.)
5. Development of ability to work with others. (Dramatic activity requires each individual to contribute, members of the group to cooperate, and all of them to feel sensitivity to each other.)
6. Stimulation of creativity and imagination. (Role-playing can require an individual to react spontaneously to the situation and to exercise imagination in enacting a role, without a script or elaborate instructions from the teacher.)

Varieties of Role-Playing. One simple form of role-playing, suitable for lower grades, consists of dramatizing a story the class is reading. Once the pupils get the hang of role-playing at this level, they may contrive their own dialogue and the teacher may ask them why they think the characters in the story behave as they do. In the middle and higher grades, dramatization may be used, for example, in English classes for better understanding of a Shakespearean play or a Dickens novel, or in history classes for comprehension of the issues at the Congress of Vienna. A social studies class might reenact the famous Scopes trial of the 1920s, when the attorney Clarence Darrow defended and the the statesman William Jennings Bryan opposed the teaching of Darwinism in Tennessee's schools.

An expanded form of story dramatization abandons the classic scripts, and exercises the pupils' imagination. The players might be asked to contrive a scene in which Tom Sawyer and Huckleberry Finn encounter Long John Silver and Captain Hook, or in which Christopher Robin joins Captain Nemo on the voyage *Twenty Thousand Leagues Under the Sea.*

In another version, involving translation of historic events into modern parallels, students might be asked to represent Thomas Jefferson and Alexander Hamilton as participants in the 1980 presidential campaign, contriving arguments for them in support of Ronald Reagan and Jimmy Carter. Or students might be invited to enact black-white confrontations in Africa in terms of American Indians and advancing European settlers.

Still another form of role-playing lends itself to exploration of students' social attitudes and personal concerns. The teacher might present this situation: Jimmy has bought Tom's old bike for $10, but he does not have the money. After a week, Tom demands his money or his bike back. Jimmy finds a wallet with $15 in it, and a card in the wallet bears the owner's name and address. Pupils designated as Jimmy and Tom discuss the problem, and members of the class propose solutions and offer moral guidance or, as may happen, immoral guidance.

Action Methods. The term *action methods* applies to dramatization that dispenses entirely with a script and encourages spontaneous exploration of ideas and concepts. The workings of a gasoline engine, for example, might be represented by one pupil as the gasoline, another as the fuel line, others as the ignition system, still others as the cylinders in which the gasoline explodes. Or a single student may portray Ulysses S. Grant and others may interview him pointedly about his career and the scandals that plagued his presidency.

Introducing Role-Playing. As a teacher, do not expect to plunge a class successfully into role-playing without a good deal of preparation, especially in the upper grades. Unlike their younger brothers and sisters, adolescents fear looking silly and do not take readily to pretense, which they dismiss as "kid stuff." Because of their developing but still uncertain consciousness of sex, they shun contrived physical contact with others; for role-playing that involves such contact, they will need a good deal of gradual *shaping*. So, start slowly. For your early dramatizations, choose simple roles that threaten no one's dignity. Work gradually toward more sophisticated material, fitting your requirements to the pupils' needs, interests, and levels of understanding.

Role-playing should be approached step-by-step (Miller, 1976):

1. The warmup. Present the situation, story, or problem in a way that evokes the pupils' interest and involves them in it.
2. Selecting role-players. Choose students who are likely to feel comfortable in their roles, and do not force anyone to take a role. A shy or withdrawn pupil may be given a minor role at first.

Role-Playing Situations

For role-playing requiring only one main character, with other students in bit parts, Chesler and Fox (1966, p. 67) suggest scenarios like these:

1. Your friend has asked you to go skating. Your mother says you must stay home. You do not want to hurt your friend. Mother is standing near.
2. You see one child teasing another.
3. A classmate tries to look at your paper during a test.
4. You meet a friend after you've heard that he has said unpleasant things about you.

For situations involving relationships between a student and adults:

5. You want to introduce your parents to your teacher (p. 68).
6. You have just had a meal at a friend's house and want to thank his parents.

For situations involving two or more main characters:

7. You have to return a borrowed object that you broke. How do you do this? (p. 69). ∎

3. Setting the stage. Have the students discuss in general outline, but not in detail, what they plan to do.
4. Coaching the audience. Encourage the nonplayers to follow the action and dialogue sympathetically, but to keep considering alternatives.
5. The enactment. Encourage the players to spontaneity (without excesses of emotion or language) and to expressing the situation as they see it. Make sure they understand that they will not be confused with the characters they pretend to be and will not be blamed for the characters' behavior.
6. Discussion and evaluation. This is an important part of the procedure. It should begin with questions to the nonplayers about the role-players' feelings, and then turn to possible alternative courses to those the role-players followed.
7. Sharing experiences and generalizing. Youngsters may *offer* personal experiences brought to mind by the enactment, but the teacher should exercise care to keep the youngsters from putting themselves in a poor light. They may also generalize about the situation they have seen acted and, if they volunteer to do so, draw conclusions.

Dos and Don'ts. Because the three Rs are back in fashion in most areas, role-playing may be frowned on by some school boards, administrators, and parents. The teacher who introduces role-playing should be prepared to defend the importance of affective education, of which role-playing is a tool. One way to keep out of trouble is to tell the administration what you are doing: an apparently covert activity is sure to be stopped once it's discovered. Another safeguard is to do a little public relations promotion work about role-playing among fellow teachers. The more confederates you have, the less likely the administration is to order: "Cut that out!"

PUPILS AS TUTORS

Earlier in this chapter, under the heading *Help from Outside the Classroom*, we cited instances in which parents and retired people assisted youngsters in learning. An even broader resource, which has been tapped increasingly in the last two decades, exists within the schools themselves: it consists of pupils as tutors. Their use is variously known as *peer tutoring, peer teaching,* and *cross-age tutoring,* and its results have been surprising, at least to nonprofessionals. One such result, discovered by teacher experience and by research, is that the tutors may benefit as much as or more than the schoolmates they tutor. For the youthful tutors, the practice appears to have these advantages:

1. It provides a sense of purpose and participation in society and develops a sense of responsibility for others.
2. It heightens their self-esteem and increases their friends' respect.

Interviewer: *You two have been helping each other out. Do you like to do that?*
Child: *It's perfect.*
Interviewer: *In what ways is it perfect?*
Child: *Because if I got it wrong, he can tell me when I get it right.*
Interviewer: *So you don't have to wait for your teacher to tell you one way or the other that things are right or wrong? Do you think this helps?*
Child: *Lots 'n lots!*
Interviewer: *Do you think you'd like to be doing this for the whole year?*
Child: *No, not for the whole year. Sometimes. For different things. It helps.*
Interviewer: *Why does it help?*

3. It involves them in working with adults, in a kind of apprenticeship for careers.
4. It gives them a better understanding of their teachers' problems, to the improvement of their own classroom behavior.
5. It permits them to put some of their own ideas into practice and to employ what they have learned.
6. It increases their own knowledge, by requiring them to master what they are teaching and to fill in gaps in their information.

Can students be teachers? What are the benefits?

For the pupils who are tutored, the benefits—apart from the acquisition of knowledge—appear to be these:

1. They receive individual instruction.
2. They develop a sense of accomplishment and an enjoyment of success, which encourage further learning.
3. They have a "teacher" closer to their own ages, rather than an awesome adult, and their "teacher" is likely to talk in language that they understand better than an adult's, making new ideas easier to absorb.
4. They relish the attention and concern of friends bigger than themselves, which nurture their own self-esteem. The resulting big-and-little-kid friendships have a side effect, as well: where tutoring programs exist, younger children are less likely to be subjected to indignities on the playgrounds, because the tutors look out for their charges.

Child: *First of all, I understand what I'm doing. Second—to be able to do it.*
Teacher's comment: *"Peer teaching has saved me. We had increases in class size this year. Can you believe it! I thought enrollments were supposed to be declining. Anyway, the children love it and it frees me for other things instead of scrambling around checking everyone's seatwork. There are still a few problems that I haven't figured out yet, like should I switch tutors around regularly? Or what to do with Reuben, who refuses to work with anyone? And some kids have trouble staying on-task. Mrs. Bryan and I have been trading tutors. We think it helps break up the in-group or in-class cliques. There are two other teachers who want to start peer teaching programs here."*

The teacher who assigns a tutor gains a student with greater understanding of the teacher's role, with better-developed leadership qualities, and usually with increased knowledge. The teacher who gets a tutor as a helper gains time to devote to the class as a whole and to individual pupils who need attention without special tutoring. The school administration gains from tutoring by expansion of its instructional resources at little cost (Lippitt, 1976).

The method is not without its drawbacks. A student assigned to tutor may worry about failing, about being given an unchallenging task, about being rejected by the youngster to be tutored, about being ridiculed by friends. The pupil to be helped may resent being identified as slow, or may be fearful of an older student, especially if the child has been bullied in the past. Teachers who contribute tutors may feel concern that the tutors will lose too much time out of class. Teachers who get tutor-helpers may be upset by extra demands on themselves for planning, for training the tutors, for arranging to share the work. If the teachers are accustomed only to younger children, they may feel unable to deal with older pupils such as the tutors.

Research studies, nevertheless, indicate considerable success for peer tutoring. Sixth graders of low achievement improved their reading ability significantly after two months in which they tutored low-achieving second graders in reading (Klentschy, 1972). Ninth graders in a remedial reading class bettered their reading comprehension significantly after they had served as paid tutors to a seventh grader who read poorly (Marascuilo, Levin, and James,

1969). Poorly motivated students who were assigned to tutor unmotivated younger children in mathematics showed an increase in the level of their motivation, improvement in self-concept, more favorable attitudes toward school, and greater achievements in math (Mohan, 1972). Under-achieving sophomores and juniors who represented disciplinary problems improved their self-concepts, their self-acceptance, and their grades—though their attitudes toward school remained unchanged—after tutoring elementary school children twice a week (Haggerty, 1971).

Is it the tutoring that improves the tutors' own schoolwork, or the extra time they spend studying in preparation for tutoring? In search of the answer, Allen and Feldman (1974) set up an experiment in which fifth graders who read poorly either tutored third graders or studied alone daily. After two weeks, the youngsters performed much better on the subject matter in which they had tutored than in material they studied alone. Tutoring itself, and not just the extra time spent studying, resulted in the improved academic achievement, Feldman, Devin-Sheehan, and Allen (1976) conclude. Tutoring requires rehearsal of the subject matter, though, so study and practice by the tutor are built into the process.

Who Makes a Good Tutor? You have probably noticed that in the studies cited the tutors all were problem pupils themselves: the research concentrated on what *they* achieved, rather than the children they helped. Why not use only the best and the brightest as tutors? The best and the brightest, teachers find, often do not succeed as tutors, presumably because they cannot understand why someone else should find learning difficult. It is evident from the research, however, that experience as a tutor may benefit a great variety of students. Whether tutored children benefit more from one kind of tutor than another remains undetermined. The crucial factor, Feldman, Devin-Sheehan, and Allen point out, may be the degree of difference in competence between the tutor and the tutored. If the tutor is clearly superior to the pupil, the tutor's rank among peers may not matter.

Neither does it matter, research by Klentschy (1972) indicates, whether or not the tutor and the tutored are of the same sex, although boys generally prefer to tutor other boys; and, the same research showed, male tutors and their male pupils gain more academically than do girl tutors and girl pupils. But race and economic status do seem to matter: black pupils improve significantly under black tutors (Brown, 1972; Coker, 1969; Freyberg, 1967; Liette, 1972), and youngsters from lower-income families do better under tutors of like background (Hamblin and Hamblin, 1972; Nichols, 1969; Snapp, Oakland, and Williams, 1972).

Some authorities on tutoring hold that tutors must be trained in both subject matter and dealing with younger children (Lippitt, 1976), and some tutoring programs require potential tutors and teachers to attend regular seminars. But evidence to support that position remains scant, and no one yet knows for sure whether or not training improves tutoring.

Starting a Tutoring Program. If you are going to use tutors, here are a few guidelines:

1. Decide on your approach. Do you want a highly structured program, with explicitly stated objectives, carefully described techniques, and formal schedules followed by evaluation? Or do you prefer informal methods?
2. Set your general goals. Is your aim to improve academic achievement? Change attitudes toward school? Change problem behavior? (Tutors can modify their pupils' behavior, Pines [1976] reports.) Encourage potential dropouts to stay in school? Whom do you want to help most, the tutor or the tutored?

What guidelines can be used to establish a peer tutoring program?

3. Choose your participants. The research cited earlier indicates that you will have a lot of leeway in pairing off the students. But don't hesitate to re-arrange the pairs if the tutor and the tutored don't hit it off.
4. Pick a place for the tutoring. The cafeteria, the library, the learning center (if your school has one), the gym locker rooms, the guidance counselor's office, even the corridors are possibilities. Then set a regular time for the tutor and tutored to meet.
5. Check frequently on progress. Give the experiment a few weeks: if it doesn't seem to be working, reconsider the arrangement.

Like lots of other new methods of instruction, tutoring probably will not solve all your classroom problems. But experience with it indicates that it often helps, and it costs nothing to try it. (Unpaid tutors, by the way, frequently do better than those who expect recompense. It's the motivation that counts.)

Peers may also be used to boost affective development, including their own. Students tutoring or being tutored sometimes confront likes and dislikes, and it may prove worthwhile to plan for some clarification of values. What will you do, for example, when Donald has trouble being a tutor because he disdains "dummies"?

VALUES CLARIFICATION

In case you already have forgotten what it is like to be a child, youngsters worry about all sorts of things and ponder all sorts of issues, personal and impersonal. Should I smoke cigarettes, even though my parents think I shouldn't? Is it okay to try pot because my friends use it? Should I keep on going to church even though I have my doubts about all that religious stuff? Is it ever right to fight in a war? How far should I go with sex? Are all people really created equal? Would I enjoy going hunting and killing something, like Uncle Joe? Is it right to read those sexy books that I get a big kick out of? Should people who live off welfare be made to get jobs and work? Should I be a Republican or a Democrat when I can vote? What kind of person do I want to be?

As a teacher, you may help your students find their own answers by *values clarification*, which has a twofold approach:

1. Direct guidance in analyzing, refining, and holding to values.
2. Indirect encouragement of an appreciation of the viewpoints of others, which, of course, is one of the explicit objectives of role-playing.

The teacher can and should define his or her own values in the course of discussion, but should not impose them on students or offer judgments of the students' values.

How do values relate to motivation?

The valuing process incorporates seven subprocesses (Raths, Harmin, and Simon, 1966):

1. *Choosing freely.* If a value is forced on you, you are unlikely to accept it consciously among your values.
2. *Choosing from alternatives.* Your freedom of choice is greater if you are given several values to choose from.
3. *Choosing after considering the consequences.* An intelligent system of values is not arrived at impulsively; it requires thought and prediction of what will result from any choice you make.
4. *Prizing and cherishing.* You should respect your own values and view them as part of you.
5. *Affirming.* Once you have arrived at values, you should be willing to announce and publicly defend them, sharing them when that is appropriate.
6. *Acting upon choices.* Your values should be apparent from your actions.
7. *Repeating.* If you act on your values, you should do so consistently; if your actions are inconsistent with your values, their relationship needs reexamination.

Why be concerned with student values? How can they be clarified?

Values clarification methods are intended to advance students through those seven subprocesses. Seventy-nine classroom activities for practice in the subprocesses are proposed by Simon, Howe, and Kirschenbaum (1972).

For *prizing*, for example, they suggest that the teacher ask students to list "twenty things you love to do," which may range from reading comics to surfing or traveling abroad. When the lists are complete, the students place symbols, intended to be self-revealing, beside each activity. A letter *R* would indicate an element of risk—emotional, physical or intellectual—in the activity. The symbol *N5* would denote an activity in which the student would not have engaged five years earlier. An *F* would mean that the student's father indulged in the same activity, and would show that father and student shared certain interests. A *P* would mark an activity that the student would publicly affirm. Then the students compare and discuss their lists, and the teacher, well into the discussion, reads his or her own.

For *choosing*, the teacher asks students to draw a flight of steps or a ladder with "the kind of person I'd least like to be like" at the bottom and "the kind of person I'd like most to be like" at the top. Again, students compare lists and defend their choices.

For *acting*, the teacher outlines a situation and asks what students would do. Some possible situations:

You are walking behind someone. You see him take out a cigarette pack, withdraw the last cigarette and put it in his mouth, crumple the package, and nonchalantly toss it over his shoulder onto the sidewalk. You are twenty-five feet behind him. What would you do?

You are driving on a two-lane road behind another car. You notice that one of its wheels is wobbling more and more. It looks as if the nuts are coming off one by one. There's no way to pass the driver, because cars are coming in the other direction in a steady stream. What would you do?

You are driving along the highway alone on a rainy day. In front of you is a hitchhiker dressed in hippie garb holding a sign lettered with the name of your destination. What would you do? (Simon, Howe, and Kirschenbaum, p. 33).

Dos and Don'ts. Listen to students explain their values but offer no judgments of right or wrong. Present your own values but do not try to impose them. Do not insist that any student participate. And, generally, apply the same cautions that go with role-playing.

THE ECLECTIC WAY

The behaviorist and the humanist, or affective, approaches to education both have contributions to make to classroom management and creation of an agreeable classroom atmosphere. Though proponents of the humanist techniques such as role-playing and values clarification rarely say so aloud, they believe implicitly that making students more humane—if that is the word—prevents classroom disruption. The behaviorist method typically attacks disruption after the fact. The two positions are usually assumed to be at opposite poles. Yet the humanist prevention and the behaviorist remediation may well be interchangeable. The humanist techniques have often been applied after the fact, and in that event are more remedial than preventive. The behaviorist techniques are designed to reduce the likelihood of an undesirable behavior's recurrence, and thus take on a preventive character.

For the future teacher, then, the reasonable course would seem to be: Pick, choose, refine, and experiment with humanist techniques as preventives. And when disruption occurs, as it inevitably will, try behaviorist techniques as treatment. But don't be afraid to use both ideas at once; that might be the strongest tonic of all.

Summary

Teachers spend vast energy attempting to control misbehavior. There are many theories about why classroom misbehavior occurs and persists, and several give direction to teachers. In developing theory and in implementing classroom management practices, teachers must be inventive and flexible; holding to a single approach will limit effectiveness.

A frequent correlate of misbehavior, especially in elementary-age boys, is termed *hyperactivity* and is typically treated with medication. Drugs may show unpleasant side effects, however, and medication for hyperactivity is beginning to give way to behavior modification methods.

Behavioral techniques may be used effectively to manage a wide range of disruptive situations. A *group contingency* requires several students—or a whole class—to display appropriate behavior before a reinforcer is awarded. Group contingencies are efficient, particularly when simple equipment is used to monitor students' behavior.

The widespread use of corporal punishment for unruly students has created much controversy. Its occasional effectiveness is offset by negative side effects, such as the development of bad attitudes among students and reciprocal aggression.

Failure on routine school tasks often results in misbehavior, and the teacher must intensify efforts to manage the classroom and create an atmosphere conducive to learning. In addition to remedial methods, which occur after the fact of misbehavior, a teacher must plan a preventive approach. Many humanist techniques aim toward prevention, using the general principles of clear structure, genuine friendliness, and successful experiences for all students.

Another preventive method requires involvement of parents in school work. Several experiments in this area have proved successful, and one of them brings even outsiders into the classroom: retired people instruct pupils in noncurricular skills such as gardening, knitting, and puzzle-construction.

Classroom climate may be improved by the *jigsaw technique*, in which pupils work in groups of half a dozen or so. Each youngster is given one part of an overall assignment, and each of the members has to contribute to the group's information if the group is to complete the assignment. In working together, they replace competition with cooperation, and students who did not like each other are led by their interdependence to become friendlier. Though the jigsaw and other cooperative techniques do not necessarily raise grades, they do help to improve attitudes toward school and to develop better self-concepts.

Another teaching tool in the affective domain is *role-playing*, in which pupils act out scenes from history or literature, or situations that present dilemmas. Role-playing is intended to increase pupils' understanding of themselves and of others, to provide opportunities for experimentation with changes of behavior and for practice of social skills, to develop a capacity for cooperation, and to stimulate creativity and imagination.

Much research has been done on the use of pupils as tutors, and *tutoring* has become widespread in the last two decades. The youngsters who serve as tutors often benefit as much as or more than the pupils they tutor. In the selection of tutors, the crucial factor, it is believed, is the difference in competence between the tutor and the tutored: a potential tutor may be close to the bottom of his or her own class yet succeed at tutoring a younger child who knows even less. Tutors preparing to instruct others fill in gaps in their own knowledge; in the affective domain, they gain in self-esteem and respect from their peers.

Values clarification is a form of classroom activity in which the teacher and pupils explore social and moral attitudes. Teachers do not impose their own values, although they reveal them.

In sum, classroom management of misbehavior may employ both the behaviorist and the humanist approaches; on occasion, they may be interchangeable.

Chapter Study Guide

CHAPTER REVIEW

1. An important outcome of role-playing, according to its advocates, is that it promotes self- _____ .

2. _____ is a term applied to dramatization that dispenses entirely with a script and encourages spontaneous exploration of ideas.

3. As a teacher, you can help your students discover much about their own beliefs and attitudes through _____ .

4. The jigsaw technique was invented primarily to improve _____ .

5. The _____ theory of misbehavior argues that early childhood experiences are paramount.

6. Students often respond to inescapable punishment by showing _____ .

7. Students may be willing to misbehave to gain _____ , a powerful reinforcer.

8. Much fidgety, troublesome behavior in classrooms may result from the learning disability termed _____ .

9. Both _____ and _____ have been used to help control hyperactivity.

Answer questions 10–22 True or False:

10. Peers may be used to help control deviant behavior.

11. A group contingency refers to letting a whole class deliver reinforcement, such as applause, to a youngster.

12. Special apparatus—lights or timers, for example—may be used effectively to operate group contingencies.

13. Although teachers and parents expect swift and fair discipline, students often resent it.

14. Behavioral methods, by definition, ignore the affective domain.

15. Corporal punishment is neither popular nor widely used in schools today.

16. The teacher cannot do much for chronically disruptive youngsters.

17. A youngster's chronic discipline problems are often part of a larger constellation of antisocial behaviors.

18. Highly permissive environments may be hazardous to psychological health.

19. By observing aggressive models, children usually learn that aggression doesn't pay.

20. It is best to get in touch with parents after report cards are issued, not before, so there is a written record of achievement.

21. Adolescents may be reluctant to get involved in role-playing.

22. In peer tutoring, the tutor often shows achievement gains.

FOR FURTHER THOUGHT

1. You are a teacher with a couple years of successful classroom experience. What misbehavior situation would make you seriously consider quitting teaching? Do you think the school could guarantee that the situation would not occur again during your career?

2. Have crime and violence in schools increased more than in other social institutions? Would it help if schools were magically transformed to one-room rural schoolhouses, with one teacher instructing 33 children across four grades?

3. Sex differences in misbehavior are beyond question and are usually attributed to social learning influences. Do you think that emerging equality of opportunity for females, federal Title IX act (equality in sports), and other related changes may change the sex balance of misbehavior?

   Develop a currently unfashionable argument: Aggression is sex-related because of genetic structure, not learning.

IMPORTANT TERMS

hyperactive
amphetamine
task analysis
baseline
group contingency
classical conditioning

corporal punishment
jigsaw methods
role-playing
action methods
peer tutoring
values clarification

SUGGESTED READINGS

ALLEN, V. L. (ed.). *Children as teachers.* New York: Academic Press, 1976. These readings provide a theoretical and historical background to peer tutoring, but also provide necessary practical information for arranging peer-teaching situations.

ARONSON, E., BLANEY, N., STEPHAN, C., SIKES, J., and SNAPP, M. *The jigsaw classroom.* Beverly Hills, CA: Sage, 1978. Description of jigsaw research and application. Big on promise, but short on evidence.

CASTILLO, G. A. *Left-handed teaching.* New York: Praeger, 1974. Nearly 150 humanist activities are described, grouped around such titles as "sensory awareness" and "building trust." Suited for the affective side of education, most activities appear to be at the elementary age level.

CLARIZIO, H. A. *Toward positive classroom discipline* (3rd ed.). New York: Wiley, 1979. A popular short book on management of misbehavior, stressing behavioral methods.

DREIKURS, R., GRUNWALD, B. B., and PEPPER, F. C. *Maintaining sanity in the classroom: Illustrated teaching techniques.* New York: Harper and Row, 1971. Dreikurs, a psychiatrist, applies his strategies to school situations. Easy reading, filled with dozens of examples and case histories of classroom difficulties.

DUKE, D. L. (ed.). *Classroom management.* The 78th Yearbook of the National Society for the Study of Education, Part II. Chicago: University of Chicago Press, 1979. Excellent collection of articles, some summarizing research and others developing theory. Management is considered broadly, from decision-making to control of misbehavior.

KIRSCHENBAUM, H., and SIMON, S. B. (eds.). *Readings in values clarification.* Minneapolis: Winston Press, 1973. A good orientation to the background and issues involved in humanistic education.

Office of Education. *Tutoring resource handbook for teachers.* Washington, D. C.: U. S. Government Printing Office (DHEW Publication No. OE 74-00103), 1974. A guidebook for teachers interested in arranging turoting experiences. Includes sample forms for such things as parents' permission and daily tutoring record.

O'LEARY, K. D., and O'LEARY, S. G. (eds.). *Classroom management* (2nd ed.). New York: Pergamon Press, 1978. This book of readings deals strictly with behavioral management strategies for teachers. Although a few articles provide general descriptions or deal with practical issues, the majority focus on research reports of what works in behavior modification.

SCHIMMEL, D., and FISCHER, L. *The civil rights of students.* New York: Harper and Row, 1975. Legal aspects of conflict in the school, stemming from Bill of Rights and due process interpreted by the courts.

SIMON, S. B., HOWE, L., and KIRSCHENBAUM, H. *Values clarification: A handbook of practical strategies.* New York: Hart, 1972. This book is practically the manual for those interested in humanistic activities for the classroom. Includes some eighty techniques, many dealing with role-playing activities.

WHALEN, C. K. and HENKER, B. (eds.) *Hyperactive children.* New York: Academic Press, 1980. Volume of readings about hyperactivity in various environments, and assortment of treatment possibilities.

ANSWER KEY

1. understanding; 2. Action methods; 3. values clarification; 4. racial acceptance; 5. bad character; 6. aggression; 7. teacher or student attention; 8. hyperkinesis *or* hyperactivity; 9. drug therapy. . .behavior modification; 10. T; 11. F; 12. T; 13. F; 14. F; 15. F; 16. F; 17. T; 18. T; 19. F; 20. F; 21. T; 22. T

PART

III

Measuring Learning Outcomes

The next two chapters, which constitute Part III of this book, deal in effect with what accountants and other people in business call *the bottom line*, the figures at the end of a firm's annual report. Those figures reveal in terms of profit or loss whether or not the company's hard work of the past year was worth the effort. For teachers and their pupils too there is a bottom line, which Bloom calls—as you may remember from Chapter 1—*learning outcomes*. Suppose that, during your teaching year, you have carefully considered your students' characteristics, in accordance with Part I, and have applied the appropriate methods of instruction discussed in Part II. But how can you determine whether or not your toil has paid off? How can you tell how much your students have learned, and how much of it was what you wanted them to learn? Why, you respond, you give them tests, of course! But teaching and learning do not lend themselves easily to addition and subtraction. There are many kinds of tests, and each kind has its drawbacks. And after you have given a test, how do you evaluate the results? Do they accurately reflect what your students have learned, or were the high and low scores partly a matter of guessing and good and bad luck?

In chapters 14 and 15, we shall consider the merits and demerits of the several ways of measuring learning. We hope that you will also find ways to make the resulting measurements understandable to yourself, to your students, and to their parents.

14

The Meaning of Measurement and Evaluation

When we began to write this chapter, which is about the uses of measurement in education, we opened our dictionary—chiefly out of curiosity—to see what it said about *measure*. Funk and Wagnalls (1946) defined the verb as "to compute or ascertain the extent, quantity, capacity or dimensions of, by applying a rule or standard." Then, for thirteen columns two and a half inches wide and ten and one-quarter inches deep, the dictionary discoursed on methods and types of measurement.

Yet we cannot measure people whole. A person's measurements do not equal the person. Measurements are not unlike photographs, which capture some aspects of the subject at the moment the camera's shutter clicks. A series of photographs may record varying aspects and indicate changes over a period of time, but still will not reproduce the subject's dimensions in full. Similarly, measurements may summarize certain characteristics, but the sum of the person always exceeds the sum of the measurements.

We use measurement to make a judgment about something, but measurement and evaluation, although they are complementary, are technically not the same: we *evaluate* on the basis of measurement. Therefore, in theory, measurement usually precedes evaluation, although in practice the two may occur simultaneously. For example, you are timing a friend, a racing swimmer, in the pool. (Measurement.) Without checking the stopwatch, you are thinking: "Hey, she's *fast*." (Evaluation.)

What is the relationship between measurement and evaluation?

You may imagine, if you wish, measurement and evaluation as a couple of swinging dance partners. Measurement wears a look of objectivity, carefully observing what's going on and making mental notes; evaluation obviously is subjective and depends on impressions that can change on the basis of measurement's comments. They start dancing a good distance apart but draw closer and closer, finally seeming inseparable—as long as the music lasts. But enough of the analogy. Because the two processes—which is what they really are—often appear inseparable, the terms measurement and evaluation may be used interchangeably in parts of the rest of this chapter. If we refer to measurement, just take it for granted that evaluation is close by.

Why Measure People?

We measure because, if we did not, all judgments would have to be subjective. (Suppose your college grades were based only on what your professors *felt* about you!) Some people object that translating human behavior into numbers affronts human dignity and deprives us of our identity. To a point, the objections may be valid. For example, we know a man who refused to accept an important piece of mail from a superefficient corporation because the letter's address omitted the name of his town, for economy's sake, and gave only its zip code. He wrote on the envelope "I do not live at 99999, I live in the village of so-and-so." (The letter came back to him properly addressed and the corporation abandoned the practice of using only zip codes.)

But the use of measurements and numbers constitutes the only fair alternative to judgments deriving from feelings and impressions. One of us once helped a teacher to determine why he was having so much difficulty getting along with a student. It seemed to the teacher that the student was always roaming around the classroom and disturbing others. Collecting baseline data in preparation for a behavior modification program (about which you read in Chapter 10), we counted the times that members of the class, including the problem child, left their seats. The troublesome lad, the tally showed, was out of his seat less often than most of his classmates. But additional observations disclosed that every time the student was out of his seat he interrupted the teacher while he was talking to other students or marking papers.

Numbers and objective observation helped us to pinpoint the real problem—the habit of interrupting. Without the first count, everyone might have agreed that the student was out of his seat a lot. The count made it clear that his wandering, when compared with that of others, was not excessive; interruption was the culprit.

A caution may be in order here. Numbers do not necessarily make observations objective, for numbers can be—and sometimes are—used arbitrarily. Even then, though, numbers can help us to think critically about our impressions and to communicate those impressions systematically to others. Once impressions are shared, we can consider them more carefully and decide whether we have been relatively objective or subjective, arbitrary or accurate.

So numbers and measurements provide a useful frame of reference for summarizing, interpreting, comparing, and explaining behaviors. They help us to be more precise than if we trust our selective, and sometimes faulty, qualitative assessments. But, again, numbers or measurements do not equal the total person. They do facilitate the handling of massive amounts of information about an individual and help to specify and clarify differences among people, especially learners.

Behind the measurements administered in schools, there is always *some* reason, although the reason may relate only vaguely to student development. Public relations, for example, may motivate administrators to give schoolwide achievement tests. If the school ranks above the national norms, the administrators look good; if the school ranks below the norms, the administrators can point their fingers at the tight-fisted school board and justify demands for bigger budgets. High school principals often measure the percentage of students who are going to college and, if the figures are favorable, send them to the local newspaper and the radio station. Increasingly, district superintendents adapt from business and industry the "systems approach" to measure what the taxpayers' money buys, for the guidance of parents and the school boards they elect. And, at the classroom level, some teachers administer achievement tests for the not-very-good reason that they believe they are expected to do so, or that teachers always have done so. But there are purposes for measurement in schools that seem more pertinent to the interests of prospective teachers, and more useful and beneficial for students.

"I use criterion-referenced tests all the time, but it took me a while to come around to them. I don't know what the problem was—they make perfect sense. I guess I was just in a rut . . . kids have been rank ordered for a zillion years, and it seemed like the right thing to do. It's more work, criterion-referenced tests, because I have to tie my test items to the class objectives, but it's worth it. I have the feeling—I can't prove this—the kids are less competitive since I switched. There's not so much status in beating out everyone else. It hasn't made evaluation less important to them. They still get tense. I can't figure out whether that's good or not. If they were casual about it, if it didn't mean much, maybe they wouldn't work so hard. I don't know. I can't experiment with it, not in this community. Parents would be on my back in a flash."

454

DECISION-MAKING

What are the roles of measurement in education?

This is the most general and comprehensive reason of all for measurement. By measuring and comparing, we enable ourselves better to decide what is and what isn't, what we should have done that we didn't, and what we should do next. Measurement helps to determine, for example:

1. Whether to pass or fail a student.
2. Whether a student needs enrichment materials, or more practice on the same material.
3. Whether a student has met the objectives and should move on to a new unit.
4. Whether your behavior modification techniques are working.
5. Whether you should change part of your lesson plan because it is not proving effective.
6. Whether changes, once you have made them, show improvement over the old methods and materials.
7. Whether you should counsel a student to apply to an Ivy League school, choose a junior college, or join the army.

Such examples of the uses of measurement in decision-making are elementary. But the measurement for decision-making has more complex purposes. One of them is feedback.

FEEDBACK TO STUDENTS

What effect does feedback have on students?

Whether or not to provide feedback to students about their progress hardly seems to involve much of a decision. Students feel that they have a right to know how they are doing, in the judgment of someone who is supposedly in a position to evaluate. From the educators' standpoint, feedback has long been regarded as motivating to students. (We discussed this point in Chapter 12.) *What* kind of feedback to provide remains, however, unresolved. This question has arisen from research on the effects of feedback. Some students, it has been found, improve their work in order to receive *positive feedback*. Some are motivated by a fear of *negative feedback*. And still others are not motivated at all by the usual school feedback of either variety. Because feedback has different reinforcement and punishment values for differing individuals, it obviously will not have an identical motivating effect on every student.

Ideally, you might devise several grading systems, each of them tailored to provide different feedback and to encourage different students' motivation, according to their needs. Practically, it would not work. Even if your school administration permitted you to set up, say, seven grading systems, you would find yourself devoting more time to arranging feedback situations than to teaching.

Yet some kind of feedback appears to be needed and appreciated by most youngsters. Early research (Page, 1958) indicated that even "canned" comments such as "Excellent" written at the top of students' papers motivated students as effectively as did personal notes such as "Good work, Cara. Keep it up!" But more recently, Stewart and White (1976) report that custom-tailored remarks, like the one to Cara, wield greater influence in improving student achievement. For the teacher, there is an incidental, useful by-product: personalized notes help to associate students' names and faces with the quality of each individual's work; thus, if you bump into Chris's father in the supermarket, you can tell him with assurance that Chris is doing exceptionally well in social studies and that you have just given him a 94. (That is feedback to parents, another plus for you, for Chris, and for Chris's dad.)

Feedback can be given in many ways. Two broad categories or systems of measurement lend themselves well to feedback, and the sections immediately following describe them.

Norm-Referenced Measurement. In norm-referenced measurement, a time-seasoned approach, students have been judged by comparing them with their classmates. The brightest students—or those who seemed brightest—got As, the dullest got Fs, and the rest fell in between. The system derives its name from the fact that each student's work is evaluated in reference to his or her relative position in class (or school, town, or state). That kind of measurement tells students where they stand among their peers. Such information can be important, but it can also be misleading. Consider a student in a French class whose immigrant family speaks French at home, or a student in a Spanish class whose family speaks Spanish. At term's end, each of them receives an A without having had to work much, or even without having learned much that they did not already know. But classmates who have rarely heard any language other than English may have acquired considerable French or Spanish, yet at term's end rank at the bottom of the class. Their rank tells them little or nothing about their specific accomplishments. The norm-referenced measurement tells us only that a student has done better or worse than others, not what he or she has done relative to his or her starting point, or what a student can or cannot do.

Is your grade in this course norm-referenced?

As the purpose of norm-referenced measurement is simply to rank students, no statement of goals or objectives is necessary. And because the system focuses on ranking, the more their scores spread out, the easier it becomes to rank them: therefore it is important to maximize the differences among them, so that teacher and students can clearly distinguish the third in rank from the fourth, and the tenth from the eleventh and so on.

Emphasis on ranking in the norm-referenced system makes it essential to know the makeup of the group being ranked. The student who speaks Spanish at home will rank differently in Spanish classes in the United States and in his family's native Spain.

How do norm-
referenced and
criterion-
referenced
measurements
differ?

Criterion-Referenced Measurement. In criterion-referenced measurement, students are evaluated by their progress toward specified objectives or criteria, so the fixing of goals becomes essential. The purpose of the system is to indicate what a student can do. It will not automatically show which students do better than others. Because criterion-referenced measurement is based on comparison to some stated criterion, scores need not be spread out. Indeed, it is possible for most of a class to demonstrate—or fail to demonstrate—mastery of the objectives. We shall say more about the teacher's use of criterion-referenced measurement in Chapter 15.

Both norm-referenced and criterion-referenced measurement involve comparisons. The former compares students with their peers; the latter compares students' progress with objectives. Either system can provide important feedback to students.

FEEDBACK TO TEACHERS ABOUT THEIR TEACHING

Measurement of students' learning provides, of course, an indirect measure of a teacher's effectiveness, but some theorists hold that students' achievement constitutes the most important index of a teacher's success—or failure. Because teaching and learning are such complex processes, however, that theory must be seasoned with several teaspoonsful of salt. The relationship between students' and teachers' performances is not so elementary as *one plus one equals two.* A student may fail to show learning for reasons beyond a teacher's control: emotional difficulties, learning disabilities, developmental lag, anxiety about tests, home environment. But if measurement of achievement suggests that a student is making little progress, the teacher still has the responsibility for seeking the problem's source and for providing whatever help is possible. (Measuring and evaluating teacher effectiveness is discussed further in Chapter 16).

HOMOGENEOUS GROUPING

Some kind of measurement is essential in the practice of homogeneous grouping, which is simply the placement together of students who share an important characteristic or attribute. One common form of grouping, known as *tracking* or *streaming*, has been practiced by schools for many years but is now highly controversial. Tracking, as you know from your own school years, involves assignment of youngsters of similar abilities to one class—the bright with the bright, the average with the average, the slow with the slow. Tracking in public schools is most frequently based on student achievement or IQ as measured by group tests.

Although widely practiced—at least three-fourths of all secondary schools use it—ability grouping has come under fire on many counts. Critics point out that tracking on the basis of IQ or achievement often results in *de facto*

"I guess I've seen—and given—the whole gamut of tests. Workbook tests. Standardized tests. Formal tests that I've made up. But personally, I've come to rely very heavily on the testing system that I've developed as part of my daily class routine. Every correct answer, every performance, gets a "tab"—a colored plastic chip. At the end of the week I record these—for math, for reading, for geography—from that kind of thing to things like 'kindness,' 'helpfulness,' 'talking in front of class.' This

segregation and argue that pupils assigned to slow classes suffer emotionally and academically (Esposito, 1973; Findley and Bryan, 1975). On the other hand, some upper-level students sense a great deal of pressure and report that they might be happier in groups of which less is expected (Starkey and Klusendorf, 1977). Other bright students favor placement in honors classes, as a recent incident in a village in New York's suburban Westchester County indicated.

Just before the school year ended in June, the principal of an elementary school began getting telephone requests from parents of youngsters who were going into the fifth grade in September. The parents wanted their children assigned to a certain teacher. Some such calls are routine; administrators get them every year, from people who want little Judy to have the teacher Jimmy had two years ago. But when the principal got his sixteenth call with the identical plea, his curiosity was aroused. The teacher was indeed a good one, but no better than the other fifth-grade teachers in that school. The next parent to call was asked the reason for the request. "I don't know," replied the mother, "Marie just asked me to ask you." Calls by the principal to the other mothers elicited similar responses. So the children themselves were asked. It transpired that they all had been grouped in a bright class in the third grade, had learned a lot, and had gotten good report cards. In the fourth grade, however, they had been scattered, and they had chafed because their teachers had had to go slow for the other kids. At the fourth grade's end, the bright ones got together and agreed to ask for a single teacher by name—they didn't care which teacher—so that they would all be in the same fifth grade class. That way, they reasoned, they wouldn't be bored.

way, every day I'm testing every area consistently. At the end of the term all I have to do is look in that book. That tells me a lot about what Barbara or Michael or whoever is capable of doing, has learned, has progressed in, and so forth. Overall I think it's a fair system—it really gives them a chance to prove themselves. On top of that, it's a great motivator. These kids don't even think of it as being tested. To them it's a reward."

How is measurement related to various student-grouping plans?

Educators' rationale for tracking is similar to that of those bright Westchester kids: tracking should increase teaching efficiency because teachers do not have to cope with broad individual differences in learning capacity in a single classroom. Also, many educators have believed, teachers would be more likely to tailor lesson plans, teaching methods, and materials to fit the needs of groups assigned on the basis of similar ability. Such expectations have not materialized. Even in homogeneously grouped classes, most teachers appear insufficiently trained or motivated to adapt their instructional techniques. They speed up or slow down the presentation of material but do not change the nature of its content (Froman and Owen, 1979). Another objection to ability grouping is that if teachers expect little of children in low-level classes their expectations may be borne out. In the case of bright children, self-fulfilling prophecy is of course beneficial. But for the first grader identified as "slow," the outcome may be disastrous. We will say more about the power of expectations in Chapter 16.

In a society where schools must, in theory at least, provide equal educational opportunity for all, the answer to the tracking issue is not easily come by. One possible solution is to continue to group pupils but to apply other standards than IQ or achievement. Suppose, for example, pupils and teachers were matched on the basis of their personalities. Or some students were assigned to *structured* classes and others to *unstructured* classes, based on their needs (Hunt and Sullivan, 1974). Whatever system may eventually replace tracking by IQ or achievement and whatever the characteristics are that determine the grouping, precise measurement will make it more likely that the grouping will prove appropriate and the method effective.

459

MEASUREMENT IN RESEARCH

The term *research* evokes images of thick-lensed scholars poring over ancient books from library cellars or doing mysterious things with test tubes in mysterious laboratories. In either case, measurement would seem to have no role. But research means *to study thoroughly,* and the more one studies a subject, the more difficult it becomes to avoid measurement.

Virtually all fields of research have adopted numerical systems for making measurements more objective and precise, and scientists generally evidence disdain for those who suggest that research can proceed without numbers and measurement. "If it exists it can be [eventually] measured," their adage goes. Speculation about a concept or a relationship is considered to be only a first step in research. Ultimately, the researcher has to produce the evidence, and the evidence must be supported by measurement. Researchers in a few specialized areas keep inventing new systems of measurement that are thought to be more accurate than older methods, and some of the new systems are way over the heads of ordinary folk like us. Fortunately, we can satisfy most of the measurement requirements of teaching by employing the old standbys described in this chapter and the next.

Collecting the Evidence

TEACHER-MADE TESTS

In Chapter 7, we discussed the setting of behavioral objectives, which provide you with a picture of what *ought* to occur. The logical next step is to measure whether or not it *does* occur. The handiest tool for that is the *teacher-made test;* i.e., one the teacher has cooked up. The teacher-made test, which is the most widely used measuring instrument in education, can provide either broad or precise assessments of progress in any of the domains, cognitive, affective, or psychomotor. Among the advantages of such tests:

1. Because you do not have to buy them from a publisher, they cost little more than the paper on which you mimeograph them and the time you spend constructing them.
2. They are available when you need them. You do not have to wait for the school to order them or for the mail to deliver them, and you can use them on the spur of the moment if you need a pop quiz.
3. They can be flexible in format, fitting the teacher's philosophy of testing, student and teacher preferences, and the level of behavior being measured. (Remember Bloom's taxonomy in Chapter 7?) A single test can include multiple-choice, true-or-false, short-answer, and essay items.
4. They can be designed to measure precisely what the teacher intends to measure.

What are advan-
tages and liabilities
of teacher-made
tests?

On the other hand, teacher-made tests often are confounded by such slips and oversights as these:

1. Teachers' failure to develop tests that constitute *representative samplings* of the domain being measured. For example, a class may have spent the last two weeks on Western Hemisphere geography. On a test, the teacher asks for an essay to answer the question "How do the exports of South America relate to the imports of North America?" But the Americas' export-import trade made up a scant 5 percent of the subject matter, so it is far from representative of what the class has studied and may know. (A representative test is said technically to have *content validity*, which we shall discuss in Chapter 15).

2. Teachers' development of tests that are unstable or inconsistent samplings of behavior. The example above applies here too. A pupil may have learned 95 percent of what the teacher taught about Western Hemisphere geography, but may somehow have missed the point about trade. So the test question does not elicit what the pupil does know, and he or she gets an F instead of an A. (*Reliability* of a test, the pertinent technical term in this case, will be examined in Chapter 15).

3. Teachers' failure to prepare a test of just the right level of difficulty. Too tough a test may suggest that the students have not learned, or that the teacher did not teach properly, whereas the fault really lies in the test itself. Too easy a test may suggest that all goes well and thus fail to disclose weaknesses in the students' learning or the teacher's method of instruction.

4. Teachers' failure to consider whether the test is intended to be norm-referenced or criterion-referenced, a distinction that affects the test's apparent difficulty. Norm-referenced tests should result in widely spread scores. Criterion-referenced tests should help to determine whether or not specific objectives have been met, and by their nature restrict the range of scores. In fact, they usually result in many high scores, which make the test questions *appear* to have been easy, when the high scores may actually indicate successful teaching.

5. Teachers may teach toward the test, wittingly or unwittingly. If such priming occurs, the test is not a valid evaluation of learning; it merely measures how well students recall selected data and not whether they have mastered some larger content area.

Suggestions for countering some of these limitations will be offered in Chapter 15. For now, it should suffice to say that teacher-made tests have strong advantages but are beclouded by limitations that can be minimized.

STANDARDIZED TESTS

Standardized tests require expertise, time, and money for development, and usually are produced by specialized corporations or independent researchers. The painstaking process by which they are constructed suggests that they should be more accurate and dependable instruments of measurement than comparable teacher-made tests. The process generally includes these steps:

1. Determine the area to be tested.
2. Write tentative or "pilot" components of the test.
3. Submit the components to experts for review.
4. Revise or discard certain items on the basis of the experts' opinions.
5. Choose a representative sample, called the *standardization sample*, of those people for whom the test is designed and give the test to that sample.
6. Determine by statistical analysis which items or parts of items are too difficult or too easy, which items do or do not help to spread the scores, and whether the test reliably and consistently measures what it is supposed to measure.

How to Help Students Take Standardized Tests

Sometimes students do well on standardized tests because they are good test-takers, not necessarily because they are bright, Masha K. Rudman (1976) argues. Rudman disapproves of such tests in their present form but concedes that changes may be a long way off, so she suggests three procedures intended to make more students good test-takers:

The Warmup. Well before a test, distribute facsimiles of answer sheets and have students practice filling in their names and other information. Give preliminary instructions in the precise language that the test manual prescribes. ("Complete the information called for at the top of this page." or "Fill in the blanks asking for your name, school, date of tests, etc. Be sure to write clearly.") Go through the routine often enough so that students will be more nearly relaxed when they confront the real test.

Practice arranging seats in the manner that test-makers usually suggest to prevent the copying of answers; in time it will become a kind of game.

Give students at least two *dull* No. 2 pencils for practicing on the answer sheets. (Dull pencils do not break easily and permit marking of answer boxes with a single bold stroke, thus saving time for the student.)

Advise students not to worry about neatness—speed is what counts on most standardized tests.

After students have had several practice sessions filling in information and marking boxes, give them a few rapid drills in which you call off right answers and students check the proper boxes.

Next, prepare a list of easy questions such as:

1. How many students are in this class?
   a. 30 b. 14 c. 18 d. 25 e. None of these
2. What season is this?
   a. Winter b. Spring c. Summer d. Fall
   e. All of the above

Have students answer on separate sheets, identical with those they will use during the actual test. This will give them practice in the dozen little motions involved in reading on one page and answering on another, a skill they may not need on regular classroom tests. It will also help to isolate performance from thought and content—an essential in test-taking.

Emphasize that the ability to mark boxes has nothing to do with students' knowledge or intelligence.

7. On the basis of the statistical analysis, repeat steps 2 through 6 if necessary.
8. Prepare a manual for giving the test and interpreting its results. The manual will, or should, include information from steps 5 and 6, with *norm tables* that show precisely how the standardization sample performed on the test.

Among the advantages of standardized tests are these:

1. They tend to have high validity (they measure what they are supposed to measure).
2. They tend to have high reliability (the scores prove stable and consistent).
3. Their manuals' norm tables permit you to compare your students' performance with that of the standardization sample.
4. All students taking the test do so under the same standard conditions (time limits, instructions, equipment).

The Dry Run. Obtain copies of old tests from the publisher to familiarize students with their appearance, the vocabulary of the directions, and the format of the questions.

Let students confer on how to cope with the questions, and advise them yourself how to skip over irrelevancies and concentrate on material for which there are answer boxes.

Scrutinize the test for the need of special skills, such as dealing with graphs and charts, and give students practice with them.

Consider the test's scoring system. If a test instructs "Do not guess," wrong answers will be subtracted from the total of right answers, so discuss with students the risks of guessing. But if you know the score will count only right answers, let students guess when necessary.

Show students how to skim for test-taking, extracting the main idea from the first or last sentence of a passage and matching it with the suggested answers. (True understanding and the ability to answer test questions are two different things.) For practice at skimming, have students read aloud and silently, stressing only key words.

After all the practice, give the students rules for test-taking.

1. Finish the whole test or a section of it as quickly as possible by answering *only* questions where you are sure of the answers.

Return to the doubtful ones later.

2. Leave a minute or two at the test's end to fill in blank boxes. This is the time for guessing (unless wrong answers are deducted from the score) and for checking to see that the number of questions asked and answers recorded match.
3. Don't waste time reading interesting passages. Just answer the questions.
4. Realize that the test's "right" answers may not be the only answers or the best ones. Don't argue with them.

The Follow-Through. Try the test yourself, to see if skimming and matching yield the right answers, and to determine how fast you can go. Then set up a timetable for your students.

Imbue the students with confidence. Emphasize that their scores will reflect only their ability to take tests: you'll judge their learning by their work during the school year. So prepare them to approach their ordeal with light hearts. ∎

Adapted by permission from *Learning, The Magazine For Creative Teaching*, February 1976. © 1976 by Education Today Company, Inc.

"I'm interested in how they feel as well as in how much they learn. I've developed a bunch of self-report questionnaires. Most of them were my own ideas, and I've got a few tips from [the school psychologist]. I've used these questionnaires to measure, oh, what time of the day, and what day of the week the kids feel most alert or most tired. I've got a little three-item job that asks how much they think they got out of any particular class. Here's one I have to get run off for tomorrow. I want to find out what sort of class discussions they think are most worthwhile—large group, small group, more frequent, with certain topics, none at all, that sort of thing. Why do I bother with all this? Yeah, it looks like kind of a hobby, doesn't it! Actually, can you imagine trying to interview each kid about each question? I wouldn't have time to do any teaching!"

What are the merits and limitations of standardized tests?

Apart from the fact that such tests are obviously hard to develop, standardized tests' disadvantages include:

1. Ordinarily the tests must be bought. (Some standardized tests, primarily those published in professional journals, may be reproduced free, if the authors' permission is obtained.)
2. Tests may cover too much ground for your purposes. Because the developers cannot know what *you* stress in your class, they make the tests comprehensive enough to provide something for everyone. But you may be interested in measuring only one small aspect of achievement or ability in a given field such as math or science rather than the whole broad area to which tests are usually directed.
3. Tests may reach to higher levels than your students have attained. A single achievement test may include items related to *knowledge, application* and *synthesis*—again, recall Bloom's taxonomy. If you have focused on material at the knowledge level, your students may not fare too well on a test that touches on application or synthesis.
4. Tests' accuracy, from your standpoint, depends on how closely your students resemble the standardization sample. If your students differ from that sample, their scores may not mean what they are supposed to mean. But you are *required* to administer and score the tests precisely as the manual

464

prescribes. Deviation makes the test unstandardized and, again, can change the meaning of the scores.

5. Most tests use only the multiple-choice format, chiefly because the answers can be scored by anybody, without subjective judgments. That may be viewed as an advantage rather than a limitation, but some people argue that requiring students to choose one best answer, when there may be several possible answers, pressures them into convergent thinking.

6. The format of the test may be much different from those of tests your students are accustomed to. If your classroom tests are generally of the essay variety, and time limits make little difference, a strictly timed, multiple-choice test may measure your students' ability to adapt to the test's arrangement rather than their knowledge of content.

7. Most standardized tests are norm-referenced rather than criterion-

Problems of Standardized Tests

You have finally located a standardized test of *schmoozing!* The test manual looks pretty good: there is a description of how the test was developed, statistical information about the consistency of the test, instructions for administration, and so on. There is even a detailed description of the standardization sample, which consisted of kids from Elito, a suburb of Los Angeles.

You administer and score the test according to the manual's instructions. To your surprise, your students from rural Pennsylvania score well *below* the entire standardization sample. Your first impression is that your students are rather dull at schmoozing. On further reflection, you have some gnawing questions about the appropriateness of this test for your students. Your call to the Elito school system confirms your doubts. Elito budgets one-fourth of its money for special schmoozing teachers, and all of their students practice the schmooze at least two hours a day. By contrast, your own students have never had any direct instruction in schmoozing, and there is no money budgeted for such education.

Because the standardization sample was so unrepresentative, you cannot make much sense out of your students' scores by comparing them to the restrictive norm tables from Elito. In an effort to salvage the whole project, you develop *local norms*, in much the same way as the original norms were produced. Now you can feel more confident of making sense of your students' scores without depending on the norms from the manual.

Postscript: Many tests accused of being "biased" suffer from problems similar to the one you encountered (although not so exaggerated); their standardization samples are not representative of a particular group of students. You could have saved yourself much anguish and energy if you had *first* dug out some published reviews of the schmoozing test.

One of the best sources for such reviews is the series of *Mental Measurements Yearbooks*. The *Yearbooks* contain very comprehensive critiques of all major published tests. Although the critiques are often filled with technical jargon, your knowledge of measurement terms plus a general impression of the reviewer's judgment will give you a good basis for selecting standardized tests. The *Yearbooks* also contain information for ordering tests (addresses, prices, grade or age levels, etc.). The suggested readings at the end of this chapter give other important sources of test descriptions and reviews. ■

referenced, for two reasons. One is that criterion-referenced measurement represents a fairly recent development; the other is that, because criterion-referencing depends on precise objectives, test-designers would find it difficult to create a test that fits your particular objectives. However, because of widespread interest in criterion-referenced measurement, test publishers are now jumping on the bandwagon.

Several of the limitations we have cited suggest that standardized tests are inflexible. But don't jump to the conclusion that that characteristic invalidates them. Most measurement specialists agree that flexibility in testing may generate even more problems than inflexibility. Tests are most fair, the specialists believe, when all students confront identical questions and receive identical instructions: varying instructions and the assignment of different questions to different students make interpretation and comparison of scores difficult.

Measuring a Self-Concept

You're a tenth-grade teacher. The principal, a concerned administrator, asks about Hermie and what your objectives are for him. Hermie's self-concept is so poor, you reply, that for the next six weeks you're going to devote as much attention to improving it as to his instruction in math. (From your answer, it seems obvious that you do not feel that Hermie's self-concept should be left to his family or the guidance counselor. Neither do you believe that it is too late to change a fifteen-year-old's view of himself and that "that's the way he is.")

The principal says: "Sounds like a good idea."

Six weeks later the principal returns. "How's Hermie doing?"

"It's amazing," you say. "We got him involved in some jigsaw learning groups and I gave him plenty of reinforcement for his progress in math. He feels a lot better about himself."

"How can you tell?"

"Oh, you always can tell. Any kid in the class would agree that Hermie's changed."

"Well, you're probably right but I still would like to know *how* you can tell. What cues [measurement] do you use to base your judgment [evaluation] on?"

"What difference does that make?"

"I think you and Mr. Flamingo [the guidance counselor] must be using different cues, because he doesn't agree about Hermie's self-concept. I'm going to see him tomorrow afternoon. Could you give me a list of your cues?"

"Uh huh. . . ."

On the next day you leave your list of cues in the principal's office:

Smiles more often.
Has made three friends in class.
Disparages himself much less than he used to.
Looks me in the eye now when speaking.
Initiates verbal exchanges.

At your lunch hour, the principal stops by and asks if you are satisfied with your list. You say defensively: "I know there *must* be more to self-concept than those behaviors but they're the only things I can come up with."

The principal replies: "There *is* more to self-concept than just observable behaviors, but when we're evaluating a self-concept, they're all we have to go on."

Can you suggest other cues that might be used to evaluate self-concept? It may help to think about what things indicate a poor self-concept as well as what indicates a good one. ■

Teacher-made and standardized tests generally focus on educational achievement, but you may be interested in measuring other areas as well—creativity, students' interests, self-concepts, attitudes, morale, preferences among the various types of reinforcers, and students' opinions of your own teaching effectiveness. For such measurements, standardized tests do exist. On the other hand, a well-thought-out teacher-made test may be easier to work with and of course permits you to ask precisely the questions to which you want answers. It also allows you to be more spontaneous in measuring and evaluating. But a test that you devise in your five-minute break may be seriously flawed.

OBSERVATION INSTRUMENTS

Certain types of measure require special knowledge and thousands of hours of work for their preparation: it is best to let the experts devise them. So-called *observation instruments* exemplify that kind of measure.

What is the function of observation instruments?

An observation instrument's purpose is to amass facts as a counterbalance to a teacher's intuitive judgments. But the facts are self-evident, many teachers protest. We *know*, they argue, how often a student responds to questions, how much lecturing and how much discussion go on, how much social contact occurs, and how many of our students express their feelings. Actually, it is impossible to attain perfect objectivity about classroom activity. Intuition, on which teachers' supposed knowledge depends, may be a crude and imprecise indicator of the truth, varying in its accuracy with teachers' characters and biases. Some teachers prove right most of the time and some almost always prove wrong. Even those teachers whose judgment rarely fails them, though, can benefit by a double check carried out more objectively.

The range of topics for which observation instruments provide a double check is immense; broad categories of such instruments, arranged by Simon and Boyer (1974), cover affective and cognitive behaviors, classroom procedure, and materials and equipment, among other things, and the same researchers have edited a collection of ninety-nine widely used observation techniques.

Steps in employing observation instruments are:

1. Decide what behaviors to observe.
2. Locate or develop an observation instrument.
3. Observe and tally behaviors into proper codes or categories.
4. Summarize the data.
5. Evaluate the summarized data.

That is the general procedure. In its application, these ground rules should be followed:

1. Record observations permanently, rather than trust them to fallible and selective memory.

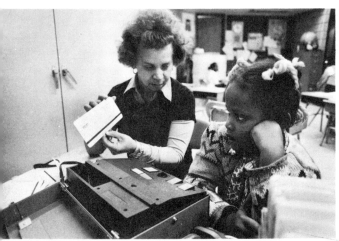

"Not many students look forward to evaluation. Humans want to be right, and evaluation usually points out some things that aren't right. It does help students learn, though, I'm sure of that. I give regular, formal exams. But I also do lots of

2. Make someone responsible for observing. Because teachers rarely can sit back and do the job themselves, an individual from outside the classroom generally has to be recruited: he or she should be familiar with the requirements of careful and uninterrupted observation and recording. A parent, a teacher's aide, a student from another class, or a senior citizen in the community is a potential observer to help collect data. As a substitute, a videotape recorder, if one is available, may be employed and its tape coded and summarized by the teacher later.

How should observation instruments be used?

3. Provide for a warmup period before recorded observation begins. The behavior to be evaluated obviously has to be typical, and students will not behave typically in the presence of an outsider or a mechanical gadget until the novelty has worn off.

4. Focus on observable behavior and rule out inferences about what may be going on in someone's head (Did the student intend to show off? Is the teacher bestowing phony praise?) because inferences flaw the accuracy of the observations.

5. Check for agreement between raters if more than one observer is used. Have the observers watch the same situation for a number of minutes and see if

informal, individual evaluation. I can soften negative feedback that way; give each child personal suggestions for improvement."

the behaviors they have recorded are the same. The extent to which they agree (or disagree) will give you an estimate of the reliability of the observations.

6. Make sure the observation instrument measures what it is supposed to measure. This may seem to be gratuitous advice, but systematic observation of people is a fairly recent development in measurement, and some instruments do not work so well as their developers assert they do. Herbert and Attridge (1975) suggest careful scrutiny of the instrument's manual to determine whether or not the instrument produces "true results." Their article, *A Guide for Developers and Users of Observation Systems and Manuals*, provides explicit information on how to judge the worth of an observation instrument.

SELF-REPORT INSTRUMENTS

When a student is asked to describe systematically his or her feelings, beliefs, attitudes, or interests, a *self-report instrument* usually is employed to collect the data. Unlike the observation instrument, which requires someone else to watch and record one's external behavior, the self-report instrument tells on introspection of one's internal behavior: it operates in accord with the old notion that each of us is the best judge of what is going on inside ourselves. Self-report instruments typically focus on the affective domain—opinions, likes and dislikes, evaluations. They come in a wide variety of forms. Some are *unstructured* and ambiguous, like the Rorschach Ink Blot test; some are *highly structured*, like multiple-choice questions in which only one answer is correct. Because unstructured instruments require a great deal of training to administer and interpret, most educators prefer simpler and highly structured instruments.

Sociometric Measures. One of the most commonly used self-report techniques is *sociometry*. It is a method typically used to determine what patterns of friendship or esteem occur in group settings. In a classroom, it can be used to find out which students are best liked or which are thought to be

---

An Example of a Sociometric Instrument

Over the past couple of weeks, you have discovered that the friendship groupings in your class are more complex than you had imagined. Jimmy, for example, likes to *play* with Fred, but does not like to *work* with him. Also, you have been picking up some cues that students may be good judges of "who's who," because they are aware of interactions that go on outside the classroom. You decide to collect some systematic evidence about the sociometric status of your students, so you give them a version of a sociometric scale, perhaps one that you have developed:

Here are names of all students in this class. First of all, circle *your* name on the list. Then write the number that best fits how you feel about each of your classmates next to their names.

Put a *1* if you like that person as a friend very much

    2 if you like that person as a friend

    3 if it does not matter if that person is your friend

    4 if you don't care for that person as a friend

    5 if you don't care for that person as a friend at all

Steven	_____	Emily	_____
Pamela	_____	Ray	_____
Joseph	_____	Kelli	_____
Daniel	_____	Gary	_____
Merle	_____	(etc.)	

You tally the total number of points for each student, and find a pretty clear ranking of liked and disliked students. Also, there appear to be about three groupings of students, with two or three students who received extremely high scores.

Questions to ponder:

Is the information from the questionnaire meaningful?

Do you think the responses might have been different if you had asked students to fill out the forms anonymously?

Do you think responses would have been different if you had asked only for positive nominations?

Can you—*should* you—intervene with some technique designed to increase the acceptance of the isolates?

Does it make sense to readminister the device *following* an intervention? Why? ■

the brightest or dullest. Since sociometry can quickly determine *who likes whom*, it identifies the popular students and the loners, or isolates, as psychologists call them. With that type of information, the teacher gains several advantages:

Should students sign their names to a sociometric instrument?

1. Groups that will work well may be established more easily;
2. Development of undesirable cliques may be inhibited by placing popular students and loners in the same group or groups;
3. Loners may be benefited by inclusion in a mixed group, because of the tendency to learning by imitation;
4. Teams that the *students* perceive as being most nearly equal in ability can be constructed for group competition in academic areas.

But go easy! If you intend to put your sociometric findings into practice, lace their application with common sense and ethics. Suppose Robert has been clearly distinguished by tests as a loner. If he indicates that he yearns for acceptance by an "in" bunch, your manipulations will be justified. If he has evidenced no dissatisfaction with his social status, consider what you know about him—besides the fact that he is a loner—before you plunge him willy-nilly into the classroom whirl. If he is highly creative, for example, he may do his best work independently and prefer things that way.

An example of a simple sociometric device of the kind you may be using appears in the box on p. 470. Some people object to such questions as 3, 4, and 5 in the box, which ask students to identify negative feelings about others. The requests *could* reinforce already existent negative feelings. To avoid that possibility, a useful technique is to concentrate on positive approaches, such as *Guess Who?* In this system, students are asked to

Guess who

is the most cheerful and friendly	_____
works well with others	_____
is always willing to help	_____
never bugs other people	_____
Etc.	_____

Interest Questionnaires. As their name implies, these questionnaires deal with students' interests and their preferences among classroom routines, kinds of instruction, free-time activities, subjects of study, and other aspects of school life. The questionnaires ask, as do all self-report instruments, that students check responses they feel are appropriate. Because it is so simple, the interest questionnaire is the easiest of all measuring devices to develop, use, and interpret. And you will probably be the best person to develop an interest questionnaire for use in your classroom, because you know what has gone on there and what activities can be arranged. An example of an interest questionnaire appears in the box on p. 472.

An Example of a Self-report Instrument

Probably the most common reason for the failure of behavior modification procedures is the use of inappropriate reinforcers. It is remarkably easy to misjudge the potency of material, social, or activity reinforcers for a given student. It is also easy to presume that a single type of reinforcer will work for the whole class.

Even if we know that everyone has differing preferences for reinforcers, how is it possible to figure out what will work best for each student?

One simple but powerful technique is the use of an interest questionnaire known as the *reinforcement menu*. With this device, students are asked to select, as though they were in a cafeteria, those items which interest them. Even more information is gathered because each student is also asked to *rate* each item.

Below is an abbreviated example of a reinforcement menu. With a little imagination, it can easily be adapted to different grade levels. In developing your own menu, be careful not to include items that are beyond the bounds of the school in terms of cost or legality. ■

Name _____ Date _____

The items in this questionnaire refer to things and experiences that you may enjoy or are of interest to you. Check each item in the column that best describes how much you like it today.

	Not at all	A little	Pretty much	Very much
1. *Beverages*				
a. water	___	___	___	___
b. milk	___	___	___	___
c. soda	___	___	___	___
d. cocoa	___	___	___	___
e. fruit juice	___	___	___	___
2. *Reading*				
a. comic books	___	___	___	___
b. sports	___	___	___	___
c. newspapers	___	___	___	___
d. adventure	___	___	___	___
e. famous people	___	___	___	___
f. travel	___	___	___	___
g. humor	___	___	___	___
h. science	___	___	___	___
3. *Being Praised*				
a. about appearance	___	___	___	___
b. about work	___	___	___	___
c. about strength	___	___	___	___
d. about athletic ability	___	___	___	___
e. about your brains	___	___	___	___
4. *Games*				
a. chess	___	___	___	___
b. checkers	___	___	___	___
c. Scrabble	___	___	___	___
d. other (list)	___	___	___	___

What could you do with an interest questionnaire?

Here are a couple of suggestions that may be useful in preparing your own classroom questionnaire:

If you ask students to list, say, five classroom activities that they have "really enjoyed," they are likely to recall—and therefore put down—those that were most recent. But if you include in the questionnaire all twenty-three, say, of the activities in which the class has engaged, the pupils will not have to depend on their memories, and the results will be more informative to you. And just in case *you* have not remembered everything, you may want to leave room at the bottom for some additional responses.

Do not ask students merely to check yes or no on each item, but give them a chance to indicate their degree of preference or distaste, as in the box. Their responses will have precision and more meaning to you.

Summary

Measurement makes our observations more systematic, objective, and precise. When measurements are converted into numbers, they provide a base for communication and expression. The numbers, however, represent a *summary* of whatever phenomena are being measured. *Evaluation* is the process of interpreting the meaning and worth of the data. In education, the broadest purpose of measurement is to facilitate decision-making. Other purposes include:

1. Feedback to students. This may be *norm-referenced*, comparing each student with other students, or *criterion-referenced*, comparing students' progress with predetermined objectives.
2. Feedback to teachers. This informs teachers about the effectiveness of their teaching procedures.
3. Guidance for homogeneous grouping. Despite criticism and research findings, grouping of students on the basis of academic ability persists. Measurement may be used for other kinds of grouping, however.
4. Research. Measurement permits researchers to confirm or disprove hypotheses.

Two kinds of tests, which of course are measuring tools, permit teachers to determine whether or not their teaching objectives have been attained. The most common testing technique is the *teacher-made test*, development of which is considered in Chapter 15. *Standardized tests*, produced by specialized publishers or independent researchers, are developed with much more rigor than most teacher-made tests, but have the handicap of measuring goals much broader than any teacher's specific objectives. Standardized tests offer *norms*, permitting comparison of test scores in a given class or school with the scores made by a representative sample of the people being tested.

Observation instruments enable teachers to record many types of classroom data, and are more precise than informal judgments. *Self-report techniques*, for which there are many instruments, ask students to reveal their feelings, attitudes, or interests. *Sociometric* devices, a special kind of self-report measurement, facilitate analysis of friendship or esteem patterns within groups. *Interest questionnaires*, another special kind of self-report measure, help to determine students' likes and dislikes and are simple to design and employ.

Chapter Study Guide

CHAPTER REVIEW

Answer questions 1–13 True or False:

1. In theory, evaluation and measurement are the same thing.

2. In norm-referenced measurement, each student's work is evaluated in reference to a norm set by state boards of education.

3. A disadvantage of norm-referenced measurement is that it fails to measure a student's progress.

4. In criterion-referenced measurement, students' progress toward specified objectives is measured.

5. Measurement of students' learning also provides a direct measure of a teacher's effectiveness.

6. Tracking has come under attack on the grounds that it often results in *de facto* segregation.

7. Norm-referenced testing should produce a wide spread of scores.

8. Standardized tests are usually linked clearly to classroom objectives.

9. Multiple-choice questions have been criticized on the grounds that they encourage divergent thinking.

10. Most standardized tests are criterion-referenced.

11. Observation instruments are designed to measure affective behavior only.

12. A self-report instrument relies on introspection of one's internal behavior.

13. Precise goal statements help to ensure accurate feedback from a criterion-referenced system.

FOR FURTHER THOUGHT

1. The box, "Measuring a Self-Concept" (p. 466), has the principal say, "There *is* more to self-concept than just observable behaviors, but when we're evaluating a self-concept, they're all we have to go on," and then adds, "Can you suggest other ways that might be used to evaluate self-concept?"

   One avenue to pursue may be artistic student self-expression, because it often indirectly reveals a person's self-image. Could you devise an assignment in writing or one of the other arts with themes that might serve this purpose? (Examples: "When I think about the future"; "Something I've overcome"; "My world.") How could you determine whether this assignment truly indicates the self-concept?

2. Devise a short criterion-referenced test to measure students' mastery of one of the activities you designed in connection with Chapter 2, 3, 7, 8, or 10.

3. It is worth noting that the *quality* of thought or performance seldom lends itself to measured evaluation. Even in mathematics, counting the number of correct answers on a test will not reveal the elegance—or lack of it—behind the thought process that produced the answer. There is no easy way to measure such qualities of writing as relevance, coherence, economy, or originality—the heart of good written expression. (Instead of trying, many teachers resort to counting mechanical errors in students' writing, which often has the effect of inhibiting expression and in any case does nothing to ensure the quality of aliveness which alone makes something worth reading.) In the absence of more refined instruments of measurement, the presence of such qualities and values must still be intuited by the teacher. Do you think the future will bring useful measures of, say, originality, or must it be left to intuition? How could you develop a test of originality in thinking? Would your test distinguish between useful ideas and signs of mental disturbance?

IMPORTANT TERMS

measurement
evaluation
norm-referenced
criterion-referenced
homogeneous grouping
teacher-made test

standardized test
observation instrument
self-report instrument
sociometric measure
interest questionnaire

SUGGESTED READINGS

CHUN, K., COBB, S., and FRENCH, J. R. P. *Measures for psychological assessment: A guide to 3,000 original sources and their applications.* Ann Arbor, MI: Institute for Social Research, The University of Michigan, 1975. As the title suggests, there are many original sources here for published tests. Sources of tests are also cataloged by "descriptors" (e.g., tests of achievement motivation).

GRONLUND, N. E. *Preparing criterion-referenced tests for classroom instruction.* New York: Macmillan, 1973. A clear, concise introduction to criterion-referenced measurement, stressing a how-to-do-it approach.

HOEPFNER, R., et al. *CSE test evaluations.* Los Angeles: Center for the Study of Evaluation, UCLA Graduate School of Education, 1970-1974. These reviews cover the entire spectrum of published tests used from preschool through high school in five volumes: Preschool-Kindergarten, Elementary School, Secondary School Grades 7 and 8, Grades 9 and 10, and Grades 11 and 12. An easy format helps work through the maze of tests, and summary "grades" (good, fair, poor) are awarded each test. An excellent resource for figuring out the suitability of tests.

JOHNSON, O. G. *Tests and measurements in child development, Handbook II.* San Francisco: Jossey-Bass, 1976. A two-volume follow-up to the Johnson and Bommarito *Handbook I.* Includes 900 additional unpublished tests and related information. The age range for these tests has been extended to 0–18.

JOHNSON, O. G., and BOMMARITO, J. W. *Tests and measurements in child development, Handbook I.* San Francisco: Jossey-Bass, 1971. Gives general description, source, technical information, and bibliography for over 300 unpublished measures. The scales cover the age range 0–12, and are chunked into the categories of cognition, personality and emotional characteristics, and perceptions of the environment. The scales themselves are *not* given.

ROBINSON, J. P., and SHAVER, P. B. *Measures of social psychological attitudes* (rev. ed.). Ann Arbor, MI: Institute for Social Research, The University of Michigan, 1973. One hundred seventeen published personality measures are given, with comments about their usability. Although the majority are intended to be used at the high school level and above, there are occasional tests for elementary level youngsters.

The following eight texts are all concerned with general issues in measurement and evaluation in education, particularly standardized testing. In each case, coverage is comprehensive and understandable.

AIKEN, L. R. *Psychological testing and assessment* (2nd ed.). Boston: Allyn and Bacon, 1976.

ANASTASI, A. *Psychological testing* (4th ed.). New York: Macmillan, 1976.

BROWN, F. G. *Principles of educational and psychological testing* (2nd ed.). New York: Holt, Rinehart and Winston, 1976.

CHASE, C. I. *Measurement for educational evaluation.* Reading, MA: Addison-Wesley, 1974.

GRONLUND, N. E. *Measurement and evaluation in teaching* (3rd ed.). New York: Macmillan, 1976.

MEHRENS, W. A., and LEHMANN, I. J. *Standardized tests in education* (2nd ed.). New York: Holt, Rinehart and Winston, 1975.

NUNNALLY, J. C. *Educational measurement and evaluation* (2nd ed.). New York: McGraw-Hill, 1972.

TENBRINK, T. D. *Evaluation: A practical guide for teachers.* New York: McGraw-Hill, 1974.

ANSWER KEY

1. F; 2. F; 3. T; 4. T; 5. F; 6. T; 7. T; 8. F; 9. F; 10. F; 11. F; 12. T; 13. T

It is your first year of teaching. You and your seventh-grade class have just completed the first math unit of the semester, and it's time to find out how well you have taught and how much your students have learned. So you face the awesome task of preparing a test. From your own high school days, you recall some pretty poor tests that your teachers slapped together, and you want to develop one that covers the ground and that is fair to your students and to you.

In this chapter, we shall first consider how to evaluate student performance and how to construct a respectable test; then we shall deal with some clues to understanding scores on the tests you make up yourself, and on the standardized tests you may be asked to administer.

Planning a Teacher-Made Test

You have never organized a test before. You may be pressed for time, as teachers usually are. At the end of each lesson, you probably forgot to jot down possible test items or ideas, so now you decide to review quickly what you have taught in the past few weeks. You reach for the students' textbook, turn to the appropriate chapter, and scan it page by page in search of ideas that will suggest test questions. When you have more or less mined the chapter, you look for questions the book's author may have included. Then you think up a few questions on your own, based on material discussed in class but not in the book. When you have enough items, you feel confident that you have a good test. You probably do not. Your test is likely to prove as accurate as a yardstick made of elastic.

How much time can you afford for measuring and evaluating achievement?

Preparation of a good test demands considerable time and planning. In fact, a recent study reported that primary school teachers spent more classroom hours monitoring and evaluating student progress than they did on direct instruction (Hiatt, 1979). A systematic approach to test construction will help you to use your time more efficiently and to be fair in grading; and as we indicated in the previous chapter, careful measurement will improve the accuracy of your decision-making.

Before writing down a single question for a test, ask yourself:

1. What is the purpose of this test? (The answer should help you shape the test as a whole and the nature of individual items. If you use behavioral objectives, the purposes of the test are at hand.)
2. What are *all* the important points I have taught? (If you omit some, the test will lack validity, which we shall consider a little farther on.)
3. How much emphasis would be given to other assigned readings? (If you test only on the material you have covered in class, you won't be able to tell whether or not students understood what they were to have read on their own—or whether they even read it.)

4. How much emphasis does each point merit? (The answer depends on your objectives.)
5. What is the level of my class? (The answer should determine the difficulty of the test items.)
6. How long should a test be? (First graders tire more quickly than sixth graders, so tests in the lower grades may have to be shorter. At the high school level, you might need to fit your test to a thirty-minute, forty-five-minute, or hour-long period.)

What preliminary testing questions must be answered?

7. Under what conditions will the test be given? (If a room is too hot or too noisy or a test is given just before the school's crucial basketball game, for example, the results could be affected. In some circumstances, it may be wise to postpone the test.)

While writing the test, keep in mind the two characteristics of good tests that every professional test developer seeks: reliability and validity.

RELIABILITY

If you give a student a test on Monday and a similar test on Friday, and the resulting scores prove the same or close, you could judge the tests to be *reliable*. If the scores differ much, you would have your doubts about the tests. To do its job, any test must provide accurate and consistent measurement, and in testing, consistency and reliability are synonymous. Teacher-made tests, in contrast with standardized tests, are by repute of low reliability. Yours need not be.

Reliability will be easier to embody in your tests if you think about basic test theory. The idea isn't complicated; it is simply this: an *obtained score*—what one gets on a test—is made up of two components, a *true score* and an *error score*. The true score reflects what a person actually knows. But we may never learn the true score because of static by the error score. Contributing to the error score are oversights, mistakes in reading a question, and basic misunderstanding of the question. Often, additions to the error score are built in when the test is put together. Too much emphasis may be placed on one topic and not enough on another. Questions may be ambiguous, confusing, or unnecessarily difficult to comprehend. The time allotted for the test may be too short or the questions too long. Each of us has probably fallen victim to common faults in teacher-made tests, and resultant distortion of the obtained score. Have you ever complained, "We never studied some of the stuff he asked on that test" or, after a multiple choice quiz, "Well, *C* may be the right answer, like she says, but I think *B* is right too, because . . ."? If you have, then you are familiar with some of the difficulties in teacher-made tests.

What may change the theoretical error and true scores?

It hardly needs to be said that the lower the error score, the closer the obtained score comes to representing what a person knows. Reliability in a test lowers the error score; furthermore, it is crucial because, as you will learn later in this chapter, a test cannot be valid (or accurate) unless it is reliable.

Measurement specialists have come up with some ground rules to help

"I was a little threatened about using a test grid—it looked like a big deal. It took a grand total of ten minutes to become expert in it! Of course, if you haven't written objectives to start with, then it will take lots longer. It was amusing when I took a couple of my old tests and plugged them into a test grid, you know, to see how the items were distributed. Wow, were they bad! It shouldn't be funny, because those tests were unfair to lots of students. The test grid has eased my conscience a little about being fair in testing and grading."

decrease error in tests and increase reliability. First, they know that tests are more reliable if they contain a number of questions—half a dozen or more—rather than only one. That is because you reduce the possibilities that some poor students will guess the right answers and that others who know the subject will flunk because they have misread one item. Consider a quiz that contains only three items and may not be very representative of the content that the student is responsible for knowing. Imagine that Tom, a good student, has studied and understands almost all the content— except, by bad luck, the small portions covered by the three test items. He will probably flunk the test, but Dick, who studied nothing until ten minutes before class, happens to remember only the three pieces of material covered by chance in the quiz. The high grade he receives will make him happy, but it won't reflect what he has learned. If the teacher gave an alternative quiz, with three different items, the grades of the two students would probably be reversed.

Asking a good number of questions rather than a few is important also when you consider the different areas of content you may want to cover. A single essay item on the function of memory might not measure reliably how much a psychology student knows about cognitive processes in general. A better alternative would be three or four short essays with fewer points assigned to each but covering more of the broad area of the cognitive domain.

A second ground rule is that clarity of test questions improves the reliability of the test score. If a question is ambiguous, a student may respond differently on different days. If an item is subject to interpretation, different students likely will interpret it differently.

On the basis of these rules, we offer two suggestions: (1) Make your test longer rather than shorter (not in inches but in items). Use several items, where possible, for each area of content because tests with limited samplings of content areas often prove unreliable. (But apply common sense and allow sufficient time for all of your students to complete the test.) (2) Carefully check each item on a test for ambiguities and other flaws before a test. Then check again after the test, asking students about each item: Was the question clear? Was it fair? Did you have trouble with it and, if so, why? Even if you never use the same items again, the students' answers should help you to avoid future problems.

Despite these suggestions, you are unlikely to eliminate all error due to unreliability on a test. Unless every student knows the subject perfectly, some answers will represent guesses, and even if the guesses are correct, they will have introduced error to the test score. Other students may get answers wrong, not because they do not know the material, but because of illness, emotional strain, or distraction by out-of-school problems. Circumstances like those are beyond your control, but it is your responsibility, and should be your goal, to make your test as reliable as possible.

VALIDITY

Let's assume that you have constructed a highly reliable test—so reliable, in fact, that if you gave various versions of it half a dozen times in a semester to the same class, every student's score would always come up virtually unchanged. You have taken the first step in building a sturdy measuring device. Your test would be defective, though, if you did not take the second step, the planning and construction of a *valid* test. A test is valid only if it measures what it is supposed to measure; it is "on target." To be on target a measurement must first be consistent, or reliable. (The relationship between reliability and validity is depicted in Figure 15.1.) Once reliability is attained, test writers seek accuracy. If a test score is inaccurate, educational planning or decisions based on it will be faulty. For example, a decision to identify a Spanish-speaking child as retarded because she scored low on an English language intelligence test would be inappropriate, because the test would have assessed language skills, not intellectual capabilities. The test might be reliable, because the child probably would always get a similarly low score, at least until she became fluent in English, but it would not be valid.

Of the various forms of validity for which test-makers strive, the most important to the classroom teacher is *content validity*. Your tests will have content validity if the items that constitute them relate directly to (1) your objectives and (2) what you have taught, and if they represent a comprehensive sampling of the subject. An exam on France's political history from 1789 to 1914 would lack validity if it included the test item: "What is the meaning of the sentence *'Honi soit qui mal y pense'?*" But the question might be valid in a quiz on medieval French.

A fair sampling is an essential to content validity as the relevancy of the

Can a test be valid but unreliable?

Can a test be reliable but invalid?

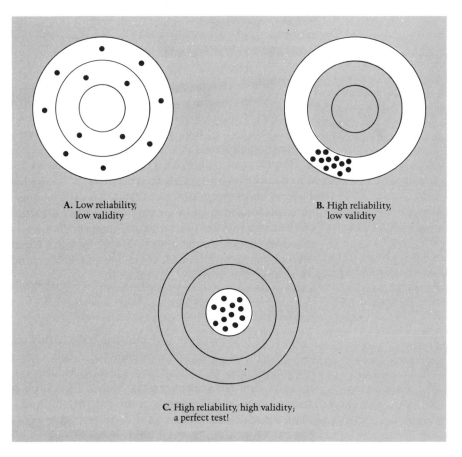

Figure 15.1. Good aim in testing takes both consistency and accuracy. In the diagrams, assume that the shots are responses to test items and the bullseye is the objective to be measured. Note that an unreliable test—one where responses are inconsistent, as in *A*—is automatically invalid. For example, an achievement test on which a student randomly guesses the response to each question gives an unreliable and invalid estimate of the student's knowledge. It is possible to achieve reliability and still miss the mark on validity, as in *B*. If a student always chooses option *A* on multiple-choice items, the score on a particular test, no matter how many times it was administered, would be consistent. But the score would not be an accurate reflection of the student's knowledge. A good test must produce a score that is both reliable and valid: in target *C*, responses are quite consistent and accurate.

items, yet even college and university professors sin on that score. In a survey of college students' complaints about tests, Milton and Edgerly (1976) came across a quiz in a course that covered 2500 years of philosophy: five of the seven questions centered on Immanuel Kant. That test, a final, lacked content validity.

Ensuring that your tests relate to your objectives and fairly sample content as a whole need not be so difficult as it may seem. Test developers have found two tools to help build content validity into tests. Understanding and using the first tool, a taxonomy, will prepare you to use the second, a table of specifications.

TAXONOMIES AND THEIR USE

A test's purpose may be merely to measure memorized knowledge, of course, and a test may be designed to that end. But a teacher interested in determining higher levels of cognition may intend a test to explore students' capacities in, say, application, and yet develop a test that examines only knowledge. A taxonomy can help avert such bloopers. The taxonomies used in education classify different types of learning and performance. When employed to develop objectives, as they often are, taxonomies help teachers plan for more than mere rote memorization by students. In test construction, taxonomies aid in avoiding the pitfall of measuring only one type of learning when measurement of many types is desired.

Several ready-made taxonomies are available. You may recall one, Benjamin Bloom's Taxonomy of the Cognitive Domain, introduced in Chapter 7. The first level of learning in Bloom's taxonomy is knowledge. After that come comprehension, application, analysis, synthesis, and, finally, evaluation (Bloom et al., 1956).

How would a taxonomy such as Bloom's be applied to preparation of a test? Suppose you are teaching a course in psychology and are faced with constructing a quiz. If you wish to determine whether or not your students have done more than memorize the material you presented, you will ask questions based on the various levels of the taxonomy, as in the following:

1. Define positive and negative reinforcement. (A student could respond here out of memory. The item taps the *knowledge* level only.)
2. In your own words and in terms of your own experiences, explain what positive and negative reinforcement mean to you. (A response requires *comprehension* in addition to knowledge because students must do more than parrot definitions.)
3. Here are several situations. Some are examples of positive reinforcement, some of negative reinforcement, and some of neither. Classify the situations. (This requires application because the student must possess the information and extend it to new or unfamiliar circumstances.)
4. Here is a situation in which a behavior needs to be changed. Determine what environmental forces contribute to the behavior and set up a program using positive reinforcement. (This item requires both *analysis* and *synthesis*. First, the student must identify the elements in an unfamiliar situation and judge the influence of each. Then the information must be synthesized or put back together again in a new pattern or structure.)
5. Johnny's teacher has designed the following behavior change program to

increase Johnny's attention span. Do you think it will work? Why or why not? (All of the previous levels of the taxonomy have been combined here, and the student has been asked to speculate and make a judgment. Evaluation is required because a new situation must be appraised and an outcome must be predicted.)

Why use a taxonomy to develop a test?

Your test, of course, need not measure each level of cognition. How much of it you devote to any level depends on your students' age and development, the material studied, and the sort of learning you have been teaching toward. It is important to remember that each level of Bloom's taxonomy subsumes the previous levels. If a student correctly answers an analysis-level question, you may fairly assume that he or she has memorized the relevant content and can comprehend and apply it. But, if the student misses, you cannot easily tell what he has learned, unless he has answered other items at lower cognitive levels.

There will be times when you feel that none of the ready-made taxonomies precisely fits your needs. In that case, you may want to compile one of your own that does. Teaching French, Spanish, or German, say, you could construct a list made up of *knowledge, comprehension,* and *ability to express ideas.* In chemistry, your list might embrace *memorization, application,* and *prediction;* i.e., the ability to estimate the consequences of an experiment.

A taxonomy, home-made or hand-me-down, simply clarifies for you the levels of student attainment that you want to measure and facilitates the selection of test items: taxonomies work for any subject on any level.

TABLES OF SPECIFICATION

Knowing what you want to measure does not in itself guarantee test validity. You must still select a representative sample of the content. It is easy to forget something or to overemphasize one area at the expense of others. To avoid such bungles, we employ the second tool of test construction—a table of specification. See the example in Figure 15.2. In the table, aspects of the subject matter, you notice, comprise a vertical list at the table's left. Aspects of behavior extend horizontally across the top. The simple figures indicate the number of questions you are asking in one area of content and on one level of behavior. The figures with # in front of them indicate the test items' position in the quiz. The table in Figure 15.2 is only a sample; if you are going to use a table, you usually will find it best to produce your own.

How does a table of specification work?

In building a table, first determine how you are going to summarize the content area; then, using a taxonomy, decide on the levels of test questions. Next, write the items. Note on the table how many of them you have for each area. You don't have to number the items, as in Figure 15.2, but many teachers find that the practice speeds the assembly of the test. A table of specification constitutes, in effect, a running scoreboard which makes it more likely you will cover the ground that you want to cover and emphasize the points that

Subject matter or area*	Types of cognition or behavior		
	knowledge	concepts	application
A.	Items #1, 8, 12	#3, 6	#2, 11
B.	#15	#18, 19	#4, 5, 10
C.			
D.			

*Can be objectives, or outline of content, or key ideas and concepts.

Figure 15.2. Table of Specification

you want to emphasize. (This is the purpose of noting the number of items in each area on your table.) A table of specification takes time to prepare. But it helps to give a test reliability and content validity (Chapter 14), and particularly to minimize a major problem of teacher-made tests (see pp. 479–480)— poor sampling of content.

Choosing Kinds of Tests

Tests, as you know from experience, fall in two broad categories, *objective* and *essay* types. The objective variety, which include *true-false, matching,* and *multiple-choice* items, gets its name from the fact that any trained examiner will come up with the same score as any other trained examiner; there is no room for subjective judgment in the scoring. The term *objective,* in this case, does not refer to an exam's planning or development, but has to do only with how a test is scored: a distorted, biased test could be objectively scored.

Recognition or production tests: Which do you prefer?

Perhaps a more accurate distinction between types of tests is *recognition* versus *production.* The first kind, of which multiple-choice tests are the most common, present possible answers to the student, who must try to recognize the best alternative. In the production category, examplified by essay or fill-in-the-blank tests, the student has to come up with his or her own response to a question. Do recognition and production tests measure different skills? Let's consider that issue as we discuss the advantages and disadvantages of both kinds starting with true-false recognition tests.

TRUE-FALSE TESTS

Because a true-false quiz presents the student with only two alternatives, the student obviously has a 50 percent chance of guessing the right answer. Such tests lack reliability if there are only a few items in the test. And remember, a threat to a test's reliability also endangers its validity. If, on a true-false test, a student gets 50 percent of the answers right by just guessing, his score does not mean he has mastered half of the content on which the test is supposed to evaluate him.

MATCHING TESTS

Tests with matching items, where a list of premises from one column must be matched with the appropriate response choice from a second column, decreases the likelihood that students will get items right by chance. The two lists to be matched can be any number of things: dates and events, points on a map, cities or countries, accomplishments, or pictures and names. The directions for matching items simply instruct students to make an association or connection between the members in the two columns. The matching activity is useful in determining if students can see relationships, make associations, or

"I've got to explain test results to the students. It isn't enough just to hand back their work with a mark on it—they look at the mark and stash it away. They need feedback on each item they miss, and some of them will need more work on those

simply remember knowledge-level information, such as the author of a particular book.

Hopkins and Antes (1979) offer several tips that will help you construct sturdy matching items. First, keep instructions simple and straightforward. Let students know if they can use a particular response more than once in the matching, or if each column choice may be used only once. It is usually best to have the number of items in the column from which the matching items or formulas are selected be greater than the number of items in the second column or list.

Would you use a table of specifications to help construct a matching test?

When selecting items to be included in the option lists, do not include wildly discrepant alternatives; a person's name in a list of dates will stand out and may give away an answer. In arranging the alternatives in column choices, if a logical order exists, it should be followed. For example, dates may be arranged chronologically, or names listed in alphabetical order. Finally, don't get carried away in developing matching tests. Keep your lists to a maximum of twelve items. Five to eight selections probably are the most efficient for students to scan for answers. If you need to include more choices, then two separate matching items might be more suitable.

MULTIPLE-CHOICE TESTS

The most commonly used of objective tests, the multiple-choice form greatly reduces the likelihood of good guessing. In a ten-item test in which each item offers four alternatives, the probability of getting seven right answers by luck, as Payne (1974) points out, is one in a thousand. But multiple-choice

concepts. Testing and grading take a lot of my time. I should have taken more courses on evaluation. Hah!"

tests are popular among test-givers for reasons other than their reliability. Among their major merits:

1. Items can be written to measure with fine discrimination almost any aspect of cognition in relation to the teacher's objectives.
2. They permit short answers to complex questions.
3. They are easily scored.
4. They allow evaluation of a wide range of content in a short time because test-takers do not have to produce responses, but only indicate the statements with which they agree.

Why are multiple-choice items so popular?

Some critics object that multiple-choice tests measure only memorized material. That generally is not true, but when it is, the fault is the writer's, not the format's. Multiple-choice items may be written to measure any level of the cognitive domain, although they are increasingly difficult to write as you move up the levels.

A multiple-choice item contains two major components, its stem and its alternative answers. The *stem*, which may be phrased as a question or a simple statement, is the part that reads, for example, "Most automobiles are propelled by...." Of the alternative responses, one is the correct answer and the others are the *distractors*, so-called because they are intended to distract or mislead students who are not certain of the correct answer. In this case, the alternative responses might be:

a. a steam engine
b. an electric storage battery
c. an internal combustion engine
d. a solar cell

The alternatives usually range in number from three to five: two would make guessing easy for the students, as in the case of true-false items, and more than five might be difficult for the teacher to find. (Good distractors can prove hard to come by.)

Writing Stems. Here are some suggestions for preparing multiple-choice stems:

Make your stem a clear and explicit embodiment of a fact or idea, as in "Printing with movable type was introduced by..." Avoid single-word stems.

Keep the stem free of nonessential details. In a stem that reads "The town of Valley Forge, *a pleasant, quiet place in southeastern Pennsylvania*, is best known as..," omit material of the kind we have italicized; it lengthens the time it takes to read the item and may confuse students.

Keep the stem free of background material. For example, in a question about the decisions reached at Yalta, avoid beginning "President Roosevelt, Prime Minister Churchill, and Josef Stalin met in the Russian resort of Yalta in World War II." Either your students should have learned that or you should not be asking the question. Your stem might simply say: "The Yalta Conference agreed that . . ."

Include in the stem all words that otherwise would require repetition in the alternative responses. For example:

Water boils when heated to
a. 32 degrees F.
b. 100 degrees F.
c. 112 degrees F.
d. 212 degrees F.

Rather than:

Water boils
a. when heated to 32 degrees F.
b. when heated to 100 degrees F.
c. when heated to 112 degrees F.
d. when heated to 212 degrees F.

Put your stems in positive rather than negative form whenever possible, avoiding *no, none, not, never* and *except*. It is better to ask "Which of these four men served as President of the United States?" than to say "None of these men served as President of the United States except." If you have to use a negative, underline it or capitalize it to lessen the chance that it will confuse students.

Scrutinize your stems for clues that give away the answer. If your stem reads "The mammal with the longest gestation period is an" and your alternative responses are

a. horse
b. jackal
c. raccoon
d. elephant
e. mouse

What are the characteristics of a good multiple-choice test?

the article *an* will point to the correct choice.

Although stems may be phrased as declarative statements or as questions, testing experts recommend the question form on the ground that the teacher is less likely to slip up and fall into ambiguities.

Writing Distractors. Good distractors are as important as good stems. Here are some guidelines for contriving distractors:

Make the distractors as plausible and as logical to students who don't know their stuff as the correct response. Avoid incongruities: if your stem reads "Christopher Marlowe was" your alternative responses should *not* be a diverse collection like this:

a. a signer of the Declaration of Independence

b. a pioneer English surgeon
c. an Elizabethan dramatist
d. an Antarctic explorer

It might be better to write the stem as "Christopher Marlowe wrote the" and offer such alternative responses as:

a. novel, *Vicar of Wakefield*
b. poem, *The Ancient Mariner*
c. play, *Dr. Faustus*
d. treatise, *The Anatomy of Melancholy*

Try to keep the right answer the same length as the distractors and in the same style. If your question reads "Which of these is a prepositional phrase?" avoid alternative responses such as:

What are important rules for writing multiple-choice items?

a. as they approached the building from South Street
b. of the plumbing system
c. now is the time for all good men to come to the aid of their country
d. after they have finished reading the assigned text

Because it stands out from the others, the right answer would be easy to guess, even for a student who could not ordinarily tell a preposition from a proposition. Better alternatives might be:

"We have 'See Me' times at various times during the day and the child can come up and talk to either of us about what the problem is. We try to make sure every child understand what the grade means, why they got it, and—most important —what they did wrong. I go over it until they understand and can do it right. We call them 'See Me' papers."

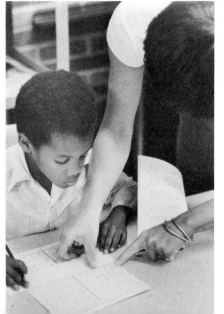

a. as they approached
b. of the plumbing
c. now is the time
d. after they finished

Alternate the position of the correct response, sometimes putting it first, sometimes last, sometimes in the middle.

When alternative responses are figures, give them in numerical order, as:

a. 10
b. 26
c. 49
d. 100

Make your alternative responses mutually exclusive, so that only one answer is correct.

Rarely use "all of the above" or "none of the above." If you do, be sure to mix up correct and incorrect instances. Using "all of the above" as a space-filler will quickly cue students not to choose it. If, on the other hand, the "all" or "none" options are consistently used as the correct responses, they will be readily chosen by the student forced to guess.

ESSAY TESTS

Proponents of essay tests contend that such tests permit students to manifest learning and creativity in ways that multiple-choice and other objective tests do not. Instead of regurgitating what they have been taught, students (the argument goes) have the opportunity to synthesize information and explore the relationships among ideas.

What are the merits of essay items?

Experts on testing, however, point to certain weaknesses of the essay test, and their cautions merit consideration. One objection has to do with content validity (Marshall and Hales, 1971). A unit of study on which you wish to test your class may embody more than a dozen important points. If you pose an essay question for each point, your test is likely to prove too long for the usual one-hour testing period. Reduce the number of questions and you reduce the content validity. You can limit this effect by incorporating several points in a single question. But attempts to ensure content validity may negate a major reason for giving essay tests, which is to avoid a mere playback of acquired information. When your test questions allow a student to go beyond the basic content of the subject and to explore relationships, the questions themselves threaten content validity. And if a student does not do well on such questions, you cannot tell whether the student does not know the fundamentals or simply cannot cope with the questions.

A second major objection concerns scoring. It takes a great deal of time to score essay examinations. If you have thirty students and devote only five minutes to each paper, you will spend two and a half hours on scoring one test.

If you have four classes of that size and give several essay tests in each grading period, time will definitely be a problem. A friend who teaches in high school tells us his enthusiasm for essay exams faded rapidly after he gave all of his English literature classes simultaneously an essay midterm. He found himself with 700 pages of hurried scrawl to be graded within four days!

In addition to being tedious and time-consuming, the scoring of essay exams can be unreliable, and that may be one of the essay test's most important limitations. In a classic study that has been repeated a number of times in recent years with similar results, 142 English teachers graded two test papers. Their scores for one paper ranged from 50 to 98 and on the other paper from 64 to 99 (Starch and Elliott, 1912). It isn't that the tests are necessarily unreliable, but that the scores are, often with good reason. (The papers that one grades at 7:00 P.M., while one is still relatively fresh, may receive very different attention from those which are read in the weariness of 2:00 A.M.)

Another problem of essay exams is that irrelevant factors may influence scoring. Judgments of essay quality are susceptible to *halo effects*, in which a single attribute or characteristic colors the whole. For example, in scoring a handwritten response to a question, a teacher may have difficulty reading the writing. Sloppy script may introduce an expectation of sloppy organization, even though all the required information is in the response. A neat, punctuation-perfect essay may gain unearned points. (More will be said about halo effects in the classroom in Chapter 16.)

How would you minimize the problems of essay tests?

So experts at testing often recommend objective rather than essay tests. But on occasion you may feel that your goals can be met only by an essay test. You will not be able to eliminate all the problems, but you may be able to cut them down to size. The guidelines that follow will help.

Writing Essay-Test Questions. In preparing an essay test, try these procedures:

Give your self plenty of time for the writing of each item. As a teacher just starting out, you may hear from your elders that essay questions are easy to prepare but difficult to grade and that multiple-choice questions have the opposite attributes. In fact, writing *good* essay questions demands time, thought, and effort.

Build questions around problems to be solved. If you are going to measure only memory, you'll be better off with an objective test.

Define the problems clearly. You want to be sure that all your students interpret each question in the same way; otherwise you may have them writing good answers to the wrong questions.

What guidelines can be used in composing essay questions?

Limit each problem. You may be tempted to give students lots of leeway, but it is better to avoid asking them to deal with broad areas of content. Decide what knowledge or skill you want specifically demonstrated by their answers, and write your question accordingly. In a psychology course, for example, the test item "Discuss reinforcement" would be far too broad. If you want to determine basic understanding, you would do better to state the problem thus: "Distinguish among positive reinforcement, negative reinforcement, and punishment." If you want to test students' knowledge of theories of reinforcement, you might request: "Compare two theories of why reinforcers work."

Avoid asking optional questions. If you include optional questions, you are giving, in effect, several different tests and thus are unable to compare students fairly. No question, as a rule, should be in a test unless it is important to measuring achievement. Every question should be important, and every student should be expected to tackle every question.

Prepare for your own use a key to each question's answer. If you have written

Holistic Evaluation of Essays

The ease of constructing essay exams (or assignments) is usually offset by the difficulty of their grading. A new scoring approach, called *holistic evaluation,* suggests a way to streamline the scoring of essays without compromising validity or reliability. Holistic evaluation differs from traditional scoring methods in a number of ways. First, it is generally done by at least two readers. In some cases a whole team of teachers grades a group of papers. The final score for a paper is the average of all the evaluators' scores. The scores are based upon the readers' impressions of the whole rather than the precise details of the paper. Holistic evaluation emphasizes attention to ideas as well as the mechanics of writing. By establishing the ground rules for scoring before reading a single paper—a requirement of the holistic approach—neither of these aspects is shortchanged.

The chart below shows an example of a holistic rating scale used in scoring English writing assignments. Notice that the ratings range from "low" to "high" with corresponding numeric values. Either a general rating of the paper may be given, using the verbal descriptors, or a point rating may be given, using the numeric system. Either rating can be easily translated to letter grades.

Because the grading is based upon the whole rather than the details, it is rapid. Once a paper

is read it should take no more than a minute or two to score. The system also has the potential to be more reliable and objective than traditional methods. The same criteria are applied to each paper. When more than one rater scores each paper there is less chance for personal bias to dramatically influence grades.

But this new approach should not be expected to replace traditional methods of evaluating students' writing. In-depth analysis of compositions is sometimes important and should not be eliminated entirely. For example, marginal notations correcting spelling or punctuation in papers help students learn to avoid those mistakes in the future. In the holistic approach, those corrections are not made. If you assign classwork, homework, or tests with essays, it may be best to use both approaches: score half of the writings with the holistic method and score the remaining essays in detail. ■

	Low		Middle		High
General Merit					
Ideas	2	4	6	8	10
Organization	2	4	6	8	10
Wording	1	2	3	4	5
Flavor	1	2	3	4	5
Mechanics					
Usage	1	2	3	4	5
Punctuation	1	2	3	4	5
Spelling	1	2	3	4	5
Handwriting	1	2	3	4	5
					Total

a question well, you should be able to identify the major points that the answer should include. The key will prove useful when you score the papers.

Reading the Answers. When you mark a test, it is a good idea to read all the answers to your first question before you tackle the second question, and so on. The procedure will help to keep you honest, because if you read all of John's paper, and then all of Jill's paper, your judgment may be subtly influenced. For example, if John muffed Question 1, you may approach his answer to Question 2 with more skepticism than it deserves. And if Jill had a superb answer to Question 1, you may tend to give her the benefit of any doubt on Question 2. Even a paper's position in the pile may affect the mark you give. A C-student's test might end up with a D if you have just finished an A paper, or with a B if you have just marked an F paper. Many teachers take the precaution of having students sign their test papers on the back of the last page rather than at the top of the first page, so that marks will be less weighted by teacher-student relationships. That works only to a degree, though, because in elementary and high school classes of ordinary size, handwriting may identify the pupil.

Dealing with Raw Scores

Once you have constructed, administered, and graded your tests, you will need to make sense of the scores. If the first paper you graded produced a score of 85, you might think that student had done pretty well. But if the next paper rates 94, and the twenty-three papers that follow score from 90 to 100, the 85 will no longer impress you. These are raw scores and provide only limited information to you and your students. For these scores to be made more useful, they will need to be examined in certain ways and interpreted more carefully. This section of the chapter will suggest some methods to use to examine the scores and will offer some clues to understanding the meanings of groups of scores.

CENTRAL TENDENCY OF SCORES

What is the meaning of *central tendency*?

Whenever you test a group of individuals, whether you are measuring their height and weight, their cognitive skills, or anything else, you will find that the results tend to cluster around one point, or sometimes, around several points. In the middle of the cluster will be one score that is most representative of all the scores. That score is the *mean* or *average score*, arrived at, of course, by adding up all the scores and dividing the total by the number of scores involved.

The habit that scores have of clustering is called *central tendency*, and focusing on a central tendency is a good way to make sense of raw scores.

Calculating a central tendency value permits comparison of raw scores with a standard.

How do the mean, median, and mode differ? When are they identical?

Besides the mean score, there are two other measures of central tendency. One of these is the *median*, which is the score in the middle when you put all the scores in order from lowest to highest. It is often used when scores pile up unevenly on one side of the arithmetic mean. The median lets us find the midpoint of the group; 50 percent of the scores fall above the median of any distribution and 50 percent fall below it, no matter how uneven the distribution looks.

The third measure of central tendency is the *mode*. The mode of any group of scores is the most frequently occurring score. It may show up anywhere in the distribution, although it is usually found toward the midpoint. When the distribution is perfectly symmetrical—an unusual event—the mean, median, and mode will be equal.

PERCENTILES AND GRADE EQUIVALENTS

How would you interpret a percentile score of 1?

Publishers of standardized tests usually try to make raw scores more informative by converting the raw scores to *percentile scores* or *grade-equivalent scores* and sometimes to both. A *percentile score* tells a student and the teacher where the student stands in relation to other people who have taken the test. A percentile score of 75 indicates that 25 percent of the other people made raw scores as good as or better than that particular student's, and 75 percent did worse. A *grade-equivalent score* tells student and teacher where the student stands in relation to schooling in general. Suppose that a raw score, whatever it is, has been converted to a *grade-equivalent score* of 6.1. That 6.1 figure represents what an *average* pupil in the first month of the sixth grade would achieve: grade-equivalent scores are arrived at by taking a representative sample of student performance each month at each grade level and averaging the resulting scores. If the raw score was made by a youngster who is indeed in the first month of the sixth grade, the pupil is performing at grade level; if the student is an eighth grader, he or she obviously is working below grade level. Knowing that is useful to a point. But you would be unwise, as a teacher, to set grade-equivalency as your target.

What limits interpretation of a grade-equivalent score?

Because most classes in American schools are grouped by student ability, as we mentioned in Chapter 14, it is likely that the average performance of a class will *not* be precisely at grade level: high-ability groups will score above their grade level, and low-ability groups below. Even if you teach in a school where students are not grouped homogeneously, do not expect all your pupils in a class to perform at grade equivalency. In almost any mixed ability class, half the students will be above and the other half below average. And students will keep moving about that average point. Some students will show bursts in learning in midyear, some at year's end. Although grade-equivalent scores tell us more than do raw scores, they should not be treated as infallible or the ultimate goal of any classroom. They are estimated from large groups of children and may not accurately reflect the circumstances unique to your class. They may be most useful and informative when interpreted in conjunction with your own teacher-made classroom tests, the tests you will probably be using to grade your students.

Grading

Grades are quite new in education's long history. For centuries students never enjoyed the satisfaction of an A or suffered the trauma of an F. As a student yourself, or as a prospective teacher, you may have wondered whether there should be any grades now. But before you crawl too far out on that limb, consider these three facts:

1. Grades represent a teacher's periodic reports on student progress and thus provide the feedback that acts as reinforcement or punishment to the student.

Why grade? Why not?

2. For most students, grades serve as incentives for motivating achievement.*
3. Most schools require some form of grading for the reasons discussed in Chapter 14.

So for you the issue is likely to be not whether to grade but *how*. That *how* may take you aback. Doesn't grading come naturally? Isn't it just a matter of common sense? The answer to both questions is no. Grading is a complex affair, and the grades you give may affect the courses of your students' lives. Knowing how to grade is an important component of knowing how to teach. Yet many future teachers receive little or no training in that aspect of their profession, and the complaints of students and parents about grades often seem justified.

METHODS OF GRADING

Grading involves evaluation, which by nature is subjective and dependent on comparisons. Of the various bases of comparison widely used in schools, none is flawless, and as a teacher you should be aware of their merits and demerits. Let's consider the most common ways of comparing and grading.

Grading on the Curve. Grading on the curve—the bell-shaped curve of statistics—simply applies the norm-referenced model, or relative, measurement described in Chapter 14. In norm-referenced evaluation, students are graded by comparing them with their peers as we indicated: the brightest get the few As, a majority get Bs, Cs, and Ds, and the few who are left Fs. Usually no rules fix the proportions of the class that are to receive each grade. But some

---

* Although it is a complicated issue, pass-fail grading has repeatedly been shown to be a less powerful incentive for achievement.

instructors decide in advance how many As, Bs, etc., to award, and where students fall in the statistical distribution becomes more important than their actual scores. That procedure can have some odd results: Hills (1976) passes on a story about a graduate school in which an instructor always gives a five-student class one A, one B, one C, one D, and one F. So a forewarned class of five hauled a vagrant off the street and hired him to attend lectures and serve as a lightning rod for the F. Still other instructors follow a normal curve distribution, so that As equal Fs in number, Bs equal Ds, and Cs outnumber them all.

What is the meaning of norm-referenced grades?

The norm-referenced model has its allurements. It rests on the assumption—often verified—that abilities and achievement are normally distributed. It saves teachers the trouble of setting standards, and its arbitrary workings demand little explanation to administrators, parents, or students.

But the norm-referenced model has its failings as well. Its interpretation is difficult because it offers a single ambiguous meaning: relative rank. It tells nothing about what a student knows or does not know, merely that he has performed better or worse than his peers. A good class with a good instructor will likely achieve only as many As and Bs as a poor class with a poor instructor; and the outside world will never know that some As were of gold and some of tin. But the good class and the good teacher know, and feel frustrated and cheated. The B or C received in their honors class would probably be a solid A in a less competitive class. Because norm-referenced evaluation demands ranking of students, it is often criticized as fostering excessive competition. When students resort to cheating and sabotage of peers' work to raise their own rank, it is time for serious consideration of alternate evaluation systems.

What is the meaning of criterion-referenced grades?

Grading by Standards. In this approach, which derives from the *criterion-referenced measurement* described in Chapter 14, teachers set standards and base grades on their attainment. If you use behavioral objectives (see Chapter 7), you already have a head start on a criterion-referenced system of evaluation. For a class in typing, the standard for an A might be forty words per minute for five 200-word pages with a maximum of four erasures. For an algebra class, the standard might be the correct completion of nine out of ten problems in twenty-five minutes. Proponents of criterion-referenced evaluation argue that where a student stands in class is less important than the demonstration of knowledge or skill, and that in the norm-referenced model an entire class might fail to reach the teacher's objectives but the top failure would still rate an A.

The criterion-referenced model presents its problems too, though. How does the teacher determine standards, which are nowhere graven in stone? Standards set too high invite excessive failures. Standards set too low bring down a hail of protest on other teachers that they are being unduly tough. Should standards once fixed be raised for unusually bright classes? Lowered for slow classes? If so, then an A in one class has a different meaning in another, one of the faults of the norm-referenced system.

Criterion-referenced evaluation does not fit easily into the style of A-through-F grading. Mastery of an objective obviously merits an A, but how much error will earn a B, and how much more will earn a C? For each objective you may have to develop several performance standards, each corresponding to a grade. But it is also possible that you will expect certain objectives to be accomplished only by A students. For a B, students might show mastery of a subset of the entire list of objectives.

How are perform- ance standards developed for criterion- referenced evaluation?

An alternative would be to tie letter grades to various proportions of the full list of objectives. It may be necessary to state the various subsets in advance. Instead, if all the objectives are equally important, mastery of a stated number of objectives would earn different grades. For example, students who master 90 percent of the total list of objectives would get an A; Bs would go to students who master 80 to 89 percent of the list, and so on. Thus, marking can be based on demonstrated knowledge and skill, and reflect different levels of mastery without falling into the traps associated with a norm-referenced system. All students or none can earn any grade (something not possible in the norm-referenced model), and students would not have to compete with each other to reach the top of the grade pile. Furthermore, students could know in advance what percentage of mastery they would have to show to earn any grade.

What are the pros and cons of some common grading systems?

Grading on Growth. Some teachers grade on the basis of educational growth between a starting point, designated Time 1, and a finish line, designated Time 2: students who demonstrate the most progress get the highest grades. The flaw here is that the student who knows most about the subject at Time 1 is penalized because he has less room to grow. Another is that growth grades are nearly impossible to interpret. Is the gain from 0 percent to 20 percent of course content equivalent to a change from 75 percent to 95 percent? Finally, when the word gets around, some loafers will hide what they know at the start, then demonstrate an enormous burst of "achievement."

Grading on Expectations. In this approach, grades are based on what the teacher believes a student can do rather than on the student's performance relative to a standard or a norm. One teacher's admonition to a pupil makes the point: "Johnny, I know you made the highest score in the class but I'm not going to give you an A because you can do a great deal more than you are doing. You have the ability and the talent but you are not using them the way you could. So I'm giving you a B and I'm going to keep on giving you a B until you're doing your very best."

But teachers often are not good judges of capability. How does Johnny's teacher really know what Johnny can do? So this method does not lend itself to general application in a classroom. A few students of our own, however, have confided that teachers like Johnny's did stir them to greater effort. Good and Brophy (1977) report that confident and generally successful students are sometimes turned off by praise, but increase their efforts when mild criticism is offered. Once in a while, then, if you have an obviously bright student whose marks are pretty good but who isn't trying hard, you may want to grade the way Johnny's teacher did.

What ethical issues are involved in grading on expectations?

Some recent research supports the possible influence of expectations on achievement. Means et al. (1979) found improvements in student work when teacher expectations differed from feedback. An example: Before the lesson, a teacher remarks, "I think you will have trouble with this," (negative expectancy) but after the lesson she praises the student's work (positive feedback). The opposite mixture also proved effective: "You should do well on this assignment," but later, "I am surprised that you haven't done better."

We do not propose that you contrive dishonest combinations of expectations and grades to boost achievement. There will be ample opportunity to express genuine surprise or disappointment. Be alert to expectation's effects, though. If it sours a student, be ready to shift to an alternative evaluation method.

Humanistic Grading. Student and teacher together determine the student's grades. This system is applicable only to the humanistic approach to education advocated by Carl Rogers (1969). In that approach, students set their

---

Grading without Objectives

Some teachers attempt to use a criterion-referenced grading system without goal statements or objectives. They specify standards (see the box on "Grading with Objectives") and then grade students on whether or not the students correctly answer a certain percentage of, say, test items. Two problems flaw this technique.

The first difficulty arises from the use of arbitrary percentages: If the test items are easy, most of the class could score 90 percent without knowing much. If the test items are difficult, the same students might score only 30 percent. The percentage alone provides insufficient feedback about learning.

The second difficulty is that without objectives it is hard to determine whether or not the test is representative of the whole content area or domain being measured. A test slanted toward one small portion of the domain will not tell much about (1) the student who has learned only that portion, and scores well, or (2) the student who has learned a good part of the whole domain but scores poorly on the biased sample of questions.*

Use of objectives or goal statements should reduce these difficulties. Precise goal statements help to maximize accurate feedback from a criterion-referenced system. Besides, goal statements can be examined and revised on the basis of their difficulty, sequence, level of required knowledge, and relevance to larger goals.■

* See pp. 481–484 for a discussion of proper content sampling in achievement testing.

Grading with Objectives

Suppose you have a class with a record of average achievement and no serious disipline problems. You decide to try out a criterion-referenced system. Incorporating some suggestions from your students, you establish a list of objectives. You are expected to continue to use the A–F grading procedure, so you draw up a chart:

A = completion of 100 percent of the objectives
B = 95 percent
C = 90 percent
D = 85 percent
F = less than 85 percent

To your surprise, no student makes it into the A-or-B range, and only three reach C level. Rather than dump your criterion-referenced system, you might look for the reasons your students did not do so well as you had expected. Some possible explanations:

1. Your objectives were too difficult.
2. The standards (percentages) were too high.
3. Your test items were too tough or too ambiguous.
4. Your teaching focused on things other than the objectives.
5. Your test items did not measure the content.
6. You failed to motivate the students or arouse their interest in the objectives.
7. You did not share the objectives with the students.

Now, let us suppose that everyone in the class achieves 100 percent of the objectives. Are you justified in assuming that everything is going perfectly? Why or why not? ∎

own objectives and measure their own progress. The teacher evaluates that progress with the student, and the two together arrive at a grade. Generally, there is little testing, and what there is of it is designed for summing up what has been learned, rather than for grading.

One sizable problem with the system is that many students are ill-prepared to set their objectives. They have not had much practice thinking about what they could learn or accomplish in a particular field of study. Consider how much training and practice in educational goal-setting you have had in your dozen or so years of schooling. Were you prepared to design your own course-work?

Is humanistic grading a realistic alternative?

Realistic goal-setting and self-criticism, essentials for grading oneself, are learned skills. If you choose a humanistic approach to grading, you must first help your students develop the abilities they will need to share in establishing objectives and assessing progress on their own. Provide plenty of opportunities for students to practice the required skills, and give them feedback as to how well they are doing. A common error is to introduce the method too abruptly. If your class is the only one in the school in which students participate in goal-setting and evaluation, you may want to apply it gradually. That way is likely to prove more successful than abrupt presentation by one teacher in one classroom for one year. Unfortunately, the one-teacher, one-year situation is common, particularly in high school.

"Grading has always been a struggle for me. It's hard to be objective, it's hard to know if I've been fair, it's hard to give negative feedback to children—especially those who try like hell and still don't accomplish much. I've decided that I simply will not grade on effort. It's such a subjective thing and I think I used to do it just to avoid giving honest marks. It seems arbitrary, but I think there are plenty of ways to reward effort in a class—just not on an academic test.

COMMON ERRORS IN EVALUATING

Whatever system of grading a teacher uses, there are several ways in which things can go wrong, usually because of faulty practices on the teacher's part. Some common errors:

1. Use of poorly constructed tests.
2. Grading without tests or careful assessment involving checklists, projects, and the like. Observation too often is based on general and vague impressions, glib speech, politeness, and other characteristics not related to academic achievement.
3. Grading on the result of a single test.

What are the major pitfalls in grading?

4. Giving too many tests, which cut into time for instruction.
5. Teaching to fit a standardized test. Such tests are designed to *sample* students' knowledge and to cover far more material than any one course can or should include. Teaching to such tests distorts evaluations.
6. Changing the difficulty of tests during the course. Some teachers give extremely difficult midterms in the hope that students will do very well on easier final exams. Others give easy midterms to provide student with experience of success in preparation for difficult final exams. The better way is to inform students what will be expected of them and keep the tests at that level.
7. Grading students on the basis of behavior such as tardiness, absences, sloppiness, failure to turn in homework, or reluctance to participate in classroom activity. Grades should reflect academic achievement, and should not be employed to enforce discipline.*
8. Grading to avoid hurt feelings or to be "democratic." Some teachers tend to give all students Cs so that the laggards will not grieve and the brighter pupils will not flaunt their success. That practice negates the purpose of grading.
9. Obscuring the criteria you use to determine grades. The commonest way to commit this *faux pas* is simply to fail to tell your students your goals or performance objectives for them. Unless they know what you expect, studying for a test or writing a critical paper may become an exercise in trying to read your mind. Then, students most adept at that guessing game will earn the highest grades, even though they may not have learned the most. Another way to err is to make an assignment or give a test without telling students how much it will count toward their total grade. Informed in advance of a project's or exam's importance, students are likely to spend more time and effort on the task than they would otherwise.

---

* The official grading policy of many schools contradicts our suggestion. When nonacademic behavior contributes to a grade, the grade becomes less reliable, less valid, and less interpretable. There is no compelling evidence that links such grading procedures with improved motivation or fewer discipline problems.

CONCLUSIONS

Grading, as we said earlier, is a complex issue. You may adopt one of the methods we have discussed or you may arrive at one of your own. In any case,

---

Suggested Questions for Self-Evaluation

Here is a self-evaluation form that one of our colleagues uses in his college classes (Stanwyck, 1977, p. 305). This type of questionnaire can be used in a traditional classroom for additional input in assigning grades, or in a humanistic classroom as the sole or primary basis for determining grades. ■

[NOTE: The *"Final Statement"* (item 8) *must* appear at the end of your self-evaluation report, and *must* be signed.]

1. What did I want from this course, professionally and personally?

2. To what extent did I get what I wanted?

3. To what extent am I personally responsible for getting—or for not getting—what I wanted? (Note: Explicit sentences can be helpful for this, e.g.: "I got X because I . . ."; and "I might have gotten Y if I had . . .")

4. To what extent did I invest myself in course requirements and activities?
   a. Did I do more than "minimum-to-get-by"? How? How much?
   b. When—and how seriously—did I begin carrying out my Project?

5. What, if anything, have I gained from this course experience which I did not expect? To what extent are these incidental gains the result of *my* investment? How?

6. In what ways, if any, have my ideas changed about:
   a. Education?
   b. Teaching?
   c. Children?
   d. Myself?

7. What, if any, changes do I expect (or plan) to make in my professional and/or personal *behavior* as direct or indirect result of this course experience? When?

8. Final Statement:
   "On the basis of my serious and honest consideration of the above question, and/or other questions as indicated, I hereby assert that I deserve a grade of _____ for aspects of my course performance which are not otherwise evaluated."

Signed)_____

you will necessarily be influenced by the policies of your school. You will have to determine early what the rules are there, but do not be surprised if you find that they are not well developed. Despite the importance that grades have in modern education and in later life, little time and effort have been devoted to creating a philosophy of grading.

Summary

On standardized tests, *percentile scores* indicate where students stand in relation to others who have taken the test: a percentile score of 75 means that the student surpassed 74 percent of those tested. A *grade-equivalent score* represents what average children in a given grade can do.

In preparing your own test, it is advisable to consider the test's purpose, the important points you have taught, how much emphasis to place on each point, the achievement level of your class, and the conditions under which the test will be given. Use of a *taxonomy*—published or drawn up by you—and the charting of a *table of specification* will help to give your test *reliability* and *validity*. Reliability ensures consistent scores. Validity means that the test accurately measures what you intend it to measure.

Tests fall into two broad categories, *objective* and *essay*, which affect how the tests are scored. Another way of viewing tests is in terms of what students are asked to do—to recognize or to produce information. The objective recognition type, which is most widely used, usually consists of multiple choices, of which one is the right answer and the others *distractors*, designed to mislead ill-prepared students. Distractors should be plausible and logical, and they demand much effort to contrive. Multiple-choice tests are easy to score. Essay tests, their proponents contend, give students more opportunity to display their learning and creativity. But it is difficult to control an essay test's reliability and validity, and such tests are difficult to score because judgments are subjective.

An understanding of the various approaches to grading is essential to teachers. In the *norm-referenced model*, students are graded on the basis of their standing in class. In the *criterion-referenced model*, grades depend on comparison of performance with standards set in advance. Some teachers grade on the amount of educational growth between a starting point and a finish line. Still others grade on the basis of what a student may be expected to achieve because of capabilities and talent, and give a bright underachiever a lower grade than the student's marks merit. In the humanistic approach to education, students and teachers set grades together.

All methods of grading have their flaws, and whatever system you adopt—one widely used or one you devise yourself—you will necessarily be influenced by the rules prevailing where you teach.

Chapter Study Guide

CHAPTER REVIEW

1. As a tenth-grade teacher you find that one of your students is reading at the 7.3 level. That would mean that the student

   a. had answered 73 percent of the test items correctly.
   b. ranked at the seventy-third percentile of those taking the test.
   c. reads at the same level as the *average* student in the third month of the seventh grade.
   d. reads at the same level as the *best* student in the third month of the seventh grade.

2. If you were an eighth-grade student and scored at the eighty-second percentile on a test, it would mean that

   a. 18 percent of the people taking the test scored equal to or better than you.
   b. 18 percent of the people taking the test scored equal to or worse than you.
   c. you performed at the same level as the *average* student in the second month of the eight grade.
   d. you performed better than eighty-two students.

3. If a teacher took the scores on a test and ranked them, assigning grades on the basis of the ordering of the scores so that most of the scores received a grade of C, which grading model would the teacher be following?

   a. central tendency
   b. norm-referenced
   c. criterion-referenced
   d. true score

4. At the end of the grading period a teacher gave each student a questionnaire that required the students to assess their own performance for that grading period. What philosophy of teaching and grading was this teacher following?

   a. cognitivist
   b. behaviorist
   c. progressive
   d. humanistic

5. If a teacher withholds an A from a student because he or she consistently scores high on tests with no apparent effort, the teacher is following the grading model known as

   a. criterion-referenced.
   b. norm-referenced.
   c. curve.
   d. expectation.

6. If a teacher awarded grades based on students' height, those grades would probably be

   a. unreliable and invalid.
   b. reliable but invalid.

c. reliable and valid.

d. unreliable but valid.

7. The _____ is the score in the middle when you put all the scores on a given test in order.

8. A system of classifying and ordering the various skills or processes involved in learning is called a _____.

9. Reliability and _____ are synonymous.

10. In order to have content validity the items on a test must show a _____ sampling of the subject.

11. One problem with essay tests is that the scoring is often _____.

12. The norm-referenced method of grading rests on the assumption that abilities and achievements are _____ distributed.

Answer questions 13–15 True or False:

13. A matching test would be termed a "production" measure because teachers must develop it.

14. Holistic evaluation is a norm-referenced system of grading.

15. Humanistic grading shifts much responsibility to the student.

FOR FURTHER THOUGHT

1. Suppose every student in the country were reading above grade level, because of some miraculous new instructional technique. The testing corporations retested students and refigured their norms; would all students now be above grade level in reading?

2. Explain the importance of using a taxonomy in designing a test; of using tables of specification.

3. It is sometimes said that tests, although they may motivate the able, discourage the poor student from trying. Tests and grades have also been known to encourage an elitist attitude among abler students. As a teacher, how would you avoid or minimize these destructive potentials of tests and grading? Consider such questions as: What should be the principal purpose of tests? of grades? Which grading model best realizes that purpose? Finally, in your opinion, are grades really necessary, or can their essential purposes be accomplished by other means?

IMPORTANT TERMS

reliability
validity
content validity
table of specification
objective test
recognition test

holistic evaluation
central tendency
mean
median
mode
raw score

production test

item stem

distractor

halo effect

percentile score (or rank)

grade-equivalent score

norm-referenced

criterion-referenced

SUGGESTED READINGS

The following twelve books are all good introductions to the use of tests and measurements in education. In general, each book discusses measurement terms, simple statistical techniques in measurement, issues in grading of student progress, and, most importantly, how to build suitable tests. Further, each book is written for the beginner, and little math background is necessary for a complete understanding of content.

AHMANN, J. S., and GLOCK, M. D. *Measuring and evaluating educational achievement* (2nd ed.). Boston: Allyn and Bacon, 1975.

GAY, L. R. *Educational evaluation and measurement.* Columbus, OH: Charles E. Merrill, 1980.

GREEN, J. A. *Teacher-made tests* (2nd ed.). New York: Harper and Row, 1975.

HILLS, J. R. *Measurement and evaluation in the classroom.* Columbus, OH: Charles. E. Merrill, 1976.

HOPKINS, C. D., and ANTES, R. L. *Classroom testing: Construction.* Itasca, IL: F. E. Peacock, 1979.

HOPKINS, C. D., and ANTES, R. L. *Classroom testing: Administration, scoring, and score interpretation.* Itasca, IL: F. E. Peacock, 1979.

LIEN, A. J. *Measurement and evaluation of learning* (3rd ed.). Dubuque, IA: Wm. C. Brown, 1976.

LINDEMAN, R. H., and MERENDA, P. F. *Educational measurement* (2nd ed.). Glenview, IL: Scott, Foresman, 1979.

MORRIS, L. T., and FITZ-GIBBON, C. T. *How to measure achievement.* Beverly Hills, CA: Sage, 1980.

SAX, G. *Principles of educational and psychological measurement and evaluation.* Belmont, CA: Wadsworth, 1980.

SCANNELL, D. P., and TRACY, D. B. *Testing and Measurement in the classroom.* Boston: Houghton Mifflin, 1975.

TUCKMAN, B. W. *Measuring educational outcomes: Fundamentals of testing.* New York: Harcourt Brace Jovanovich, 1975.

ANSWER KEY

1. c; 2. a; 3. b; 4. d; 5. d; 6. b; 7. representative; 8. taxonomy; 9. consistency; 10. comprehensive *or* representative; 11. unreliable; 12. normally; 13. F; 14. F; 15. T

PART

IV

The Call for Accountability

In Part IV we consider some of the ways in which education is responding to the public's call for accountability, or the assignment of responsibility for the outcomes of teaching. The response to accountability pressures takes two forms—innovations that are tried and tested on a national scale, and more modest efforts by individual teachers. In both forms the same questions arise: What strategies will enhance (or inhibit) the quality of instruction? How can I determine the value of a particular strategy?

16

Being Accountable

The Demand for Teacher Accountability

A few years ago, the *New York Times* reported that the parents of a high school graduate had sued their school district for $5 million on the ground it had failed to educate their son (January 20, 1977). The youth had his diploma but, his parents' lawyer said, he read at the fourth-grade level and could not add or subtract. The judge dismissed the actions, ruling that the parents had not proven their son's academic problems resulted from poor teaching, but the case exemplified the public's growing dissatisfaction with the outcomes of schooling.

How did the movement for accountability in the schools get started?

That lawsuit was not the first of its kind. Neither is it an entirely new idea to hold instructors accountable for the quality of their instruction: back in the 1400s, students at the University of Bologna fined their professors for straying off course. But through the 1970s the pressures for *teacher accountability* became greater for a number of reasons which we shall discuss shortly. In this chapter we will consider, among other topics, the public's increasingly questioning attitude toward the schools and the tendency to place the responsibility for students' inadequacies on educators. We will address those new directions in educational accountability on two levels. On one level, the issues arise largely from judicial decisions, legislation, and the national philosophy. The second level, which derives from research and common sense, involves you personally and your effect on your students.

The insistence on educators' accountability results from:

1. Evidence that students are learning less than they used to. Scores on the Scholastic Aptitude Test (SAT) and the American College Test (ACT) have declined dramatically in the last decade or so. University and college professors complain that their students write atrociously, and blame the students' high school English teachers, who blame the elementary school teachers, who blame the students' homes. (At least a dozen theories have been suggested to explain declining scholarship; the explanations range from academic irrelevance to agnostic irreverence.)
2. Rising school taxes and college tuition charges. In an era of consumer activism, taxpayers and parents have become more insistent on knowing what they are getting for their money in education as in everything else.
3. Increasing crime and violence in the schools. Staffs are "too easy," critics complain, on disruptive and law-breaking youngsters.
4. Broadened political power of racial minorities. Their voting strength and increased participation in civic affairs win them respectful hearings when they charge that schools shortchange minority children.
5. The fairly new premise that virtually any child can learn anything, given sufficient time and instruction.

Accountability in education sounds as simple and as reasonable as accountability in business or industry. When you buy an automobile or a washing machine, you expect the manufacturer and the dealer to stand behind their product and to make good if something proves wrong with it. Why should not educators provide the warranties for what they sell? But teachers are not retailing appliances, and the characteristics of the customers have a great deal to do with how the product performs. Children spend only part of their waking hours in school; the rest of the time they are influenced by their home environments, their peers, and television. It would be absurd to expect the school, then, to make every pupil an achieving citizen who is also trustworthy, loyal, helpful, friendly, courteous, kind, obedient, cheerful, thrifty, brave, clean, and reverent.

THE EFFECTS OF THE DEMAND

Sometimes a demand for accountability really represents a demand for control over what is taught and who is to be hired to teach it. (Frequent targets: sex education and controversial library books.) But on balance, accountability seems to have had beneficial effects on education. Teachers, administrators, researchers, and theorists have been prompted to question what they have been doing, to refine old techniques, and to experiment with new ones. Let's look at some of the changes and trends that have resulted.

Research on Effective Teaching. In the 1960s, research on teaching was characterized by ambiguity and contradiction. A few researchers tried to organize the many diverse studies, and slowly, their work began to shed new light on what makes teaching successful. Encouraged, researchers have shown heightened interest in teaching processes, and experimentation is under way. It will be years before they can speak with confidence, but some of the latest findings are reviewed in this chapter.

A Return to the Basics. Philadelphia school officials announced plans in the spring of 1976 for an experiment in Fitler Elementary School that would stress reading, writing, and arithmetic, maintain strict discipline, assign lots of homework, and promote pupils only if they passed their examinations. The school would require pupils to arrive in class clean and neatly dressed—no jeans, no sneakers—and to salute the flag and recite the pledge of allegiance each day before classes begin. Pupils who misbehaved would be tossed out. Fitler School is in North Philadelphia, in an area of broken windows and boarded-up, abandoned houses; it accommodates about 500 students, from kindergarten through sixth grade.

What is the goal of the return-to-basics movement?

Well before the start of the fall term, when the experiment was to begin, school officials were deluged with applications from so many parents—most of them black or Hispanic—for enrollment of their children that seventeen school buildings, rather than one, had to be made available. In the Fitler School, at least, achievement is now markedly higher than in most of the city's schools. The Philadelphia return to basics exemplifies an apparently nationwide desire to concentrate on the fundamentals of education and to eliminate what their critics call "frills." (When taxpayers vote on school budgets, music, art, and athletic activities are often categorized as frills.)

Minimum Competency Testing. Advocates of minimum competency testing, who sound like behaviorists, insist that students be required to demonstrate that they have learned at least the fundamentals of basic subjects. Most states recently have made such testing a matter of law, and the remaining states are headed in the same direction (Pipho, 1978).

What started out as an evaluation of students' skills before the award of diplomas has funneled down to earlier grades. Minimum competency tests now are often given at early elementary school levels, and students must pass them to go on to the next grade. Legislation in New York State even requires testing of students before they enter public school. If a child cannot show reading readiness, he or she is not admitted to first grade.

What minimum competencies should school be responsible for?

The movement has not been without difficulties. Some critics warn that emphasis on the bare bones of essential material may lessen students' and teachers' motivation toward more advanced pursuits. Further, the legislation may indeed have outrun teacher and school preparation: educators have not settled on *what* competencies to require, *how* to measure competencies and develop remedial programs, and *where* to get the time and the money for the

"The first day in school I explain the whole routine of getting credit in school. I tell them, 'Now you're going to get credit for everything you do in class. I don't want any guesswork when the report card comes along.' I explain to them, 'You will get everything you have earned. You will not get anything you haven't earned. Any awards—merit, honor roll, school spirit—that you get you take the pats on the back. You did it. It's not the teacher.' Because they just think teachers sit down and just take numbers and give them marks! So I keep a very accurate record. Every day. Every week. That's an awful lot of work—it is! But I work them hard, so that's fair—because otherwise a lot of it's left to guesswork. . . . Three

programs. And, finally, the question of *how* to set standards and *who* should set them remains. Some argue that each community should fix its own, since it knows its students best and bears most of the financial burden of providing education. Others press for statewide standards so that diplomas awarded to graduates of Smith High School in Connecticut, for example, will mean as much as those from any other high school in the state. The logical extension of this would be national standards. Then, the shaky argument goes, we could know what any student at any grade level can do regardless of where he or she went to school.

Do specific objectives improve accountability?

Setting Goals. Behavioral objectives, introduced by Robert Mager in 1962 (Chapter 7), have become increasingly important as a result of the public demand for visible evidence of accomplishment. More teachers than ever before are employing the technique voluntarily and in some school systems teachers are being *required* to specify their teaching goals in writing. As specific objectives become more common, resistance to their use appears to be waning. Boykin and Pope (1977) asked 202 students who were halfway through their student teaching what they thought of the statement "Teachers should use behavioral objectives." Eighty-nine percent agreed, 7 percent were undecided, and only 4 percent disagreed. One of us recently asked social

months after school has opened it becomes a very subjective process when you make out a report card—unless you have a very specific, accurate record. And you know, teacher's reputations precede them. There are children who don't want to come in here because this is the room where you get all the homework—this is the room where you have to work too much—this is the room where you have to obey at lunch. But once they get in here they see that I run a fair class. I give them responsibility, and credit and freedom. That's important to me—that's the way I like to approach teaching. We're accountable to each other."

studies student teachers to specify the most useful information from their educational psychology course taken two years earlier. "Behavioral objectives!" they chorused.

Mastery Learning. In most classrooms, as you are all too well aware, a few students get As, and the rest range from Bs to Fs. If every student could rate an A, a teacher would have the perfect response to accountability. Mastery learning, which was devised by Benjamin Bloom in the 1960s, is based on the premise that virtually all students (except for some "exceptional" children) can learn virtually anything; it just takes some students longer than others. So in a classroom where mastery learning is in effect, every pupil would theoretically show minimum competency, and the teacher would feel no anxiety about accountability.

The technique of teaching for mastery is quite different from conventional teaching techniques. In the usual classroom method, all students are exposed to the same amount of material for the same length of time, and they are expected to absorb it to varying degrees. In teaching for mastery, the amount of material to be learned thoroughly remains the same for all the students, but the time allotted for learning varies with each student's needs. Thus, student ability, the factor traditionally viewed as crucial for achievement, lessens in importance, whereas *time spent* on instruction becomes more important.

Aina O'Malley, who employs the mastery learning method in teaching grammar, has reported how it works in her classes at Milwaukie High School in Milwaukie, Oregon. "If only half the class passed the test the first time, I have the students who did pass explain it to those who didn't. They can use work sheets, alternate texts, or listen to a tape recorder. Sometimes just hearing it from a peer instead of myself makes the difference" (Fiske, 1976, p. 9E). The second time around, most students pass the test and the class moves ahead, while the few who failed get special attention from the teacher—and she keeps at it until they pass. Emmett L. Jones, teaching introductory biology at Olive-Harvey College, a Chicago community college largely attended by impoverished minority students, found that 88 percent of his class got As or Bs under the mastery learning approach, compared with 35 percent in a nonmastery control group.

Requisite to teaching for mastery, Bloom (1976) has pointed out, are:

1. Careful attention to students' cognitive and affective entry characteristics and adaptation of instructional techniques to those characteristics.
2. More individualized instruction, implicit in the first requisite, with smaller classes, teacher aides, and peer tutors.
3. Adequate time for instruction, skillfully manipulated to keep slow and fast learners occupied.

What is the role of testing in the mastery approach?

The most important component of the mastery method, Bloom (1980) advises, is diagnostic or *formative* testing; it takes place regularly during instruction, and each test covers only a single unit or small portion of the material studied. Its purpose is to pinpoint areas of mastery and nonmastery, and the results are not used for grading. If the student has mastered a unit, he or she may move on to the next; if the student has not, an alternative plan for attaining mastery should be put to work. Bloom does not recommend repetition of the same old stuff if Joey has not caught on; rather, applying innovation and ingenuity, you should come up with materials and methods that fit Joey's style.

When several units—or the entire course—have been completed, a *summative* test is given, to determine whether the whole area has been mastered. If the formative tests have been precise, if remedial materials and methods have been appropriate, and if students have been given enough time, the summative test should demonstrate mastery. Grades are based, usually, only on the summative test; Block (1977) recommends that A be used to indicate mastery, the remaining grades for differing levels of partial mastery, and a mark of "Incomplete" for failure. (Your principal may need some persuasion on that last suggestion.)

One objection frequently raised to mastery learning is that the slow learners retard the fast learners. Supporters of the technique agree that that proves true at the beginning of a term, but contend that the pace of the whole class is soon accelerated by enhanced learning ability all around. O'Malley says: "Some of the slow ones may have never done well before. Each time they master one building block, they gain confidence to master others. They develop good feelings about themselves" (Fiske, 1976, p. 9E). Since she adopted the mastery technique, she reports, both the fast and the slow learners have covered more ground.

An important practical problem of the mastery model is that few teachers have the time or energy to implement it fully. If you try the approach, consider developing it by successive approximations.

Does mastery learning benefit all? A quite different objection is made by Daniel J. Mueller. In an article entitled "Mastery Learning: Partly Boon, Partly Boondoggle," Mueller says:

> My indictment is not that the high level of performance of slower learning students on the pre-specified instructional objectives is being purchased at the expense of the performance of faster learning students on the pre-specified objectives. In fact, mastery proponents and researchers have strongly emphasized that under mastery learning both slow and fast learning students are brought to a high level of performance on the pre-specified objectives. My indictment is rather that the faster learning students could be learning more. If faster learning students could be motivated to spend as much time studying as are slower learning students, they could learn more than the pre-specified objectives; in some cases two or three or four times more. By pre-specifying a finite number of learning objectives and concentrating instructional efforts on bringing all students to this level, not only does the mastery model not facilitate the maximization of learning for faster learning students, it actually precludes it (1975, p. 4).

A good many teachers who favor the mastery learning approach but who see validity in Mueller's objection have found their own solution: they divide their classes into fast and slow groups and apply the mastery technique within each. Bloom and some fellow theorists disapprove of that practice. The issue is a practical and philosophical one that you will have to decide for yourself. Of course, a powerful alternative to ability grouping is peer tutoring, discussed in Chapter 13. Nevertheless, Bloom and his colleagues have provided substantial evidence over a decade that teaching for mastery can help teachers demonstrate accountability in the most convincing of manners—by showing that their students have mastered their studies.

The Voucher System. In this approach to accountability, which is still virtually untried, "you pay your money and you take your choice." The "money" would consist of vouchers distributed by school districts to the parents of schoolchildren; the parents then would choose their children's schools—public, private, or parochial, profit or nonprofit—and pay for their tuition with the vouchers. The vouchers, convertible by the schools into cash, would constitute the schools' only income in most cases, so the schools would have to compete to survive: parents dissatisfied at year's end with the results at the school they picked could take their business elsewhere next year. The voucher system represents free enterprise at work in education; the consumer controls the market by affecting the success or failure of the product. The system might also broaden opportunities for the poor: in the 1960s, at least 15 percent of school-age children attended private schools (Campbell, Cunningham, and McPhee, 1965), but few children of the poor were among them. The voucher system could well change that.

Should parents make decisions allowed by the voucher plan?

Education under the GI Bill of Rights already operates in somewhat similar fashion. Otherwise, there has been no full-scale test of the scheme, but a limited demonstration occurred in the early 1970s in the community of Alum Rock, adjacent to San Jose, California. The demonstration was limited because it embraced only public schools, and teachers' jobs and the schools' survival were guaranteed, as they would not be in a true test. Fourteen of the district's twenty-four schools were "voucher schools" and each voucher school was required to offer at least two distinct programs, called minischools. In a single year, the fourteen schools provided fifty-five such minischools.

The minischools' programs were devised by the teachers, often in consultation with parents, and each school was required to provide annually a description of its philosophy and methods. The descriptions were incorporated in a pamphlet distributed to parents to help them choose. Scores of children in the voucher schools did not differ significantly from those of pupils in the nonvoucher schools, but a substantial majority of the district's students enrolled in the voucher schools. "Perhaps the most striking outcome of the project," Joel Levin, its director, has written,

> has been its ability to mobilize teacher enthusiasm and commitment. Teachers feel that the programs they have designed are "theirs" and consequently, they feel a vested interest and professional pride in making them successful. Teachers have been working longer hours and extra days of their own volition to

improve their minischools. Peer pressure has been mobilized frequently by teachers in a program when they have felt that one of their members was not doing his or her share. In short, the teachers feel an "ownership" of their mini-schools which can best be compared to the proprietary feeling and commitment to success of the owner of a small neighborhood store (Warren, 1976, p. 14).

Widespread adoption of the voucher system appears unlikely, however, because of strong opposition to it on varied grounds. One major objection is that inclusion of parochial schools would violate the Constitutional principle of separation of church and state. Another is that if half the parents in a district chose to send their children to private schools, the public schools would be left empty, half their teachers would be left jobless, schools would be consolidated, and their buildings would become surplus. But the expanding private schools would need additional facilities and additional teachers. They could take over the abandoned schools and hire the jobless teachers; the only change would be that public schools had become private schools. Still another objection is that a student influx to private schools would foster segregation.

Perhaps the objections are, for the most part, unfounded—though the church-and-state issue would certainly present a serious problem. In any case, the voucher system represents a provocative idea.

Vouchers and magnets—is choice the answer to accountability?

Magnet Schools. Somewhat similar to the voucher plan but much more broadly adopted is the magnet school approach; it involves the development of specialized schools intended to attract students with special interests, skills, and needs. Whereas the voucher plan was inspired by the desire to decentralize control of schools and to give students and parents more options, the magnet school idea was proposed as an alternative to busing to achieve desegregation; most magnet schools are in big cities. Theoretically, a school that emphasizes science and math, say, should draw a healthy mixture of ethnic groups.

The Performing Arts School in Cincinnati represents a good example. Its 500 students—and a waiting list as long—constitute a racial mix close to that of the city's entire school population. Candidates for enrollment are given auditions in singing and improvised acting, and are tested in drawing and for physical coordination: acceptance in the school depends on artistic promise. The curriculum provides two hours daily of instruction in the performing arts and somewhat more time for regular academic subjects. Except for mathematics, students are not placed in lock-step grades; they are grouped by their needs and by their demonstrated achievement (Eardley, 1976).

Magnet schools are free of the careful budgeting required by the voucher plan. But they are not without problems. The cost per pupil is often higher than that in traditional schools. The per pupil cost at Houston's High School for the Performing and Visual Arts, for example, is ten times the cost in a back-to-basics high school (Special Report, 1979).

Among Cincinnati's fourteen magnet schools, several are racially unbalanced, and the long-range effect on desegregation is undetermined. Teachers and administrators worry about what may happen to their jobs should the experiment end. Many innovative curriculum plans are squelched because of states' rigid certification requirements (Barber, 1979). Nevertheless, the magnet school plan is off to a stronger start than the voucher plan.

The Collapse of Performance Contracting. Some educational innovations generate widespread interest because of their theoretical potential, but fail in practice. Performance contracting exemplifies an approach to accountability that did not fulfill the enthusiastic prophecies of its early advocates. Performance contracting attempted to apply the methods of business and industry to teaching, and in the 1969–70 school year, the school systems of Texarkana, Texas, and Portland, Oregon, gave it a try.

They contracted with private corporations to take over instruction in such subjects as reading and arithmetic, with payments to the corporation based on the improvement, if any, in pupils' scores. The method in effect transfers accountability from the educators to the outsiders.

Other school systems followed Portland's and Texarkana's lead. Various contracting firms employed various educational approaches, including behavior modification's reinforcement procedures. Some dispensed entirely with professional teachers; others retained a few professional teachers and replaced the rest with their own technicians and with parents of pupils.

By 1975, despite its seeming promise, performance contracting was dead. A number of reasons contributed to its failure:

Teachers' unions, which are increasingly potent politically, opposed the idea as a threat to jobs.

How to measure students' gains, if any, engendered controversy: debates raged over methods of measurement, over who should do the measuring, over what types of scores to employ.

What killed performance contracting?

School boards grew impatient with lengthy contract negotiations.

Most damaging of all, it is likely, was an Office of Economic Opportunity study of 25,000 low-achieving students in school districts where performance contracting was in effect. The study found performance contracting little better than traditional methods (Office of Economic Opportunity, 1972).

TO INNOVATE OR NOT TO INNOVATE?

Education's recent history is profusely punctuated with innovations that have been largely abandoned, among them closed-circuit television, teaching machines, team teaching, and the open classroom (Hechinger, 1976). Why do they fail when, as with performance contracting, they have great support, energy, and resources behind them? Sometimes the reasons are clear: in Leonia, New Jersey, for example, the Alternative High School recruited scholars of prestige to teach courses voluntarily but the Leonia Education

Association thwarted the plan in a series of legal battles (Karant, 1977). But usually the causes of failure remain obscure: even in the case of performance contracting, other reasons have been advanced besides those we cited, and there is little agreement about them. And if hindsight is beclouded, how can we ever predict whether an innovation is likely to succeed or fail?

Does that mean, then, that all innovations are doomed and that we should steadfastly maintain the status quo?

The evidence indicates the answer is an emphatic no! Hechinger (1976) points out that though many novel ideas have faded, they have left a legacy of related and more promising innovations. The teaching machines of the 1950s, for example, have evolved into programmed, self-instructional materials. And generally rejected innovations survive in some schools and school systems because they meet their needs: a survey by Aslin and DeArman (1976) of more than 3000 high schools in the north central states found that virtually all innovations of the last twenty years still flourish somewhere. (Table 16.1 illustrates the dynamic and complex picture of innovative development at the high school level.) For the most part, Aslin and DeArman report, schools are likely to stick with inexpensive, simple, and easily manageable programs and to toss out the costly and complex.

What role should innovation play?

A good way to look at innovations is to consider them as experiments rather than as positive answers. All innovations presumably begin with the hunch that they will improve education—by helping to individualize instruction, by heightening student achievement, by making for greater accountability. But the hunch must be tested in practice. If the innovation proves no better than the procedure it replaced (few innovations appear to have impeded student progress) then a decision is in order: Should you scrap the whole thing and go back to the old way? Or should you adopt parts of the program that work and skip the rest of it? (The second choice often is the better.)

Formal and Informal Innovation. Innovations are not always handed down from on high; they often originate with teachers. So innovations can be classified as formal and informal, as Weber (1977) does with individualized instruction practices. *Informal* innovation describes the myriad inventions and little experiments of the individual teacher. If Mr. Fredrikson decides to try to motivate Jim to read by providing Jim with comic books, he is engaged in informal and perhaps unstructured innovation. But if Mr. Fredrikson decides to move Jim into Individually Prescribed Instruction (Talmadge, 1975), a highly structured, sequenced, and sophisticated program, he is resorting to *formal* innovation. Informal innovations usually are much more flexible than the formal variety and lack the latter's polish and prior testing, but they don't have to be purchased, as their counterparts generally do, and they constitute a potent component of classroom practice. Both kinds work side by side: even when a whole school system adopts a formal innovation, teachers continue to improvise.

Table 16.1 Status of 33 Selected Innovations in Responding Schools

Innovation	Have tried but abandoned		Was never used	
	#	%	#	%
PSSC physics	304	9.3	2,040	62.4
Harvard physics	37	1.1	2,643	80.9
ESCP physical science	58	1.8	2,727	83.4
SSSP physical science	24	0.7	3,122	95.6
IPS physical science	105	3.2	2,222	68.0
Humanities	211	6.5	1,966	60.2
Career education	18	0.6	1,568	48.0
Independent study programs	92	2.8	1,189	36.4
Mini-courses	99	3.0	1,586	48.6
Learning packages	67	2.1	1,825	55.9
HSGP geography	14	0.4	3,014	92.3
IPI	8	0.2	2,788	85.4
SRSS sociology	7	0.2	2,990	91.5
Ethnic studies	60	1.8	1,911	58.4
Television instruction	121	3.7	2,505	76.6
Programmed instruction	138	4.2	2,113	64.7
Teaching machines	59	1.8	2,577	78.8
Telephone amplification	33	1.0	2,941	90.0
Simulation or gaming	18	0.6	1,169	35.8
Data processing equipment	112	3.4	1,492	45.7
Computer assisted instruction	46	1.4	2,290	70.1
Flexible scheduling	146	4.5	2,667	81.6
Team teaching	389	11.9	1,157	35.4
College credit courses	60	1.8	1,880	57.5
Nongraded programs	15	0.5	2,649	81.0
Teachers' aides–paraprofessionals	106	3.2	1,250	38.2
Differentiated staffing	9	0.3	2,872	87.8
School-within-a-school	19	0.6	3,093	94.6
Cultural enrichment program	24	0.7	2,536	77.6
Optional class attendance	27	0.8	3,008	92.0
Extended school year	8	0.2	3,191	97.6
Action learning	24	0.7	1,403	42.9
Early leaving plan	19	0.6	1,358	41.5
Total	2,477	2.3	73,742	68.4

Are all teaching practices little experiments? What is an experiment?

A conservative approach to innovation suggests that teachers must await theoretical and research support before launching informal experiments. But Goodlad (1979) argues that teachers should experiment routinely, without necessarily waiting for a theorist's stamp of approval. The efforts of scholars do help to foster new practices, of course, but sometimes teachers have more

Fully implemented and operating		Being tried on limited basis		Before 1965		Year adopted			
						1965–69		1970–74	
#	%	#	%	#	%	#	%	#	%
678	20.7	246	7.5	179	14.5	767	62.3	285	23.2
400	12.2	186	5.7	8	1.3	242	38.9	372	59.8
325	9.9	160	4.9	19	3.5	274	50.6	248	45.8
70	2.1	50	1.5	9	6.3	63	43.8	72	50.0
732	22.4	208	6.4	28	2.7	348	33.2	671	64.1
792	24.3	296	9.1	79	6.1	687	52.9	532	41.0
607	18.6	1,071	32.8	55	3.2	143	8.4	1,496	88.3
741	22.7	1,245	38.1	54	2.6	486	23.4	1,535	74.0
821	25.1	759	23.2	12	0.7	330	19.6	1,339	79.7
353	10.8	1,020	31.2	27	1.9	218	15.1	1,194	83.0
132	4.0	104	3.2	13	5.2	83	33.2	154	61.6
126	3.9	343	10.5	9	1.9	47	9.9	419	88.2
138	4.2	133	4.1	10	3.6	96	34.5	172	61.9
771	23.6	528	16.1	16	1.2	206	15.2	1,135	83.6
234	7.2	409	12.5	57	7.5	193	25.2	515	67.3
234	7.2	783	24.0	80	6.9	281	24.3	796	68.8
209	6.4	426	13.0	55	7.9	206	29.7	433	62.4
84	2.6	209	6.4	23	7.0	75	22.8	231	70.2
716	21.8	1,366	41.8	32	1.5	267	12.7	1,802	85.8
1,330	40.7	330	10.1	154	8.7	1,058	59.5	565	31.8
564	17.3	369	11.3	10	1.0	263	26.9	704	72.1
334	10.2	120	3.7	21	3.5	297	48.9	289	47.6
669	20.5	1,054	32.2	152	7.2	903	42.8	1,056	50.0
706	21.6	662	19.0	160	11.5	326	23.4	905	65.1
206	6.3	400	12.2	18	2.9	105	16.9	500	80.3
1,021	31.2	892	27.3	69	3.4	921	45.6	1,029	51.0
153	4.7	237	7.2	32	8.0	78	19.5	289	72.4
82	2.5	76	2.3	19	10.6	43	24.0	117	65.4
270	8.3	440	13.5	63	8.6	156	21.3	514	70.1
47	1.4	186	5.7	4	1.5	45	17.2	212	81.2
48	1.5	23	0.7	7	8.9	17	21.5	55	69.6
1,087	33.3	753	23.0	194	10.4	489	26.2	1,184	63.4
1,148	35.1	744	22.8	97	5.1	514	26.9	1,300	68.0
15,828	14.7	15,790	14.6	1,765	5.2	10,227	30.0	22,120	64.8

immediate needs. They are in classrooms *now,* and if a simple shift in seating arrangement cuts down disturbances or improves attention, it does not need much additional justification.

Like all innovations, informal innovations should be judged by one criterion: Have things improved, and is the improvement worth the effort? As a

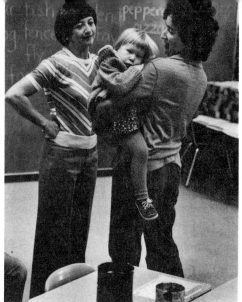

"How do I know if I'm effective? It's little things. Like when parents act relaxed during a conference. When a child lights up after solving a hard problem. Or when

teacher, don't forget to make the judgment. Formal innovations always are assayed because of their cost and visibility. But teachers often neglect to evaluate the procedures they contrive themselves. Without evaluation, you may lose sight of the purpose and even of the innovation.

Teacher Effectiveness

Certain teachers, it seems, have an artful touch in producing high achievement and positive attitudes among their students. For eighty years, research has aimed to make a more precise and scientific statement about how to be artful in the classroom. But only recently has teacher effectiveness research begun to provide clear direction. Part of the problem has been the persistent myth that teaching and learning are ruled by a few major, undiscovered principles. Today we know that teaching and learning are extremely complex acts, and the governing principles change according to the teacher's personality, the subject taught, and the characteristics of the students. The effective teacher applies scientific principles and shifts to equally valid principles when the situation warrants.

Does correlation mean causation?

To discover important principles, much research has compared behaviors of successful and unsuccessful teachers. Success is usually defined by students' high achievement. For forming hypotheses about effectiveness, this is a good beginning, but without additional evidence it is reckless to assume that particular behaviors of effective teachers *cause* success. If a researcher found that millionaires smile more often than do poor folk, he could not seriously propose that to get rich one should smile more often. An alternate hypothesis is as plausible: having wealth makes one more sociable.

everyone in the lounge is complaining and you don't have to join in because it's been a good day. Yeah, I'll take credit for those things."

A more complex educational example: Successful teachers are usually found to be organized and businesslike (Rosenshine, 1976), but it does not automatically follow that practicing organization will help deficient teachers. Organized teachers may be effective not because they are organized but because they are more intelligent, a trait difficult to alter. Whether training in specific skills will profit teachers and their students is answered by experimental studies, which are scarce. But their number grows, and they do provide direction for improving teaching.

DIRECT INSTRUCTION

In a recent experiment, Clark et al. (1979) found that sixth-grade students showed higher achievement when their teachers were trained to

Ask a high proportion of knowledge level questions (see Bloom's Taxonomy, chapters 7 and 14).
Give prompt and precise feedback during recitation.
Provide explicit lesson structure by stating objectives, outlining the lesson, reviewing and summarizing main ideas, and signaling which portions are most important.

Good and Grouws (1979) and Ebmeier and Good (1979) found improvements in fourth-grade students' math achievement when teachers followed a systematic, straightforward approach. Teachers practiced behaviors previously observed in effective instructors, including

Keeping momentum through the period.
Being enthusiastic.

Increasing the pace of instruction, as long as most recitation questions are answered successfully.

Assigning uninterrupted seatwork; students are accountable for showing evidence of work.

Holding weekly and monthly review sessions.

What is direct instruction?

Similar results have been found in studies of junior high and high school classes (Brophy, 1979a). A strong theme runs through much of this research; Rosenshine (1979) has termed it *direct instruction*. Direct instruction means that the teacher *directs* the class toward specific goals. The teacher is clearly the leader and the authority. Little reliance is placed on discussion, student ideas, discovery learning, or other types of *indirect* teaching. This teaching style is becoming increasingly fashionable for promoting achievement in the basic skills.

Here, in summary, are the main features of direct instruction:

1. Academic goals are spelled out and aimed toward.
2. Virtually all goals involve basic academic skills. Nonacademic issues and personal concerns are handled outside the classoom.
3. Instruction is usually done in large groups (i.e., whole classes). When seatwork is assigned, it is monitored continuously to make sure students are engaged.
4. Factual, convergent teacher questions predominate during recitation, and they are easy enough for at least three-fourths of the class to answer correctly.
5. Praise for genuine accomplishment and correct responses is bestowed liberally.
6. The pace is rapid and steady, with little time lost to organization, directions, or discipline. Compare this idea to Hiatt's (1979) finding that in most elementary classrooms, a mere 20 percent of the time is devoted to instruction.

Direct instruction seems to become less powerful as learning tasks increase in complexity (see Figure 16.1), and as students become more mature. By junior high school, for example, student contribution of ideas may enhance achievement (Evertson et al., 1978). Of course, even in teaching basic skills to young children, direct instruction does not always work. In his review of teacher effectiveness, Brophy (1979b) cautions: "There do not appear to be any universal teaching competencies (i.e., specific behaviors such as praising or asking higher level questions) that are appropriate in all teaching circumstances. . . . Teachers must not only master particular skills but know when to use them" (p. 735).

Maintaining Flow. The use of momentum in direct instruction is extremely important. It not only keeps students on task but reduces classroom disruption. Arlin (1979) observes that off-task behavior nearly doubles when momentum falters. Some of Arlin's pointers for sustaining momentum:

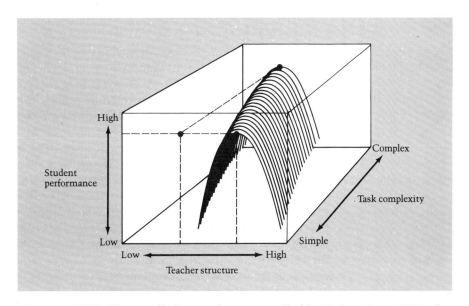

Figure 16.1. This diagram links two factors studied by Robert Soar (1977): the complexity of learning tasks and teacher structure. Teacher *structure* or *direction* refers to direct instruction, where the teacher closely monitors student performance, controls the type, frequency, and amount of recitation, gives prompt feedback to students, and ensures that students are actively engaged with tasks. First, it can be seen that extremes of control—too much teacher direction or too little—produce the least learning. Optimum structure occurs between the extremes. Second, the point of optimum structure depends on the nature of the learning task. Simple tasks, such as those requiring rote memorization or following of directions, are best performed under moderately high teacher structure. As task complexity increases, "students will need increasing freedom to explore and interact with subject matter" (Soar, 1977, p. 99).

How can momentum be sustained?

1. Apply smooth transitions between lessons or activities. Alert teachers know when the end of a lesson or period approaches, and they avoid choppy endings.
2. Signal clearly when a transition approaches. Successful teachers alert students before a shift in activities: "We'll turn to math in five minutes, so wrap up your projects."
3. Establish momentum patterns early in the school year. When teachers rehearse signals—"Materials must be returned before the class is dismissed"—and are consistent in their use, students learn the signals rapidly. After a while, activities themselves signal transitions, and teachers do not have to prod and nag to keep the lesson flowing.
4. Avoid chatter about nonacademic affairs and reduce attempts to persuade students that learning is a good idea. Beginning teachers, especially, are

anxious to please students, and much time is spent cajoling them or listening to self-appointed critics.

About the importance of planning for momentum, an experienced band teacher has this advice: "Always make sure the kids have an instrument in their mouth, so they can't spit at each other, and something in their hands so they can't throw anything. You can't bog down or you'll pay for it" (Arlin, 1979, p. 53).

Time on Task. A major purpose of using momentum is to ensure that students are actively engaged in learning. Why do we stress the matter? Teachers have always been expected to pursue classroom topics actively and to make sure students are attentive. Careful observation of teachers weakens that expectation. The amount of time *allocated* to basic academic subjects varies enormously, even among teachers in the same school (Dishaw, 1977). Predictably, increased time spent on a topic produces higher student achievement, as long as not too many objectives are used (Borg, 1979).

How are allocated time and engaged time related?

But even when *allocated* time is constant, different students do different things. In a forty-five-minute period, one student may be attentive for thirty-five minutes, another for only five. So a much stronger predictor of student achievement is *engaged time*, or *time on task*, during which a student is actively listening, reading, practicing, or reciting. Teachers have considerable control over time on task through careful preinstructional planning and by supervision during instruction. Do not plan to grade papers or write objectives while your students are doing seatwork or working in small groups; they need attention, steering, and feedback.

Are small groups the most productive?

Group Size. Although Rosenshine (1979) argues for large-group instruction, new research shows that work in small groups may enhance learning under certain conditions. The most apparent of those conditions is student ability. In particular, small groups—about four persons—often favor high-ability students, whereas low-ability students tend to profit more from large groups (Peterson and Janicki, 1979). Small groups give able students opportunity to do spontaneous peer tutoring, a worthwhile activity in its own right (Allen, 1976). Low-ability students, who probably do not have sufficient grasp of the material to teach it to peers, require more structure and direction from the teacher. Also, with less able students in a large group, the teacher can attend to the whole class at once and give prompt, individual assistance and feedback. When six small groups are operating, the teacher cannot monitor the direction and progress of all students.

Should students decide whether to work in large or small groups? Usually not; arranging instruction according to student preferences is not positively related to their achievement and attitudes, and is sometimes detrimental (Cronbach and Snow, 1977). This is particularly true when their preferences tend toward whatever approach promises the least effort.

Brophy (1979a) notes that large-group instruction has withstood perennial attempts to discredit it, not because teachers are stuck in a rut, but because it works. Compared to small-group instruction or individualization, it is easier to organize, provides good opportunity to learn by imitation, allows close monitoring of students, and reduces pecking orders created by ability grouping.

EFFECTIVE AFFECT

What affective teacher behavior invites success? Commitment, Stephens (1967) proposes. Learning and teaching come naturally, and we can learn and teach spontaneously, Stephens theorizes. But we are not all equally good at them, and the disparities result from the differences in our degrees of commitment.

Can an unenthusiastic teacher be effective?

Certainly no one would disagree that commitment—to children, to teaching, to our own methods of teaching—is important. *But what do committed teachers do differently from less committed teachers?* Partial answers are beginning to appear: *warmth* and *enthusiasm*, engendered by a teacher's sense of commitment, seem to be major factors (Rosenshine, 1970). Warm and enthusiastic teachers, as perceived by students and professional observers, improve classroom climate, enhance academic achievement, and—not surprisingly— are rated more highly by their students (Rosenshine and Furst, 1971).

Warmth and enthusiasm heighten effectiveness in two ways:

1. Students enjoy and imitate warm teachers (Portuges and Feshbach, 1972), and are infected by their enthusiasm.
2. Teachers communicate their expectations of students, it is becoming clearer, through their behavior (Brophy, 1979a).

Successful teachers are not dry, stuffy folk. They use affective behaviors to motivate and sustain achievement. A warm and enthusiastic teacher presumably conveys the conviction that classrooms are places where individuals are to be respected and valued, and where students should perform and enjoy their tasks. An important sign of respect is the use of authentic praise (Evertson et al., 1980). Brophy (1979b) points out that praise is sometimes misused in attempts to be positive toward an unmotivated student, or as a "consolation prize" for the child who fails repeatedly. Students are sensitive to such blunders.

Genuine warmth, enthusiasm, and praise do not always work miracles. No matter how hard we try to be engaging, our captive audience may occasionally sit on its hands. So teaching can sometimes be boring and exasperating, complicating our expectancies.

TEACHER EXPECTANCIES

If you are like most experienced teachers, you believe that high-ability students are more controllable than are low-ability students, and that interactions with high-ability students have greater probability of success (Cooper et al., 1979). Will your expectations make any difference in the classroom?

Studying teacher effectiveness, investigators at the University of Texas Research and Development Center for Teacher Education have pursued for

"It's very hard to keep momentum going. There are hundreds—no, thousands—of chances to get bogged down during a school day. When that happens, kids will right away find something else to do—fiddle around, make faces at their pals, daydream, whatever. Then you've got the double problem of getting their attention back plus trying to get back on track with the lesson. There are several things I do that help with momentum. One is that when we have recitation, I use simple questions that everyone can answer. It doesn't sound very challenging, but everyone succeeds, so there's a lot of reinforcement. Whenever I ask a brainbuster [a high-level question], there are big pauses, students sit down low in their seats or pretend to be taking notes so I won't call on them. If only one or two students can answer the question, I've lost momentum for everyone else in the room. It's not worth it."

a decade their own inquiries and reviewed others' research about teacher expectancies. Their work has included observation of how teachers communicate low expectations to a segment of a class. Typically, that segment embodies the low achievers and the least motivated. Teachers' beliefs about such students help to generate a vicious cycle, as we suggested in Chapter 11. When little Fred, poorly motivated and a low achiever with a dim view of school, enters a new class he does not start afresh. His new teacher may accept Fred's status as an unchangeable fact of life and signal to Fred that she does not expect much of him. To put it in technical terms, she responds to the existing motivation and achievement pattern by forming low expectancies and then communicating them to Fred. Her signals come in so strong, often enough, that Fred has little choice but to respond as she expects. Classical and higher-order conditioning, of course, help to explain some of Fred's poor responses. If teacher and student both expect failure and failure indeed follows, it should surprise no one that Fred's feelings about school grow even darker.

Now let's consider several teacher behaviors that communicate low expectancies and hinder the cognitive and affective growth of children like Fred. Among those behaviors, which have been summarized by Jere Brophy and Tom Good, originally of the University of Texas center (Brophy and Good, 1974), are:

Allowing low achievers less time to answer questions. Teachers evidently find pregnant pauses harder to accept from low achievers and tend to answer questions themselves, or to move on quickly to another student. With high achievers, teachers wait longer, prompt the student or rephrase the question, or ask another question. In one case, the implication is "You don't know it, do you?" In the other it is "I think you can get it."

How do teacher expectancies affect student learning?

Criticizing low achievers' wrong answers. Incorrect responses from low achievers elicit more obvious irritation from teachers than do such responses from good students. If criticism serves as punishment, then learning theory suggests that low achievers will become less likely to attempt a response. Perhaps out of sympathy and good intentions, teachers sometimes *reinforce* low achievers in their errors, praising them when praise is unwarranted. That approach may increase inaccurate response and encourage a false sense of competence. If students are to acquire skills, the skills must be real.

Paying less attention to low achievers. Teachers call on them, smile at them, and look them in the eyes less frequently than they do better students. What's more, teachers sometimes seat low achievers away from where the action is (Adams and Biddle, 1970), probably increasing their sense of isolation from the rest of the class.

Heller and White (1975) examined the frequency of approval and disapproval in junior high schools. When they compared high- and low-ability classes, they found no differences in the frequency of approval statements, but more disapprovals delivered in low-ability classes. Rosenshine (1971) has noted that high rates of disapproval seem to lower achievement; teachers thus help to stack the deck against low-ability students.

Teachers' nonverbal behavior, too, favors bright students. Teachers emit more smiles and nods, have more eye contact, and lean toward able students more (Chaiken et al., 1974). Students do not idly receive these signals. When they think a teacher is ineffective, they send back similar messages, generally appearing less attentive and interested (Feldman and Prohaska, 1979). When students expect competence, they act more positively and appear to learn more. The teacher, Feldman and Prohaska (1979) observe, reciprocates with enthusiasm and thoroughness. When positive expectations rule, classrooms are places for fun. When expectations sour, all participants grow bitter. These are complex interactions, and it may be impossible to unravel exactly *who* is responsible for *what*. No matter; *you* will be in charge of the classroom, and when low expectations arise, you must initiate a change.

In sum, teachers behave differently to low and high achievers, in accordance with their expectations. Their contrasting approaches appear to help high achievers to continue to succeed and low achievers to continue to fail. But the principles of expectancy communication, like other principles considered in this book, are *general* and apply to *groups* of teachers. An individual teacher's behavior and interactions with students may not fit the mold. You may indicate high expectations to a low-achieving student, treat him or her fairly, provide the environment for success, and still see the student fail. But the Brophy and Good observations serve as important guidelines toward improving your effectiveness, if you apply them with sensitivity. Brophy and Good point out, for example, that changing the behaviors we listed won't do much good if other signals of low expectations still go out. Imagine a teacher who decides to grant low achievers more time to respond—and taps his toe or twiddles his thumbs waiting for their answers.

Can a teacher *not* communicate expectations?

Why Do Teachers Communicate Expectations? The answers are complex and mostly speculative, but Brophy and Good offer some possible explanations. One is that student achievement rewards teacher behavior: we all expect that if we are effective in class, our effectiveness will be reflected in our students' cognitive and affective growth. Their growth will imply that we are doing our jobs well; their failure to grow will suggest that we are not. Another possibility is that teachers may be aware that expectancies can influence students, but they may be unaware that they are communicating their expectancies. That is understandable: Jackson (1965) notes that an elementary school teacher engages in 650 private interactions with students *per day*. At that pace, there isn't much time to contemplate what we're up to. Both colleagues and students can help on that.

Still another factor: low achievers, Brophy and Good argue, may seem unattractive and unpleasant to some teachers, and the reason may be more complex than the fact that low achievement implies teacher failure. Back in Chapter 10, we outlined some of the possible side effects of punishment, among them increased antisocial aggressiveness. If student failure serves as punishment, then it is predictable that low achievers will often face teachers with sullenness and hostility. And angry, obdurate youngsters aren't fun.

The Influence of Physical Appearance on Expectancy. One of the most interesting—and saddening—issues in teacher expectancy concerns another type of student unattractiveness: their physical appearance. Growing research evidence suggests that the way children look influences teachers' attitudes toward them, and vice versa (see Goebel and Cashen, 1979). Of course, almost everyone is repelled by ugliness, and teachers are no exceptions. In a psychology experiment, one of us donned a grotesque head mask and wandered through the aisles for a few minutes at the start of a class made up chiefly of prospective teachers. Among their comments later were:

> I felt that poor man would never have a chance in life because of his physical appearance. . . . At first it was disgusting and then when I knew who it was it was funny but still disconcerting. I don't like physical atrocities and I can't stand to look at them.

> I was pretty revolted by the sight, which would have been a pretty terrible impression if it had been a real person who looked like that.

How such repugnance manifests itself in school has been shown by various investigators. After a review of several studies, Berscheid and Walster (1972) concluded that teachers are prone to regard attractive students as brighter, more interesting, more responsive, more poised, and more honest than their unattractive peers. The same researchers reported on a University of Minnesota experiment in which students in the teacher certification program were given fictitious reports of youngsters' misconduct. To each report was attached a photograph of a child, previously categorized as attractive or unattractive. As the reported misconduct grew increasingly serious, the prospective teachers were found, generally, to judge the unattractive children more harshly than their better-looking counterparts.

Are teachers influenced by their students' looks?

In a similar study, Clifford and Walster (1973) sent to more than 400 fifth-grade teachers a comprehensive report card of a high-achieving fifth grader. Each copy of the card was accompanied by a photograph—of an attractive boy, an attractive girl, an unattractive boy, or an unattractive girl. The teachers were asked to judge the student's IQ and peer relationships, the parents' attitude toward school, and how far the student would go in school. To all four questions, the answers favored the attractive students.

If we grant, then, that students' appearance influences teachers' expectations, does it in turn affect teachers' behavior? A study by Adams and Cohen (1974) suggests that is does indeed: observing teacher-student interactions, they found that the teachers' own ratings of their students' facial attractiveness influenced the patterns of interaction.

Can the cycle of negative expectations be reversed? Some suggestions by Good, Biddle, and Brophy may help:

Private conversations with students.
Solicitation of students' ideas.
Integration of students' ideas into the curriculum.
Explanations of why suggestions are rejected or action on them delayed.
Modeling of respect for individuals and interest in learning (1975, p. 205).

Now let's assume that you try to govern your expectations and exert care in communicating them to students. How will you judge whether or not your efforts have been effective? How can you make yourself accountable to yourself? In the rest of this chapter we shall address the question of evaluating your behavior, by others and by yourself.

Evaluating the Teacher

Whatever it is that makes a teacher effective, it is a certainty that what proves effective with one student or one class need not work equally well with others. Yet, in this era of accountability, it is increasingly likely that you as a teacher will be *evaluated*, perhaps again and again. Some teachers object strongly to evaluation on the ground that it remains a game without rules. Others argue, philosophically, that no human being should or can judge another—although their philosophy rarely inhibits them from evaluating their pupils.

There are practical problems, too. The greatest problem is to define effective

"I always try to leave enough time at the end for them to get back in their seats and settled down. And I'll just very quickly go straight through again and review everything—including answering the pretest questions, and pointing out to everyone what some of them found out, discovered, or wanted to know about.

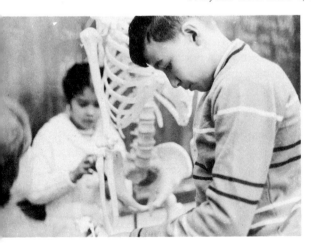

teaching. After centuries of experience in teaching, it remains difficult to say what methods are best, what characteristics good teachers should possess, or how much students should be expected to learn from those thought to be "good" teachers. Reflect for a moment on the teachers you have judged to be effective. Were they all alike? Probably not. The problem becomes more complex as we try to identify teachers who are effective for a whole class of students, all with different needs and personalities.

Can effectiveness be measured validly?

Even though teacher evaluation is flawed and difficult to do well, it serves two important purposes. It helps administrators to weed out the obviously incompetent or ineffective teachers and allows the shining stars to be rewarded with promotion and merit raises in pay. The second and extremely useful purpose is to provide feedback to teachers. As you recall from Chapter 14, feedback gives learners a sense of how well they are doing, shows where they still need improvement, and motivates them to keep trying. Because teachers as well as their students are learners, teacher evaluation feedback can help instructors correct their own failings, keep doing the things which are productive for their students, and encourage efforts to keep improving instruction.

Informal evaluation of teachers goes on all the time, of course. Parents form judgments on the basis of their children's remarks, on their impressions at Back-to-School Night, on gossip at PTA meetings. Administrators evaluate during casual conversations and by glancing into classrooms through open doors as they walk down the corridors. None of these methods is particularly accurate.

There are more formal ways.

The whole time I try to keep in tune with the kids, make sure I have them, you know, have their curiosity up—and I'll just keep going over and over it until they've got it. Somehow that doesn't bother me, I guess, because I really love my work. I just love watching them learn."

To Conform or Not to Conform

Individuality and independence often characterize the genius and other superior human beings, and as a future teacher you may possess those attributes. However admirable those traits may be, they are not always considered desirable by employers, including school boards and district superintendents. How much of them you will want to display will be for you to decide. The following evaluation of a famous teacher has been presented by John Gauss (1962); it may help you to make up your mind, but we present it without recommending any course for you. ■

Teacher Evaluation

TEACHER: *Socrates*

A. PERSONAL QUALIFICATIONS

	Rating (high to low)	Comments

	1	2	3	4	5	Comments
1. Personal appearance	☐	☐	☐	☐	☑	Dresses in an old sheet draped about his body
2. Self-confidence	☐	☐	☐	☐	☑	Not sure of himself — always asking questions
3. Use of English	☐	☐	☐	☑	☐	Speaks with a heavy Greek accent
4. Adaptability	☐	☐	☐	☐	☑	Prone to suicide by poison when under duress

B. CLASS MANAGEMENT

	1	2	3	4	5	Comments
1. Organization	☐	☐	☐	☐	☑	Does not keep a seating chart
2. Room appearance	☐	☐	☐	☑	☐	Does not have eye-catching bulletin boards
3. Utilization of supplies	☑	☐	☐	☐	☐	Does not use supplies

C. TEACHER-PUPIL RELATIONSHIPS

	1	2	3	4	5	Comments
1. Tact and consideration	☐	☐	☐	☐	☑	Places student in embarrassing situation by asking questions
2. Attitude of class	☐	☑	☐	☐	☐	Class is friendly

D. TECHNIQUES OF TEACHING

	1	2	3	4	5	Comments
1. Daily preparation	☐	☐	☐	☐	☑	Does not keep daily lesson plans
2. Attention to course of study	☐	☐	☑	☐	☐	Quite flexible—allows students to wander to different topics
3. Knowledge of subject matter	☐	☐	☐	☐	☑	Does not know material—has to question pupils to gain knowledge

E. PROFESSIONAL ATTITUDE

	1	2	3	4	5	Comments
1. Professional ethics	☐	☐	☐	☐	☑	Does not belong to professional association or PTA
2. In-service training	☐	☐	☐	☐	☑	Complete failure here — has not even bothered to attend college
3. Parent relationships	☐	☐	☐	☐	☑	Needs to improve in this area—parents are trying to get rid of him

RECOMMENDATION: *Does not have a place in Education. Should not be rehired.*

THE PROCESS APPROACH

In the *process approach*, which teachers refer to as "being observed," a principal or other administrator sits in a classroom for a while and, in theory at least, notes what the teacher does, what the students do, and how their behaviors interact. That kind of observation has its flaws. For one thing, the observer sees only an extremely limited and possibly contrived sample of classroom procedures.

If the observer arrives unannounced (an unlikely occurrence since most teachers' unions require advance notice of observation by an administrator) the teacher may become flustered and give a bad performance. Or the administrator may arrive in time to see quiet students engaged in seatwork and not have a chance to see active group instruction. If the observation is announced, the lesson still may not be representative of what routinely occurs in the classroom. Most teachers are careful to present their best instructional techniques and classroom skills for observation.

Can halo effects benefit a teacher?

Another limitation of the process approach is that it depends on general impressions, which are subject to the *halo effect*. The halo effect, as described in Chapter 15, occurs when a single attribute or characteristic colors our impression of the whole. If a teacher is understandably nervous during the principal's visit, the halo effect could create an impression that the teacher is ineffective. At the opposite extreme, an observer may watch a teacher successfully maintain quiet in the classroom and imagine the teacher effective in all aspects of instruction, not only classroom management.

In a systematic and efficient use of the process approach, the principal or other administrator employs an objective observation schedule or checklist, on which behaviors are summarized and checked off every few seconds, as they occur. Even better—although more costly and likely to be employed only in affluent school districts—is the practice of calling in a trained outside observer to make the checklist record. Either of these practices reduces the influence of a halo effect on objectivity.

THE PRODUCT APPROACH

The *product approach* looks at the end result, not the process. That result, of course, is student growth and achievement. In the past few years, many educators, researchers, and parents have come to believe that the single most important index of teaching effectiveness is student achievement. Their argument sounds reasonable enough.

What are some problems of teacher evaluation?

But some problems arise in putting the product approach into practice. What measure of student achievement do you use? The grades that the teacher gives? They can be manipulated to make the teacher *seem* effective. Standardized tests? Perhaps. But some teachers favor one test, others another. And even if all the teachers agreed on a single test, the results would not necessarily be a fair evaluation of your effectiveness. Suppose, for example, that your class begins the school year with slightly less capability than other classes in the same grade. And suppose that, at the end of the school year, the class is still behind the other classes, as evidenced by a standardized test. Does the result prove that you are slightly less effective as a teacher than your colleagues are? On the other hand, teachers who know they are to be judged on the basis of their students' performance on a standardized test may *teach toward the test*, and wittingly or unwittingly indicate to students what they will be tested on. If you and Mr. Gustafson down the hall both have classes in American history, and you coach yours a bit for the upcoming examination, are you a better teacher because your students do better than Gus's?

Another problem of the product approach is that it virtually ignores one whole area of student growth—the affective domain. Although educators pay lip service to the importance of building good character, responsibility, citizenship, and moral stature, few ever treat these qualities as products that should be measured. Certainly it is difficult to find good measures of honesty or virtue, but that does not mean that those outcomes of education should be overlooked. If a teacher can encourage an interest in learning or a healthy community attitude among the students in his or her class that product should be recognized and valued by the schools. As the product approach stands now, such recognition is difficult to come by.

STUDENT RATINGS

How many students participate in teacher evaluation?

One increasingly popular idea is to have students evaluate their teachers. Student ratings may be considered as an informal process approach, discussed earlier. Although it lacks the rigor of systematic observation, students see their teachers every day of the school year, not for an occasional forty-five minutes. Furthermore, they are the consumers of the teacher's product, and if you want to know how good an automobile is, you don't ask the car dealer, you ask the person who drives one. Understandably, though, the procedure strikes some teachers as preposterous. How can inexperienced, immature youngsters judge whether or not I am competent? they object. The answer to that is: It depends on the kinds of questions they are asked. A college senior may be expected to reply fairly to "Did the teacher display any mannerisms or traits that inhibited your learning?" A second grader could not even comprehend the question, but could answer this one: "How do you usually feel in this class? (a) worried; (b) good; (c) nervous; (d) smart; (e) dumb" You can get sensible, useful answers from your students about your effectiveness if you put your questions in terms they can understand.

Administrators rarely want to see the results of student ratings, particularly when the students are below the high school level. But teachers do want to see them, their own as well as others' ratings. When one of us developed a rating scale to be used at the middle school level, the payoff to teachers who gave up class time to collect ratings was that summaries of their students' responses (and descriptions of the ratings given by students in other classes in the school) would be provided. The teachers reported that the ratings were useful in identifying things their students found bothersome or particularly pleasant in the class. Where the teachers considered criticisms justifiable, they focused their efforts on making improvements. Seeing how other teachers in the school were rated, they could judge how they stacked up in their own class. If they felt they had one or two areas that needed attention, they then asked around among other teachers to find out how things were handled in different classes.

But research studies show that teachers' behaviors do not always improve because of feedback of their students' ratings (Froman and Owen, 1980). One reason is that not all teachers want to improve. And if teachers don't trust students' ratings feedback will have little credibility. Another reason why teachers do not always improve after they receive feedback could be that the rating scales used are sometimes imprecise. For example, a typical rating scale might look like this:

Teacher attitude: 1   2   3   4   5   6   7   8   9   10

                   poor   average   excellent

Ratings on this scale present an overall impression of a teacher's attitude, but they hardly specify what was wrong. If you rated between poor and average, how would you know what to do to develop a better attitude? The concept *better attitude* is not easily translated into a single question that will elicit an informative answer. But in a process similar to task analysis, you can break down attitude into its components. Here are some aspects of teacher behavior that compose and help to clarify attitude:

1. smiles
2. uses sarcasm
3. makes me feel important
4. is courteous
5. tells me when I do a good job
6. makes fun of some students
7. pays attention to students

None of these aspects of behavior in itself equals attitude. But as a group, they can indicate how you can improve your attitude.

Do student ratings measure perceptions or teacher behaviors?

Now, one point is likely to occur to you. Even if you want to do things right, and even if you have prepared your questions carefully, how seriously do you have to take your students' answers? Like adults, youngsters have their bad days. A poor grade on a test, a quarrel with a best friend, a disappointment at home, may influence their judgments of you. Why should you trust their diagnoses?

You may have between twenty and a hundred and fifty students, and their impressions will balance out. If you haven't been getting on too well with Jennifer for the last two months, her rating of you is likely to reflect the antagonism. On the other hand, Andy just scored an A + on an exam, and he may be a little too enthusiastic about you. Skip the extremes at either end.

Teachers on teaching: *"Know your subject. Have your rules. Let the kids know your rules. Organization is important—and motivation. Be up to date. And try to relate their day-to-day living with the classroom. . . . But you know I really like what I'm teaching—so I guess it's easy if you like what you're teaching. It really helps, because then you're motivated!"*

"We have ten minutes in the morning and ten minutes in the afternoon, and those are always pandemonium: Get your coats off! Get your books! Whatever you have to do—just do it! Take the attendance . . . scurry around passing out lunch tickets . . . it's a real zoo. But—you know—it's enjoyable. It gets you going. In the morning it gets everybody rev'd up. . . . And I kind of like the noise. . . . If I ever had to teach in an institution of, say, adults—well—I taught adults one year in night school and I really didn't like it. Much too quiet. And everybody did their work and there's no challenge."

"I say to them, 'I'm not a teacher who's going to tell you I know everything, because I'd only be kidding you. I'm going to make mistakes and when I do I want you to tell me—because I want to learn from you as much as you learn from me. It's a two-way deal.' It takes time to build up their confidence, but there are years when you have classes that take this by the horns and do a great job with it. I mean from the morning—8:30—right through the end of the day."

Calculate a mean or a median for all the ratings, and you will get a pretty good idea of what your students think of you, how effective you are as a teacher, and where your efforts at improving instruction may be best spent.

Summary

Parents and taxpayers in general are increasingly insisting that educators must be held accountable for the quality of education. As a result, school personnel have been stimulated to reconsider traditional approaches and to examine possible new ones. Among recent developments are:

1. A return to emphasis on the fundamentals, reading, writing, and arithmetic.
2. A trend toward setting behavioral objectives.
3. Pressure for schools to document, through measurement, that students are attaining minimum competencies.
4. Renewed interest in research on teaching effectiveness.

An extremely important change in teaching techniques has taken place in the form of *teaching for mastery*, which is based on the theory that almost any child can learn anything, given the time and patient corrective feedback. Another apparently thriving innovation is the specialized *magnet school*, designed to reduce racial segregation by attracting students of varied ethnic heritage with curricula that appeal to their particular interests. Such schools are operating in many urban regions. An even more radical approach to accountability is the yet-to-be-tested *voucher system*, which would permit parents to choose any school, public or private, for their children and to pay for tuition with school district funds. Under this system, schools would have to compete for pupils and, in theory, would have to be more responsive to parents' and pupils' requirements. Thus far, the system has been put into operation only in part, and only in one California school district. It has not bettered pupils' attainments, but has won the support of parents and participating teachers.

In recent decades, several innovations have come and more or less gone. One striking failure was *performance contracting*, in which corporations or other agencies outside the school system contracted to take over some teaching functions and to be paid on the basis of gains in student achievement. Such failures inspired the superficial view that educational innovations represent fads that will prove counterproductive to good schooling. But a closer look reveals that new products and procedures may lead, at the very least, to more durable and more useful inventions. Teachers' *informal* innovations invaluably complement school-wide or system-wide *formal* innovations, but both varieties must be evaluated and their usefulness determined.

Teachers may be effective without stressing innovative ideas and practices. Research is beginning to uncover behaviors associated with improved student achievement. Some of these factors are affective—showing *warmth* and *enthusiasm*—whereas others are procedural, such as monitoring and reviewing content. *The direct instruction* model, in which goals are specified, recitation is factual and brisk, and little time is wasted on nonacademic matters, may boost achievement in basic areas. Although students' time on task is always important, teacher control of time becomes less important as subject matter grows complex. When teachers communicate high academic expectations to students, effective classroom management increases, and accountability becomes less worrisome.

A further development in teacher accountability is the measurement of effectiveness, for which there are various procedures. In one of those procedures, the *process approach*, teachers are observed at work by principals, administrators, or on occasion by trained outsiders. The method is most effective when the observer uses an observation schedule or checklist, and notes a teacher's actions and omissions every few seconds. In a second procedure, the *product approach*, one evaluates a teacher on the basis of student achievement. Both methods are designed to inform administrators about a teacher's effectiveness. A third system, in which teachers question their students, helps teachers to gain insight into their own weaknesses and strengths.

Chapter Study Guide

CHAPTER REVIEW

1. One important cause of the movement to make educators accountable for student learning is evidence that students are learning _____ than they used to.

2. _____ and _____ , engendered by a teacher's sense of commitment, seem to be major factors in a teacher's success.

3. According to Bloom, the most important component of the mastery method of teaching is _____ testing.

4. _____ requires students to demonstrate by performance that they have learned at least the fundamentals of basic subjects.

5. Evidence shows that teachers behave differently toward high and low achievers in accordance with their _____ .

6. _____ is based on the premise that virtually all students can learn virtually anything.

7. In the _____ approach to teacher evaluation, the administrator observes the ongoing behavior of teacher and students.

8. Performance contracting
   a. has spread quickly throughout school systems.
   b. is an example of a failure of an innovation.
   c. favors high ability students.
   d. was developed because of conflict between business and education.

9. Minimum competencies are
   a. defined by parents.
   b. based on the lowest levels of achievement in a school.

c. impossible to determine.

d. difficult to compare from school to school.

10. The major purpose of magnet schools is to

a. foster desegregation by attracting students of different races.

b. overcome poor teaching.

c. provide more resources in special areas such as science or art.

d. arrange a more valid way of measuring achievement.

Answer questions 11–16 True or False:

11. Innovative plans are best left to researchers.

12. Direct instruction encourages the use of student comments and ideas.

13. Momentum is an important part of direct instruction.

14. Engaged time and allocated time are usually different.

15. Teacher expectations may be transmitted verbally or nonverbally.

16. The product approach to teacher evaluation focuses on teacher behaviors.

FOR FURTHER THOUGHT

1. The "back-to-basics" movement in education has usually focused on the skills of reading, writing, and arithmetic. But in a fast-changing world threatened by its own technologies and by a lack of conviction about values, it can be argued that the real basics must begin with the ability to think flexibly and independently and to develop personal values—to be able to ask, rather than to answer, questions.

   If you were asked to design a minimal competencies test, what competencies would you assign priority to? How would you defend your choice?

2. Which elements in the mastery learning method, as described by Bloom on pp. 516–518, do you think are most responsible for the successes of that teaching method. Do you think the method has any drawbacks? As a teacher, would you want to use the system?

3. If expectations may be transmitted unwittingly, how will you know when you do it? Are there occasions when it is important to purposely show expectations?

4. If you were teaching, how would you prefer to be evaluated—by the product or the process approach? Why? To what extent might you make use of student ratings?

IMPORTANT TERMS

accountability	direct instruction
minimum competency testing	momentum
mastery learning	allocated time
formative testing	engaged time
summative testing	time on task
voucher plan	teacher expectancy

magnet school	process approach
performance contracting	product approach
formal innovation	halo effect
informal innovation	student ratings

SUGGESTED READINGS

BLOCK, J. H., and ANDERSON, L. W. *Mastery learning in classroom instruction.* New York: Macmillan, 1975. This short volume stresses a practical, step-by-step approach to organizing a mastery system in any classroom. Particularly helpful is the last chapter, consisting of frequently asked, tough questions about the mastery model.

BLOOM, B. S. *Human characteristics and school learning.* New York: McGraw-Hill, 1976. Here Bloom develops his theory of school learning (presented in Chapter 1 of this text) and shows how mastery learning serves to complement the theory. Includes summaries of related research.

BROPHY, J. E., and GOOD, T. L. *Teacher-student relationships.* New York: Holt, Rinehart and Winston, 1974. An enormous review of the literature related to teacher and student influence in the classroom. Much of the review is centered on the effects of teacher expectancy on the class environment.

COGAN, M. L. Educational innovation: Educational wasteland. *Theory into Practice,* 1976, *15*(3), 220–227. A scathing critique of change for the sake of change.

DOYLE, K. O. *Student evaluation of instruction.* Lexington, MA: Lexington Books, 1975. Doyle, an educational researcher, discusses the meaning and methods of student ratings of teacher effectiveness.

DUNKIN, M. J., and BIDDLE, B. J. *The study of teaching.* New York: Holt, Rinehart and Winston, 1974. A well-written review of what research has uncovered about classroom dynamics. A summary chapter (Findings for Teachers) pulls together the major research outcomes and translates them into sensible teaching practices.

EVANS, E. D. *Transition to teaching.* New York: Holt, Rinehart and Winston, 1976. A small paperback for the prospective teacher, with honest discussions of what to expect in the classroom. Includes a section on teacher effectiveness and teacher evaluation.

GAGE, N. L. (ed.) *The psychology of teaching methods.* The 75th Yearbook of the National Society for the Study of Education, Part I. Chicago: University of Chicago Press, 1976. A variety of reviews of recent research on decision-making, direct instruction, holding discussions, and so on.

GOOD, T. L., and BROPHY, J. E. *Looking in classrooms* (2nd ed.) New York: Harper and Row, 1978. An examination of how to pay attention to classroom dynamics, for the purpose of improving management. Deals as much with preventive issues as with after-the-fact remedies.

HECHINGER, F. M. Where have all the innovations gone? *Today's Education,* 1976, *65*(3), 81. Hechinger, an education critic, examines innovations of the last two decades and the reasons for their failure.

INSEL, P. M., and JACOBSON, L. F. (eds.). *What do you expect?* Menlo Park, CA: Cummings Publishing Co., 1975. A collection of readings on expectancy in human affairs, including teaching. Articles range from research to opinions.

PETERSON, P., and WALBERG, H. (eds.). *Research on teaching: Concepts, findings, and implications.* Berkeley, CA: McCutchan, 1979. Recent collection of research reviews; some articles have implications for easy transition from journals to the classroom.

ROSENTHAL, R., and JACOBSON, L. F. *Pygmalion in the classroom: Teacher expectation and pupils' development.* New York: Holt, Rinehart and Winston, 1968. A lively introduction to the self-fulfilling prophecy and teacher expectancy. Covers the historical aspects of self-fulfilling prophecy, the famous Oak School experiment, and implications for teaching.

ANSWER KEY

1. less; 2. Warmth . . . enthusiasm; 3. diagnostic *or* formative; 4. Minimal competency testing; 5. expectations; 6. Mastery learning; 7. process; 8. b; 9. d; 10. a; 11. F; 12. F; 13. T; 14. T; 15. T; 16. F.

Bibliography

ABIDIN, R. R., JR. What's wrong with behavior modification. *Journal of School Psychology*, 1971, 9 (1), 38–42.

ADAMS, G. R., and COHEN, A. S. Children's physical and interpersonal characteristics that affect student-teacher interactions. *Journal of Experimental Education*, 1974, 43 (1), 1–5.

ADAMS, R., and BIDDLE, B. J. *Realities of teaching: Explorations with videotape.* New York: Holt, Rinehart and Winston, 1970.

ALEXANDER, C., and STRAIN, P. S. A review of educators attitudes toward handicapped children and the concept of mainstreaming. *Psychology in the schools*, 1978, 15 (3), 390–396.

ALLEN, V. L. (ed.). *Children as teachers.* New York: Academic Press, 1976.

ALLEN, V. L., and FELDMAN, R. S. Learning through tutoring: Low-achieving children as tutors. *Journal of Experimental Education*, 1974, 42, 1–5.

ALLPORT, F. H. *Social psychology.* Boston: Houghton Mifflin, 1924.

ALSCHULER, A. S. *Developing achievement motivation in adolescents.* Englewood Cliffs, NJ: Educational Technology Publications, 1973.

ALVINO, J., and WIELER, J. How standardized testing fails to identify the gifted and what teachers can do about it. *Phi Delta Kappan*, 1979, 61 (2), 106–109.

AMERICAN EDUCATION. Education of the handicapped today. June 1976.

AMERICAN PSYCHIATRIC ASSOCIATION. Planning psychiatric services for children in the community mental health program. Washington, DC: American Psychiatric Association, 1964.

AMES, C., and FELKER, D. W. An examination of children's attributions and achievement-related evaluations in competitive, cooperative, and individualistic reward structures. *Journal of Educational Psychology*, 1979, 71 (4), 413–420.

ANASTASI, A. *Common fallacies about heredity, environment, and human behavior.* ACT research report #58. Iowa City: American College Testing Program, 1973.

ANDERSON, R. C., and KULHAVY, R. W. Learning concepts from definitions. *American Educational Research Journal*, 1972, 9, 385–390.

ANDERSON, R. C., REYNOLDS, R. E., SCHALLERT, D. L., and GOETZ, E. T. Frameworks for comprehending discourse. *American Educational Research Journal*, 1977, 14, 367–381.

ARENDS, R., and FORD, P. M. *Acceleration and enrichment in the junior high school: A follow-up study.* Olympia, WA: State Superintendent of Public Instruction, 1964.

ARLIN, M. Teacher transitions can disrupt time flow in classrooms. *American Educational Research Journal*, 1979, 16 (1), 42–56.

ARNOLD, J. E. Useful creative techniques. In Parnes, S. J., and Harding, H. F. (eds.), *A source book for creative thinking.* New York: Charles Scribner's Sons, 1962, pp. 251–275.

ARON, I. E. Moral philosophy and moral education: A critique of Kohlberg's theory. *School Review*, 1977, 85, 197–217.

ARONSON, E. *The jigsaw classroom.* Beverly Hills, CA: Sage, 1978.

ARONSON, E., BLANEY, N., SIKES, J., STEPHAN, C., and SNAPP, M. Busing and racial tension: The jigsaw route to learning and liking. *Psychology Today*, 1975, 8 (9), 43–50.

ASLIN, N. G., and DE ARMAN, J. W. Adoption and abandonment of innovative practices in high schools. *Educational Leadership*, 1976, 33 (8), 601–606.

ATKINSON, R. C., HERMANN, S. J., and WESCOURT, K. T. Search processes in recognition memory. In Solso, R. L. (ed.), *Theories in cognitive psychology: The Loyola symposium.* Potomac, MD: Lawrence Erlbaum, 1974.

AUSUBEL, D. P. A new look at classroom discipline. *Phi Delta Kappan*, 1961, 43 (1), 25–30.

AUSUBEL, D. P. *The psychology of meaningful ver-*

bal learning. New York: Grune and Stratton, 1963.

AUSUBEL, D. P., NOVAK, J. D., and HANESIAN, H. *Educational psychology: A cognitive view* (2nd ed.). New York: Holt, Rinehart and Winston, 1978.

AYLLON, T., and AZRIN, N. H. *The token economy: A motivational system for therapy and rehabilitation.* New York: Appleton-Century-Crofts, 1968.

AYLLON T., and RAINWATER, N. Behavioral alternatives to the drug control of hyperactive children in the classroom. *The School Psychology Digest,* 1976, 5 (4), 33–39.

AYLLON, T., and ROBERTS, M. D. Eliminating discipline problems by strengthening academic performance. *Journal of Applied Behavior Analysis,* 1974, 7, 71–76.

BAER, D. M. Stimulus response: Let's take another look at punishment. *Psychology Today,* 1971, 5 (5), 32–37.

BAHRICK, H. P., BAHRICK, P. O., and WITTLINGER, R. P. Those unforgettable high-school days. *Psychology Today,* 1974, 8 (7), 50–56.

BALLER, W. R. A study of the present social status of a group of adults who when they were in elementary schools were classified as mentally deficient. *Genetic Psychology Monographs,* 1936, 18, 165–244.

BALLER, W. R., CHARLES, D. C., and MILLER, E. L. Mid-life attainment of the mentally retarded: A longitudinal study. *Genetic Psychology Monographs,* 1967, 75, 235–329.

BANDURA, A. Social learning through imitation. In Jones, M. R. (ed.), *Symposium on motivation.* Lincoln, NE: University of Nebraska Press, 1962, pp. 211–269.

BANDURA, A. Behavioral psychotherapy. *Scientific American,* 1967, 216 (3), 78–86.

BANDURA, A. Vicarious and self-reinforcement processes. In Glaser, R. (ed.), *The nature of reinforcement.* New York: Academic Press, 1971.

BANDURA, A. Behavior theory and the models of man. *American Psychologist,* 1974, 29, 859–869.

BANDURA, A., ROSS, D., and ROSS, S. A. Imitation of film-mediated aggressive models. *Journal of Abnormal and Social Psychology,* 1963a, 66, 3–11.

BANDURA, A., ROSS, D., and ROSS, S. A. Vicarious reinforcement and imitative learning. *Journal of Abnormal and Social Psychology,* 1963b, 67, 601–607.

BANDURA, A., and WALTER, R. H. *Social learning and personality development.* New York: Holt, Rinehart and Winston, 1963.

BARATZ, S. S., and BARATZ, J. C. Early childhood intervention: The social science base of institutional racism. *Harvard Educational Review,* 1970, 40, 29–50.

BARBER, L. W. Review of *Magnet schools* by Estes and Waldrip. *Educational Evaluation and Policy Analysis,* 1979, 1 (5), 79–80.

BARCLAY, J. R. Sociometry: Rationale and techniques for effecting behavior change in the elementary school. *Personnel and Guidance Journal,* 1966, 44, 1067–1075.

BAROFF, G. S. *Mental retardation: Nature, causes, and management.* New York: John Wiley, 1974.

BARTLETT, F. C. *Remembering: A study in experimental and social psychology.* Cambridge: Cambridge University Press, 1932.

BARTLETT, I., FENTON, E., FOWLER, D., and MANDELBAUM, S. *A new history of the United States.* New York: Holt, Rinehart and Winston, 1969.

BATES, J. A. Extrinsic reward and intrinsic motivation: A review with implications for the classroom. *Review of Educational Research,* 1979, 49 (4), 557–576.

BEILIN, H. Teachers' and clinicians' attitudes toward the behavior problems of children: A reappraisal. *Child Development,* 1959, 30, 9–25.

BENHAM, B. J., GIESEN, P., and OAKES, J. A study of schooling: Students' experiences in schools. *Phi Delta Kappan,* 1980, 61 (5), 337–340.

BEREITER, C., and ENGELMANN, S. An academically-oriented preschool for culturally deprived children. In Hechinger, F. M. (ed.), *Education of the disadvantaged.* New York: Doubleday, 1966, pp. 105–135.

BEREITER, C., and SCARDAMALIA, M. The limits of natural development. *The Researcher,* 1977, 16 (1), 1–16.

BERNSTEIN, B. Social structure, language, and learning. *Educatiional Research,* 1961, 3, 163–176.

BERNSTEIN, B. A sociolinguistic approach to socialization. In Gumperz, J. J., and Humes, D. (eds.), *Directions in sociolinguistics.* New York: Holt, Rinehart and Winston, 1972, pp. 472–497.

BERSCHEID, E., and WALSTER, E. Beauty and the best. *Psychology Today,* 1972, 5 (10), 42–46.

BIELBY, D., and PAPALIA, D. Moral development and perceptual role-taking egocentrism: Their development and interrelationship across the life-span. *International Journal of Aging and Human Development,* 1975, 6, 293–308.

BINET, A. *The measurement of intelligence.* Translated by Lewis M. Terman. Boston: Houghton Mifflin, 1916.

BINET, A. The education of intelligence. In Torrance, E. P., and White, W. F. (eds.), *Issues and advances in educational psychology* (2nd ed.). Itasca, IL: Peacock Publishers, 1975, 73–82.

BINET, A., and SIMON, T. *The development of intelligence in children.* Baltimore: Williams and Wilkins, 1916.

BLOCK, J. H. Conceptions of sex roles: Some cross-cultural and longitudinal perspectives. *American Psychologist,* 1973, 28, 512–526.

BLOCK, J. H. Individualized instruction: A mastery learning perspective. *Educational Leadership,* 1977, 34 (5), 337–341.

BLOCK, N. J., and DWORKIN, G. IQ, heritability, and inequality. In Block, N. J. and Dworkin, G. (eds.) *The IQ controversy.* New York: Pantheon, 1976, 410–540.

BLOOM, B. S. *Stability and change in human characteristics.* New York: John Wiley, 1964.

BLOOM, B. S. Learning for mastery. *UCLA-CSEIP Evaluation Comment,* 1968, 1 (whole no. 2).

BLOOM, B. S. *Human characteristics and school learning.* New York: McGraw-Hill, 1976.

BLOOM, B. S. The new direction in educational research: Alterable variables. *Phi Delta Kappan,* 1980, 61 (6), 382–385.

BLOOM, B. S. et al. *Taxonomy of educational objectives, handbook 1: Cognitive domain.* New York: David McKay, 1956.

BLOOM, B. S., and BRODER, L. J. *Problem solving processes of college students.* Chicago: University of Chicago Press, 1950.

BOEGLI, R. G., and WASIK, B. H. Use of the token economy system to intervene on a school-wide level. *Psychology in the Schools.* 1978, 15 (1), 72–78.

BOGEN, J. E. Some educational aspects of hemispheric specialization. In Wittrock, M. C., et al., *The human brain.* Englewood Cliffs, NJ: Prentice-Hall, 1977.

BORG, W. R. Teacher coverage of academic content and pupil achievement. *Journal of Educational Psychology,* 1979, 71 (5), 635–645.

BORING, E. G. Intelligence as the tests test it. *New Republic,* 1923, 35, 35.

BOURNE, L. E., JR., EKSTRAND, B. R., and DOMINOWSKI, R. L. *The psychology of thinking.* Englewood Cliffs, NJ: Prentice-Hall, 1971.

BOWER, G. H. Organizational factors in memory. *Cognitive Psychology,* 1970, 1, 18–46.

BOYKIN, A. O., and POPE, C. Teacher, take a test on grading. *Phi Delta Kappan,* 1977, 58 (7), 561–563.

BRAINE, M. D. S. The ontogeny of English phrase structure: The first phase. *Language,* 1963, 39, 1–13.

BRANDWEIN, P. F. et al. *The social sciences: Concepts and values.* New York: Harcourt Brace Jovanovich, 1970.

BRIGHAM, T. A. Self-control: Part II. In Catania, A. C., and Brigham, T. A. (eds.), *Handbook of applied behavior analysis.* New York: Irvington Publishers, 1978, 259–274.

BRODINSKY, B. Back to the basics: The movement and its meaning. *Phi Delta Kappan,* 1977, 58 (7), 522–526.

BROLIN, D. *Vocational preparation of retarded citizens.* Columbus, OH: Charles Merrill, 1976.

BROOKS, R. Contrast between teachers' and clinicians' perceptions of secondary school children's behavior. *Educational Research,* 1978, 21 (1), 63–64.

BROPHY, J. E. *Advances in teacher effectiveness research.* Occasional paper # 18. East Lansing, MI: Institute for Research on Teaching, Michigan State University, April 1979a.

BROPHY, J. E. Teacher behavior and its effects. *Journal of Educational Psychology,* 1979b, 71 (6), 733–750.

BROPHY, J. E., and GOOD, T. L. *Teacher-student relationships: Causes and consequences.* New York: Holt, Rinehart and Winston, 1974.

BROPHY, J. E., and PUTNAM, J. G. Classroom management in the elementary grades. In Duke, D. L. (ed.), *Classroom management. The 78th yearbook of the national society for the study of education: Part II.* Chicago: University of Chicago Press, 1979, 182–216.

BROUDY, H. S. Ideological, political, and moral considerations in the use of drugs in hyperkinetic therapy. *School Review,* 1976, 85 (1), 43–60.

BROWN, J. C. Effects of token reinforcement administered by peer tutors on pupil reading achievement and tutor collateral behavior. *Dissertation Abstracts International,* 1972, 32 (7-A), 3775.

BROWN, R. *Social psychology.* New York: The Free Press, 1965.

BROWN, R. Development of the first language in the human species. *American Psychologist,* 1973, 28, 97–106.

BROWN, R., and HERRNSTEIN, R. J. *Psychology.* Boston: Little, Brown, 1975.

BRUININKS, R. H., and RYNDERS, J. E. Alternatives to special class placement for mentally retarded children. *Focus on Exceptional Children,* 1971, 3, 1–12.

BRUNER, J. S. *The process of education.* Cambridge, MA: Harvard University Press, 1960.

BRUNER, J. S. *The process of education* (paper). New York: Vintage Books, 1963.

BRUNER, J. S. *Toward a theory of instruction.* Cambridge, MA: Belknap Press, 1966.

BRUNER, J. S. Learning the mother tongue. *Human Nature,* September 1978, 283–288.

BRUNER, J. S., GOODNOW, J. J., and AUSTIN, G. A. *A study of thinking.* New York: John Wiley, 1956.

BRYEN, D. N. Teacher strategies in managing classroom behavior. In Hammill, D. D., and Bartel, N. R. (eds.), *Teaching children with behavior and learning problems.* Boston: Allyn and Bacon, 1975, 123–153.

BUREAU OF EDUCATION FOR THE HANDICAPPED. Number of pupils with handicaps in local public schools, Spring 1970. Washington, DC: Dept. of Health, Education, and Welfare, 1970.

BUROS, O. K. (ed.). *The eighth mental measurements yearbook.* Highland Park, NJ: Gryphon Press, 1978.

BUROS, O. K. (ed.). *The seventh mental measurements yearbook.* Highland Park, NJ: Gryphon Press, 1972.

BURTT, H. E. An experimental study of early childhood memory. *Journal of Genetic Psychology,* 1941, 58, 435–439.

BUTLER, L., MIEZITIS, S., FRIEDMAN, R., and COLE, E. The effect of two school-based intervention programs on depressive symptoms in preadolescents. *American Educational Research Journal,* 1980, 17 (1), 111–119.

CALLAHAN, R. C. A comparison of opinions held by urban and surburban students on inner-city schools. *Phi Delta Kappan,* 1980, 61 (7), 492–493.

CAMPBELL, R. F., CUNNINGHAM, L. L., and MCPHEE, R. F. *The organization and control of American schools.* Columbus, OH: Charles Merrill, 1965.

CARLSEN, R. G., TOVATT, A., ALM, R. S., and CARLSEN, R. C. (eds.) *Encounters.* New York: McGraw-Hill, 1967.

CARROLL, J. B. A model of school learning. *Teachers College Record,* 1963, 64, 723–733.

CARROLL, J. B. (ed.). *Language, thought, and reality: Selected writings of Benjamin L. Whorf.* Cambridge, MA: MIT Press, 1956.

CARROLL, J. B., and MAXWELL, S. E. Individual differences in cognitive abilities. In Rosenzweig, M. R., and Porter, L. *Annual review of psychology,* vol. 30. Palo Alto, CA: Annual Reviews, Inc., 1979, 603–640.

CATTELL, R. B. Theory of fluid and crystallized intelligence: A critical experiment. *Journal of Educational Psychology,* 1963, 54, 1–22.

CAWLEY, J., and FITZMAURICE, A. M. *The individualized educational program in mathematics.*

Tulsa, OK: Educational Development Corp., 1976.

CHAFFIN, J. D. Will the real mainstreaming program please stand up! (Or, should Dunn have done it?) *Focus on Exceptional Children,* 1974, 6 (5), 1–17.

CHAIKEN, A. L., SIGLER, E., and DERLEGA, V. J. Nonverbal mediators of teacher expectancy effects. *Journal of Personality and Social Psychology,* 1974, 30, 144–149.

CHARLES, D. C. Ability and accomplishment of persons judged earlier mentally deficient. *Genetic Psychology Monographs,* 1953, 47, 3–71.

CHARLES, D. C. A historical overview of educational psychology. *Contemporary Educational Psychology,* 1976, 1 (1), 76–88.

CHESLER, M., and FOX, R. *Role-playing methods in the classroom.* Chicago: Science Research Associates, 1966.

CHOMSKY, N. Review of Skinner's *Verbal behavior. Language,* 1959, 35, 26–58.

CHOMSKY, N. *Aspects of the theory of language.* Cambridge, MA: MIT Press, 1965.

CHRISTIE, P. R. Does the use of tangible rewards with individual children affect peer observers? *Journal of Applied Behavior Analysis,* 1975, 8, 187–196.

CLARIZIO, H., and MCCOY, G. *Behavior disorders in children* (2nd ed.). New York: Crowell, 1976.

CLARK, C. M., GAGE, N. L., MARX, R. W., PETERSON, P. L., STAYROOK, N. G., and WINNE, P. H. A factorial experiment on teacher structuring, soliciting, and reacting. *Journal of Educational Psychology,* 1979, 71 (4), 534–552.

CLEMENTS, S. D. Minimal brain dysfunctiion in children. *NINDB Monograph No. 3, Public Health Service Bulletin No. 1415.* Washington, DC: U.S. Department of Health, Education, and Welfare, 1966.

CLIFFORD, M. M., and WALSTER, E. Effect of physical attractiveness on teacher expectations. *Sociology of Education,* 1973, 46, 248–258.

CLINE, C. B., CROFT, R. G., and COURRIER, L. Desensitization of children to television violence. *Journal of Personality and Social Psychology,* 1973, 27, 360–365.

COKER, H. An investigation of the effects of a cross-age tutorial program on achievement and attitudes of 7th grade and 11th grade students. *Dissertation Abstracts International,* 1969, 29 (10-A), 3319.

COLEMAN, J. S. *Equality of educational opportunity.* Washington, DC: U.S. Department of Health, Education, and Welfare, Office of Education, 1966.

COLEMAN, J. S. Recent trends in school integration. *Educational Researcher,* 1975a, 4 (7), 3–12.

COLEMAN, J. S. Racial segregation in the schools: New research with new policy implications. *Phi Delta Kappan*, 1975b, 57 (2), 75–78.

COMBS, A. W. *Educational accountability: Beyond behavioral objectives*. Washington, DC: Association for Supervision and Curriculum Development, 1972.

COOPER, H. M. and BARON, R. M. Academic expectations and attributed responsibility as predictors of professional teachers' reinforcement behavior. *Journal of Educational Psychology*, 1977, 69 (4), 409–418.

COOPER, H. M., BURGER, J. M., and SEYMOUR, G. E. Classroom context and student ability as influences on teacher perceptions of classroom control. *American Educational Research Journal*, 1979, 16 (2), 189–196.

COOPER, H. M., and LOWE, C. A. Task information and attributions for academic performance by professional teachers and roleplayers. *Journal of Personality*, 1977, 45, 469–483.

COOPERSMITH, S. A method for determining self-esteem. *Journal of Abnormal and Social Psychology*, 1959, 59, 87–94.

COVINGTON, M. V. and OMELICH, C. L. Effort: The double-edged sword in school achievement. *Journal of Educational Psychology*, 1979, 71 (2), 169–182.

CRONBACH, L. J. *Essentials of psychological testing*. New York: Harper and Row, 1970.

CRONBACH, L. J., and SNOW, R. E. *Aptitudes and instructional methods*. New York: Irvington, 1977.

CRUICKSHANK, W. M. Some issues facing the field of learning disability. *Journal of Learning Disabilities*, 1972, 5, 380–388.

CULATTA, R., and CULATTA, B. Communication disorders. In Blackhurst, A. E. and Berdine, W. H. (eds.), *Introduction to special education*. Boston: Little, Brown, 1981.

CULLER, R. E., and HOLOHAN, C. J. Test anxiety and academic performance: The effects of study-related behavior. *Journal of Educational Psychology*, 1980, 72 (1), 16–20.

CUSICK, P. Holistic evaluation of writing: Quick and reliable. *Primary Activities* New York: Scott, Foresman, Fall 1979, 1.

DARCH, C. B., and THORPE, H. W. The principal game: A group consequence procedure to increase classroom on-task behavior. *Psychology in the Schools*, 1977, 14 (3), 341–347.

DAVIES, S. P., and ECOB, K. G. *The mentally retarded in society*. New York: Columbia University Press, 1959.

DAVIS, G. A. Training creativity in adolescence: A discussion of strategy. In Davis, G. A., and Scott, J. A. (eds.), *Training creative thinking*. New York: Holt, Rinehart and Winston, 1971, 261–269.

DAVIS, G. A. *Psychology of problem solving*. New York: Basic Books, 1973.

DeCECCO, J. P., and CRAWFORD, W. R. *The psychology of learning and instruction*, second edition. Englewood Cliffs, NJ: Prentice-Hall, 1974.

DeCHARMES, R. From pawns to origins: Toward self-motivation. In Lesser, G. (ed.), *Psychology and educational practice*. Glenview, IL: Scott, Foresman, 1971, 380–408.

DEIKER, T., and MATSON, J. L. Internal control and success orientation in a token economy for emotionally disturbed youngsters. *Adolescence*, 1979, 14 (53), 215–220.

DENNEY, N. and DENNEY, D. Modeling effects on the questioning strategies of the elderly. *Developmental Psychology*, 1974, 10, 458.

DENNIS, W., and DENNIS, M. G. The effect of cradling practices upon the onset of walking in Hopi children. *Journal of Genetic Psychology*, 1940, 56, 77–86.

DENNY, J. P. Effects of anxiety and intelligence on concept formation. *Journal of Experimental Psychology*, 1966, 72, 596–602.

DENO, E. N. *Educating children with emotional, learning, and behavior problems*. Minneapolis: University of Minnesota, National Support Systems Project, 1978.

DEWEY, J. *The child and the curriculum: The school and society*. Chicago: University of Chicago Press, 1956.

DISHAW, M. *Descriptions of allocated time to content areas for the A-B period*. Technical Report IV-2a. San Francisco: Far West Laboratory for Education Research and Development, July 1977.

DiVESTA, F. J. *Language, learning, and cognitive processes*. Monterey, CA: Brooks/Cole Publishing Co., 1974.

DiVESTA, F. J., and PALERMO, D. S. Language development. In Kerlinger, F. N., and Carroll, J. B. (eds.), *Review of research in education*, vol. 2. Itasca, IL: F. E. Peacock, 1974, 55–107.

DIXON, B., SHAW, S., and BENSKY, J. The administrator's role in fostering the mental health of special services personnel. *Exceptional Children*, 1980, 47 (1), 30–36.

DOUGHERTY, E. H., and DOUGHERTY, A. The daily report card: A simplified and flexible package for classroom behavior management. *Psychology in the Schools*, 1977, 14 (2), 191–195.

DUCHASTEL, P. Learning objectives and the organiza

tion of prose. *Journal of Educational Psychology*, 1979, 71 (1), 100–106.

DUNN, L. M. Children with mild general learning disabilities. In Dunn, L. M. (ed.), *Exceptional children in the schools* (2nd ed.). New York: Holt, Rinehart and Winston, 1973, 127–188.

DWYER, C. A. Sex differences in reading: An evaluation and a critique of current theories. *Review of Educational Research*, 1973, 43, 455–467.

DYER, H. S. The discovery and development of educational goals. *Proceedings of the 1966 invitational conference on testing problems*. Princeton, NJ: Educational Testing Service, 1967, 12–24.

EARDLEY, L. Cincinnati's magnet schools. *Integrated Education*, 1976, 14 (5), 14–20.

EBEL, R. L. *Measuring educational achievement*. Englewood Cliffs, NJ: Prentice-Hall, 1965.

EBEL, R. L. And still the dryads linger. *American Psychologist*. July 1974, 485–492.

EBMEIER, H., and GOOD, T. L. The effects of instructing teachers about good teaching on the mathematics achievement of fourth grade students. *American Educational Research Journal*, 1979, 16 (1), 1–16.

EINSTEIN, A., and INFELD, L. *The evolution of physics*. New York: Simon and Schuster, 1938.

EISENBERG, L. Future threats or clear and present dangers? *School Review*, 1976, 85 (1), 155–165.

ELAM, S. (ed.). *The Gallup polls of attitudes toward education 1969–1973*. Bloomington, IN: Phi Delta Kappan, 1973.

ELKIND, D. Egocentrism in adolescence. *Child Development*, 1967, 38, 1025–1034.

ELKIND, D. Educational psychology. In Mussen P., and Rosenzweig, M. R. (eds.), *Psychology: An introduction*. Lexington, MA: D.C. Heath, 1973, 420–445.

ELROD, W. T. Paddles still swing in Indiana schools. *Hartford Courant*, April 1, 1979.

ERIKSON, E. *Childhood and society* (2nd ed.). New York: W. W. Norton, 1963.

ERON, L. D., HUESMANN, L. R., LEFKOWITZ, M. M., and WALDER, L. O. Does television violence cause aggression? *American Psychologist*, 1972, 27, 253–263.

ESPOSITO, D. Homogeneous and heterogeneous ability grouping: Principal findings and implications for evaluating and designing more effective educational environments. *Review of Educational Research*, 1973, 43 (2), 163–179.

EVANS, R. *Dialogue with Erik Erikson*. New York: Harper and Row, 1967

EVERTSON, C., ANDERSON, L., and BROPHY, J. *Texas junior high school study: Final report*, vol. 1, Report 4061. Austin, TX: Research and Development Center for Teacher Education, University of Texas, 1978.

EVERTSON, C. M., ANDERSON, C. W., ANDERSON, L. M., and BROPHY, J. E. Relationships between classroom behaviors and student outcomes in junior high mathematics and English classes. *American Educational Research Journal*, 1980, 17 (1), 43–60.

FAIRCHILD, T. N. Home-school token economies: Bridging the communication gap. *Psychology in the Schools*, 1976, 13 (4), 463–467.

FEDERAL REGISTER. Public Law 94–142. Washington, DC: Government Printing Office, 1976.

FELDHUSEN, J. F. Problems of student behavior in secondary schools. In Duke, D. L. (ed.), *Classroom management. The 78th yearbook of the national society for the study of education: Part II*. Chicago: University of Chicago Press, 1979, 217–244.

FELDMAN, R. S., and DEVIN-SHEEHAN, L. Children tutoring children: A critical review of research. In Allen V. L. (ed.), *Children as teachers*. New York: Academic Press, 1976, 236–249.

FELDMAN, R. S., and PROHASKA, T. The student as Pygmalion: Effect of student expectation on the teacher. *Journal of Educational Psychology*, 1979, 71 (4), 485–493.

FELKER, D. W. *Building positive self-concepts*. Minneapolis: Burgess, 1974.

FESTINGER, L. The motivating effect of cognitive dissonance. In Lindzey, G. (ed.), *Assessment of human motives*. New York: Holt, Rinehart and Winston, 1958.

FINCHER, J. *Human intelligence*. New York: G. P. Putnam's, 1976.

FINDLEY, W., and BRYAN, M. *The pros and cons of ability grouping*. Bloomington, IN: Phi Delta Kappa Education Foundation, 1975.

FISKE, E. B. Mastery teaching: Until all are caught up. *New York Times*, 29 August 1976, p. 9E.

FLANAGAN, J. C. The first 15 years of project TALENT: Implications for career guidance. *Vocational Guidance Quarterly*, September 1973, 8–14.

FLANAGAN, J. C., TIEDEMAN, D. V., and WILLIS, M. B. *The career data book*. Palo Alto, CA: American Institutes for Research, 1973.

FLAVELL, J. H. *The developmental psychology of Jean Piaget*. Princeton, NJ: D. Van Nostrand, 1963.

FODOR, E. M. Resistance to social influence among

adolescents as a function of level of moral development. *Journal of Social Psychology*, 1971, 85, 121–126.

FOSTER, G., and YSSELDYKE, J. Expectancy and halo effects as a result of artificially induced teacher bias. *Contemporary Educational Psychology*, 1976, 1 (1), 37–45.

FRANCIS, E. W. Grade level and task difficulty in learning by discovery and verbal reception methods, *Journal of Educational Psychology*, 1975, 67, 146–150.

FREEMAN, R. D. Minimal brain dysfunction, hyperactivity, and learning disorders: Epidemic or episode? *School Review*, 1976, 85, (1), 5–30.

FREMONT, T. S., SEIFERT, D. M., and WILSON, J. H. *Informal diagnostic assessment of children*. Springfield, IL: Charles C. Thomas, 1977.

FREMONT, T. S., and WALLBROWN, F. H. Types of behavior problems that may be encountered in the classroom. *Journal of Education*, 1979, 161 (2), 5–24.

FREYBERG, J. T. The effect of participation in an elementary school buddy system on the self concept, school attitudes and behaviors, and achievement of fifth-grade Negro Children. *Graduate Research in Education and Related Disciplines*, 1967, 3, 3–29.

FROMAN, R. D., and OWEN, S. V. *A review of research on the impact of homogeneous grouping*. Storrs, CT: Bureau of Educational Research, University of Connecticut, 1979.

FROMAN, R. D., and OWEN, S. V. Influence of different types of student ratings feedback upon later instructional behavior. Paper presented at the annual meeting of the American Educational Research Association, April 1980, Boston, MA.

FURTH, H. G., and WACHS, H. *Piaget's theory in practice: Thinking goes to school*. New York: Oxford University Press, 1975.

FYANS, L. J., and MAEHR, M. L. Attributional style, task selection, and achievement. *Journal of Educational Psychology*, 1979, 71 (4), 499–507.

GAA, J. P. The effect of individual goal-setting conferences on academic achievement and modification of locus of control. *Psychology in the Schools*, 1979, 16 (4), 591–597.

GAGNÉ, E. D. Long-term retention of information following learning from prose. *Review of Educational Research*, 1978, 48, 629–665.

GAGNÉ, R. M. and WHITE, R. T. Memory structures and learning outcomes. *Review of Educational Research*, 1978, 48, 187–222.

GALLUP, G. H. Seventh annual Gallup poll of public attitudes toward education. *Phi Delta Kappan*, 1975, 57 (4), 227–241.

GALLUP, G. H. Eighth annual Gallup poll of the public's attitudes toward the public schools. *Phi Delta Kappan*, 1976, 58 (2), 187–200.

GALLUP, G. H. Twelfth annual Gallup poll of the public's attitudes toward the public schools. *Phi Delta Kappan*, 1980, 62 (1), 33–36.

GARDNER, H. *The arts and human development: A psychological study of the artistic process*. New York: John Wiley, 1973.

GARDNER, J. *Excellence*. New York: Harper and Row, 1961.

GARIBALDI, A. M. Affective contributions of cooperative and group goal structures. *Journal of Educational Psychology*, 1979, 71 (6), 788–794.

GAUSS, J. Teacher evaluation. *Saturday Review*, 21 July 1962, 47.

GAZZANIGA, M. Review of the split brain. In Wittrock, M. C., et al., *The human brain*. Englewood Cliffs, NJ: Prentice-Hall, 1977.

GEISMAR, M. (ed.). *Mark Twain and the three R's*. Indianapolis: Bobbs-Merrill, 1973.

GETZELS, J. W., and CSIKSZENTMIHALY, M. From problem solving to problem finding. In Taylor, I. A., and Getzels, J. W., *Perspectives in creativity*. Chicago, IL: Aldine, 1975, 90–116.

GETZELS, J. W., and DILLON, T. J. The nature of giftedness and the education of the gifted. In Travers, R. M. W. (ed.), *Second handbook of research on teaching*. Chicago: Rand McNally, 1973, 689–731.

GEWIRTZ, J. L. The roles of overt responding and extrinsic reinforcement in "self" and "vicarious-reinforcement" phenomena and in "observational learning" and imitation. In Glaser, R. (ed.), *The nature of reinforcement*. New York: Academic Press, 1971, 279–309.

GIBSON, E. *Principles of perceptual learning and development*. New York: Appleton-Century-Crofts, 1969.

GIL, A. (ed.). *In the words of Piaget*. New York: W. W. Norton, 1971.

GINSBURG, H., and OPPER, S. *Piaget's theory of intellectual development* (2nd ed.). Englewood Cliffs, NJ: Prentice-Hall, 1979.

GLASER, R. Components of a psychology of instruction: Toward a science of design. *Review of Educational Research*, 1976, 46 (1), 1–24.

GOEBEL, B. L., and CASHEN, V. M. Age, sex, and attractiveness as factors in student ratings of teachers. *Journal of Educational Psychology,* 1979, 71 (5), 646–653.

GOLDSTEIN, H. Social and occupational adjustment. In Stevens, H. A., and Heber, R. (eds.), *Mental retardation: A review of research.* Chicago: University of Chicago Press, 1964.

GOOD, T. L., BIDDLE, B. J., and BROPHY J. E. *Teachers make a difference.* New York: Holt, Rinehart and Winston, 1975.

GOOD, T. L., and BROPHY, J. E. *Educational psychology: A realistic approach.* New York: Holt, Rinehart and Winston, 1977.

GOOD, T. L., and GROUWS, D. A. The Missouri mathematics effectiveness project: An experimental study in fourth-grade classrooms. *Journal of Educational Psychology,* 1979, 71 (3), 355–362.

GOODALL, K. Shapers at work. *Psychology Today,* 1972, 6 (6), 53–63, 132.

GOODLAD, J. I. Perspectives on theory, research, and practice, In Duke, D. L. (ed.), *Classroom management. The 78th yearbook of the national society for the study of education: Part II.* Chicago: University of Chicago Press, 1979, 391–412.

GOODMAN, L., and MANN, L. *Learning disabilities in the secondary school.* New York: Grune and Stratton, 1976.

GOTTLIEB, J. Attitudes of Norwegian and American children toward mildly retarded children in special classes. *Journal of Special Education,* 1974, 7, 313–319.

GOWAN, J. C. Background and history of the gifted-child movement. In Stanley, J. C., George, W. C., and Solano, C. H. (eds.). *The gifted and the creative.* Baltimore: Johns Hopkins University Press, 1977, 5–27.

GREENWOOD, C. R., HOPS, H., and WALKER, H. M. The program for academic survival skills (PASS): Effects on student behavior and achievement. *Journal of School Psychology,* 1977, 15 (1), 25–35.

GRINSPOON, L., and SINGER, S. Amphetamines in the treatment of hyperkinetic children. *Harvard Educational Review,* 1973, 43, 515–555.

GRONLUND, N. E. *Stating behavior objectives for classroom instruction* (2nd ed.). New York: Macmillan, 1978.

GROSSMAN, H. J. (ed.). *Manual on terminology and classification in mental retardation.* Washington, DC: American Association on Mental Deficiency, 1973.

GUR, R. E., GUR, R. C., and MARSHALEK, B. Classroom seating and functional brain asym-

metry, *Journal of Educational Psychology,* 1975, 67 (1), 151–153.

HAAN, N., SMITH, M. B., and BLOCK, J. Moral reasoning of young adults: Political-social behavior, family background, and personality correlates. *Journal of Personality and Social Psychology,* 1968, 10 (3), 183–201.

HAGGERTY, M. The effects of being a tutor and being a counselor in a group on self-concept and achievement level of under-achieving adolescent males. *Dissertation Abstracts International,* 1971, 31, (9-A), 4460.

HALL, E. M. A conversation with Jean Piaget, *Psychology Today,* May 1970, 27–30.

HALL, E. M. Bad education—a conversation with Jerome Bruner. *Psychology Today,* December 1970, p. 50.

HALL, R. V., AXELROD, S., TYLER, L., GRIEF, E., JONES, F. C., and ROBERTSON, R. Modification of behavior problems in the home with a parent as observer and experimenter. *Journal of Applied Behavior Analysis,* 1972, 5, 53–64.

HAMBLIN, J. A., and HAMBLIN, R. L. On teaching disadvantaged preschoolers to read: A successful experiment. *American Educational Research Journal,* 1972, 9, 209–216.

HAMBLIN, R. E., HATHAWAY, C., and WODARSKI, J. Group contingencies, peer tutoring, and accelerating academic achievement. In Ramp, E. A., and Hopkins, B. L. (eds.), *A new direction for education: Behavior analysis 1971,* vol. 1. Lawrence, KS: University of Kansas, Department of Human Development, 1971.

HARRIS, V. W., and SHERMAN, J. Use and analysis of the "good behavior game" to reduce disruptive classroom behavior. *Journal of Applied Behavior Analysis,* 1973, 6 (3), 405–417.

HARROW, A. J. *A taxonomy of the psychomotor domain: A guide for developing behavioral objectives.* New York: David McKay, 1972.

HARTLEY, J., and DAVIES, I. K. Preinstructional strategies: The role of pretests, behavioral objectives, overviews, and advance organizers. *Review of Educational Research,* 1976, 46 (2), 239–265.

HARTSHORNE, H., and MAY, M. A. *Studies in the nature of character: I. Studies in deceit.* New York: Macmillan, 1928.

HATTIE, J. Should creativity tests be administered under testlike conditions? An empirical study of three alternative conditions. *Journal of Educational Psychology,* 1980, 72 (1), 87–98.

HAVIGHURST, R. J. Choosing a middle path for the use of drugs with hyperactive children. *School Review*, 1976, 85 (1), 61–77.

HAVIGHURST, R. J., and NEUGARTEN, B. L. *Society and education* (4th ed.). Boston: Allyn and Bacon, 1975.

HAVILAND, J. M. Teachers' and students' beliefs about punishment. *Journal of Educational Psychology*, 1979, 71 (4), 563–570.

HEBER, R. F., and DEVER, R. B. Research on education and habilitation of the mentally retarded. In Haywood, H. C. (ed.), *Social-cultural aspects of mental retardation*. New York: Appleton-Century-Crofts, 1970, 393–427.

HECHINGER, F. N. Where have all the innovations gone? *Today's Education*, 1976, 65 (3), 81–83.

HELLER, M. S., and WHITE, M. A. Rates of teacher verbal approval and disapproval to higher and lower ability classes. *Journal of Educational Psychology*, 1975, 67 (6), 796–800.

HENRY, S. E., MEDWAY, F. J., and SCARBRO, H. A. Sex and locus of control as determinants of children's responses to peer versus adult praise. *Journal of Educational Psychology*, 1979, 71 (5), 604–612.

HERBERT, J., and ATTRIDGE, C. A guide for developers and users of observation systems and manuals. *American Educational Research Journal*, 1975, 12, 1–20.

HERBERT, J. J., and HARSH, C. M. Observational learning by cats. *Journal of Comparative Psychology*, 1944, 37, 81–95.

HERON, W. Cognitive and physiological effects of perceptual isolation. In Solomon, P., Kubzansky, P. E., Leiderman, P. H., Mendelson, J., and Wexler, D. (eds.), *Sensory deprivation*. Cambridge, MA: Harvard University Press, 1961.

HERSON, M., EISLER, R. M., and MILLER, P. M. Historical perspectives in behavior modification: Introductory comments. In Herson, M., Eisler, R. M., and Miller, P. M. (eds.), *Progress in behavior modification*, vol. 1. New York: Academic Press, 1975, 1–17.

HERTZ-LAZAROWITZ, R., SHARAN, S., and STEINBERG, R. Classroom learning style and cooperative behavior of elementary school children. *Journal of Educational Psychology*, 1980, 72 (1), 99–106.

HEWETT, F. M., and BLAKE, P. R. Teaching the emotionally disturbed. In Travers, R. M. W. (ed.), *Second handbook of research on teaching*. Chicago: Rand McNally, 1973, 657–688.

HEWETT, F. M., TAYLOR, F. D., and ARTUSO, A. A. The Santa Monica project: Evaluation of an engineered classroom design with emotionally disturbed children. *Exceptional Children*, 1969, 35, 523–529.

HIATT, D. B. Time allocation in the classroom: Is instruction being shortchanged? *Phi Delta Kappan*, 1979, 61 (4), 289–290.

HIGHET, G. *The art of teaching*. New York: Vintage Books, 1950.

HILL, K. T., and SARASON, S. B. The relation of test anxiety and defensiveness to test and school performance over the elementary school years. *Monographs of the Society for Research in Child Development*, 1966, 31 (2), 1–76.

HILL, S. H., and LIEBERT, R. M. Effects of consistent or deviant modeling cues on the adoption of a self-imposed standard. *Psychonomic Science*, 1968, 13, 243–244.

HILLS, J. R. *Measurement and evaluation in the classroom*. Columbus, Ohio: Charles Merrill, 1976.

HODGKINSON, H. What's right with education? *Phi Delta Kappan*, 1979, 61 (3), 159–162.

HOMME, L., CSANYI, A. P., GONZALES, M. A., and RECHS, J. R. *How to use contingency contracting in the classroom*. Champaign, IL: Research Press, 1973.

HOPKINS, C. D., and ANTES, R. L. *Classroom testing: Construction*. Itasca, IL: F. E. Peacock, 1979.

HORNBLUM, J. N., and OVERTON, W. F. Area and volume conservation among the elderly: Assessment and training. *Developmental Psychology*, 1976, 12, 68–74.

HORNER, M. S. Toward an understanding of achievement-related conflicts in women. *Journal of Social Issues*, 1972, 28, 157–175.

HULL, C. L. *Principles of behavior*. New York: Appleton-Century-Crofts, 1943.

HULSE, S. H., DEESE, J., and EGETH, H. *The psychology of learning*. New York: McGraw-Hill, 1975.

HUMPHREYS, L. Seminar III (behavioral genetics). In Davis, B. D., and Flaherty, P. (eds.), *Human diversity: Its causes and social significance*. Cambridge, MA: Ballinger, 1976, 97–143.

HUNT, D. E., and SULLIVAN, E. V. *Between psychology and education*. New York: Dryden Press, 1974.

HUNT, E. Varieties of cognitive power. In Resnick, L. (ed.), *The nature of intelligence*. Hillsdale, NJ: Lawrence Erlbaum, 1976, 237–259.

HUNT, J. McV. Traditional personality theory in the light of recent evidence. In Janis, I. L. (ed.), *Current trends in psychology: Readings from American Scientist*. Los Altos, CA: Wm. Kaufmann, 1977, 218–225.

INSTITUTE FOR SOCIAL INQUIRY. *Connecticut poll #4, release #3.* Storrs, CT: Univ. of Connecticut, March 4, 1980.

JACKS, K. B., and KELLER, M. E. A humanistic approach to the adolescent with learning disabilities: An educational, psychological, and vocational model. *Adolescence,* 1978, *13* (49), 59–68.

JACKSON, P. E. "Teacher-pupil communication in the elementary classroom: An observational study." Paper read at the annual meeting of the American Educational Research Association, 1965.

JACOBSON, L. I. "Intelligence—myth and reality." Paper read at the Urban Life Center Conference, March 1976, Georgia State University.

JAMES, W. *Talks to teachers on psychology: And to students on some of life's ideals.* New York: H. Holt, 1899.

JAMES, W. *The principles of psychology.* New York: Dover, 1950 (reprint of the 1890 edition).

JENNINGS, F. G. Jean Piaget: Notes on learning. *Saturday Review,* 1967, *50* (17), 81–83.

JENSEN, A. R. How much can we boost IQ and scholastic achievement? *Harvard Educational Review,* 1969, *39* (1), 1–123.

JENSEN, A. R. *Educability and group differences.* New York: Harper and Row, 1973.

JENSEN, A. R. *Bias in mental testing.* Riverside, NJ: Free Press, 1979.

JOHNSON, D. *Educational psychology.* Englewood Cliffs, NJ: Prentice-Hall, 1979.

JOHNSON, D., SKON, L., and JOHNSON, R. Effects of cooperative, competitive, and individualistic conditions on children's problem-solving performance. *American Educational Research Journal,* 1980, *17* (1), 83–93.

JOHNSON, R., RYNDERS, J., JOHNSON, D. W., SCHMIDT, B., and HAIDER, S. Interaction between handicapped and nonhandicapped teenagers as a function of situational goal structuring: Implications for mainstreaming. *American Educational Research Journal,* 1979, *16* (2), 161–167.

JOHNSON, R. A., KENNEY, J. B., and DAVIS, J. B. Developing school policy for use of stimulant drugs for hyperactive children. *School Review,* 1976, *85* (1), 78–96.

JONES, R. L. (ed.). *Mainstreaming and the minority child.* Reston, VA: The Council for Exceptional Children, 1976.

JUNG, C. G. *Man and his symbols.* New York: Doubleday, 1964.

JUSTMAN, J. Personal and social adjustment of intellectually gifted accelerants and non-accelerants in junior high schools. *School Review,* 1953, *61,* 468–478.

KAGAN, J. *Understanding children: Behavior, motives, and thought.* New York: Harcourt Brace Jovanovich, 1971.

KAMIN, L. J. *The science and politics of IQ.* Potomac, MD: Erlbaum, 1974.

KARANT, V. I. Socrates denied: A defeat for community resource people in the public schools. *Phi Delta Kappan,* 1977, *58* (8), 639–641.

KARNES, F. A., and COLLINS, E. C. State definitions of gifted and talented: A report and analysis. *Journal of the Education of the Gifted,* February 1978, 44–62.

KAZDIN, A. E. Self-monitoring and behavior change. In Mahoney, M. J. and Thoreson, C. E. (eds.), *Self-control: Power to the person.* Monterey, CA: Brooks/Cole, 1974, 218–246.

KAZDIN, A. E. *History of behavior modification: Experimental foundations of contemporary research.* Baltimore: University Park Press, 1978.

KELLEY, J. F., and HAKE, D. F. An extinction-induced increase in an aggressive response in humans. *Journal of Experimental Analysis of Behavior,* 1970, *14,* 153–164.

KELLY, T. J., BULLOCK, L. M., and DYKES, M. K. Behavior disorders: Teachers' perceptions. *Exceptional Children,* 1977, *43,* 316–318.

KERSHNER, J. R. Cerebral dominance in disabled readers, good leaders, and gifted children: Search for a valid model. *Child Development,* 1977, *48* (1), 61–67.

KESS, J. F. *Psycholinguistics.* New York: Academic Press, 1976.

KIBLER, R. J., BARKER, L. L., and MILES, D. T. *Behavioral objectives and instruction.* Boston: Allyn and Bacon, 1970.

KINTSCH, W., KOSMINSHY, E., STREBY, W. J., MCGOON, G., and KEENAN, J. M. Comprehension and recall of text as a function of content variables. *Journal of Verbal Learning and Verbal Behavior,* 1975, *14,* 196–214.

KIRK, S. A. *Educating exceptional children* (2nd ed.). Boston: Houghton Mifflin, 1972.

KLAUSMEIER, H. J. Instructional design and the teaching of concepts. In Levin, J. R., and Allen, V. L. (eds.), *Cognitive learning in children.* New York: Academic Press, 1976, 191–217.

KLAUSMEIER, H. J., and ALLEN, P. S. *Cognitive development of children and youth.* New York: Academic Press, 1978.

KLAUSMEIER, H. J., GHATALA, E. S., and FRAYER, D. A. *Conceptual learning and development.* New York: Academic Press, 1974.

KLAUSMEIER, H. J., and GOODWIN, W. *Learning and human abilities* (4th ed.). New York: Harper and Row, 1975.

KLAUSMEIER, H. J., and HOOPER, F. H. Conceptual development and instruction. In Kerlinger, F. N. (ed.), *Review of research in education*, vol. 2. Itasca, IL: F. E. Peacock, 1974, 3–54.

KLENTSCHY, M. P. "The effect of sixth-grade tutors on the word attack attainment of second graders." Paper read at annual meeting of the California Educational Research Association, November 1972, San Jose, CA.

KOCH, L., and KOCH, J. Now teenagers want tougher schools. *Parade*, March 30, 1980, 24–26.

KOESTLER, A. *Act of creation.* New York: Dell, 1966.

KOHLBERG, L. The development of children's orientations toward a moral order: I. Sequence in the development of moral thought. *Vita Humana*, 1963, 6, 11–33.

KOHLBERG, L. Stage and sequence: The cognitive development approach to socialization. In Goslin, D.A. (ed.), *Handbook of socialization theory and research.* Chicago: Rand McNally, 1969, 347–480.

KOHLBERG, L. Continuities in childhood and adult moral development revisited. In Baltes, P. B., and Schaie, K. W. (eds.), *Life-span developmental psychology: Personality and socialization.* New York: Academic Press, 1973, 179–204.

KOHLBERG, L., and KRAMER, R. Continuities and discontinuities in childhood and adult moral development. *Human Development*, 1969, 12, 93–120.

KÖHLER, W. *The mentality of apes.* New York: Harcourt Brace Jovanovich, 1925.

KOUNIN, J. S. *Discipline and group management in classrooms.* New York: Holt, Rinehart and Winston, 1970.

KRAMER, R. B. Changes in moral judgement response patterns during late adolescence and young adulthood: Retrogression in a developmental sequence. Ph.D. dissertation, University of Chicago, 1968.

KRASNER, L., and KRASNER, M. Token economies and other planned environments. In Thoreson, C. E. (ed.), *Behavior modification in education. 72nd yearbook of the National Society for the Study of Education*, part I. Chicago: University of Chicago Press, 1973, 351–384.

KRATHWOHL, D. R. et al. *Taxonomy of educational objectives, handbook II: Affective domain.* New York: David McKay, 1964.

KRYSTAL, S., and HENRIO, S. *PREP report no. 35, educational accountability and evaluation.* Washington, DC: U.S. Department of Health, Education, and Welfare, 1972.

KUMAR, V. K. The structure of human memory and some educational implications. *Review of Educational Research*, 1971, 41 (5), 379–417.

LABOV, W. Academic ignorance and black intelligence. *Atlantic Monthly*, 1972, 229 (6), 59–67.

LARSON, M. E. Humbling cases for career counselors. *Phi Delta Kappan*, 1973, 54 (6), 374.

LAVOIE, J. C. Aversive, cognitive, and parental determinants of punishment generalization in adolescent males. *Journal of Genetic Psychology*, 1974, 124, 29–39.

LAWRENCE, J., and LEE, R. E. *The night Thoreau spent in jail.* New York: Bantam Books, 1972.

LAYCOCK, F. *Gifted children.* Glenview, IL: Scott, Foresman, 1979.

LEE, B. N., and MERRILL, D. *Writing complete affective objectives: A short course.* Belmont, CA: Wadsworth, 1972.

LEVINSON, D. J. Toward a conception of the adult life course. Unpublished manuscript, August 1979.

LEVINSON, D. J., DARROW, C. N., KELIN, E. B., LEVINSON, M. H., and MCKEE, B. *The seasons of a man's life.* New York: Alfred A. Knopf, 1978.

LEWIS, W. W. Continuity and intervention in emotional disturbance: A review. *Exceptional children*, 1965, 31, 465–475.

LIETTE, E. E. Tutoring: Its effects on reading achievement, standard setting, and affect in mediating self-evaluation for black male underachievers in reading. *Dissertation Abstracts International*, 1972, 32 (8-A), 4244.

LINDSLEY, O. R. Can deficiency produce specific superiority—the challenge of the idiot savant. *Exceptional Children*, 1965, 31, 225–232.

LIPPITT, P. Learning through cross-age helping: Why and how. In Allen, V. L. (ed.), *Children as teachers.* New York: Academic Press, 1976, 157–167.

LOCKE, E. A., and BRYAN, J. F. Cognitive aspects of psychomotor performance: The effects of performance goals on the level of performance. In Singer, R. N. (ed.), *Readings in motor learning.* Philadelphia: Lea and Febiger, 1972, 286–292.

LOCKE, J. *John Locke on education.* Edited by Peter

Gay. New York: Bureau of Publications, Teachers College, Columbia University, 1964.

LOCKWOOD, A. L. The effects of values clarification and moral development curricula on school-age subjects: A critical review of recent research. *Review of Educational Research*, 1978, 48 (3), 325–364.

LOFTUS, E. F., and PALMER, J. C. Reconstruction of automobile destruction: An example of the interaction between language and memory. *Journal of Verbal Learning and Verbal Behavior*, 1974, 13, 585–589.

LURIA, A. *The mind of a mnemonist.* New York: Basic Books, 1968.

McCAFFREY, E., and CUMMING, J. *Behavior patterns associated with persistent emotional disturbances of school children in regular classes of elementary grades.* Onondaga County, NY: New York State Department of Mental Hygiene, Mental Health Research Unit, 1967.

McCANDLESS, B. R. *Children.* New York: Holt, Rinehart and Winston, 1967.

MACCOBY, E. E., and JACKLIN, C. N. *The psychology of sex differences.* Stanford, CA: Stanford University Press, 1974.

McDANIEL, T. R. Exploring alternatives to punishment: The keys to effective discipline. *Phi Delta Kappan*, 1980, 61 (7), 455–458.

McDOUGALL, W. *An introduction to social psychology.* London: Methuen, 1908.

McGEE, C. S., KAUFFMAN, J. M., and NUSSEN, J. L. Children as therapeutic change agents: Reinforcement intervention paradigms. *Review of Educational Research*, 1977, 47 (3), 451–477.

McGUINNESS, D., and PRIBRAM, K. The origins of sensory bias in the development of gender difference in perception and cognition. In Bortner, M. (ed.), *Cognitive growth and development: Essays in honor of H. G. Birch.* New York: Brunner/Mazel, 1978.

MacMILLAN, D. L. *Mental retardation in school and society.* Boston: Little, Brown, 1977.

McMILLAN, J. H. Effect of instructional procedure and pupil locus of control on achievement and attitudes. *Psychology in the Schools*, 1980, 17 (1), 123–127.

MADDI, S. R. *Personality theories.* Homewood, IL: The Dorsey Press, 1968.

MAGER, R. F. *Preparing instructional objectives.* Palo Alto, CA: Fearon Publishers, 1962.

MAGER, R. F. *Developing attitude toward learning.* Palo Alto, CA: Fearon Publishers, 1968.

MAGER, R. F. *Goal analysis.* Belmont, CA: Fearon Publishers, 1972.

MAHONEY, M. J., and THORESON, C. E. *Self-control: Power the person.* Monterey, CA: Brooks/Cole, 1974.

MAIER, N. R. F. Reasoning in humans: On direction. *Journal of Comparative Psychology*, 1930, 10, 115–143.

MALOTT, R., TILLEMA, M., and GLENN, S. *Behavior analysis and behavior modification: An introduction.* Kalamazoo, MI: Behaviordelia, 1978.

MALOTT, R. W. *Contingency management in education.* Kalamazoo, MI: Behaviordelia, 1972.

MARASCUILO, L., LEVIN, L., and JAMES, H. *Evaluation report for the Berkeley Unified School District's remedial reading program*, 15 September 1969, Berkeley, CA.

MARLAND, S. P. *Education of the gifted and talented.* Report to the Congress of the U.S. by the U.S. Commissioner of Education, and background papers submitted to the U.S. Office of Education. Washington, DC: U.S. Government Printing Office, 1972.

MARSHALL, J. C., and HALES, L. W. *Classroom test construction.* Reading, MA: Addison-Wesley, 1971.

MARTENS, R. Effect of an audience on learning and performance of a complex motor skill. In Singer, R. N. (ed.), *Readings in motor learning.* Philadelphia: Lea and Febiger, 1972, 381–390.

MASLOW, A. H. *Toward a psychology of being* (2nd ed.). Princeton, NJ: D. Van Nostrand, 1968.

MASON, E. P. Some correlates of self-judgments of the aged. *Journal of Gerentology*, 1954, 9, 324–337.

MAURER, D., LIEGEL, L. S., LEWIS, T. L., KRISTOFFERSON, M. W., BARNES, R. A., and LEVY, B. A. Long-term memory improvement? *Child Development*, 1979, 50 (1), 106–118.

MAW, W. H., and MAW, E. W. Self-concepts of high and low curiosity boys. *Child Development*, 1970, 41, 123–129.

MEANS, V., MOORE, J. W., GAGNÉ, E., and HAUCK, W. E. The interactive effects of consonant and dissonant teacher expectancy and feedback communication on student performance in a natural school setting. *American Educational Research Journal*, 1979, 16 (4), 367–373.

MEDWAY, F. J. Causal attributions for school-related problems: Teacher perceptions and teacher feedback. *Journal of Educational Psychology*, 1979, 71 (6), 809–818.

MEHTA, M. Charting the grandperson galaxy. *Phi Delta Kappan*, 1976, 58 (3), 244–247.

MEICHENBAUM, D., and CAMERON, R. The clinical potential of modifying what clients say to themselves. In Mahoney, M. J., and Thoreson, C. E. (eds.), *Self-control: Power to the person.* Monterey, CA: Brooks/Cole, 1974, 263–290.

MELTON, R. F. Resolution of conflicting claims concerning the effect of behavioral objectives on student learning. *Review of Educational Research,* 1978, 48 (2), 291–302.

MERCER, J. R. *Labeling the mentally retarded.* Berkeley, CA: University of California Press, 1973.

MERRILL, M. D. Necessary psychological conditions for defining instructional outcomes. *Educational Technology,* 1971, *11,* 34–39.

MERRILL, M. D., and TENNYSON, R. D. *The effects of types of positive and negative examples on learning concepts in the classroom.* Washington, DC: U.S. Department of Health, Education, and Welfare, Office of Education, Bureau of Research, 1971.

MESSÉ, L. A., CRANO, W. D., MESSÉ, S. R., and RICE, W. Evaluation of the predictive validity of tests of mental ability for classroom performance in elementary grades. *Journal of Educational Psychology,* 1979, 71 (2), 233–241.

MICHAELS, J. W. Classroom reward structures and academic performance. *Review of Educational Research,* 1977, 47, 87–98.

MILGRAM, S. *Obedience to authority: An experimental view.* New York: Harper and Row, 1974.

MILLER, G. A. The magical number seven, plus or minus two: Some limits on our capacity for processing information. *Psychological Review,* 1956, 63, 81–96.

MILLER, J. P. *Humanizing the classroom.* New York: Praeger, 1976.

MILLER, R. V. Social status and socioempathic differences among mentally superior, mentally typical, and mentally retarded children. *Exceptional Children,* 1956, 23, 114–119.

MILLS V. BOARD OF EDUCATION. 348 F. Supp. 866. (DCC), 1972.

MILNE, A. A. *Winnie-the-Pooh.* London: Methuen, 1926.

MILNE, A. A. *The world of Pooh.* New York: E. P. Dutton, 1957.

MILTON, D., and EDGERLY, J. W. *The testing and grading of students.* New Rochelle, NY: A Change Publication, 1976.

MISCHEL, W. A social-learning view of sex differences in behavior. In Maccoby, E. (ed.), *The development of sex differences.* Stanford, CA: Stanford University Press, 1966.

MOHAN, M. Peer tutoring as a technique for teaching the unmotivated. Teacher Education Research Center, research report. State University College, Fredonia, NY, March 1972.

MOORE, G., and STEPHENS, B. Two-year gains in moral conduct by retarded and nonretarded persons. *American Journal of Mental Deficiency,* 1974, 79, 147–153.

MORISHIMA, A. Another Van Gogh of Japan: The superior artwork of a retarded boy. *Exceptional Children,* 1974, 41 (2), 92–96.

MOSS, H. A. Early sex differences and mother-infant interaction. In Friedman, R. C., Richart, R. M., and VandeWiele, R. L. (eds.), *Sex differences in behavior.* New York: Wiley, 1974, 149–163.

MOWRER, O. H. *Learning theory and behavior.* New York: Wiley, 1960.

MUELLER, D. J. Mastery learning: Partly boon, partly boon-doggle. *Teacher Education Forum,* 1975, 3 (whole no. 11).

MURRAY, F. B. Two models of human behavior and reading instruction. In Gallagher, J. McC., and Easley, J. A. (eds.), *Knowledge and development,* vol. 2. New York: Plenum Press, 1978, 177–197.

MURRAY, H. A. *Explorations in personality.* New York: Oxford Univerity Press, 1938.

MYERS, P. I., and HAMMILL, D. D. *Methods for learning disorders.* New York: Wiley, 1976.

NASH, R. Pupils' expectations of their teachers. In Stubbs, M., and Delamont, S. (eds.), *Explorations in classroom observation.* New York: Wiley, 1976, 83–98.

NATIONAL ADVISORY COMMITTEE ON HANDICAPPED CHILDREN. *First annual report, special education for handicapped children.* Washington, DC: U.S. Office of Education, 1968.

NATIONAL INSTITUTE OF EDUCATION. *Violent schools—safe schools: The safe school study report to the Congress.* Washington, DC: U.S. Dept. of Health, Education, and Welfare, 1978.

NEISSER, U. Self-knowledge and psychological knowledge: Teaching psychology from the cognitive point of view. *Educational Psychologist,* 1975, *11* (3), 158–170.

NEUGARTEN, B. L. The awareness of middle age. In Neugarten, B. L. (ed.), *Middle age and aging: A reader in social psychology.* Chicago: University of Chicago Press, 1968, 93–98.

NICHOLS, W. A study of the effects of tutoring on the self-concept, reading achievement and selected attitudes of culturally disadvantaged children.

Dissertation Abstracts International, 1969, 29 (9–A), 2898.

OFFICE OF ECONOMIC OPPORTUNITY. *An experiment in performance contracting: Summary of preliminary results.* Washington, DC: Office of Planning, Research, and Evaluation, 1972 (OEO Pamphlet 3400-5).

O'LEARY, K. D. The operant and social psychology of token systems. In Catania, A. C., and Brigham, T. A. (eds.), *Handbook of applied behavior analysis.* New York: Irvington Publishers, 1978, 179–207.

O'LEARY, K. D. Pills or skills for hyperactive children. *Journal of Applied Behavior Analysis,* 1980, 13 (1), 191–204.

OLWEUS, D. *Aggression in the schools: Bullies and whipping boys.* Washington, DC: Hemisphere Publishing Corp., 1978.

OSBORN, A. F. *Applied imagination* (3rd ed.). New York: Charles Scribner's Sons, 1963.

PACKARD, R. G. The control of "classroom attention." A group contingency for complex behavior. *Journal of Applied Behavior Analysis,* 1970, 3, 13–28.

PAGE, D. P., and EDWARDS, R.P. Behavior change strategies for reducing disruptive classroom behavior. *Psychology in the Schools,* 1978, 15 (3), 413–418.

PAGE, E. B. Teacher comments and student performance: A seventy-four classroom experiment in school motivation. *Journal of Educational Psychology,* 1958, 49, 173–181.

PAIVIO, A., and YUILLE, J. C. Changes in associative strategies and paired-associate learning over trials as a function of word imagery and type of learning set. *Journal of Experimental Psychology,* 1969, 74, 458–463.

PAPALIA, D. E. The status of several conservation abilities across the life-span. *Human Development,* 1972, 15, 229–243.

PAPALIA, D. E., and BIELBY, D. Cognitive functioning in middle and old age adults: A review of research based on Piaget's theory. *Human Development,* 1974, 17 (6), 424–443.

PARKE, R. D. Punishment in children: Effects, side effects, and alternative strategies. In Hom, H. L., and Robinson, P. A. (eds.), *Psychological processes in early education.* New York: Academic Press, 1977.

PAVLOV, I. P. Experimental psychology and psychopathology in animals. In Pavlov, I. P. *Selected works.* Moscow: Foreign Languages Publishing House, 1955.

PAYNE, D. A. *The assessment of learning: Cognitive and affective.* Lexington, MA: D.C. Heath, 1974.

PAYNE, J. S., POLLOWAY, E. A., SMITH, J. E., and PAYNE, R. A. *Strategies for teaching the mentally retarded.* Columbus, OH: Charles E. Merrill, 1977.

PEASE, G. A., and TYLER, V. O. Self-regulation of timeout duration in the modification of disruptive classroom behavior. *Psychology in the Schools,* 1979, 16 (1), 101–105.

PETERSON, L. R. Verbal learning and memory. In Rosenzweig, M. R., and Porter, L. W. (eds.), *Annual review of psychology,* vol. 28. Palo Alto, CA: Annual Reviews, Inc., 1977, 393–415.

PETERSON, P. L., and JANICKI, T. C. Individual characteristics and children's learning in large-group and small-group approaches. *Journal of Educational Psychology,* 1979, 71 (5), 677–687.

Phi Delta Kappan. L. A. schools begin spanking to restore eroded discipline. 1980, 61 (8), 515.

PIAGET, J. *The moral judgment of the child.* Translated by M. Gabain. New York: Harcourt, Brace and World, 1932.

PIAGET, J. *The origins of intelligence in children.* Translated by Margaret Cook. New York: International Universities Press, 1952.

PIAGET, J. *The construction of reality in the child.* Translated by Margaret Cook. New York: Basic Books, 1954.

PIAGET, J. The definition of stages of development. In Tanner, J., and Inhelder, B. (eds.), *Discussions on child development,* vol. 4. New York: International Universities Press, 1960.

PIAGET, J. *Origins of intelligence in children.* New York: W. W. Norton, 1963.

PIAGET, J. *On the development of memory and identity.* Translated by E. Duckworth. Barre, MA: Clark University Press, 1968.

PIAGET, J. Intellectual evolution from adolescence to adulthood. *Human Development,* 1972, 15, 1–12.

PIAGET, J., and INHELDER, B. *The psychology of the child.* New York: Basic Books, 1969.

PIATT, R. G. An investigation of the effect the training of teachers in defining, writing and implementing educational behavioral objectives has on learner outcomes for students enrolled in a seventh grade mathematics program in the public schools. *Dissertation Abstracts International,* 1970, 30, 3352.

PIERSEL, W. C., and KRATOCHWILL, T. R. Self-observation and behavior change: Applications to academic and adjustment problems through behavioral consultation. *Journal of School Psychology*, 1979, 17 (2), 151–161.

PINARD, A., and SHARP. E. I.Q. and point of view. *Psychology Today*, 1972, 6 (1), 65.

PINES, M. How children learn to talk. *Redbook*, November 1979, 35, 217–221.

PINES, M. B. "Peers as change agents and teachers." Paper read at the annual meeting of the New England Educational Research Organization, May 1976. Bureau of Educational Research and Service, School of Education, University of Connecticut.

PIPHO, C. Minimum competency testing in 1978: A look at state standards. *Phi Delta Kappan*, 1978, 59 (9), 585–587.

Planning psychiatric services for children in the community. Washington, DC: American Psychiatric Association, 1964.

PORTUGUES, S., and FESHBACK, N. The influence of sex and socioethnic factors upon imitation of teachers by elementary schoolchildren. *Child Development*, 1972, 43, 981–989.

PRATT, R. E., and OWEN, S. V. The use of elementary-age students as modifiers of teacher behavior. Paper read at the annual meeting of the Northeastern Educational Research Association, Ellenville, NY, October 1974.

PREMACK, D. Toward empirical behavior laws: 1. Positive reinforcement. *Psychological Review*, 1959, 66, 219–233.

PRESSLEY, M. Increasing children's self-control through cognitive interventions. *Review of Educational Research*, 1979, 49 (2), 319–370.

PRESTON, R. C. Reading achievement of German and American children. *School and Society*, 1962, 90, 350–354.

RACHLIN, H. Self-control: Part I. In Catania, A. C., and Brigham, T. A. (eds.), *Handbook of applied behavior analysis*. NY: Irvington Publishers, 1978, 246–258.

RATHS, L., HARMIN, M., and SIMON, S. *Values and teaching: Working with values in the classroom.* Columbus, OH: Charles Merrill, 1966.

REDL, F., and WATTENBERG, W. *Mental hygiene in teaching*. New York: Harcourt Brace Jovanovich, 1959.

REID, D. K. Genevan theory and the education of exceptional children. In Gallagher, J. McC., and Easley, J. A. (eds.), *Knowledge and development*, vol. 2. New York: Plenum Press, 1978, 199–241.

RENSTROM, R. The teacher and the social worker in stimulant drug treatment of hyperactive children. *School Review*, 1976, 85 (1), 97–108.

RENZULLI, J. S. *The enrichment triad model: A guide to developing defensible programs for the gifted and talented.* Mansfield Center, CT: Creative Learning Press, 1977.

RENZULLI, J. S. What makes giftedness? Reexamining a definition. *Phi Delta Kappan*, 1978, 60 (3), 180–184; 261.

REYNOLDS, M. A framework for considering some issues in special education. *Exceptional Children*, 1962, 28 (7), 368.

REYNOLDS, M. C., and BIRCH, J. W. *Teaching exceptional children in all America's schools.* Reston, VA: Council for Exceptional Children, 1977.

RICE, B. Brave new world of intelligence testing. *Psychology Today*, Sept. 1979, 27, 41.

RICKS, J. H., JR. *On telling parents about test results.* Test service no. 54. New York: The Psychological Corporation, 1959.

RIEGEL, K. Dialectic operations: The final period of cognitive development. *Human Development*, 1973, 16, 346–370.

RINGNESS, T. A. *The affective domain in education.* Boston: Little, Brown, 1975.

ROBINS, L. N. *Deviant children grow up.* Baltimore: Williams and Watkins, 1966.

ROCHE, A. F., LIPMAN, R. S., OVERALL, J. E., and HUNG, W. The effects of stimulant medication on the growth of hyperkinetic children. *Pediatrics*, in press, 1980.

RODEN, A. H., and HAPKIEWICZ, W. G. Respondent learning and classroom practice. In Klein, R. D., Hapkiewicz, W. G., and Roden, A. H. (eds.), *Behavior modification in educational settings*. Springfield, IL: Charles C. Thomas, 1973.

ROGERS, C. R. *Client-centered therapy.* Boston: Houghton Mifflin, 1951.

ROGERS, C. R. A theory of therapy, personality, and interpersonal relationships. In Koch, S. (ed.), *Psychology: A study of science*, vol. 3. New York: McGraw-Hill, 1959, 185–256.

ROGERS, C. R. *Freedom to learn.* Columbus, OH: Charles Merrill, 1969.

ROSEKRANS, M. A. Imitation in children as a function of perceived similarity to a social model and vicarious reinforcement. *Journal of Personality and Social Psychology*, 1967, 7, 307–315.

ROSENBAUM, A., O'LEARY, K. D., and JACOB, R. G. Behavioral intervention with hyperactive children: Group consequences as a supplement to individual contingencies. *Behavior Therapy*, 1975, 6, 315–323.

ROSENSHINE, B. Enthusiastic teaching: A research review. *School Review*, 1970, 78, 499–514.

ROSENSHINE, B. Teaching behavior related to pupil achievement: A review of research. In Westbury, I., and Bellack, A. (eds.), *Research into classroom processes: Recent developments and next steps.* NY: Teachers College Press, 1971.

ROSENSHINE, B. Recent research on teaching behaviors and student achievement. *Journal of Teacher Education*, 1976, 27 (1), 61–64.

ROSENSHINE, B. Content, time, and direct teaching. In Peterson, P., and Walberg, H. (eds.), *Research on teaching: Concepts, findings and implications.* Berkeley, CA: McCutchan, 1979.

ROSENSHINE, B., and FURST, N. Research on teacher performance criteria. In Smith, B. O. (ed.), *Research in teacher education: A symposium.* Englewood Cliffs, NJ: Prentice-Hall, 1971.

ROSENTHAL, R. *Experimenter effects in behavioral research.* New York: Appleton-Century-Crofts, 1966.

ROSS, A. O. *Psychological aspects of learning disabilities and reading disorders.* New York: McGraw-Hill, 1976.

ROTTER, J. B. Generalized expectancies for internal versus external control of reinforcement. *Psychological Monographs*, 1966, 80, 1–28.

ROUSSEAU, J. J. *Emile.* Translated by Barbara Foxley. New York: E. P. Dutton, 1961.

RUBIN, J. Z., PROVENZANE, F. J., and LURIA, Z. The eye of the beholder: Parents views on sex of newborns. *American Journal of Orthopsychiatry*, 1974, 44, 512–519.

RUBIN, K., ATTEWELL, P., TIERNEY, M., and TUMULO, P. The development of spatial egocentrism and conservation across the life-span. *Developmental Psychology*, 1973, 9, 432.

RUDMAN, M. K. Standardized test taking: Your students can do better. *Learning*, 1976, 4 (6), 76–82.

RUMELHART, D. E. *Introduction to human information processing.* New York: John Wiley, 1977.

SALZBERG, C. The development of freedom and responsibility in elementary school. Paper read at Kansas Conference on Behavior Analysis in Educaton, Lawrence, KS, May 1972.

SCHAIE, K. W., and WILLIS, S. L. Life-span development: Implications for education. In Shulman, L. S. (ed.), *Review of research in education*, vol. 6. Itasca, IL: F. E. Peacock, 1978, 120–156.

SCHMID-KITSIKIS, E. Piagetian theory and its approach to psychopathology. *American Journal of Mental Deficiency*, 1973, 77, 51–63.

SCHMID-KITSIKIS, E. The cognitive mechanisms underlying problem-solving in psychotic and mentally retarded children. In Inhelder, B., and Chipman, H. H. (eds.), *Piaget and his school.* New York: Springer-Verlag, 1976, 234–255.

SCHMIDT, G. W., and ULRICH, R. E. Effects of group-contingent events upon classroom noise. *Journal of Applied Behavior Analysis*, 1969, 2, 171–179.

SCHULTZ, C. B., and SHERMAN, R. H. Social class, development, and differences in reinforcer effectiveness. *Review of Educational Research*, 1976, 46 (1), 25–29.

SCHWARTZ, B. *Psychology of learning and behavior.* New York: W. W. Norton, 1978.

SEARS, P. S., and BARBEE, A. H. Career and life satisfactions among Terman's gifted women. In Stanley, J. C., George, W. C., and Solano, C. H. (eds.), *The gifted and the creative: A fifty-year perspective.* Baltimore: Johns Hopkins Press, 1977, 28–65.

SEARS, R. R. Sources of life satisfactions of the Terman gifted men. *American Psychologist*, 1977, 32 (2), 119–128.

SENESH, L. *Our working world families at work.* (2nd ed.). Chicago: Science Research Associates, 1973.

SERBIN, L. A., and O'LEARY, K. D. How nursery schools teach girls to shut up. *Psychology Today*, December 1975, 57–58; 102–103.

SHIFFRIN, R. M. Short-term storage: The basis for a memory system. In Restle, F. R., Shiffrin, R. M., Castellan, N. J., Lindman, H. R., and Pisoni, D. B. (eds.), *Cognitive theory.* Hilldale, NJ: Lawrence Erlbaum, 1975, 193–218.

SIMON, A., and BOYER, E. G. (eds.). *Mirrors for behavior III: An anthology of observation instruments.* Wyncote, PA: Communication Materials Center, 1974.

SIMON, H. A. Information processing models of cognition. In Rosenzweig, M. R., and Porter, L. W. (eds.), *Annual review of psychology*, vol. 30. Palo Alto, CA: Annual Reviews, Inc., 1979, 363–396.

SIMON, S., HOWE, L., and KIRSCHENBAUM, H. *Values clarification: A handbook of practical strategies.* New York: Hart Publishing Co., 1972.

SIMPSON, E. J. The classification of educational objectives in the psychomotor domain. In Ely, D. P., et al. *The psychomotor domain.* Washington, DC: Gryphon House, 1972, 43–56.

SJOGREN, D., and TIMPSON, W. Frameworks for comprehending discourse: A replication study. *American Educational Research Journal*, 1979, 16 (4), 341–346.

SKINNER, B. F. *The behavior of organisms: an experimental analysis.* New York: Appleton-Century, 1938.

SKINNER, B. F. *Walden two.* New York: Macmillan, 1948.

SKINNER, B. F. *Verbal behavior.* New York: Appleton-Century-Crofts, 1957.

SKINNER, B. F. Why teachers fail. *Saturday Review*, 16, October 1965, 80.

SKINNER, B. F. *Beyond freedom and dignity.* New York: Alfred A. Knopf, 1971.

SKINNER, B. F. *About behaviorism.* New York: Alfred A. Knopf, 1974.

Skinner's utopia. Panacea, or path to hell. *Time*, 20 September 1971, 50.

SLAVIN, R. E. Separating incentives, feedback, and evaluation: Toward a more effective classroom system. *Educational Psychologist*, 1978, 13, 97–100.

SLAVIN, R. E. Effects of biracial learning teams on cross-racial friendship. *Journal of Educational Psychology*, 1979, 71 (3), 381–387.

SLAVIN, R. E., and MADDEN, N. A. School practices that improve race relations. *American Educational Research Journal*, 1979, 16 (2), 169–180.

SLOANE, H. N., YOUNG, K. R., and MARCUSEN, T. Response cost and human aggressive behavior. In Etzel, B. C., LeBlanc, J. M., and Baer, D. M. (eds.), *New developments in behavioral research.* Hillsdale, NJ: Lawrence Erlbaum, 1977, 531–542.

SLOBIN, D. I. *Psycholinguistics.* Glenview, IL: Scott, Foresman, 1971.

SMITH, H. A., BLECHA, H. K., and PLESS, H. *Modern science level one.* Atlanta: Laidlaw Brothers Publishers, 1974.

SNAPP, M., OAKLAND, T., and WILLIAMS, F. C. A study of individualizing instruction by using elementary school children as tutors. *Journal of School Psychology*, 1972, 10, 1–8.

SOAR, R. S. An integration of findings from four studies of teacher effectiveness. In Borich, G. D. (ed.), *The appraisal of teaching: Concepts and process.* Reading, MA: Addison-Wesley, 1977.

SOLOMON, R. W., and WAHLER, R. G. Peer reinforcement control of classroom problem behavior. *Journal of Applied Behavior Analysis*, 1973, 6 (1), 49–56.

SONTAG, L., and KAGAN, J. The emergence of intellectual achievement motives. *American Journal of Orthopsychiatry*, 1967, 37, 8–21.

SOWELL, T. New light on IQ. *New York Times Sunday Magazine*, March 27, 1977, 87–89.

SPECIAL REPORT/EDUCATION. A new approach to classroom education. *U.S. News and World Report*, September 10, 1979, 37–39.

SPRAGUE, R. L., and GADOW, K. D. The role of the teacher in drug treatment. *School Review*, 1976, 85 (1), 109–140.

STANFORD, G., and ROARK, A. E. *Human interaction in education.* Boston: Allyn and Bacon, 1974.

STANLEY, J. C. Rationale of the study of mathematically precocious youth (SMPY) during its first five years of promoting educational acceleration. In Stanley, J. C., George, W. C., and Solano, C. H. (eds.), *The gifted and creative: A fifty-year perspective.* Baltimore: The Johns Hopkins University Press, 1977, 75–112.

STANLEY, J. C. On educating the gifted. *Educational Research*, 1980, 9 (3), 8–12.

STANWYCK, D. J. Teaching for personal growth and awareness. In Triffinger, D., Davis, J. K., and Ripple, R. E. (eds.), *Handbook on educational psychology.* New York: Academic Press, 1977.

STARCH, D., and ELLIOTT, E. C. Reliability of the grading of high school work in English. *School Review*, 1912, 20, 442–445.

STARKEY, R., and KLUSENDORF, A. M. Students' attitudes toward tracking. ED146056. Educational Resources Information Center, 1977.

STEPHENS, J. M. *The process of schooling.* New York: Holt, Rinehart and Winston, 1967.

STERNBERG, R. J. Stalking the IQ quark. *Psychology Today*, September 1979, 42–54.

STEWART, L. G., and WHITE, M. A. Teacher comments, letter grades, and student performance: What do we really know? *Journal of Educational Psychology*, 1976, 68 (4), 488–500.

STOKES, I. N. P. *Iconography of Manhattan island*, vol. 4. New York: Robert H. Dodd, 1922.

SUEDFELD, P. The benefits of boredom: Sensory deprivation reconsidered. In Janis, I. L. (ed.), *Current trends in psychology: Readings from American Scientist.* Los Altos, CA: Wm. Kaufmann, 1977, 281–290.

SURATT, P. R., ULRICH, R. E., and HAWKINS, R. P. An elementary student as a behavioral engineer. *Journal of Applied Behavior Analysis*, 1969, 3, 85–92.

SWANSON, H. L., and REINERT, H. R. *Teaching strategies for children in conflict.* St. Louis: C. V. Mosby, 1979.

TAFFEL, S. J., and O'LEARY, K. D. Reinforcing math with more math: Choosing special academic activities as a reward for academic performance.

Journal of Educational Psychology, 1976, 68, 579–587.

TALMADGE, H. (ed.) *Systems of individualized education*. Berkeley, CA: McCutchan, 1975.

TERMAN, L. M. *Genetic studies of genius: Mental and physical traits of a thousand gifted children*, vol. 1. Stanford, CA: Stanford University Press, 1925.

TERMAN, L. M. The discovery and encouragement of exceptional talent. *American Psychologist*, 1954, 9, 221–230.

TERMAN, L. M., and ODEN, M. H. *Genetic studies of genius: The gifted child grows up: Twenty-five years' follow-up of a superior group*, vol. 4. Stanford, CA: Stanford University Press, 1947.

TERMAN, L. M., and ODEN, M. H. *Genetic studies of genius: The gifted at mid-life: Thirty-five years' follow-up of the superior child*, vol. 5. Stanford, CA: Stanford University Press, 1959.

THORNDIKE, E. L. The principles of teaching. In Joncich, G. M. (ed.), *Psychology and the science of education*. New York: Bureau of Publications, Teachers College, Columbia University, 1962, XL, 20–26.

TITCHENER, E. B. *A text-book of psychology*. New York: Macmillan, 1910.

TOBIAS, SHEILA. *Overcoming math anxiety*. New York: W. W. Norton, 1978.

TOBIAS, SIGMUND. Anxiety research in educational psychology. *Journal of Educational Psychology*, 1979, 71 (5), 573–582.

TORRANCE, E. P. Creatively gifted and disadvantaged gifted students. In Stanley, J. C., George, W. C., and Solano, C. H. (eds.), *The gifted and the creative: A fifty-year perspective*. Baltimore: Johns Hopkins University Press, 1977, 173–196.

TORRANCE, E. P., and WHITE, W. F. (eds.). *Issues and advances in educational psychology*. Itasca, IL: Peacock, 1975, 73–82.

TRAVERS, R. M. W. *Essentials of learning*. New York: Macmillan, 1972.

TRICKETT, E. J., and MOOS, R. H. Personal correlates of contrasting environments: Student satisfactions in high school classrooms. *American Journal of Communication Psychology*, 1974, 2 (1), 1–12.

TUMERMAN, L., and MEDVEDEV, Z. A. A Soviet scientist, now in Israel, tells of nuclear disaster. *New York Times*, 9 December 1976, p. 8.

TURIEL, E. An experimental test of the sequentiality of developmental stages in the child's moral judgements. *Journal of Personality and Social Psychology*, 1966, 3, 611–618.

TURNBULL, A. P., and SCHULZ, J. B. *Mainstreaming handicapped students*. Boston: Allyn and Bacon, 1979.

TWAIN, M. Corn-pone opinions. In Geismar, M. (ed.), *Mark Twain and the three R's*. Indianapolis: Bobbs-Merrill, 1973, 214–218.

VACC, N. A. Long term effects of special class intervention for emotionally disturbed children. *Exceptional Children*, 1972, 39, 15–22.

VERNON, W. M. *Motivating children: behavior modification in the classroom*. New York: Holt, Rinehart and Winston, 1972.

VIDLER, D. C. Achievement motivation. In Ball, S. (ed.), *Motivation in education*. New York: Academic Press, 1977, 67–89.

VYGOTSKY, L. S. *Thought and language*. Cambridge, MA: MIT Press, 1962.

WALKER, H. M., and BUCKLEY, N. K. Programming generalization and maintenance of treatment effects across time and across settings. *Journal of Applied Behavior Analysis*, 1972, 5, 209–224.

WALLACE, G., and KAUFFMAN, J. M. *Teaching children with learning problems* (2nd ed.). Columbus, OH: Charles Merrill, 1978.

WALLAS, G. *The art of thought*. New York: Harcourt Brace Jovanovich, 1921.

WARREN, J. Alum Rock voucher project. *Educational Researcher*, 1976, 5 (3), 13–15.

WATSON, J. B. Psychology as the behaviorist views it. *Psychological Review*, 1913, 20, 158–177.

WATSON, J. B. *Behaviorism*. New York: W. W. Norton, 1925.

WATSON, J. B., and RAYNER, R. Conditional emotional reactions. *Journal of Experimental Psychology*, 1920, 3 (1), 1–14.

WATTENBERG, W. W., and CLIFFORD, C. Relation of self-concepts to beginning achievement in reading. *Child Development*, 1964, 35, 461–467.

WAY, B. *Development through drama*. New York: Humanities Press, 1967.

WEBER, G. The cult of individualized instruction. *Educational Leadership*, 1977, 34 (5), 326–329.

WECHSLER, D. *The measurement and appraisal of adult intelligence* (4th ed.). Baltimore: Williams and Wilkins, 1958.

WEINER, B. Attribution theory, achievement motivation, and the educational process. *Review of Educational Research*, 1972, 42, 203–215.

WEINER, B. Achievement motivation as conceptualized by an attribution theorist. In Weiner, B. (ed.), *Achievement motivation and attribution theory.* Morristown, NJ: General Learning Press, 1974, pp. 3–48.

WEISS, B. H., ROSENBAUM, P. S., SHAW, A. M., and TOLBERT, M. J. *Great waves breaking.* New York: Holt, Rinehart and Winston, 1977, 492.

WESMAN, A. Standardizing an individual intelligence test on adults: Some problems. *Journal of Gerontology,* 1955, *10,* 216–219.

WEST, M., and AXELROD, S. A 3D program for LD children. *Academic Therapy Quarterly,* 1975, *10,* 309–319.

WESTERMARCK, E. *The history of human marriage* (5th ed.), vol. 3. New York: Allerton Book Company, 1922.

WHEELER, R., and RYAN, F. Effects of cooperative and competitive classroom environments on the attitudes and achievement of elementary school students engaged in social studies. *Journal of Educational Psychology,* 1973, *65,* 402–407.

WHELAN, R. J. The relevance of behavior modification procedures for teachers of emotionally disturbed children. In Knoblock, P. (ed.), *Intervention approaches in educating emotionally disturbed children.* Syracuse, New York: Syracuse University Press, 1966, 101–109.

WHITE, G. D., NIELSON, G., and JOHNSON, S. M. Timeout duration and the suppression of deviant behavior in children. *Journal of Applied Behavior Analysis,* 1972, *5,* 111–120.

WHITE HOUSE CONFERENCE ON CHILD HEALTH AND PROTECTION. Report of the committee on special classes. Gifted children. In *Special education: The handicapped and the gifted. Education and training.* Section 3. New York: Century, 1931, 537–550.

WHITEHURST, G. J. Observational learning. In Catania, A. C. and Brigham, T. A. (eds.), *Handbook of applied behavior analysis.* New York: Irvington Publishers, 1978.

WICKMAN, E. K. *Children's behavior and teachers' attitudes.* New York: Commonwealth Fund, 1928.

WILLIAMS, J. W. Discipline in the public schools: A problem of perception? *Phi Delta Kappan,* 1979, *60* (5), 385–387.

WILLIAMS, R. L. The silent mugging of the black community. *Psychology Today,* May 1974, p. 32.

WILLIAMS, R. L., and ANANDAM, K. *Cooperative classroom management.* Columbus, OH: Charles E. Merrill, 1973.

WILSON, C. W., and HOPKINS, B. L. The effects of contingent music on the intensity of noise in junior high home economics classes. *Journal of Applied Behavior Analysis,* 1973, 6 (2), 269–275.

WILSON, G. M. The social utility theory as applied to arithmetic, its research basis, and some of its implications. *Journal of Educational Research,* 1948, *41,* 321–337.

WINETT, R. A., BATTERSBY, C. D., and EDWARDS, S. M. The effects of architectural change, individualized instruction, and group contingencies on the academic performance and social behavior of sixth graders. *Journal of School Psychology,* 1975, *13* (1), 28–40.

WINETT, R. A., and WINKLER, R. C. Current behavior modification in the classroom: Be still, be quiet, be docile. *Journal of Applied Behavior Analysis,* 1972, *5,* 499–504.

WISSINK, J. F. A procedure for the identification of children with learning disabilities. Ph.D. dissertation, University of Arizona, 1972.

WITTROCK, M. C. The generative processes of memory. In Wittrock, M. C., et al., *The human brain.* Englewood Cliffs, NJ: Prentice-Hall, 1977, pp. 153–184.

WITTROCK, M. C. The cognitive movement in instruction. *Educational Psychologist,* 1978, *13,* 15–29.

WITTROCK, M. C. and LUMSDAINE, A. A. Instructional psychology. *Annual Review of Psychology,* 1977, *28,* 417–459.

WOLF, M. M., HANLEY, E. L., KING, L. A., LACHOWICZ, J., and GILES, D. K. The timer game: A variable interval contingency for the management of out-of-seat behavior. *Exceptional Children,* 1970, *37,* 113–117.

WOMEN ON WORDS AND IMAGES. *Dick and Jane as victims* (2nd ed.). Princeton, NJ: Author, 1975.

WORCESTER, D. A. *The education of children of above-average mentality.* Lincoln, NE: University of Nebraska Press, 1956.

WRIGHT, E. L. Effect of intensive instruction in cue attendance on solving formal operational tasks. *Science Eduction,* 1979, *63* (3), 381–393.

WUNDT, W. *Physiological psychology,* fifth edition. New York: Macmillan, 1910.

ZACH, L. The IQ debate. *Today's education,* 1972, *61* (6), 40.

ZAJONC, R. B. Social facilitation. *Science,* 1965, *149,* 269–274.

ZEILBERGER, J., SAMPEN, S. E., and SLOANE, H. N. Modification of a child's problem behaviors in the home with the mother as therapist. *Journal of Applied Behavior Analysis,* 1968, *1* (1), 47–53.

ZEILER, M. D. Principles of behavior control. In Catania, A. C., and Brigham, T. A. (eds.), *Handbook of applied behavior analysis.* New York: Irvington Publishers, 1978, 17–60.

ZIEHL, D. C. An evaluation of an elementary school enriched instructional program. Ph.D. dissertation, State University of New York at Buffalo, 1962.

ZIMMERMAN, B. J., and ROSENTHAL, T. L. Observational learning of rule-governed behavior by children. *Psychological Bulletin*, 1974, 81, 29–42.

Glossary

ability grouping: Sometimes called "homoge-neous" grouping, the practice of arranging classrooms so that students are grouped according to mental ability. For example, a high school might have a "college prep" class, a "business" class, and a "vocational" class. Ability grouping is discredited in research literature but still widely practiced.

acceleration: Allowing *gifted* students to "skip" a grade or two, or to compress a year's work into a shorter time period.

accommodation: The development of and change in cognitive structures as a result of encounters with experience. For Piaget, accommodation meant a change in schema. A child alters his or her schema of animals as only four-legged creatures to include animals with only two legs. Compare to *assimilation*.

accountability: Being responsible for something. In education, administrators and teachers are answerable for the quality of instruction and for student achievement.

achievement motivation: A hypothesized need to excel in achievement-related situations (i.e., business, school).

action methods: In *role playing*, a spontaneous exploration of a topic by a student or students with little or no structure imposed by the instructor.

adaptation: Piaget's term for the processes of *assimilation* and *accommodation*.

adaptive behavior: A criterion for determining *educable mental retardation*; refers generally to social skills and survival functions (e.g., acquiring clothing, food, shelter).

affect: The feelings and emotions of a person. *Self-concept* is an example of an affective variable.

affective characteristics: See *affective entry characteristics*.

affective domain: The area of human behavior that includes feelings, values, interests, attitudes, and emotions. Compare to *cognitive domain* and *psychomotor domain*.

affective entry characteristics: Student affective attributes that are brought to the learning situation, including self-concept, feelings, and values. See also *affective domain*.

age of reason: The point in the child's life, around six or seven years of age, when it was traditionally assumed the child began to think in the same way that adults do.

allocated time: The amount of clock time devoted to a particular topic or lesson in school. Shows a modest relationship with achievement: As time allocated increases, achievement tends to increase. Compare to *time on task*.

amphetamine: A generic term for a class of stimulant drugs. In many children the drug shows a paradoxical effect (that is, acts as a depressant), and is often used in the treatment of *hyperkinesis*.

Army Alpha Test: Intelligence test devised for recruits during World War I; notable because it was the first *group test* available for use in screening and placement.

assimilation: Incorporating information and experience into existing ideas. For Piaget, a child assimilated a new creature seen at the zoo into his or her "animal" schema. Compare to *accommodation*.

association: In learning, a general term referring to the connection of a stimulus and response. In memory, a theoretical retrieval mechanism that involves a search among *schemas*.

attribute listing: In creativity training, analyzing all attributes and features of a problem or object and systematically varying each attribute in turn.

attribution theory: An extension of *locus of control*. Attribution theory, like locus of control, seeks the source of responsibility for outcomes of behavior; it tries to discover why we attribute behavior to one cause or another. This theory of motivation deals with four perceived causes of success or failure in achievement situations: ability, effort, task difficulty, and luck.

aversive stimulus: In behavioral terms, an event that is annoying or unpleasant, and whose presentation prompts escape or avoidance behavior.

baseline: In *behavior modification*, the frequency of a behavior before any modification is begun. The purpose of baseline data is to evaluate the modification program by comparing where the student was to where the student is after modification.

behavior disorder: A phrase often used synonymously with *emotional disturbance*. Some prefer to use *behavior disorder* because it focuses on observable problems, while *emotional disturbance* hints at deep, mysterious causes.

behavior modification: The manipulation of observable behavior based on empirical principles. The term sometimes has negative overtones of authoritarian control and has even been used to indicate brainwashing, psychosurgery, and control by pharmaceutic drugs.

behavioral objective: Sometimes termed "instructional objective," an explicit, observable, and measurable outcome. For example, given five problems, students will correctly convert Fahrenheit temperatures to Celsius temperatures. Compare to *educational goal*.

behavioral programming: A *self-control* procedure that involves changing consequences of one's own behavior.

behaviorism: The study of behavior as behavior. A deterministic philosophy of learning. Behaviorism avoids speculation about any internal, unobservable process and focuses on measurable, overt actions. Compare to *cognitive psychology*.

black English vernacular: Abbreviated as BEV, the speech patterns used by black persons throughout the United States.

Bloom's taxonomy: An abbreviated form of *The Taxonomy of Educational Objectives: Cognitive Domain*, authored by Benjamin Bloom and others. The taxonomy gives a hierarchy of cognitive behaviors and sample objectives for each level of the hierarchy. See also *cognitive domain*.

Bloom's Theory of School Learning: A model of the learning process that includes the assessment of student characteristics, the matching of those characteristics with instructional goals and methods, and the evaluation of student accomplishments.

brainstorming: A procedure meant to enhance creative thinking in groups. A problem is presented and the group generates many possible solutions; evaluation of solutions is deferred until a later time.

Buros's *Yearbooks*: *See Mental Measurements Yearbook.*

central tendency: The clustering of scores around a central point of a distribution. Measures of central tendency are the *mean, median*, and *mode*.

checklist: In creativity training, checklist questions are used to devise *divergent* answers. For example, in a creativity exercise one could ask children, "If we wished to modify a calculator, how could we make it smaller? larger? Can it be combined with other machines?"

chronological age: Representation of age in years and months; used with *mental age* to compute the *intelligence quotient*.

classical conditioning: The repeated pairing of an unlearned stimulus with a neutral stimulus, to make the neutral stimulus evoke an automatic response. See also *higher order conditioning, conditioned stimulus*, and *unconditioned stimulus*.

cognition: Thinking and learning; the study of cognition focuses on how humans and other organisms acquire, organize, store, and use information.

cognitive characteristics: See *cognitive entry characteristics*.

cognitive development: The acquisition of thinking skills and intelligence. Development results from the interaction of genetic potential and environmental experiences and is thought to occur in a naturally unfolding sequence.

cognitive dissonance: Occurs when new information conflicts with existing ideas, forcing a person to adjust his or her ideas or opinions. Humans generally reduce dissonance by rationalizing, ignoring the new information, or changing beliefs.

cognitive domain: The area of human behavior that involves thinking, knowing, understanding, and comprehending. Compare to *psychomotor domain* and *affective domain*.

cognitive entry characteristics: Cognitive attributes that students bring to the learning situation, including ability to recall relevant facts, ability to form abstract concepts, and understanding written material. See also *cognition*.

cognitive psychology: The study of *cognition*, the processes of thinking, concept learning, and memory. Compare to *behaviorism*.

cognitive structure: Roughly synonymous with *schema*, cognitive psychologists' term for the basic unit of mental functioning.

Coleman Report: Officially titled *Equality of Educational Opportunity*, this government-sponsored project sought to determine the extent of racial segregation in schools, how much educational imbalance exists, and the relationship between racial mixture of school and achievement.

communication disorder: Any of a variety of difficulties in speaking or understanding the spoken word.

components: From Robert Sternberg's adaptation of *information processing* theory, a portion of intelligence responsible for carrying out acts selected previously. Compare to *metacomponents*.

concept: A grouping of objects, events, or ideas that share one or more common characteristics. Apples, pears, and oranges share common attributes that fit them into the concept of "fruit."

concept analysis: A term for several activities used in preparation for teaching a concept, including defining, listing attributes, specifying relationship with other concepts, etc.

concept attribute: A characteristic necessary to define a grouping of stimuli; the characteristic is required of each stimulus within the group.

concept example: One of the stimuli within a concept grouping. For the concept "natural cheese," Jarlsberg and Gorgonzola are examples. Compare to *concept nonexample*.

concept nonexample: A stimulus lacking one or more *defining* attributes of a particular concept, used to help illustrate the boundaries of a concept being taught. For the concept "natural cheese," American cheese and cheese spread are nonexamples because they lack several of the defining attributes of "natural cheese" (i.e., unpasteurized; no added water, salt, gels, and emulsifier). Compare to *concept attribute*.

concrete operational period: The third of Piaget's periods of cognitive development, extending from the ages of six or seven to about eleven or twelve. During this period the child can deal with concrete facts logically but cannot yet think abstractly. The concrete operational child can perform *decentration*, *reversibility*, and *conservation*.

conditioned reinforcer: Sometimes termed "secondary reinforcer," or "generalized reinforcer," equivalent to a *conditioned stimulus* in *classical conditioning*. A stimulus whose reinforcing power has been learned, presumably because of its association with a *primary reinforcer*. Money is a common conditioned reinforcer, its potency resting on its association with food, shelter, and other goals.

conditioned response: A response evoked by a conditioned stimulus. The conditioned response is very similar to the *unconditioned* (unlearned) *response*, but is paired with a learned stimulus. See also *classical conditioning*.

conditioned stimulus: A stimulus that was once neutral and is now associated with a particular response. The stimulus has become learned, or conditioned, because of its pairing with an *unconditioned stimulus*, or with another potent conditioned stimulus. See also *classical conditioning* and *higher order conditioning*.

conditioning: Learning that a particular *stimulus* is associated with another stimulus, or with a particular *response*, as the result of practice and *contiguity*. See also *classical conditioning* and *operant conditioning*.

connotative meaning: The personal meaning a word carries in addition to the strict dictionary definition. Connotative meaning is the result of the experiences a person has with the word. For example, the meaning that the word "friend" has to a person is influenced by his or her friendships. See *denotative meaning*.

consequence: In operant conditioning, the stimulus that follows a response, and that is said to control the strength or frequency of that response. See also *reinforcement* and *punishment*.

conservation: Piaget's term for the realization that quantity does not change with a change in shape. Jill complained that she was the only one with a little glass. After getting a larger glass she poured her milk from the small glass into the larger, but then was upset because she only had a little bit of milk in her large glass.

construct: A term for an internal, hypothetical process. The existence of a construct can only be inferred from observable performance; examples include intelligence, motivation, and learning.

content validity: A test has content validity if it accurately represents the body of knowledge it claims to be measuring.

contingency contracting: An agreement, usually in writing, between a teacher and a student outlining each person's responsibilities.

Commonly, the arrangement focuses on student accomplishment and on the consequences of the student's completion of a task.

contiguity: In learning, an adjacent stimulus and response, or an adjacent stimulus and stimulus. If stimulus and response do not occur together and contiguity is lost, learning will diminish.

conventional level: Kohlberg's middle two stages of *moral development*, focusing on pleasing others and on maintaining established rules or laws. See also *preconventional level* and *postconventional level*.

convergent production: Sometimes termed "convergent thinking," the invention of a single best response to a problem or question. Compare to *divergent production*.

convergent thinking: See *convergent production*.

corporal punishment: An *aversive stimulus* delivered to a person in an attempt to reduce some behavior. Outlawed in many Western and Communist countries, it is practiced widely in the United States.

creativity: The production of a unique or novel response to a problem. Most definitions, but not all, include the requirement that the unique response be culturally useful.

criterion-referenced measurement: Assessing performance by comparing it to an established standard. A person's standing in no way depends on the performance of peers but rather on whether or not the criterion has been met. Compare to *norm-referenced measurement*.

cross-age tutoring: See *peer tutoring*.

crystallized intelligence: According to Cattell's theory, intelligence resulting from experience and education. Compare to *fluid intelligence*.

cultural bias: The accusation that standardized tests are written for the benefit of white, middle-class, urban people and that they discriminate against minority cultural groups. In rural areas of western states where hunting and fishing are highly regarded activities, youngsters asked to name the four seasons, a question on a certain intelligence test, are very likely to answer "dove season, pheasant season, deer season, and fishing season." Because of cultural bias, this response would be marked wrong.

culture-fair test: A measuring device that shows no inherent bias against or in favor of any particular ethnic, racial, or cultural group. Culture-fair tests are nonexistent and appear to be impossible.

decentration: According to Piaget, the kind of reasoning involving the child's ability to consider two or more characteristics of an object or event at the same time. For example, a child who can simultaneously consider both the depth and width of a container is decentrating.

defining attribute: A characteristic of a concept that distinguishes its members. For example, a defining attribute of the concept "variable mortgage" is an interest rate which may change over the term of the loan.

denotative meaning: The dictionary definition of a word, independent of one's own personal meaning for it. Compare to *connotative meaning*.

desensitization: Modification of a strong emotional response to a weaker response; occurs by repeated presentation of an aversive stimulus (e.g., observing violent acts repeatedly), or by linking a weak response to successively stronger stimuli (e.g., thinking about a theater, then thinking about a stage, then thinking about a politician speaking on that stage, then thinking about you giving a speech on that stage, then thinking about your mother watching your speech, and so on).

deviation IQ: A replacement for the flawed *ratio IQ*, this intelligence quotient uses a similar formula but includes yearly variations in scores, so that an IQ of 94 at age ten is supposed to be equivalent to the same score at age fourteen.

dialectic operations: Riegel's hypothesized fifth period of cognitive development in which an adult may be aware of contradictory ideas and acknowledge both as possible. For example, the existence of *behaviorism* does not invalidate *cognitive psychology*.

direct instruction: A group of teaching behaviors that clearly identifies someone as authority and leader and directs learners to specific instructional goals. Compare to *indirect teaching*.

disability: Usually synonymous with disorder or dysfunction, the imperfect functioning of a body limb or organ.

discovery learning: In general, an instructional process placing greater responsibility on the learner for finding information or problem solutions. Types of discovery learning range from leaving the student almost entirely on his or her own—called unguided discovery—to a more cooperative relationship, or guided discovery.

discrimination: The ability to distinguish among two or more stimuli; the ability to respond differently to similar stimuli.

discriminative stimulus: Abbreviated S$_d$, a stimulus that cues a particular response. For instance, a stop sign is an S$_d$ that prompts pressing the brake.

distractor: In multiple-choice test items, those responses that are plausible and incorrect, meant to distinguish test-takers who know content from those who do not.

distributed memory: Hunt's *information processing* approach to thought. Memory, the key to intellectual behavior, is hypothesized to operate in several stages, analogous to the working of a computer.

disuse theory: An explanation of forgetting, once discredited and now revived in altered form. The early version explained that "time" caused forgetting: the longer a memory stayed dormant, the more it was forgotten. This explanation was discredited when it was discovered that time is a measuring device that does not cause anything. Today, the disuse theory depends upon the idea that memory proteins metabolize if they are not strengthened by occasional use.

divergent production: Sometimes termed "divergent thinking," the development of more than one possible response to a problem or question. Believed to be a central characteristic of *creativity*. Compare to *convergent production*.

divergent thinking: See *divergent production*.

E.D.: See *emotional disturbance*.

educable mentally retarded (EMR): A subgroup of mentally retarded persons composed of those who as students are capable of mastering fundamental academic skills. As adults, former EMRs are usually self-sufficient and independent. An approximate IQ range for this group is 50 to 70.

Education for All Handicapped Children Act: A federal law that became effective September 1978; it guarantees equal educational opportunity for handicapped students. A major feature of the law is that handicapped children must be placed in an educational setting that is the least restrictive environment. Other features are the right to due process, which protects an individual from erroneous classification, capricious labeling, and denial of equal education; protection against discriminatory testing in diagnosis; and the establishment of individualized educational programs.

educational goal: A broad, general purpose in education; for example, teaching students to speak and reason effectively. See also *behavioral objective*.

educational psychology: The study of human learning and instruction, and the evaluation of those processes using the theories, findings, methods, and instruments of psychology for educational purposes.

egocentrism: In Piagetian theory, the dependence on subjective patterns of thought at the beginning of each period of *cognitive development*. As growth in each period occurs, the focus shifts from subjective—egocentric—thought to objective thought. For example, early in *formal operations*, an adolescent becomes able to think abstractly about other peoples' abstract thought. But egocentrism compels the adolescent to imagine that others are critically considering the small wart on his left hand. As objective thought grows, there will be a gradual realization that others have blemishes, too, and that most concerns of others are about more substantial matters than a small wart.

eg-rule: An instructional pattern for concept teaching in which examples are first given and then grouped with a concept definition (or rule). *Discovery learning* commonly uses the eg-rule procedure by presenting stimuli and requiring a search for an explanatory principle or definition.

elaborated code: Taken from Bernstein's analysis of social class differences in language, the grammatical structure corresponding to middle-class usage, marked by complicated and subtle rules and meanings. Compare to *restricted code*.

elaboration: The ability to fill in detail or embellish; used in the measurement of creativity.

emotional disturbance: Often abbreviated E.D., a handicapping condition of the *affective domain*. Includes inappropriate emotional responses to common stimuli; for example, hysterical crying or rage on the discovery of a fly sitting on a desk.

EMR: See *educable mentally retarded*.

enactive mode: The first of Bruner's modes of representation, extending from birth to about age three, during which children's physical actions form the basis for their understanding of the environment.

encoding: In *information processing*, the transformation and storage in memory of incoming stimuli.

engaged time: See *time on task*.

engineered classroom: An instructional arrangement employing behaviorist techniques, usually meant for the education of *emotionally disturbed* youngsters.

enrichment: Generally, offering additional learning resources to *gifted* students.

entry characteristics: See *student entry characteristics.*

environmental planning: A type of self-control in which conditions that precede a problem behavior are altered. For example, if I wish to stop munching peanuts as I type, I could either remove the peanuts from the typing area or move the typewriter somewhere else.

equilibration: An attempt to balance assimilation and accommodation; according to Piaget, equilibration is a major force behind cognitive growth.

Erikson's stages: A theoretical series of eight levels of personality development, from infancy through adulthood. The stages are built on a psychoanalytic framework, and each stage involves the resolution of a conflict *(identity crisis)* between competing needs.

error score: The portion of a test score beyond an individual's control, resulting from mistakes, oversights, misunderstanding, good luck, and bad guesses. See also *true score* and *obtained score.*

evaluation: In education, the process of placing a value on a measured outcome of instruction. For example, Mr. LaHoya evaluates a test score of 90 as good achievement.

example: See *concept example.*

example matching: A method of concept teaching in which an *example* and a *nonexample* are paired; both have the same *irrelevant attribute,* but the nonexample lacks the concept's *defining attribute.* For instance, in learning the concept of "wine acescency," two wines may be matched for their sourness. Both share the irrelevant attributes of being a bottled liquid made from fermented grapes. But they differ on the defining attribute because one smells like vinegar, the other like grape.

exceptional: A child whose ability or performance deviates from normal. While much attention goes to children with handicaps, the *gifted* or *talented* youngster is also exceptional.

expectancy: A prediction; in education, informal and sometimes unwitting prophecy of student achievement. In practice, teacher expectancy may lead to the unintentional communication of the prediction to a student. For example, belief that a student will do poorly may cause the teacher to provide less reinforcement, spend less time, avoid eye contact, and so on.

expressive difficulty: A group of *communication disorders* which impair clear communication to others; for example, stuttering or lisping.

external locus of control: See *locus of control.*

extinction: Withholding a reinforcing event until the behavior that once produced the reinforcer has been eliminated. At the outset of extinction, the behavior will temporarily increase as the organism increases its attempts to regain the reinforcement. Ultimately, as it becomes obvious that no reinforcer will appear, the behavior will cease.

extrinsic motivation: Movement toward a goal for the purpose of receiving external reward. Compare to *intrinsic motivation.*

Family Educational Rights and Privacy Act: Also called the "Buckley Amendment," or the "Right-to-Know Law," a law which guarantees parents the right to inspect their children's files and to challenge erroneous information.

fixed ratio schedule: abbreviated FR, a pattern of *reinforcement* in which a specific proportion of all appropriate responses is reinforced. For example, in an FR:4 schedule, every fourth appropriate behavior is reinforced. Compare to *variable ratio schedule.*

flexibility: In the measurement of creativity, the number of categories or different concepts produced by a series of problem solutions.

fluency: A component of creativity; the capacity to come up with alternative solutions to a problem in a fast and steady-flowing stream.

fluid intelligence: One of Cattell's forms of intelligence, encompassing an individual's brightness or adaptability. See also *crystallized intelligence.*

formal innovation: In education, the large-scale process of inventing, producing, testing, and marketing an instructional tool. Compare to *informal innovation.*

formal operations period: The fourth of Piaget's periods of cognitive development, extending from the ages of eleven or twelve to about fifteen or sixteen, during which the child acquires the ability to think abstractly. The child is able to develop and test hypotheses and symbolic meanings and generalize from imaginary situations.

formative testing: Assessment of progress during the instructional period for the purpose of providing feedback to students and diagnosing difficulties. Compare to *summative testing.*

functional fixedness: The inability to recognize that objects may be used for other than their conventional uses. Functional fixedness is thought to impair problem solving. See also *response set.*

generalization: The capability of similar stimuli to produce the same response. For example, if a child has learned to dislike the dog that bit him, he will possibly generalize his dislike to other similar dogs.

gestalt: Broadly, a configuration, pattern, or the "whole" picture. As a theory of psychology, the forerunner to present day *cognitive psychology.*

gifted: A general term for demonstrated superior abilities, often determined by intelligence testing. See also *talented.*

goal analysis: A process of breaking a vague desire into specific, observable components; helpful in the development of *behavioral objectives.*

grade equivalent score: A score designed to translate raw scores into an index of grade performance. A grade equivalent score of 3.5 would mean that the student's raw score on a test was equivalent to the *average* score made by students in the fifth month of the third grade.

grandma's law: Another term for the *Premack principle,* often stated in grandmotherly terms; for example, if you eat your peas, you may have your cake.

group contingency: A behavior modification plan that requires each member of a group to demonstrate a specific act before a consequence is delivered. An illustration: "When all the tests are handed in, the answer keys will be passed out."

grouping: See *ability grouping.*

group intelligence test: A measurement device ordinarily used with more than one person at a time. More widely used than *individual intelligence tests* because of economy and efficiency of testing.

group test: See *group intelligence test.*

habit-family hierarchy: In problem-solving, a series of possible solutions ranked from most to least probable. Based on a behaviorist formulation of problem-solving.

halo effect: An unwarranted generalization based on limited evidence. For example, a teacher assumes Nancy is bright because she sits in the front row and nods at appropriate moments. A negative halo: Tom has been misbehaving. In grading his unit exam, the teacher is unusually critical of his spelling and penmanship.

handicap: An environmental obstacle exaggerated by a physical disability. For example, being confined to a wheelchair is a handicapping condition when stores do not have wheelchair access.

hearing impairment: Any of a range of difficulties in hearing, usually modifiable.

hemispheric specialization: The adaptation of each half of the brain to particular, specialized functions. In humans, the left hemisphere specializes in cognitive, abstract reasoning, while the right hemisphere organizes perceptual and spatial stimuli. See also *split-brain.*

higher order conditioning: The linking of a neutral stimulus with an established *conditioned stimulus,* to make the neutral stimulus evoke the same response as the conditioned stimulus. See also *classical conditioning.*

holistic evaluation: A method of grading essay examinations in which at least two readers mark the same exam in terms of general categories rather than specific points.

holophrastic stage: In language development, the use of single words to convey the meaning of entire phrases, usually occurring between one and two years of age. For example, using "Mine!" to mean "That's my doll—please hand it over!"

homogeneous grouping: See *ability grouping.*

hyperactivity: See *hyperkinesis.*

hyperkinesis: Also called hyperactivity, a motor learning disorder, characterized by rapid, flighty movement; inability to sit still and pay attention. Often treated with *amphetamines* and *behavior modification.*

hypoactivity: An uncommon learning disorder in which a child is overly sluggish and resistant to physical movement or exercise.

iconic mode: The second of Bruner's modes of representation, extending from about age three to seven or eight, during which children use images in thinking.

identification: The perceived similarity of a learner to the model in *imitation learning.*

identity crisis: In *Erikson's* theory of personality development, a conflict occurring at each stage. If the conflict is not resolved properly before moving to the next stage, emotional difficulties may result.

IEP: See *individualized education program.*

imitation learning: Sometimes called *modeling*

or *observational learning*, learning by observation and imitation of a model. Overt practice and reinforcement are believed to be less important in imitation learning than in other types of learning.

impairment: Diseased or defective organs that result in some form of disability.

incompatible behavior: In *behavior modification*, a behavior contrary to, or opposite to, a targeted behavior. For instance, it might be possible to decrease social isolation by increasing an incompatible behavior—social interaction.

indirect teaching: A style of instruction sometimes characterized as "student-centered"; that is, it encourages students to share in classroom dialogue.

individual intelligence test: A measurement device used with only a single person at a time. Believed to be somewhat more *valid* and *reliable* than *group intelligence tests*. A specialist is required to administer and interpret the individual test, and this increases its cost.

individualized education program (usually abbreviated **IEP**): A provision of the *Education for All Handicapped Children Act* that requires schools to create a statement of specific plans for each handicapped student, to be developed with parents' asistance.

individual test: See *individual intelligence test.*

individuation: Jung's psychoanalytic term for the process of freeing oneself from pressures for social approval; usually occurs around middle adulthood.

informal assessment: Screening for impairment or disability without standardized, structured measures; usually performed by teachers.

informal innovation: In education, a teacher's individual and sometimes private use of novel instructional methods. Compare to *formal innovation.*

information processing: A theory about the receipt, coding, storage, and transformation of data, modeled after computer functions. A recent offshoot of *cognitive psychology.*

inner consistency: Richard Lecky's term to describe the natural striving for mental balance between's one's self-concept and one's own perception of the environment.

insight: In cognitive psychology, the realization—often abrupt—of a possible solution to a problem.

instructional objective: See *behavioral objective.*

intelligence: A vague, general characteristic composed of an assortment of mental behaviors valued by a particular culture.

intelligence quotient (abbreviated **IQ**): A measurement term for scores derived from an intelligence test. IQ scores above the mean score of 100 are believed to show higher intelligence, while those below 100 represent less intelligence. See also *ratio IQ* and *deviation IQ.*

intentional forgetting: A psychoanalytic explanation of forgetting which says that painful memories are quickly forgotten. Sometimes called "repression."

interest questionnaire: A type of *self-report instrument*, designed solely to tap a person's interests.

interference: The explanation that most forgetting is the result of old or new knowledge interfering with attempts to remember something. See *retroactive* and *proactive inhibition.*

internal locus of control: See *locus of control.*

intrinsic motivation: Purposeful behavior that presumably reinforces itself and does not depend on external reward. Compare to *extrinsic motivation.*

IQ: See *intelligence quotient.*

irrelevant attribute: A stimulus characteristic that does not help identify the stimulus as a member of a particular concept. For example, for the printmaking concept of "artist's proof," size and cost are irrelevant attributes. Compare to *concept attribute.*

item stem: In test development, especially with multiple-choice questions, the premise or introduction to the question. The remainder of the question consists of the correct answer and two or more *distractors.*

jigsaw technique: An instructional method originally devised to combat racism. Students are given portions of a problem or a lesson and must cooperatively share the information in order to solve the problem or progress to the next lesson.

language: A patterned, organized set of symbols used to communicate.

law of effect: Either of two principles developed by psychologist Edward L. Thorndike. The earlier version stated that a pleasurable stimulus would increase the behavior that produced it, while an aversive stimulus would decrease the behavior that produced it. The modified law of effect acknowledged that *punishment* did not have the opposite effect of *reinforcement.*

L.D.: See *learning disability.*

learning: A hypothetical process within the organism, inferred by observing lasting changes in performance.

learning disability (usually abbreviated **L.D.**): A broad class of symptoms that show difficulty in mastering one or more school subjects. Commonly, a learning-disordered youngster shows normal intelligence, but sub-average performance in certain tasks (often reading).

learning disorder: See *learning disability.*

learning outcomes: Measurable student achievement following a teaching unit. Can occur in the psychomotor, affective, or cognitive domain. Believed by some to be an indirect measure of teacher effectiveness.

least restrictive environment: An important portion of the *Education for All Handicapped Children Act*, requiring that exceptional students be placed in a situation as close to normal as possible. For most forms of disability the regular classroom is considered least restrictive, but for severe disorders, placement in a regular classroom may actually increase restriction.

level of performance: A component of a *behavioral objective* that further specifies the behavior to be demonstrated. The level of performance may indicate how much, how well, how often, or how fast a behavior should occur; for example, "... will solve the differential equations *with no more than two errors.*"

life space interviewing: A nonbehavioral technique used with *emotionally disturbed* children. It is a form of therapeutic assistance in which the teacher and the child discuss the events associated with a child's problem in school. The intent is to strengthen the child's ability to cope with problems.

link method: A system of aiding memory by associating words with mental images.

loci method: A system of aiding memory by associating verbal material to be learned with a familiar physical structure.

locus of control: A general perception of responsibility for consequences of behavior. With an *external* locus of control, one assumes that the environment is responsible for outcomes of behavior; an *internal* locus suggests that the person himself is responsible. See also *attribution theory.*

long-term storage: Permanent storage of information in the memory. See also *short-term storage.*

magnet school: An educational alternative to court-ordered busing, meant to improve racial

mixtures at segregated schools. A magnet school generally focuses on a specific curriculum (e.g., art and music) and is intended to attract children of all ethnic groups.

mainstreaming: The placement of exceptional youngsters in a regular classroom for all or part of the school day. Mainstreaming is an abstract educational goal and may occasionally conflict with the *least restrictive environment*, as when a seriously disturbed child cannot cope with a regular classroom environment.

Maslow's need hierarchy: Abraham Maslow's humanist theory of motivation. The individual is believed to be innately motivated to progress from the simplest needs (e.g., survival) to the most complex needs (e.g., creativity).

mastery learning: A model of instruction built on the assumption that most school-age children are capable of accomplishing most of the school's objectives. In practice, use of the mastery model generally translates into allowing more or less time for mastery of objectives and careful, continuous evaluation of progress.

matching
(in *concept teaching*): See *example matching.*
(in *test development*): A *recognition test* in which a list of premises must be joined to a list of possible responses.

maturation: Developmental change thought to be relatively free of environmental influence and primarily controlled by genetic structure.

mean: The arithmetic average, computed by adding up all the scores and dividing the sum by the number of scores. Used as measure of central tendency.

meaningful verbal learning: Connecting or associating new information with knowledge the learner already possesses. See also *rote learning.*

measurement: In education, determining the outcomes of instruction by comparison based on a common standard.

median: A measure of central tendency, figured by rank-ordering scores and locating the middle score.

mediation: In learning theory, the intervention of mental processes between stimulus and response. Presumably, a stimulus can be perceived, processed, coded, and perhaps stored in memory before an overt response is made. These internal events *mediate* between stimulus and response.

memory: A hypothetical *construct* used to explain the storage of information in the brain.

mental age: A concept used in the measurement of intelligence. Tests are *standardized* so that a high score represents a mental age beyond one's *chronological age*; a low score means that measured mental age is below chronological age.

Mental Measurements Yearbook: A series of volumes that critically reviews practically all published tests and lists the publisher's address, the cost, and the purpose of the test.

metacomponents: In Sternberg's *information processing* theory, that level of intelligence responsible for the selection of problem-solving strategies.

minimum competency testing: An arrangement in which students must demonstrate mastery of specified skills in order to move to the next grade level or to graduate.

mode: The most frequently occurring score in a distribution.

modeling: Loosely synonymous with *imitation learning*; technically, the display of behaviors meant to be imitated by an observer.

modes of representation: See *enactive*, *iconic*, and *symbolic*.

momentum: In the *direct instruction* model, setting a brisk teaching pace by keeping attention focused on academic objectives and by making smooth transitions between activities.

moral development: The process by which humans acquire a sense of morality. Broadly, the learning of such affective characteristics as morality, values, and honesty.

motivated forgetting: See *intentional forgetting*.

motivation: A hypothetical *construct* to explain why behaviors appear to be goal-directed.

nature-nurture: The aged and unresolvable argument about the primary origins of intelligent behavior—inherited or learned.

need to achieve: A *construct* referring to an *intrinsic motive* to perform one's best in achievement situations, such as school or business.

negative reinforcement: Using a *negative reinforcer*; removing an aversive or annoying stimulus in order to increase escape or avoidance behavior.

negative reinforcer: An *aversive stimulus* whose removal strengthens the behavior that removed it. For example, on a hot, muggy day (aversive stimulus), I will turn on a fan. If I am successful in decreasing the heat, my fan-operating behavior will have been strengthened. Compare to *positive reinforcer*.

neobehaviorism: Any of several schools of learning that stress the importance of observable, measurable behavior but, unlike *behaviorism*, do speculate about internal events.

neurometrics: Measuring intelligence by examining changes in brain wave patterns in response to visual or auditory stimuli.

nonexample: See *concept nonexample*.

nonspecific transfer: The form of learning involving a continual broadening and deepening of knowledge in terms of basic and general ideas. For example, an instructor advises a student on studying for and taking exams, and the student applies the general rules to all his classes. Sometimes called "transfer of principles." Compare to *specific transfer*.

norm: A standard or model for behavior in a group. In testing, norms are scores obtained from a large and representative sample of a population. The scores then are used as benchmarks for comparing the performance of others on similar tests.

norm-referenced measurement: Assessing performance by comparing all scores, so that a person's standing depends on his or her relative rank among peers. Compare to *criterion-referenced measurement*.

norm table: A table listing actual scores from a *standardization sample*, so that scores can be compared with those of other persons of the same age, grade level, or ability level.

object permanence: A characteristic of *cognitive development* that grows during Piaget's *sensorimotor period*; the awareness that an object removed from sight still exists.

objective test: A measure of scoring which is highly reliable, that is, the score is not influenced by the person grading the exam.

observation instrument: A measuring device relying on direct observation of behavior.

observational learning: See *imitation learning*.

obtained score: The raw score that a person receives on a test. The obtained score is the sum of the *true score* and the *error score*.

operant behavior: Behavior whose strength or frequency is controlled mostly by its consequences.

operant conditioning: Linking a response to a reinforcing stimulus. This type of learning involves responses that appear to be voluntary and that are maintained by *reinforcement*. Examples include waving, reading, and talking. Compare to *classical conditioning*, in which a stimulus is linked to another stimulus, and the response is apparently involuntary.

operation: In Piagetian terms, the central mental action. In cognitive development, a major advance occurs when the child moves from action in reality to action in imagination. The primary feature is reversibility: an individual can consider possibilities and return to the original point to determine the validity of those possibilities.

organization: Piaget's term for the natural tendency of humans (and other animals) to arrange their processes into efficient systems. In humans, organization deals mainly with the logical arrangement of experiences into *schemas*.

originality: In the measurement of creativity, the infrequency or rarity of a response.

origins: In motivation theory, a term used by Richard deCharms to indicate individuals with an *internal locus of control*. Compare to *pawns*.

overgeneralize: In concept learning, to mistake a *nonexample* as an example. For instance, overgeneralization occurs when a child claims that a packet of non-nutritive sweetener is sugar.

overlearning: Study and practice of material beyond the point of mastery; said to result in learning that is more resistant to forgetting.

overt practice: Rehearsal of an obvious, measurable behavior. Covert practice occurs when a skill or idea is practiced mentally; it is an important part of *imitation learning*.

pawns: In motivation theory, deCharms's term for individuals with an *external locus of control*. Compare to *origins*.

peer teaching: See *peer tutoring*.

peer tutoring: Also termed "peer teaching" and "cross-age tutoring," an instructional method that uses a peer as a major teaching resource.

peg method: A system of aiding memory by using rhymes and images.

percentile score: A score that reveals a person's relative standing among peers. The percentile score shows that a person did as well as, or better than, that percent of the group taking the test. For example, a percentile score of 75 indicates that the score is as good as, or better than, 75 percent of the remaining scores.

perception: The interpretation of sensations received by the sensory organs.

performance: Any observable, measurable behavior.

performance contracting: Hiring educational services outside the school system, typically done under a legal contract. At the height of its popularity (around 1970), contracted work ranged from simple consulting to taking over the entire educational arrangement for a school.

perseveration: A learning disorder characterized by repetition of movements or, more commonly, of words and phrases.

personal fable: Exemplifying *egocentrism* early in *formal operations*, the idea that principles of human behavior are valid only for other people. For example, your infatuation at age 14 was true love that would last forever, even if no one else, not even the object of your affection, believed it. (Do you recall clothing and popular music you knew you would never get tired of?)

personality: A vague assortment of hypothetical *constructs* meant to explain causes of behavior. Most personality attributes are located in the *affective domain*.

person approach: A two-step method of analyzing creativity. First, researchers establish the elements of personality and biography that are common to persons judged to be creative. Others are then compared to the profile of characteristics to determine whether they are creative. See also *product* and *process approaches*.

positive reinforcement: Using a *positive reinforcer*. Responding to a behavior in a way that will increase or strengthen that behavior.

positive reinforcer: A stimulus presented to strengthen the behavior that produced it. Compare to *negative reinforcer*.

postconventional level: The two uppermost stages in Kohlberg's theory of *moral development*, characterized by attention to the "good of the people" and reliance on one's own conscience. See also *preconventional level* and *conventional level*.

preconventional level: In Kohlberg's scheme of *moral development*, the lowest two stages, in which moral reasoning revolves around issues of authority, reward, and punishment. See also *conventional level* and *postconventional level*.

predictive validity: The extent to which a test score accurately predicts some future outcome. For example, if a reading test accurately predicts later school achievement, it would have predictive validity.

Premack principle: Named after David Premack, it is the use of a preferred activity to reinforce a less preferred activity. For example, if you spell 90 percent of the quiz words correctly, you are exempt from the final exam. Here, being excused from an exam (preferred activity) is used to reinforce a less preferred activity, studying spelling words.

preoperational period: The second of Piaget's periods of cognitive development, extending roughly from age two to age six, during which the child begins to use *operations*, or mental activities, in the process of combining and transforming information. In this period, mental operations increasingly depend on the child's use of language.

prepotent need: In *Maslow's need hierarchy*, the need that dominates attention and energy at a particular time.

primary reinforcer: An unlearned stimulus that will naturally strengthen a behavior (e.g., food, water, shelter). Equivalent to an *unconditioned stimulus* in *classical conditioning*. Compare to *conditioned reinforcer*.

principle: In learning theory, a group of concepts linked in a meaningful way. For example, we may arrange these concepts—paste, with, rag, a, soft, wax, apply—into a purposeful rule: apply the paste wax with a soft rag. Principles allow the solving of *problems*.

proactive inhibition: An explanation of forgetting in which old knowledge interferes with learning new information. Compare to *retroactive inhibition*.

problem: A sensed gap in knowledge; a goal with no immediate solution.

problem-finding: A rarely practiced skill of locating a problem that is not readily apparent; should be applied to areas that wreak social or ecological havoc when discovered too late.

process approach

(to analyzing creativity): Investigation of mental processes involved in creative problem solving. Compare to *product approach*.

(in evaluating teaching): Inspection of how students and teachers behave in the classroom, usually by direct observation. Compare to *product approach*.

product approach

(to analyzing creativity): Assessing a person's creativity by judging his creative products, such as a work of art, a publication, or an invention. Compare to *process approach*.

(in evaluating teaching): Judging teacher effectiveness on the basis of student growth or achievement gain. Compare to *process approach*.

production test: A measure that requires the testee to supply responses to items, such as an essay exam. Compare to *recognition test*.

psychomotor characteristics: See *psychomotor entry characteristics*.

psychomotor domain: The area of human behavior that encompasses motor behavior, or bodily movements, including fine and gross physical skills. Compare to *cognitive domain* and *affective domain*.

psychomotor entry characteristics: Student skills of movement that are brought to a learning situation and that influence the nature of instruction. For example, in teaching typing, fine motor coordination is an important entry characteristic. See also *psychomotor domain*.

Public Law 94–142: See *Education for All Handicapped Children Act*.

punisher: In lay terms, an aversive or annoying event. In scientific terms, a stimulus that suppresses the behavior that produced it.

punishment: Application of a stimulus that reduces the likelihood of some behavior.

ratio IQ: The original intelligence quotient, calculated by dividing *mental age* by *chronological age* and multiplying by 100. Its use has been abandoned in favor of *deviation IQ*.

raw score: The score made by an individual on a test before it is converted to a derived score (such as a percentile or IQ score).

recall method: Measuring learning by requiring the individual to recall information without the aid of cues. An essay test is an example of testing memory by recall. Compare to *recognition method* and *savings method*.

receptive difficulty: A type of *communication disorder* in which a person has trouble comprehending language or other stimuli from the environment.

recognition method: Measuring learning by requiring a person to recognize and distinguish previously learned material when it is mixed with new or unfamiliar material.

recognition test: A measure whose answers are provided within the question; testee must select an answer from several given possibilities. Compare to *production test*.

reconstruction: In memory retrieval, the unintentional filling in of forgotten bits, to make a remembrance seem more coherent.

reduction of uncertainty: An explanation of attention to unusual or improbable events. Confronted with strange stimuli, we experience uncertainty and are *intrinsically motivated* to resolve the uncertainty. Attention helps to search for familiar features or recognizable patterns.

reinforcement schedule: The pattern in which reinforcers are delivered. See also *fixed ratio* and *variable ratio schedule.*

reinforcer: In lay terms, a pleasurable or rewarding event. In scientific terms, a stimulus that increases or maintains the strength of a response associated with it.

reliability: A test property based on consistency of measurement. In any test the items should be consistent with each other, and they should give consistent results each time the test is administered. See also *validity.*

repertoire: In behavioral psychology, all behaviors or skills an individual is capable of demonstrating.

response: A general term usually referring to an observable performance. Commonly used in association with *stimulus.*

response set: The tendency to respond in a single, stereotyped pattern to different stimuli. For example, on a multiple-choice test, a student tends to mark answer "a" whenever he guesses on an item. Using response sets tends to impede problem-solving. See also *functional fixedness.*

restricted code: From Bernstein's analysis of social class differences in language, the grammatical structure corresponding to lower social classes; characterized by simplicity and predictability. Compare to *elaborated code.*

retroactive inhibition: An explanation of forgetting in which new information is said to interfere with old knowledge. In a history class in which both world wars are studied, and learning World War II material interferes with the learning of World War I material, retroactive inhibition has occurred. See also *proactive inhibition.*

reversibility: In Piagetian terms, the ability to reverse or undo mental activity in either a real or imaginary sense.

role playing: Placing students into simulated situations where they must act out their own ideas. Used mainly to increase awareness of the student's own feelings, others' attitudes, and interpersonal relationships.

rote learning: The memorization of material, usually without reference to its meaningfulness or its relation to prior knowledge. Compare to *meaningful verbal learning.*

rule-eg: In concept teaching, the familiar sequence of presenting first a concept definition, then giving several illustrations. Compare to *eg-rule.*

savings method: Measuring learning by studying the relearning of material. The effort or time spent on the two occasions is compared; little effort on the second occasion suggests great savings.

schema: Piaget's term for the way knowledge is represented cognitively, roughly similar to a concept. According to Piaget, schemas are organized, logical mental patterns of the external world. In cognitive psychology, schema has become the basic unit of *information processing,* referring to a *cognitive structure* in which data are coded and stored.

selective attention: Paying attention to some sensations or stimuli and ignoring others; occurs without conscious effort.

self-concept: The effective variable that refers to the view one has of one's self. A person with a positive self-concept considers himself or herself worthwhile; a negative self-concept means the person feels worthless.

self-control: *Neobehaviorist* term for the ability to pass up an immediate, probable reinforcer for a long-range, less probable reinforcer. For example, self-control by a person wishing to study for an exam might be avoiding the phone, television, doorbell, and other immediately reinforcing distractions. Methods of self-control include *self-observation, environmental planning,* and *behavioral programming.*

self-observation: First step in *self-control,* involving monitoring and recording of one's own behavior to establish a *baseline.* Sometimes self-observation alters behavior on its own, so that other self-control steps need not occur.

self-report instrument: A measuring device relying on a person's judgment about himself or herself. Usually used to measure personal characteristics in the *affective domain,* such as interests, attitudes, feelings, and self-concept.

sensorimotor impairment: Any of a variety of disorders relating to the *psychomotor domain* or to sensory reception (i.e., hearing, sight, touch).

sensorimotor period: The first of Piaget's periods of cognitive development, extending roughly from birth to two years of age. In this period the infant explores the world primarily with senses and motions.

sensory storage: Memory storage that holds information for only fractions of a second. See also *short-term storage* and *long-term storage.*

sex-role stereotype: See *sex-typed behavior.*

sex-typed behavior: Behavior stereotypically linked to one or the other sex. Examples: playing "house" is traditionally a female game, while domineering, aggressive behavior is sex-typed as masculine.

shaping: Reinforcing steps that go successively closer to a goal. As each preceding step is mastered, reinforcement is withheld until the next step is taken.

short-term storage: Memory storage that holds information just long enough to sort it out and determine if it should go into long-term storage.

situation-specific reinforcer: A reinforcer that strengthens or maintains a particular response. Commonly applied to classical conditioning. For example, the pain from a baseball hitting the head will *only* strengthen fear. See also *transsituational reinforcer*.

social learning theory: One of a variety of *neobehaviorist* models of learning. Focuses on the social environment as responsible for much learning, particularly with the processes of observation and *imitation learning*.

social transmission: In *cognitive developmental* theory, a major mechanism for experiencing the world. Broadly, learning from interacting with and observing others.

sociometric measure: An instrument generally used to measure friendship patterns in a school setting. Scores are established by asking students to "rate" everyone else according to how well they like them.

special conditions: In *behavioral objectives*, a component that states any unusual circumstances under which a behavior must be demonstrated; for example, "using a map," or "without a calculator."

specific transfer: Learning specific skills that can be applied to similar tasks. See also *nonspecific transfer*.

spiral curriculum: Bruner's model of education in which a student is exposed to the same ideas throughout his schooling. Each exposure, however, is geared to the student's particular level of development in depth of material presented.

split-brain: Refers to the two hemispheres of the brain; often used in reference to brain research or to specialization of the two hemispheres.

spontaneous recovery: Occurs during extinction; it is a temporary increase in the rate or strength of a behavior, as though it "recovered." The increase rarely pushes the behavior as high as its original level.

standardization: Developing a measure on which the conditions are said to be equal in all cases. For example, a standardized test provides the same questions, the same apparatus, the same directions, and the same time limits to all persons who take the test. It also has a *norm table* for comparison of scores.

standardization sample: Persons used to establish the *validity* and *reliability* of a standardized test. Their scores are generally published in a *norm table*, which allows comparisons of scores.

standardized test: A measure that has been rigorously developed, which allows comparisons of current scores with those of a *standardization group*. Standardized tests presumably have better *reliability* and *validity* than do teacher-made tests. See also *standardization*.

Stanford-Binet test: The classic *individual intelligence test*, originally translated and adapted from French by L. M. Terman, a Stanford University psychologist. Revised in 1972.

stimulus: A situation or event that prompts behavior.

structure of intellect: Psychologist J. P. Guilford's theory that intelligence is composed of many elements. He suggested that there were some 120 elements of intelligence, in each of which the three major dimensions of operations, products, and content of intelligent behavior interact.

student entry characteristics: Those attributes of students that are important enough to influence teaching techniques (e.g., prior experience in subject matter, intelligence).

student ratings: Questionnaires meant to measure student impressions of teacher behavior.

subsume: Ausubel's term for including and categorizing information into a permanent mental or cognitive system. According to him, it is the way new information becomes part of a person's existing knowledge.

successive approximations: In *behavior modification*, stepwise and systematic movements toward a goal. See *shaping*.

summative testing: Assessment following the presentation of an instructional unit (e.g., a final exam). Compare to *formative testing*.

symbolic mode: The third of Bruner's modes of representation, which begins at about age seven or eight. In this mode children use symbols to think abstractly.

table of specifications: Also termed "test grid," a two-dimensional outline used to help organize a test and ensure its *content validity*. One dimension describes areas of content to be measured, the second gives types of behavior or cognition to be measured.

talented: Usually refers to persons of superior skills who do not necessarily show high intelligence. See also *gifted.*

targeting: In *behavior modification,* the pinpointing of an observable and measurable behavior that is to be strengthened or weakened.

task analysis: Breaking up a large goal into smaller subgoals, and putting the subgoals in sequence.

teacher expectancy: See *expectancy.*

teacher-made test: A measuring device developed and scored by a teacher. See *standardized test.*

telegraphic speech: In language development, the use of sparse phrases which omit unnecessary words; for example, "Dig it!" to mean "I agree with your comment."

terminal behavior: A component of a *behavioral objective* describing expected performance in observable, measurable terms.

time on task: The length of time that a student spends attending to a scheduled activity. Compare to *allocated time.*

time out (abbreviated **TO**): In *behavior modification,* removing a child from a reinforcing environment (compared to removing a portion of the environment from the child). Generally used in modifying disruptive classroom behavior.

token economy: In *behavior modification,* an exchange system in which neutral tokens (e.g., poker chips, check marks, slips of paper) are awarded for appropriate behavior. The tokens are accumulated and "cashed in" for objects or activities that work as reinforcers.

transfer of principles: See *nonspecific transfer.*

transformational grammar: A principle in Noam Chomsky's theory of language development. In perceiving and using language, a person is thought to operate on language with internal rules of grammar; a person "transforms" the language into his or her own individual meanings and thinking.

transitions: In Levinson's theory of adult personality, periods of change between major *eras* of development.

transsituational reinforcer: A reinforcing event that can be used to strengthen many different behaviors. Commonly applied to *operant conditioning.* For example, praise can be used to reinforce many operant behaviors. See also *situation-specific reinforcer.*

true score: The portion of an *obtained score* that accurately reflects what a person actually knows. See also *error score.*

two-factor theory of intelligence: Spearman's theory in which one factor (g) represents general intelligence, and the second factor (s) represents specific abilities.

unconditioned response: An unlearned, involuntary reaction to an unlearned stimulus. For example, an unlearned or *unconditioned stimulus* of an electric shock will automatically evoke an unconditioned response, fear or avoidance.

unconditioned stimulus: A stimulus that requires no learning in order to evoke a response. Its automatic action is presumably innate and genetically organized. For example, the stimulus of tickling a small child will naturally create laughter and squirming.

undergeneralize: In concept formation, the inability to perceive one or more members of a given concept. For example, undergeneralization occurs when a learner declares that mental retardation and emotional disturbance are types of exceptionality but that giftedness is not. Compare to *overgeneralization.*

validity: The extent to which a test measures what it is supposed to measure. See *content validity* and *predictive validity.*

values clarification: A series of activities meant to help students clarify their own feelings, attitudes, and values.

variable ratio schedule (abbreviated **VR**): A pattern of reinforcement in which responses are reinforced intermittently or at random. A VR:10 schedule means that *on the average* every tenth occurrence of the desired response is reinforced; actually, it might be the eighth response, then the twenty-third response, and so on. Compare to *fixed ratio schedule.*

verbal ability: A cluster of related cognitive skills, usually measured by speaking responses. Most tests of intelligence are heavily weighted toward verbal ability.

vicarious reinforcement: Imagining that someone else's reinforcer will be yours if you perform a similar behavior. The empathic identification with a model being reinforced, generally associated with *imitation learning.*

visual impairment: Difficulty in sight processes.

visual-spatial ability: Skill in perception and comprehension of shapes, patterns, and arrangement in space.

voucher (system): A plan to increase educational opportunity by providing parents with vouchers that may be used to "purchase" education at a school of choice.

Wechsler Intelligence Scale for Children-Revised: Abbreviated WISC-R, an *individual intelligence test* for persons ranging in age from five to sixteen years. Revised in 1974.

Wechsler tests: A group of tests developed to measure intelligence, the most popular of which is the *Wechsler Intelligence Scale for Children-Revised.*

Whorf's hypothesis: Named after Benjamin Whorf, the notion that language's meanings are responsible for individual perceptions of the world. According to Whorf, language determines reality, not the other way around.

WISC-R: See *Wechsler Intelligence Scale for Children-Revised.*

work personality: A set of attitudes toward occupational behavior, such as feeling that it is important to please the boss, to arrive at work on time, and so on.

Index